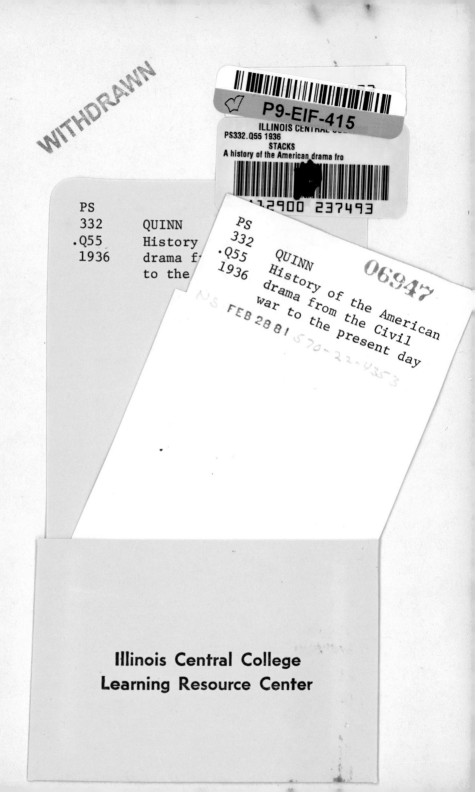

A HISTORY OF
THE AMERICAN DRAMA

FROM THE CIVIL WAR
TO THE PRESENT DAY

With all best wishes,
Sincerely, Eugene O'Neill.

[From the bust by Edmond Quinn]

A HISTORY OF

THE AMERICAN DRAMA

From the Civil War to the Present Day.

BY

ARTHUR HOBSON QUINN

*Author of "A History of the American Drama from
the Beginning to the Civil War"*

ILLUSTRATED

Revised Edition

APPLETON-CENTURY-CROFTS, INC.

NEW YORK

PREFACE

IN THIS survey of our native drama from the beginning of modern playwriting to the present day, I have had three objects. The first has been to paint a picture of the drama, not only in its loftiest moments, but also in those no less significant stretches of achievement in which it has been one of the most potent forces in our social history. The second has been to point out among the playwriting of the period the prevailing types and tendencies so that some coherent progress might be apparent. The third has been to indicate the relative merits of the dramatists, not only from my own point of view but also from that of the effect of their plays upon the discriminating criticism of their time. I have not indulged to any degree in quotations from that criticism; it has seemed to me my duty to absorb it and to pass it to my readers, mellowed by the judgment of time.

I have been faced by the difficulty which any historian encounters who dares to treat of the contemporary. But the great importance of recent dramatic achievements in America demands attention, and while I recognize that it is not possible to write of the playwrights of today with the same finality as those of yesterday, I have made a compromise which by a happy accident is reflected approximately in the division of the two volumes of this book.

From Augustin Daly to Clyde Fitch, I have tried to treat the dramatists historically, as well as critically, and to record completely the result of their achievement. How difficult this has been, owing to the fact that so many of the plays remain in manuscript, literally hidden by authors and managers, owing to the inadequacy of the copyright laws, I need not emphasize. From the death of Moody to the present day I

PREFACE

have been more selective, but even here I have omitted, I trust, no important work. Sometimes the playwrights have been treated in separate chapters, sometimes they have been grouped according to the kind of play for which they have been distinguished. Usually, their work has been treated as a unit, but in some cases, it has been assigned to different chapters, when the variety of their plays demanded it. In no case have I let the dragon of uniformity keep my readers from any information which I felt should be at their service. I have laid myself open perhaps in consequence to criticism for omissions or inclusions, but I shall not defend myself in detail against it.

It is necessary, however, to explain my general principle of selection. I have treated the drama as a living thing, written for the professional theatre, and I have made no effort to consider the hundreds of dramatic poems which are for reading only, or the thousands of plays upon which the amateur practices his skill. I have tried to set the plays against the background of the stage and to explain dramatic conditions in terms of the American theatre. It seemed unnecessary, therefore, for example, to treat the dramas of Henry James, written for the English stage, and failing on it, however interesting they may be to read. On the other hand, I have written a history of the drama and not of the theatre and I have had to omit any detailed discussion of Little Theatres, Community Theatres, and kindred projects, except in so far as they contribute to establish dramatic opportunity.

I have felt it best to omit any discussion of the one-act play as a type, but rather to treat the short plays of each author under the discussion of his work as a unit. I cannot feel the distinction between the one-act play and the full length play as I do the difference between the short story and the novel. Nearly all our really significant playwrights have made use of the one-act play as a preparation for more important productions, but the condition of our professional stage holds still no great inducement to the writer of the short play. Valuable as these one-act plays are to the beginner in school or college, or to the Little Theatre group, they seem to lie outside my province. Here again, I have made one exception, in the work of Howells, for reasons which need not be repeated here.

I have had such cordial assistance in the progress of this work that it is hardly possible to record my appreciation. From the relatives and friends of the earlier playwrights I have experienced invariably courtesy and confidence, in granting me the opportunity of reading manuscripts as well as providing me with accurate information. Especially from Mrs. James A. Herne, Miss Julie Herne, Mrs. William Vaughn Moody, Miss Mildred Howells, Mr. Edward A. Daly, Dr. Anthony H. Harrigan, and Mr. R. C. Campbell have I received invaluable assistance. I can hardly estimate fully the generous interest of Miss Virginia Gerson and Mrs. J. H. Edmonds, in aiding me to make my discussion of Clyde Fitch authentic. From those in intimate touch with our dramatic past and present like Mr. and Mrs. Otis Skinner, Dr. Horace Howard Furness, Mr. Daniel Frohman, Mr. Hamlin Garland, Mr. William Seymour, Dr. John L. Haney, Mr. Barrett Clark, Mr. Arthur Hornblow, Mr. Kenneth Macgowan, Mr. T. A. Curry, and Mr. George B. Berrell, of California have come constant assistance and encouragement. To the intelligent interest of Miss Alice Kauser, Mr. T. R. Edwards and Mr. F. J. Sheil, of Samuel French, Mr. Howard Rumsey and Mr. R. J. Madden of the American Play Company and Mr. Louis Sherwin of the Charles Frohman office I owe the securing of manuscripts without which my work would have been at a stand still.

If I should thank the living playwrights who have furnished me with information it would simply be to repeat the table of contents, for I have been, I am afraid, ruthless in laying them under contribution. I must mention, however, Mr. Augustus Thomas, Mr. William Gillette, and Mr. David Belasco, who have been particularly cordial in loaning me manuscripts and permitting quotations to be made from their published and

PREFACE

unpublished plays. And it has been an especial pleasure to be able to give my readers the benefit of the correspondence which reveals authentically the artistic purpose of Mr. Eugene O'Neill.

Among correspondents in other places, Mrs. Lillian A. Hall of the Shaw Theatre Collection, Miss Jessie L. Farnum of the Library of Congress, Professor George C. D. Odell of Columbia University, Dr. Napier Wilt of the University of Chicago have been especially helpful. My greatest debt has been, however, to my friend, Professor Brander Matthews, who read the manuscript as far as Chapter XII and whose unfaltering memory and wide knowledge of the drama made his advice invaluable.

Among my own colleagues, Professor Schelling has as always been fruitful of counsel. I am grateful for the interest of Provost Penniman, who arranged the leave of absence which permitted the completion of the work, and the help of Professor Baugh, Professor Bradley and Professor Musser has been given unsparingly. Professor Crawford, Professor Doernenburg, Professor Weigand and Professor Scholz have been cordial in helping me solve the vexed questions of foreign sources for American plays.

I wish to acknowledge here also the courtesy of Richard Badger, Walter H. Baker, Boni and Liveright, Brentano's, Dodd, Mead and Company, Samuel French, Henry Holt and Company, The Houghton Mifflin Company, A. A. Knopf, Little, Brown and Company, The MacMillan Company, and Charles Scribner's Sons, in granting permission to quote from plays published by them. I am indebted to the courtesy of Miss Virginia Gerson and Mr. Montrose J. Moses, editors of *The Letters of Clyde Fitch*, for permission to reprint certain extracts from them.

Finally I wish to record the informal but zealous assistance of my wife and children, whose interest is reflected in the play list and in countless other ways.

A. H. Q.

University of Pennsylvania, 1927.

FOREWORD TO THE REVISED EDITION

In preparing this revision in one volume, it has seemed best, for practical reasons, to preserve the text of the two volumes as I wrote them in 1927. In order to bring the history up to the present day, however, I have added a chapter, which I have called "The New Decade," dealing with the highly interesting developments from 1927 to the present day. In this survey, I have naturally laid most stress upon the work of those playwrights like Eugene O'Neill, Philip Barry, Maxwell Anderson, Sidney Howard, George Kaufman and Marc Connelly, who were becoming established in 1927, but I have also treated those members of the younger generation who either seem to me to have marked promise for the future, or whose work has attracted such attention that it becomes necessary to discuss it. If I have differed sharply in certain instances from the usual critical judgments concerning the most recent playwrights, it is perhaps because the historian is trained to see the drama in a longer perspective than the contemporary critic, and plays may seem of greater or of less importance to him than to those whose memories are shorter or whose enthusiasm is less resilient. While I am concerned only with plays that have seen the stage, and I do not share with purely academic criticism a scorn of the popular test of drama, I also know that some of the finest examples of American playwrighting in this decade have failed by commercial tests, and completely negligible products have enjoyed long runs, often by appeals to sensational methods. It is the province of a critical historian to remain unimpressed by any standards but those which are based, not only upon a knowledge of the drama, but also by a love of the theatre at its best.

While the main text has remained unaltered except for the

FOREWORD TO THE REVISED EDITION

correction of misprints and obvious errors of fact, the Bibliography and the Play List have been completely revised and re-
set, so that all the work of a playwright may be found in one
place. For invaluable help in this revision I am indebted to
Mr. Barrett H. Clark, Dr. John L. Haney, Mr. Edward H.
O'Neill, Dr. Sculley Bradley and to my daughters, Helen Cloyd
Honneus and Kathleen Carberry Quinn. I wish also to acknowledge a grant by the Faculty Research Committee of the
University of Pennsylvania.

I wish to acknowledge here also the courtesy of Mr. Eugene
O'Neill for permission to print extracts from his letters written
to me; of Mr. Maxwell Anderson, Mr. Sidney Howard, Mr.
Marc Connelly and Mr. Philip Barry for permission to quote
from their plays and of Samuel French, Charles Scribner's Sons
and Farrar and Rinehart for the right to print material published by them.

University of Pennsylvania, March, 1936.

CONTENTS

CONTENTS

Edward Harrigan dramatizes the types of city life—
The song, the duet, the dialogue and then the play—
The Mulligan Cycle, and *Squatter Sovereignty*—Irish,
German, Negro and Italian types—The adventurer
in *Major Gilfeather*—*Riley and the Four Hundred*—
Charles Hoyt's farces of the city and the small town—
Wide variety of his types—*A Tin Soldier, A Midnight
Bell, A Texas Steer*—*A Trip to Chinatown* establishes
a record of performances in New York—Other type
plays—*The Senator*—*The Dictator*.

The progressive nature of the frontier—Murdoch's
Davy Crockett in Tennessee—Plays of the Far West—
Bret Harte's *Two Men of Sandy Bar*—His collabora-
tion with Mark Twain in *Ah Sin*—Harte's success in
Sue—Mark Twain and *The Gilded Age*—Joaquin Mil-
ler's *The Danites in the Sierras*—Bartley Campbell's
My Partner—His other plays—The passing of the
frontier.

The growing emphasis on character—Steele Mac-
Kaye's work in the theatre—*Hazel Kirke*—Denman
Thompson's *Old Homestead*—The great significance of
Herne's work—His beginning with Belasco in melo-
drama—*Chums* becomes *Hearts of Oak*—Its advance
over its British source—Historical drama in *The Min-
ute Men*—The increasing fidelity to truth in *Drifting
Apart*, leading to the stark realism of *Margaret Flem-
ing*—Herne's association with Howells and Hamlin
Garland—*Shore Acres*—Reality and the Civil War in
Griffith Davenport—*Sag Harbor*—Difference between
Herne and the European realists.

Belasco's beginning in California—His association
with Herne—*La Belle Russe* introduces him to the

CONTENTS

East—Stage manager at the Madison Square and the Lyceum—He and W. C. De Mille collaborate in *The Wife, Lord Chumley, The Charity Ball* and *Men and Women—The Girl I Left Behind Me* with Franklin Fyles—His best period, in association with John Luther Long, produces *Madame Butterfly, The Darling of the Gods* and *Adrea*—Long's other plays—Belasco's plays of the West—His artistic triumphs in stage lighting—*The Return of Peter Grimm*—The real contribution of Belasco as a playwright.

Revival of the heroic play under influence of Barrett, Mansfield, Sothern and Skinner—William Young's *Pendragon, Ganelon* and *Ben Hur*—Henry Guy Carleton—Richard Mansfield as a playwright—Thomas Bailey Aldrich—His *Mercedes*, and *Judith of Bethulia*—Ernest Lacy's *Chatterton*—Mrs. Burnett and Francis Marion Crawford—His *Francesca da Rimini* for Bernhardt—The dramatization of novels at the end of the century.

The playwright-actor states his case—Early adaptations, *Esmeralda* and *The Private Secretary—Held by the Enemy*, the first successful play of the Civil War—*A Legal Wreck*—Farces from the French and German—*Too Much Johnson*—His great contribution, the cool determined man of action—The vivid interplay of motives in *Secret Service—Sherlock Holmes—Clarice*, a play of South Carolina—His later plays.

Thomas's training as a playwright in the newspaper and the theatre, in St. Louis—*Editha's Burglar* and other one-act plays—Joins the Madison Square—*Alabama* establishes his reputation—The theme of our re-united country—The middle West of *In Mizzoura*—Finance and politics in *The Capitol*—The real West

CONTENTS

in *Arizona*—Picturesque history in *Oliver Goldsmith*—
Light comedies, *The Earl of Pawtucket, The Other Girl*
—The play of occult forces in *The Witching Hour* and
The Harvest Moon—Thomas's fine play of toleration,
As a Man Thinks—His sane treatment of the "double
standard"—*The Copperhead* dramatizes the patriot-
ism of the average American—Attack on prohibition
in *Still Waters*—The significance of Thomas's plays in
the struggle to preserve the liberty of the individual—
His constructive criticism of life.

The college-trained playwright—Mansfield gives him
his opportunity in *Beau Brummell*—Fitch shows in
his first play his knowledge of social values and his
ability in dialogue—Adaptations from French and
German—Vivid historical drama in *Nathan Hale* and
Barbara Frietchie—Enters on his best period with *The
Climbers* and *The Girl with the Green Eyes*—The failure
of *Major André*—Powerful melodrama of *The Woman
in the Case*—International contrasts in *Her Great Match*
—Brilliant character portrayal of *The Truth*—Its appreciation abroad—*The City*, produced after his premature death—Fitch's best characters the incarnation
of one virtue or vice—The reversal of critical opinion
in his case.

VOLUME TWO

Changes in the drama and theatre with the turn
of the century—The effect of the "syndicate" upon
dramatists—Projects for betterment—The new dramatic generation—Moody's leadership in the celebration of the individual protest against standardization of life—His verse dramas and their emphasis
upon human dignity—The contrast between East

CONTENTS

CONTENTS

CONTENTS

CONTENTS

The O'Neill myth—His love of adventure—Acting and reporting—One-act plays and the Provincetown Players—The drama of the sea in *The S. S. Glencairn*—Reality of his characters—*Ile*—*Beyond the Horizon*, the tragedy of frustrated dreams—*The Straw*, a powerful study of unquenchable hope—*Anna Christie*, a drama of fate and regeneration—O'Neill's own interpretation of the ending—In *The Emperor Jones*, O'Neill establishes the new unity of impression—Social satire in *The First Man*—Symbolism of *The Hairy Ape*, a drama of misguided power—*Welded*, and the torment of mutual passion—Romantic symbolism in *The Fountain*, in which O'Neill begins a new period in his art—*All God's Chillun Got Wings*, another tragedy of frustrated aspiration—*Desire Under the Elms*, the ironic treatment of passion—Triumph of symbolism in *The Great God Brown*, the protest of the creative artist—O'Neill's interpretation of the symbolism—The brilliant satire of modern commercialism in *Marco Millions*—The world artist strikes the universal note in *Lazarus Laughed*—O'Neill's statement of his philosophy of composition—His place in our literature—The nobility of his conception of humanity—O'Neill the mystic—His Celtic heritage—Hawthorne and O'Neill; their sympathy with sinners—The poet of aspiration.

The effect of the War upon drama in sharpening the scrutiny of life and institutions—The attempt to deal sincerely with character—Zona Gale and Susan Glaspell, examples of the drama of revolt—The domestic drama reaches a high point in *The Hero* by Gilbert Emery—His other plays—Owen Davis leaves melodrama for better things—The domestic comedy of Kaufman and Connelly—George Kelly's shrewd observation of life—The imaginative touch in Sidney Howard and Maxwell Anderson—Other playwrights of the domestic drama.

CONTENTS

CONTENTS

ILLUSTRATIONS

ILLUSTRATIONS

WILLIAM VAUGHN MOODY . . . . *facing p.* 12

PERCY MACKAYE . . . . " 30

RACHEL CROTHERS . . . . " 50

LANGDON MITCHELL . . . . " 62

JESSE LYNCH WILLIAMS . . . . " 70

PHILIP BARRY . . . . " 84

EDWARD SHELDON . . . . " 92

OWEN DAVIS . . . . " 110

FACSIMILE OF LETTER FROM EUGENE O'NEILL . . . " 198

GILBERT EMERY . . . . " 212

GEORGE KELLY . . . . " 226

SIDNEY HOWARD . . . . " 232

A SCENE FROM *The Scuffletown Outlaws,* A PLAY OF
   THE NORTH CAROLINA MOUNTAINEERS . . . . . " 242

A HISTORY OF
THE AMERICAN DRAMA
VOLUME ONE
FROM AUGUSTIN DALY TO THE
DEATH OF CLYDE FITCH

❧

CHAPTER I

Augustin Daly, Constructive Artist of the Theatre

MODERN American drama begins with Augustin Daly. While Dion Boucicault was a greater playwright and I have elsewhere [1] paid tribute to his influence, it was individual and partially destructive. Daly was a constructive artist and through the transition decades of the sixties and seventies he laid the foundations of the days to come. He was aware, too, how through the apparently tangled skein of our dramatic history runs the clear thread of its consistent progress. He knew how firmly laid were the foundations in domestic and social comedy, in the plays of the frontier, in the drama which had revivified our great historical figures and reflected the struggles that founded and established the nation. He recognized, too, the spirit of our fine romantic tragedies and comedies. More than once he decries the general lack of knowledge of what our playwrights had already accomplished, and chooses for special mention *Brutus, Charles II, Francesca da Rimini, The Gladiator, The Broker of Bogota,* and *Jack Cade,* and suggests the revival of the plays of Mrs. Howe and Mrs. Mowatt. How he would have enjoyed the revival of *Fashion* at the Provincetown in 1924! He was hospitable to new playwrights, as we shall see. And one of his most significant criticisms, possibly aimed at Bronson Howard's *One of Our Girls,* suggests that if a contrast is desired between a "wild whooping American girl" and a conservative family, why should an American playwright lay his scene in a foreign country, when "a respectable New York, Boston or Philadelphia family would be equally amazed and distressed by such a

[1] *History of the American Drama from the Beginning to the Civil War,* Chap. XIII.

1

A HISTORY OF THE AMERICAN DRAMA

girl." Most important is his prophecy that "our national drama will be established without restriction as to subject or plot. The coming dramatist will be indifferent on that score. Neither Shakespeare nor any of his contemporaries, nor Corneille nor Racine, nor Schiller nor Goethe made the national drama of their native lands by the delineation of national character only. . . . We must not exact of American dramatists more than has been demanded of its dramatists by any country. The present masterpieces of the stage, in every tongue, are pictures of the passions of mankind in general, rather than attempts at national portrait painting." He recognized that notwithstanding the realistic tendency in our literature, the theatre, which by its very nature reverts to the unusual and the heroic, can never entirely lose the flavor of romance. Not all his prophecies came true, but his picture of "the silent brooding, observant boy sitting in the gallery" who is to write the play of the future, was to be fulfilled.

This is an account of our drama and not of our theatre, yet before we discuss the creative work of Augustin Daly it is necessary to portray in brief the theatrical situation in the United States during the decade from 1860 to 1870, in order that we may understand the paucity of playwriting during this transition period. It was an epoch of changing and of disturbed conditions. Before the Civil War it had been the custom for large cities and even smaller towns to have their stock companies. Stars, both native and foreign, visited these towns and were supported by the local companies. While the invention of the traveling company with one play, eventually broke down this system, the transition was gradual. In 1872 Lawrence Barrett took his company but not the scenery of his plays, but in 1876 when J. G. Stutz took out *Rose Michel*, the scenery accompanied the play. The season of 1878-79 marked the end of the stock company at the Walnut Street Theatre in Philadelphia, and Otis Skinner, who was then a member of it, attributes the change to the desire of the public to see new faces and costumes. He believes that the stock system led

2

to versatility rather than supreme excellence, but that on the whole it provided a training for the actor which the traveling company did not furnish. In New York, the situation differed from that of the rest of the country and stock companies continued until the close of the century. Obviously the effect upon the theatre would be the emphasis laid upon New York City as the origin or the goal of successful plays.

On the drama it had at first a destructive effect, as it limited the opportunity of playwrights in Philadelphia, Boston, Baltimore, Charleston, Chicago, Cincinnati, and even Mobile or New Orleans, of having their plays produced in those cities. It meant that playwrights would go to New York, as Bronson Howard did, and that for our purpose the record of the New York stage becomes, much more exclusively than in the earlier period, the background of the professional drama. The character of the New York audiences and the preferences and artistic sense of the producers becomes therefore of more and more significance. The increase in the foreign element in New York City spelled little good to the drama of American life and the attitude of such a leading manager as Lester Wallack, who though American born was much more British in his tastes and sympathies even than his English father, was unfavorable to the production of native plays. Even more striking is the fact that New York, though the producing center, did not often develop playwrights who would reveal the drama that lies inherent in its multiform civilization. Augustin Daly was born in North Carolina, Bronson Howard in Detroit, Steele MacKaye in Buffalo, William Gillette in Hartford, David Belasco in San Francisco, Clyde Fitch in Elmira, Augustus Thomas in St. Louis, Langdon Mitchell and John Luther Long in Pennsylvania.

The effect of the Civil War upon the theatre was at first disturbing, but was not of long continuance. Niblo's Garden was closed from April 29 to December 23, 1861. The Bowery Theatre was dilapidated by military occupation in May, 1862. The Boston Theatre closed on April 6, 1861, after a short season of only sixteen weeks. But by 1862 the theatres in New York, Philadelphia and Boston seem to have been playing to good business, and while according to Rhodes,[1] the *Richmond Enquirer* of October 10, 1863, inveighs against the theatre, the Richmond Theatre, which had burned in 1862, was reopened in February, 1863. Of much greater importance was the shifting in the center of population in New York City which resulted in the closing of the old Broadway Theatre in 1859, the destruction of the Chatham Theatre in 1862 and the transfer of the Wallacks, father and son, from the Lyceum to the new Wallack's Theatre in 1861. "Wallack's" continued as the leading theatre in New York, but it was devoted largely to the production of British comedy except when John E. Owens played his character parts in *Self* or *Solon Shingle*. There was a competent company at Niblo's Garden, but here British plays were performed almost exclusively, except during the visits of Edwin Forrest and J. H. Hackett. Forrest kept in his repertory the romantic tragedies of the earlier days, such as Bird's *Gladiator* and *Broker of Bogota*, Stone's *Metamora* and Conrad's *Jack Cade*, while Hackett was still playing *A Kentuckian's Trip to New York* and *A Yankee in England*. Edwin Booth played Payne's *Brutus* at times, though his interest lay in other fields.

But it was not only the personal preference of a great actor that preserved the earlier drama. I notice, during the sixties, performances at the New Bowery Theatre of old favorites such as *Brutus, The Poor of New York, Paul Jones, Putnam, The Octoroon, Horse Shoe Robinson, Moll Pitcher, The New York Fireman, Nick of the Woods, A Glance at New York*, and *The Surgeon of Paris*. Noah's *She Would Be A Soldier* was played at Barnum's Museum in 1866, and J. S. Jones' *Paul Revere* was put on at the Boston Museum in 1876. Of the American plays of an earlier period, the tragedies of Robert Montgomery Bird and Robert T. Conrad and the comedies of Joseph Stevens Jones were to show the most vitality, with the

[1] *History of the United States.* V, 425.

4

exception of the composite *Rip van Winkle,* and the supreme creation of the early drama, Boker's *Francesca da Rimini,* which was to last until the present century.

Although no great play arose from the Civil War during the period of conflict, the theme was by no means neglected. Few of these acted dramas were printed and we can in general judge of their contents and their effect only by theatrical history. As early as January 16, 1861, an anonymous play, *Our Union Saved, or Marion's Dream* was played at the Olympic Theatre in which "the President" was played by D. J. Maguire. On February 11, 1861, George H. Miles inserted "a second act of national tableau" entitled "Uncle Sam's Magic Lantern," into a spectacle called *The Seven Sisters,* which had formerly nothing to do with the Civil War, but which filled Laura Keene's Theatre for one hundred and seventy-seven nights. The interpolated patriotic scene had a delightful mixture of characters, including Uncle Sam, Disunion, Diogenes, Massachusetts, South Carolina, Virginia, Columbia and Liberty. The older Revolutionary drama was revived at the Boston Museum, *Our Flag is Nailed to the Mast* being given on April 30, 1861, and a Civil War episode was added to *The Liberty Tree* in June.

The speedy dramatization of events during the War of 1812 was paralleled during the Civil War by the industry of Charles Gayler, the dramatist who supplied the New Bowery Theatre. Bull Run was fought on July 21, 1861, and on August 15, *Bull Run, or the Sacking of Fairfax Courthouse* was on the stage. It ran for four weeks and was afterward revived. Gayler also wrote *Hatteras Inlet, or Our Naval Victories,* put on at the New Bowery, November 2, 1861, three months after the event. His speed in dramatization was outclassed, however, by that of Harry Seymour, whose *Capture of Fort Donelson* celebrated at the New Bowery Theatre, on February 22, 1862, Grant's triumph on February 16, in what was really the first great Union victory of the war.

John T. Raymond appeared in *The National Guard* at

Niblo's Garden in 1862 and another anonymous play, *How To Avoid Drafting*, at the Bowery Theatre in the same year sounds like a comedy. There seems to have been a lull in the Civil War plays in New York during 1863, but in January, 1864, *The Unionist's Daughter, or Life in the Border States* was put on at the Bowery. At the Tremont Temple in Boston, the comic opera of *Il Recrutio*, in which seventy members of the Forty-ninth Massachusetts took part, reveals in the program of its one performance how comedy entered into the conception of the war, even in 1863.

These plays were hastily written and their disappearance is hardly to be regretted. One of the few survivals, *Off to the War* by Benjamin E. Woolf, whose *Mighty Dollar* was later to make a great popular success, was played in Boston in 1861. It is a one-act farce comedy which reflects the impatience of the public at the contradictory news from the front and satirizes the attitude of the colored contrabands. Another survival, *A Supper in Dixie*, written by William C. Reynolds under the name of James Triplet, and played in Chicago in 1865, is a farcical treatment of the situation in Richmond in February of that year. There is a ring of truth, however, in the description of the difficulties that strolling actors found in obtaining food, which makes the play appealing in spite of its farcical character.

Of much greater interest is the melodrama, *The Guerillas*, by James D. McCabe, Jr., for, according to the preface, it was the first original drama to be produced in the Southern Confederacy. It was performed for the first time at the Richmond Varieties, on December 22, 1862, and had a successful run of a week. As a drama its merits are not high, but there is a certain vigor in the intensity of the patriotic feeling which appealed to a Southern audience. The destruction of homes and other property by the guerillas or irregular troops who operated in the western portion of Virginia, forms the motive of the play. The hero is the youngest of three generations, the eldest of whom is a veteran of the Revolution, and the author dwells upon the note so often struck in Southern literature, that of the purity of their descent from the older American stock. General Frémont is one of the villains of the play, and is the center of an incident reminiscent of *Measure for Measure*. The negro character, Jerry, represents the loyalty to his master which was later to provide so appealing a motive in *Secret Service*, and in the novels of Thomas Nelson Page and Francis Hopkinson Smith.

At the end of the war the plays began to multiply. *Grant's Campaign, or Incidents of the Rebellion* by John F. Poole at the New Bowery in December, 1865; *The Union Prisoner* by Milnes Levick at Barnum's Museum in December, 1867; *British Neutrality* by T. B. De Walden at the Olympic in July, 1869; *Ulysses, or the Return of U. S. Grant* at the Union Square Theatre in September, 1871, and *The Returned Volunteer* at the Academy of Music in October, 1871, indicate perhaps sufficiently the nature of the themes treated. The Battle of Gettysburg forms the scene of the third act of Augustin Daly's *Norwood* (1867), and there is some vigor in the picture of the battle scene, even if it is conventional. Dion Boucicault's *Belle Lamar*, produced at Booth's Theatre, August 10, 1874, has been earlier described and was probably the first Civil War play that can be considered seriously. After its comparative failure, the motive was to wait until the eighties to be brought to popular approval with William Gillette's *Held by the Enemy*.

The Color Guard by Colonel Alfred R. Calhoun is said to have been popular with the Union soldiers after the war. The author, who had an interesting political career, wrote from experience, but his play has little dramatic structure. Its appeal came doubtless from the courage of the hero, Louis Ludlow, who preserved the colors of his company, in defiance of the probabilities, even in Libby Prison. To a reader of today the greatest interest lies in its reflection of the loyalty of the Tennessee mountaineers to the Union, dramatized in the words of Father Allen, who dies satisfied that "the flag has

7

come back to Tennessee." *The Color Guard* was played as far west as San Francisco, where General Grant is reported to have witnessed the performance in 1879 at the California Theatre.

But to return to the first significant figure in the record of our drama after the Civil War. Augustin Daly was born in Plymouth, North Carolina, July 20, 1838, the son of Captain Denis Daly, a sea-captain and ship owner, and of Elizabeth, daughter of Lieutenant John Duffey, of the British army. His mother, early left a widow, brought her two boys to New York City, where they soon became frequent attendants at the theatres and were members of the amateur groups, which under such names as the "Burton Association" or the "Murdoch Association" were the precursors of the Little Theatre movement of the present day. Joseph Francis Daly, in his authoritative life of his brother, tells us that Augustin rarely if ever acted. His interest from the beginning lay in the creation and production of plays, and he began his career as a manager in 1856 in Brooklyn by hiring the one available hall and boldly attempting a varied performance, including scenes from *Macbeth* and *The Toodles,* with all the artistic and financial difficulties that might have been expected. At the beginning of his career, Augustin Daly showed the unfaltering courage, the fertility of resource and the optimism under discouraging circumstances which were to carry him through years of struggle and apparent defeat to the ultimate goal of his desires. In many of his qualities and in certain of his experiences he presents a striking parallel to our first playwright and producer, William Dunlap. In their ardent love of the beautiful, in their keen sense of the theatrically effective, in their determination to improve the conditions of the playhouse, they were alike. Alike too they were in their introduction of the contemporary drama of France and Germany and their use of native themes for their own plays. But while Dunlap failed, under the intolerable burden imposed upon him by circumstances, Daly organized a company that was to become the

8

standard of artistic achievement for this country, established his own theatre in London and even invaded the Continent in 1886 and carried an English-speaking company to Germany for the first time in three centuries.[1]

At the age of twenty-one, Daly became the dramatic critic for the New York *Courier*, retaining his connection with this paper for ten years and writing also at times for the *Sun*, the *Times*, the *Express* and the *Citizen*. Among the shifting conditions in the theatre of the early sixties and the disturbed state of New York City in the days of the draft riots, Daly attentively studied plays, which he criticized honestly and with growing skill.

His career as a dramatist began with *Leah the Forsaken*, an adaptation from the German melodrama, *Deborah*, written in 1850 by Salomon Hermann von Mosenthal, a North German playwright, then living in Vienna. Daly did not translate the play himself and indeed throughout his entire career he seems to have depended upon others for the first drafts of his foreign adaptations. *Leah the Forsaken* was first produced at the Howard Athenæum in Boston, December 8, 1862, with Kate Bateman in the title role, and then in January, 1863, at Niblo's Garden. It had a great success in both places. The theme is the persecution of the Jews and the scene an Austrian village in the Eighteenth Century. The repudiation of Leah by her Christian lover, her consequent misery and her final acceptance of fate, provided a medium in which Kate Bateman starred in England and which had a long stage life. Daly's adaptation was quite a free one. The blank verse of the original, perhaps necessarily, became prose, and many of the speeches were cut. Sometimes Daly's alterations seem improvements, as in the scene in which Father Hermann protects Leah by simply holding up the Cross. At the end, however, where Daly adds a scene and brings in Nathan, a renegade Jew, to represent persecution, Mosenthal's conclusion seems

---

[1] Edwin Booth had acted in Germany in 1881, but was supported by a German company.

simpler and more artistic. Critical judgment as well as popular taste greeted *Leah* with approval in New York and Boston. George William Curtis [1] wrote enthusiastically of it. Daly was to turn once more to Mosenthal for his inspiration. In 1873 he adapted a tragedy bordering on the melodrama, *Madeleine Morel*. It is a powerful play, somewhat after the manner of Dumas, in which a young girl who, through her loss of natural protectors, has become the mistress of an Englishman, Lord Durley, and is forced to leave her lover, Count Julian Dalberg, who has offered to marry her. The final scene, in a cathedral, in which Madeleine, who is about to take the veil, recognizes Julian, about to be married to another, and goes mad, provided Clara Morris with an opportunity for effective acting. One scene of this play, in which Lord Durley enters Madeleine's reception room from an inner apartment with his coat and hat and indicates thereby his relation to her, points forward perhaps to a similar situation, much praised for its adroitness, in Pinero's *Iris* and Walter's *The Easiest Way.*

The success of *Leah the Forsaken* led to several commissions for Daly, mainly adaptations from the French and German, which have come down only by title. With some assistance he wrote a play on a Biblical theme, *Judith,* in 1864, in which the career of the Jewish heroine is brought up to the death of Holofernes. He next turned to the field in which he was to score several popular successes, the dramatization of the British and American novel. The managers of the New York Theatre suggested to him in the fall of 1866, that he adapt Charles Reade's powerful study of jealousy, *Griffith Gaunt.* Daly constructed a play which made full use of the dramatic scenes of the novel, especially in the trial in the last act. The English law in the Eighteenth Century forbade a person accused of murder the benefit of counsel, and Kate Gaunt, who

---

[1] *Harper's Weekly*, VII (March 7, 1863), 146. Curtis drew a parallel between the persecution of the Jews in Europe and the race prejudice against the negroes which, he claimed, was the cause of the War. He said, "Go and see *Leah* and have the lesson burned in upon your mind, which may help to save the national life and honor."

is falsely accused of the murder of her husband, is compelled to defend herself. This gave Rose Eytinge, whom Daly had chosen for the part, a fine opportunity of which she seems to have taken full advantage. Daly altered the plot at this point, certainly in the interest of theatrical effectiveness, by bringing Griffith Gaunt in person to the trial scene.

Up to 1867 Daly had been experimenting in the arrangement of material already clothed in literary form by other hands. He attempted in his first original play he produced to deal with real life in New York City. So far as the setting of *Under the Gaslight* is concerned, he succeeded. The home of Laura and Pearl Courtland, with its atmosphere of comfort, the basement to which Laura flies when the secret of her birth is discovered, the police court in which she is given into the custody of the blackmailer Byke, the pier on the North River from which she is thrown, were all elements in a stage reality which goes back of course to Benjamin A. Baker's *A Glance at New York* in 1848, and perhaps more immediately to Boucicault's *The Poor of New York*. Daly developed a scene which he claimed was suggested by the railroad crossing over which he passed daily. Snorkey, the wounded soldier, who watches over the heroine, is bound to the railroad track by the villain, Byke. But Laura, who has escaped from both her captors and the North River, is in a near-by signal house where she has been locked at her own request. When the audience has been worked up sufficiently, Laura breaks out and saves Snorkey from an approaching train. This situation wa copied almost immediately by Boucicault in *After Dark* and the court proceedings which ensued established Daly's exclusive rights in this stage property for the United States.

It has been suggested that Daly owed this scene to *The Engineer*, produced at the Victoria Theatre in London in 1865, and the existence of a copy of *The Engineer* among the Daly manuscripts indicates that he knew of the play.[1] But the circumstances are entirely different. Randall Matthews,

[1] Correspondence in the Daly files proves he knew of it only in 1892.

the villain of *The Engineer*, has taken a rail out of the track over which his rival is speeding. The engine comes on the stage and kills him instead, but without employing effectively that principle of suspense which animated the scene in *Under the Gaslight*, and which was not beneath the notice of the playwright who sounded the summons of the Scottish thanes which waked the porter in *Macbeth*.

While *Under the Gaslight* is realistic in its setting, its characters are conventional. Snorkey, probably the most enjoyable, is modeled directly on the comic servant of the French *mélodrame*, although he is used to criticize the failure of the United States Government to take care of its wounded soldiers. The account of Laura's early life is reminiscent of Sardou's *La Perle noire*, a play Daly was to use again in *A Flash of Lightning*. What remains, however, to Daly's credit is a compact structure, with interesting dialogue at times and at least an attempt at realism, even if he produced only its skeleton. The great success of the play was especially pleasing to him, for it was his first real effort as a producer. He had leased the New York Theatre for the summer season and selected his own company, which appeared for the first time on August 12, 1867. The play has often been revived, and proved to be one of the most popular melodramas written in English. It was not only played in London in 1868 under its own name, but it was also adapted as *London by Gaslight*.[1]

Augustin Daly wrote, altered or adapted from British and American novels, from French or German dramas, or from earlier British plays, about ninety productions which actually saw the stage. Many of these have been known only by title for Daly published very few of his plays. Fortunately I have been able to examine the manuscripts remaining until recently in the hands of his executors, and while these are not complete, they contain the most important of his productions. The most profitable way to study his work is first, to discuss those plays which are usually referred to as his original dramas, next to examine his adaptations from English fiction and from foreign

[1] See Play List.

languages, with some reference to his alterations of earlier British drama.

Under the first group are to be included *Under the Gaslight*, *A Flash of Lightning*, *Horizon*, *Divorce* and *Pique*, *Roughing It* and probably *Judith*, *The Red Scarf*, and *The Dark City*. *A Flash of Lightning* was produced at the Broadway Theatre, June 10, 1868. It was another sensation drama of the type of *Under the Gaslight*. The main plot, concerned with the accusation of the theft of a gold chain by an innocent girl and the discovery that a flash of lightning had destroyed the chain and carried it into a coal scuttle, was based upon Sardou's *La Perle noire*, in which Christianne is accused of the theft of a locket and a necklace of pearls. The complicated relations of the Fallon family, however, have little connection with the incidents of the French drama, which is primarily a satire upon the methods of detection employed by the burgomaster, M. Tricamp. The climax of Daly's play was the burning of a Hudson River steamboat through the furnace room catching fire in the effort to race with another boat. The heroine, who has been chained to the bed in one of the staterooms, is of course saved in the nick of time. In the *Life of Daly* it is stated that the playwright had unwittingly disclosed a source of danger in the construction of furnaces that was usually overlooked. *A Flash of Lightning* was successful, running till August third and was later revived. But it is a melodrama, and marks no improvement upon Daly's earlier work. Nor was *The Red Scarf*, a story of life on the Aroostook among the New England mills, of any real significance. This play is attributed to him by Judge Daly, and the manuscript, though not autograph, is signed by him on the title-page. Yet it does not read like his work and it may be a joint product. It is a sensational play, and the principle of suspense, so well used in *Under the Gaslight*, is again employed in the final scene. Gail Barston, the hero, is trapped by his rival, Harvey Thatcher, the owner of the Dark Falls Mills, who binds him to a log that is to be sawed in two. Then he sets fire to the mill so that all trace of Gail will be lost and he will be supposed to have deserted May Hamilton, whom both men love. She arrives in time to save him, of course. *The Red Scarf* was first played at Conway's Park Theatre in Brooklyn in 1869, and was repeated at the Bowery Theatre, where it was quite at home.

The next play, however, was a great advance. *Horizon*, first produced at the Olympic Theatre on March 21, 1871, begins in New York City but is speedily transported to the West of Bret Harte. Med, the girl who has been brought west by her worthless father, and Loder, the bad man who protects her after her father's murder, are representatives of that moral contrast which Bret Harte loved to draw. But Med is not too bright or good by any means and Loder renounces his claim upon her affections, in favor of her Eastern lover, in a scene which for simplicity of language and restraint of passion goes far to establish Daly's claim to be the first of the modern realists in American playwriting. Sundowne Rowse, "a distinguished member of the Third House at Washington," is a vividly drawn character and the prototype of many a stage lobbyist, even if he is a bit reminiscent of Jefferson S. Batkins in J. S. Jones' *A Silver Spoon*. The Indian attacks by night on the boat[1] and later on the stockade seem to have been very effective. Competent critics like Brander Matthews and Laurence Hutton and rival managers like A. M. Palmer testify to the merit of the play on the stage, and certainly a reading of it reveals Daly's power of character drawing and his ability in writing straightforward and interesting conversation. *Horizon* ran for two months.

Horizon, though a better drama, was outdone in popular favor by *Divorce*, which began its run of two hundred nights at the Fifth Avenue Theatre, on September 5, 1871, and was later played throughout the country. In *Divorce*, Daly borrowed the idea of the lengths to which a man's unreasoning

---

[1] Daly used a panorama probably repainted from that of the *Midsummer Night's Dream* at the same theatre a few years earlier.

jealousy may lead him from Anthony Trollope's novel, *He Knew He Was Right*. The cause of the jealousy, the attentions of an older man who is a philanderer, is the same, as is also the resulting derangement of the husband, his abduction of their child, and the visit of the wife to his retreat to secure the return of the boy. But the outcome of the play is very different from that of the novel, and the character drawing is quite dissimilar. Louis Trevelyan is an English gentleman of wealth whose passion is for having his own way and his mental trouble is carried through three volumes until he dies of it. Alfred Adrianse, in *Divorce*, is not by any means so insane and yet he is placed under restraint and is cured so that the family may be reunited. His wife, Fanny Ten Eyck, is more culpable, at least of encouraging Captain Lynde's attentions, than is Emily Trevelyan, yet the natural independence of the American woman makes her handle her affairs better and Daly changed entirely the almost abject attitude which, despite her stubborn opposition, Mrs. Trevelyan was perhaps forced by the English law to assume. This difference between the position of husband and wife in England and America is only one of the aspects of life in which the play differs from its source. Trollope's novel is shot through with social and financial contrasts and he carries on several love stories, only one of which is even faintly reflected in Daly's play. There is no social contrast in the drama, and our interest lies in the study of the relations of the married couples, one serious and one almost burlesque. The detective is most like his British counterpart, but Adrianse does not employ him in the first place; Burritt is brought to the home of Mrs. Ten Eyck by Lu, Fanny's sister, who is bored by her husband and represents the silly woman who plays with the idea of divorce for the sake of excitement.

Of the twenty-four characters in Daly's play, only six are taken from the novel. Mrs. Kemp, who tries to bring Alfred and Fanny together, is perhaps suggested by Lady Milborough, but she is an entirely different person. Daly uses none

15

of the language of Trollope and the manner in which he has sharpened the action of the episodes he has taken can be appreciated only by those who have read the leisurely pages of *He Knew He Was Right*. The play may be considered as one of his original productions, less significant than *Horizon*, but more truly his own than *Pique* and dealing with an institution that was becoming a menace to the social life of America. Daly shows truly that the only happy marriages are those based on mutual forbearance, due to the conception of the married relation as a permanent one between equals. He shows, too, the futility of divorce as a cure for the difficulties of married life. With this problem the British novel was scarcely concerned, for divorce is hardly considered as a way out and Trollope had the conventional attitude of his country that the real happiness of a wife lay in obedience to her husband. The very title of Daly's play indicated the thorough domestication of the drama.

Between the production of *Divorce* and *Pique*, Daly the producer had been very active. On January 1, 1873, the Fifth Avenue Theatre burned. Daly immediately leased the old New York Theatre and called it Daly's Fifth Avenue Theatre, which he opened on January 21, 1873.

In the same year Daly brought together a number of managers of New York City to form an association for the conduct of their business, to loan players to each other and in general to avoid the disadvantages that come from competition. Fechter, Booth, Wallack, Palmer, Jarrett and Daly were members. Perhaps the "theatrical trusts" of later days may date the beginning of their career from this apparently useful and natural alliance.

In 1873 the New Fifth Avenue Theatre was built on Twenty-eighth Street near Broadway, where once had stood the St. James Theatre in which Steele MacKaye displayed his Delsarte system of acting. On December 3, 1873, this theatre was opened. At about this time Daly gave up the Grand Opera House and the Broadway Theatre, as the old New York

Theatre had come to be called, and confined his attention to the new house. He continued in its management until the failure of *The Dark City* in 1877 forced him to relinquish it. After his trip abroad, which laid the foundations for his later associations with the foreign theatres, he transformed the old Broadway Theatre into Daly's Theatre—opening it on September 18, 1879. This theatre was long associated with his name.

It was at the New Fifth Avenue Theatre in Twenty-eighth Street that *Pique* was presented for the first time on December 14, 1875. It ran for two hundred and thirty-eight nights and was afterward played in various places and by various actors. The original part of Mabel Renfrew was created by Fanny Davenport, who with it began her career as a star. There are two main elements of interest in *Pique*,—Mabel Renfrew loves Raymond Lessing, who cares for her but cares more for money and so proposes marriage to her young stepmother, Lucille. Out of pique, Mabel accepts the hand of Captain Arthur Standish but when she is forced to live with his family she revolts and there is consequent unhappiness. This theme, which is developed throughout the first two Acts and part of the third, was taken from a British novel, *Her Lord and Master*, by Florence Marryatt. The scene is transferred to this country and some changes are made in the plot and characters. Added to the latter are Dr. Gossit, a guardian angel, and Thorsby Gill and Sammy Dymple, comedy parts, the first played by John Drew. In both stories the husband departs after a scene in which the wife tells him that she does not love him and the lover offers her his protection only to be refused. Through this scene the wife begins to realize that she does care for the man she has married. At times Daly has even borrowed the language of *Her Lord and Master*. He has omitted, however, the tiresome religious discussions of the novel and there is no social difference to add to the wife's dislike in *Pique* as there is in the British source.

The second theme is the rescue of Mabel's child who has been

17

stolen by two thugs who have taken him to "Beggars' Paradise." Here Daly left the novel entirely and created a scene which must have been as thrilling as anything of recent years. Both the den and an attic above it are shown and in the attic Thorsby and Dymple conceal themselves while the grandfather, Matthew Standish, risks his life to bring the ransom; the mother comes in disguised as old Mother Thames, one of the decoys, and the father descends through the trap door to apparently certain death to hunt for his little son. In the meantime Dymple has escaped from the attic *via* the window to call the police! The child is finally returned by Raitch, a character of Daly's creation who is a reformed if illiterate member of the gang.

This theme was probably suggested to Daly by the abduction of Charlie Ross and while it is treated melodramatically, the characters of Matthew, Mabel, and Mary, the girl whom his family wished Arthur to marry, are well drawn. The play is not as original as *Divorce* but it is better constructed. Neither, however, is of the same significance as *Horizon* for in that play we had an original theme and setting, fine construction, natural language and character drawing of indisputable veracity.

The Dark City, produced at the Fifth Avenue Theatre on September 10, 1877, was a melodrama with conventional situations, revolving around the suppression of a will which disinherited an elder daughter in favor of her stepsister. Daly had hoped for great results from the realistic effects of this play, and one of the scenes, in which the villain cuts the rope from which the hero is descending from the roof of Sybil's lodging house, seems to hold fine possibilities as a thrilling episode. But the play failed and it brought Daly's career at the Fifth Avenue Theatre to an end.

It is not easy to draw any helpful distinction between *Pique* and *Divorce* on the one hand and those more definite dramatizations of fiction which followed *Griffith Gaunt*. In November, 1867, at the request of the Worrell sisters, he dramatized *A*

Legend of Norwood, or Village Life in New England, by Henry Ward Beecher. The play was not a success. It is, however, much better reading than the novel, for the action is quicker and the humor, provided by Peter Sawmill, whom Daly changed from a white man to a negro, and the "boy from Hardscrabble" who becomes a drummer boy, seems to be largely original with the playwright. The conversation between these two on the art of war is even yet worth reading and it secured what little success the play achieved. Daly used the language of the novel at times, but he changed the plot considerably in order to bring all the principal characters together on the field of Gettysburg. While many of the characters are conventional there is in the first two Acts a realistic picture of New England life before the war.

The last play Daly wrote for the old New York Theatre, in January, 1868, was his dramatization of *Pickwick Papers*. He cleverly made the most of the apparently hopeless profusion of incident in the novel, introducing in four acts and twelve scenes the most important elements of the comedy. In the first scene the four Pickwickians are introduced at Wardle's House, Tupman is shot by Winkle and Jingle persuades Rachel to elope. Sam Weller comes on in scene two and there is a delightful scene at Mrs. Bardell's home. Acts II and III include the adventure of the lady in yellow curl papers and the trial scene of Bardell *versus* Pickwick.

One of the most striking successes of Daly's early days as a manager at the Fifth Avenue Theatre was his adaptation of Wilkie Collins' *Man and Wife*, first produced September 13, 1870. In this effort Daly succeeded in producing a successful dramatization where Wilkie Collins himself had failed. He altered the order of incidents, placing first the interview between Geoffrey and Julius Delamayn, which gives Geoffrey the alternative of deserting Anne Sylvester or being disinherited by his father, and skillfully compressed the many complicated scenes of *Man and Wife* into five stirring acts. Daly's sure dramatic instinct showed not only in what he put in, but even

19

more clearly perhaps in what he left out. The foot race is omitted and the long interval between the flight of Anne and the conference at Lady Lundie's, in which Anne proves that she is Geoffrey's wife, is bridged over admirably. The scene of the attempted murder is also a good example of compression. Daly proved again that what carries a play is fine characterization, and the part of Anne Sylvester gave Clara Morris her first great opportunity to portray the woman who saves another woman by proving her own marriage to a man she despises. Mrs. Gilbert played the part of Hester Dethridge, the apparently dumb woman, with real distinction. Of the other dramatizations of Wilkie Collins' novels, *No Name* was a failure and *The Woman in White* seems not to have been performed.

Roughing It has been described as a dramatization of Mark Twain's novel but it is not. The first two Acts are an amusing satire on the sentimental romantic play with the scene laid in New York City but with an unmistakable French flavor. When MacDuffie, the stern father, takes the center of the stage and proclaims to Antoinetta, "I am your father—you are my daughter," the heroine looks at him naïvely and replies, "Father, you terrify me!" In the third Act the characters are sent off to Simpson's Bar and a burlesque on the Western life of Bret Harte and Mark Twain follows. We meet the "Amiable Arkansas," the "pale fire-eater, Slade," to say nothing of the chief of the Goshoots who wants to marry Antoinetta, who circumvents him by dancing the tribe into submission. It is all very amusing and seems to have been successful.

It would not be possible, even were it desirable, to compare critically all of Daly's definite adaptations from the French and German, nor is it wise to indulge in hasty generalizations concerning them. Daly varied greatly in the fidelity with which he followed his models, and actual comparison of those extant plays of which the originals are also available, is necessary to reveal his varying methods.

The earliest of the adaptations of French drama that has

survived was his version of Victorien Sardou's *Le Papillon* (1862), played as *Taming a Butterfly* at the Olympic Theatre, February 25, 1864. Among the Daly manuscripts is a printed version of this play, in which the French scene is preserved. It has, however, been altered extensively; the scene has been changed to New York City and it has been given a new title, *Delmonico's, or Larks up the Hudson,* under which it appeared in June, 1871, at the Fifth Avenue Theatre. This is the only case so far as Daly's translations of Sardou are available, in which he transferred the scene to America. Sardou remained his favorite among French playwrights. One of the most interesting of the translations from this skilful constructor of plays was *Hazardous Ground,* produced at Conway's Park Theatre in Brooklyn, March, 1867. It is based upon Sardou's comedy of *Nos Bons Villageois,* which had been performed at the Théâtre du Gymnase in Paris in 1866.[1] The adaptation is quite free. Daly preserved the central situation in which a young visitor from the city makes love to the wife of the baron and mayor of the town and, being discovered in her grounds at night, feigns that he is a thief. The characters are reduced in number and the first Act is practically omitted. The language at times follows the original closely and at other times, especially at the end, is radically changed. The result is a gain in unity and it is significant that these early scenes which Daly omitted were probably written in by Sardou to lengthen the piece and thus avoid the production of another play on the same night, with a consequent loss of receipts to the author.

When Daly leased the Grand Opera House in the fall of 1872, he opened it with a free rendering of Sardou's *Le Roi Carotte* (1872), under the title of *King Carrot.* It was a spectacle, with music by Offenbach, and dealt with the Krokodynes, a people who discarded their monarch in favor of a king from the kitchen garden, with unhappy results. Other adap-

---

[1] An adaptation of *Nos Bons Villageois* by A. W. Young, under the title of *A Dangerous Game,* had been played at Wallack's Theatre, February 4, 1867.

tations of Sardou were *Folline*, from *La Maison Neuve* (1866),[1] in 1874, a satire on the new generation in France who were breaking away from the older standards of family and commercial life, *Odette* in 1882 and *The Golden Widow* in 1889 from *La Marquise*.[2]

Next to Sardou, Alexandre Dumas was Daly's most frequent source of inspiration from the French. An example of his free treatment of French drama was his adaptation of Dumas' *Monsieur Alphonse*, played in Paris in 1873, and produced by Daly at the Fifth Avenue Theatre, April 25, 1874. In this adaptation one notices first, the loss in distinction of style, and second, the addition of characters to suit the members of the Daly Company. In one case at least this addition added to the dramatic effectiveness. Octave, who is known as Monsieur Alphonse, has deceived Madame Raymonde Montaglin some years before her marriage, and on the eve of his own brings their child to her to be brought up. Dumas gives us this information in a conversation between Octave and Raymonde. Daly introduces the plot through two peasant women, probably to provide a part for Mrs. Gilbert, but the change results in bringing the child Adrienne into the presence of Captain Montaglin without any warning to Raymonde and forces her therefore to take Adrienne, with the consequent danger of discovery. Daly provides Octave with a cynical but effective speech at the end which is not in the original, and he omits, probably wisely, certain observations about life and morals in France. Bijou Heron's performance of Adrienne seems to have been a notable one.

The American, adapted from Dumas' *L'Etrangère* in 1876, while it proved no great success on the stage, is very readable and was a comparatively free translation of the original. The

---

[1] *La Maison Neuve* had been adapted in 1867 by L. R. Shewell and Fred Williams, as *The Old Cockade* and played at the Boston Museum. Clyde Fitch adapted it in 1893 as *The Social Swim*.

[2] Neither *Fernande* (1870) nor *The Fast Family* (1874), from *La Famille Benoiton*, both played at the Fifth Avenue Theatre, is an autograph MS. and no claim is made that he had any share in their adaptation.

contrast of two Americans, husband and wife, with French society was the main motive of the play. In his other adaptation from Dumas, father and son, which included *The Royal Youth (The Youth of Louis XIV)* from the elder and *Denise* from the younger, he preserved the French scene.

One of his most important adaptations from the French, *Frou-Frou*, by Henri Meilhac and Ludovic Halévy, had been produced at the Théâtre du Gymnase in Paris in 1869, and on February 15, 1870, Daly placed his adaptation on the stage of the Fifth Avenue Theatre. *Frou-Frou* is a powerful drama of contrasted character. Gilberte Brigard, the apparently frivolous woman, who marries her serious husband at the advice of her sister, Louise, who herself loves him, has been interpreted by many actresses, including Sarah Bernhardt. Agnes Ethel took the part in Daly's production and made a great success of the moving scene in which Gilberte, or Frou-Frou, returns after her flight with de Valreas, to die in her husband's arms. This scene had been shortened by Daly with a gain in effectiveness and in general the changes made in the adaptation seem to be improvements, especially the omission of the last scene of Act IV, in which Baron de Cambri tells Frou-Frou that her husband has wounded her lover in a duel, for this excision concentrates the attention of the audience upon the relations of the husband and wife. The most interesting of Daly's additions are the observations upon the art of acting which he makes through a dramatic coach who is training Frou-Frou for private theatricals. According to M. Pitou's instructions, an actor should not be natural on the stage but must be in keeping with the artificial character of the scene. He tells his pupil that people will be bored if she is entirely natural. It is not clear whether Daly is quite sincere or in part sarcastic in these expressions, but they accord well with that combination of realistic stage-setting, theatrical illusion and heightened character portrayal, which makes him the transition playwright of our stage.

When Daly's adaptations from the French are considered

chronologically, two significant facts appear. He continued to adapt Sardou and Dumas throughout his career, and with one exception preserved the atmosphere of the original. With the twenty or more plays which are founded on the work of other French dramatists, a change came about 1880. Previous to that date, when he adapted *Frou-Frou; Alixe*, almost a literal translation of *La Comtesse de Somerive* by Baroness de Prevois and Théodore Barrière; *The Two Widows*, from Mallefille; *Article 47*, a dramatization of Adolphe Belot's novel of the same name, with a part augmented for Fanny Davenport; *What Should She Do?* from Edmond About's *Germaine; The Princess Royal*, from *L'Officier de Fortune*, or *Vesta*, a tragic play from Parodi's *Rome Vaincue*—he preserved the original European scene. Sometimes he changed the nationality of his characters and not always happily. Professor Brander Matthews called to my attention the fact that in *Serge Fanine*, which Daly adapted in 1883 from Georges Ohnet, he ruined a strong situation. In the original, a Frenchwoman of the middle class, who has successfully conducted a business after her husband's death, finds that her son-in-law, a Polish Count, is a worthless bankrupt and hands him a pistol with which he may relieve the situation by removing his worthless self. When he declines to do so, she shoots him and calmly informs the characters who are attracted by the shot that the Count has committed suicide. Daly turned the French bourgeoise to whom, with her keen sense of commercial honor, such an action would have been possible, into an American woman of society, Mrs. Belyew, to whom the avoidance of scandal was the first consideration. She offers him a chance to escape, which he does not take, and it is really not clear, from the manuscript, whether he is shot by the officers of the law off stage or shoots himself.

Of these adaptations, one of the most attractive was *The Princess Royal*, which is a stirring romantic play with the scene laid in Germany, with good situations and with a slant toward a satire of the absurdities of the romantic drama. It was based on the love story of Baron Trenck and Princess Amalie of Prussia, and the hairbreadth escapes point forward to the moving picture of to-day.

Delmonico's, in 1871, was an early and an exceptional instance among the adaptations from the French in which the scene was changed to New York. But from 1879 when *Love's Young Dream*, a clever one-act comedy, was produced, Daly seems to have decided that with the exception of the plays of Sardou and Dumas, he could be more successful if he changed the atmosphere entirely and made as little of the original setting as possible. On the program of the first performance of *Love's Young Dream* it is stated that the play is by "Joseph Francis," a testimony to the share which Judge Daly took in the writing of the plays and which was in many cases much greater than has been usually supposed.

Whether the growing sense of the importance of American plays being laid in America caused this change in Daly's method of adaptation is a matter of speculation. Certainly it cannot be said that the change resulted in greater drama, although it led to the production of some clever plays.

Love in Harness from Albin Valabrègue's *Bonheur Conjugal*, was produced in November, 1886. This domestic comedy is a study of the married relations of the three daughters of Jeremiah Joblots, and while it was a stage success, it bears evidence of being a hasty production. *Love in Tandem*, a free adaptation of *Vie à Deux* by Henri Bocage and Charles de Courcy, is a better comedy. Its motive, that of a wife who tires of her husband but insists upon selecting her successor before the separation, has obvious possibilities. This play, which was first produced in February, 1892, may have been the source for A. E. Thomas' *Her Husband's Wife*. Two clever one-act plays, *Wet Blanket* (1886) and *A Sudden Shower* (1886), were adaptations of the work of playwrights like Bilhaud, Levy and Bessier.

The production of *The Lottery of Love* in 1888, from *Les Surprises du divorce* by Bisson and Mars, afforded an opportunity to compare the Daly Company with the best of French actors in their interpretation of comedy, for Coquelin was acting in the French original at the same time in New York City. *The Lottery of Love* is a most amusing play, with complications based on a young husband being provided with a mother-in-law not only by his own action but by that of his father-in-law. The dialogue is extremely clever and the play can be read now without regard to its foreign origin.

In his adaptation of German drama, Daly also turned to the work of contemporary playwrights, and he found no one of the rank of Sardou or Dumas. Yet he provided from the comedies of Gustav von Moser, Franz and Paul von Schönthan, Julius Rosen and others, plays which delighted audiences of those days and can still be performed with success. This group of playwrights, who occupy a progressively diminishing place in the histories of German drama, differ somewhat in their material and methods and Daly also differs in the freedom with which he treats their work. In his earlier adaptations of the tragedies of Mosenthal, he had kept the foreign atmosphere, but in the comedies, with one exception, *Countess Gucki*, he transferred the scene to this country.

He began in 1875 with *The Big Bonanza*, the title given to his adaptation of *Ultimo* (1873), in which von Moser had satirized the rage for speculation that came after the Franco-Prussian war. Daly adapted the play to the somewhat similar conditions in New York City in the seventies and produced an amusing comedy, bordering at times on farce. The contrasting types, Jonathan Cadwallader, the banker and broker, and his cousin Professor Cadwallader, who thinks he is able to teach the broker how to speculate, are well established. For the young lover, Bob Ruggles, who in the original had been sent to New York to lose his money, John Drew was brought over from his mother's stock company in Philadelphia to play opposite Fanny Davenport. It was the beginning of a long association between manager and actor. While there are no vital differences in plot, Daly shortened the original from five to four acts and the drama gains in unity and construction. The play ran from February 17 until the end of the season. Von Moser next provided Daly with a rapidly moving farce-comedy in *Harun al Raschid*, which was produced in 1879, as *An Arabian Night, or Haroun al Raschid and his Mother-in-Law*. In this play, dealing with a young New York man who has a liking for adventure, John Drew scored a triumph as Alexander Spinkle. The play is fairly well naturalized.

Von Moser had begun in his *Veilchenfresser* in 1876 the drama which glorified the German officer caste. It was partly the consequence of the Franco-Prussian War, but it was also, consciously or unconsciously, a dramatic expression of the national social and political impulses, then in embryo, which were partially responsible for the War of 1914. Von Moser, born in Spandau in 1825, had been an officer from 1843 to 1856. *Krieg im Frieden*, by von Moser and Franz von Schönthan, was produced in 1880 and Daly's adaptation, *The Passing Regiment*, was first performed November 10, 1881. In adapting *Krieg im Frieden*, Daly followed his original closely. The characters correspond exactly, and the arrangement of scenes is the same. The main difference lies in the transfer of the scene to Narragansett Pier from a provincial town in Germany and the modification of the rigidly regulated relationship of a German cavalry regiment to the more comradely relations of the New York National Guard. That this is done well is due partly to Daly's skill but also perhaps to the universal feminine admiration for the military which is the ostensible motive of the play. Read to-day, *The Passing Regiment* has no foreign flavor. It is an amusing farce comedy, in which Narragansett Pier is pictured before the days of its glory. The officers of the Excelsior Regiment of the National Guard of New York, from the Colonel down, capture the hearts of the girls. The leading characters, played by John Drew and Ada Rehan, are Adjutant Paul Dexter and Telka Essoff, a Russian heiress, niece of Linthicum Winthrop, "the amiable representative of one of the F. F. V.'s of Narragansett Pier." A typical change in the adaptation occurs in the second Act. In the German, Dr. Schaeffer, the regimental surgeon, who is supposed to be a bachelor, tells the General about his marrying Agnes at her father's deathbed. This scene is not badly done and it has the advantage of dramatic contrast in the positions of the two men, one all powerful and the other entirely dependent upon his superior officer's good will. This becomes in *The Passing Regiment* an interview between two men who have been friends at school, one of whom is simply better off than the other and is willing to help his friend to a hospital appointment.

Von Moser wrote a sequel to *Krieg im Frieden* under the title of *Reif von Reiflingen* which became the model of Daly's *Our English Friend*, played in November, 1882. The extent of Daly's alterations may be judged by the fact that in the printed versions there is no relation at all between *The Passing Regiment* [1] and *Our English Friend*. In the first he makes comparatively little change in the structure, though he alters the atmosphere entirely. In *Our English Friend* he makes radical changes in the structure of the play, alters the position of some scenes and rewrites others, but more important, by his substitution of Digby de Rigby, an Englishman, for Reif von Reiflingen, he turned Gustav von Moser's glorification of the German lieutenant into an international compliment. At a time when Anglomania and Anglophobia were both in the air, he represented the English gentleman as a good fellow with high standards of conduct, with unfailing courtesy, and with a certain stupidity, and yet with a promptness in action which made him a picture of at least one kind of Englishman and not a caricature. Daly thought of him as an eccentric character, however, and cast James Lewis for the part, instead of John Drew, who played Paul Spender, the husband and host at a house party at Cutty Corners in Northern New York. Daly

[1] In the MS. version it is indicated that Daly had intended to use Paul Dexter as the husband in *Our English Friend*, but changed his mind.

made *Our English Friend* more strictly social comedy, omitting most of the fourth and some of the second Acts, which represent the lieutenant in his relations as guardian angel to the household of the farmer and the apothecary. He thereby secured unity of scene and he made more prominent the part of Darbie Vaughn, played by Ada Rehan.

Daly next turned to the work of Franz von Schönthan, the collaborator with von Moser in *Krieg im Frieden*, and adapted two clever farces, which to-day are probably the best known of his plays. *Seven-Twenty-Eight, or Casting the Boomerang* is a close adaptation of *Der Schwabenstreich*. The scenes are the same and practically the only changes are in the conversation, especially in the last scene. "Der Schwabenstreich" in the original is the foolishness that everyone must commit at some period of his life. Daly makes this a boomerang which everyone throws at some period of his life and which returns to plague him. Launcelot Bargiss is retired and his wife Hypatia secretly sends his verses to a magazine conducted by Gasleigh, who is playing upon the vanity of unknown authors. Bargiss is delighted. She then has Gasleigh print a volume of the verses of her husband, which he had sent when courting her, but which unfortunately had been copied from Shakespeare, Jonson and others. The daughter of Bargiss, Florence, has had her portrait painted and exhibited No. 7-20-8, and this leads to her pursuit by a lover, Courtney Corliss, who finally wins her.

A Night Off, produced in March, 1885, follows its source, *Der Raub der Sabinerinnen* by Franz and Paul von Schönthan, quite closely in plot but the language is idiomatic in its American quality. The play is concerned with the efforts of Justinian Babbitt, who is a school-teacher in the original, but whom Daly promotes to a college professorship, to have his play produced. Marcus Brutus Snap, the manager of a wandering company, puts on the play with dire results.

The Railroad of Love, adapted by Daly from *Goldfische*, by Franz von Schönthan and Gustav Kadelburg, and per-

A HISTORY OF THE AMERICAN DRAMA

formed in November, 1887, was, according to J. F. Daly, one of the daintiest as well as the strongest comedies that had been played at Daly's Theatre. *Goldfische* was a satire on the "Mitgiftjägerei" or hunters of money, but *The Railroad of Love* contains more characterization than is usual in the type, and Daly carries over from the original the sense of high standards of honor. In one sense he improves upon *Goldfische*, for while he closely follows it in plot and scene, he omits some of the lines which represent that glorification of the army which was found in von Moser's plays. He therefore presents characters who secure our sympathy in their efforts to live up to standards of conduct which are imposed by themselves rather than by the traditions of a caste.

The Great Unknown, an adaptation of *Die Berühmte Frau* by von Schönthan and Kadelburg, played in October, 1889, is an example of free adaptation and was one of the most successful of the comedies. In October, 1890, came *The Last Word*, a modern comedy, received with great approval both at home and abroad, in which Daly transferred the scene to Washington and gave a fairly accurate picture of official life there. The best character was that of the Baroness Vera von Bouraneff, played by Ada Rehan. Daly changed the language of *Das Letzte Wort* radically and an example of his dramatic sense may be found in the climax of the first Act, when Faith Rutherell blocks her father's schemes by announcing her engagement to Boris Bouraneff. The long curtain speech of the original is omitted with distinct advantage.

The final adaptation from von Schönthan is interesting for two reasons. It is practically unique among Daly's adaptations from German comedy, in preserving the original scene. This change in Daly's method was due probably to the fact that the German dramatist wrote the play for Ada Rehan, providing her with a charming part in the Countess Hermance Trachau, known as "the Countess Gucki," from whom the play takes its name. Daly probably felt indisposed to alter the

30

play radically as he had so often done with the other plays and indeed with the inspiration that von Schönthan had had, it was not necessary. *The Countess Gucki* is a clever comedy, with real characters, especially the central one, a capable, impulsive widow who directs two appealing love episodes with genuine skill.

From Julius Rosen, who in real life was Nikolaus Duffek, born in Prague in 1833, Daly adapted a lighter form of comedy verging on farce. Of these the first was *Lemons*, a bright and successful social comedy, played in 1877, having for a plot the complications caused by the guardianship of two uncles over one niece. In *Needles and Pins* he showed how the good but romantic intentions of an heiress confuse the affairs of those she tries to help. In 1886 he transferred the scenes of Rosen's *Halbe Dichter* to New York under the title of *Nancy and Company*. This is a farce in which a joint authorship of a play is complicated by disappearances into adjoining rooms and rapid changes of stage positions with consequent hilarity. Rosen's work is not up to the standard of the von Schönthan plays, but in the hands of the Daly Company it was evidently irresistible. *Nancy and Company* was very much changed in the adaptation, to the advantage of the character drawing.

Among other adaptations from the German, probably the best are *Dollars and Sense*, produced in 1883, and *Love on Crutches*, played first in 1884. *Dollars and Sense* was derived from *Die Sorglosen* (1882) by Adolph L'Arronge. It is an amusing comedy, quite well naturalized, with its scene laid in Washington. It reveals a couple who are spending too much money, in order to satisfy the wife's ambitions, another couple in which the wife rules, and a pair in which the husband is seeking an affinity. *Love on Crutches* was from Heinrich Stopitzer's *Ihre Ideale*, which itself is based in part on Sardou's *Les Pattes de Mouche*, which in its turn glances back to Poe's *Purloined Letter*. The central character, that of the woman who takes upon herself the blame of having written a compromising letter in order to shield a wife from the suspicion of her husband, suffers quite a change in the transit through three languages. It seems to have been the opportunity of Edith Kingdon, who scored a substantial success. Otis Skinner, who played Guy Roverly, the lover, tells how, when Pinero's *Lords and Commons* was failing, Daly put *Love on Crutches* in rehearsal before his adaptation was finished and describes the night rehearsals, "while succeeding acts of the new comedy came from Daly's private office, where, through the midnight hours of the deserted theatre, he worked unwearied." [1] From this and other testimony we may be assured that the adaptations of Augustin Daly were not dashed off hastily.

Toward the end of his career, Daly turned for material to the work of Oscar Blumenthal. *After Business Hours* (1886) is an amusing satire on the craze for money, dress and speculation. *Little Miss Million* (1892), in which the central character is a young widow whose husband's family resent her marriage, had a more serious note than *A Test Case* (1892), which is almost pure farce.

In 1892 he became interested in the new movement in Germany and I found among the manuscripts an adaptation of Sudermann's *Die Ehre*, by Jerome K. Jerome and himself, which, however, seems not to have been played. The scene is laid in England.

Daly's one adaptation from the Spanish was a failure from a popular standpoint, yet was so well received by competent critics and has been the subject of so much conjecture by those who have not had access to the manuscript, that it deserves attention.[2] On December 5, 1874, he produced his version of *Un Drama Nuevo* (1867) by Tamayo y Baus, one of the most significant of contemporaneous Spanish dramatists. As usual, he had the play translated and from the stiff and

[1] *Footlights and Spotlights*, p. 146.
[2] See *A New Drama*, translated by J. D. Fitzgerald and T. H. Guild. The Hispanic Society, New York, 1915, and "Un Drama Nuevo on the American Stage," *Hispania*, VII (1924), 171–176. In the latter the editor establishes by inductive evidence that there are probably two American versions.

literal translation he made a free and vigorous adaptation. *Un Drama Nuevo* has a special interest for us because Shakespeare is a character and it is at his theatre that the drama is partly laid. Yorick, the comedian of the theatre, aspires to play tragedy and when a new play is to be produced he begs Shakespeare to permit him to play the part of Count Octavio, whose wife is unfaithful to him and is the lover of Manfredo, his protegé. While rehearsing the play Yorick accuses his wife of being unfaithful to him and his real wife, Alicia, misunderstands him and by calling out "Mercy" raises his suspicions. Alicia and Edmundo, who is to act the part of Manfredo in the new play, are in love with each other, but not in a guilty fashion. Edmundo, however, decides that they must elope and writes a letter to her fixing the time of their departure for the next day. Walton, the tragedian of the company, who is jealous of Yorick, conceives in revenge the idea of revealing to Yorick the love affair between Alicia and Edmundo. He does this by handing to Yorick at an appropriate time in the play the letter from Edmundo to Alicia. Under the influence of his jealousy Yorick has been acting magnificently and, spurred on by the letter, he surpasses Walton as a tragedian, since he is really acting a natural part. In the original play he falls down after killing Edmundo. Shakespeare explains to the audience the death of Edmundo and also states that Walton has been killed in a duel.

Daly made certain changes in the play, whose principal result was the decreased emphasis laid upon the character of Shakespeare, with a consequently greater stress upon Yorick. At the end of the third Act, Yorick, roused to fury after the duel with Edmundo, tries to stab Alicia. She takes refuge in Shakespeare's arms. Yorick falls. The prompter brings in word that the physician gives hope of Edmundo. Yorick seems to go out of his head, saying, "It is the last call!" and dies after asking his master, Shakespeare, if he is there. Instead of making the final announcement himself, Shakespeare tells the prompter to inform the people of the tragedy and that Walton has thrown himself on his own sword.[1]

Daly's career as a director belongs to theatrical rather than to dramatic history, but at least the outlines must be sketched. In 1884 he took his company to London, opening at Toole's Theatre in *Seven-Twenty-Eight*. The most successful performance was Cibber's *She Would and She Would Not*, Daly's adaptation of the Eighteenth Century comedy being recognized as a fine interpretation. Daly visited London again in 1886, playing *A Night Off* and *Nancy and Company*, and on the 19th of August, 1886, the first English-speaking company in nearly three hundred years was seen on a German stage under his direction. Six plays were given at the Wallner Theatre, in Berlin: *A Night Off*, *Nancy and Company*, *A Woman's Won't*, *Love on Crutches*, *A Country Girl*, and *She Would and She Would Not*.

The reception was at first not enthusiastic, on the part of the German critics, but it gained in warmth with the production of the English comedies and of *Love on Crutches*. The audiences were made up of American and British residents; the Germans simply did not come. The experiment at Paris was not so fortunate, for the conservatism of the French critical mind when dealing with foreign art showed itself definitely.

The third foreign trip began in April, 1888. The most important event was the production in London of *The Taming of the Shrew* on May 29, the first performance of a Shakespearean comedy by an American company in Europe. On August 3, the comedy was produced at Stratford, probably for the first time. Daly, nothing daunted by his earlier experience in France, took *The Taming of the Shrew* to Paris, where it was only mildly praised. But the discriminating British critics recognized the significance of the restoration of the Induction and of the sub-plot of Bianca and her suitors.

The foreign triumph of *The Taming of the Shrew* was re-

---

[1] For an account of Howells' more successful adaptation of the same play see Chapter III.

peated when in 1890 Daly produced at the Lyceum Theatre in London *As You Like It.* Miss Rehan played Rosalind, not as the theatrical tradition pictured her, a restrained princess in disguise, but as Shakespeare drew her. The changes which Daly made in *As You Like It* are typical of his adaptations of Shakespeare's comedies. He cut some of the speeches, as at the entrance of "the clown" in Act I, Scene 2, or restored lines to a character, such as those describing Jaques, originally spoken by the first Lord, but often placed in Jaques' own mouth. He rearranged the order of the scenes, especially in the second and fifth Acts. The changes seem not to be productive of any profound alterations, but to conduce to simpler stage arrangement and unity of place. He preserved all but two of the twenty-five speaking parts.

During Daly's third visit to Paris, in August, 1891, he produced *As You Like It, The School for Scandal, A Night Off, The Taming of the Shrew,* and *The Lottery of Love.* The reception this time in Paris was much more cordial, due partly, no doubt, to the superior quality of the plays produced.

Encouraged by his cordial reception in London, Daly built a theatre there, the corner stone being laid in October, 1891. He also began to adapt for his use Tennyson's pastoral comedy, *The Foresters,* which was produced on March 17, 1892, at Daly's Theatre. Notwithstanding the undramatic qualities of the play, the production was a thing of beauty. *Twelfth Night* was revived in February, 1893, and practically saved the London season for Daly when he took his company to his own playhouse in that city. Daly found that he had to create a public for his theatre and it took his adaptation of Shakespeare to do it. *Twelfth Night* ran for one hundred nights.

Among the later revivals of Shakespeare, which include *Much Ado About Nothing* in 1896 and *The Merchant of Venice* in 1898, *The Tempest* in 1897 remains in my memory, at least, as the most effective. The setting was like fairyland and more important the true poetic quality of the play was brought out.

A HISTORY OF THE AMERICAN DRAMA

The last years of Daly's life were not altogether happy. The public was fickle; new and good plays seemed to him hard to obtain; and from the death of his two boys he never quite recovered. Difficulties with the lessor of his London Theatre made it necessary for him to go abroad in 1899 and on June 7 he died in Paris.

To one who has been privileged to examine the manuscripts of Augustin Daly, the strongest impression is that of his great knowledge of the theatre, and of his selective power. He had scores of foreign plays translated of which he apparently made no use. But by his constant study of Shakespeare, of British comedy and of these continental models, he was making himself master of a technique which resulted in productions that became a standard of theatrical merit in this country at least. That his original work as a playwright belongs to the early portion of his career is to be regretted, but it was perhaps natural that his creative faculty should be checked as his critical knowledge developed. But there is much of Augustin Daly the playwright even in his foreign adaptations,— how much can be appreciated only through a comparison with his originals. When the constant dependence upon foreign inspiration which has been a characteristic of the English drama from the days of Shakespeare and his predecessors is remembered, and when the scrupulous care which Daly exercised in calling attention to his models on the title-pages of his privately printed plays is also noted, the derivative nature of his plays becomes less of moment. Much more apparent is his courageous struggle against great odds to establish the art both of the drama and of the theatre in a period when conditions of post-war days meant a general confusion of ideals, artistic and commercial. How well he succeeded, how much he encouraged other playwrights, like Bronson Howard, how inflexibly he insisted on the dignity of his profession, how he lifted the standard of good taste in this country, a reading of the fascinating biography by his brother and co-worker will reveal.

AUGUSTIN DALY, ARTIST OF THE THEATRE

Among the dramatic species that are associated with Daly's name, the one that showed most persistence dealt with low life in the large city. During the sixties and seventies, playwrights like Charles Foster, the stage manager of the Old Bowery Theatre, produced at least fifteen plays, of which two titles, *New York Burglars, or Wedded by Moonlight,* and *Bertha, the Sewing Machine Girl,* are sufficient to indicate their nature. In October, 1859, the year of the opening of the New Bowery Theatre, we find such anonymous plays as *New York and Brooklyn, or the Poor Sewing Girl,* while *New York in 1860, or a Hit at the Times* has at least an author's name, that of W. Petrie, attached to it. Charles Gayler, who dates back to an earlier period, continued to write melodramas, like *Out of the Streets* which appeared at the New York Theatre in 1868, and he has thirty plays to his credit after 1870. The status of such playwrights was probably similar to that of the Englishman, J. B. Howe, who was engaged by James Lingard, the manager of the New Bowery, as house dramatist at a salary of eight pounds a week and who on his arrival in this country found that "dollars" had been substituted for "pounds" in his contract! Certainly none of the playwrights who devoted their attention to this phase of drama during this period demand our continued attention. Their work has perished and probably justly, for they seem to have made no effort to portray life sincerely.

In his adaptation of fiction, Daly had at least one successful rival. Lester Wallack's *Rosedale,* which was first performed at Wallack's Theatre in 1863, was one of the most popular plays of its time. It is an interesting comedy, verging on melodrama, based upon a novel, *Lady Lee's Widowhood,* by Edward B. Hamley, with one of its most effective scenes, in which the hero, Elliot Grey, escapes from the clutches of Miles McKenna, taken from Bulwer's *What Will He Do With It? Rosedale* held the stage for more than twenty years and was revived in 1913 at the Lyric Theatre in New York. That its popularity was not due entirely to Lester Wallack's own fine performance of Elliot Grey is proved by its success in other hands. It is a pity that Lester Wallack's play upon American life, *Central Park*, produced in 1861, has perished, for it also was a success on the stage and was played as late as 1886.

In the field of social comedy, Augustin Daly was to provide opportunity and probably inspiration for Bronson Howard. *Saratoga* was produced by him in 1870, to be followed by *Moorcroft* and *Wives*. It was he, too, who produced the somewhat abortive attempts of Edgar Fawcett in *Americans Abroad* and *Our Best Society* and of Olive Logan Sykes in *Newport* and *Surf* to establish a vogue of social satire in this country.

His best play, *Horizon*, was a pioneer in the frontier drama and here, too, he provided an opportunity for the work of Mark Twain and Bret Harte.

CHAPTER II

THE significance of the work of Bronson Howard does not
lie, as has so often been stated, in the production of
Saratoga in 1870. That play marked no great advance over
social comedies of an earlier period like W. H. Hurlbert's
Americans in Paris (1858), but it is just because Howard so
well illustrates, in the broadening of his own grasp of dramatic material and the refinement of his own skill, the development of American playwriting during the period of his creative achievement from 1870 to 1906, that his work becomes
of such significance. He represents also the establishment of
the profession of the dramatist in this country. He was not,
of course, our first professional playwright. William Dunlap,
John Howard Payne, Joseph Stevens Jones, Augustin Daly
and others were professionals in the sense that they were not
amateurs, and remembering Shakespeare and Molière, their
association with the theatre as actors or managers does not
prevent the inclusion of the American playwrights in the professional class. Even in a stricter sense, Robert Montgomery
Bird and George Henry Boker had preceded Howard. Both
were eager to devote their lives to the production of plays and
Bird actually did attempt to make a living by this means until
the untoward circumstances of the time drove him into other
fields of writing. But the great difference lies in the fact that
where they had failed Howard succeeded. When he had established the possibility of a playwright in the United States
making a good living by his art, a new era began in the history
of the drama in America.

Bronson Crocker Howard was born in Detroit, Michigan,

A HISTORY OF THE AMERICAN DRAMA

October 7, 1842, the son of Charles Howard, a merchant and afterward Mayor of the city. His family had long been native, his great-grandfather, Seabury Howard, having fought both in the French and Indian War for Great Britain and in the Revolution for his adopted country, falling at the Battle of Monmouth. After Bronson Howard's schooling in Detroit was completed, he prepared for Yale, but owing to an affection of the sight he was prevented from entering college, and returning to Detroit, began his preparation for playwriting in a school from which many dramatists have graduated, that of the newspaper. His first writing seems to have consisted of humorous sketches for the *Detroit Free Press* and it was in Detroit that his first play was produced in 1864. This was *Fantine*, a dramatization of the tragic episode of Cosette, in *Les Misérables*.[1]

Realizing that the first essential to success as a playwright was contact with the theatre, Howard came to New York in 1865 and supported himself, while writing more than one play which never saw the stage, by reading exchanges and doing other work for the *Tribune* and the *Evening Post*. Finally success came with *Saratoga*, which was produced by Augustin Daly at the Fifth Avenue Theatre on December 21, 1870. It ran for one hundred and one nights and was later revived. *Saratoga* is a farce comedy, with clever situations but with no significance of plot and with characters that are types rather than real people. Bob Sackett, a New York man, becomes involved with Effie Remington, Olivia Alston, Lucy Carter and Virginia Vanderpool. As all four women go to Saratoga, where Bob also arrives, many complications ensue, including several abortive duels. Bob Sackett is a likeable fellow and the audience is in sympathy with him in his efforts to triumph over the circumstances. Howard succeeded in being amusing without being vulgar and even the scene in Sackett's parlour, where all the women come at the same time,

[1]Mawson, H. P., "A Brief Biography," in *In Memoriam, Bronson Howard*. N. Y. 1910, p. 51.

40

to save either him or their lovers, avoids the easy possibilities of the indecent. This reticence, which has remained a characteristic of a certain portion of our playwriting, makes all the more unfair such criticism as that leveled at *Saratoga* by the late William Archer in his *English Dramatists of To-day* (1886). In speaking of the feminine characters, he says, "Ordinary modesty, not to say delicacy of feeling, is apparently a thing unknown and undreamt of among them" and then quotes a passage which is certainly vulgar enough but which is not to be found either in the printed copies of *Saratoga* or in the original manuscript. The explanation lies in the fact that *Saratoga* was "adapted" for the English stage by Frank Marshall under the title of *Brighton,* Charles Wyndham appearing in the part of Bob Sackett, which James Lewis had played so successfully at Daly's Theatre; and Archer was solemnly criticizing an American for vulgarity which had been inserted by the British adaptor. Wyndham produced *Brighton* at the Court Theatre in 1874 and it was put on for a long run afterward at the Criterion. Wyndham also produced the play in Germany under the title of *Seine Erste und Einzige Liebe* and Howard witnessed the performance although he was not able to understand his own work. It was probably the first American play performed in translation in Germany.

With all its imperfections, *Saratoga* showed Howard's skill in the handling of situations and the writing of dialogue.[1]

Diamonds, which was a comedy of manners, laid in New York City and in a villa on Staten Island, was written definitely for the company of Augustin Daly, who produced it at the Fifth Avenue Theatre on the opening night of the season, September 3, 1872. While it ran until October 28, it was not considered by Howard as one of his important plays, but it revealed again a skill in the technical handling of situation. *Moorcroft,* produced also by Daly, on October 17, 1874, ran

---

[1] In several places the suggestion has been made that it was based on *Les Eaux* [?], by Scribe. There is certainly no resemblance between the play and Scribe's *Les Eaux du Mont-Dor,* and there is no Gallic flavor about *Saratoga.*

only until November 3. It exists now only in the autograph manuscript. The play begins in 1840 at the Moorcroft mansion near Savannah. Russell Moorcroft, who is in financial difficulties, decides to sell his half brother, Cyril, into slavery. Katherine Mordaunt, a neighbor who loves Cyril, buys him for $15,000, but he elopes with Virginia St. John. After an interval of eighteen years the brothers meet at Newport. Russell's son, John, and Cyril's daughter, Marie, fall in love. Katherine Mordaunt, who has nursed her hatred for Cyril, tells him she owns him and can demand his return as a fugitive slave. A reading of the scene between these two, with its exaggerated expression of emotion, shows clearly how Howard grew in power through experience and failure. The love scenes are not bad and the confident belief of Marie that her father will give her a husband just as he has given her everything else she wanted, is even charming. But the final act, in which Russell calmly tells Cyril that he has really no stain of negro blood and is not his half brother since the will which stated that fact is a forgery, and in which the two men shake hands and pair off their children, is absurd.

Moorcroft is interesting as an illustration of Howard's literary honesty. On the program he states, "As the author of *Moorcroft* I wish to acknowledge my obligation to Colonel John Hay for a strikingly dramatic idea, of which I made use. An admirable short sketch by that gentleman, entitled 'The Foster Brothers,' originally published in *Harper's Magazine*, March, 1859 [September 1869], was brought to my attention about three years ago. In that sketch may be found in outline the relations existing between four of the sixteen characters of the play, namely, Cyril Moorcroft, his half brother Russell and their two children, who fall in love with each other. With the exception of the peculiar relation in which these four characters stand to each other, there is nothing in common between the play and the story referred to. . . . I cheerfully acknowledge the very great obligation under which I am placed."

BRONSON HOWARD
[From the portrait in possession of Mr. Thomas R. Edwards]

BRONSON HOWARD

Brander Matthews is authority for the statement that John Hay would never have suspected his own share in the work if Bronson Howard had not called attention to it.[1] Howard turned the tragedy of *The Foster Brothers* into melodrama. In Hay's story, the scene is the city of Moscow, on the Mississippi River, in Illinois, and the main interest is centered in the love story of Clarence Brydges of New Orleans and Marie Des Ponts, the daughter of a French Creole, who corresponds to Cyril Moorcroft but who is really a negro and an escaped slave and is not connected by any ties, real or supposed, to his master, Victor Brydges. The latter comes to the wedding in ignorance of the facts and is saved from drowning after his steamer has caught fire, by his former slave. After a powerful scene in the open boat between the two men, Des Ponts drowns Brydges in order to save his own daughter from disgrace and dies with his former master at the bottom of the river.

Howard's next play, *The Banker's Daughter*, has a singular interest for students of the drama since the playwright has given an account of its development in his *Autobiography of a Play*, delivered first as a lecture at Harvard University in 1886 and published in the Bronson Howard Memorial Volume in 1910. *The Banker's Daughter* was first produced in 1873 at Chicago as *Lillian's Last Love*. In the original form, Lillian Westbrook has married John Strebelow, a man older than she, partly to save her father from financial ruin and partly because of a quarrel with her lover, Harold Routledge. Five years later, in Paris, Routledge returns and Lillian's love is revived, but she remains true to her husband on account of the passionate devotion she feels for their child. Count de Carojac also loves her and a duel occurs between Routledge and the Count in which Routledge is supposedly killed and at which Lillian reveals to her husband by her outcry that she has never loved him. He takes their child away, and in the final scene, in

---

[1] "An Appreciation," reprinted from the *North American Review* in the Memorial Volume, p. 37.

America, she dies heartbroken, although the child really has been returned to her, too late.

Howard offered the play to A. M. Palmer and it was put on, November 30, 1878, at the Union Square Theatre, and became one of the most appealing plays of the time. The account of the changes made in the meantime is given so admirably by Howard that a paraphrase would be an impertinence, but it can be reproduced, of course, only in part:

A dramatist should deal, so far as possible, with subjects of universal interest, instead of with such as appeal strongly to a part of the public only. I do not mean that he may not appeal to certain classes of people, and depend upon those classes for success; but, just so far as he does this, he limits the possibilities of that success. I have said that the love of offspring in woman has shown itself the strongest of all human passions; and it is the most nearly allied to the boundless love of Deity. But the one absolutely universal passion of the race—which underlies all other passions—on which, indeed, the very existence of the race depends —the very fountain of maternal love itself, is the love of the sexes. The dramatist must remember that his work cannot, like that of the novelist or the poet, pick out the hearts, here and there, that happen to be in sympathy with its subject. He appeals to a thousand hearts at the same moment; he has no choice in the matter, he must do this; and it is only when he deals with the love of the sexes that his work is most interesting to that aggregation of human hearts we call the audience. This very play was successful in Chicago; but, as soon as that part of the public had been exhausted which could weep with pleasure, if I may use the expression, over the tenderness of a mother's love, its success would have been at an end. Furthermore—and here comes in another law of dramatic construction—a play must be, in one way or another, "satisfactory" to the audience. This word has a meaning which varies in different countries, and even in different parts of the same country; but whatever audience you are writing for, your work must be "satisfactory" to it. In England and America, the death of a pure woman on the stage is not "satisfactory," except when the play rises to the dignity of tragedy. The death, in an ordinary play, of a woman who is not pure, as in the case of *Frou-Frou*, is perfectly satisfactory, for the reason that it is inevitable. Human nature always bows gracefully to the inevitable. The

44

BRONSON HOWARD

only griefs in our own lives to which we can never reconcile our-selves are those which might have been averted. The wife who has once taken the step from purity to impurity can never rein-state herself in the world of art on this side of the grave; and so an audience looks with complacent tears on the death of an erring woman. But Lillian had not taken the one fatal step which would have reconciled an audience to her death. She was still pure, and every one left the theatre wishing she had lived. I yielded, there-fore, to the sound logic, based on sound dramatic principle, of my New York manager, Mr. A. M. Palmer, and the piece was altered.

I have called the play, as produced in New York and afterward in London, the "same play" as the one produced in Chicago. . . .

[But] the play which finally takes its place on the stage usually bears very little resemblance to the play which first suggested itself to [the author's] mind. . . . The first duty of a dramatist is to put upon the stage the very best work he can, in the light of whatever advice and assistance may come to him. Fair acknowl-edgment afterward is a matter of mere ordinary personal honesty. It is not a question of dramatic art.

So Lillian is to live, and not to die, in the last act. The first question for us to decide—I say "us"—the New York manager, the literary attaché of the theatre, and myself—the first practical question before us was: As Lillian is to live, which of the two men who love her is to die? There are axioms among the laws of dramatic construction, as in mathematics. One of them is this—three hearts cannot beat as one. The world is not large enough, from an artistic point of view, for three good human hearts to continue to exist, if two of them love the third. If one of the two hearts is a bad one, art assigns it to the hell on earth of disappointed love; but if it is good and tender and gentle, art is merciful to it, and puts it out of its misery by death. Rout-ledge was wounded in a duel. Strebelow was supposed to be lost in the wreck of a steamer. It was easy enough to kill either of them, but which? We argued this question for three weeks. Mere romance was on the side of the young artist. But to have had him live would have robbed the play of all its meaning. Its moral, in the original form, is this: It is a dangerous thing to marry, for any reason, without the safeguard of love, even when the person one marries is worthy of one's love in every possible way. If we had decided in favor of Routledge, the play would have had no moral at all, or rather a very bad one. If a girl marries the wrong man, she need only wait for him to die; and if her lover waits, too, it'll be all right. If, on the other hand, we so reconstruct the whole play that the husband and wife may at last come together with true affection, we shall have the moral: Even if a young girl makes the worst of all mistakes, and accepts the hand of one man when her heart belongs to another, fidelity to the duty of a wife on her side, and a manly, generous confidence on the part of her husband, may, in the end, correct even such a mistake. The dignity of this moral saved John Strebelow's life, and Harold Routledge was killed in the duel with the Count de Carojac.

All that was needed to effect this first change in the play was to instruct the actor who played Routledge to lie still when the curtain fell at the end of the third Act, and to go home afterward. But there are a number of problems under the laws of dramatic construction which we must solve before the play can now be made to reach the hearts of an audience as it did before. Let us see what they are.

The love of Lillian for Harold Routledge cannot now be the one grand passion of her life. It must be the love of a young girl, however, sincere and intense, which yields, afterward, to the stronger and deeper love of a woman for her husband. The next great change, therefore, which the laws of dramatic construction forced upon us was this: Lillian must now control her own passion, and when she meets her lover in the second Act she must not depend for her moral safety on the awakening of a mother's love by the appearance of her child. Her love for Harold is no longer such an all-controlling force as will justify a woman— justify her dramatically, I mean—yielding to it. For her to depend on an outside influence would be to show a weakness of character that would make her uninteresting. Instead, therefore, of receiving her former lover with dangerous pent-up fires, Lillian now feels pity for him. She hardly yet knows her own feelings toward her husband; but his manhood and kindness are gradually forcing their way to her heart. Routledge, in his own passion, forgets himself, and she now repels him. She even threatens to strike the bell, when the Count de Carojac appears, and warns his rival to desist. This is now the end of the second Act, a very different end, you see, from the other version, where the little girl runs in, and, in her innocence, saves the mother from herself.

Here let me tell a curious experience, which illustrates how stubbornly persistent the dramatic laws are, in having their own way. We were all three of us—manager, literary attaché, and author— so pleased with the original ending of the second Act (the picture of the little girl in her mother's arms, and the lover bowing his head in its presence of innocence) that we retained it. The little girl ran on the stage at every rehearsal at the usual place. But no one knew what to do with her. The actress who played the part of Lillian caught her in her arms in various attitudes; but none of them seemed right. The actor who played Routledge tried to drop his head, according to instructions, but he looked uncomfortable, not reverential. The next day we had the little girl run on from another entrance. She stopped in the center of the stage. Lillian stared at her a moment and then exclaimed: "Mr. Howard, what shall I do with this child?" Routledge, who had put his hands in his pockets, called out, "What's the girl doing here, anyway, Howard?" I could only answer, "She used to be all right; I don't know what's the matter with her now." And I remember seeing an anxious look on the face of the child's mother, standing at the side of the stage. She feared there was something wrong about her own little darling who played the part of Natalie. I reassured her on this point; for the fact that I was in error was forcing itself on my mind, in spite of my desire to retain the scene. You will hardly believe that I am speaking literally, when I tell you that it was not until the nineteenth rehearsal that we yielded to the inevitable and decided not to have the child come on at all at that point. The truth was this: now that Lillian saved herself in her own strength, the child had no dramatic function to fulfill. So strongly did we all feel the force of a dramatic law which we could not, and would not, see. Our own natural human instinct—the instinct which the humblest member of an audience feels, without knowing anything of dramatic law—got the better of three men, trained in dramatic work, only by sheer force, and against our own determined opposition.

The third step, in the changes forced upon us by the laws of dramatic construction, was a very great one; and it was made necessary by the fact, just mentioned, that the child, Natalie, had no dramatic function to fulfill in the protection of her mother's virtue. In other words, there is no point in the play now where sexual love is, or can be, replaced by maternal love, as the controlling passion of the play. Consequently, the last two Acts in their entirety, so far as the serious parts are concerned, disappear, one new scene and a new act taking their place. The sad mother, playing with a little shoe or toy, passes out of our view. The dying woman, kissing the hand of the man she has wronged; the husband, awe-stricken in the presence of a mother's love; the child clasped in Lillian's arms; her last look on earth, a smile, and her last breath, the final expression of maternal tenderness—these scenes belong only to the original version of the play, as it lies in its author's desk. With an author's sensitive interest in his own work, I wasted many hours in trying to save these scenes. But I was working directly against the laws of dramatic truth, and I gave up the impossible task.

The fourth great change—forced on us, as the others were— concerns the character of John Strebelow. As he is now to become the object of a wife's mature affection, he must not merely be a noble and generous man; he must be something worthy of the love which is to be bestowed on him. He must command a woman's love. When, therefore, he hears his wife, kneeling over her wounded lover, use words which tell him of their former relations, he does not what most of us would do, but what an occasional hero among us would do. Of course, the words of Lillian cannot be such as to close the gates to all hopes of love, as they were before. She still utters a wild cry, but her words merely show the awakened tenderness and pity of a woman for a man she had once loved. They are uttered, however, in the presence of others, and they compromise her husband's honor. At that moment he takes her gently in his arms and becomes her protector, warning the French *roué* and duelist that he will call him to account for the insults which the arm of the dead man had failed to avenge. He afterwards does this, killing the count—not in the action of the play; this is only told. John Strebelow thus becomes the hero of the play, and it is only necessary to follow the workings of Lillian's heart and his a little further, until they come together at last, loving each other truly, the early love of the wife for another man being only a sad memory in her mind. There is a tender scene of explanation and a parting, until Lillian's heart shall recall her husband. This scene, in my opinion, is one of the most beautiful scenes ever written for the stage. At the risk of breaking the tenth commandment myself, I do not hesitate to say, I wish I had written it. As I did not, however, I can express the hope that the name of Mr. A. R. Cazauran, who did write it, will never be forgotten in connection with this play as long as the play itself may be remembered. I wrote the scene myself first; but when he wrote it according to his own ideas, it was so much more beautiful than my own that I would have broken a law of dramatic art if I had not accepted it. I should not have been giving the public the best play I could, under the circumstances. Imbued as my own mind

Lilian ~~Her Love~~

A Drama in Five Acts,
By
Bronson Howard.

Characters

<u>Archibald Strebelow</u> — An American Gentleman

<u>Le Comte de Carojac</u> — A French Gentleman

<u>Owen Routledge</u> — Successful in Art; — unfortunate in Love.

<u>Lawrence Westbrook</u> — A victim of prosperity.

G. Washington Phipps. N.Y. U.S.A.

<u>Babbage</u>; Mr. Westbrook's senior partner.

<u>Montvillars</u>; or Nothing, although critical.

<u>Brown</u> — Millionaire. Winter mistakes itself for Summer.

M. le Docteur Beaumarchais; — ~~strictly impartial to both parties.~~

Dr. Mildwinter — a family physician.

Thomas

<u>Lilian Westbrook</u>

<u>Florence St Vincent</u> — Brown. Very Aristocratic in taste. accepts Widowhood with Christian cheerfulness.

<u>Aunt Fanny</u> — Gentle in nature and subdued by Sorrow.

—rette. ~~A series of the Bell—~~

—lie — A.B.C. ~~X.Y.Z.~~

was, with all the original motives of the piece, it would have been impossible for me to have made changes within a few weeks without the assistance Mr. Cazauran could give me; this assistance was invaluable to me in all parts of the revised piece. In the fifth Act the husband and wife come together again, the little child acting as the immediate cause of their reconciliation; the real cause lies in their own true hearts.

The scene for which Howard thanks Cazauran probably owed its original inspiration to the interview between Rodolphe and Armande in Boucicault's *Led Astray*, but the tone was altered. *The Banker's Daughter*, revised by Howard with the aid of James Albery, was played with success in London as *The Old Love and the New*. It was played in stock as late as 1914 in this country.

Howard's careful workmanship is revealed also in a comparison of his *Baron Rudolph* with its earlier form, *Only A Tramp*, which was copyrighted in 1877 and belongs distinctly to his earlier manner. Written originally for Mr. and Mrs. W. J. Florence but not played by them, it became the property of Mr. and Mrs. George S. Knight, who seem to have performed it first at Hull, England, August 1, 1881. It was a moderate success in this country for a few seasons, but when revived at the Fourteenth Street Theatre in 1887 after some revision by David Belasco, it met with failure,[1] attributed by Belasco to Knight's acting as the tramp.

Only a Tramp is a melodrama, in which we are invited to sympathize with a weak but amiable man, Tom Goddfroy, who has squandered his fortune and who is unable to support his wife and child, both in danger of starvation through the strike of the employees of Whitworth Lawrence, the president of an iron manufacturing concern. Rhoda Goddfroy leaves Tom, drunken and hopeless, and divorces him, to marry Lawrence. Years later Tom returns, a tramp, debonair if still

[1] For detailed reports, with obvious contradictions, see Brown II, 362, 622, and 496, and Winter, *Life of Belasco*, I, 321-6. Both state that it was purchased by Knight from Howard in 1886, yet Knight played in *Baron Rudolph* at the Grand Opera House in New York, September 12, 1881, and at the Windsor Theatre on October 17.

willing to drink, joins apparently in a robbery of Lawrence's home in order to protect his daughter, and kills Lawrence in the consequent struggle. He is convicted of murder and sentenced to be hanged, then pardoned by the governor, who as one of the characters has provided the comedy element, which centers around a young widow. In the revised form,[1] Howard changed his hero from an American to a German baron, who passes through the same decline and misery, but there is no murder or trial scene, and Lawrence commits suicide on account of his own defalcations. Instead of being tried for his life, Baron Rudolph inherits a large estate and returns from Europe to bless his daughter's love affair, which is stressed much more than in *Only a Tramp*. *Baron Rudolph* is less sentimental, the comedy is much more sure in tone, and both characters and situations are more natural in their conception and arrangement. Howard recognized apparently that his forte lay not in melodrama but in comedy.

Hurricanes, a three-act farce comedy, played first in Chicago in 1878, has just been published. It was laid in New Rochelle, near New York, and it belonged to the type of *Saratoga*. When it was brought to the Park Theatre, New York, on August 31, Howard wrote as a curtain raiser a charming one-act play, *Old Love Letters*, in which Agnes Booth and Joseph Whiting scored a distinct success. Edward Warburton, a diplomat of forty, calls upon Florence Brownlee, a widow of thirty-two, to return a packet of love letters which she had written him during their engagement, broken after a quarrel thirteen years before. The revival of old memories brings about a renewal of their earlier love. Howard showed his skill in the way he used the rainy day outside to sharpen the contrast with the cozy interior of Mrs. Brownlee's apartment, in which the reunited pair begin to feel the unquenched fire of their early passion. His deftness is apparent also in the natural way in which Mrs. Brownlee sends her maid for

---

[1] First revision, autograph MS. in possession of Samuel French. A later revision is indicated in an autograph manuscript memorandum dated March 2, 1882.

BRONSON HOWARD

Warburton's letters while she really has them in her bosom at the time. Howard knew well one secret of the skillful playwright—to take the audience into his confidence and by imparting to them information which has been withheld from some of the characters, identify them with the progress of the play.

In *Wives*, produced at Daly's Theatre in October, 1879, Howard cleverly combined Molière's *L'Ecole des maris* and *L'Ecole des femmes* into a bright comedy whose success is described entertainingly by one of the cast.[1] Howard took from *L'Ecole des maris* the story of two brothers, Sganarelle, who has brought up his ward, Isabelle, in the strictest manner, intending her to be his wife, while his brother, Ariste, has allowed her sister, Léonor, many liberties. Isabelle in consequence deceives Sganarelle and marries Valère, while Léonor is content to wed the man who trusted her. With this plot he interwove the story of *L'Ecole des femmes*, in which Agnes, who is being reared by Arnolphe as an innocent fool, in order that she may be a perfect wife, deceives him completely by carrying on an affair with Horace. Howard saw clearly what indeed the criticism of Molière's own day had indicated, that the plot of *L'Ecole des femmes* is too slight for an entire play. In his hands it amplifies admirably the earlier comedy and by making the leading characters friends the combination was easily achieved. Howard treated his material freely. The verse of Molière is translated into effective prose and the speeches are cut judiciously to make room for the added situations and dialogue. The most important change was the substitution for Valère of Captain Fièremonté, who is made a bit stupid in his love-making in order to heighten the comic effect and to strengthen the character of his valet, Dorival, who takes the place of Ergaste in the original. In the third Act, Horace informs the group of male characters of his intention to carry off Agnes that night. Arnolphe departs to prevent it but the remainder agree to help Horace, Ariste pledg

[1] *Diary of a Daly Débutante*, pp. 38–45 and 49–54.

51

ing himself to obtain an order from Mazarin to transfer the person of Agnes to the King's protection. The scene in which this is later accomplished by the King's troops under Captain Fièremonté, notwithstanding the arrest of Horace by the city guard, forms the striking climax of the fourth Act and effectively welds the two plots together through the introduction of material of Howard's own creation. The incident in which the innocent Agnes, having been directed by Arnolphe to throw a stone at her lover, wraps a love note around it, is only described by Molière but is brought on the stage in an amusing scene in *Wives*. Indeed, so effective did it prove that an addition in the prompt copy indicates that Agnes, in her anxiety to carry out her guardian's instructions completely, returns to her window and precipitates her flower pot, intended for the lover, on Arnolphe's own devoted head. It is worth noting that this addition, which is farcical, is not in Howard's own handwriting.

Fun in a Green Room, a farce comedy with music, dealing with a broken-down tragic actor, was first produced as *Faun-of-the-Glenn* in 1882 and was fairly successful.

Up to this time, Howard had been ornamenting clever situations by amusing dialogue and in one play, *The Banker's Daughter*, had drawn two human beings whose happiness was frustrated for a time by the operation of human weakness. In *Young Mrs. Winthrop* he placed on the stage for the first time in America a group of characters whose actions are determined by the power of social laws and the interruption of social distractions without making the prevailing note one of satire. There had been native gentlemen and gentlewomen on our stage before this, as early, in fact, as our first comedy, *The Contrast*, but that play was written to satirize our affectation of foreign customs, and so was *Fashion* in 1845. *Young Mrs. Winthrop* is shot through with a consciousness of social values, but there is no effort made to establish the security of the positions of the characters; it is taken for granted. Douglas Winthrop and his wife Constance are drifting apart. He is immersed in business and she in social affairs. On the night of their little daughter's birthday he asks her not to go to a ball at the house of a Mrs. Warrington of whose standards he does not approve. She has decided to stay at home, when Mrs. Dick Chetwyn, who represents concretely the power of rumor in shaping our destinies, comes to take her to the ball and casually mentions the fact that Douglas has been seen calling at the home of Mrs. Dunbar, one of the set who frequent Mrs. Warrington's house. He has gone there on business but the circumstances lend color to his wife's suspicion of his fidelity. She goes to the ball and while both of them are away the child is taken ill and Constance comes home too late to see her alive. Husband and wife separate but are reunited through the efforts of a fatherly old lawyer, who makes a rather sentimental appeal to them in the last Act. Howard relieved the tension of his main situation by clever comedy, expressed chiefly by Mrs. Chetwyn, who confuses her husbands, past, present and to come, in an amusing manner. But after all, it is the real significance of the main theme, the growing complication of social and professional life in America, which interferes in the happiness of a man and a woman who really love each other, that carried the play to success. It was first performed at the Madison Square Theatre, October 9, 1882, and after its run there was played for years in stock.

Another indication that Howard was broadening in the selection and treatment of his material lies in the fact that while his earlier plays had been "adapted" for the British stage and he had himself altered *Hurricanes*, under the title of *Truth*, before its presentation in London, *Young Mrs. Winthrop* was played there without any modification. Farcical treatment, unless it be strongly marked burlesque, like our earlier Yankee plays, is often unintelligible to a foreign audience, but the gentleman and gentlewoman of one race appeal immediately to those of another and Douglas and Constance Winthrop needed no interpretation to British audiences.

A HISTORY OF THE AMERICAN DRAMA

It was perhaps Howard's recognition of this development which prompted him to write his first international contrast, *One of Our Girls*, which ran for two hundred nights, beginning November 10, 1885, at the Lyceum Theatre. The scene is laid in Paris and its suburbs and against the background of the Fonblanque family, who are "mentioned in Froissart," and who are arranging a marriage between their daughter Julie and the Comte de Crebillon, a roué and an accomplished duelist, Howard sets the figure of Kate Shipley, the daughter of an American millionaire, whose frank and self-respecting nature brushes aside the French standards which have wrecked her cousin's life and under which a marriage has been planned between her and the Duc de Fouché-Fonblanque. Captain John Gregory, of the British army, wins Kate and becomes her protector in the complications that follow Julie's flight to her lover, Henri Saint-Hilaire. In this climax of the play, at Henri's rooms, where Kate has followed Julie to prevent her eloping with her cousin, the essential conservatism of the American girl reveals itself. Of course, the model for this scene lay in a similar situation in Sardou's *Les Pattes de Mouche* (1860) in which Suzanne tells Vanhove that she is concerned in an affair with Prosper in order that she may save Clarisse, who has taken refuge in Prosper's room. But a comparison of the scenes will show how well Howard adapted the situation to the character of Kate, just as still later Wilde used it in a British setting in *Lady Windermere's Fan*. Helen Dauvray made an appealing Kate and the lines undoubtedly presented her with many opportunities. But it is capacity rather than charm which is the most definite impression and that innate refinement of imagination which has carried so many of her compatriots through much more trying situations on the Continent. The French characters are frankly conventional stage types, but Howard has represented quite accurately their utter inability to comprehend the essential decency of the relations of American young men and women, and Kate Shipley is like a breath of fresh air in a hothouse. She is much more real than Daisy Miller, in whom Henry James had confused two different types of American girl, and in the Englishman, Captain John Gregory, Howard created a character in which E. H. Sothern made a distinct hit.

The uncertainties of the theatre were strikingly illustrated in the failure of Howard's next play, *Met by Chance*, although Miss Dauvray and Mr. Sothern were again the leading members of the cast. It was a social comedy with an international contrast laid partly in the Adirondacks. According to Daniel Frohman, the difficulty lay in the fact that the subsidiary characters usurped interest to the exclusion of the principal motive. This failure, however, was atoned for by the success of *The Henrietta*, which began its career at the Union Square Theatre on September 26, 1887. It was written for Stuart Robson and William H. Crane and in their hands it achieved one of the greatest popular triumphs of its day. In sixty-eight weeks it drew the sum of $497,852, an object lesson to the managers as to what could be accomplished by the union of a skillful playwright and capable actors, in a play dealing with native conditions. It is a study of a strong, grasping, yet singularly human capitalist, Nicholas Vanalstyne, who is opposed in his domination of Wall Street by his son, Nicholas, Junior, who has ambitions of his own. The younger son, "Bertie, the lamb," played by Robson, is looked upon by his father as a fool. He is a satire on the club man of the period and yet he has won the love of Agnes Lockwood, the sister of Rose, the wife of Nicholas, Junior, and in his quiet but complete contempt for the feverish life which his father and brother live he wins the sympathy of the audience from the start. In the climax of the second Act, a packet of letters written by Nicholas, Junior, to a woman he has betrayed and abandoned, is about to fall into Rose's hands, when Bertie quietly puts them in the fire and assumes the blame in order to save Rose from knowing of her husband's guilt.

The most vivid scene on the stage was that in the broker's

office. Vanalstyne, Senior, is absent and his son attempts to wrest the control of the market from him, even robbing the safe of the securities upon which his father is depending. When the "Old Bull" returns and finds that his fortune is swept away he meets the event with courage, but on learning who it is that has ruined him he attacks his son and then leaves brokenhearted. Bertie arrives just about this time and, with a happy chance that comes as a turn to melodrama, saves the day with the five hundred thousand dollars which his father had given him as his share of the huge fortune he was expecting to leave in its entirety to his elder son. Nicholas, Junior, dies of heart failure while the inexorable stock ticker grinds out its monotonous message as the curtain falls. Bertie wins Agnes in the end, of course, and continues his successful operations on the stock exchange by buying and selling on the toss of a coin. This last is not by any means the only farcical touch in the play. Lady Mary, Nicholas' daughter, and her husband, Lord Arthur Trelawney, while amusing are burlesque, and when the play is read in cold type absurdities appear which pass unnoticed in the rapid action and clever dialogue of the performance.

Howard acknowledged, with his usual scrupulous care, that for one episode in the play, he was indebted to a chapter in *Vanity Fair*.[1] He probably referred to the self sacrifice of Dr. Parke Wainwright, who has loved Rose silently and has concealed his knowledge of her husband's relations with the other woman. Even after his death, Wainwright allows her to preserve her illusions, but Mrs. Cornelia Opdyke, a widow whom Nicholas, Senior, is pursuing, finally tells Rose the true state of affairs. The long service of Major Dobbin to Amelia in *Vanity Fair* and the way in which Becky Sharp finally reveals George Osborne's perfidy, may have suggested this portion of the plot of *The Henrietta*, but the theme is treated so differently that Howard might safely have left the debt unacknowledged. Bertie's placing of the letters in the fire is indeed much

---

[1] Matthews, Brander. "An Appreciation." *In Memoriam*, p. 37.

more definitely reminiscent of Henry Esmond's sacrifice of his birthright to save Lady Castlewood pain.

The Henrietta is definitely a satire upon the rush and the heartlessness of financial and social life, and being a satire it does not rise to the significance of *Young Mrs. Winthrop* or *Shenandoah,* yet it has a heartiness of humor, a rapidity of action and a prodigality of interesting situations and characters which put many a more sophisticated play to shame. It was played for years by Robson to whom it went after the separation of the partners in 1889, and in 1913 it was revised by Winchell Smith and Victor Mapes, and William H. Crane resumed his role of Nicholas Vanalstyne. The changes, which included the turning of Vanalstyne's son into his son-in-law and the omission of Lady Mary and her husband, seemed to mark no improvement on the original. But to at least one auditor the play still compared favorably with its modern rivals. It shines still more in comparison with *Knave and Queen,* which Howard wrote in collaboration with Sir Charles Young about 1887 but which was never played. It is a melodrama, laid in the English countryside, with a conventional plot and little characterization.

It may have been the success of William Gillette's *Held by the Enemy* or it may have been Howard's recognition of the essentially native quality of his art which prompted him to take a comedy of his early days, produced at Macauley's Theatre in Louisville about twenty years before and laid during the Civil War, and build upon it the most successful play of his career. Brander Matthews has called attention to a characteristic action of Howard in his early days of struggle in New York. He took *Drum-taps* to Lester Wallack but that manager was distrustful of a play on an American theme, and inquired of Howard whether he could not lay the scene in the Crimea. But Howard declined to ruin the play and waited for the right occasion. It came in 1888 when *Shenandoah* was produced at the Boston Museum by Montgomery Field.

At first the play was received with little favor,[1] either by the critics or by Field himself, and it was withdrawn. But a young producer who had been among the New York managers who had witnessed the Boston production had faith in the play and Charles Frohman produced it, after certain changes had been made, on September 9, 1889, at the Star Theatre in New York. The ensuing success established Charles Frohman and brought fortune to Bronson Howard. Nor was the success due fundamentally to the fine cast, which included Wilton Lackaye as General Haverill, Henry Miller as Colonel Kerchival West, Viola Allen as Gertrude Ellingham and Effie Shannon as Jenny Buckthorn. After its first long season, it went on tour and has been played by many different companies, and it could be produced to-day with little revision. For while it has no one outstanding character of the vigor of Nicholas Vanalstyne, the main motives, those of love, of patriotism and of self-preservation, are the most universal in their appeal and lift the play to a dignity of sincerity to which no satire can reach. All the leading characters are individualized with Howard's constantly growing skill, and the balance of sympathy between the North and the South is artfully kept without in any way weakening the appeal of patriotism to a generation long enough removed from the Civil War to view it with interest as a theme for artistic treatment.

From the moment when the play opens in Charleston, on the night of the firing on Fort Sumter, the note of conflict is struck. The two friends, Kerchival West and Robert Ellingham, make concrete at once the different points of view of the North and the South. When Ellingham says, "Every loyal son of Virginia will follow her flag. It is our religion," West replies, "My state is New York. If New York should go against the old flag, New York might go to the devil. That is my religion." But Howard never for a moment loses sight

---

[1] H. P. Mawson. *Bronson Howard*, p. 56. But see enthusiastic letter from Boston by Henry Whitby, *Theatre*, IV (1888), pp. 465–7. "*Shenandoah* has captured the town."

of the personal relations of his characters in the discussion of points of view. Kerchival West and Gertrude Ellingham are separated by the fortunes of war, but at the end of each act the action centers upon their love story. In fact Howard car-- ries four love stories through *Shenandoah*, three of them closely intertwined. The love of General Haverill for his young wife and his suspicion of her relations with Kerchival are woven skillfully into the second Act, in the valley of the Shenandoah, with the war drawing nearer every instant. The natural way in which the letter from Mrs. Haverill and her portrait come into West's possession through the capture of the spy who has in turn taken the portrait from the son of General Haverill, the finding of them on Colonel West when he lies wounded, and the proper transfer of the apparently incriminating evidence to his commanding officer, pass on the stage as the art that conceals the art. But in a closer study of the play they reveal the deftness with which Howard makes use of the functions of war to advance the plot. He understood too that when Ger- trude Ellingham is brought face to face with the inevitable choice between her lover and her country she will choose the former and it was a sure dramatic instinct which made How- ard build the climax of his play on the scene in which she cheers on her wounded lover to fight for his cause and urges on her own horse as he dashes by with Sheridan upon him. For deeper than patriotism and deeper than loyalty is the in- stinct to which she is responding, the instinct that keeps the race alive.

But it was not only the stirring quality of *Shenandoah* which carried it into success. It is, to use Howard's own phrase, employed in his analysis of *The Banker's Daughter*, a "satisfactory" play. The audience is keenly interested in the central motive, the love of Kerchival and Gertrude, and the author never lets them doubt for a moment the importance of that motive. But with a prodigality which has before been mentioned, he brings in a touching scene of tragedy in which General Haverill pays mutely the last tribute to his dead son, who goes unrecognized and unforgiven to his grave, and he created that scene of beauty upon which the curtain rises in the third Act, in which Jenny Buckthorn, in her suit of army blue, sounded the trumpet signal to her father's battalion. It is many years since I saw that curtain rise but the scene still lives in my memory with a charm that defies both analysis and time.

Howard never wrote hastily. Augustus Thomas tells us that in his workshop in New Rochelle he would be satisfied if a day's labor produced a dozen lines with which he could be satisfied. His next play, *Aristocracy*, was first performed at Palmer's Theatre, November 14, 1892. It is a deliberate contrast of the rich American from California, the New York family of long-established position and the European patrician. It is evident that Howard's sympathy lies with the first group. He created in Jefferson Stockton a Western capitalist who has real power and self-respect, who has already seen the East and Europe and is under no illusions concerning them. His young wife, Diana, is socially ambitious and he explains to her carefully that the way to conquer New York is *via* London. So he rents a London house, including its titled owner, and everything proceeds according to schedule. His daughter, Virginia, has been engaged to Stuyvesant Laurence of New York but the latter's father has crossed the continent to explain to Stockton the undesirability of the alliance from the point of view of New York, so the engagement is left in abeyance. This conversation is absurd and the entire Laurence family are simply caricatures. We see the Stocktons next in London and when Howard begins to develop the personal relations of his characters he is on surer ground. Mrs. Laurence has succeeded in separating Stuyvesant and Virginia and it is not unnatural that upon the day when she believes her faithless lover is to be married to another girl, Virginia should accept out of pique the urgent suit of the Prince Emil von Haldenwald, of Vienna. The Prince is a caricature also but at least he is more real than the Laurences or than the other examples of European nobility who appear in the drama. He is in pursuit of Diana Stockton and the most natural scene in the play is the one in which the power of his fascination for her, even against her own will, brings about a deadly struggle between Stockton and his son-in-law. The play ends in a weak fashion with the Stocktons established in New York City and with the news of the Prince's death in a duel with his friend the Duc de Vigny-Volante, who has been converted to a startling state of virtuous indignation at his friend's vices by the chastening influence of Virginia. *Aristocracy* was moderately popular but has not held the stage, although it was seen recently in the moving pictures, where it was turned into a sordid and suggestive picture of depravity which would have made its author turn in his grave. It is certainly one of the weakest of his plays.

Peter Stuyvesant, the last of Bronson Howard's plays to be produced, was written in collaboration with Brander Matthews, who contributed the main plot, and in particular the central character, that of the choleric old governor of New Amsterdam. This character was created for William H. Crane and portrayed the governor as a lovable but tyrannical matchmaker, who fails in his attempt at ordering the lives of two young couples, who insist upon arranging them to suit themselves. This love interest had as a background the attempt of the English to capture New Amsterdam with the help of Connecticut. The sense of the period was well established and the play was distinctly better as a piece of literature than *Aristocracy*. It had only a moderate appeal, however, and was withdrawn four weeks after its production at Wallack's Theatre, October 2, 1899.

Howard wrote but one more play, *Kate*, which has not been performed, probably because the nice adjustment of parts, which would have been rendered necessary by the even distribution of interest among the characters, called for a stock company which was not then available. It was published in 1906 in a form midway between the drama and the novel, so that we do not have it as it was originally written for the stage. It is a comedy of social life in England, with the last scene in New York. While it is an international contrast, and the heroine, Kate Hardenbeck, who is the daughter of a rich American, becomes engaged to be married to Earl Catherst without love on either side, the play is not primarily a satire and the tone is more sincere and the treatment firmer than in *Aristocracy*. Lord John Vernor, who has become a rector to keep the living in the family, his *fiancée*, the saintly Dorothea Catherst, and the other English characters are much better drawn than Howard's French or Viennese noblemen; and there are strong scenes in the play such as that between Lord John and Kate in the second Act, in which their growing interest in each other is shown and in which he tells her that he despises her for marrying a man whom she does not love.

From *Saratoga* in 1870 to *Kate* in 1906 Bronson Howard's progress was steady if not entirely constant. The strongly marked caricatures in black and white which disport themselves through the conventional situations in the earlier plays bear little resemblance to the subtler studies of a more settled social order in which the characters take their rightful places as the dominating forces of the drama. Just as Augustin Daly was a transitional force in the theatre of his time so Howard, watching and profiting by the lessons which the deepening art of the drama of his day both at home and abroad could teach him, himself led that transition with a liberal conservatism which was never too old to learn. It was in the expression of his art rather than in the choice of his material that his development came, once the farce of *Saratoga* and the melodrama of *Moorcroft* had been put aside. One must not be confused by the fact that the summit of his success as a dramatist was reached with *The Henrietta*, a play of business and *Shenandoah*, a war play. From first to last, Howard was interested in men and women moving in social relations and he never let his background of finance or war obscure the personal relations of his characters. On the contrary he made that background bring out in sharper relief the great power of social laws and conventions in shaping the lives of human beings. His realism shows perhaps at its best in the restraint which the pursuit or the possession of good form imposes upon a character. It is the inarticulate quality of Bertie Vanalstyne's self-sacrifice which made the instant appeal to an audience and it is the chivalry rather than the personal courage of Kerchival West that made him a hero. Bronson Howard left to others the depiction of the proletariat; he was concerned with the gentleman and gentlewoman. When he wrote of a Western type, he did not select a bad man or a card sharp, and his portrait of Jefferson Stockton is much more true to life than many a more famous character in our fiction or drama. It is the reticence of good breeding which makes even the Prince von Haldenwald almost endurable as a stage creation and this ability of Howard to draw a patrician, by birth or instinct, makes all the more surprising his failure with the Laurence family in *Aristocracy*. That it was the playwright rather than the social observer who erred is proved sufficiently by the existence of *Young Mrs. Winthrop* and *Kate*.

It was not only as an artist but also as a leader of his craft that Bronson Howard assisted in the establishment of the profession of playwriting in the United States. In 1891 he founded the American Dramatists Club with the purpose of giving a sense of solidarity to those who were writing for the stage. Eventually they were to take steps for their professional advancement and protection. He made the initial occasion a luncheon to Charles Gayler, a now forgotten playwright who antedated the Civil War in his efforts in melodrama, and it is interesting to note that among the thirty-five guests, only seven, Clyde Fitch, David Belasco, Franklin Fyles, Paul M. Potter, Henry C. de Mille, Maurice Barrymore, and Sydney Rosenfeld, are remembered to-day. As president of the club, which later became the Society of American Dramatists and Composers, Howard took the leading part in amending the copyright laws to make the piracy of a play a misdemeanor and punish, for the first time, the theft of a playwright's labor by imprisonment.[1] During the close of his career he was fully recognized as the representative dramatist of his time. He met the gradual approach of death through an affection of the heart with the dignity that was his strongest personal characteristic, and during his inactive later years he encouraged and sustained the efforts of younger writers with unfailing generosity. He died on August 4, 1908, at Avon-by-the-Sea, New Jersey, bequeathing his dramatic library to the society he had founded.

Howard, of course, was not alone in his treatment of social contrasts upon the stage. One of the most successful international contrasts of social types came from Howard's collaborator in *Peter Stuyvesant*. Brander Matthews, assisted by George H. Jessop, wrote *A Gold Mine* for John T. Raymond, who produced it in Cincinnati in 1887. Raymond's death did not prevent its further performance, for the part created for him, Silas K. Woolcott, of Grass Valley, California, was afterward played with great effect by Nat C. Goodwin. Woolcott, who has a gold mine to sell, is contrasted with a group of British characters at Sir Everard Foxwood's house at Kew. His sacrifice of his mine to save young George Foxwood is made without heroics, and his wooing of the Honorable Mrs. Meredith is as convincing as it is brief. Sir Everard is the combination of snob and shrewd business man not unknown in the British gentry, and the young Irish barrister, contributed by Jessop, himself an Irishman, is real. The acting of Goodwin when he realized his mine was gone and he must begin the world again, justified his claim to be more than a comedian.[2] *On Probation* (1890), also the joint product of Matthews and Jessop, is a cosmopolitan comedy in which the central character, Jonathan Silsbee, played by William H. Crane, is traveling through Europe with his sister, his niece and her governess, Mary Marlowe, to whom he is secretly engaged. Due to his philan-

[1] *In Memoriam, Bronson Howard*, p. 66
[2] See review of play, *Theatre Magazine*, V, 245.

dering, Mary has placed him on probation, and he has lapses with Lady Frank Brock and Señora Oliveria y Duarez, which are amusing and are deftly woven into a plot that carries the somewhat brittle characters successfully.

Matthews' one-act plays, among which *This Picture and That* (1887) and *The Decision of the Court* (1893) are the best, belong to the same species as Howells' comedies. The first is a clever depiction of the second wooing of a widow, with the background of the Civil War. The second, in which a husband who is about to be divorced calls on his wife to apologize for the conduct of his attorney in the divorce suit, is sharpened in its contrast by making the husband an Englishman. Their reconciliation, after the receipt of the telegram announcing the verdict in her favor, is swift and telling. At a recent production in Philadelphia, the comedy seemed as fresh as ever. Brander Matthews, however, passed from creative work to criticism and interpretation of the drama, native and foreign. For many years he has been the inspiration of students who have learned not only the history but also the principles of play writing from one whose wide knowledge has made him aware of what is permanent and what is passing in the laws of the art.

CHAPTER III

WILLIAM DEAN HOWELLS AND THE APPROACH TO REALISM

O NE of the common errors in the discussion of American
drama is to assume its divorce from the main currents of
our literature. I have shown in my survey of the playwriting
before the Civil War how Irving, Willis, Bird, Boker, Long-
fellow, Mrs. Howe and others were associated with the rise of
the romantic drama at a time when the literature in general
was following the romantic fashion. It was the untoward circumstances that surrounded the production of plays by native
playwrights that prevented or cut short their connection with
the theatre. The slow improvement in these conditions which
began in the seventies led to the attempts of Mark Twain,
Bret Harte, William Dean Howells, Thomas Bailey Aldrich
and others to write plays, and while their success in most cases
lay rather in the providing of dramatic material than in the
shaping of it, this was due to no disregard of the drama, for
which indeed all had a profound attachment. Their contributions will be discussed in the appropriate places, but among
them Howells demands special treatment, on account both of
his achievement and of his influence upon others. The leader
in the realistic treatment of familiar life, his example and his
critical judgments and inspiration, guided and encouraged
Harrigan, Herne, Thomas and Fitch, who have expressed their
obligation to him directly and implicitly.[1] From his editorial
chair on the *Atlantic Monthly* and from his "Editor's Study"
and "Easy Chair" in *Harper's Magazine*, during a period ex-
tending with but a few intermissions from 1866 to 1920, he

---

[1] Thomas, *The Print of My Remembrance*, p. 78; *Clyde Fitch and His Letters*, 47, 257.
258· see also chapter on Herne in this volume.

preached the doctrine of truth to life in all art, and when he touched the drama his judgment was sane and discriminating.[1] But his creative work, of course, surpasses his critical articles in permanent importance. To have done one thing extremely well is enough to justify any dramatist, and Howells is surpassed by no one who has written in English in the creation of the farce comedy, which depends for its effect upon the delicate contrast of domestic and social values. The fact that the one-act plays of Howells were acted chiefly by amateurs has obscured their significance. They were written by a master playwright, whose longer plays were successful on the professional stage, and the fact that there was almost no market for the one-act play unless it were distinctly written for the variety stage restricted their vogue to the amateur. In every sense of the word they are professional plays, as is proved by the performance of *The Mouse Trap* by Mrs. Kendal in London [2] and of *The Garroters*, played under the title of *A Dangerous Ruffian* at the Avenue Theatre, London, in November, 1895. William Archer speaks appreciatively of this performance, noting especially the opportunity which the character of Mrs. Roberts gave to a competent actress.[3] Bernard Shaw also paid tribute to the merits of this performance.[4]

Howells published his farces first in the *Atlantic Monthly*, then in *Harper's Weekly* and finally in *Harper's Magazine*,

[1] See especially "The Recent Dramatic Season," *North American Review*, CXLII (1901), 468-80.

[2] Howells states definitely in a letter to J. Henry Harper, printed in *The House of Harper*, p. 320, "One of them enjoyed a most noble distinction in London, where *The Mouse Trap* was twice played with an all-star cast for a charity which naturally and rightly did not include the author; he thought it riches to have his play done by Miss Ellen Terry and Mrs. Kendal." No record of the performance by Miss Terry can be found and in a letter from Mrs. Kendal to Miss Howells (August 10, 1926) she states that her own performance was given at Queen's Hall, "many years ago" and that "Miss Ellen Terry did not appear in your father's farce of *The Mouse Trap*." That Howells was in receipt of some return from the professional performances of his farces is evidenced also in a letter to Mark Twain (April 26, 1903) in which he speaks of his agent arranging for the production of "one of my farces on the London stage" and transmitting to him "22 pounds on account of farce."

[3] *Theatrical World*, Nov. 30, 1895, p. 373.

[4] *Dramatic Opinions and Essays*, I, 265-6.

where they became one of the attractions of the Christmas number, advance sheets being in demand months before their publication.[1]

In *The Parlor Car* (1876) the qualities that make these comedies fresh and vital even to-day are at once apparent. First of all comes naturalness. Beginning with the choice of scene, a place in which people may easily meet, we meet probability everywhere, from the catching of the heroine's polonaise in the window to the jar that throws her into the hero's arms at the proper moment. The dialogue is never "literary"—it is just that compromise between actual conversation and perfect English which is suitable for the stage. Next we notice the rigid economy of the reader's attention. Not a word is wasted, and if retort follows retort with a cleverness that no rival has surpassed, there is no oversubtlety to confuse. Finally, the situation, even when it dominates, never overshadows the characters. These qualities are not so vivid in *The Parlor Car* as they became later, but they are real and Howells' knowledge of the feminine nature in its ability to escape the consequences of its inconsistencies is already apparent.

Howells' first dramatic effort to be produced professionally was, curiously enough, in the field of the heroic play. It was a translation of *Sansone* by Ippolito d'Aste, made for Charles P. Pope, who produced it first at the Olympic Theatre in St. Louis on October 5, 1874, apparently with success.[2] Howells seems to have followed the structure of the Italian play closely but his blank-verse rendering of the Italian is free and shows his intuitive sense of the distinction between dramatic and epic blank verse. He was able too to enter into the spirit of a play based upon passion, revenge and the fate of a great soul who pulls down his enemy's temple, content to be crushed himself within the ruins. Howell's version was used in 1889 by Tomasso Salvini.

In 1877 Howells wrote two longer comedies, *Out of the*

[1] Harper, J. H., *The House of Harper*, p. 320.
[2] Letter from Pope to Howells, October 9, 1874.

WILLIAM DEAN HOWELLS

Question and *A Counterfeit Presentment*. The latter was produced by Lawrence Barrett at the Grand Opera House in Cincinnati, October 11, 1877. It is to be regretted that *Out of the Question*, the first of these to be written, should not have had an opportunity upon the professional stage, although there can be no doubt that of the two it is less suited for the theatre. In this play Howells had a theme that he loved to treat, the contrast of the natural gentleman with the girl who is the product of generations of breeding, and who is held back by her traditions, made concrete by her family, but who triumphs over them. It was a theme which Bret Harte also treated, but from a sentimental point of view. Howells approached the situation from the satiric angle, and some of his best shafts at the artificial standards of human conduct are contained in this almost forgotten comedy.

A Counterfeit Presentment departs from the normal in the central situation. Bartlett, an artist who is painting at the Ponkwasset Hotel, is naturally disconcerted when three new arrivals, General Wyatt, his wife and his daughter Constance, betray the greatest abhorrence upon meeting him. This is explained by the extraordinary resemblance Bartlett bears to a scoundrel who had been engaged to Constance and who has been forced by General Wyatt, upon the discovery of his crimes, to break the engagement. General Wyatt prefers to conceal the real nature of his daughter's lover from her, hoping that her pride will bring her through the ordeal. But she drops instead into nervous collapse, which is naturally not improved by her meeting with Bartlett. This situation is presented to us by the most uncompromising realist of his day without apology, and his defense might well be that he provides a dramatic situation which, once the initial difficulty is surmounted, is developed logically enough. Of course Bartlett falls in love with Constance, and the attraction and repulsion of the man with his temperamental nature and the woman struggling out of a nervous breakdown caused by disappointed love provide some scenes which give opportunities for clever

69

acting. *A Counterfeit Presentment* is not farce. The characters carry the main interest, and the dialogue reveals Howells'
powers of implication. When Mrs. Wyatt assures Constance
that Bartlett does not know of her earlier engagement, the
scene proceeds:

Mrs. Wyatt: But what made you think he knows?
Constance: (*Solemnly*) He behaved just as if he didn't.
Mrs. Wyatt: Ah, you can't judge from that, my dear. (*Im-
        pressively*) Men are very different.
Constance: (*Doubtfully*) Do you think so, mamma?
Mrs. Wyatt: I'm certain of it.

According to Barrett's letter to Howells, October 13, 1877,
The Counterfeit Presentment was a genuine and pronounced
triumph. Barrett asked, however, for certain changes, and a
new first Act was written by Howells and performed in December to Barrett's satisfaction. Howells in consequence began
the adaptation of *Un Drama Nuevo* by the well-known Spanish
playwright, Tamayo y Baus, and while Daly's adaptation had
failed, that of Howells succeeded.[1] In a letter written January 14, 1916, in response to an inquiry of mine, Howells said:

Yorick's Love is not my play, though I tampered with a masterpiece in making some slight additions to it. . . . I translated it
for Lawrence Barrett, who, against my entreaties, called it mine
in his advertisements.

Howells was too modest in speaking of his changes. In the
first Act he introduced the author and the prompter to explain
the situation and he cut the longer speeches occasionally. He
also changed the prose at times to blank verse. The most serious change was the substitution of Heywood for Shakespeare.
This change was made by Barrett probably in order that the
part taken by Shakespeare should be reduced in importance
in favor of the star part of Yorick. Howells seems to have
acquiesced in this alteration, however, for among the manu-

[1] See for plot of *Un Drama Nuevo* and discussion of the Daly version, pp. 32-4.

WILLIAM DEAN HOWELLS

scripts of the play are found later revisions in his hand, in which the word "Heywood" appears.

But the changes in the final scene of the play are most important. Yorick kills Edmund, who is defending Alice, and Yorick goes out of his head and begins to babble tragically over Edmund's body. For this scene, Howells provided, in flexible and moving blank verse, a picture of the love of an older man for the boy he had cherished. As Howells' version remains unpublished, the beginning of the scene is quoted:

Yorick: My boy, my boy, my boy! Why! Look you, Master,
He was a little lad when first I saw him,
Tattered, and wan with hunger, with such eyes,
Full of such silent histories of sorrow,
Of orphanage, and all the world's unkindness,
They went straight to my heart. I took him home
And there I have kept him ever since; nor love
Nor hate, nor even murder, could
Dislodge him. There he lieth dead, within
My heart. O I could tell you things, of how
I used to watch him in the night, and rise
And creep and kneel beside his little bed
Where we had prayed together ere he slept
And listen to his breathing, feel his pulse,
To know if any sickness threatened him.
If he were hurt, I suffered worse than he;
His childish joys made me a happy child.
You all can bear me witness how I loved him:
My love has made me many a time the laugh
Of all of you.

    . . . .

(*After a pause*)
And when he grew a man, he grew a man
After my heart, so generous, true and bold,
So faithful and so loving—

    . . . .

(*to Shakespeare*)
Master, how ill a thing it is to be
Revenged! Ay, vengeance is too much
For us weak mortals—the blood makes us drunk,
It makes us mad! Ay, vengeance is the Lord's:

71

"Vengeance is mine; I will repay," He said.
He will repay; He will repay, He said.
Canst thou imagine how I could kill my boy?
It must have been an accident, methinks;
A slip o' the foot, an error of the hand,
That did so often bless him.   I would fain
Know how it chanced.   Lend me thy sword good master.
Since he hath worn my point within his heart,
I—cannot touch it.
(*Shakespeare shrinks back but Yorick snatches his
sword from its sheath*)
                        Why, be not afraid!
You are thinking of that blackamoor of Venice,
And surely not of this poor, merry Yorick,
That never yet was apt for tragedy.
I shall not harm myself: I am past all harm!
It must have happened thus.
(*As he turns the point on his breast, they start toward
him; he laughs and uncovers it.*)
                        Nay, do not fear:
If I should pass this rapier through my breast,
It would not hurt me; I am dead within.

Yorick's Love was first performed at the Euclid Opera
House in Cleveland, Ohio, October 25, 1878, and it retained a
regular place in Barrett's répertoire as late as 1891, the year
of his death, when he produced it at the Broadway Theatre.   The
effect on a competent judge may be seen in the letters of John
Hay to Whitelaw Reid and to Howells.   "It was a very different play," he said, "from the one I saw at the Fifth Avenue
Theatre some years ago, improved almost beyond recognition."
He also approved of "keeping Shakespeare behind the flies,"
saying that "he was almost grotesque in the original." [1]   In
the opinion of other critics, *Yorick's Love* gave Barrett an
opportunity to show real ability in characterization, and to
advance from theatricality to adequate power in interpreting
dramatic action.   *Yorick's Love* was played at the Lyceum
Theatre in London, April 14, 1884.   It was revived by Lewis
Morrison in 1895 in Boston.

[1] Thayer, W. R.   *The Life of John Hay*, i, 398–402.

WILLIAM DEAN HOWELLS

Howells' professional attitude is evidenced by his dramatization of *Miles Standish* for Barrett in 1879, with which the actor planned to open his season, though it apparently was not produced.

His versatility as well as his inventive ability is shown in the delightful libretto for *A Sea Change or Love's Stowaway*. It was to have been produced at the Bijou Theatre in Boston, November, 1884, with musical accompaniment by George Henschel, but owing to the death of the manager it never saw the stage. Howells calls the published version a "lyricated farce," and indeed the supple and varied lyrics rival Gilbert, from whom the general inspiration came. But *A Sea Change* is not directed at any current craze or foible; it satirizes the capricious, inconsequent type of American girl who rejects a lover for no reason, finds him on the steamer, "a Retarder," on which they each have taken refuge, and promptly demands that he go ashore. The captain solemnly suggests his transfer to a floating iceberg, and Howells then introduced a dream scene of ingenious incongruity in which nearly all the passengers decamp on to the iceberg to join the Ice Princess and her maidens. It is fooling of a priceless quality—the absurdities of comic opera are woven into the plot with a skill that causes us to wonder again why Howells made only one attempt in this field. For example, when Muriel first comes on board this conversation follows:

Captain: And what can I do for you, miss?
Muriel: Nothing. But the man at the wheel makes me giddy, turning it round so.
Captain: (*Through his trumpet to the man at the wheel*) Lash your wheel!
Man at the wheel: (*Obeying*) Ay, ay, sir! (*Attempting to sing*) I am the——
Captain: (*Sternly*) Belay that! (*To Muriel*) Anything more, miss?
Muriel: No,—only the ship seems to tremble a good deal.
Captain: (*To the man at the wheel*) Tell the officer on duty to send me the engineer.

Man at the wheel: Ay, ay, sir! (*Down speaking tube*) Engineer!
Engineer: (*Appearing instantly, and attempting to sing*) I am
      the—
Chorus: Oh, stow it!
        We know it.
Captain: We've had enough of explanation and we'll show it.

Of the lyric that ensues one stanza will illustrate his capacity:

> If you are a statesman or ward politician,
> A man with a grievance, a maid with a grief,
> An agent, a dentist, a soul with a mission,
> Beware how you turn to your friends for relief.
>   I'll be frank with you all:
> The right way for you is to hire a hall!
>   Yes, hire a hall!

Howells also dramatized his novel of *A Foregone Conclusion* and it was produced at a matinée performance at the Madison Square Theatre on November 18, 1886. Alexander Salvini played the part of Don Ippolito, the priest who falls in love with an American girl. The theme is at best an unpleasant one and the novel is hardly one of Howells' best efforts. The drama did not secure a place upon the stage, although it was played in Boston in November, 1889, at the Tremont Theatre.

It was, however, in 1883, when Howells was at the height of his creative power, that he introduced in *The Sleeping Car* the characters which were to delight two generations. Mrs. Agnes Roberts is incomparable. From the moment she begins her tireless communion with the world, giving expression to every thought as it rises to the surface of her mind, she is a perfect fountain of humor. With a skill that is positively uncanny, Howells never allows her to become merely a caricature; she is a living woman whom we have all known and heard, thinking aloud in private and public. Her husband, the absent-minded Edward Roberts, and her brother, Willis Campbell, whose advent from California provides her with conversa-

WILLIAM DEAN HOWELLS

tion through the enlivening hours while she scatters relentlessly
the silence of the sleeping car, are merely introduced in this
opening farce. But in *The Elevator* (1885) Willis Campbell
reveals his practical nature in saving the guests of the Roberts, who are imprisoned in the elevator which has come to rest
between the fourth and fifth floors. The gathering of the
guests, the wonder at the lateness of the missing ones, is carried just to the point when one actually feels the nervous tension
of Mrs. Roberts, then we are transferred to the elevator in
which all the prisoners, from Aunt Mary to the elevator boy,
reveal themselves by their reaction to supposed danger. The
device of making this second scene contemporaneous with the
first brings the next action on at just the right moment, for
the anxiety of the prisoners makes them react to the well-
meaning but stupid inquiries of Roberts, Mrs. Roberts, Dr.
Lawton and the others, which are spoken through the grating
of the elevator shaft. Then Campbell arrives and inquires
why they do not try running it *down* since it will not go *up*.
The art with which Howells has kept the reader or hearer from
making the same suggestion can be appreciated only when he
carefully studies the subtle suggestions by which the conversation in the elevator directs his thoughts away from the obvious
solution.

The Elevator requires two changes of scene and *The Garroters* (1886) one, but after all it is not as one-act plays that
these farces are important. Every sentence in *The Garroters*
tells, from the moment Roberts arrives in his drawing room
dishevelled and worn out after his supposed encounter with a
robber on the Common, to be met with a torrent of sympathy
and admiration from his wife for his courage in recapturing
his property. The sickening moment when he realizes that
his watch has never left his dressing table and that the tousled
Mr. Bemis has been his victim is matched only by the futile
effort of Roberts, at Campbell's suggestion, to carry the matter off as a joke. Archer rightly selected Mrs. Roberts as the
most promising character when the play was produced at the

Avenue Theatre, for her amplitude of conversational vibration envelops the action.

To this group Howells next added Mrs. Amy Somers, a young widow, the heroine of *Five O'Clock Tea* (1889) and *The Mouse Trap* (1889). She is more clever than Agnes Roberts, yet just as feminine, and Howells never confuses their functions. The sophisticated skirmish between Campbell and Amy Somers which takes place in the intervals of a tea-party is masterly in its revelation of deeper feeling beneath. There is finer art here than in *The Mouse Trap*, but the picture of the ladies perched upon the furniture in dread of the mouse that exists only in Campbell's imagination is unforgettable. It leads up also to a climax that must have given Mrs. Kendal a fine opportunity, for the dialogue between Mrs. Somers and Campbell after the rest have fled contains in epitome the eternal masculine and feminine, until she guides the action by declaring:

Mrs. Somers: Nothing. But if I were a man—
Campbell: Well?
Mrs. Somers: Well, in the first place, I wouldn't have got you wrought up so.
Campbell: Well, but if you had! Suppose you had done all that I've done, and that I was up there in your place standing on a chair, and wouldn't let you leave the room, and wouldn't get down and walk out, and wouldn't allow myself to be carried, what should you do?
Mrs. Somers: (*Who has been regarding him attentively over the top of her fan, which she holds pressed against her face*) Why, I suppose if you wouldn't let me help you willingly—*I should use violence.*
Campbell: You witch!
(*As he makes a wild rush upon her, the curtain, which in the plays of this author has a strict regard for the covenances, abruptly descends.*)

In *A Likely Story* (1889) the conversation between Mr. and Mrs. Willis Campbell reaches almost the high-water mark of

Howells' effortless ease. The incidents here, however, are not so capably handled and the ending is therefore weaker. *The Albany Depot* is amusing, if a bit more obvious, for there is a distinction in social values which seems to come in and go out with Amy Somers, and she is absent except as the impelling motive of Mrs. Roberts' urgent necessity for a cook. The social cleavage which separates Mrs. McIlheny from her cousin Maggie, the cook, is, however, a subtle hit at the artificialities of all social rifts.

The perfection of Howells' art in the farce came with *A Letter of Introduction* (1892) and in the comedy with *The Unexpected Guests* (1893). In the first, Edward Roberts, longing to be rid of a traveling Englishman, has given him a letter of introduction to his uncle in New York and has written to his uncle privately, telling him his opinion of the visitor. He asks the Englishman to mail the latter missive and returns to his writing, to be interrupted by Mrs. Roberts' verbal flow of sympathy for his wasted time and by the visit of Willis and Amy Campbell. Of course Willis suggests that Roberts has misplaced the letters in their respective envelopes, and when the Englishman returns with an inquiry as to a possible mistake, the conversation in which they all try to placate him before he mildly reveals his envelope with nothing in it, is delightful.

In *The Unexpected Guests* the same group assemble for dinner, as in *The Elevator*, but this time they are at the home of Amy Campbell. Again they come late, but Mrs. Campbell meets the delay with much more ease than Mrs. Roberts did and she rises to the supreme necessity for social falsehood on the arrival of the Belforts, whom she believes have declined her invitation. Despite her skill, the guests one by one become aware of the situation, while as a chorus to their fibs the phonograph in the next room chants "Truth crushed to earth shall rise again." Finally the Belforts re-enter and then the stentorian voice of the man below calling the Iroquois Club to send a dozen more quails for the unexpected guests ends her attempts at concealment. But she meets the blow with her flag flying, and even the disclosure that her hasty misreading of Mrs. Belfort's note of acceptance has been the cause of all the difficulty only brings out her reserves, which leave her mistress of the situation as the curtain falls.

In *The Unexpected Guests* Howells passes out of the category of farce into the comedy of manners, but in *Evening Dress* (1893) he once more allows us to revel in the domestic difficulties of Roberts, left by his wife to dress and follow her to a musicale. Her conversation, as she floats out of the apartment while she urges him to think of something else she should remember to tell him, is a little classic of married life, but the search for his dress suit is pure farce and never rises above it. *A Masterpiece of Diplomacy* (1894) and *The Smoking Car* (1900) are amusing, but somehow we wish we had said good-by to the inimitable quartet in one of their great moments. With the disappearance of the Campbells and the Roberts the best period of comedy was over. It corresponds naturally to the greatest period of Howells in the novel, which began with *A Modern Instance* and ended with *The World of Chance*, but just as it was with his fiction, an occasional effort of his later period almost rivals his finest work. In fact, *Bride Roses* (1893), his one serious prose play, belongs to the great creative moments, and its poignant tragedy is intensified by the contrast between the typical indecision of the First Lady, who is selecting flowers for her tea at which a young girl is to pour, and the swift choice of the Second Lady, who selects the same roses for the funeral of the girl, who has suddenly died. Social consciousness is here in its real sense, but *Bride Roses* is allied more closely to such a dramatic sketch in verse as *The Mother and the Father* (1909) than it is to the other prose plays. These become lighter through *A Previous Engagement* (1897) and *Room Forty-Five* (1900), *An Indian Giver* (1900), and *Parting Friends* (1911). We remember the situations but not the characters, and indeed in certain of the farces which have had only magazine publication, Howells passes from satire of life to a satire on the stock figures of melodrama. *Saved; an Emotional Drama* (1908) brings on the stage at night the burglar, the child who finds him, the wife who is about to elope with her lover, the lover, the wife's sister who takes him away from her, and the husband and father who desires above everything a cup of coffee. In *A True Born Hero* (1909) Howells presents us with the conventional situation of the youthful hero who is planning to sacrifice himself to save a worthless woman who is trying to use him as a screen for her intrigue. But Howells makes him take the sensible course of declining to be a sacrifice, and expresses through one of the other characters the hope that some day such a hero will be present in plays and novels. Further than this, satire could hardly go, though Howells, in *The Impossible; a Mystery Play* (1910), made a not very successful attempt to preach a moral with the aid of a supernatural telephone.

It is only by a consideration of his work historically as well as critically that its importance and its variety become apparent. We have seen how the great realist was one of the prime movers in the revival of romantic plays on the stage, and it must not be forgotten that *A Counterfeit Presentment* was played by Lawrence Barrett before Bronson Howard had passed out of melodrama into comedy. How much more permanent is Howells' work in its essential quality of timelessness can be appreciated most quickly by comparing this play with *The Banker's Daughter, Old Lavender* or *The Danites.* His sense for the permanent is shown in his choice of those modern improvements, many new in his day, for the scene or the mechanics of his plays. He chooses the elevator, the sleeping car, the phonograph, the telephone, never the bicycle or any passing fad. Consequently they can be played or read to-day with little sense of outworn fashion. Of course they are based on eternal motives, love, marriage, the insistent clutch of the feminine upon the direction of personal affairs, the masculine carelessness or absentmindedness in Roberts, the masculine love of teasing in Campbell. Dwelling upon similar motives so often, it is surprising how little he repeats himself.

It is indeed this variety in his material and method which is usually disregarded. He began in *The Parlor Car, The Sleeping Car* and *The Register* with domestic farce. With *The Garroters* and *The Elevator* the social scene becomes a background but the complications are still external. In *The Mouse Trap* Amy Somers takes her place as the central figure, and with her entrance the rules and inhibitions of social life begin to be the directing forces of the plays. They remain so in *Five O'Clock Tea, A Likely Story, A Letter of Introduction* and *The Unexpected Guests*, and the progress of Howells' social consciousness cannot better be exemplified than in a comparison between *The Elevator* and *The Unexpected Guests*. Both have a dinner party as their setting, but in the first, laid at Mrs. Roberts' apartment, social laws have no bearing upon the plot, while in *The Unexpected Guests*, which takes place in Mrs. Campbell's drawing room, the whole significance of the play depends upon her maintenance of a social illusion. In *The Elevator* the danger is physical and is sufficiently serious; in *The Unexpected Guests* there is no danger except to the social susceptibilities of the hostess, and yet the art of the playwright holds our attention more closely and with more real interest. For Howells has drawn deftly characters who determine the action and are living beings. It is therefore comedy of manners and not farce at all. That is why *Five O'Clock Tea*, which is also comedy, rises with *The Unexpected Guests* above the level of the farces. For in *Five O'Clock Tea* there is also the interplay of character rather than the precipitation of action by accident.

The form of both comedies and farces reflects the exterior arrangement into scenes which Howells learned from his study of French drama. But there is little that is foreign in his atmosphere or form. Usually, outside of his definitely longer plays, the form is that of the one-act play. But the scene changes in several, and Howells was satisfied with the higher unity of action. In his earlier plays he introduces his characters by delightful touches of description in which he anticipated both Barrie and Shaw, to mention only two of his many successors. For as Clyde Fitch well said, the eighties and nineties were "the Howells age," and many who do not acknowledge it were affected by his unending struggle for truth in art. His plays taught manners and social values to thousands who played in them or saw them on the amateur stage. That they were played professionally so seldom was a loss to our stage which can hardly be estimated.

CHAPTER IV

Harrigan, Hoyt, and the Comedy of Types

WHILE Bronson Howard was placing on our stage his studies of men and women moving in social relations, there was developing a drama wrought out of the lower life of the larger Eastern cities, written by a playwright native to New York, and significant because of the fidelity with which the types of character are portrayed.

Edward Harrigan was born in New York City, October 26, 1845. His family came to Canada in the Eighteenth Century and Cape Harrigan, on the northern coast of Labrador, was named for an ancestor of the playwright. William Harrigan, his father, a native of Newfoundland, was a sea captain and shipbuilder. This relation to the sea is reflected in several of Edward Harrigan's plays.

His connection with the theatre began about 1867. He had run away from home, on account of his father's second marriage, and gone as far as Panama by sea. Reaching San Francisco, he joined the company of the well-known comédienne, Lotta, and remained in San Francisco, playing in comedies, melodramas and farces, mainly at the Bella Union Theatre. Forming a partnership with Sam Rickey, a comedian, he made his way East, playing in Chicago and appearing first in New York at the Globe Theatre, November 21, 1870, where the partners produced a sketch entitled *A Little Fraud*. But his marked success came with his union with Anthony Cannon, whose stage name was Tony Hart, and whom he met during a later trip to Chicago. They varied their road tours with occasional appearances at the Union Square and Bowery Theatres, and became established in New York, when on December 2, 1872, they appeared at the Theatre Comique at 514

Edward Hanna

HARRIGAN, HOYT, AND THE COMEDY OF TYPES

Broadway in *The Day We Went West* and *The Big and Little of It*. They withdrew in July, 1875, but became managers in August, 1876, and made the house one of the best known in New York City. Here were produced some of their most successful plays, like *The Mulligan Guard Ball*. In April 1881, the house was torn down. They then refitted the old Globe Theatre, at 728 Broadway, as the New Theatre Comique, and it was opened August 29, 1881, with Harrigan's play, *The Major*. Here *Squatter Sovereignty* and *Cordelia's Aspirations* first saw the stage. This theatre was destroyed by fire December 28, 1884. Not daunted by this misfortune, for the insurance had lapsed, Harrigan leased the Park Theatre at Thirty-fifth Street and Broadway, which he conducted with slight interruptions as Harrigan's Park Theatre, until April 13, 1891. In the meantime he and Hart had parted company. In 1890 he built a new theatre on Thirty-fifth Street near Sixth Avenue, which he leased to Richard Mansfield in March, 1895, and which is now the Garrick Theatre. Harrigan continued to act, especially in his own characters, such as *Old Lavender*, his last appearance in regular drama being in *His Wife's Family* at Wallack's Theatre, October 6, 1908, although he took part in a public Gambol of the Lambs, at the Metropolitan Opera House in 1909. He died June 6, 1911.[1]

Harrigan's plays grew out of the vaudeville sketches in which he as the male character and Hart as the female, impersonated the types of city life which delighted the audience of the Theatre Comique with their humor and fidelity to life. But fortunately, no question as to joint authorship disturbs the historian of the drama, for after the separation of the partners in 1885, the plays went on and Hart made no attempt at drama. Record can be found of over eighty vaudeville sketches composed by Edward Harrigan between 1870 and 1879, and while these are duplications in some cases, the va-

---

[1] The details of Harrigan's life, which differ from printed accounts in several instances, have been furnished by his son, Dr. Anthony Hart Harrigan.

riety of treatment is indicated by the titles, which take in politics, baseball, life insurance, the army, the militia, and deal with the negro and the Irish, German, Italian and other immigrant types. In their first stages, these sketches returned, curiously enough, to the primary conception of French *vaudeville:* a popular song composed and sung by the Provençal troubadours to ridicule some well-known personage.

The development from this song to the articulated play is a significant one for the history of the theatre in America. The song led to the duet, the duet to a dialogue. In the early sixties, the Theatre Comique presented a variety show with a more or less permanent company. F. S. Chanfrau was still appearing in *A Glance at New York* (1848), which reveals the continuity of our dramatic history. In 1872 Josh Hart, the manager, engaged Harrigan and Hart to give their songs and dialogues as part of a variety show. The programs of the Theatre Comique show how gradually the share of Harrigan and Hart in the entertainment grew from one number to several, and how even before they assumed the management of the theatre in 1876, a short play of from one to seven scenes like *The Blue and the Gray*, a Civil War sketch, and *Down Broadway*, a local burlesque, won their right to the coveted position at the end of the program. Harrigan's success was not confined to this country. A program of the variety theatre, the St. James Hall in Piccadilly, London, for November 7, 1877, reveals "an entirely new musical sketch, . . . by Edward Harrigan, Esq., entitled 'Walking for dat Cake,' " which is made a feature of the evening.

Another phase of Harrigan's development is illustrated by the various forms of *The Doyle Brothers.* As early as August, 1874, a three-act play by that name was produced at the Theatre Comique. This was probably the anonymous melodrama which, according to the manuscript, was "written for Harrigan and Hart," and which is simply an old-fashioned murder and arson play, laid in New Orleans. During its progress two actors, Darby and Lanty Doyle, rescue the hero,

Jerold, from prison. It is evident from the changes made in Harrigan's autograph manuscript of *The Doyle Brothers* how cleverly he used older material and adapted it to his own needs and talents. In its new form it is still a play in three acts, but Darby and Lanty have become the heroes, and in the court scene in which they rescue Jerold they occupy the center of the stage. Indeed, the old melodrama has become a vehicle for the character acting of the two partners. Harrigan took three parts, Darby Doyle, an Irish actor, old Pete, a loyal negro, and Italian Joe, a peanut vender. Hart played in three also, Lanty Doyle, Luke, a minor character, and Johanna, the heroine, who is beloved by Jerold. The old murder and arson play had become simply a means of giving Harrigan and Hart time to change their make-up for the new character part. The play reappears in their répertoire for several years, either as *Darby and Lanty* or under its original name.

Obviously it is difficult to assign a beginning to the original full-length play by Harrigan. One of the earliest, which also showed the longest vitality, was *Old Lavender*, first produced at the Theatre Comique, September 3, 1877, and growing out of a vaudeville sketch, *Old Lavender Water or Round the Docks*, played earlier in the year. Old Lavender is the genial drunkard, the descendant of Rip Van Winkle and the ancestor of "Lightnin' " Bill Jones. As the cashier of a bank he takes the blame for the misdeeds of others, and his degradation brings us to the docks of the river and to the lower form of sailors' boarding houses in New York. It held the stage for many years and was a favorite part of its creator, who undoubtedly filled its traditional outlines with life. But it did not reveal any original characterization.

While the Mulligan cycle was slowly maturing, Harrigan was also experimenting in the Irish play of the school of Boucicault. Possibly the earliest of these was *Iascaire*, a play in nine scenes, produced November 20, 1876, at the Theatre Comique. It is called a romantic play by its author, and it has certain elements of romance. Harrigan played the character

A HISTORY OF THE AMERICAN DRAMA

of Michael Delany, a misshapen foundling whose father, Cornelius Lynch, is the villain of the piece—the stock figure of the lawyer who grinds the poor. The conception of Michael is not bad, however. He turns at last on his father and persecutor and after saving Jerold Sullivan, the Irish rebel, kills Lynch in a desperate struggle. Hart played Shaun O'Kelly "the best fisherman in Galway." Another imitation of Boucicault came in 1878, in *The Lorgaire*. It was first a vaudeville sketch, then a three-act play, an interesting drama of the older fashion, laid in a fishing village on the west coast of Ireland. The Lorgaire is a detective from Scotland Yard and he solves the traditional situations, which involve the missing heir, a murder and a false accusation.

That Harrigan was influenced by Boucicault's dramas of Irish life cannot be doubted, for we find him playing in a sketch called *Arrah-na-Brogue* in 1873. But his conception of Irish character, while it vied in reality with that of Boucicault, was of a different nature. Boucicault's contribution, as I have indicated,[1] lay in his treatment of the Irish villager and the Irish gentry, on their native soil. With equal insight, Harrigan treated the Irish immigrant who had come to this country after the famine of 1848, and who had remained in the cities of the East. He did not touch the generation that had come before that time, the younger sons of the gentry, or of the commercial class, who had become assimilated into our national life. For the purposes of vivid contrast, he chose the keeper of the corner grocery, Dan Mulligan, who had fought in the Civil War with "the Sixty-ninth," and who is a leader of his clan. He is honest, courageous, loyal, impulsive, irrational, likely to become drunk and disorderly at slight provocation, and while irascible and quarrelsome, is forgiving and generous even to his enemies. His mate, Cordelia, is his counterpart, and yet she is individualized. She is at the beginning of the cycle his prudent and frugal helpmeet, she looks up to him and is at once a wife and a mother to him. But

[1] *History of the American Drama from the Beginning to the Civil War*, pp. 373–86.

86

HARRIGAN, HOYT, AND THE COMEDY OF TYPES

later she becomes affected by the itch for social distinction and
one of the best of the plays, *Cordelia's Aspirations*, tells the
story of her rise and his fall, to his financial ruin. The quiet
courage with which he returns to his corner grocery and she
takes boarders to pay their debts, and the stoicism of both, are
most appealing.

But the Irish characters are not Harrigan's only creations.
As a contrast to the Celtic temperament of Dan Mulligan, he
drew Gustave Lochmuller, the German butcher, his arch enemy
and rival; and the instinctive antipathy of Celt and Teuton
flourishes in comedy on American soil. They dislike each
other for their very virtues; and their utter inability to comprehend each other's point of view makes for real comedy.

Even more vividly drawn than the German were the negro
types, Rebecca Allup, the widow who cooks for the Mulligans;
the Reverend Palestine Puter, who disappears with the treasury of the Full Moons, "a secret order formed to keep the Irish
off the street cars"; Captain Primrose, the barber; and the
rest. They are almost perfect pictures of the guerillas of life,
hanging on the skirts of the other races and in their reckless
gayety, improvidence, impudence and superstition, adding almost unlimited possibilities to the human comedy.

The name of Mulligan first appears in the sketch and song
of *The Mulligan Guard*, produced at the Academy of Music
in Chicago, July 15, 1873, and later, September 8, at the Theatre Comique in New York. It was a burlesque upon the target
excursions of the military organizations, named after local politicians, which sprang up in the wards of New York City.
After paying their respects to the ward leader, these companies marched to the depot or steamer landing, en route to
the picnic ground where the target, carried in the rear by a
negro, was to be placed. These excursions sometimes concluded
with a small riot, in which people were killed or wounded. In
a letter written in 1874, Harrigan states that he wrote the
sketch as a burlesque upon this "nuisance." In 1875 the contrast between the Irish and negro races appeared in *The Mul-*

ligan Guards and the Skidmores. The slow development by which a song with casual dialogue slowly grew into a coherent play, with occasional songs, is illustrated by the two forms of *The Mulligan Guard Picnic.*[1]

The first form, which took about forty minutes to play, appeared on the stage of the Theatre Comique, September 23, 1878. Harrigan describes it on the manuscript as "an outrageous sketch," and with the instinct of a playwright he took it off after a short run, because he wished to give more body to it. It is little more than the amplification of the picnic in *The Mulligan Guard,* although there is a slight plot concerning the disappearance of Dan Mulligan and the desire of Cordelia, his wife, to marry a dancing master. In its second form (1880), the apparent drowning of Lochmuller and the projected marriage of his widow is set against a background of the continued rivalry of the Skidmores and the Mulligans.

But it was in *The Mulligan Guard Ball,* which began January 13, 1879, at the Theatre Comique, and made a tremendous hit, running one hundred nights, that the outlines of the Mulligan cycle became established. Dan and Cordelia Mulligan are disturbed by their son Tom, who wishes to marry Katrina Lochmuller, the daughter of Gustave and Bridget Lochmuller, the latter herself an Irishwoman. The story is an old one, as old as *Romeo and Juliet,* but in the hands of a capable playwright it is of perennial interest. It is mingled in a medley that at times becomes uproarious, with a contest between the Mulligan Guards and the Skidmore Guards, a negro organization. The theme was suggested to Harrigan by the rage for militia companies; and the lines,

> Our captain's name is Hussey,
> A military man,

were suggested by the popularity of Jack Hussey, a policeman who was also noted as a life saver. The Skidmore Guards, in

[1] In giving the titles of the Mulligan plays, I have followed Harrigan's spelling in the original manuscripts. This is not consistent, in the use of "Guard" or "Guards," but he evidently thought of the organization at times as individuals and at times as a unit.

their individual capacities, serve the Mulligans as waiters or
barbers, but once clothed in their regalia, they admit of no
inequality. In fact, they rent the same hall at the same time
for their meetings, and the resultant collision becomes farce
when the Skidmores, having taken the room upstairs, under
protest, come through the ceiling. In the meantime Tom Mulligan and Katrina Lochmuller elope, Tom urging her not to
weaken, "for many a noble family came from a marriage like
this." There are other types introduced, among them Rosen-
felt, the tailor, who demands his rent for the cutaways of the
Mulligans, but the main theme is the contrasted race pride of
the Irish and the German with the vivid background of the
negro. *The Mulligan Guard Chowder* takes the Mulligans and
the Skidmores over to New Jersey, for a clam bake. In the
Mulligan Guards' Christmas appear the McFudds. Planxty
McFudd is Bridget Lochmuller's brother and he has just married Diana, Cordelia Mulligan's sister, at Albany. Cordelia
departs for Albany to bring them down, and Dan seizes the
occasion to go off with the Mulligan braves to a shooting
match. Of course all arrive, together with the Skidmore
Guards, at the Mulligan home for Christmas dinner. The conflict between the German, the Irish and the negro is epitomized
in the scene in which Bridget Lochmuller declines to drink
with Rebecca Allup, the cook, and the latter remarks, "I admire an Irishwoman but a German woman never can lay a
hand on me!" Bridget Lochmuller rolls her sleeves up, saying, "Don't you call me a German!" and proceeds to conflict.
There is some clever conversation in this play and Montgomery
Jangles, the crazy man who strikes attitudes representing historical characters, such as "Socrates leading Marie An-
toinette to Execution" and "Pocahontas bathing at Coney
Island," satirized the Felicia Hemans' vogue in verse and other
forms of art that had not yet passed out of popular favor.

   The Mulligan Guard Surprise (1880) is a forerunner of a
better play, *Cordelia's Aspirations*, and is concerned with the
moving uptown of the Mulligans and their return. Harrigan

was accustomed to the reworking of his material, and his alterations invariably are improvements. *The Mulligan Guard Nominee* (1880) is an amusing satire on politics, on women's organizations, and on the British fear of American interposition in Irish affairs. When the play opens they are at the Cunard docks waiting for Bridget Lochmuller to come home. Oliver Bullwinkle, an English spy, comes on the same ship. He is trying to obtain evidence of Irish conspiracies here and in Sligo. There is a delightful meeting of the Nightingales, "a society of Irish ladies who are working for Irish freedom." Bridget Lochmuller has brought back a cipher letter and Bullwinkle is very anxious to get it. There is a contest on for Alderman-at-large, and Dan Mulligan and Lochmuller are rival candidates. Mulligan's crowd meet in Lyric Hall; there is a speech and a fight with the Lochmuller contingent, till the police come, and Rebecca tells them loftily, "I'm a member ob de Baptist church—don't push me!" It is not only farce. There is a scene appealing in its revelation of affection between Dan and Cordelia when he finds her at the negro ball and at first pretends to give her in charge, and her cry— "Oh, Dan, Dan, you're as young as ever!"—lingers in the memory. In the seventh scene, at Primrose's Barber Shop, one of Dan's men, McSweeney, raises a fight and is arrested, and the feudal organization that governs us still is reflected in this conversation:

Dan.   Raylease that man!
Officer.   He's been making a disturbance at the polls.
Dan.   Raylease him! I'm 200 votes ahead of Lochmuller and I'll say no more.
Officer.   Anything, Mr. Mulligan, to oblige *you.*

In *The Mulligans' Silver Wedding* (1881) other types are introduced, such as Washington Irving Crumbs, an author, and Edgar de Angelles, an actor, who hurl at each other epithets like "the shade of Burns" and "the fringe of John McCullough." But Cordelia and Dan remain the central characters—"twenty-five years married and wid niver an angry word, only what passed between ourselves." In the ninth scene, Cordelia, having found a letter apparently from an actress to Dan, decides to take poison. She drinks from a whiskey bottle which Dan has labeled "Rat Poison" in a praiseworthy effort to keep Rebecca Allup from drinking it. When Cordelia tells him that she is dying, he looks at the bottle and then at her lovingly, and saying, "Cordelia, we'll die together," he drinks, himself. So touched is she by his devotion, that she forgives him his apparent infidelity.

The Mulligan cycle had perhaps its best expression in *Cordelia's Aspirations* (1883) and *Dan's Tribulations* (1884). Cordelia, having saved money, decides to go to Europe and takes with her Rebecca Allup as a lady's maid. She returns with her relatives Planxty, Diana, Ellen and Rosey McFudd, some of whom had belonged to Bridget Lochmuller in *The Mulligan Guards' Christmas*. She makes Daniel sell the house in Avenue A and move to Madison Avenue, which gives rise to an affecting scene when the old furniture is sold. The second Act reveals Dan and Cordelia in their new house, at a reception, in which Dan, of course, makes blunders. There is more plot than usual, centering in Planxty's efforts to obtain control of the property and separate Dan and Cordelia. Their reconciliation is brought about by the same incident of the "rat poison," arranged even more deftly. Dan decides to move back to Avenue A and there is much comedy in consequence, some of which is built on earlier material in *The Mulligan Guard Surprise*. The main characters are well done, although the Irish relatives are intentionally burlesqued and Harrigan wisely does not individualize the supposed society at the reception. They simply furnish the room. The conversation between the negroes is as usual amusing. Rebecca tells Simpson, "Mister Mulligan's been flirting wid some other woman." Simpson replies, "You don't say!" then gives utterance to the profound truth, "You can't tell from where you sit how far it is to where you're going. Man's liable at any time ——"

In *Dan's Tribulations*, Dan and Cordelia have returned to Mulligan's Alley, Dan keeping his grocery once more and Cordelia teaching French to regain some portion of the savings, lost through her extravagance. Rebecca is as amusing as ever. She has married a negro, Clinton, to revenge herself for Simpson Primrose's defection, and is once more a widow. "Twice a widow, third time a ghost," she explains, and having sold the corpse to "a colored doctor" she is keeping the empty coffin in Mulligan's ice box, preparatory to burying it at night, so as to avoid discovery of her action. She passes off a bogus dollar on Bridget Lochmuller, who has also come down in the social scale. Cordelia is dunned by debtors and Dan transfers, against his better instincts, the little house he still owns to Bridget Lochmuller, to avoid his creditors. Of course, when Bridget later turns against them, the transaction is vitiated by the counterfeit dollar. The last act, laid at "Madame Mulligan's Académie Française," in which Cordelia conducts a French class and in which Tom and Kitty return to pay off the debts, is mingled comedy and hearty sentiment without burlesque. The concealment which Tom practices on his father, till he finds out the real situation, thereby saving his father's pride and self-respect, is well arranged and the revelation comes at last through Tom's taking a fall out of Dan by a trick known only to them both. Harrigan closed the Mulligan cycle with a play which leaves one with a feeling of satisfaction at the high heart and quiet philosophy of a character who was the product not only of observation but also of imagination.

Harrigan did not confine himself to the Mulligan family in his treatment of Irish life. In *Squatter Sovereignty* (1882) he dramatized the conflict between the legal owners of the rocky land lying adjacent to the East River and the "squatters" who had taken possession and who had lived there unmolested while the land had little apparent value. The play was laid, in the author's mind, in the district east of First Avenue and at the foot of East Seventy-second Street. The Widow Nolan

EDWARD HARRIGAN AS DAN MULLIGAN IN *CORDELIA'S ASPIRATIONS*

and Felix McIntyre decide that her daughter Nellie and his son Terence shall marry, although Nellie and Fred Kline, the son of Captain Kline, the legal owner of a portion of Shantytown, have decided otherwise. The bargaining between the parents as to the contributions of the two families is richly humorous, and when the two clans, the McIntyres and the Maguires, to whom the Widow belongs, are brought into collision, the delicate shades of social distinction among the inhabitants of Shantytown are productive of real comedy. Never for a moment do the McIntyres let the Maguires forget the condescension which alone permits the alliance, and the audiences recognized the difference between the two clans. The best-drawn characters are those of Felix and the Widow, and their love-making in the last act is very amusing. *The Leather Patch* (1886), while successful on the stage, seems to be of less significance than the Mulligan plays or *Squatter Sovereignty*. It capitalized the rivalry between funeral directors and apparently led to the introduction of the "male quartet" at funeral services through the enterprise of one of the cast who represented that innovation in the play. But the finer shades of characterization are lost in a welter of fights, disguises and scenes of low life.

Much better from the point of view of characterization is *The Major*, which opened the New Theatre Comique in 1881. The central figure, Major Gilfeather, is well conceived. He lives on his wits, his vocabulary is extensive, and he emerges from situations by his cleverness in hoodwinking other people. Some of the phrases of this play, such as "You may take it and keep it forever," are still current in popular speech, and Mrs. Miranda Biggs, the keeper of a lodging house in Bleecker Street, whose father "was a Seminal Indian," revealed Harrigan's ability as a sketcher of types other than the immigrant.

The Muddy Day (1883) is a mélange of Quaker, Irish and negro types. The central character is the Widow O'Leary, who insists on remaining thirty-five years of age, and quotes as authority for her desire to be remarried the example of her father, "who lived to be eighty and had four wives, a Hogue, a Logue, a Wogue and a Brogue." She is wooed by Captain Roger McNab, owner of the schooner *Muddy Day*. *Are You Insured?* (1885) reflected a current interest. *The O'Regans* (1886) contained an attractive philosopher who is interested both in the doctrine of evolution and in Home Rule.

Of the later plays, *Reilly and the Four Hundred* (1890) was one of the most popular. It relates the love story of the son of a pawnbroker and the niece of Commodore Toby Tow, who is supposed to be among "the Four Hundred" but gives little evidence of social security and was probably intended to be simply a caricature. The knowledge of the sea which was Harrigan's inheritance is brought into the play and the lines at times are crisp and telling, but while the play had a long stage life, it seems less vital than the Mulligan cycle.

Waddy Googan (1888) introduced the Italian types; Antonio Ronzani, the clever but unscrupulous Italian lawyer, Bianca Gillano, the waif, and the lower types like Carlo Donetto, but they seem less real than the Irish or German characters. Harrigan played Waddy Googan and also Joe Cornello, a half-witted Italian, in a successful performance. Here again Harrigan's knowledge of the wharves came in, and also his acquaintance with restaurants in New York. There is evidence that toward the end of his career he was seeking for new fields, for an unproduced play, *In the North Woods*, is laid rather vaguely in the lumber regions. The heroine, Hattie Moffit, is described as being "of the M'liss type," and evidently the success of the play of the frontier made him ambitious to draw characters in another fashion. But the play is interesting only as proving that his real strength lay in a different field. Few of these later plays have the imaginative quality of *Pete* (1887), Harrigan's play of Southern life, which ran for five months at the Park Theatre. This is also a melodrama, and the main plot, concerning the abandonment of the child, May Coolidge, before the war, and her salvation afterward, is the-

EDWARD HARRIGAN AS "MAJOR GILFEATHER" IN *THE MAJOR*

atrical rather than dramatic. But Pete, the negro servant, played by Harrigan, is very appealing in his devotion to the daughter of his old master, and in his description to May of her father's death at Malvern Hill or his revelation of her identity, which he has kept from May for her own safety, can be recognized the skill which made Harrigan's plays so effective. The playwright who could put into Pete's mouth the line, "A child's memory and a very old man's belong to dreams," had a real vein of poetic feeling. Pete, as a character, goes back to the early days of *The Doyle Brothers* or *Down in Dixie*.

Harrigan's sense of discrimination remained with him to the last, and in *Under Cover* (1903) he drew characters from the lower ranks of the sporting fraternity with an accompaniment of Irish, German and negro types. His touch, while not quite so firm as in the early days, had not lost its individual quality, and the critical response was enthusiastic. His gift for song writing would need special treatment to do it justice; and the music of "Dave" Braham was set to sentiment and humor which delighted thousands.

Harrigan wrote of real people and studied his audiences closely to note the effect, sitting incognito among them. He said in 1889 [1] in an interesting statement of his dramatic principles that he had confined his work to the depiction of life among the common people, because "their trials and troubles, hopes and fears, joys and sorrows are more varied and more numerous" than those in other walks of life. The appeal is consequently greater and he was unconsciously following the example of Dickens. Human nature, he continued, was much the same the world over and he tried to portray types that were not merely accidental and local but had a touch of the universal. In the same article he added that whenever he portrayed a "type" he was applauded and so he devoted his art to the development of the New York "boy," the Irish-American and the negro. As these grew in popularity, he added

---

[1] *Harper's Weekly*, Feb. 2, 1889. Supplement, pp. 97–8.

other types, which were not confined to New York, but existed in the other large cities of the United States; the Englishman, the Chinaman, the German, the Italian and the Southern darky. The reason he emphasized the Irish and negro types lay in the fact that they are the two races who care most for song and dance.

After a revival of some of his plays comparatively late in his career, he remarked to a friend that the new generation knew nothing of the people depicted in *The Mulligan Guard* or *Cordelia's Aspirations*. It is true that other waves of immigration have pushed Dan and Cordelia and Gustave Lochmuller out of their habitations, and since the races they represent have risen in the economic and social scale, their types are not so easily to be recognized, while Rebecca Allup and Palestine Puter, not having progressed, are still as much alive as ever. But just because Harrigan saw the dramatic quality inherent in the foreign races that are to-day integral elements of the civilization of the United States, his plays take on a real significance as social history.

While Edward Harrigan was amusing audiences with the types which reflected the street life of New York, Charles Hoyt was delighting thousands with his farce comedies dealing with varied scenes and characters, and depicting the East and the West, the city, the country and the small town. The clergyman, the clubman, the newspaper editor and reporter, the squire, the baseball player, the politician, the railroad agent, the undertaker, the plumber, the "sporty widow," the woman's rights advocate, innumerable waiters, bartenders and tramps, jostle one another in his plays, all highly colored but with real vitality and drawn with a skill which even the manuscript reveals, but which demands actual stage performance for its proper exhibition.

Charles Hale Hoyt was born in Concord, N. H., July 26, 1860. At eighteen years of age he became associated with a newspaper at St. Albans, Vermont, and shortly after joined the staff of *The Boston Post*, acting as dramatic and musical critic as well as sports editor, and becoming one of the first "columnists" in this country. His newspaper work brought him into connection with the theatre and he studied attentively the negro minstrels who performed at the Howard Athenæum, especially the company of Rich and Harris.

Cezalia, his earliest extant play, was a comedy, put on at the Globe Theatre in Boston in 1882. The figures are conventional and the language is stilted and has none of the vigor of his farces. It was not successful. The next, *A Case of Wine*, was tried out first in the South. It was some years after revised as *A Texas Steer* and became one of the most popular of his plays.

His first substantial success was *A Bunch of Keys, or Where There's A Will, There's A Play*, although this was revised before it met with popular approval. It opened in December, 1882, at Newark, New Jersey, and came into New York at the San Francisco Music Hall, in March, 1883. The cast was headed by Willie Edouin, who seems to have collaborated, and included James T. Powers and Julian Mitchell, to become the stage manager of Hoyt and later a producer on his own account. He is authority for the statement that while Hoyt produced his own plays and made a fortune, he did not usually direct them or even attend rehearsals, but was constantly watching his audiences and making suggestions to his stage directors. *A Bunch of Keys* is farce of the broadest kind. Three sisters, Rose, Teddy and May Keys, have been made a grim jest by an uncle who has left them a hotel property on condition that it shall go to the one who is declared to be the homeliest, by a traveling salesman then staying in the hotel. They each decline to take the property under these conditions, and the consequent endeavors of their *fiancés* to persuade them to accept it, make the play.

A Parlor Match (1884), written for the comedians Evans and Hoey, is a satire on spiritualism and the search for buried treasure. While it can hardly be said to compare with the contemporary treatments of spiritualism in the novel such as

A HISTORY OF THE AMERICAN DRAMA

Howells' *The Undiscovered Country*, it has some very amusing scenes, laid in a seaport village.

A Rag Baby (1884) portrays vividly the small town. Christian Berriel, a prominent undertaker, separated from his wife, comes to place his child in Miss Pratt's school, and Tony Jay, his brother-in-law, buys the drug store in order that he can send the wrong medicines to Christian Berriel and keep him ill. Tony wishes to obtain possession of his niece in order to return her to his sister. The drug store, in which two acts are laid, is the scene of hilarity, on account of the methods of Tony Jay and his assistant, Old Sport, who is inspired by the fact that in shaking hands with his employer he "can grasp the hand that grasped Sullivan's."

A Tin Soldier (1886) is laid in New York City, apparently, for locality meant little to Hoyt. He was concerned with types rather than local color. Brooklyn Bridge, "a gentleman of high position," has gone to a fancy-dress ball as a tin soldier, and Rats, a scamp who has taken his costume, gets into difficulties with a woman who insists upon Bridge making her reparation. But this plot is lost in a whirlwind of farce consequent upon the invasion of the house by Vilas Canby, a practical plumber, who is paid four dollars an hour and who employs Rats as his helper. The latter learns fast, for upon being sent on his first job he says, "I might go over and see it and shut off the water and bring away the faucets and connections and the meter—that will hold the job for us till we are ready to attend to it." Vilas Canby is a real character, and the servant from next door, Carry Story, who comes in to borrow supplies, has a vitality in her capacity for irritation that is positively creepy.

Hoyt was a master in selecting situations in which a large number of people could be brought naturally to the stage. *A Hole in the Ground* (1887) is laid in a railroad station, and nearly every event that happens to traveling and suffering humanity while waiting for delayed trains is portrayed. The agent is as thoroughly disagreeable a person as can be con-

98

ceived and when the Stranger, who is the leading character, asks him why he cannot be "halfway decent" he promptly replies, "Then no one would know I was the agent."

The Brass Monkey (1888) is perhaps best described in Hoyt's own words:

> *The Brass Monkey* is a somewhat desultory reference to a variety of subjects having no particular relevancy to what little plot there may be in the play. There is an endeavor to make a little mild fun on the 1001 petty superstitions of the day which everybody derides and secretly believes in, more or less. There is an attempt to illustrate the sincerity of obtrusive grief and to show the difficulties that may beset an inexperienced man in running an auction room. In Birdie, the correspondent of *The Society Gazette,* the author has attempted to satirize the guerillas of journalism, who by their outrages upon truth and decency have managed to create more or less prejudice against an honorable profession (in which they only occupy the place of hangers-on), and have made the approach of an interviewer more terrible than the coming of a pestilence.

Hoyt describes his next play, *The Midnight Bell* (1889), as "a legitimate comedy." "It is a legitimate comedy," he continues, "because it is in four acts and farce comedies are always in three." . . . "If when the agony is over, it has been found that the characters, scenes and incidents have been presented in an amusing fashion, the author will be satisfied." Hoyt evidently felt the criticism that his work was farcical in nature and his defense is that he tried first to be amusing. That he succeeded is beyond question. The leader of the theatre orchestra in Philadelphia was often almost unable to conduct, so infectious was the humor of the plays, although he had witnessed them very many times. Perhaps it was on account of this criticism that Hoyt attempted a more serious plot in *A Midnight Bell,* dealing with the sacrifice of Ned Olcott, a young bank teller, to save Squire Olcott, his uncle, from a charge of dishonesty, and the courage of a clergyman in a rural community in defying the petty malice of the women of his congregation against a young school-teacher who, he believes, is in love with Ned. The types, however, are conventional though somewhat affected by the realism which Herne's creations were bringing to the stage. With *A Texas Steer* (1890) Hoyt's art entered into its best period. Maverick Brander, who has been made a Congressman from Texas, on account of the desire of Mrs. Brander and their daughter Bossy to visit Washington, heads a family who are real people. The adventures of the Branders in the Capital are of course exaggerated and the army officers, one of whom Bossy captures, seem less real than the Texans, for their characters, being more restrained, lend themselves less to caricature. But there have not been many more amusing scenes on our stage than the climax of the second Act when Brander is victimized by a feminine blackmailer, whose mother "had been kissed by Daniel Webster" and who leads the embryo statesman into a position where a concealed camera puts him in her power. His curtain speech—"Did it cost Daniel Webster one hundred dollars to kiss your mother?"—echoes even now in the moving pictures. In this play Caroline Miskel, afterward Mrs. Hoyt, took a leading part.

A Trip to Chinatown opened at Hoyt's Madison Square Theatre, November 9, 1891, and ran 650 times, until August 17, 1893, up to that time the longest consecutive run of any play given in the United States. It was revived February 12, 1894, and the 700th performance took place March 26, 1894. As usual, the title had little to do with the play. The scene is laid in San Francisco. Ben Gay, a wealthy bachelor, wishes to go to a masked ball, and when his niece, Tony, and her friends tell him they are going on a trip through Chinatown, he allows her to go in order to cover his own tracks. Of course they all meet at the ball with consequent comedy, in which a widow from Chicago figures largely. She is the best-drawn character, though Welland Strong, a companion of Ben Gay, who comes West for his health, is an amusing creation. This part was acted by Harry Conor, who played in it for eleven years.

HARRIGAN, HOYT, AND THE COMEDY OF TYPES

Hoyt had an almost uncanny sense for human weakness and usually played upon the surface of life. But in *A Temperance Town* (1893) he seemed to be more serious in his attack upon hypocrisy and cruelty. He chose a village in Vermont in the early days when Prohibition was still a local issue, and made his central character the village drunkard, Launcelot Jones. In "Mink" Jones, Hoyt portrayed the genial vagabond who attends to anyone's business but his own, and who neglects his family to help others. He is almost a certain source of success for a playwright, for he is endowed with qualities which usually do not belong to a drunkard in real life and he appeals to that innate sympathy which is felt for the character whose mingled vices and virtues allow the sober citizen to indulge vicariously in those weaknesses he chooses for reasons of his own to forego. Mink Jones and Fred Oakhurst, who conducts a saloon, are the only honest men in a town whose leading citizens are typified by the Reverend Earnest Hardman and Kneeland Pray, the local druggist "who will sell on prescription." They persecute the honest and upright lawbreaker who is saved by the return of the son of the minister. There are many humorous scenes, but there is a serious undercurrent which makes the play of more permanent worth.

A Milk White Flag (1893) is once more pure fooling—the Ransome Guards, which consists of unlimited officers and one private, is good farcical material, but no more. *A Runaway Colt* (1895) is a defense of the professional baseball player, in which Hoyt proceeded to the unusual lengths of introducing as a central character Captain Adrian Anson of the Chicago "Colts," who is contrasted much to his advantage with clergymen and bank cashiers. *A Black Sheep* (1896), laid in Tombstone, Arizona and in New York City, is not so convincing as the farces that precede or follow it. *The Contented Woman* (1897) reveals more earnestness of purpose. It dramatizes the contest between man and woman for their respective spheres of life. Benton Holme and his wife, Grace, run against each other for Mayor of Denver. There is some clever satire—Grace wishes to know what to wear at a rally of her party just as Benton wishes to know what to say, and the toast, "To woman, once our superior, now our equal," has been revived in recent years with effect. In fact, many of the clever sayings of Hoyt are used to-day in ignorance of their origin.

The Stranger in New York (1897) is also of more interest than many of the earlier plays. It is laid in New York City and pictures the life in hotels and at a French ball with vivid if highly colored scenes. The stranger who preserves his incognito among trying circumstances is the cool, quiet man of resource who is always an appealing character.

In *A Day and a Night in New York* (1898), Hoyt represented theatrical life and modified the theme of *David Garrick* by having an actress pretend that she is *not* one in order to protect her mother, who has concealed her daughter's profession from her second husband. During the progress of the play at the Garrick Theatre, Mrs. Hoyt died. Hoyt's mind seems to have been affected by grief, and his next play, *A Dog in the Manger*, already shows signs of mental deterioration, though it is at times clever. Hoyt was committed to a sanitarium in July, 1900, but was released on petition of friends, and placed under medical care until his death, November 20, 1900.

Hoyt's plays, like Harrigan's, were interspersed with songs, not, however, always of his own creation. But also like Harrigan's, the plays were not merely musical comedies. There is always a plot, slight though it be, and the characters, though types, have some reality. No one rises in the memory with the tenacity of Dan Mulligan or Cordelia or Rebecca Allup, possibly because Hoyt wrote no cycle of plays, but gave new names to his creations, who indeed are different human beings. The very names of Hoyt's characters, while adding by their clever incongruity to the sum of our amusement—Rashleigh Gay, Welland Strong, Manley Manners, Phil Graves, the undertaker, and so on forever—forbid almost at the start our se-

CHARLES H. HOYT

CHARLES H. HOYT

rious consideration of their possessors. And yet on running over the lists, one finds how few are chosen outside of the actual surnames with which we are familiar. It is only a reminder of the metaphorical processes by which these family names began.

Harrigan's art was a finer one than Hoyt's. It was based on a long study of the stage, especially of Molière. And when Brander Matthews took Coquelin back to talk to Harrigan in his dressing room, the latter conducted the conversation in French. There is an imaginative quality in his plays which came perhaps from his Celtic strain, which Hoyt's rougher and broader strokes did not reveal. With the gradual disappearance of the audiences who saw them, there likewise passes away the memory of a humor which had in it nothing sordid or debasing, but which nevertheless held thousands spellbound. The manuscripts can only faintly reflect the steady sparkle of the humor that was Harrigan's and the wit that was Hoyt's, and the best of their plays should be revived in printed form. For America is not rich enough in the records of her art to lose what they have contributed to her vanished hours of joy.

The example set by Harrigan and Hoyt was followed during the eighties and nineties by many playwrights, but few deserve mention here. Popular successes, written for actors like W. H. Crane and Nat Goodwin, were wrought out of similar material. One of the best of these was *The Senator* (1889), by David Demarest Lloyd, in which Crane made a great hit as Senator Hannibal Rivers. Even now the character of the impetuous, lovable Senator, while verging always on farce, comes out of the pages of the manuscript with a freshness that years can hardly dim. It is to be noted also that the cheapest elements, like the Chinaman, were put in by Sydney Rosenfeld. Lloyd did not live to see *The Senator* produced. He had other stage successes to his credit like *For Congress*, written for Raymond and afterward rewritten for Roland Reed by Rosenfeld under the title of *The Politician*. His political plays show, however, the essential weakness of the type play, when we compare, for example, *The Senator* with

A HISTORY OF THE AMERICAN DRAMA

Thomas's *The Capitol,* written five years later. We have not had many serious studies of our politics, largely because of managerial dread of controversial topics.

It was much simpler to take our politicians to a South American State, as Richard Harding Davis did in *The Dictator* (1904) and substitute for Colonel Bowie, the real consul, a young American of the romantic type Davis knew how to draw so well. Of his other long plays *The Galloper* (1906) was a clever picture of the various types of war correspondents, American and English, operating in the front during the Greco-Turkish war of 1897. Davis's dramatic work, however, while it extended into the twentieth century, began in the early nineties with one-act plays, of which *The Other Woman* (1893) was quite well done, and *The Disreputable Mr. Reagan* (1895) provided E. H. Sothern with a congenial rôle. These were dramatizations of Davis's own stories and they give one the same impression as his fiction, a sense that they come near to being first rate but just lack the element of artistic truth. But certainly his earlier one-act plays ring more truly than *The Galloper* or *The Dictator.* Perhaps this is due to the fact that Davis seems to belong to the nineteenth century, or at least he may be considered as a writer of the transition which in the case of the type play is practically a continuous process.

CHAPTER V

THE DRAMA OF THE FRONTIER

THE very essence of the frontier is its progressive nature. To the earlier playwrights Kentucky was the land of the pioneer, and when Paulding drew Nimrod Wildfire in 1831, or when Louisa Medina dramatized Bird's novel, *Nick of the Woods*, in 1838, the hero either came from that State or at least had scalped Indians within its borders. This tradition persisted perhaps because of the continued popularity of *Nick of the Woods*, and one of the best of the plays of the seventies was laid apparently in Tennessee.

The next step in the development of the frontier was the crossing of the Mississippi and a play of the transition period, *Kit the Arkansas Traveler* (1870), by T. B. DeWalden, deals with the pioneer who represented one further step westward. This play was popular for many years and the character of Kit Redding became, in the interpretation of F. S. Chanfrau, the standard pioneer. After his death Henry Chanfrau continued it in his répertoire as late as 1894. The elder Chanfrau had made a great success with his portrayal of Mose, the New York fireman, in 1848, and his power as a character actor was shown in his ability to interpret the wronged husband and father who is seeking the wife and child that had been taken from him.

A much better play, *Davy Crockett*, was the work of a nephew of the actor, James E. Murdoch, who allowed his name to be added to that of the playwright and actor, who became known as Frank Hitchcock Murdoch. He did not see *Davy Crockett* produced, as he was acting in Philadelphia, when it was first performed at Rochester, New York, September 23, 1872. Hitchcock died November 13, 1872. Owing to an error in Hut-

A HISTORY OF THE AMERICAN DRAMA

ton's *Curiosities of the American Stage*, a romantic story has grown up of Hitchcock's death on account of the unfavorable criticism of *Davy Crockett*.[1]

Frank Mayo, who created the character and produced the play, had confidence in *Davy Crockett* and, undaunted by its first cold reception, continued it successfully for many years. It was played later by his son, Edwin Mayo; and by a grim accident, Harry Hitchcock, the playwright's brother, was apparently negotiating for the purchase of the dramatic rights, when he met his tragic death at the Brooklyn Theatre fire.

Davy Crockett is based apparently on the tradition of the Tennessee trapper and hunter, who "found out what was right and went ahead," and whose autobiography is a significant document in our social history. He was certainly a less idyllic character than his stage descendant. The scene of the play is a frontier settlement, not named, but probably in Tennessee, and since Crockett died in defense of the Alamo in 1836, the action presumably takes place before that time. The character of the trapper, strong, simple, unable to read, but with a keen sense of right, is contrasted with that of the young girl, Eleanor Vaughan, whom he had known as a child, but who has been educated abroad. She returns with her guardian, Major Royston, to be married to Neil, the nephew of Oscar Crampton, a neighboring Squire, who has a hold over the Major through some notes of the usual dubious quality familiar to the finance of the stage. The plot, however, is negligible; the complications which keep Davy and Eleanor apart are brushed aside as soon as it is necessary by his simple expedient of carrying her off on the swiftest horse in the neighborhood. The literary inspiration of *Davy Crockett* is from Walter Scott and Hitchcock made no secret of that inspiration. In the second Act, which takes place in Davy's hut, Eleanor is saved from freezing by Davy's courage and decision, and while

[1] But see Brander Matthews, "The American on the Stage," *Scribner's Monthly,* XVIII (July, 1879), pp. 327–8. From members of Hitchcock's family I learn that his death was due to causes unconnected with his plays.

they sit by the fire she reads to him the ballad of Young Lochinvar. In Davy's vernacular, "A nod's as good as a wink to a blind horse," but just then the howl of approaching wolves is heard and the Act ends:

(Interior of Crockett's hut.)

Eleanor:	What is it?
Davy:	Keep still and listen. (*A howl is again heard.*)
Eleanor:	I hear a long, low cry as of some animal in distress.
Davy:	Ah, you hear it then. I was right, wasn't I? Thar it is again.
Eleanor:	What is it?
Davy:	That's wolves.
Eleanor:	Wolves— (*Screams.*)
Davy:	Don't be scared—
Eleanor:	But—is there no danger?
Davy:	Ain't I here?
Eleanor:	Yes, but they are so dreadfully near.
Davy:	Yes, they tracked you in the snow and smell blood.
Eleanor:	Blood!
Davy:	Take it easy, girl. This door is built of oak, I built it—and—blazes, the bar's gone.
Eleanor:	Gone? (*Wolves howl all round cabin.*)
Davy:	Yes, I split it up to warm you and your friend— Rouse him up. The pesky devils is all around the house.
Eleanor:	(*Goes to Neil.*) Neil—help! help! (*The wolves throw themselves against the door and bark.*)
Davy:	Quick there, I can't hold the door agin 'em—
Neil:	I tell you, uncle, if the girl says no, there's an end of it—
Eleanor:	My God—he is delirious—
Davy:	What!
Eleanor:	'Tis true—nothing can save us.
Davy:	Yes, it can.
Eleanor:	What?
Davy:	The strong arm of a backwoodsman.

(Davy bars the door with his arm. The wolves attack the house. Their heads are seen through the opening in the hut and under the door.)

CURTAIN

The very incident goes back to Scottish history, but the quotation will show the direct speech and the quick, if melodramatic, action. On the stage it is quite effective, for the climax grows naturally out of the situation. What makes *Davy Crockett* of significance, however, is the way in which Hitchcock created and Mayo interpreted the character of a man of few but strong traits, loving naturally a girl whose education and breeding had not blinded her to the innate nobility of his nature, and who saw him in surroundings which brought back the fragrance of a childhood's friendship. It is old-fashioned romance set in a newer stage technique and Mayo acted the part in such a quiet restrained manner that he made the romance seem possible. It is an idyll, in a way, of the pioneer life, with the crudity toned down; and the author chose wisely a contrast which from *Othello* to *The Great Divide* has never failed to appeal to human sympathy. In a way it showed progress, for there were no Indians, no tomahawking, and no shooting except of the wolves, and it may be said to mark the transition from the cult of "the natural man" to the study of the natural gentleman.

As Professor Paxson has shown, the frontier is either a line, a region, or a process.[1] For the purpose of drama, it is a region, and when the standardizing process which turns the frontier into a stable civilization has become apparent, the contrasts which are the life of drama become less vivid. What made *Davy Crockett* a success was the direct current which flowed between the opposite poles of two natures, one strong and one charming.

Davy Crockett inspired no school of play writing. But in 1871 Augustin Daly had seen the greater theatrical possibilities of another frontier, that of California, and *Horizon* is the first of a series of plays which owe their inspiration to Bret Harte. It was a different frontier, less primitive and more sophisticated, much more varied in its elements, and almost too rich in striking incidents. That it became melodrama was

[1] Paxson, F. L. *History of the American Frontier*, p. 43.

inevitable, for life itself was melodrama. *Horizon* has already been discussed and its directness of dialogue and vivid characterization noted. There can be no question, however, that the two most important characters, Panther John Loder, the "bad man," who rises naturally to the greatness of self-sacrifice, and "Med" Van Dorp, the untutored product of the Western plains, are the combination of romance in conception and realism of treatment which made Bret Harte the creator of a popular school of fiction. In *Horizon* are to be found also "the Heathen Chinee" and other definite imitations of Harte, and the play, while laid ostensibly "near Fort Jackson," is really placed in that land of romance which Harte created through his observation and imagination. California objected to Harte's pictures of its life as exaggerated in their lawlessness and crudity, but the stage adopted his standards without question, for Harte's genius had seen the picturesque in the new civilization of the frontier and for his purposes the picture was more important than the photograph. His ambition was to write successful plays and he began his dramatic effort with an attempted collaboration with Dion Boucicault in a play, *Kentuck*, for Augustin Daly. But for reasons which become apparent from Boucicault's letters to Daly,[1] the two men could not work together. Bret Harte must have modified his original conception or perhaps he simply rejected Boucicault's suggestions, for the outline of the play as given in Daly's biography bears little relation to the finished product, *The Two Men of Sandy Bar*, which was produced at the Union Square Theatre, August 28, 1876. While not an absolute failure, it was hardly successful on the stage, though it went on tour after its brief run in New York. The play was based on Bret Harte's story, *Mr. Thompson's Prodigal*, which tells with mingled pathos and humor of the search of a repentant father who has driven his son from home, and who, having been converted to an emotional form of religion, seeks his son and apparently finds him. But at the dinner he gives to celebrate the prodigal's re-

[1] Daly, J. F. *The Life of Augustin Daly*, pp. 170–6.

turn the real Charles Thompson appears, hopelessly drunk, and the impostor departs. It may have been the quiet gentlemanly way in which this impostor plays his game, even at the end, which suggested to Bret Harte that he bring his favorite creation, John Oakhurst, the gambler, into the play in a similar situation. Likewise, he took the love story of Sandy Morton and Miss Mary, the central characters of *The Idyll of Red Gulch*, and made the first take the place of Charles Thompson. Finally he superimposed Colonel Starbottle, who had nothing to do with the original story, upon the plot and made him the star, to be acted by Stuart Robson. The result is a confused melodrama, with brilliant dialogue at times, but with no real coherence. Judge Daly suggests that the peculiar utterance of Stuart Robson, "which was not only not Western —but not like anything known to civilization"—killed the play.

A minor part in *Two Men of Sandy Bar*, that of Hop Sing, had been taken by C. T. Parsloe, and his performance had been so acceptable that Bret Harte and Mark Twain built a play around the character of the Chinaman, Ah Sin, who was famous as the "Heathen Chinee" of Harte's poem. It was first put on at the National Theatre, Washington, May 7, 1877, before a brilliant audience, and was sufficiently successful to induce Augustin Daly to produce it in New York, on July 31, at the Fifth Avenue Theatre. *Ah Sin* provides an interesting study of the two great exponents of Western life, working together for the first and last time. It reveals the unwholesome result of the star system. The part of the Chinaman is made prominent at the expense of probability and construction, and as a background he is provided with a conglomeration of miners, and visiting townspeople, male and female, over whose complications he presides and whom he outwits with ease. His mingled shrewdness and stupidity are not badly represented. The relative contributions of Bret Harte and Mark Twain are difficult to distinguish, for the height-

THE DRAMA OF THE FRONTIER

ened contrasts of rough miners with the types of San Francisco
women, young and old, who are evidently intended to represent refinement and breeding, are reminiscent of both writers.
If any distinction is to be made, the men seem to be more
definitely Bret Harte's creation, while certainly Mrs. Plunkett
and her daughter are the product of Mark Twain. The former is Mrs. Malaprop translated to the West, and some of her
speeches, like, "Here we stand, two lonely, friendless, dissolute
women," or, "I cannot think of him without going into ecsta-
sies of sensibility, perfect ruptures of emotion," have earmarks
of his own. The play lasted about five weeks, then was withdrawn for lack of support. The most successful episode connected with its production was Mark Twain's curtain speech
at the first night in New York.[1] One paragraph will show its
quality:

I wish to say also that this play is didactic rather than anything else. It is intended rather for instruction than amusement.
The Chinaman is getting to be a pretty frequent figure in the
United States, and is going to be a great political problem, and
we thought it well for you to see him on the stage before you had
to deal with that problem. Then for the instruction of the young
we have introduced a game of poker. There are few things that
are so unpardonably neglected in our country as poker. The
upper class know very little about it. Now and then you find
Ambassadors who have a sort of general knowledge of the game,
but the ignorance of the people at large is fearful. Why, I have
known clergymen, good men, kind-hearted, liberal, sincere and all
that, who did not know the meaning of a "flush"; it is enough to
make one ashamed of one's species. When our play was finished,
we found it was so long, and so broad, and so deep—in places—
that it would have taken a week to play it. I thought that was
all right; we could put "To be continued" on the curtain, and run
it straight along. But the manager said no; it would get us into
trouble with the general public, and into trouble with the general
government, because the Constitution forbids the infliction of
cruel or unusual punishment; so he cut out, and cut out, and the
more he cut out the better the play got. I never saw a play that
was so much improved by being cut down; and I believe it would

[1] See *Life of Daly*, pp. 234–5.

have been one of the very best plays in the world if his strength had held out so that he could cut out the whole of it.

Harte's letters reveal how earnestly he desired to write successful plays and how he turned aside from more secure engagements to dramatize *Jeff Briggs' Love Story*, *Thankful Blossom*, *The Luck of Roaring Camp*, *Clarence*, and *A Blue Grass Penelope*, none of which saw the stage. In *The Luck* the heroine was educated by the wealthy members of the camp and brought to Paris, where, Harte hoped, "this mingling and contact of these rough men with this high-super-civilized Old World" might produce dramatic effect. Harte had undertaken this play at the suggestion of Boucicault and a version by the latter was performed at the Empire Theatre, New York, May 14, 1894, but there is no indication that Harte had any share in it.

Bret Harte's only substantial success came years later, with *Sue*, in which he collaborated with T. Edgar Pemberton, and which is a dramatization of Harte's story, *The Judgment of Bolinas Plain*. Other characters were introduced and it was first played on September 15, 1896, at Hoyt's Theatre, New York. On October 12 it started on tour, and it was produced in London at the Garrick Theatre, June 10, 1898, where Annie Russell scored a distinct personal success.[1] Sue marries Ira Beasley, the owner of Bolinas Farm, a man much older than herself. She becomes fascinated by a circus acrobat, Jim Wynd, and starts to run away with him, but is prevented from going by Parson Davies. The plot is not so important, though there is a certain cleverness in the stage management so that Jim Wynd and Ira fire at the Sheriff and each believes that he has killed him. But the character of Sue, who has never had the joys of childhood or girlhood, and who reacts instinctively to her one hope of pleasure, was a real Bret Harte figure, unmoral rather than immoral, and was drawn with the sense of the dramatic which, notwithstanding his stage failures,

[1] See *Letters of Bret Harte*, pp. 424–35 and 449–55, and *Life* by Pemberton, pp. 269–74.

THE DRAMA OF THE FRONTIER

Harte possessed. This gift was recognized by Clement Scott in his intelligent analysis of the play in the *Daily Telegraph* on the morning after the first performance in London. "The dramatic gift, the poetic gift, the realistic gift are seldom combined. But Bret Harte possesses them all."

It is true that his works teem with dramatic situations, but the limitations which, while allowing him to become one of the great writers of short stories, prevented him from becoming a successful novelist, also prevented him from becoming a practical playwright. If the one-act play had been at that time a profitable branch of theatrical art, Bret Harte might have succeeded in it. But his sense of construction was lacking for a broader structure, as the failure of *Gabriel Conroy*, his one full-length novel, proved. It was partly the very wealth of his material, as it was with Dickens, which stood in his way. Others could select and reject and win success as Clay Greene did with *M'liss*,[1] in which Annie Pixley starred, or as Paul Armstrong did with *Salomy Jane* (1907), played by Eleanor Robson, but the author himself could not cut out relentlessly all that was not contributory to the real essence of the plot. There is enough in *Two Men of Sandy Bar* to carry three plays, but under the star system in vogue in 1876, the very excellence of John Oakhurst, of Sandy Morton, militated against the success of a play whose star was Colonel Starbottle. More than that, Bret Harte's characters had become almost like historical personages, and even he could not take liberties with them. Playgoers who had formed their conception of John Oakhurst, of Sandy Morton, of Miss Mary, of Colonel Starbottle, from the fine art of a short story where they flashed into being through the deft description and narration of a master of the form, did not relish seeing these same characters altered by their own creator on the stage. It must be remembered, too, that Bret Harte, even at his best, is constantly

[1] Bret Harte's own adaptation of this story remained unacted. He was unable to prevent the unauthorized use of his material in this country, but he stopped the plays in England.

skirting the edge of danger in his treatment of the sentimental, and the touch that heightened his characters for the footlights was in some cases fatal. But if he could have worked harmoniously in collaboration with a trained playwright, he might have produced significant plays, for his great contribution to modern literature, the portrayal of moral contrasts in human beings from an objective, unmoral point of view, is in itself essentially dramatic.

Mark Twain's one success as a playwright was in a certain sense associated with the frontier, but it was the frontier of the older region. The play of *The Gilded Age* seems to have disappeared, and we have only the character as revealed in the novel and the tradition of the remarkable performance of John T. Raymond as Colonel Mulberry Sellers. The first dramatization was made by Gilbert S. Densmore, a newspaper man, in San Francisco and the play was produced by John T. Raymond at the California Theatre, April 23, 1874.[1]

Mark Twain at once challenged the right to dramatize the book and an amicable arrangement was made between him and Densmore, by which the latter relinquished any share in the play. Mark Twain wrote a version, which contained some of the elements of Densmore's plot, but the character of Colonel Sellers, which carried the play as Raymond acted it, was the creation of Mark Twain, with some contribution, including the name itself, from Charles Dudley Warner. The revised play was put on at the Park Theatre, New York, September 16, 1874, and ran for one hundred and nineteen nights. The frontier of *The Gilded Age* was, of course, a fairly stabilized region, and the play carried its hero to Washington and the lobbying of the post-war period. Yet Colonel Sellers has in him the quality of perennial youth and the spirit of adventure which have made the frontier a progressive process in our history.

[1] See Paine, A. B., *Mark Twain*, pp. 517-19, Winter, William, *The Life of David Belasco*, I, pp. 64–8, and Matthews, Brander, "Mark Twain and the Theater" in *Playwrights on Playmaking*, pp. 168–75, for discussion of the relative shares of Clemens and Densmore in the play.

THE DRAMA OF THE FRONTIER

Mark Twain's interest in the stage was keen and constant, however, and he was a capable actor. After the failure of *Ah Sin*, he made an attempt at a play dealing with a detective, but gave it up. He conceived of *The Prince and the Pauper* first as a drama, and while he wisely chose to write it in its present form, he dramatized the story later and offered it to various managers without result. The version with which many theatre goers are still familiar was made by Abby Sage Richardson in 1890, and arranged for the stage by David Belasco. *Pudd'nhead Wilson* also saw the stage through other hands. Frank Mayo, who had played *Davy Crockett* so long, dramatized Mark Twain's novel in 1895 and it was a substantial success.

A comparison of the novel with the play reveals the instinct of the trained actor for stage effects. Mayo cut the long speeches of Pudd'nhead Wilson, even in the trial scene, remorselessly. He made a climax of one act the revelation to Tom Driscoll that Roxy the slave is his mother, but he created out of "Chambers," the real heir to the Driscoll estate, who had been deprived of his birthright by Roxy when she changed the babies in their cradles, a real person instead of a mere foil to Tom. By cleverly indicating a protecting care of Chambers by Rowena, the niece of Pudd'nhead Wilson, he prepared the way for a love story when Chambers turns out to be white, and he therefore secured a wider sympathy in the audience.

Mark Twain and William Dean Howells revived Colonel Sellers in *The American Claimant, or Mulberry Sellers Ten Years Later*, in which the Colonel is represented as more wildly extravagant than ever and is also a claimant to an English earldom. This play actually saw the stage for about a week out of town and was put on at a matinée performance in New York, but it is not important. Yet it is at least an interesting circumstance that both Bret Harte and Mark Twain should have made such efforts to become practical playwrights. The successful dramatization of their fiction by other hands reveals its essentially dramatic quality. It was with Mark Twain as with Bret Harte, a lack of constructive sense and an inability to discard material which detracted from the unity of stage presentation.

The regret which Bret Harte and Mark Twain felt at their frequent failures was probably not lessened by the success of their chief rival in the delineation of Western life. Just as *Ah Sin* was withdrawn from Daly's Theatre, *The Danites in the Sierras*, by Joaquin Miller, was produced at the Broadway Theatre on August 22, 1877, and proved to be one of the most popular of the plays of the Frontier. The plot and characters are definitely based on Miller's conception of the West as a place of strong passions and emotions, of quick thinking and acting, of lurid lights and sharp shadows. The influence of Bret Harte is clear, but after all Miller knew his material. He drew vivid contrasts, not only moral but also racial and religious. The shadow of the Danite or Mormon vengeance pursuing the young girl, Nancy Williams, who is disguised as a boy and lives alone in a cabin in the Sierras to avoid their pursuit, is a dramatic theme. The character of Sandy McGee is lifted bodily from Bret Harte. He is the strong man who is animated by the desire to protect the weaker of either sex and who marries "the widow" and lives happily with her until she is murdered by the Danites, and then marries equally happily Nancy Williams, when she resumes her feminine attire. The Chinaman, the women with a past, who reform and become pillars of society, are all equally conventional stage figures. But there is a directness in the dialogue, a sense of action and a pulsing humanity felt at times in Miller's lyric poetry, which are not by any means negligible.

The play was at first the joint product of Miller and an "alert actor" in London who helped Miller put together two of his short stories, *The First Woman in the Forks* and *The Last Man of Mexican Camp*, and it was published under the name of *The First Families of the Sierras*. It was revised by Alexander Fitzgerald, an actor in Philadelphia, for Mr. and Mrs. McKee Rankin (Kitty Blanchard), and the first cast

included Louis Aldrich and Fitzgerald himself. The printed
version of the drama differs from the play as it was performed,
but Miller has omitted some of the more melodramatic elements. *The Danites* was popular for many years,[1] being
played at the California Theatre in 1878, and was the play
selected by McKee Rankin when he took a complete American
company to the Sadler's Wells Theatre, London, opening April
2, 1880. Rankin claimed that he was the first actor and manager to take a complete American company abroad,[2] and the
venture was successful. He and Mrs. Rankin became identified with the production of the frontier play.

Forty-nine, Miller's second play, was produced by them at
Haverly's Theatre, New York, on October 1, 1881. It has the
theme which Miller used in his verse more than once—that of
the Argonaut, the pioneer who sticks to his tunnel even after
hope is gone, and who wins gold at last. The character of
"Forty-nine," played by Rankin, is in a sense an epic figure,
and when he takes the blame of a supposed robbery to shield
his son, who is ignorant of his parentage, he achieves a certain distinction. Carrots, the girl whom he is protecting, and
who turns out to be an heiress, was played by Mrs. Rankin,
and is an amusing figure. The remainder of the plot is negligible, but the scene in which the old negro, Sam, identifies
Carrots by the song he sang her in her infancy, is real drama.

Tally Ho! was founded according to Miller on Horace Greeley's account of his crossing the Sierras with Hank Monk, the
dashing stage driver. "Joe Jefferson," he continues, "was its
godfather; John Sousa wrote the music, and the present leading member of Congress from San Francisco played a part."
Tally Ho! is another play in which the central character, Hank
Monk, attempts to sacrifice himself for another, this time his
wife, who is accused of murder. It is less veracious than *The
Danites*, but has a certain vigor and directness of language.

[1] See *Plays of the Present*, pp. 80–2, and Introduction to *The Danites* in Joaquin
Miller's *Poems*, Vol. 6, San Francisco, 1910.
[2] Brown. *History of the New York Stage*, II, 363.

A HISTORY OF THE AMERICAN DRAMA

An Oregon Idyll was his own favorite among his plays, because it dealt with the woods and the characters were known to him. It has the usual plot, with the exception that the hero, John Logan, is part Indian, and his misfortunes have a racial as well as a personal appeal. The insertion of the Boston types, Archie Shuttlebuck and Margaret Hutchinson, who are caricatures, marks Miller's one attempt at sectional contrasts.

The varying appeal of the frontier drama illustrates clearly how jealous a mistress is the art of playwriting. Bret Harte, Mark Twain, Joaquin Miller were writers of fiction and poetry who approached the stage at times, but whose main achievement lay elsewhere. The best plays of the frontier were written by either an actor like Hitchcock, a producer like Daly, or by Bartley Campbell, who represents with Bronson Howard the professional playwright, who devoted himself entirely to his craft.

Bartley Campbell was born in Pittsburgh, August 12, 1843. He began his career as a newspaper man on the Pittsburgh *Post* and, after serving on the Louisville *Courier Journal* and the Cincinnati *Enquirer*, he became founder and editor of the *Southern Monthly Magazine* in New Orleans in 1869. When he began playwriting in 1871 he retired from journalism, as he held that once a man writes a play, especially an unsuccessful one, he should never again write dramatic criticism for a newspaper. He began playwriting in 1871 with a sensational drama, *Through Fire*, and in 1872 wrote for E. L. Davenport a social comedy, *Peril, or Love at Long Branch*. In the same year he assisted R. M. Hooley to transform Hooley's Opera House, which had been the home of minstrelsy in Chicago, into Hooley's Theatre, which should produce legitimate drama in opposition to McVicker's Theatre. Bartley Campbell organized the company and directed the plays, many of which were his own. Among these were *Fate*, a domestic drama, and *Risks, or Insure Your Life*, written to give John Dillon a leading comedy part. It had for its theme a study of life insurance,

118

which was at that time increasing in popularity. The leading character, George Washington Pembroke, was afterward played by John T. Raymond in New York and in California. Among the plays Campbell wrote while in Chicago were *The Virginian*, *Gran Uale*, *My Foolish Wife*, and *On the Rhine*, a story of the Franco-Prussian War.

In the summer of 1875, the company at Hooley's Theatre played a summer season at Maguire's Opera House in San Francisco. While there, Bartley Campbell adapted Von Moser's comedy, *Ultimo*, under the title of *Bulls and Bears*, and it was performed in San Francisco with great success on June 7 just before Daly's company arrived with his adaptation of the same play, *The Big Bonanza*, performed on July 19. For the first time Bartley Campbell came in contact with California life. He became a member of the Bohemian Club and knew Bret Harte and Joaquin Miller. It was this Western experience that was to provide him with the material for his finest play, *My Partner*. In 1876, he made his first trip to England, and in November of that year produced *The Virginian* at the St. James Theatre, with Mrs. John Wood and Sam Piercy in the cast. While in London he wrote *A Heroine in Rags* and *How Women Love*. The latter was first produced at the Arch Street Theatre in Philadelphia, May, 1877, and was afterward rewritten as *The Vigilantes, or the Heart of the Sierras*. It was a play laid in 1856 in and around San Francisco and the Yosemite Valley.

That Campbell was not unmindful of the criticism of the seventies, which urged the revival of the drama that is of permanent literary worth, is proven by his writing *Clio* in verse. It is a dramatic spectacle laid in Italy in the Twelfth Century, played first in Pittsburgh and Chicago in 1878. In 1885 he revised the play and it was produced on a great scale at Niblo's Garden with music by Operti. These early plays seem to be non-extant.

My Partner, produced at the Union Square Theatre, September 16, 1879, represents the drama of the frontier in its most impressive form. It is the dramatic treatment of the theme of the friendship of two partners broken by the love of the same woman, whose epic was written by Bret Harte. Harte's influence is seen clearly in the general atmosphere, but Campbell had been on the ground, and the play is the result of observation of actual life rather than of reading about it. Joe Saunders, the hero, is the large-hearted type of miner, rough in manner but gentle in spirit, and with a personal dignity which comes perhaps from his creator's avoidance of the tempting opportunity, which Harte seldom resisted, of providing his hero with a besetting weakness. Campbell preferred to endow Ned Singleton, Joe's partner, with that unmoral attitude which causes him to betray Mary Brandon under promise of marriage. Joe overhears their conversation and makes Ned promise to marry her. In the second Act, which is laid in the cabin of Joe and Ned, the play reaches its climax. The stage direction which indicates definitely that the cabin is *not* to be made of unplaned logs, shows how Campbell realized that the frontier of which he was writing had become stabilized. Yet even in 1869, in which year the action is supposed to occur, it remained essentially a man's country, and the dramatic value of the situation rests upon the close bond made by the friendship of two partners, and the essential sense of justice which allows them to act fairly to each other even when they are parting forever. Joe tells Ned that they must separate, "for the old confidence is gone," and they divide the gold they have held jointly. After the division, Ned turns away for a moment and Joe secretly adds a portion of his own share to his partner's stock. Yet he refuses to shake hands with Ned, for the hurt has gone too deep, and he leaves the cabin. Almost immediately Scraggs, a man who nurses a grudge against the Brandons, enters and attempts to persuade Ned that he should not marry Mary, since she had been Joe's mistress. Ned attacks him as a slanderer, and in the ensuing fight Scraggs stabs him with Joe's knife. In a few moments Joe returns and speaks to his dead partner, who is apparently sitting at the table with his back to Joe.

There he is! My partner, and he hasn't stirred yet.—Say—Ned—Ned.

Well you see, I've come back!—I couldn't go away without a feeling that we parted friends – – – When I got down thar in the canyon – – where we worked together: I set down to take a look at the old familiar spot. The dry leaves were a-dancing in the wind, the birds singing in the branches, and the creek laughing among the boulders, as if there were no such thing as pain or part-ing. Everything came back to me. The days we worked together, the plans we used to lay for the time we had made our pile, and could afford to let the pick grow red and rusty in the mine. All your good acts came a-crowding around me, making me ashamed of myself, that I'd refused a hand, I'd often been glad to grasp, when I warn't able to help myself – – and so – I'm here – here to offer ye my hand, and to ask yer pardon. – – Before I go away forever.

(He extends his hand.)

What, ye won't take it? All right, remember I offered it! That's all I can do.

(He goes to the door.)

Oh! darn it, Ned – – we mustn't part like this – – Look up and speak – – Ned – Ned – You ain't sick, are you, partner? Say, partner, what's the matter?

(He takes Ned's hand and comes around in front.)

What's this, Ned? Cold and rigid. Dead! No! No! – Ned – Partner – – look up! Don't sit staring there like that. Only speak to me once more – – Only say, say you forgive me – – Oh, my God, he's dead – – dead – – dead.

The remainder of the play, in which Joe is accused of the murder and is saved by Wing Lee, the Chinaman, is reminiscent of *Ah Sin*. Yet there are some very effective scenes—Joe's proposal of marriage to Mary, under the shadow of his approaching execution, is simple and sincere. Quite appealing, too, is the spectacle of Joe, practically under sentence of death, released by the Sheriff on parole, because he is "square." The apparent paradox of a supposed murderer being worthy of trust was in fact based upon the real conditions of the frontier. The pioneers in California developed laws and customs based on practical necessity and the standards of right and wrong became either confused or more clear according to the point of view. But there is no question that *My Partner* is true to the life it portrayed, and there is even less doubt of its dramatic excellence. It was played by Louis Aldrich for many years. It was translated into German and was played for about fifty nights, beginning September 15, 1884, at the Residenz-Theater in Berlin, Campbell attending the rehearsals. It had been performed in London April 10, 1884, at the Olympic Theatre. The profits of *My Partner*, in which he had only the author's share, were so large that Campbell determined to produce his own plays, and for a time he was successful. *The Galley Slave*, which opened the season of 1879 at the Chestnut Street Theatre in Philadelphia, is a melodrama, laid in Europe, well constructed and vigorous, but conventional. The climax of the second Act, in which Sidney Norcott, being found in Cicely Blaine's apartment at night, allows himself to be arrested as a thief, is reminiscent of Sardou's *Nos Bons Villageois*. The subtitle is "A Reflex of American Society Abroad," but the interest is not social but emotional. This may have accounted for its success in Berlin, where it ran for eighty-three nights at the Wilhelm-Theater in 1881. In fact, wherever the scene of Campbell's plays were laid the emotional relations were stressed. *Siberia* (1882), his other extant play of foreign life, is an improvement on *The Galley Slave* and its complicated plot forbids retelling. Yet at the end of each of the six acts comes a swift and telling climax, and the sense of peril to the exiles from Russia is ever present. *Separation* (1884) is a melodrama, laid partly in New York and partly in Normandy. Its theme is the puritanical prejudice against the theatre, made concrete by the enforced separation of a mother from her child when she refuses to obey her husband who forbids her to sing for charity at even an amateur performance. Again the curtain descends upon emotional crises

THE DRAMA OF THE FRONTIER

when the mother sees her daughter after a lapse of fifteen years, or when later for the girl's own sake she declines to recognize her. If Campbell had drawn the scenes in which the latent love of mother and child come into being with the same skill with which he drew the manly affection in *My Partner,* he might have made something out of *Separation,* for the plot after all turns upon the contrasted characters of the husband and wife. Twice at least Campbell laid the scenes of his play in the South. *Fairfax* was played first in New York on December 29, 1879. It is a melodrama, in which the author has produced several effective scenes and has portrayed Southern character in its romantic aspects, but without any especially significant picture of Southern conditions. He has, however, provided an appealing heroine in Mrs. Marrigold, a young wife who is brutally treated by her husband, and who believes she has killed him in a struggle over their child. She becomes the governess of Edwin Fairfax's child, and he and she fall in love with each other. Dr. Guy Gaylord, the friend of Fairfax, who knows of her past life, believes he should prevent the marriage, but she convinces him of her rectitude. This quiet, unenthusiastic observer, who at first is suspicious but later refuses to believe even Gladys' own testimony against herself, is the best character in the play. It was written for Lester Wallack, but there was a disagreement about some proposed changes and Campbell walked out of the theatre with his play. Later, when Abbey produced it, the part was taken by Frederick Robinson with success.

The White Slave (1882) is a vivid melodrama, laid in Kentucky, near the Mississippi River. It is based definitely on *The Octoroon,* but perhaps anyone who took from Boucicault felt justified. Liza, the supposed octoroon, turns out to be white, however, and there is sufficient difference in the plot to make a striking melodrama. In the third Act occur the lines which even yet are remembered for their theatrical quality. Lacy, the brutal owner of Liza, says to her: "I can send you to the fields to work all day among the common niggers, a hoe

123

in your hands, rags upon your back," and Liza answers, "Rags are royal raiment when worn for virtue's sake, and rather a hoe in my hands than self-contempt in my heart." Campbell deliberately planted these lines for their effect.

Paquita, produced at the Fourteenth Street Theatre, August 31, 1885, under his own management, was his last play. It is laid in the Southwest and is based on a situation in which a surgeon is called upon to perform an operation upon his wife's lover that saves the life of the latter. Campbell's end was tragic. In May, 1886, he became mentally disordered and he was committed to the State Hospital for the Insane at Middletown, New York, in November. He died there July 30, 1888. Financial difficulties, due to his effort to act as author, director and producer of plays, seem to have been the cause of his breakdown. In his incessant activity he wore himself out. In little more than ten years he had made and lost a fortune. That his plays have not gained him lasting reputation is not surprising, for none has been published, and with the exception of *My Partner*, probably none can be considered as real contributions to dramatic literature. But his plays read even in manuscript are interesting, and to have succeeded in producing a play of the frontier which shares the primary honors with *Davy Crockett* and *Horizon* is no inconsiderable claim to remembrance. For the frontier is in some respects the most significant element in American history, and to have caught and reflected its spirit is an achievement whose importance will grow rather than diminish with time.

CHAPTER VI

James A. Herne and the Realism of Character

I T WOULD be clearly an error to attribute to any one playwright that development of our drama which gradually substituted, for the strongly accentuated type, the well-rounded natural character who dominated the situations, instead of being created for them, and whose moral, spiritual or emotional conflict provided the central motive of the play. It has become the custom to call the widespread tendency in English literature which began in the thirties and became supreme in the sixties, by the name of realism, and while much confusion has been caused by a failure to distinguish between the selection of familiar material and the realistic method of treating it, it would be idle to object to the term itself. In the late sixties and early seventies the realistic method had become well established in this country in fiction with the work of Elizabeth Barstow Stoddard, of William Dean Howells and Henry James. In their work, it was associated usually with the selection of familiar phases of life, and the influence of the novels of Howells and of Miss Wilkins upon the plays of Herne is clear. Yet Daly had used the methods of realism in dealing with romantic material in *Horizon* as early as 1871, and even at the height of the romantic impulse of the earlier period, we see in the work of Bird, of Boker, of Conrad and Willis, that sincerity of portrayal and surety of touch which produced real characters upon the stage.

The problem of tracing the development of the newer realism of the seventies and eighties is sufficiently difficult when we are dealing with a literary medium like the novel, which is entirely in the control of its creator. With the drama, the difficulty is increased by the fact that it is an art depending upon

125

an interpreter as well as a creator. James Steele MacKaye (1842-94) was a pioneer in a sense, in bringing the quiet restrained quality of Delsarte's method of acting to the American stage, but of MacKaye's plays unfortunately only six are available. Steele MacKaye is more significant in the history of the theatre than in the history of the drama,[1] but in the former his valiant struggles for naturalness helped in the general movement toward realism. His plays were usually French adaptations, like *Rose Michel*, or melodramas, such as *Won at Last*. *Hazel Kirke*, produced first on February 4, 1880, at the Madison Square Theatre, was a revision of an older play of MacKaye's, *An Iron Will* (1879). It is a domestic drama laid in England, and the plot, dealing with the expulsion from her home of Hazel Kirke by her stubborn father, who objects to her marriage with an English nobleman; the false marriage, her return to her home, and attempted suicide, belong to a species of British drama long familiar to the stage. What distinguishes *Hazel Kirke* from its dramatic ancestors is the quiet natural dialogue, and the absence of the usual stage villain. There is a fine climax, too, when Dunstan Kirke, blind, hears his daughter's voice calling for help and cannot save her. *Hazel Kirke* proved to be one of the most popular plays of its time. It had a consecutive run of about two years at the Madison Square Theatre, continuing on the stage for over thirty years and being produced in England, Australia, Japan and Hawaii.

The only other play of MacKaye's of real significance is *Paul Kauvar* (1887), a play of the French Revolution. This is a fine melodrama, intense in its situations, with a plot too complicated in its constant surprises for retelling. MacKaye skillfully kept the love story of Paul Kauvar and Diane de Beaumont the central interest, but contrasted its fidelity and purity with the clash and terror of the Revolution. As the Republic is to triumph, Paul Kauvar is made a republican,

---

[1] *Epoch*, the life of Steele MacKaye by Percy MacKaye, to my regret, appeared too late to be of service to me.

STEELE MAC KAYE

but inasmuch as the sympathy of the audience will always be with the royalists, he is made an advocate of liberal measures, rather than of anarchy. The realism of *Paul Kauvar* lay in the settings and in the acting. The characters are types and the play could have had no such effect in the direction of naturalism as *Hazel Kirke*.

MacKaye's work was frequently the adaptation of foreign or native material. That he drew pictures of life with sincerity is evidenced by the criticism of *A Fool's Errand* (1881), a dramatization of one of Judge Tourgee's novels.[1]

It is gratifying for once to see on the stage Southern people who are possessed of about the same faults and virtues as the rest of the world and no more, and to witness at the same time the usual Northern contrast without the accompaniment of suspenders and catarrh.

It is a matter of regret that MacKaye's plays are not available for study, in order that his share in the movement might be fully determined.

It is not hard, however, for one who views our dramatic progress from the historical standpoint, to see the roots of the newer realism, as far back as *The Contrast* of 1787. Jonathan, the Yankee "waiter," and Charlotte, the girl of the period, are both as real as Maria, the sentimental heroine, is unreal. But it was in the period from 1825 to 1860 that we find in the Yankee plays, like Woodworth's *Forest Rose* and Jones' *Silver Spoon*, the certain if crude ancestors of Uncle Nathaniel Berry of *Shore Acres*. Grandmother Rigglesty in *Neighbor Jackwood* (1857),[2] by John T. Trowbridge, is as vivid a portrait of disagreeable old age as our stage has seen, and his other play, *Coupon Bonds* (1876), places a real family, the Ducklows, in a native homely setting with a fidelity that quite matches many more widely known examples of the realistic rural drama. Both these plays were dramatizations of Trow-

---

[1] Philadelphia *North American*, October 27, 1881.
[2] For plot, see *The American Drama from the Beginning to the Civil War*, pp. 289–90.

bridge's own stories, and he was essentially a novelist, but they are of interest as showing the continuity of our dramatic impulses. Indeed, if theatrical conditions had been more favorable, Trowbridge might have made a career as a playwright, for his work is far above the usual sentimental melodrama of the time.

Before the first important play of Herne had been written, Denman Thompson (1833-1910) had developed from the most lowly of dramatic origins a real character and a play which held the stage as long as he could produce it. In the early seventies, Thompson, who was a variety actor in cheap playhouses like the Columbia Opera House in New York, or the old Club Theatre in Philadelphia, known as "wine rooms" or "free and easies," was acting in a one-act skit, *The Female Bathers*. It was a lineal descendant of *A Glance at New York* (1848), for it introduced a Yankee farmer to the seamy side of New York life. Various stories are told about the inception of *Joshua Whitcomb*,[1] but the best authenticated seems to be that J. M. Hill, of Chicago, was so much impressed by Thompson's acting that he persuaded him to write or have written by George W. Ryer, a four-act play in which the character of a farmer, Joshua Whitcomb, based on a real person, Joshua Holbrook, of Swansea, New Hampshire, became the center of a more dignified if a more sentimental drama. *Joshua Whitcomb* was apparently acted first in New York at the National Theatre on April 3, 1876, and continued in Thompson's hands to be a highly popular vehicle for ten years. In 1878, when he was playing in California, he met Herne, but that Herne was prompted toward the realistic rural drama by witnessing *Joshua Whitcomb* is unlikely. As will be seen later he had other inspiration. In 1886 *Joshua Whitcomb* had become *The Old Homestead*, with an augmented cast.[2] By this time

[1] A half-hour sketch under that name was acted at Harry Martin's Varieties in Pittsburgh, in February, 1875.

[2] The program of the Boston Theatre for April 5, 1886, reads, "DENMAN THOMPSON will present his new play by Denman Thompson and George W. Ryer, THE OLD HOMESTEAD, A Sequel to 'Joshua Whitcomb.'"

HERNE AND THE REALISM OF CHARACTER

Thompson had undoubtedly learned something from Herne, of whose plays he was a great admirer, and indeed it would be idle to deny the possibility of mutual influence. *The Old Homestead*, so far as plot is concerned, is negligible. What remains from the stage performance is the character of a simple, lovable old farmer. But its significance belongs to the theatre rather than to the drama. Thompson's acting made the play, and his interpretation was so natural that it is reported that one of his New England audiences demanded the return of their money, since he gave them nothing but what they could see any day. The persistence of *The Old Homestead* is perhaps, after all, its chief claim to notice, although it shares with *Hearts of Oak* and *Hazel Kirke* the credit of inspiring the great vogue of rural plays in the last decades of the century.

What makes the plays of Herne more important than those of Trowbridge on one side, or of Thompson on the other, is that he began with work of the older fashion, that he grew above it and that in him appeared the combination of the playwright and the actor. As a playwright he developed steadily, from *Hearts of Oak* to *Griffith Davenport*, in the reality of his characters and situations; as an actor he progressed also in the reality of his interpretation. Moreover, he was a conscious artist; his theories grew out of his experience and he was willing to sacrifice, for the sake of what he saw was truth, a competence, even a fortune.

James A. Herne was born February 1, 1839, at Cohoes, New York. The name was originally Ahearn, but the first letter became an initial. He never authorized the use of Alfred as a middle name, though it has been ascribed to him. His first appearance on the stage was at the Adelphi Theatre in Troy in 1859 as George Shelby in *Uncle Tom's Cabin*. After playing two seasons there he went to Baltimore and joined the company at the Holliday Street Theatre. In 1866 he married Helen Western and was a member of her company for one season, when they separated by mutual agreement. Later he be-

129

came the leading man for her sister, Lucille Western, and played in a variety of parts, including Sir Archibald Levison in *East Lynne*, Bill Sykes in *Oliver Twist*, and Dan Peggotty in *Little Em'ly*. His first visit to California, in 1868, was with Miss Western's company. When he returned to California as a star he played at Maguire's Bush Street Theater in a répertoire which included Caleb Plummer, Dan'l Peggotty, Captain Cuttle and other characters of Dickens.

Herne has told us [1] how strong was the influence of Dickens upon him, how he learned from him the great significance of humanity as a motive in art. It was the humanity also in the work of Boucicault that attracted him and taught him the quickness in appeal of that art which speaks directly from the heart of the playwright to the sympathy of the audience.

During his career as stage manager at Maguire's New Theatre in San Francisco in 1874, Herne was beginning to adapt novels such as *Oliver Twist* and *Charles O'Malley*, probably reshaping older material. In the latter he played the character of Micky Free. About this time he also made a version of *Rip Van Winkle*, highly praised by David Belasco for its fidelity to the Dutch quality in the character.

When the Baldwin Theatre, first called Baldwin's Academy of Music, was opened March 6, 1876, Herne became stage manager and leading character actor. Here we find him acting in a great variety of parts, from Solon Shingle in *The People's Lawyer*, with its reflection of an earlier stage realism, to romantic characters such as the Count de Clairnot in a dramatization of Gaboriau's *Within an Inch of His Life*. This play, produced February 17, 1879, at the Grand Opera House, is of interest as the first instance of collaboration of Herne and Belasco. Herne outlined the main plan of development of the plot. With the idea of giving dignity to the play, Herne as stage director announced it simply as "Gaboriau's *Within an Inch of His Life*," and it was seriously criticized as a drama by the French writer of mystery stories. Later Belasco's name

---

[1] "Art for Truth's Sake in the Drama," *Arena*, February, 1897.

was attached to it, and undoubtedly his share in it was large, especially in the mechanical effects.

In 1877 there was studying with a well-known actress, Julia Melville, a girl by the name of Katharine Corcoran. Mrs. Melville, feeling sure of her pupil's talent, wished to have Herne's judgment, and a rehearsal lesson was arranged on the stage of the Baldwin Theatre. Herne became interested in Miss Corcoran's work, and shortly after offered her the part of Peg Woffington in a benefit performance of *Masks and Faces*. After this they toured the Pacific Coast in a stock starring engagement, and were married on April 2, 1878. It was only after the marriage that Mrs. Herne joined the Baldwin Theatre Stock Company.[1] It would be difficult to overestimate the importance of this marriage upon Herne's career both as a playwright and as an actor. As will be seen later, his most important plays were written definitely with her in mind as the leading woman, and her advice in the reshaping of plot and character is seen at its best, perhaps, in *Griffith Davenport* and *Margaret Fleming*.

His association with David Belasco at the Baldwin Theatre was intermittent and their relative shares in the early plays which they wrote together, such as *Marriage by Moonlight*, performed June 30, 1879, are now difficult to assign. A romantic play was needed for the company which included Rose Coghlan, James O'Neill, and "Katharine Corcoran," and Herne and Belasco took the melodrama, *Camilla's Husband*, by Watts Phillips, produced in London in 1862, and revised it to suit the company and the changing fashions of the theatre. The second Act of the manuscript of *Marriage by Moonlight* is missing, so that an exact comparison with its original is not possible. The first Act has been entirely rewritten, and the central situation, the marriage of the heroine, Lady Clarisse Calthorpe, to Lorraine, a wandering painter, in order to prevent her forced marriage to her cousin Harold, whom she dis-

---

[1] This statement, differing widely from printed accounts of their first meeting, is given on the authority of Mrs. Herne.

likes, takes place at Calthorpe Park at night instead of in the village inn. The text was probably Herne's, but in the climax with its background of the moonlight scene Belasco's touch may be recognized. It is essential to the plot that Lorraine, who has married Lady Calthorpe in a half stupor, for the money he badly needs, should not recognize her when he returns later in the play, a well-known artist. In *Camilla's Husband*, Maurice, the artist, fell in love with Lady Camilla Hailstone at first sight and married her for that reason, saved her life at a picnic and nobly renounced her and her wealth in the second Act. Herne and Belasco omitted much of this melodrama, and substituted a motive which is more appealing. Clarisse, already predisposed to favor Lorraine, sees in a picture gallery his painting, "The Innocent Convict"—described by a minor character as "A young man with strangely handsome, half-crazed, half-poetic face, bending beneath the weight of a crime never committed." It is his own portrait and reflects the effect upon him of the treachery by which Harold Calthorpe has had him convicted of the theft of the money Clarisse had given him.

This shame is made use of again quite effectively in the last Act, which takes place in his studio. A duel has been arranged between Lorraine and Harold, but Lorraine, under the stress of emotion caused by his discovery of Clarisse's love for him, has promised her he will not fight. This situation is taken from *Camilla's Husband*, but the scene is made much more powerful, indeed almost tragic, by the mingled emotions of love and shame which force Lorraine to hold himself in check under Harold's insults until Clarisse, who has been concealed in the studio, can stand them no longer and releases Lorraine from his promise. Much of the language is changed, but even when that of the earlier play has been used, there is presented the interesting case of playwrights employing exactly the same words to express much deeper feeling on account of qualities which they have written into the nature of the character earlier in the play. It is also significant that the part Herne played, "Peeping Tom," the wandering cockney-gypsy, through whom

Lorraine's real parentage is discovered, is much cut down in the revision, while that of Hazel, played by Mrs. Herne, is emphasized through a charming little love scene at the opening of the last Act.

The second joint effort of the two playwrights which has survived, has been made the subject of so much contradictory discussion that it is necessary to give a fairly detailed account of its origin and progress. In the summer of 1879, Belasco brought to Herne the second Act of a play which he called *Chums.* Apparently Belasco did not confide to Herne that the play was based upon an earlier English drama, *The Mariner's Compass*, by Henry J. Leslie, which had been acted for the first time in America at the New Bowery Theatre, May 22, 1865. Herne consented to collaborate with Belasco in building up a play out of the material offered. The first performance of *Chums* occurred on September 9, 1879, at the Baldwin Theatre, with Herne as Terry Dennison, Katharine Corcoran as Chrystal, Annie Adams as Aunt Betsy, and Maude Adams as Little Chrystal. After a run of two weeks, *Chums* was withdrawn, but although it had not met with a favorable reception both Herne and Belasco had confidence in the play, and at Mrs. Herne's suggestion it was decided to make an eastern tour. *Chums* seems to have been a failure in Salt Lake City and other western towns until it reached Chicago. The leading managers in that city, McVicker and Hooley, declined to produce the play, but when it was finally put on at Hamlin's Theatre, on November 17, 1879, it was successful. It was rechristened *Hearts of Oak*, and after a tour was brought out again in Chicago at Hooley's Theatre in March, 1880. The vagaries of law, as applied to the rights of a dramatist, are illustrated by the suit which followed Hamlin's attempt to produce *The Mariner's Compass* at his theatre under the title of *Hearts of Oak*. The courts solemnly decided that anyone could play *The Mariner's Compass*, as it was a British play, but that the title of *Hearts of Oak* belonged to Herne and Belasco. If the attorneys for Hamlin had only read *The Mariner's Com-*

pass, they would have discovered that the title "Hearts of Oak" was taken from a sailors' chorus in that play!

Hearts of Oak was played for the first time in New York, March 29, 1880, at the New Fifth Avenue Theatre. During a later engagement in Philadelphia the partners had a disagreement and Herne purchased Belasco's rights in the play. Notwithstanding its failure to meet with popular success in its early stages, *Hearts of Oak* became a valuable dramatic property and was acted by Herne and Mrs. Herne for many years. As it is the first play of Herne's that has survived in complete form, a comparison with *The Mariner's Compass* reveals certain important facts concerning Herne's methods of adaptation.

The Mariner's Compass is a domestic melodrama, first produced at Astley's Theatre, London, March 4, 1865. Silas Englehart, a coast guard, has brought up Ruby Dayrell, a sailor, and Hetty Arnold, both orphans. He loves Hetty, while she and Ruby care for each other. The play opens just before Ruby's return from sea and Silas asks Hetty to marry him. She agrees, and then comes the shipwreck of Ruby's sloop and Ruby's rescue by Silas, though he has discovered that his foster child is his rival. Silas has made up his mind to go away, but Hetty convinces Ruby it is their duty to give up their own happiness, and they persuade Silas that their love is fraternal. After a year, the married pair are shown in their happy state, and then Ruby returns. In a melodramatic scene at Margate Jetty, Hetty shows Ruby that she has determined to be true to Silas. Silas leaves for the Arctic regions, after Hetty has upbraided him roundly for leaving her and their child.

Up to this point *Hearts of Oak* follows in plot rather closely the outlines of *The Mariner's Compass*, although a comic subplot is omitted entirely, and the character of Owen Garroway, a lovable sailor, which was suggested by Dan Peggotty, was created by Herne. The relations of Terry Dennison to Ruby Darrell and Chrystal in *Hearts of Oak* are established, from a superficial point of view, in about the same way as in the earlier drama. But the difference can be appreciated only in a careful reading of both plays, for it lies partly in the closer fidelity to the natural language of human beings and partly to a deft change which deepens the tenderness of the affection existing among Terry, Chrystal and Ruby [1] while it lessens the theatrical intensity of its expression. The scene in *Hearts of Oak* on Whaler's Wharf, in which Chrystal and Ruby reveal their unchanged love for each other, clutches at the sympathy of the audience and is a distinct advance over the corresponding episode in *The Mariner's Compass* in which Hetty flings her unused wedding ring into the sea.

The most vital change came in the fifth and sixth Acts of *Hearts of Oak*, which replace Act IV of *The Mariner's Compass*. The violent reactions of Silas when he returns to find his wife just married to Ruby, the attempted suicide of Hetty in the mill race, her rescue from the mill wheel by Ruby, who dies in the act, and the final picture of the returned husband clasping his dripping wife in his arms, are replaced by two scenes, quiet in action and touching in their human appeal. Terry returns, blind and white-haired, to find Chrystal and Ruby married. He dies after his little daughter has called him "father"—at his request and under the impression that he has brought a message from her real father who has died in the Arctic regions, and it is only after Terry's death that Chrystal recognizes him. The scene leaves Ruby and Chrystal together, and their mutual love which they have done their best to conquer is to be rewarded. *Hearts of Oak* is by no means one of Herne's best plays, and the last scene might in incompetent hands seem sentimental, but in Herne's performance the dignity of Terry's self-sacrifice secured the sympathy of his hearers. How much of the credit for the improvement in *Hearts of Oak* is due to Herne and how much to Belasco will probably never be known. Herne was entirely responsible for the first, third and last Acts as the play now stands,[2] including the homelike scene at the supper, which is not in *The Mariner's*

[1] Changed to Ned Fairweather in later versions.
[2] Statement of Mrs. Herne.

135

Compass, and the introduction of the baby, who is only hinted at in the British play.

The Minute Men of 1774-75, played first at the Chestnut Street Theatre, Philadelphia, April 6, 1886,[1] while not a popular success, is of interest since it is Herne's first original play that has survived. It illustrates, too, how his skill was developing, for it is uneven in merit and at times is reminiscent of a much older manner. The scenes are laid in Dorchester Heights and the neighboring forest, and the battles of Lexington, Concord and Bunker Hill are brought in as dramatic pictures after the curtain has fallen on the second and third Acts. This is, of course, poor art, for the historical episodes are thereby separated from the main action, and while in the first instance an opportunity is given for the heroine, Dorothy Foxglove, to rally the men at Lexington Common, this is the only occasion in which the characters of the drama really have any relation to historical events that is not obviously forced upon them. Herne had not learned what Bronson Howard and William Gillette were to illustrate immediately afterward in *Held by the Enemy* and *Shenandoah*, that audiences are not interested in historical episodes for their own sake. The personal relations must form the climax of the action, and in any case the scene at Lexington Common scarcely admits of the introduction of a heroine who, every schoolboy knows, was not present.

Herne speaks of the character of Dorothy Foxglove, which was written for Mrs. Herne, as "glorious," and it is indeed charming. In the same account of his work he tells us that he could not write stage comedy, but the comedy scenes in which Dorothy appears are the bright spots of the play. The plot is not remarkable. Dorothy Foxglove has been brought up by Reuben Foxglove as his daughter. She is really the child of Sir Frederick Shelton, who is commanding his Majesty's Eighteenth Grenadiers, and the discovery of her parentage

[1] The play was announced for April 5, but owing to extensive preparations, it was postponed. Philadelphia *Public Ledger*, April 6 and 7, 1886.

JAMES A. HERNE

Taken in his study on Convent Avenue, New York, shortly before the production
of *Griffith Davenport*

through her locket is made in the old conventional way. Her lover, Roanoke, who is supposed to be an Indian and who is really the son of Captain Winslow, a Colonial officer, is no nearer reality than Metamora, and the love story of Rachel Winslow and Ned Farnsworth, which is obstructed at every convenient point by Dyke Hampton, the villain, is carried on by stage figures rather than real people. The language at times is stilted and the sentiment exaggerated.

Yet on the other hand, whenever Dorothy Foxglove enters there seems to be blown into the action a breath of inspiration. The scenes in which she makes Lieutenant Smollet, the British officer, assist her in her cooking; the later scene in which she captures him at the point of his own pistol, when he has been sent to bring her back to Sir Frederick; her tender treatment of Reuben, her foster father, half daughterly, half maternal— all build up a picture of young womanhood that remains vivid even after a mere reading of the manuscript. What they must have been, when clothed with life and color by Mrs. Herne, it is hard to overestimate.

It was perhaps natural that the next best part to that of Dorothy should have been Reuben Foxglove, played by Herne. The simple, natural farmer is contrasted skillfully with Sir Frederick Shelton, especially in the scene in which he refuses payment for his years of care of his foster child and tells Sir Frederick, "There's some things that can't be paid for, and love's one of them." Herne made Lieutenant Smollet a likeable British gentleman, instead of the villain that so often decorated the play of the Revolution. Yet the atmosphere of the War for Independence is well caught, and the indomitable spirit that animated the women of that time is expressed not only in Dorothy but also in Ann Campbell, who handles a gun as well as her male compatriots, and is no doubt an accurate portrait of a pioneer of her type.

The next step forward in the direction of natural character drawing was *Drifting Apart*, originally called *Mary, the Fishermen's Child*, which was first produced at the People's Theatre, New York, May 7, 1888. The scene is laid in Gloucester, among the seafarers. Jack Hepburne, an attractive sailor with a weakness for drink, is married at the close of the first Act to Mary Miller, who as a foundling has been brought up by the fisher folk. In the second Act a domestic interior reveals their mutual trust and happiness. Jack goes to the village for Christmas presents and returns, to his wife's horror, in a drunken condition. In Acts III and IV the future is revealed to him in a dream which includes a powerful scene in which Mary and her child are starving. The child dies on her mother's lap, of cold and hunger, and Jack in desperation rushes out of the house with Mary in his arms. The audience is not aware that this is all a dream until the last Act, when the household is shown after Jack's return to sobriety, and the play ends upon a note of forgiveness and repentance, expressed with simplicity and with fidelity to the inarticulate quality of such natures.

The final form of *Drifting Apart* has perished and the manuscript of *Mary, the Fishermen's Child* reveals again how Herne made alterations in plots and characterization. The language of the earlier form is at times overwrought and Herne himself very truly described Silas and Hester, in whom the stagestruck girl and her lover were burlesqued, as its weakest feature. How thorough was his work in revision is revealed in his correspondence with Hamlin Garland.[1]

Drifting Apart was not very successful in popular appeal. Mrs. Herne, who acted Mary Miller, attributes the failure to the early use of what is now known as the "cut back" in the dream scenes. She feels that the audiences resented the discovery that their emotions had been harrowed by what was after all unreality, while the tragedy was too keen for it to be appreciated for its own sake. The play made a lasting impression, nevertheless, upon competent judges like Howells and Hamlin Garland, and it led to Herne's association with the group of novelists who were leading the realistic movement in

[1] Letter of June 4, 1889.

fiction. He was encouraged to continue his struggle to represent the lives of real people, and his work took on the color of a crusade against the meretricious in drama. He has himself expressed it [1] as "Art for Truth's Sake" in an article which is a significant document in our dramatic history. The philosophy of his playwriting is expressed in this passage:

Art for art's sake may be likened to the exquisite decoration of some noble building; while art for truth's sake might be the building itself. Art for truth's sake is serious. Its highest purpose has ever been to perpetuate the life of its time. The higher the form of expression, the greater the art. Vereschagin uses his masterly art to express truth. There is none of the "pomp and circumstance of glorious war" in his battle pictures. They reproduce war as it is. Tolstoy uses his art for truth's sake; so do Howells and Enneking and Hardy and Sudermann; and so does Whitcomb Riley. And so did Browning and Lanier and other great masters of the art. But in expressing a truth through art it should be born in mind that selection is an important principle. If a disagreeable truth is not also an essential, it should not be used in art. Mr. Howells has the art of selection in a remarkable degree. Mr. Enneking says: "The Ideal is the choicest expression of the Real." Truth is the essential of all art. I do not well see how there can be art without some truth. I hold it to be the duty of the true artist to state his truth as subtly as may be. In other words: if he has a truth to manifest and he can present it without giving offense and still retain its power, he should so present it, but if he must choose between giving offense and receding from his position, he should stand by his principle and state his truth fearlessly.

In his emphasis upon reality of portraiture Herne was not simply following the example of the novelists of his time. He was convinced of the importance of character drawing by his stage experience. In a letter to Hamlin Garland [2] he says:

Character *business*, as we call it, is *the* business of to-day in the theatrical profession. *Mansfield* is a character actor; Irving is a character actor; Wm. Warren was a character actor; Stoddart,

[1] See *The Arena*, February, 1897, pp. 361–70.
[2] Dated "Monday," written probably in 1889.

LeMoyne, Couldock, Jefferson, all these are character actors. Character acting means the finest of all parts built upon *broad* lines. It embraces facial expression, dialect, comedy and pathos. You will see in *Hearts of Oak* what I mean by character acting. Terry Dennison, Owen Garroway, Uncle Davy, in this play are character parts,—Ned Fairweather a *straight* part. Now character acting (to be perfect) can be only acquired by *study*, with of course as I say above a fair amount of undoubted dramatic instinct. The straight acting can be done by any person whom nature has favored with personal qualifications.

In the same letter he suggests the dramatization by Howells and Garland of *The Rise of Silas Lapham.*

Herne was not simply exploiting a theory. He had proved his sincerity by sacrifice. *Hearts of Oak* had brought him a fortune, nearly all of which he had lost in attempting to carry his theory into practice. *Drifting Apart* ran on tour for over two hundred and fifty performances, but it made no money. And yet Herne, undaunted, wrote *Margaret Fleming*, which was more daring in its fidelity to truth and much less likely to appeal to the public.

It was first tried out at Lynn, Massachusetts, for three performances beginning July 4, 1890, in which Herne acted Philip Fleming. Herne endeavored to secure a theatre in New York and Boston without success, and finally rented Chickering Hall, a small auditorium on Tremont Street, holding about five hundred people, where the play was produced on May 4, 1891, and ran for two weeks, creating a distinct artistic sensation. Herne was supported in his efforts by an open letter urging him to produce the play and signed by W. D. Howells, Hamlin Garland, Mary E. Wilkins, and other leaders of the movement toward realism in fiction and the first performance, largely through the enthusiasm of Hamlin Garland, became a confession of faith of the realistic movement in America. The play was received with critical approval, but was too far ahead of its time for a popular success. On October 5, 1891, it was revived for three weeks in Boston and a matinée performance took place at Palmer's Theatre, New York, on

HERNE AND THE REALISM OF CHARACTER

December 9, 1891; but the critics of that city failed to appre-- ciate the play. Herne lost several thousand dollars, but he had won recognition, no longer simply as an actor, but as an artistic pioneer and a literary craftsman. Even more pronounced was the appreciation of Mrs. Herne's acting as Margaret Fleming. *Margaret Fleming* was revived in 1894, and was performed in 1907 with Chrystal Herne in the title rôle, and again in 1915 with Julie Herne as Margaret.

Herne's experiment was one of the earliest efforts at an independent theatre and a call was issued by Thomas Bailey Aldrich, James A. Herne, Hamlin Garland, B. O. Flower, Ralph A. Cram, and others, for a meeting on May 21, at Pierce Hall, Boston, "to consider plans for the establishment of a distinctively American Theatre. In general," the notice states, "it is designed to forward the building of a theatre on the co-operative plan, and to open a Stage whereon the Drama shall be considered a Work of Art, and produced as such— independent of cheap popularity, and where Americanism and modernity shall be the prime requisites. We invite your co-operation at the meeting named above, believing that a Theatre of this general scope must have a great influence upon our literature and especially upon the development of Dramatic Art."

Margaret Fleming is the study of a woman's character. For a revelation of the nobility inherent in the cultivated American gentlewoman, it ranks with the portraits of Lina Bowen in Howells' *Indian Summer* and Isabel Archer in Henry James' *The Portrait of a Lady*. As a contrast to her there is established the character of her husband, Philip Fleming, in whose office the first Act is laid. His prompt decision is shown in the handling of the business attendant upon the conduct of his mill, and by the way in which, after the disclosure by Dr. Larkin that Lena Schmidt has had a child by Philip, he braces himself to attend to urgent matters of detail. He is drawn with great skill; he is not a mere sensualist or a weakling, but a man with a charm that is heightened, perhaps, by a light carelessness, and he has no difficulty in distinguishing his real love for his wife from the sensual passion he has had for Lena. Indeed, he has never troubled to deceive Lena into a belief that he loves her. The first scene closes upon a perfectly normal conversation between Philip and his superintendent. No attempt is made at the old-fashioned climax.

In the second scene there is a charming picture of Margaret in her home life with their baby daughter Lucy. There is no sentimentality, but the little touch by which she closes her dress as the curtain rises prepares the way for the climax of the third Act. The relation by Maria, Margaret's maid, of the serious trouble into which Lena, her sister, has fallen at the hands of some unknown lover is brought in quite simply and prepares the way for the coming disaster. Already the major relationships are established, with an economy of the personnel that reveals Herne's skill. When Philip returns from the office after some delay, there is a charming scene of wifely devotion, and the utter happiness of Margaret makes the approaching tragedy all the more poignant.

In the second Act the disclosure of the danger of blindness for Margaret through approaching glaucoma is established through the conversation of Dr. Larkin. Philip's light-heartedness and ability to forget his cares are consistently portrayed, and the comedy scenes between Maria and her husband, Joe, are used to draw Philip from the stage and permit Maria to make her request to Margaret to come with her to see Lena. The light touch of confidence and comfort with which Margaret leaves Philip is secured with the apparent ease of art.

The third Act takes place in Mrs. Burton's cottage, where in a room off the stage Lena lies dead. Dr. Larkin tries to prevent Margaret from learning the facts, but she comes first in contact with the little baby, a boy, and is attracted to him. Then the disclosure of Philip's fatherhood is made by the letter Lena has left, which Maria brings on with her. The reading of the letter by Maria serves two purposes beside the obvious one of informing the audience. It shows Margaret's growing

Cordially yours
Katharine C. Herne

James A. Herne

JAMES A. HERNE AS JOE FLETCHER AND KATHARINE CORCORAN HERNE AS "MARGARET"

IN *MARGARET FLEMING*

dimness of vision and also proves that Philip was not the ordinary seducer, for Lena writes that she knew he never loved her, although she loved him. Margaret's reaction to the terrible truth is masterly. Instead of breaking down at once, she dominates the situation, forces Maria to give up the idea of shooting the seducer, transfers at once the sympathy of the audience from the dead girl to the injured wife:

You think I am—happy—because I am his—wife? Why, you poor fool! That girl never in all her life suffered one thousandth part what I have suffered in these past few minutes. Do you dare to compare her to me? I have not uttered one word of reproach, even against her, and yet she has done me a wrong that not all the death-bed letters that were ever written can undo. I wonder what I have ever done to deserve this! (*She loses control of herself and sinks, sobbing, in the chair; her arms upon the table; her head dropping upon them.*)

After this brief loss of control she sends for Philip without wasting a word; she parries the doctor's last desperate effort to stop her by his warning that she may endanger her sight by the shock. And then the child begins to disturb her; and the Act proceeds to its close:

Margaret: What is the matter with that child? (*Her voice seems remote. Her expression remains fixed.*) Why don't you keep it quiet?

Mrs. Burton: (*In a hushed voice*) It's hungry.

Margaret: (*In the same mood, but her voice is a little querulous*) Well, then, why don't you feed it?

Mrs. Burton: I can't get nothing for it. I've tried everything I could think of, but it's no use. (*She rises and places the child upon the sofa.*) There, be still, you poor little critter, an' I'll see what I ken get fer ye.

(*As she goes out the door at the back*)

Margaret: Bring a lamp; it's getting dark here.

(*There is silence, then the child's wail arouses her. She half turns her head in its direction and tries to quiet it.*) Hush, child, hush. (*Then she reaches out her hand as if to pat it.*) There, there, poor little thing. Don't fret—it's no use to

143

fret, child—be quiet now, there, there now. (*She turns and slowly gropes her way to the sofa; sits on the edge of it, feels for the child and gently pats it, murmuring softly*) Hush, baby, go to sleep.

(*There is silence. A pitying half smile plays across her face. She utters a faint sigh and again drifts away into that inner consciousness where she is evidently at peace. Again the child is restless—it arouses her, and hopeless of comforting it, she takes it in her arms. After a moment, she rises to her feet and stumbles towards the table. She knocks against the low chair. At the same moment, Philip Fleming dashes breathless into the room through the door at the right. He pauses in horror as Margaret raises her head, her eyes wide open, staring into his, her face calm and remote. She hushes the child softly and sits in the low chair. Philip stands in dumb amazement watching her. The child begins to fret her again. She seems hopeless of comforting it. Then scarcely conscious of what she is doing, suddenly with an impatient swift movement she unbuttons her dress to give nourishment to the child, when the picture fades away into darkness.*)

In this scene Herne revealed the strength of that dramatic action in which, while few or no words are spoken, the relations of human beings are developed or revealed with the fatal swiftness which is the essential quality of great dramatic moments. The essence of such action is quiet natural expression through word, gesture, or that repose which becomes in itself active. It is shown again in the last scene in *Shore Acres*. It differs radically from the intense brief sentences of melodrama in which the object is not revelation of character but intensification of situation.

In the first form of the play there was an interval of five years, and then in the fourth Act there were scenes on Boston Common and in a small shop at the North End. The boy had died and Maria had stolen Lucy out of revenge. There was also a certain amount of comedy here. Then came the final scene in a police station to which Philip and Margaret had gone in search of Lucy, and here she said good-by to her husband, refusing forgiveness to him. The effect of this ending, in which Margaret stood alone, her figure gradually disappearing as the curtains came together noiselessly, was, according to those who witnessed the Chickering Hall performance, something new in dramatic art.

In the present form, which was acted later by Mrs. Herne, there is an entirely different close. Margaret is blind, the shock having produced the effect Dr. Larkin dreaded, but she faces the future calmly. Philip returns and she receives him with a noble reticence, with forgiveness but with an indication that she cannot again be his wife. She learns that he has attempted suicide, has been rescued and has been advised by his nurse in the hospital to return to his wife. Then the play proceeds:

Margaret: Then you must do something for your child.
Philip: Yes, our dear child.
Margaret: No, not our child—not Lucy. Your son.
Philip: My son?
Margaret: Yes.
Philip: Where is he?
Margaret: Here.
Philip: (*Resentfully*) Who brought him here?
Margaret: I did.
Philip: (*Amazed*) You brought that child here?
Margaret: Yes, where else should he go?
Philip: You have done that?
Margaret: What other thing was there for me to do? Surely if he was good enough to bring into the world, he is good enough to find a shelter under your roof.

Then after he tells her about his attempted suicide, she urges him to go to the mill and pick up his life again. He starts to do so, then says:

I'd like to see Lucy. Where is she?
Margaret: (*At table occupied with the flowers*) They are both out there. (*Indicating with a turn of the head*) In the garden.
(*Philip goes quickly to the door opening upon the garden and gazes out eagerly. Margaret pauses in her work, gives*

145

*a long sigh of relief and contentment; her eyes looking into
the darkness; a serene joy illuminates her face. The picture
is slowly faded out as Philip steps buoyantly into the
garden.)*

Mrs. Herne believes the present form of the play is more
unified and preserves the tone more securely. She is the best
judge, for the changes were made through the results of her
experience. Certainly the present form proceeds logically.
Margaret is not drawn as unrelenting, and no artistic purpose
is secured by the mere fact of unhappiness, unless that unhappiness is inevitable. Margaret and Philip represent the eternal contrast between character and personality. Her final joy
rises out of the triumph of character over fate and circumstances. It comes best through sacrifice, and the mere personality through whom the sacrifice is brought about will return
inevitably to the haven of character, which will just as inevitably receive it.

Herne's next play was directly inspired by his contact with
the natives of Lemoine, a town on Frenchman's Bay in Maine,
where he spent his summers. As early as 1889 he had had
the idea of a drama based on the contrasted characters of two
brothers, and after his disappointment with *Margaret Fleming*, he returned to *The Hawthornes*, as it was first called.
Under the influence of the natural beauty of that region between the pine hills and the sea, Herne tells us how *The Hawthornes* "sloughed off its old skin and took on new form and
color. Its stage people began by degrees to assume the character and affect the speech of the typical men and women of
Maine. Stage traditions vanished. *The Hawthornes* lost its
identity, and emerged a survival of the fittest, and Mrs. Herne
called it *Shore Acres*." [1] Mrs. Herne played Helen Berry,
Martin's daughter.

The record of *Shore Acres* is one of the many examples of
the accidental happenings in stage history. One of the most
successful plays of its time struggled hard for a chance of pro-

[1] *Arena*, February, 1897, p. 368.

duction. It was first performed at McVicker's Theatre, Chicago, May 17, 1892, as *Shore Acres Subdivision*, and after two weeks the title was changed to *Uncle Nat* at McVicker's suggestion. It ran for four weeks, with general critical approval, but it was not considered to be a financial success. Only an unexpected vacancy at the Boston Museum caused the manager, R. M. Field, to put on the play in February, 1893. It ran for one hundred and thirteen performances, instead of the two weeks he had arranged, but even then its fate hung on a thread. Field took the play to the Fifth Avenue Theatre in New York, where it opened on October 30, 1893. During the first two weeks it seemed about to fail and only a fortunate clause in the contract, which guaranteed the production of the play for four weeks, saved it from being taken off. By that time it had become a pronounced success both with the critics and with the public, and after transfer to Daly's Theatre, it ran for the entire season. It restored Herne's fortune, and is still being acted in stock.

Shore Acres is again a character study. Nathaniel Berry, or "Uncle Nat" as he is called, acted by Herne, is a lovable creature, who has built his life up apparently of little things, since he has let the great things pass him by on the way to others. His younger brother, Martin, has married the girl Nat loved, and even the property which they jointly own has passed into Martin's control. In order to enter into a real estate operation, Martin wishes to sell the land on the knoll, looking out to sea, where their mother is buried. How difficult it is to depict any situation in which the memory of a dead mother is made the motive can only be appreciated after a mental review of the many overwrought scenes for which it is responsible! But hoping to prevent the sale, Uncle Nat, with his quaint phraseology, draws a vivid picture of their mother's all-night vigil on the knoll when their father had been lost at sea. This is most effective on the stage.

Uncle Nat watches over the love story of his niece Helen and Dr. Sam Warren, to whom Martin objects on account of his "free-thinkin' ideas." Helen is well drawn, for the stubborn quality in Martin is revealed in her nature, mingled with the intolerance of youth, as his is deepened by the prejudice of age. Nat is the philosopher who is liberal to all opinion; perhaps because the greater joys of life have not been his, he is determined that Helen shall not lose them. The advanced opinions of Dr. Warren, which do not seem very advanced to-day, alarm Nat not a bit, nor is he unduly impressed by them. Herne brought on the stage the age-long conflict between the tory and the radical, expressed in the brief conversation between Martin and Sam:

Martin. I don't want to know nothin' and I don't want her to know nothin' that I don't want her to know.

Sam. Why, you see, Mr. Berry—you can't help—

Martin. I'm a bringin' up my family, and I don't want any interference from you, nor Darwin, nor any of the rest of the breed. What book's that yeh got there now?

Helen. One of Sam's books, Father.

Martin. Well, give it right straight back to Sam; I don't want nothin' to do with him nor his books.

Sam. It's my book, Mr. Berry, but it was written by a man—

Martin. I won't hev you a-bringin' them books here, a-learnin' my daughter a pack of lies, about me and my parents a-comin' from monkeys—

The "book" is Howells' *A Hazard of New Fortunes,* and while at first glance the whole discussion seems old-fashioned, recent developments have proved that it is not an outworn struggle and also that Herne selected for his example of Helen's reading one of the truly permanent contributions to the literature of that period. Howells must certainly have been amused to find himself quoted as an example of "advanced ideas." His philosophy more nearly approaches that of Nat, who is the eternal liberal, the force that keeps the world moving, while tory and radical both obstruct progress with recurrent fashions in morals and science.

Nat believes that life is too short for unhappiness, and he

acts promptly in helping Helen and Warren to run away upon Captain Ben Hutchins' boat. This leads to a theatrically effective if melodramatic struggle in the third Act, in the lighthouse, in which Martin in his desperate anger tries to prevent Nat from igniting the beacon, hoping thereby to wreck the *Liddy Ann,* in which Helen and Warren are eloping. Nat's spirit flares up and he tells Martin his long years of self-effacement have ended, and he drives his brother away from the stairway leading to the light. The curtain descends upon his apparently futile effort to reach the light in his weakened condition, but in the next scene, on the deck of the *Liddy Ann,* we learn that she has been saved by the sudden appearance of the light.[1]

This act is much less artistic than the ones which precede and follow it, in the farmhouse kitchen. In the first, the Christmas dinner is redolent of reality, and in the last scene, after Helen and Warren have returned with their child and everything has been straightened out naturally, Nat puts the house to bed. Nothing is said, but by the expression in his face, one reads his thoughts.

Uncle Nat has been locking up, and seeing to the fire. He takes the candle and starts upstairs. The wind howls outside; the stage darkens slightly as he gets to the foot of the stairs; he looks off where the others have gone. He smiles and thinks to himself during the remainder of the scene, without speaking:

Uncle Nat. Well, everything's all right again. I wonder how long Nell 'n' Sam's going to stay. A month'r two anyway. By George, it's going to be pooty hard work to get the ol' farm inter shape again. Well, hard work never skeered me. I wonder if I locked that door. (*He goes and tries it.*) Gracious, what a night. (*He looks out of the window.*) Snow'll be ten foot deep in the morning. Ol' Berry's all right. Tim's there. (*As he mounts the stairs*) Bless that baby. (*Smiles off at it*) I wonder what the young uns'll say in the morning. It'll be better'n a circus here when Millie sees that baby.

[1] In the manuscript play *Light House Cliffs,* by Frank Hitchcock Murdoch, there is a scene from which Herne, who had acted in *Light House Cliffs,* derived this situation. But in the earlier play, it is not the brother who renews the light; the ship is wrecked and there are other differences.

(*As he disappears the stage is dark, only the firelight flickering through the chinks of the stove. The cuckoo clock strikes twelve and the curtain slowly descends.*)

Anton Chekhov has been praised justly for the final scene in *The Cherry Orchard*, in which the old servitor closes the house after the family have left it, without a word spoken. But the historian of the drama notes that *Shore Acres* antedates *The Cherry Orchard* by twelve years.

This ending did not close the play in its original production in Chicago. Here the curtain went down on the confusion caused by the explosion of a gun with which Nat, as a veteran of the Civil War, was going through the manual of arms, prompted by the receipt of his arrears of pension. This bit of fooling was put in at the request of the management. Herne preferred the quieter ending at all times.

My Colleen, a romantic play in which the pathos and humor of Irish character seem to have been adequately treated, was written for Tony Farrell, a comedian, in 1891. Both Mr. and Mrs. Herne acted in it during the season at McVicker's Theatre in which *Shore Acres* was produced.

In January, 1893, *The New South*, by J. R. Grismer and Clay Greene, was produced. Herne acted the part of Sampson, a negro murderer, and in a powerful scene represented the growing effect of fear in a negro's mind. It may be that this suggested to him the motive of slavery, but the direct source of *The Reverend Griffith Davenport* was the novel, *An Unofficial Patriot*, by Helen H. Gardener. Herne changed the incidents and characters of this loosely constructed story into a unified drama to which the calmest critical judgment has given a high place among the playwriting of the time. It was first performed at the Lafayette Square Theatre in Washington, January 16, 1899, and later at the Herald Square Theatre, in New York, from January 31 to February 10.

The scenes of the play are laid in Virginia and in Washington, before and during the Civil War. Griffith Davenport is a member of an old Virginia family, who has become a

Methodist circuit rider. Naturally devout, his communings with God and nature have made him almost a mystic. To him slavery is inconsistent with Christianity, and he has vowed never to buy or sell a slave. By inheritance, however, he owns a large plantation and a number of slaves, and when he marries, his wife Katharine brings him others. To her his scruples are incomprehensible, for she represents the point of view of the patrician. In the play, their eldest son, Beverly, sides with her, while Roy shares his father's feelings. In the novel both had been strong Union men and this change adds to the dramatic element of conflict, and makes the struggle of Griffith more lonely and difficult.

The first act shows the garden of the Davenport estate; the negroes are living in a peaceful condition typical of many Virginia plantations. Into this idyllic state a personal note of tragedy is struck when Sally, Katharine's maid, enters to beg "Marse Griff" to buy her husband, John, who is to be sold by his master on the next plantation. He resists at first all appeals, even those of his wife, but finally yields to Sally's dramatic plea. This scene, which occurs in the novel, is reinforced in the play by another scene which reflects the misery of the free negro Jim and also the cruelty of a neighboring planter Nelson, who has just captured Sampson, a runaway slave. These are introduced to make clear the difficulty of the problem. If Davenport simply frees his slaves he does them an injury rather than a benefit. He must therefore leave his home if he persists in his attitude, and he can see no other solution.

In the second Act, which takes place in the stately drawing-room, Griffith frees his slaves. In a scene not in the novel, Beverly and Roy represent the family tragedy that occurred so often during the Civil War.

"Roy," the former says, "if this thing ever comes to a war between the North and the South, which side are you going to fight on?"

"On my side," replies Roy, laughing.

Beverly looks at him thoughtfully. "Roy," he continues,

"if I ever met you in a battle, I believe I'd kill you quicker than I would a real Yankee."

Roy takes a deep breath, and then adds, "I'm sorry, Bev, but I'm afraid I'll have to give you the chance."

The negroes, assembled in the hope of presents from the master, are stupefied at the manumission papers, which degrade them into the class of "free niggers" who belong to nobody. Suddenly Nelson's negro, Sampson, bursts into the room, a broken chain dangling from his ankle, a pruning knife in his hand. Nelson is at his heels with his dogs and men, and without an apology to Mrs. Davenport, he orders his men to take Sampson. Sampson holds up his knife.

"Ef you come neah me, I'll cut ma throat," he says quietly. Griffith, aghast, calls out, "I'll buy him, Nelson."

"I won't sell him," replies Nelson, and starts toward Sampson. But the negro plunges the knife into his throat and falls dead before them.

From this point Herne took even greater liberties with his material. A strong scene was made of the announcement of Lincoln's election, the growing hatred of his neighbors for Griffith being made concrete in Nelson's denunciation of him, and Katharine's quiet but bitter reply, "We will go." Driven from home, Griffith becomes affected by the spirit of the martyr and, gathering his family around him, he prays fervently for help and guidance in the new life which they must face, and for the safety of his country.

In the novel, Davenport went to Indiana after a brief stay in Washington. For the sake of unity Herne kept the scene of the fourth Act in Washington, in the humble home in which they are living during the war. Beverly is in the Confederate army and Roy enlists in the army of the Union. Then occurred one of the most important changes in the play. In the novel, Lincoln had sent for Davenport and asked him to guide the Union forces through Virginia. The interview, which is the best piece of writing in the novel, was at first used in the drama. Something, however, seemed to be wrong. Herne worked upon the scene for a long time and became so discouraged that he was about to give up the play. Then Mrs. Herne, who acted Katharine, saw the difficulty. It was an error in technique to bring into the most important scene in the play a character who became to the audience of more interest than the hero. Lincoln naturally dominated the scene and it was decided to indicate his influence through Governor Morton of Indiana, who had, in real life, persuaded Mrs. Gardener's father to enter the service, but who had only been mentioned in the novel. Morton shows Davenport how Lincoln has heard of him, and by displaying the map of Virginia reveals how sadly in need of guidance is the Union army. Then Morton asks him to war against his own people:

Gov. M.: He's going to send a corps of engineers down there to make a new map of that country. He wants you to lead that corps. You can go in your character of chaplain or—
Griffith: No. If Ah do this thing Ah'll do it outright. Ah've nevah seen it as yo've made me see it to-day. If Ah go Ah'll ride in the lead, not as a chaplain nor as suttlah, but as just what Ah shall be—God help me—a gov'ament guide.

While Griffith rebels at the idea of being a spy, Morton produces the telegram:

Order your man Davenport to report to me immediately.
A. LINCOLN.

Through the climax of the Act, in which is developed the conflict between Griffith and Katharine, who begs him not to betray their State, the influence of Lincoln is portrayed in a more vital manner than if he had been present, and yet the interest remains centered upon the characters upon the stage. Katharine has begged him not to leave her and he replies:

Griffith: Katharine, (*Pointing to picture*) that is Abraham Lincoln, the President of the United States, after his inauguration March 4, 1861. (*Taking cabinet photo of Lincoln from top of bookcase*) This is Abraham Lincoln March 1, 1862.

Do yo' see the change in the face? No human being has evah suffered in a lifetime what this man has suffered in one sho't yeah. Men think it is a great thing to be the president of a great nation; and so it is, in time of peace; but ah! Katharine, in time of wah! President Lincoln hasn't got a man he dare trust to map this country. (*Shows map.*) Look at that. (*Getting excited*) He turns to me, and he says, "Davenpo't, I need *you*. Ah answered when yo' all needed me. Now when I need yo'—" He points his accusing fingah at me and says, "Theah is but one way to sho'ten this wah, to lessen the awful slaughter, the carnage and suffering, on *both* sides. Theah is but one man who knows how to do this, and that man is (*Pointing to himself*) yo'. And yo' have not done yo'ah duty to yo'ah country. No sah, nor to yo'ah God, until yo' have done that." (*Falls into a chair overcome with his emotions, and buries his face in his arms.*)

Katharine: (*Almost heart-broken*) Ah know—Ah know—But ah! To think of yo', mah husband, guiding an a'my against—

Griffith: Look at that bridge. Do yo' remembah that bridge on the 22nd of last July? (*Points out of window in direction of Long Bridge*) Do yo' see young sons like yo'rs dragging bleeding limbs across it? Do yo' see terror-stricken ho'ses trampling down those wounded boys?

Katharine: (*Horrified*) Don't, Griffith! Fo' God's sake, don't! *Griffith:* It is fo' God's sake—Ah pray to mah God that Ah may nevah see anothath such day in mah life. If Ah knew how to prevent a railroad accident— What would yo' think of me if Ah did not prevent it?

Katharine: Yo' have sacrificed so much already, Griffith. Yo' have impoverished yo'rself—

Griffith: Ah know, Ah know—

Katharine: The people down theah loved yo' so befo'. Ah hoped that after all pe'haps we might some day go back theah again, but now— (*Shakes her head*) Every man, woman and child in Virginia will hate—and despise yo'—

Griffith: The people down theah nevah unde'stood me. But yo', yo' do—would yo' evah have loved me—had I been different?

Katharine: (*Going to him. Firmly*) No.

Griffith: Will yo' respect me now, if Ah do not respect mahself?

Katharine: No.

Griffith: Then kiss me, and tell me to go.

HERNE AND THE REALISM OF CHARACTER

Katharine: Do yo' realize what yo' ask of me?

Griffith: Yes.

Katharine: Is there no othah way?

Griffith: Ah see none.

Katharine: Ah, Griffith! How can Ah say it? Suppose anything should happen to you? That yo' should be taken? (*Breaking down*) Ah'd nevah forgive mahself. Ah believe Ah'd kill mahself. (*Recovering herself*) Griffith, Ah have made sacrifice aftah sacrifice for yo'. Now yo' come to me and ask me to make the supreme sacrifice of mah life. Ah rebel; Ah cannot do it. (*Decisively*) Ah *will* not do it. (*Changing her tone*) Ah, Griffith! mah husband, yo' awe all Ah have. Ah love yo'; Ah tell yo' Ah love yo'. Ah cannot give yo' up.

Griffith: Katharine, this is not a question of yo'ah life or mah life, or of our love fo' each othah. The life of the nation is at stake. Abraham Lincoln calls out to me, "Help me to save the nation. Help me to save this nation." Ah can't shut mah ears to his pitiful cry.

Katharine: You solemnly believe it your duty to go, do you?

Griffith: Yes, Katharine. It is a duty Ah owe mah fellow men on both sides of Mason and Dixon's line. It is a duty Ah owe to the man Ah helped to make responsible for this war. It is a duty Ah owe the government undah which Ah live, and of which Ah am an infinitesimal paht.

Katharine: (*Seeing that argument is useless*) Well, then—go! (*This last with a supreme effort.*)

Griffith: (*Relieved*) Ah knew Ah could depend on you. Yo' awe the bravest little woman in the wo'ld.

In the first scene of the fifth Act, Griffith is seen leading the troops through his native mountains until they approach his own home, when he declines to go further. In the play he is then captured by the Confederates under his son Beverly and is accused of being a spy. The last scene, which is entirely different from the novel, is laid back at the old Davenport mansion. Griffith has been searched and his commission found on him, so that he becomes a prisoner of war. He is allowed to speak to Katharine before he is taken to prison, and the play ends as they are sitting together on the steps of the porch in the moonlight, renewing their vows of love and faith.

Katharine asks him to sing an old song of their courtship days, and he begins:

"Oh, if I were king of France——" as the curtain falls.

But the plot of *Griffith Davenport* cannot even suggest the sweep and color of the play, with its diversity of characters, each one a distinct portrait. That it was not a popular success remains among the unsolved problems of the stage.[1]

Sag Harbor, Herne's last play, was produced at the Park Theatre in Boston, October 24, 1899. It is a revision of *Hearts of Oak*, the main theme being the contrasted love of two brothers, Ben and Frank Turner, for the same woman, Martha Reese, who marries Ben, the older, on account of the gratitude she feels for him, while she really loves Frank. The central character, however, was not the husband, as had been the case in *Hearts of Oak*, but Captain Dan Marble, a guardian angel of everyone, played by Herne himself. The situation is a bit more keen in its sense of conflict, for the two lovers are brothers instead of foster father and son, and Frank urges Martha to run away with him, when he returns two years after her marriage to Ben. There is no Arctic voyage, although Ben threatens to go to the Klondike, and the relations are straightened out largely by the story Captain Marble tells them on Easter Sunday, of a wife who finds that after sending her husband off to war in a similar situation she has really loved him best. Curiously enough, this story follows in its main outlines the plot of Belasco's *May Blossom*, which had appeared between the productions of *Hearts of Oak* and *Sag Harbor*.

There is a certain advance in naturalness in *Sag Harbor*. Striking situations are avoided and the more insistent urge of Frank's passion for Martha, while less ideal than Ruby Darrell's sentiment, is more true to human nature. There is a

---

[1] The unique complete MS. of *Griffith Davenport* was burned. Act IV survived among the papers of the late William Archer and came into the possession of Dr. Brander Matthews, through whose courtesy the foregoing extract has been made. The analysis of the play is also based upon the scenario, furnished through the courtesy of Miss Julie Herne, who acted Emma West, the *fiancée* of Roy, and through the oral accounts of Mrs. Herne, who acted Katharine Davenport.

Addenda to Act IV

May or May not be used.

Katherine

When are you to see your President?

Griffith

"Starting up from a reverie — looks at watch" Now! — Now — Gracious — He's a half hour late — "Seizes hat and starts for door"

Katherine

Wait — one minute — When you see him — Tell him he must send me and make his household through his lines — "Pause" She goes to him — and puts both of her hands on his shoulders — Griffith — this means everything to me now — You must help me to get back to Virginia — Promise me that you will do nothing for him until he agrees to do this for me —

Griffith

"After Pause" All. promise —

Katherine

Thank you" — — Good bye —

Griffith

Won't you kiss me

Katherine

Yes. "Kisses him warmly"

Griffith

Good bye — Katherine sometimes

A PAGE FROM THE ORIGINAL "LOST MANUSCRIPT" OF
GRIFFITH DAVENPORT

closer approach to reality, too, in the portrayal of Martha's love for Ben, and the relations between Captain Marble and his wife are delicately expressed. Several entirely new characters are introduced, especially Jane Cauldwell, a young music-teacher who comforts Frank at the end. This part was played by Chrystal Herne, and the heroine, Martha Reese, by Julie Herne.

Sag Harbor was a very substantial success. It ran until January 20, 1900, in Boston, and opened the Republic Theatre in New York on September 27, 1900, with practically the same cast, except that Lionel Barrymore played Frank Turner. After Herne's death on June 2, 1901, several changes were made in the cast.

When Herne's work is considered as a whole, it will at first seem that it represents several different species, leaving aside the early romantic melodrama, like *Marriage by Moonlight*, or the vanished Irish play, *My Colleen*. These are the domestic melodrama of *Hearts of Oak;* the domestic comedies of *Shore Acres* and *Sag Harbor;* the domestic tragedies (for no matter what the endings may be they are tragedies) of *Drifting Apart* and *Margaret Fleming;* and the historical dramas, *The Minute Men* and *Griffith Davenport*. Yet the very effort to so classify his work reveals the essential artificiality of the attempt. The significant fact which arises from the effort is that Herne's popular successes lay in the field of domestic melodrama and comedy. In *Hearts of Oak, Shore Acres* and *Sag Harbor* he was dealing with the characters of primitive people, and the motives of love, loyalty and family affection are those of most universal appeal. The reality of character and conversation is set against a background in which effective devices to secure human interest are employed. The famous supper scene, for example, which began in *Hearts of Oak*, continued to please the audiences who saw *Shore Acres* and *Sag Harbor*. Their pleasure was due to their recognition of familiar objects, and recognition is the result of an easier mental effort than any reaction which comes from a stimulus given to the imagination.

The Minute Men and *Griffith Davenport* are both historical plays, it is true, but the first relates as a piece of dramatic art much more closely to *Hearts of Oak*, as a melodrama, and the really helpful classification of Herne's play is a progressive one. He began with romantic melodrama in association with David Belasco in *Marriage by Moonlight*, and in the various forms which *Chums* and *Hearts of Oak* assumed he was working his way out of melodrama into something more assured. At first he apparently felt that the material was all important, and he turned to the Revolution for facts and atmosphere that would lend verity to his work. Yet *The Minute Men* is still tinged with the stilted language of an earlier stage epoch, though it redeems itself partly by the firmer drawing of the central characters. His own tastes led him to the study of simple natural people, and it is not strange that when he combined this selection of familiar material with the realistic treatment of it, in *Drifting Apart* and *Margaret Fleming*, that he should progress rapidly toward the summit of his creative achievement. It was at this time that his art became more conscious, under the inspiration of men like Hamlin Garland, while his reading of foreign playwrights and novelists, like Ibsen, Sudermann, Hardy and Zola, strengthened his own predilection toward realism. The result was less popularity and financial loss, but our drama gained a landmark. Howells was quite right when he called *Margaret Fleming* an epoch-marking rather than an epoch-making play. It produced no immediate effect and founded no school. But on looking back we can see that 1890 seems now the beginning of an era. One has only to compare *Men and Women*, of Belasco and De Mille, with *Margaret Fleming*, to see the difference between a play distinctly of that period and the work of Herne. The Scandinavian drama influenced him little, and the German less. He may have learned some lessons in naturalism by reading Ibsen, but he could hardly have seen any of his plays before 1890. According to Hamlin Garland, he learned from Ibsen to dispense with the "asides" and other artifices of the older stage. He mentions Sudermann in his article written in 1897, before quoted, but if any influence came to Herne from the author of *Frau Sorge*, which indeed he read, it was passed through an artistic consciousness which was aware of the dignity of decency and the value of reticence in permanent art.

It was with Herne in drama as it was with Howells in the novel. He was at first subconsciously in sympathy with an impulse which was dominating Europe, and he and Mrs. Herne struggled toward an expression, in drama and on the stage, of a simpler and more sincere form of realistic art. In this they were ahead of their time, so far as America is concerned. Later, when their efforts began to receive the appreciation of Howells and Garland, they recognized their part in this movement and their efforts became more conscious. But they were authorized rather than inspired by the continental realists.

One marked difference between Herne and the European naturalistic movement lay in the humanitarian aspect of his work. He became vitally interested in social reform and, becoming convinced of the justice of Henry George's theory of the single tax, he talked in public on the subject in many of the principal cities of the Union. It became, in fact, a life work with him, and influenced his later writing, especially *Shore Acres*.

The advance in *Margaret Fleming* and in *Griffith Davenport* lies in the less obvious material and the finer subtlety of motive. Herne speaks of *Margaret Fleming* as "the epitome of a powerful but savage truth." But while its central motive, the rebellion of a wife against an action that strikes at the roots of family life, represents the most primitive impulse of our natures, it was just because Margaret Fleming was a refined and cultured woman that the climax of the third Act is so telling a piece of dramatic art. How much less effective would such a scene have been if the woman had been drawn

159

from the personnel of *Hearts of Oak!*[1] But when a gentle-woman, whose every instinct is in open rebellion at the discovery of her husband's liaison with the sister of her servant, finds the impulses of repulsion checked and conquered by the flood of feelings that spring from the universal motherhood within her, we have that shock of conflict which comes only with great drama. Audiences of 1890, however, were not ready for the shock which arises from the relapse into the primitive.

Nor apparently did they understand the combination of patriot and mystic in *Griffith Davenport*. Perhaps the failure of that play to win popular success may have been due to a subconscious feeling that a man should remain true to his own people, as the universal hero worship of Robert E. Lee has indicated. But whatever may have been the causes which led to the failure of Herne's best plays, there can be no question that it was due to the difference of theme rather than the method of treatment. For between *Margaret Fleming* and *Griffith Davenport* had come *Shore Acres*, his greatest popular success, and the fineness of art which reflects an emotion in a glance or a movement of the hand is revealed in that play in a masterly fashion.

And finally and most important, of course, comes the revelation of character. Both from the script and the stage there emerge Margaret Fleming, Philip Fleming, Uncle Nathaniel Berry, Martin Berry, Ann Berry, Griffith Davenport, Katharine Davenport, Captain Dan Marble, Dorothy Foxglove, Mary Miller, to speak of only the leading characters among many. They are not types: they are individuals. They remain in the memory—real people—for us to speculate upon their merits and defects, to wonder whether they really did the things their creator made them do, in short to become citizens of that world which is the product of close observation and

[1] Winter, in his *Life of Belasco*, I, 200, says that "this incident occurs, by the way, under other circumstances, in the fourth [*sic*] chapter of *Hide and Seek*, by Wilkie Collins, published in 1854." The implication is unfair, since the scene in the sixth chapter of *Hide and Seek* has to do with the nursing by a circus woman of the child of a poor girl, with whom neither she nor her husband has any relation.

powerful imagination, in which they may meet the creatures of another great human realist, Charles Dickens, whose characters Herne loved to represent upon the stage.

It is not unworthy of note that both in Herne and Mrs. Herne that quality of imagination which is primarily Celtic had a racial origin. Hundreds of plays upon rural life had their rise during this period, following Herne's success, and few remain worthy of serious consideration. They were usually simply photographic representations of eccentric types and pleased for the moment by their obvious appeal to the faculty of recognition. But in Herne's plays there is a quality of devotion which rises like a flame in the natures of Margaret Fleming and Griffith Davenport, the wife and the patriot, in their greatest hours of trial. This note of loyalty, the prevailing quality that lives in the song and story of Scotland and Ireland, is struck in every play of Herne's from *Chums* to *Sag Harbor*. And there is also a charm, indefinable, but present in the domestic scenes of happiness of *Margaret Fleming* and *Griffith Davenport* before the tragedy comes; throughout all the fisher plays; in the comedy scenes in *The Minute Men*, when Dorothy Foxglove is on the stage; which are as different from the horseplay of the rural drama of Herne's imitators as Conn the Shaughraun is from the average stage Irishman. That they are often associated with the parts played by Mrs. Herne, who was born in Ireland, raises a final problem which the historian cannot solve—to what extent the plays as they now exist were the joint product of the dramatist and the actress to whom Herne has frequently paid his tribute for her inspiration.[1]

It would serve no purpose to chronicle the many imitations and reproductions of the scenes and characters of rural life which owed their inspiration to the popularity of *Hearts of Oak* and *The Old Homestead*. As has been indicated, they are not a new development in our drama, and in many cases

---

[1] Hamlin Garland, who was in close contact with Herne, tells me that Mrs. Herne constantly suggested "scenes, lines, and stage business."

belong in material and treatment to the same species as *The Silver Spoon* of J. S. Jones. They rise or fall in significance as they caught the new spirit of the natural, and perhaps two examples will illustrate the difference between the real and the false notes in the rural chorus.

The County Fair, by Charles Barnard and Neil Burgess, first performed at Proctor's Twenty-third Street Theatre, March 5, 1889, was one of the great popular successes of its time, for it continued its life at the Union Square Theatre in November, 1889, and ran practically continuously until May 31, 1890. Its success was undoubtedly due to the acting of Neil Burgess as Miss Abigail Prue, the old maid who is the feminine counterpart of Joshua Whitcomb and Uncle Nat. Miss Abby has a sharp tongue, but she has a warm heart for Tags, the waif who turns out to be her own sister's child, and she is sentimental, too, over Otis Tucker, who has been courting her mildly for fourteen years. The plot is conventional where it is not negligible, but the dialogue is bright and the atmosphere is sincere.

Way Down East, by Lottie Blair Parker, on the other hand, was a "pastoral drama," which pointed backward rather than forward in the development of realism. It has all the old conventional figures, beginning with the stern father who will not let his son marry the drooping stranger who totters on the stage, having left her child in the graveyard, and not forgetting the burlesque of the college professor who makes comic love to the farmer's daughter. The lessons of simplicity and sincerity which Herne had taught were neglected, and yet the play was a great popular success, beginning at the Manhattan Theatre on February 7, 1898, a long run of three hundred and sixty-one performances in New York.

But as has been sufficiently pointed out, the rural drama was not Herne's most significant contribution; it was the establishment of character.

CHAPTER VII

David Belasco and His Associates

O F ALL the playwrights who form the subject of this study, David Belasco presents the most difficult problem. He has written so often in collaboration with others, the plays bearing his name present apparently so many different aspects both as to selection of material and method of treatment, and his career has been so long and fruitful as playwright, producer and director, that generalizations become at first glance almost impossible. It will be best to consider his work as a series of stages, in which, often with the aid of others, he has passed through various phases of dramatic fashion, sometimes determining it, and sometimes following. After this survey perhaps a certain consistency will become apparent. This method will permit also of the treatment of other playwrights of importance who did their best work in association with Mr. Belasco, and of whom pressure of space will forbid separate discussion.

David Belasco was born in San Francisco, July 25, 1853, both his parents being English Jews, although the family seems to have been originally Portuguese. In 1858 they moved to the trading post, Victoria, and here he was educated, partly in a monastery under the guidance of a Catholic priest, whose influence remained for many years upon Belasco, even in the severity and uniformity of his dress. The theatre, however, was in his blood, for his father had been connected with the London playhouses as a harlequin and his parents associated with the people of the stage. He was used indeed for children's parts, in all probability as early as 1858, but he certainly acted as the Duke of York in Charles Kean's performance of *Richard III* at the Victoria Theatre in 1864. Return-

163

ing to San Francisco about 1865, he entered the Lincoln Grammar School, where he remained until 1871. His education was, however, quite as much derived from extensive reading and his observation of life, and his indomitable energy, spurred on by the very moderate circumstances of the family, led him to such engagements as he could obtain in the minor offices of the theatre. In 1869 he played a newsboy in Augustin Daly's *Under the Gaslight* at Maguire's Opera House in San Francisco, and he may be said to have definitely adopted the stage as a profession when he took part in F. G. Marsden's *Help* in 1871 at the Metropolitan Theatre.

He began, too, his dramatic efforts, his first play, *Jim Black, or the Regulator's Revenge,* being written when he was but twelve years of age, and being produced on the road. In the official list of his productions, fifteen titles are recorded prior to 1872. The names[1] will indicate the nature of the plays sufficiently, their significance lying simply in the precocity of the boy and the unmistakable impulse toward romance. His life was a precarious one, and his early plays, all of which have disappeared, consisted probably of the re-shaping of fiction, poetry or other plays for an immediate market. Thus he seems to have produced and acted in a version of the Enoch Arden story, made for Annie Pixley about 1876, which is of interest on account of the later use of a similar situation in *Chums.*

During an engagement at Piper's Opera House in Virginia City, Nevada, in 1873, Belasco came under the influence of Dion Boucicault, and the lessons he learned from that master of technique have remained with the pupil in the keen sense of what is theatrically effective and in that combination of romantic material and realistic treatment which is one of the reasons for Belasco's success.

In 1874 began his association with James A. Herne at Maguire's New Theatre, where he acted a dwarf in Herne's production of *Rip Van Winkle.* He was employed as actor, as-

[1] See List of Plays.

sistant stage manager, and even prompter with Bartley Campbell and the Hooley Comedy Company, during their visit to California, never scorning to take even the humbler positions if thereby he could learn something of value. His own list of productions, the list given by Winter in his *Life of Belasco*, and the accounts in *My Life's Story* are contradictory, but out of all the bewildering mass of material there emerges the figure of a hard-working actor and playwright, learning his profession in a school which developed Herne, Harrigan and other dramatists, the highly colored life and theatre of California in the seventies. Of all who worked in that atmosphere, Belasco seems to have been most deeply affected by it, as was perhaps natural since it was his native soil, and while the others saw it from the point of view of the theatre, it had been part of his education. He continued apparently to adapt plays, especially from the novels of Dickens and Wilkie Collins, but does not even claim these in his own list.

His second association with Herne began at Baldwin's Academy of Music in 1876, but it was intermittent. Meanwhile he adapted *Article 47*, under the title of *The Creole*, for Eleanor Carey, and this was produced at the Union Square Theatre in New York in 1881. During the spring of 1877 he wrote and directed eight plays, nearly all in one act, which were performed at Egyptian Hall in San Francisco, and in which he acted as well. To judge from the casts that have survived, they were either moral melodrama, like *The Prodigal's Return*, or else were built up upon a stage device known as "Gardner's Egyptian Mystery," a variant of the once-famous "Pepper's Ghost"—an optical illusion again appealing to Belasco's love of the bizarre. Even before this time he had been experimenting with new effects in stage lighting. By use of colored silks he had anticipated his own gelatine slides, and there can be no doubt that Belasco in his theatres in California was developing that remarkable sense of the part played by lighting in the illusion of the stage, in which he anticipated more widely known efforts of foreign directors and which led eventually to the marvelous construction of the Belasco Theatre in New York.

His wanderings took him to Oregon, but he was soon back at the Baldwin Theatre to direct such plays as *Saratoga* and *The Danites*, a connection which took him on tour in the spring of 1878, and culminated in a deserved tribute to his skill.[1] His position at the Baldwin led him to the dramatization of novels such as *The Vicar of Wakefield*, and the quick imitation of Eastern successes, such as *The Banker's Daughter*, under the title of *The Millionaire's Daughter*. The delightful confusion of such adaptations is indicated by the fact that a character by the name of Adam Trueman, the farmer in *Fashion*, was inserted in the play and that Belasco defended himself from the charge of plagiarism on the ground that his most effective scene, that of the duel, was taken from *The Corsican Brothers*!

His association with Herne in *Marriage by Moonlight* and in *Chums* and *Hearts of Oak* has been analyzed sufficiently.[2] The separation was inevitable, for dramatic rather than personal causes. Herne went on developing a form of drama with which Belasco was really not in sympathy, and the latter returned to the Baldwin Theatre, in April, 1880, as actor and dramatist. Here he produced such melodrama as *Paul Arniff*, laid in Russia, or *The Eviction*, in which he seized the current interest in the difficulties between landlord and tenant in Ireland.

Meanwhile he was nursing his ambition to gain a footing in the East. Believing that if he could attract Wallack's attention the way would be opened, he secured Osmond Tearle and Gerald Eyre from Wallack's company for a summer engagement at Baldwin's Theatre, and also persuaded Maguire to engage Mary Jeffreys-Lewis, who was in San Francisco, for the leading part in a play to be written by him. *La Belle Russe* was first presented at the Baldwin Theatre on July 18,

[1] Winter. *Life of Belasco*, I, 106.
[2] Pp. 133-6.

1881. It is based on two plays, *Forget Me Not*, by Herman Merivale and Charles Groves, and *The New Magdalen*, by Wilkie Collins, both of which had been acted under Belasco's management.[1] It is a sensational melodrama of English social life, in which an adventuress attempts to impersonate her twin sister, even carrying her efforts to the point of taking that sister's place as the wife of her long-lost and re-found husband. The play was announced as "from the French," as San Francisco shared with the other American cities a distrust of home talent, and only when it proved a success was Belasco's name attached to it. He went to New York with Maguire to place the play, but through the latter's insistence upon dealing with other managers, he was prevented from selling it directly to Wallack, though the latter eventually secured it. It was produced at Wallack's Theatre on May 8, 1882, with Rose Coghlan as Beatrice, and scored a popular success, being put on at the Pavilion Theatre, London, April 17, 1886. Nearly forty years later, at a dinner given to Belasco, Rose Coghlan paid her tribute to the possibilities which the part afforded an actress in a strong emotional rôle.

Back in San Francisco, he continued his work at the Baldwin Theatre until a meeting with Gustave Frohman not only occasioned the last production of a play by Belasco in San Francisco—the melodrama, *American Born*—but led also to his final departure for New York. In the fall of 1882, through the Frohmans, he became stage manager at the Madison Square Theatre, succeeding Steele MacKaye, who had broken relations with the owners, the Mallory brothers, after making the Madison Square Theatre well-known through his plays and his stage devices. Belasco signalized his advent in the East by the production of Bronson Howard's *Young Mrs. Winthrop*, and he showed his ability at the direction of a different kind of play from that which he had been writing and directing in San Francisco. It was a potent organization to which he had come. The Mallorys had a policy of encourag-

[1] Winter, I, 231.

ing American playwrights, like Howard and Gillette; they had in Daniel Frohman one of the shrewdest business managers in America, and the company headed by George Clarke, Mr. and Mrs. Thomas Whiffen, Agnes Booth and W. J. Le Moyne was a splendid one.

Belasco's first effort as a playwright under his new conditions was produced on April 12, 1884, and ran until September 27. *May Blossom*, which was an alteration of an earlier play by Belasco, *Sylvia's Lovers*, produced in 1875 in Virginia City, is a variant of the story of *Hearts of Oak*, with the returned wanderer a lover instead of a husband. Richard Ashcroft and Steve Harland are both in love with May Blossom, and she accepts the former. Ashcroft, who is a Confederate sympathizer, very naturally, since the play is laid in Virginia during and after the Civil War, is arrested by the Federal authorities and begs Harland to tell his *fiancée*. Harland, hoping to marry May, allows her to believe that Ashcroft is dead, and they are married after a year. Ashcroft returns in about two years and demands that May elope with him. She refuses, partly on account of her child and partly since she has apparently begun to love Harland. Ashcroft departs. Of course May upbraids her husband and Steve joins the Confederate army, returning in about six years, having gone on a whaling trip after the war is over. May becomes reconciled to him. This play, which for many years was the only published example of Belasco's work, can hardly be looked upon as one of his best. The characters are inconsistent, especially that of Harland, who is represented as being an honorable man and yet is capable of unspeakable treachery. In feminine psychology, however, Belasco made no mistake, for it is extremely likely that a wife would forgive a crime prompted by her husband's overpowering love for her. The one-thousandth performance of this play was made the occasion for a tribute to the author.

Belasco remained in association with the Madison Square Theatre for only two years, then resigned. After various

DAVID BELASCO

experiences, including an association with Lester Wallack, for whom he adapted Sardou's *Fernande*, a brief return to San Francisco, in 1886, to direct a stock company at the Baldwin Theatre, which numbered among it such actors as Mantell, Henry Miller, and Maurice Barrymore, he became stage manager of the Lyceum Theatre, in 1886, then under the direction of Daniel Frohman.

This position led to the second important period of Belasco's playwriting, that in which he was associated with Henry C. DeMille (1850-93). DeMille, who had been a school-teacher and a play reader at the Madison Square Theatre before he became a playwright, had written a social comedy, *John Delmer's Daughters*, which had been produced at the Madison Square Theatre in 1883 and had failed. His frontier play, *The Main Line or Rawson's Y*, had been no more successful when put on at the Lyceum Theatre in 1886, and the description of it implies that it was of no especial significance.[1]

The combination of Belasco and DeMille produced four of the most successful plays of their day. *The Wife*, which was produced November 1, 1887, at the Lyceum Theatre, was written definitely with the stock company led by Herbert Kelcey and Georgia Cayvan in mind. The central idea was an old one. Robert Grey and Helen Freeman, though lovers, have parted because Lucile Ferrant, who had been jilted by Robert, tells Helen of their earlier relation. Helen marries, out of pique, the Hon. John Rutherford, who in due time becomes aware of the situation. Here Belasco, under the inspiration of Howard's *The Banker's Daughter*, suggested that Rutherford, instead of behaving as the stage husband usually did under those circumstances, should endeavor to win his wife's love, having too much pride to acknowledge that an early girlish passion must necessarily be more powerful than her reaction to his own love and confidence. Rutherford finally succeeds, not without some inner struggles. The play is significant in studying Belasco's development, for it is the least effective

[1] *Theatre Magazine*, II, 24-5.

of this series. It is artificial, and the early motives and actions are quite obvious in their relations to later scenes. The main theme is so padded out with comedy at the beginning of each act that it seems as though material were lacking. The audience, too, has to be told everything, and "asides" are plentiful. In short, it belongs to the fashion of that day.

The relative shares of Belasco and DeMille are best indicated by a description of their methods of collaboration. According to Daniel Frohman,[1] DeMille wrote most of the play. After it had been developed to a certain point, they brought it to the Lyceum Theatre. DeMille sat at a desk near the empty stage and Belasco acted upon the stage the scenes of the drama. If the result was not satisfactory to Belasco, DeMille changed lines, cut out or added scenes and otherwise modified the play, always with a view to stage effectiveness. If the heroine had been introduced upon the left side of the stage when her entrance would have been more telling upon the right, and the script forbade the change of position, then the script had to be altered. When the authors handed over the manuscript, the labor was only half done. Every scene had to be adjusted to the stock company, whose very excellences in some cases proved embarrassing. Grace Henderson, who played Lucile Ferrant, the adventuress, had a peculiarly sympathetic voice. According to the play she was to indicate by her intonation that she was lying to Helen in her revelation of the earlier relation between Robert Grey and herself. But her voice was so appealing that the audience refused to sympathize with anyone but her. So the melodramatic line, "Robert Grey, I'll bring you back to me, no matter what was the cost," was inserted, and she said this to the audience as an aside.

This incident is illuminating in its revelation of the difficulty of appraising justly the work of playwrights of this period. The line in question was added at the instigation of Daniel Frohman, and he was probably justified from the point of view of stage effect. Read in manuscript, it is a blot on the play.

[1] Statement to the present writer.

There can be no question that this was only one of hundreds of cases where the necessities of a stock company rather than the will of a playwright determined the final form of a drama. Such incidents may well have been contributing causes to the decline of the stock companies. Weak and at times commonplace as it was, *The Wife* proved a financial success, receiving two hundred and thirty-nine consecutive performances and leading to the production of other plays by the two playwrights.

Lord Chumley, their second effort, was produced at the Lyceum Theatre, August 21, 1888. It was written for E. H. Sothern, and the hero is not without a certain resemblance to Lord Dundreary, his father's successful part. *Lord Chumley,* like many interesting and successful plays, is made up of situations and characters that are not strictly original. But the central character, that of a young English nobleman who, apparently stupid, vapid and inane, is really brave, acute and above all loyal in love and friendship and willing to sacrifice himself for the sake of friend and lover, remains after nearly forty years, a vivid and delightful memory. The part was just suited to Sothern, and he was provided with lines which are a decided improvement upon those in *The Wife.*

During the interval between *Lord Chumley* and *The Charity Ball,* Belasco directed a production of the *Electra* of Sophocles, in which, as has been pointed out,[1] "the much admired and highly extolled 'modern novelties' of simplicity in stage settings and lighting displayed by Mr. Granville Barker, in 1915, were used by Belasco—twenty-eight years earlier." *The Charity Ball* was produced at the Lyceum Theatre, November 19, 1889. It is a strong play, of intense feeling at times, in which a successful attempt is made to bring sin and suffering into vivid contrast with the brighter phases of social enjoyment. The Reverend John van Buren, a fine type of clergyman, is contrasted with his weak and selfish brother, Dick, who has seduced Phyllis Lee and abandoned her on account of his

[1] Winter, I, 355.

A HISTORY OF THE AMERICAN DRAMA

desire to marry Ann Cruger, an heiress, who is really in love with John. The relations of Dick and Phyllis become known to John and Ann during the Charity Ball, and that night Phyllis comes to appeal to John for comfort. He has become fascinated by her physical beauty, but he crushes this feeling, and on Dick's return home demands that he immediately marry Phyllis, offering to perform the ceremony. The quarrel between the brothers, intense yet subdued, was heightened by the entrance of their mother, who, blind but watchful, has heard a disturbance and enters at the height of the scene. Her simple words of gentle reproof, "My boys, my boys," which quiet them, spoken by Mrs. Thomas Whiffen in the original cast, were an example of the use of the family relation as a theme for drama which it would be hard to excel. The marriage is performed, and later John and Ann discover that their love, if a bit placid, is sufficient for happiness.[1]

The last play in which DeMille and Belasco collaborated was *Men and Women*, produced at Proctor's Theatre, October 21, 1890. The germ of the play was furnished to Belasco by a recent banking scandal, in which the father of a young man who had speculated with the funds of his bank is said to have exclaimed, "I'll save the bank, if it costs me a million a day." *Men and Women* is a compound of the themes of banking, speculation, love and family affection. The partners recognized that in the intense moments of anxiety which come to those who are carrying on financial operations which bring them within the shadow of the law, there are fine opportunities for drama. William Prescott, a bank cashier, has taken bonds belonging to the bank and loaned them to Arnold Kirke, a broker, who fails. Suspicion falls on Edward Seabury, the assistant cashier, who is engaged to Dora Prescott, William's sister. At a midnight meeting of the directors of the bank, Seabury is accused of theft. He denies the charge but is

[1] I wondered at the reason which had led to the insertion of the proposal scene with its involved reference to the love story of David Copperfield and Agnes Wickfield, to find at last, from Daniel Frohman, it was inserted to give Georgia Cayvan, the leading lady, an opportunity to resume the stage, from which she had been absent too long!

172

arrested. Agnes Rodman, the *fiancée* of Prescott, who has been told by Mrs. Kirke that William is the culprit, begs her father, Governor Rodman of Arizona, to save the bank, if Seabury is released. But Calvin Stedman, counsel of the bank, declines to let Seabury go, for he loves Dora and wishes to disgrace his rival. Rodman's offer is accepted, however, by the directors, and then Stedman denounces Rodman as a former convict and therefore untrustworthy. Pendleton, one of the directors, saves the bank, using the phrase which had inspired the play, but he is not interested in Seabury. Then comes a daring but successful climax when Prescott, finding that Agnes knows his guilt, confesses by putting on himself the handcuffs which are waiting for Seabury. The last Act falls decidedly in interest: Prescott is looking for a position, which Pendleton eventually gives him.

What held the audience was the vivid picture of moral and emotional conflict, especially in the characters of Prescott and Agnes. The language when read in the manuscript seems at times stilted and overwrought, but in the fine performance of the original company, which included Sydney Armstrong as Agnes, Maude Adams as Dora, Frederic de Belleville as Cohen, William Morris as Prescott and Orrin Johnson as Seabury, these defects were not noticeable. What remains most clearly is a picture of the normal life of people with real standards without much stress being laid upon them. The peace and comfort of such life makes the tragedy, when it comes, more striking, and the ball given while the bank is under its strain was well conceived and executed.

Belasco had withdrawn from his association with the Lyceum Theatre in March, 1890, in order to secure his independence. He had succeeded as a playwright and as an actor, but he knew that his greatest strength lay in the field of production and direction. DeMille, before his death in 1893, adapted *Das Verlorene Paradies* of Ludwig Fulda which as *The Lost Paradise* was successful. Those who saw *Men and Women* and *The Lost Paradise* recognized that they belong to the same species—the domestic drama which was eminently "satisfactory" to the audience, which had progressed quite far from the sickly sentimentality of *The Stranger*, and whose limitations it is quite possible to overstress. A comparison of the two plays indicates also the large share which DeMille must have had in the verbal expression of the plays in which he collaborated with Belasco.

Though Belasco's efforts to establish Mrs. Leslie Carter as a star led ultimately to success, they engrossed his attention at this time with financial loss and anxiety, and they led at first to no important drama. *Miss Helyett* (1891), a comic opera, is negligible, and *The Girl I Left Behind Me* was produced, not for her, but for the opening of the Empire Theatre in 1893. In collaboration with Franklyn Fyles, then dramatic critic of the New York *Sun,* he constructed one of the most vivid plays of Indian and army life which our drama contains. The time was ripe, for the death of Sitting Bull and the successful operations of General Miles were in the public memory. The scenes were laid in an army post near Fort Assinniboine, in the Sioux Country. General Kennion, who is in command, is visited by his daughter Kate, and a ball is given in her honor. Throughout the gayety there is suggested an impending danger of Indian uprising, under the leadership of Scarbrow or John Ladru, the chieftain of the Blackfoot Sioux. This is accomplished by the constant receipt of telegrams from Fort Assinniboine. Inside the post, the personal relations are also strained. Kate is engaged to be married to Lieutenant Parlow, and finds too late that she loves his colleague, Lieutenant Hawksworth. Parlow had some time before seduced and abandoned the wife of Major Burleigh, one of the officers, who is ignorant of the name of her betrayer. The first crisis occurs when the telegrams which have been coming from the fort suddenly cease, and the savage whoops outside indicate the approach of the Indians. Hawksworth volunteers to go to the fort and bring succor.

In the third Act occurs a striking episode, expressed briefly but forcibly. The situation grows desperate and General Kennion stoops to treat with Ladru. The audience sees the stockade, with the whites behind it, and Ladru rides up, unseen, his voice alone being heard. Some time previous, his daughter, Fawn Afraid, who is in love with Hawksworth, had come into the stockade to bring water to the whites, and has been shot, although this is not known to those within the post, who believe she is living. Then follows this scene:

Kennion: (*His eyes fall on Fawn. With an inspiration.*)
    Ladru, your child is here. What shall I do with her?
Ladru: Fawn is with her own people. (*Fawn kneels.*)
Kennion: (*Pointing toward Fawn*) She is with us. I will be more
    merciful than you. (*Deliberately*) The first shot you fire
    on this Post, I will give the order to—kill her.
Ladru: (*With a cry of intense feeling.*)
    Ah!
Burleigh: That reached his heart.
                        (*A pause*)
Ladru: If Fawn is with you, show her to me.
    (*Kennion turns to Burleigh. As Burleigh starts to bring
    Fawn to the parapet, she sinks to the ground. Dr. Pennick
    goes quickly to her, opens her blanket and examines her.*)
Dr. Pennick: She is dead.
    (*All stand aghast. Kennion remains motionless on the para-
    pet, not daring to show his despair to Ladru. A pause.*)
Ladru: My soft-eyed Fawn is not there to protect you.
Kennion: I give you my solemn word—she is here.
Ladru: Then let me hear her voice.
    (*The sun by this time has fully risen and the sky is illumined,
    the light falling on the hopeless faces of the group.*)
    She cannot stay my hand again!

The constant anxiety of an army officer for the safety of his wife and daughter which Belasco had suggested to him by the description of Mrs. George Crook, widow of General Crook, a veteran of Indian warfare, was dramatized in the scene in which General Kennion, when hope has been abandoned, is about to kill Kate to save her from worse than death. According to one school of criticism, he should have discarded this

A HISTORY OF THE AMERICAN DRAMA

idea, because Sheridan Knowles had in *Virginius* taken a simi-lar motive from Roman history. The playwrights should probably have silenced also the clear bugle notes of the rescuing cavalry which Kate, with her attentive faculties keyed to the highest pitch, naturally hears first, because Boucicault had written *Jessie Brown*. But our drama would have missed one of its best portrayals of deep but repressed emotion, when civilized men and women are brought into peril from a foe whose savage standards make desperate resistance the only cause of action.[1] *The Girl I Left Behind Me* ran from January to June, 1893, a second company remaining at the Empire Theatre while the first company went to Chicago during the Columbian Exposition.

Belasco, in his autobiography, speaks of the principle of suggestion employed in this play, through which the audience hear the Indians chanting and the soldiers galloping, but are unable to tell whether there are ten or ten thousand at hand. He states also that such scenes were new in the East. Leaving aside the question of novelty, there is no doubt about the effect, for it is due to a principle greater than that embodied in any one play, the principle of suspense.

After a dismal failure in his effort to adapt *Schlimme Saat* under the title of *The Younger Son*, Belasco produced *The Heart of Maryland*, with Mrs. Leslie Carter as Maryland Calvert, in October, 1895. His adventures before he succeeded in finding and retaining financial backing read like a romance, but at last he secured an established position as dramatist and producer, for the play proved an abounding success. It is a melodrama of the Civil War, not as significant as *Shenandoah* (1888) or *Secret Service* (1895), but it moves quickly despite a complicated plot. Belasco had visited Maryland to study the situation and the Southern atmosphere is well portrayed. The liking of the audience is caught at first

[1] See Winter, I, 403–21 for an exhaustive and enthusiastic analysis of the play. His one criticism, that it is impossible that Kate, "though she loves Hawksworth, has promised to marry Parlow," is a curious error, since Kate was engaged to be married to Parlow before meeting Hawksworth.

176

DAVID BELASCO AND HIS ASSOCIATES

by the Northern officer, Alan Kendrick, and since his success means the salvation also of Maryland Calvert, who has risked her life and forsaken her own cause to save him, the audience is led cleverly to transfer its sympathy from the Southern side to the side that must win. The play is marred, however, from the point of view of permanent worth, by the situation in which Maryland swings out from a tower holding on to the clapper of a bell which was to have been the signal for the lover's doom.

Neither Belasco's adaptation of *Zaza* (1899), nor his farce, *Naughty Anthony* (1899), is of significance to us. Yet, the latter, being too slight to fill the requirements of an evening's entertainment, led to the production of one of his finest plays. Looking for material with which to construct a one-act play, he read the story of *Madame Butterfly* by John Luther Long and saw its great dramatic possibilities. The resulting collaboration which produced the play of *Madame Butterfly*, ushered in the period of Belasco's career when his most permanent contributions to dramatic art were made. His instinct had always been for the romantic, and in Long he found a collaborator whose creative power far surpassed that of any other playwright with whom Belasco had been associated, with the exception of Herne. But Herne's best work was done with the material of familiar life; Long's taste was for the exotic, and to the exotic every instinct of Belasco, even his Oriental extraction, responded. It was one of those singularly happy combinations that are rare in dramatic history, and it gave to dramatic literature three masterpieces.

Madame Butterfly, first performed at the Herald Square Theatre, March 5, 1900, is a tragedy of Japan, but the motive is a universal one. Cho-Cho-San, a Japanese girl of good stock, is an orphan, whose father, an officer in the Imperial army, has committed suicide on account of his inability to carry out the commands of his Emperor. Her relatives have persuaded her to form an alliance with an American naval officer, Lieutenant B. F. Pinkerton, who looks upon the matter as a temporary affair, as indeed it is considered by everyone but

Madame Butterfly, as Pinkerton calls her. The very choice of the name is an inspiration on Long's part. It strikes the note of tragedy, for upon this careless lover, who has been away for two years, who has told her he will come back "when the robins nest again," and who has in reality married legally an American wife, Madame Butterfly has lavished a love so strong, so enduring that it lifts her into greatness. To others the form of marriage through which they had gone was an idle tribute to custom—to her it was the symbol of her devotion. Long caught well the spirit of Bushido, the Japanese noblesse oblige. Madame Butterfly preserves the dignity due not only to her blood but to her assumed position as "Mrs. Leftenant B. F. Pinkerton," and hides under her habit of courtesy her breaking heart. Sharpless, the consul, cannot bear to tell her all the truth and so Butterfly believes that Pinkerton, whose ship has arrived in port, is to come home to her the next day. It was necessary, therefore, to show the passage of time, and here Belasco's art intervened and in a striking scene he showed the approach of night, the circuit of the stars and the stealing in of the morning, with the servant, Susuki, and the little child asleep, but with Madame Butterfly standing by the window, in the chill terror of the gray dawn. Pinkerton returns, but they do not meet, for she has gone to the "liddle lookout place" to see him sooner, and as he stands gazing at the playthings on the floor we hear her voice singing the song he had taught her, in his arms:

> "Rog'-a-bye-bebby,
> Off in Japan,
> You just a picture
> Off of a fan."

He cannot face her and he leaves Sharpless with money for her, to tell her of his marriage. She takes the blow bravely but is hardly conscious when Kate, his wife, enters and the air becomes electric with the brief interchange of words:

Kate: Is this? (*Sharpless nods and goes. There is a short pause, while the two women look at each other; then Madame*

178

Butterfly, still seated, slowly bows her head.) Why, you poor little thing—who in the world could blame you—or call you responsible—you pretty little plaything.
(*She takes Madame Butterfly in her arms.*)
Madame Butterfly: (*Softly*) No playthin'—I am Mrs. Leftenant B. F.—No—no—now I am only—Cho-Cho-San, but no playthin'. . . .

Madame Butterfly gives up her child that he may be brought up in his father's country and she kills herself with her father's sword. Pinkerton enters just in time for her to die in his arms; plucky to the last.

The play follows the story quite closely, almost completely so far as the language is concerned. In the story, Pinkerton does not return to the house but leaves money with Sharpless, which she refuses. Kate and she meet in the consul's office and Madame Butterfly, after attempting suicide, decides to live for the child's sake. The changes make far more striking situations, and here Belasco's hand is evident. But the conception of character and the central situation belong to John Luther Long and these are the two qualities of *Madame Butterfly* which have given it a place in the literature of the world. The part of Madame Butterfly was created in America by Blanche Bates, and the rôle was assumed at the Duke of York's Theatre in London, April 28, 1900, by Evelyn Millard. In both cases it was recognized as a distinguished work of art. Giacomo Puccini was present at the first night in London, and though he was unable to understand the words, he saw its dramatic value and at once requested permission to compose an opera on the basis of the play. *Madama Butterfly* was first performed in New York in English, November 12, 1906. But its greatest production was in Italian, at the Metropolitan Opera House, February 11, 1907, when Geraldine Farrar sang Cio-Cio-San; Louise Homer, Susuki, and Enrico Caruso, Pinkerton. The opera is naturally enlarged, but follows the lines of the play in general. It has now taken its assured place among operas of the first rank.

A HISTORY OF THE AMERICAN DRAMA

From the point of view of dramatic history it will be best to treat together the plays in which Long and Belasco collaborated, omitting for the moment the theatrical history which intervened. Belasco, on looking for a play with which to fill his new theatre, naturally turned to Long for assistance. The partners proceeded logically. Certain themes, they reasoned, had been successful on the stage. What were they? Long made a study of those dramas which had become classic, and he found that the three themes, heroism, patriotism and love, seemed to be the widest in their appeal. So it was decided that all three should be put into the new play. The result was *The Darling of the Gods*, produced first at Washington, November 17, 1902, and brought to the Belasco Theatre in New York, December 3, 1902.

The story of *The Darling of the Gods* centers again about a woman. The Princess Yo-San, played by Blanche Bates, is betrothed to a courtier whom she does not love, and to postpone the evil day she makes a provision that before she marries him he will capture a notorious outlaw, Prince Kara.[1] Kara is but a name to her, but in reality she had been saved from danger by him and he had promised to come to her father's palace. When he appears, he has been wounded in his attempt to break through the cordon of the war minister, Zakkuri, a remarkable character whose fiendish nature was represented brilliantly by George Arliss. Yo-San conceals him in her apartments. She is suspected by her father, the Prince of Tosan, and Migaku, a spy of Zakkuri has traced Kara to his sanctuary. Inu, a mute giant, who guards her, takes care of Migaku effectively and the scene proceeds to the climax of the second act.

[1] The statement in Winter's *Life of Belasco*, II, 71, that *The Darling of the Gods* is based on an old play, *The Carbineer*, the manuscript of which was "turned over to Long" is without foundation. Long never saw such a play, according to his written statement to me. In Long's study of Japanese history, he was attracted by the heroic defense of Saigo, a leader in the rebellion of 1868, against the Imperial army in its attack on Satsuma. Saigo and thirty of his followers committed suicide. At Belasco's suggestion, the "two-sword men" were reduced to ten in the play to make the struggle more tragic.

Yo-San: Father!

Prince of Tosan: (*Horrified*) Yo-San!

(*Kugo crosses the bridge, but lingers beyond the center half, turning—his head and the lantern just showing.*)

Yo-San: Forgive my appearing here. No Kimono (*She modestly draws her robe about her as a veil.*) —no veil—but I am much frightened . . . while I slept a man looked through my shoji. . . . Inu killed him—there! (*She points down the steps. Inu holds up the body of Migaku from the lotus by the moat—as though it had drifted nearer shore.*)

Inu: Ugh!

(*The water drips from Migaku's face—as Kugo, reaching over the bridge, holds up his lantern to throw the light in Migaku's face—All look*)

Prince of Tosan: (*To Zakkuri*) Is this one of your spies?

Zakkuri: (*Puzzled—but with craft*) He deserved his miserable death—if he were not killed for what he saw!

(*Inu drops Migaku's body into the water.*)

Prince of Tosan: The zealous Zakkuri dared to say that an out-law—Kara—sought shelter behind your shoji. . . . Answer. . . .

Zakkuri: Upon oath . . . before Shaka!

(*All kowtowing, save the Prince, who resents the insult.*)

Prince of Tosan: Zakkuri!

Zakkuri: (*Craftily*) I am but a servant of the Emperor, who must have the truth—

Prince of Tosan: (*To Yo-San*) Before Shaka! (*All kowtow.*)

Yo-San: (*Holding up the incense*) Before Shaka, God of Life and Death—to whom my word goes up on this incense—I swear, hanging my life on the answer—I have not seen this Kara! (*Simply*) With much shame, I ask you, how could I? Since I am dressed for sleep?

(*Setsu at a look from Yo-San appears—takes the lantern and exits into the house.*)

Prince of Tosan: (*Stands looking at Zakkuri*) You hear!

Zakkuri: Lord of Tosan, I was too zealous for the Emperor! (*Fawning to Yo-San*) May the Gods give you good sleep! (*He crosses up to the bridge—turns, looks at Yo-San—then snaps his fingers for his spies to precede him. Zakkuri and Tonda-Tanji and Kugo disappear from bridge. The Prince of Tosan has ignored his kowtowing.*)

Prince of Tosan: (*Raising his hand*) My daughter! The goddess of good dreams visit you! (*He goes off.*)
Yo-San: (*Without moving, wiping the tears from her impassive face with her fingers*) It is better to lie a little than to be unhappy much.

For forty days Kara stays with her; then he hears from his band and must go. The scene of parting is memorable for its expression:

Kara: Answer . . . how long since the night I was brought in behind this shoji?
Yo-San: (*Monotonously*) Say but two days.
Kara: Oh!
Yo-San: (*Quickly*) Four days . . . then. . . .
Kara: Setsu! (*She does not come from behind the screen.*) Setsu! (*Setsu comes down timidly.*) How long?
Setsu: August Prince, I think to-day is Friday.
Yo-San: (*Kneeling*) You think too rapidly . . . it is earlier . . . Monday.
Kara: Yo-San, answer!
Yo-San: (*Frightened*) It is set out on the tablet of time, my Lord and Master.
Kara: (*Demanding it*) The tablet! (*Setsu stands a moment, then takes the calendar from the table and comes slowly down*)
Kara: (*Angrily*) Ah! (*He starts to take it.*)
Yo-San: (*Still on her knees, throws herself between him and Setsu.*) Aie, aie! He takes such beautiful moments as we have had . . . and calls them days . . . hours. . . . Aie! They will look longer than they were.
Kara: (*After taking the tablet from Setsu . . . counting*) . . . Forty days . . . Shaka!
Yo-San: Ah no, belovèd, it is still the night you came!

They are, however, discovered. She is an outcast and he is doomed to torment, unless she betrays the hiding place of his followers. At first she refuses; then when she is made to see through the trapdoor what awaits him, she gives the information. But both are tricked by Zakkuri, and when she finds her way to Kara's citadel, it is only to watch him die with honor, surrounded by the dead bodies of his Samurai. It is an exquisite scene, as she begs him, "Let me slip by the judgment gods with you . . . in the dark." He forgives her and she is left, to follow him after she has been purged by a thousand years of her punishment in hell for the betrayal—because she loved much. The production was made on a lavish scale, and the impression was one of continuous beauty. It ran for two years, was produced by Beerbohm Tree in London, December 28, 1903; at the Theater des Westens in Berlin in May, 1903, and also in Italy and Australia.

On December 26, 1904, in Washington, D. C., Belasco produced the tragedy of *Adrea*, the third play written in collaboration with John Luther Long. The theatre was built especially for this purpose as Belasco was shut out of the theatres controlled by the Trust. On January 11, 1905, it was produced at his theatre in New York and continued until May 4, 1905. It was played the next season also, alternating with *DuBarry* and *Zaza*.

Adrea is a romantic tragedy laid in the fifth century A.D. on an island in the Adriatic Sea. Long invented the situation, which is based upon the condition of disorder that prevailed in the Roman Empire after the fall of Rome in 476. Adrea is a princess, the oldest daughter of the late King Menethus. It is a law in that kingdom that no one shall succeed to the throne unless he or she is physically perfect. Adrea is blind, so she cannot rule and her younger sister, Julia, is about to be crowned. She is unpopular on account of her character and Adrea is greatly beloved by the people. Kaeso, a neighboring prince, is to marry Julia in order to rule the kingdom. Adrea had met him some years before in Arcady and he had promised to marry her, but he forgets his love in his ambition and Julia demands that he shall tell Adrea all is over. He tries to do so but is carried away by his memories and Adrea believes that he is going to marry her. Julia, with the hatred of the woman who possesses the lover for the woman who keeps the love, takes a terrible revenge upon her sister by betraying her into the arms of the court jester, Mimus, who puts on Kaeso's armor and who has long lusted for Adrea. They are married, and Mimus, who can imitate Kaeso's voice, does not allow her to suspect the truth until the morning. Shortly after the opening of the second scene, she comes down the steps of the palace, calling:

Adrea: O Father! O Father! What is this monstrous thing I dare not name? . . . Father! Awake! I am Adrea! Alone . . . afraid in the dark! I . . . I have been kissed by lips I do not know . . . horrible lips . . . horrible lips that blistered mine . . . and held my arms that . . . Ah! Father! Give me sight . . . give me sight . . . give me sight, and lead me to one man . . . that I may know who . . . I am numbed . . . I dare not think . . . I dare not think . . . no, no, no, no, . . . God, give me sight! God, give me sight . . . give me sight!

Mimus: (*Who has come down stealthily from the palace and is now at the bargeman's side. The bargeman has stepped out from the darkness. Apart to him*) We are the two who go forth . . . she and I. (*He points to her with a finger and motions to the bargeman, who passes off.*)

Adrea: God! God! Give me sight! (*As though she would tear the veil from her eyes.*)

Mimus: (*Taking a step forward, no longer speaking in Kaeso's voice, but softly, persuasively, to Adrea*) Dawn breaks. . . . The time decreed for us to go . . .

Adrea: (*Turning at the altar. In a voice frozen with terror . . . almost in a whisper*) Ah! Who speaks . . . who is this man they gave me to? Answer! Answer!

Mimus: (*Taking her outstretched hand*) Come. . . .

Adrea: (*As though breaking away from the very thought*) No . . . No . . . (*She starts to stagger back from him, then turns as though to run.*)

Mimus: (*Who has picked up the leading strings which trail across the scene, speaking savagely, and attaching the strings to Adrea's wrist, then winding them tightly about his own several times*) Come! Come! Thou art mine . . . come . . . (*He drags Adrea toward him by the strings. She totters, staggers forward, calling out,* No! No! No! *grasps the altar as she is being dragged past it, and clings to it, calling* Father! *and as Mimus would go toward Adrea, a stream of lightning, accompanied by a sudden roar of thunder, darts from the dark sky and strikes down Mimus. He lies flat on the floor at a little distance from Adrea, the guiding strings still wound about his wrist. The altar is overturned; Adrea totters, still clinging to it, and falls lying on it. The fallen brazier's light still shines. The rumble of thunder dies away, but the stage is still dark; a storm cloud seems to hang over the city, surrounding it. Adrea, stunned, her eyes closed, puts her hands to her head, dazed, then opens her eyes, then opens and shuts them, looks about and vaguely comprehending that she sees, passes one hand before her face, staring at it.)*

Adrea: I see! I see! *(Then she looks again, seeing something she had never known before, then stares about at all the strange scene and the mystery of it. Suddenly finding on looking down that her guiding strings are still held, the memory of the past night comes over her. With terrible anticipation, she tracks the strings until they lead her to the figure on the floor)* You! . . . *(On her hands and knees she stares at Mimus. Then still on her knees, with a mad impulse lifting up the unconscious body until her face peers into his, the brazier light shining past her, falling on his face. In a whisper)* God! God! *(She lets him drop. Then with a low cry of horror, shuddering, her eyes staring, her outstretched fingers stiffened, she draws in a long breath of terrible realization, swaying where she kneels.)*

Adrea goes to die in the Tower of Forgetfulness, but hearing the cries of the wedding procession, especially Kaeso's laugh of triumph, and being warned by the shadow of her father that she is to reign, she decides to take the throne in order to revenge herself upon Kaeso. She is crowned and Kaeso is brought before her and acknowledges his wrong but pleads only his ambition to rule the world. She condemns him to be whipped publicly through the city. At the end of the coronation festivals three days later, the Queen sends for Kaeso again, to condemn him to death—then begins to relent. She finds, however, that Mimus is still alive and at sight of him all her rage breaks forth and she condemns Kaeso to be torn to pieces by wild horses. The senators at first object to this so that she tells them the story of his wrong to her. "I shall not bear

a child to sit this throne—for I should fear to see its face—
lest it be red and white—I bring none after me—this lost ac-
cursed thing he made—this wanton of a fool is Queen of
Adrea!"

In witnessing Kaeso's remorse she begins to relent, but the
senators hold her to her word and she finally stabs Kaeso to
save him from the wild horses.

In the Epilogue fourteen years later, she sends for the son
of Kaeso and Julia, a boy, Vasha, who is to reign in her place.

Adrea: (*Looking back at the boy*) Ay? To-day thou goest to my
dear land. Nay! Nay! 'Tis in the playing. . . . Think
of me often here in Arcady.
Vasha: I go to—Adrea?
Adrea: Yea . . . and think of me as one who dwells here, happy
. . . and if, when thou dost weary of thy ruling, thou
wouldst play again . . . steal back—Nay—nay—'tis in the
playing still—steal back and kiss me . . . so. (*She kisses
him. He looks at her warily, half converted.*) And lead me
with thy gentle hands along the ways of old . . . perchance
one day thou wilt not come alone, sweet Prince . . . Oh,
build thy throne upon love . . . for only love endures. . . .
Garda!
(*Enter Garda and the Herald of the Senate. Garda carries the robe, the Herald of the Senate follows with the crown
and the scepter on a gold cushion. Adrea takes the robe
from Garda and wraps Vasha in it. He lays his little shield
at the foot of the throne steps.*)
Vasha: But why dost thou wrap me in this robe?
Adrea: It is a little . . . a little game we play. We play at be-
ing King. (*The Herald of the Senate and Garda exeunt.*)
Thou the Prince, and I, the Queen, who being blinded may not
rule. (*She offers the crown.*)
Vasha: (*Rejecting it*) But I would not have a throne for which
a queen must give her eyes.
Adrea: 'Tis in the playing . . .
Vasha: Oh . . . then! (*He allows her to put on the crown.
Adrea leads Vasha to the throne. As Vasha sits, his little
legs are not long enough to reach the platform.*)
Adrea: Come . . . come . . . now turn thy head . . . (*She turns
his face from the window*) so . . . thou mayst not look . . .

DAVID BELASCO AND HIS ASSOCIATES

until I speak the word . . . that makes thee King . . . and makes me (*Falters*) only happy Adrea again. . . . (*She puts the scepter in his hand. He kisses her in childish fashion, puts his arms about her, happy because he is having his own way.*)

Vasha: Ha! I love this playing! (*He is tempted to look.*)

Adrea: Dost thou? (*Puts his hands over his eyes.*) Put thy hands so . . . look not. . . . wait the word . . . I wish thee joy, dear little Prince. (*She retreats to the window, facing the child, who sits on the throne, crowned and robed.*) Think of me in the Spring when all is green in Arcady . . . happy, peaceful, wishing thee well . . . and do not forget me. (*Vasha turns.*) Nay . . . Nay . . . 'Tis in the playing . . . look not. Live long, love long, and see dear children at thy feet. May the gods keep thy heart young, thy faith pure, thy soul at peace, O child of Kaeso! (*As he tries to peep*) Nay . . . nay . . . look not! (*Adrea, at the casement, takes her last look at Vasha, peering at him, smiling.*) So let me see thee last . . . so let me see thee last . . . at play. Nay . . . look not. (*She pulls down the covering of skin at the window.*) O Sun, who took my sight at birth . . . I give thee back . . . I give thee back thine own! (*She turns and opens the window. She stands, a golden figure in the flood of dazzling sunlight. After a pause during which she has been looking into the sunlight, she turns, blinded, and comes down, groping her way to the throne.*) Long live the King! (*She kneels at the feet of Vasha on the throne, the sun pouring in.*)

Adrea is the finest of the plays written by Belasco and Long and it has so far not been excelled in its own species, the romantic tragedy, by any play acted in English in the Twentieth Century. The spirit of the age is caught wonderfully —whether it is accurate or not does not matter—it satisfies the auditor as a fit background for great, unrestrained passions and emotions. The character drawing of Adrea is magnificent. All through the play she is dominated by her great love for Kaeso. She hates terribly because she loves greatly. The crown is merely a means to her to be revenged on him for his betrayal. Julia she forgets—because Julia was not loved by

187

her, but in a speech in the fourth Act she utters the cry of the woman who has lost her belief in the love of the man she loves, as well as it has been put in modern drama.

In contrast with her, Kaeso's main passion is ambition. He sacrifices her to it, and when he has been beaten and is facing death he loses our sympathy by his apparent weakness. She keeps the sympathy, always. Fate has played her evil tricks, and she has met them with the patrician spirit that came from her Roman ancestors. Life to her and to her age was cheap in comparison with the satisfaction of the passions of love and revenge. The sense of patriotism was local, but she could feel also responsibility for her country; and something of the royal sense of the fitness of things attributed to Elizabeth is indicated in her relinquishing the scepter to a man-child who above all is Kaeso's son.

After *Adrea*, Belasco and Long produced no plays under their joint authorship. Long made several essays alone, the most successful being his dramatization of his own short story, *Dolce*, produced by Mrs. Fiske in 1906. It is the story of an artist who has painted the picture of a little Italian girl in New Orleans, then loses sight of her until some years later she comes, a countess, to his studio in Florence and demands that he sell her picture, which, of course, he refuses to do. Their recognition and reunion made an appealing climax to a play based upon the fragrance of youthful memories. *Kassa*, written for Mrs. Carter (1909), was a rather turgid drama laid in Austro-Hungary and was not successful, though it provided Mrs. Carter with a mad scene at the end of the play.

Crowns, which was produced at the Provincetown Theatre in November, 1922, is a romantic tragedy, laid about the time of Christ, somewhere in Palestine. But, as in *Adrea*, locality is not important. The theme is the contest of love and ambition. Ardan and Yolan are left at their respective fathers' deaths contesting heirs to a kingdom which is conquered by Sargon. They are spared and live in an olive garden shut in from the outside world till they are grown to young manhood and

Photo by Wm. Shewell Ellis

John Luther Long —

womanhood. But the leaders of their factions will not let them be and, after murdering Sargon, the captains plant the seeds of ambition in their minds, separate them, and by lies and stratagems bring on a war between them. Long draws in a highly poetic way the lust of power and the passion for war in all their tragic meaning. Ardan and Yolan still love each other, but through misunderstanding believe themselves enemies. Yolan's troops win, for Ardan goes mad after he kills Elfer, the loyal servant who had reared them, and the moment of her crowning is to be the signal for his death. But because her love is the greater, she kills herself, and he is brought in shackles to her chamber of death, his mind cleared of its madness. As he is led to the throne, he presses to his brow the crown of thorns she had made for herself. *Crowns* is perhaps too subtle for popular approval, and it did not succeed on the stage. But it is the product of imaginative power, and the tragedy is poignant with the agony of frustrated love.

Belasco's energies had been divided during this period between his work with Long and his establishment as an independent producer. He had devoted himself also to the training of Mrs. Leslie Carter, who achieved in the character of Adrea the summit of her artistic career, and to the development of David Warfield from a variety actor to a leading part in melodrama like *The Auctioneer*. The struggles of Belasco against the "Theatrical Syndicate" belong to the history of the theatre rather than to that of the drama, although they have profoundly affected the methods and the opportunities of production. It was the growth of the "Theatrical Syndicate," which brought under its own control the main theatres throughout the country, and hence was able to dictate terms to any producer of a play, which spurred on Belasco to have a theatre of his own. In 1900 he secured a lease of the Republic Theatre and began to alter it to suit his purposes. The possession of the theatre made him secure so far as New York was concerned, but his fight against dictation continued.

Meanwhile, he was revising a play upon the courtesan,

Madame DuBarry, the mistress of Louis XV, which had been written by Jean Richepin, and which Belasco found unsuitable for his purposes. After *DuBarry* was produced, on December 12, 1901, at Washington, suit was brought by agents of Richepin to compel Belasco to share the receipts of the play. Belasco had already paid the French dramatist $3,500 for the manuscript which he stated before the court he had not used. The suit was allowed to lapse and while Richepin's play was produced in London in 1905 it has not been possible for me to compare the versions. *DuBarry* was a gorgeous dramatic spectacle, in which Belasco indulged his fancy in conceiving of situations in which violent passions rose, triumphed and fell. The most striking scenes were those in which DuBarry conceals her lover in her own bed while her master, the King, and also her enemies, are searching for him, and the final passage of Du-Barry through the dirty streets to the guillotine, howled at by the mob. Contrasts are plentiful, and Mrs. Carter made good use of them. The skill of the playwright was shown most clearly in the way by which he secured the sympathy of the audience, not so much for the courtesan, as for the woman the courtesan might have been. This was done by painting her, in cheerful disregard of history, as a woman who really regretted the life of peace and honor she might have lived with the lover of her youth. Yet she was not made so heroic or so virtuous that the same audience might not be completely reconciled to her doom.

Belasco next made out of a novel, *The Bath Comedy*, by Agnes and Egerton Castle, a charming light comedy, *Sweet Kitty Bellairs*, which was produced on November 23, 1903, at Washington. It was a very different Eighteenth Century from that of *DuBarry*. The effect was one of charm rather than of splendor and the central character, a coquette with a warm heart, with a gift for intrigue, but with a soul a bit above her heartless companions, was well portrayed by Henrietta Crosman. The original story was artificial and so was the play, but it proved a success and was played in 1907 in London.

For the next period of his playwriting, Belasco turned from the gorgeous spectacles of history to the vivid panorama of Western life in America. In both he selected incidents and characters that were out of the ordinary. *The Girl of the Golden West* was prepared with the capabilities of Blanche Bates in view and a heroine who is at once pure, courageous, loyal and passionate, who keeps a saloon and is able to cope with any situation which presents itself, appears to a modern auditor so utterly impossible that he ceases to criticize her from that point of view at all, which is of course what the artful dramatist who produced the play foresaw would happen. The climax of the drama is an illustration of Belasco's skill. "The Girl" having resisted the advances of all comers, falls in love with Dick Johnson, a picturesque, if overclean, outlaw. He is pursued by the sheriff, Jack Rance, who traces him to her cabin, where, unchaperoned, she has retained the respect of the neighborhood. Johnson has been wounded by Rance before reaching the cabin and is concealed by the girl in a loft. Rance enters, looks everywhere but in the obvious place of conceal-ment, and then the girl challenges him to play a game of poker with her, on the understanding that if he wins, she is the stake and if she wins, he will discontinue his efforts to find her lover. She cheats him by an old card trick, and he is about to leave when a drop of blood falls from the wounded man upon his handkerchief. The drama hardly seems to be capable of going further in the direction of improbability. Yet Belasco has told us in detail in his autobiography how he based this scene upon an incident which was witnessed by his father.

Belasco has also recorded the fact that the character of Jake Wallace, "a traveling camp minstrel," was an exact photo-graph of a Jake Wallace whom he knew and that when nego-tiations were under way between Puccini and himself prelim-inary to the writing of *La Fanciulla del West*, it was this singer of camp songs who provided the theme upon which the

Italian composer based his opera. Belasco is too experienced a dramatist, of course, not to know that the mere fact that a certain event happened is no presumptive evidence of its probability. But perhaps after all both Harte and Belasco realized the probabilities of the West better than those who know that life only at second hand. He was justified in one sense, by the popularity of the play, which ran three years after its performance at the new Belasco Theatre in Pittsburgh, October 3, 1905. The opera by Puccini was produced at the Metropolitan Opera House, December 10, 1910, with Emmy Destinn as Minnie, the girl, Enrico Caruso as Dick Johnson and Pasquale Amato as Jack Rance. It was the first grand opera to be written on an American theme.

The Rose of the Rancho (1906) in which Belasco continued his presentation of Western life, was based on an earlier play, *Juanita*, by Richard Walton Tully, which Belasco revised. It is an interesting study of an important if disgraceful period in American history, that of the occupation of California by the settlers from the United States. The Spanish owners, who had occupied the land for centuries, were dispossessed by land jumpers, because they were either too proud or too ignorant of the situation to file claims in the American land offices. The play is concerned with the love of Robert Kearney, who has been sent by the government to investigate the land cases, and Juanita Kenton, the "Rose," whose grandmother, Doña Petrona Castro, is owner of the Rancho. Kearney is endeavoring to block the movements of Kincaid, who with a band of ruffians is forcibly taking possession of the estates. Juanita's mother announces her engagement to Don Luis de la Torre, a wealthy young man from Monterey, but Juanita declines him. She is then horrified to find Kearney apparently in Kincaid's band, which he has joined in order to protect her. She repudiates him, but of course all ends happily. The character of Juanita is more consistent than that of Minnie, and the Spanish race pride and the way in which they react to an appeal to their courtesy was well portrayed. The production, like that of *The Girl of the Golden West,* was sumptuous. The pictures of the scenery of southern Califorania were marvelous, and every device which could represent that region as it was known to Belasco was lavished by him upon the stage production. If there is really Portuguese blood in him, it showed in the sympathy with which he entered into the interpretation of Latin-American civilization. This play introduced Frances Starr as a leading woman.

In December, 1906, he laid the corner stone of his new theatre, first called the Stuyvesant and now the Belasco Theatre. In it are contained the results of years of experiment, and it is not exaggeration to say that from the point of view of stage mechanism, it is complete. Probably the devices for lighting are the most remarkable. Belasco has had as his associate in this field Louis Hartman, who has installed and remodeled a system of lighting which is exactly fitted to its purpose, the concealment of the means and the securing of the effect. Belasco has been a student of lighting since the early seventies. He was present at what was probably the first attempt to use electric light for stage illumination, at the California Theatre, February 21, 1879,[1] and he has labored constantly to bring light as it is brought in nature, from above rather than below. As early as 1879, when he directed the Passion Play in San Francisco, he had experimented with the abolition of footlights and in 1917 he did away with them entirely. Light comes from various sources, especially from a great iron hood, which hangs behind the proscenium, and from lights attached to each sliding scene. In the balcony, light streams from a panel which is apparently ornamental, but which consists of small doors, which are controlled by the great switchboard that stands on the stage. These doors open and shut so gradually that to the audience the light is fading or increasing in brilliancy, from an unknown source. Belasco spares nothing in his desire to reach perfection in this regard. For each play, new "dimmers" by which the light is shaded, are provided, and one glance at the

[1] Winter, II, 245.

collection of lamps, used once and once only, in his stage settings, illustrates the prodigality of Belasco's methods.[1]

The Stuyvesant Theatre was opened October 16, 1907, with *The Grand Army Man*, the joint product of Belasco, Pauline Phelps and Marion Short. The central character of this play, which is not especially significant, is that of Wes' Bigelow, who has brought up the son of a former sweetheart and who finds the boy dishonest. Nor need Belasco's adaptation of *Le Lys* by Pierre Wolf and Gaston Leroux, produced in December, 1909, detain us. It has to do with the revolt of a daughter against parental tyranny for the sake of her younger sister.

The Return of Peter Grimm, first produced at the Hollis Street Theatre in Boston, January 2, 1911, while it owes its inception to Cecil DeMille, the son of Belasco's former collaborator, deals with just the kind of theme which the romantic fancy of Belasco would find congenial. Peter Grimm is an old bachelor, a practical botanist, gentle but stubborn. He expects to be succeeded in the business by his nephew, Frederik, a selfish and immoral person, whose real nature has been concealed from his uncle, for Peter extracts from Kathrien, a girl he has brought up and loves dearly, a promise that she shall marry Frederik. She is in love, however, with James Hartman, one of Peter's employees. Peter has also taken charge of a little boy, William, who is the grandson of old Marta, the cook, and is really the illegitimate son of Frederik by a woman who does not appear. Peter has joked with an old friend, Dr. MacPherson, about the possibility of the dead returning but has taken a sceptical attitude toward such reappearances. At the end of the first Act, Peter dies suddenly.

The remainder of the play consists of Peter Grimm's efforts to undo the wrong he has done to Kathrien. He appears not as a wraith but exactly as he had looked in real life, and he

---

[1] The subject of stage lighting cannot be adequately treated here. The above statements are based on my inspection of the Belasco Theatre under the guidance of Mr. Hartman.

makes fervent attempts to communicate with his friends. None
of them see him, though Frederik, to whom he makes one of his
strongest appeals, believes for a moment that he sees his uncle's
ghost. But he is present as an influence upon Kathrien and
Frederik and, most potently, upon William, who speaks to him
and who goes willingly when Peter Grimm carries him off to
the other world at the end of the play. Peter Grimm reaches
the child most easily because he loves him and because William,
through his illness, is already nearing the other world. In
William's feverish condition his reactions are most probable,
also, from the human point of view. It is this careful avoidance of the spectacular in dealing with the supernatural which
makes the play so artistic. The occult and the real are blended
with so skillful a hand that the line which separates the known
and the unknown presents no difficulties for the auditor to
cross. One can believe that William simply remembered, under
the sharpening influence of fever, that the man who had come
to see his mother was Frederik, and thereby showed Kathrien
that her promise need not be kept. Or if he prefers, he can
believe that Peter Grimm spoke to the boy through the invin-
cible power of love. But the dramatist who called back the soul
of Peter Grimm had no thesis to prove except the quotation
which begins the play: "Only one thing counts—only one
thing—love." Skillfully, too, does he avoid any description of
the future life. Peter Grimm is happy there evidently so that
the death of the child is felt to be a release for him. As Peter
puts it:

Before your playing time is over—you're going to know the
great secret. No coarsening of your child's heart, until you stand
before the world like Frederik; no sweat and toil such as dear
old James is facing; no dimming of the eye and trembling of the
head such as the poor old Doctor shall know in time to come; no
hot tears to blister your eyes; tears such as Katie is shedding
now; but in all your youth, your faith—your innocence, you'll
fall asleep.

One of the most effective bits of stage management was the creation of the bridge of light which seemed to connect Peter to the living. Very little light was thrown on him, but there was a distinct rose color in the light on the living characters, which made him seem less vivid in contrast, without making him spectral.

Interest in the occult probably led to the production of *The Case of Becky* written by Edward Locke and revised by Belasco, which dealt with a girl of double personality. The staging of this play, especially those scenes in which Dorothy or Becky, the heroine, is so conscious of the unseen presence of her stepfather who exercises an evil control over her that it throws her into hypnosis, excited the admiration of the medical profession.[1]

Since *Peter Grimm*, Belasco the dramatist has become secondary to Belasco the producer. *The Governor's Lady*, the joint product of Belasco and Alice Bradley, on the theme of a woman who does not advance in mental growth with her husband and who is supplanted in his affections by a younger woman, is a melodrama with one strong situation in which the younger woman calls on Mrs. Slade, to persuade her to agree to a divorce. But in his desire to provide reality of stage setting, Belasco placed an utterly absurd last Act in a restaurant which was scrupulously photographic to the last spoon and fork.

Van der Decken, which was based on the myth of the "Flying Dutchman," was tried out at Wilmington in 1915 but has not yet been produced in New York and cannot be said to be in a finished state. *The Son Daughter* (1919), written with George Scarborough, is a Chinese melodrama laid in New York City, with an absurd plot, on which Belasco wasted some striking lighting effects, especially in the scene of the death of the patriot leader who poisons himself in order to avoid being tor-

---

[1] See Reichert, Edward Tyson, M. D.: "'Dr. Jekyll and Mr. Hyde,' and 'The Case of Becky,' as staged by Mr. David Belasco, together with actual instances of Dual Personalities." *Lectures of the University of Pennsylvania.* Vol. for 1914–5.

tured for his secrets. Since 1920, Belasco has with one exception contented himself with adaptations of foreign plays. *Kiki*, from the French of André Picard, gave Lenore Ulric an opportunity to represent a coquette who became, with a wrench, a "good girl" at the end of the play. *Laugh, Clown, Laugh,* from Fausto Martini's *Ridi, Pagliaccio* was a more significant production, with some scenes of real sincerity, as was also *The Comedian* of Sacha Guitry. In these plays, Belasco translated successfully foreign aspects of the theatre. The sense of the responsibility of the actor to his audience was especially well carried over from the French original in *The Comedian.*

Belasco's production of *The Merchant of Venice* in 1922 belongs to our theatrical rather than our dramatic history, yet it was in a sense the crowning achievement of his career. For admirable as was Warfield's representation of racial revenge, it was the production which was of most significance. Belasco translated to a modern audience the beauty with which the imagination of the Elizabethans endowed the performances of Shakespeare, and which our flabbier fancies do not create.

No final judgment upon Belasco as a playwright is possible. So intangible is that contribution which takes an idea from experience, from observation, from the fiction, the poetry, even the plays of others and by a process explainable only in terms of genius, translates them into successful drama, that it would be idle to pretend to finality in critical judgment. But in viewing his work historically, over a period of sixty years, certain general facts emerge. He began with a predilection for what was unusual, intense and even bizarre, and his consistency in this preference has been remarkable. To him the drama is not the representation of familiar life. Incidents are selected, even in domestic drama like *May Blossom*, from among the unusual episodes of an ordinary life. His characters are not those with which we are normally familiar, and if his collaborators, like Herne or DeMille, lead him into the placing of such characters upon the stage, one of two things happens. If like Herne, the other playwright is his equal, there is an inevitable separation. If Belasco is the dominant force, as was the case with DeMille, the plays show the definite trend away from the calmer scenes of *The Wife* to the intense, almost melodramatic climaxes of *The Charity Ball* and *Men and Women*. If his collaborator is himself predisposed to romantic situation, Belasco's love for the colorful and the sensational runs unchecked, and the result is *The Rose of the Rancho* and *The Girl of the Golden West*. Once only among his many associations, did he meet with a collaborator whose imagination was more powerful than his own, who provided him with great characters, not normal and not familiar. It was to Belasco's credit that he recognized the genius of John Luther Long, and that he treated the material provided him in *Madame Butterfly*, *The Darling of the Gods*, and *Adrea* with the respect which a creator of one kind feels for a creator of another. The result is romance which scorns restriction, which has the high courage that soars beyond the provincial, to deal with universal passions and emotions, which rides right at the five-barred gate of probability, knowing that if it fails, it falls into the ditch of nonsense, but if it rises triumphant, it outlines against the sky the imperishable figures of literature. It is a grim commentary on our artistic recklessness, that two of the noblest creations of our romantic drama live still only in the memories of the audiences who saw them and the few who have read them in manuscript.

It is not necessary to deal here with the discussions that have raged over the questions of plagiarism in Belasco's acknowledged plays. Frequently these disputes have led to lawsuits which have invariably ended in his favor. Dealing only with those plays which are available in print or manuscript, this apparent paradox appears. Leaving aside *The Return of Peter Grimm*, his most important work was the acknowledged result of collaboration with James A. Herne, William C. DeMille, Franklyn Fyles, and John Luther Long. This work exceeds in value *May Blossom*, *The Heart of Maryland*, and *The Girl of the Golden West*.

Yet with the exception of Herne, none of these four collaborators has been able to write a successful play. Long has written imaginative and interesting dramas, but they have not held the stage. To the historian who has met the term "derivative" till he is weary of it, the conclusion is obvious.

If Belasco has no great invention, as seems probable, he has what is of more importance in drama, a keen sense of the instinctive motor and emotional reactions of an audience. To him a play is a living thing; it is a compound of playwright, actor, director, and auditor. With every instinct tingling with the love of romance, he has sought to make that necessary compound tangible by lavishing upon his productions every known device by which stage realism is secured. He conducted for many years a struggle, at first against overwhelming odds, for the right to his artistic independence, and his position as the foremost director of the United States was recognized by the spontaneous tributes tendered him in 1921 by the dinners given in his honor by the Society of American Dramatists and Composers and by the Society of Arts and Sciences. No one who was present can forget the sincerity of the appreciation of those he had directed. If more emphasis was laid upon his achievement as producer and director than as a playwright, his failure to print his plays is perhaps responsible.

Note to Revised Edition

David Belasco died May 15, 1931, in New York City. John Luther Long died October 31, 1927, in Philadelphia.

CHAPTER VIII

The Indian Summer of Romance

WHILE the general tendency toward the treatment of actual American life upon the stage was being established, the heroic play based upon universal themes was not by any means neglected. The Drama of the Frontier and the work of Belasco and his associates were not the only evidences of the ever-present desire for romance. Romantic tragedy had seemed, indeed, to pass from favor during the sixties, but it rose again into a flowering in the seventies, largely under the inspiration of Lawrence Barrett. The heroic or romantic play has usually depended upon the interest of an actor to whom the character of a hero, defying fate or his enemies, has strongly appealed. This romantic tradition of the stage, while it had its great period from the thirties to the sixties, nevertheless has persisted in the succession of which Barrett, Mansfield, Sothern and Skinner are perhaps for us the foremost examples. These actors turned frequently to Shakespeare or to other English and even to continental drama, but their biographies reveal their constant search for American playwrights who could furnish them with material. The result was sometimes achieved by the excursion of a realist into an alien field. We have seen how Howells furnished Pope and Barrett and Salvini with successful adaptations of Spanish and Italian drama.[1] It was Barrett who revived Boker's *Francesca da Rimini* in 1882 and showed for the first time the possibilities of that masterpiece. He inspired Boker, too, to write *Nydia* and *Glaucus*, although he did not produce them.

William Young (1847-1920), whose plays with two exceptions remain in manuscript, provided Barrett with two of his

[1] See pp. 68-72.

leading parts. *Pendragon,* produced first at Chicago, in 1881, is a blank-verse play in five acts dealing with the Arthurian story. Barrett played King Arthur, and Young made of him a man less frigid than the traditional figure. Launcelot, played first by Louis James and later by Otis Skinner, is more human, too, than is usual, and Guinevere is a strong figure. Modred drives the tragedy on through Vivien, his tool, and brings it to a high point in the Queen's chamber when Arthur, after Launcelot has been condemned for his treachery, shows how death is easy compared with his living fate of knowing how his best friend has betrayed him. The climax of Barrett's acting, however, came in the fourth Act at Almesbury, when Arthur takes leave of Guinevere:

Arthur: Woman—for thou art woman—I am man.
    Never again, upon this brink of time,
    Shall we two meet—hear then my last confession!
    Yea, though I know that every wanton drop
    That makes thee smooth and fair hath played me false —
    That thou hast sold me for a lecher's kiss,
    To endless shame—still—still, despite it all,
    I love thee—love thee! Dost thou hear? I love thee!
    Let men hereafter gibe at me, and say:
    "This is that Arthur, who once thought to match
    His puny strength against the bulk of Rome,—
    Yet could not win and keep one woman's heart!"
    Despite it all, I care not, still I love thee—
    And in that word take thou thy full revenge!
    Slight, though thou art, yet art thou conqueror!
    And, O, should'st thou not well be satisfied?
    'Tis I, at last, who burn, whilst thou art cold,
    'Tis I, at last, who plead, whilst thou art voiceless!
    Self-signed and sealed, a madman, or a knave,
    I quit this world, in which I hoped so much,
    Without a hope. And thou for whom I suffer—
    Now—even now—at this last hour thou wilt not
    So much as say "God bless thee!" Then, will I!
    God bless thee, and forgive thee! Yea, forgive,
    As I forgive. God make thy pillow soft,
    As thou hast made mine hard—thine end as sweet,

As thou hast made mine bitter!—shield—protect thee
From every harm—from shame, from pain, from sorrow!
Give thee love, fortune, friendship, length of days—
And at the last receive thee to that Heaven,
Whose gate this hand hath shut against my soul!

Ganelon, written in 1888 and produced in New York in 1891, has apparently perished, but according to Winter it gave Barrett one of the finest opportunities of his career. Certainly the conception was a truly tragic one. Ganelon is the son of the traitor who betrayed Roland at Roncesvalles, and Young portrayed the burning desire of the knight to redeem his name. After saving a Corsican city from the Saracens, he is defrauded of his reward and when his attempted suicide places him in their hands, he, maddened by a sense of injustice, repeats the treachery of his father and betrays the town to the enemy. Death comes after his repentance, fighting again for his own people. The impression made by Barrett's impersonation of a proud spirit, stung by injustice to madness, and passing from one emotional state to another, was apparently tremendous. Young published only two plays, *The Rajah* and *Ben Hur.* *The Rajah,* produced at the Madison Square Theatre, June 5, 1883, ran for two hundred and fifty performances. It is a romantic comedy, laid at an English country house, with a conventional plot, but with extremely clever conversation and well-established characters, especially Harold Wyncot, the "Rajah," who has been a captain in the East India Service and who inherits the estate. Young's most popular play was his dramatization of Lew Wallace's novel of *Ben Hur,* which was first given at the Broadway Theatre on November 29, 1899, and after running through three seasons in New York, Philadelphia and Boston, became a perennial of the theatre. Young had good material with which to work and used it to distinct advantage. He was a skilful artist, working sincerely and capable of writing a blank verse flexible and at times distinguished. His plays, with the exception of *Young*

America (1896), seem to have been upon foreign themes, but twice at least he touched the universal note of tragedy.

Barrett constantly made changes in the texts of the plays he controlled, and in the case of Richard Mansfield this dictation of the actor-manager went much further.[1] Mansfield as will be seen, wrote plays himself. His first real success as an actor came in the part of Baron de Mersac in Henry Guy Carleton's (1856-1910) *Victor Durand* (1884), a romantic melodrama of artificial quality, in which he impersonated a villain who imperils his own safety by bringing about the recapture of the husband of the woman he loves. Carleton began his play writing with a tragedy, *Memnon* (1881), partly in verse, which Booth and McCullough seem to have considered producing. It is the only one of his plays deserving the name of dramatic literature, and at times it rises to a considerable height. It is laid in Thebes, and in the character of Memnon, the arch-prophet of Egypt, Carleton drew a heroic figure, surrounded by the jealousy of conspirators at home and the pressure of Persian ambitions. Discouraged apparently by his failure to secure an audience for his sincere attempt at romantic tragedy, Carleton turned to the production of *A Gilded Fool* (1892) for Goodwin, an absurd play; *The Butterflies* (1894), a more adroit farce comedy, in which John Drew and Maude Adams made a stage success; and *Colinette* (1899), an adaptation from the French of Lenôtre and Martin, which was skilfully made for Julia Marlowe.

Mansfield was himself driven to writing *Monsieur*, his first play (1887), by the paucity of material to suit his special talent. It is a romantic drama, laid in New York City, with a central character of André de Jadot, or "Monsieur," a French gentleman, who endeavors to live by the teaching of music. Contrasts are provided by his appearance at the house of a wealthy patron, and his collapse on account of hunger. In its plot, which provided a happy ending tinged with the sentiment of love triumphant, it is reminiscent of an older school, but

[1] See account of the composition of *Beau Brummell*, pp. 266-9.

Mansfield's performance of André de Jadot was gallant and was comparatively successful. Upon *Don Juan* (1891) he lavished a great deal of effort, but the public did not respond. He kept it in his répertoire, however, for some time. His conception of the eternal lover, brought up with the most rigorous care, and breaking into life with a zest for adventure that carries him finally to his death, has some reality and power. It is built, however, upon Byron, Dumas and Molière, and does not deserve the extravagant praise Winter gives it. The best scene is that in the oratory of the Duchess, in which Donna Julia, Lucia and Geralda reveal their love for Don Juan in various ways. There is also some sharp satire upon the attitude of the public toward actors. Mansfield's part in the production of *Beau Brummell* (1891) belongs more properly under the discussion of the plays of Clyde Fitch.

Thomas Russell Sullivan, who had made the adaptation of *Dr. Jekyll and Mr. Hyde* (1887) for Mansfield, wrote an original play for him upon the life of Nero (1891) which was a failure, but which seems to have provided a powerful tragic climax in the Emperor's death. In 1896, Mansfield was again the inspiration for a play called *Napoleon Bonaparte*, by Lorimer Stoddard, which is really a series of scenes representing the Emperor at various points in his career, the first act being laid in his tent at Tilsit and later acts including a prelude to Waterloo, and his death at St. Helena. The scenes, for it is hardly a play, are written to make Napoleon the center of attention, and Kings and Queens, ministers and corporals, confide to the audience their private and public affairs in the orthodox manner of one form of the romantic drama.

Mansfield was sensitive to a mistaken criticism which objected to his joint work as playwright and actor, so when he and J. I. C. Clarke dramatized *The First Violin* (1898) by Jessie Fothergill, he assumed the name of Meridan Phelps. The play, which is itself of no great importance, marks his passage into that phase of the romantic movement which brought upon the stage the dramatization of novels, and which led to his production of *Beaucaire* in 1901. But while other interests claimed his attention, it must be remembered to his credit that he encouraged American playwrights in his own way, if that way was not always to their liking.

It is an illuminating exercise in the discrimination between what is permanent and what is passing in dramatic literature to compare such plays as Carleton's stage successes with the work of Thomas Bailey Aldrich (1856-1907). Aldrich had a real dramatic sense and also a keen desire to write for the theatre. His early correspondence records his rueful regret when his plays were returned unopened by the actors to whom he sent them, and this may have caused his hesitation in allowing *Mercedes* to be produced, when A. M. Palmer urged him to permit it. But while much of the romantic work of the period seems hopelessly old-fashioned, Aldrich's dramas are to-day as fresh and vital as when they were written and produced. *Mercedes,* published in 1884 and produced with Julia Arthur, selected by Aldrich himself, for the title rôle, at Palmer's Theatre, May 1, 1893, is a prose tragedy in two acts laid in Spain in 1810 during the Napoleonic campaign. In the dialogue between Captain Louvois and his lieutenant Laboissière, we learn that they have orders to massacre the inhabitants of the village of Arguano, where Louvois had been nursed back to life by Mercedes, and had grown to love her. In the second Act, laid in a stone hut in Arguano, Mercedes has stayed to protect her old grandmother and her child, Chiquita, at the risk of her own life, when the rest have fled. Before going they have poisoned some wine and hidden it. Laboissière enters the hut and while Mercedes is quietly defying him, the soldiers appear with the wine. Then Aldrich showed his power to write telling dialogue:

Laboissière: Open it, some one, and fetch me a glass.
(*To Mercedes*) You will drink this.
Mercedes: (*Coldly*) When I am thirsty I drink.
Laboissière: Pardieu! this time you shall drink because *I* am thirsty.

Mercedes: As you will. (*Empties the glass*) To the King!

Laboissière: That was an impudent toast. I would have preferred the Emperor or even Godoy; but no matter—each after his kind. To whom will the small-bones drink?

Mercedes: The child, señor?

Laboissière: Yes, the child; she is pale and sickly-looking; a draught will do her no harm. All the same, she will grow up and make some man wretched.

Mercedes: But, señor ——

Laboissière: Do you hear?

Mercedes: But Chiquita, señor—she is so little, only thirteen months old, and the wine is strong!

Laboissière: She shall drink!

Mercedes: No, no!

Laboissière: I have said it, sacré nom ——

Mercedes: Give it me, then. (*Takes the glass and holds it to the child's lip.*)

Laboissière: (*Watching her closely*) Woman! your hand trembles.

Mercedes: Nay, it is Chiquita swallows so fast. See! she has taken it all. Ah, señor, it is a sad thing to have no milk for the little one. Are you content?

Laboissière: Yes; I now see that the men may quench their thirst without fear. One cannot be too cautious in this hospitable country! Fall to, my children; but first, a glass for your lieutenant. (*Drinks.*)

The child dies and Laboissière draws his sabre just as Louvois enters and there follows a deeply moving scene of recognition under the shadow of approaching death for both of them as the wine slowly does its work. In this drama, intense and swift in movement, there is the quality of reticence, which made Aldrich's lyrics so exquisite. Only one brief gesture of Padre Josef in Act I hints at Louvois' fatherhood of the child; it deepens the tragedy but Mercedes does not tell him in the few moments they face certain death together. Although his dramatic dialogues date from *The Set of Turquoise* in 1858, Aldrich's work crossed the new century. In 1865 he had published his narrative poem, *Judith,* which he revised in 1896 as *Judith and Holofernes.*

THE INDIAN SUMMER OF ROMANCE

Out of this he made a tragedy in four acts, acted by Nance O'Neill at the Tremont Theatre in Boston in 1904, and later on tour. Aldrich made a loving human woman out of the Biblical heroine, whom he describes as "a beautiful cold-blooded abstraction." In the camp of Holofernes she is saved not only by the power of her undaunted soul triumphing over the natural weakness of a woman, but also over the attraction which the royal attributes of Holofernes have for her own lofty nature. Her cry is from her heart:

> Oh, save me, Lord, from that dark cruel prince,
> And from mine own self save me! for this man,
> A worshipper of senseless carven gods,
> Slayer of babes upon the mother-breast,
> He, even he, hath by some conjurer's trick,
> Or by his heathen beauty, in me stirred
> Such pity as unnerves the lifted hand.
> Oh, let not my hand fail me, in Thy name!

It is to be noted, however, that the blank verse is end-stopped, and suffers from the lack of flexibility which was a characteristic of the Victorians, and which partially accounts for the failure of some of the verse plays of the Nineteenth Century. Their authors wrote about romantic subjects but their form was affected by the restraint which the period bred in them. No one who is familiar with Aldrich's poetry, especially the dialogues like *Pauline Palovna,* can fail to realize his sense of the dramatic. His mastery over the art of suspense is shown in his short stories, of which *Marjorie Daw* is only one brilliant example. The stage lost a playwright through the existence of conditions against which a man of letters like Aldrich did not care to struggle.

The heroic tradition was handed on by many actors, for during the nineties there rose a wave of interest in romance which revealed itself in the novel and in poetry as well as in drama. Julia Marlowe was one of those whose talent lay in this field and while she acted usually in plays of foreign authorship, she was seeking, like all the stars, for native plays that suited her. In *Chatterton* by Ernest Lacy (1863-1916), a Philadelphian, she found a one-act tragedy of exquisite pathos and of telling dramatic effect. Lacy had made a long study of the life of the poet, and he presented a picture of Chatterton in his garret, burnt out by a flame of aspiration too great for his mind and body to support, until in the terror of approaching madness, he takes his life. Lacy afterward elaborated the theme into a five-act tragedy, *The Bard of Mary Redcliffe*, for E. H. Sothern, but the combination of Sothern and Marlowe in a program of Shakespearean plays prevented its production. Lacy's second play, *Rinaldo, the Doctor of Florence*, was produced by Joseph Haworth in 1895, first in Boston and later in Montreal and on tour. It is a five-act tragedy in blank verse, with some real poetry but with constant interruption of the dramatic action by comments upon life and self-introspection. The last scene, in which Rinaldo dies of remorse, in the presence of the body of the woman who has loved him, brought in to be a subject of his knife, represents the virtues and defects of the romantic tragedy.

Owing its inception to the same desire for romance, but with an appeal to a different audience, the dramatization of novels progressed throughout our entire period and rose to a climax toward the end of the century. This phenomenon was much less important in the history of drama than in that of fiction, but even if only for its unfortunate effect upon the opportunities of playwrights, it must have its place in our record. Daly's work in this field has already been mentioned and the share of Frances Hodgson Burnett (1849-1924) in providing material for the early plays of Thomas and Gillette, calls attention to the dramatic quality of many of her novels. She dramatized her story, *Little Lord Fauntleroy* (1887), and made a success of it, though the play does not skirt the edge of the sentimental so successfully as does the novel. Mrs. Burnett was, of course, international rather than American, and *Little Lord Fauntleroy* had its first production in England,

where a lawsuit consequent upon an attempted piracy established the right of a novelist to protect himself against an
unauthorized dramatization of his book.[1] Mrs. Burnett's later
plays are nearly all upon English subjects. She was more successful than another novelist, also international in scope, who
made persistent efforts to write for the stage. Francis Marion Crawford (1854-1909) attempted to dramatize *Dr. Claudius* in 1897, but it was a failure. Later he tried to invert the
usual process and planned *In the Palace of the King* (1900)
first as a play, consulting Viola Allen, whom he had selected
as the heroine, in its construction. He then wrote the story
and the final dramatization was put in shape by Lorimer
Stoddard. Certain changes were made, and additional characters like the Cardinal Luis de Torres were added. The English
version of *Francesca da Rimini* (1902), written originally for
Sarah Bernhardt, reveals Crawford's real skill as a dramatist.
It is the simplest and the most direct of all the dramatic treatments of the story, and while it has not the great sweep of
Boker's play, it follows the historical facts more closely. It
is laid fourteen years after the marriage between Giovanni and
Francesca, and their daughter, Concordia, is an unconscious
instrument in bringing on the tragedy. Crawford's understanding of the Italian patrician is shown in his use of Paolo's
neglected wife as a dramatic motive, which brings about the
climax of the second Act. Francesca at first thinks she is a
woman of the people, and she is revolted at the thought that
Paolo has been unfaithful to her with such a rival. But when
Paolo confesses that it is his wife, a noblewoman, to whom he
has been unfaithful, and in whose death he is an accessory,
Francesca's love is restored. The last scene is swift and powerful. Giovanni, who has been led to suspicion by Concordia's
artless prattle and by a spy he has employed, comes into Francesca's room and finds the lovers together. Francesca throws
herself between Paolo and his sword and is mortally wounded

[1] See William Archer's "Review of the Season of 1887-8" in *The Dramatic Year.*
Ed. by Edward Fuller, Boston, 1889, pp. 28–31.

before Paolo is killed. Then after her cry to Paolo—"Wait for me one little moment!"—she turns to Giovanni and strikes at him with her weapon as he has struck her with his: "I would not kill you if I could, lest I should see your face in hell. It is not large enough to hold your soul and ours." And she mocks him as she kisses Paolo passionately. "This is what you have asked for in vain and I have refused—what you shall never have of me!" Francesca is at all times the central character. She is the passionate medieval Italian, as are all the characters, and they proceed with that simplicity and singleness of purpose which Crawford and Boker alone, among the writers of English versions of the story, have understood and interpreted.

The work of industrious playwrights like Paul M. Potter, Edward E. Rose, Paul Kester and others, who arranged for the stage the most popular of the romantic historical novels that swarmed during the close of the Nineteenth and beginning of the Twentieth Centuries, needs no analysis. Some of the novelists whose work they dramatized tried to share in their rewards. For example, Winston Churchill, whose *Richard Carvel* had been adapted by Rose, himself wrote a stage version of *The Crisis* for James K. Hackett. But none of this work is of permanent value.

It is difficult to limit this romantic impulse to any definite period for not only Belasco, but also Gillette, Thomas, and Fitch were affected by it to some extent. There is, however, a certain homogeneity in the work of the playwrights discussed in this chapter, if only in their treatment of universal rather than native themes, and in their frequent choice of verse as a medium. In one sense it was a survival of an older impulse, and its relative lack of popular success was partly due to this quality, while the romances of American life like *Secret Service, Arizona, Nathan Hale,* and *The Heart of Maryland* were packing the theatres. But in view of the popularity of *Ben Hur* even this explanation falters. Perhaps, after all, the distinction, more clear then than to-day, between the professional and the amateur offers the best explanation. Yet from the point of view of its permanent place in our dramatic literature some of the products of this late flowering of romance, like *Mercedes* and *Chatterton*, rank with the best of the products of the Nineteenth Century.

CHAPTER IX

WILLIAM GILLETTE AND THE REALISM OF ACTION

IN CONSIDERING the drama as a living thing, one of the most insistent problems is the proper estimation of the relative values of words and action. The student of the drama as literature is naturally prone to lay greater stress upon the former, for to him the word is the permanent factor and he is so conscious of the temporary quality of the history of the theatre as compared with the history of the drama, that his constant danger lies in underestimating the significance of those accompaniments of the verbal expression which have in many cases been responsible for its survival.

In a letter accompanying a revision of *Secret Service*, which he was good enough to make for a volume of plays I was editing, William Gillette expressed a point of view worthy of the attention of those who are willing to accept the word of a creative artist as of more significance than that of the critic:

> I thank you for incorporating the Acting Directions with the actual words spoken, in the case of *Secret Service*, notwithstanding your evident opinion that the words constitute the play. We differ there in a marked degree—for even in book form,—to be read only, I would much prefer that people read what my characters *do*—how they *behave*—and what is in their minds—than to merely get the words they utter.

It is to be noted that Gillette is speaking of the action which springs from the playwright as creative artist, not the interpretation which an actor may put upon both words and action. He allies himself here with the position of Herne, which led to the striking scenes in *Margaret Fleming* and *Shore Acres*, already discussed, in which no words are spoken. But while

With highest regard
and best of wishes for the work
William Gillette

GILLETTE AND THE REALISM OF ACTION

Gillette stands in our dramatic history for the development of action, it is for action which reveals character as well as action which develops striking situations.

William Gillette was born in Hartford, Connecticut, July 24, 1855, his father, Francis Gillette, being at one time Senator of the United States. As early as 1875 he acted professionally in *Across the Continent* in New Orleans, and appeared as Guzman in *Faint Heart Never Won Fair Lady*, at the Globe Theatre in Boston. His first appearance in New York was at the Park Theatre in 1877 in *The Gilded Age*, where he acted as Foreman of the Jury, and his "entire vocal effort," as he expresses it, was "We have!" and "Not guilty." He was, in other words, learning his profession gradually. Gillette differs, however, from his contemporaries who were equipping themselves, during the seventies, for their dramatic careers. While acting at the Park Theatre, he was attending classes at the College of the City of New York, and later, when playing small parts in Boston, he made arrangements for special classes at Harvard and the Massachusetts Institute of Technology, and was a regular student at Boston University. None of these courses led to a degree, but they probably helped in that development of the sense of form which Gillette so markedly possesses. The fact that Gillette's taste led him in such a direction is of more significance perhaps than the results of his labors, for it reveals a desire for a broader outlook than the theatre alone can give. It was a natural result from the cultivated surroundings in which he had grown up in Hartford.

His first striking success as an actor came at the Boston Museum as Prince Florian in Gilbert's *Broken Hearts*, and he progressed so steadily in critical approval and popular favor that his reputation as a playwright has been somewhat obscured by his success in the interpretative field.

His first play, *The Professor*, produced at the Madison Square Theatre, June 1, 1881, is a character study of Professor Hopkins, who is a middle-aged teacher, admired by a bevy

of girls and in consequence badgered by the younger lovers
of the maidens. Gillette acted in the leading part and it was
a distinct success, running for one hundred and fifty-one consecutive performances, and later being taken on tour as far
west as St. Louis, where Augustus Thomas records his impression of its charm.[1]

In his first published play, *Esmeralda*, Gillette collaborated
with Mrs. Frances Hodgson Burnett, whose story of *Esmeralda* had appeared in *Scribner's Monthly* for May, 1877.
Mrs. Burnett, who was born in England but who was profoundly interested in certain phases of American life, discovered in the mountaineers of North Carolina dramatic
material which has recently been rediscovered. Only one act,
however, of the play is laid in North Carolina. The Rogers
family, headed by Mrs. Lydia Ann, who has dominated both
her husband and her daughter, Esmeralda, is determined to sell
the farm and is unwittingly about to close the bargain for five
hundred dollars with Drew, a speculator, when Dave Hardy,
a young neighbor, prevents the sale. Dave loves Esmeralda
and suspects that Drew has discovered ore on the land. Lydia
Ann is shrewd and when she sees the opportunity of wealth
she wastes no time in resentment but drives a good bargain
with Drew and just as relentlessly tells Dave they are through
with him. Dave at first defies her, but again she presents the
one argument that could win him, the appeal to his generosity
to let Esmeralda have a chance of comparing him with other
men before she marries him. There was of course in 1881 a
sentimental flavor to the family discussion, but even yet there
is a vivid contrast between the dominant woman who has been
a school-teacher at the county town and the man whom she
had married "for a whim," a gentle lovable soul, inarticulate
in his joy or sorrow.

Esmeralda is taken abroad and in Paris Mrs. Rogers arranges a marriage between her and the Marquis de Montessin.
Dave comes over, of course, and it turns out that the ore is

[1] *Print of My Remembrance,* 137.

really on his land. The sub-plot is unimportant but the scenes in the third Act, in which Esmeralda defies her mother, are quite vigorous. Even better is the "old man's" assertion of his right to be the head of the house, trembling all the while, but nerving himself to "go through with it."

The original story had been laid in Paris and was told by a French teacher of languages, who helps Esmeralda and her father in their loneliness and struggle against Mrs. Rogers, the latter appearing only in the background. To Mrs. Burnett is due the creation of the four main characters, but in the play they become active rather than passive figures. Gillette laid out the plan, Mrs. Burnett wrote the dialogue and then Gillette revised it, so that the drama may be looked upon in a real sense as a collaboration.

Esmeralda ran continuously from October 29, 1881, until October 7, 1882, and held the stage as long as 1900. Annie Russell and later Viola Allen played Esmeralda, and John E. Owens made the part of Elbert Rogers memorable. When it was played as *Young Folks' Ways* in London, John Hare took the part of Rogers, and Mr. and Mrs. Kendal were in the cast. Gillette's first two plays helped to establish the fortunes of the Madison Square Theatre as a place in which American dramatists would have an opportunity, and the Mallorys reaped a large reward for their sagacity.

The stage history of *The Private Secretary*, in which Gillette turned to the comedy of *Der Bibliothekar* (1878), by Gustav von Moser, illustrates the difficulties of passing critical judgment upon the drama of that period. *Der Bibliothekar* was adapted by both Gillette and Charles Hawtrey, an English playwright. On September 29, 1884, Gillette opened at the Comedy Theatre, New York, with his version, called *Digby's Secretary*. On the same evening, A. M. Palmer produced Hawtrey's version, under the title of *The Private Secretary*, at the Madison Square Theatre. Palmer tried to prevent Gillette from performing his play, but as Gillette had obtained von Moser's permission and was paying him a royalty while

Hawtrey was not, Palmer proposed a compromise. After playing his own version for a few months, Gillette continued under Palmer's management, making a new adaptation, founded upon his own, but using certain features of Hawtrey's play. It was in that composite production that Gillette appeared for five seasons.[1]

Gillette kept the plot of *Der Bibliothekar* in its main outlines, but there are many changes in details, owing to the increased importance given to the part of the Rev. Robert Spaulding, played by Gillette. In the German he is a minor character, does not appear in the second Act, and in the last Act is brought on just at the end. The comedy is broad farce in both cases. Robert Spaulding has been engaged as a private secretary by Turner Marsland, a country gentleman at Edgington, in England. Marsland's nephew, Harry, persuades his friend Douglas Cattermole, who is beset with duns, to go down to Marsland Manor with him, and represent himself as the private secretary. They persuade Spaulding, who is a guileless creature in rubbers, to stay in Cattermole's rooms for a time, but of course he follows them down to the Manor and a series of very comic situations develop. Gillette added to the low comedy by the addition of a wife and children for the clergyman, who are at first accredited to Douglas Cattermole, with a consequent misunderstanding between Edith Marsland and himself. Gillette amplified the slight references to spiritualism in the original by making the Reverend Mr. Spaulding appear as a medium. In this amplification there is reflected the current interest in spiritualism, in 1884.

In his next play Gillette wrote the first important drama of the Civil War. It was indicated in an earlier chapter that the writing of plays laid in the Civil War was practically continuous. Most of them were, however, of a hopeless quality. Boucicault's *Belle Lamar* (1874) has already been discussed. There are some vigorous moments in *Allatoona*, by Major General Judson Kilpatrick and J. Owen Moore, especially dur-

[1] Letter from Mr. Gillette, January 7, 1916.

ing the "battle in the clouds." It is truly a chronicle play, beginning at West Point, where the hero, Harry Estes, and his classmate, Charles Dunbar, take opposite sides, and proceeding to General Sherman's headquarters at Atlanta and General Corse's stubborn defence of his position. The latter is made one of the characters in the play, and Moore, who probably wrote nearly all of it, claims in the introduction historical accuracy.

But it is not accuracy which spells success in historical drama. There must be no flagrant distortion of well-known facts, but the audience is primarily interested in the personal relations of the characters and the conflict between the North and the South must be symbolized in a hero and heroine who represent the dramatic struggle in such a way that our sympathy is secured for them both. Boucicault had attempted this in *Belle Lamar,* but he had not recognized the greater appeal of the war play if it presents the tense moments when the imminence of tragedy is set against a background of domestic life. The characters must have courage and decision and the danger of the hero is intensified if it is reflected to the audience by the love and anxiety of the heroine.

These qualities were all present in *Held by the Enemy,* which began its career at the Criterion Theatre, Brooklyn, February 22, 1886, and came into the Madison Square Theatre in August. The action takes place in "a Southern city which has been captured and occupied by Northern forces," and in the first act Gillette established the atmosphere of refinement and comfort in the home of the McCreerys, aunt and nieces, while outside the war is raging. Eunice is betrothed, by a family arrangement, to her cousin, Lieutenant Gordon Hayne, who is in the Confederate army. But Colonel Harvey Brant, and Brigade Surgeon Fielding, of the Union army, are also in love with her, and the play centers on the efforts of Fielding to win her, by force, if necessary. The attempt of Hayne to enter the city as a spy, to make plans of the fortifications, and Brant's capture of him, give Fielding his opportunity. At

Hayne's court-martial, Fielding is judge advocate and cleverly directs the evidence to prove that Brant is animated by his rivalry with Hayne to convict the Confederate spy. Eunice plays into his hands by bursting out, in forgetfulness of all save her desire to protect her cousin, that no one but Brant has seen the incriminating paper which has been taken from Hayne. Brant when questioned, declines for her sake to testify against Hayne, and then Hayne to save him from the charge of dishonor acknowledges he is a spy and is proud of it. It is a conflict of honor between two men who love the same woman, and through Hayne, Gillette expressed in vigorous language the pride of the spy in his secret mission.[1]

Gillette here expressed the idea he was to bring to more complete development in *Secret Service*—the heroism of the spy. Hayne almost escapes from his prison in the next Act through the destruction of the walls by a timely shell, but is shot. In the fourth Act, laid in a military hospital, Gillette produced a scene which for sheer intensity of emotional appeal has rarely been exceeded. The McCreerys have secured from the commanding general a permit to bring Hayne's body through the lines. He is not really dead, and how the examining surgeon was deceived is never made clear, but in the whirl of incident that is forgotten. The sense of danger of discovery, of the great pressure of time, is well expressed, and largely through clever comedy, which prevents the situation from becoming too tense. Thomas Beene, a Northern war correspondent, and Susan McCreery, a younger sister, provide the comedy. Beene, a part later played by Gillette, is a preliminary sketch of the cool, quick-thinking and acting man, which is the playwright's favorite character. Fielding, returning, suspects that Hayne is not dead, and the efforts of Eunice and of Brant, who is unaware of the deception, to prevent the body from being examined, build up a skillful piece of stage arrangement. It is one of those situations which, under analysis, fall into

[1] See *Theatre*, II, 178, for the effect made upon the audience by this scene as acted by J. E. Kellerd in the part of Hayne.

pieces, and read coldly in type, seem almost absurd, and yet in action appear probable. For as a matter of fact, Gillette had studied the psychology of military discipline. To a civilian, it may seem impossible that Brant should order Fielding to desist from having the body examined, yet the soldier knows that the possession of an order from the commanding general made even the brigade surgeon's interference an intrusion. The soldier is accustomed to obey orders and ask no questions, and also to allow no one else to ask questions. Then when General Stamburg comes on the scene, Brant, in order to justify himself, asks the General to order the body to be examined. Eunice glides near him and whispers that Hayne is alive. From this point until the curtain there is an opportunity to study a series of rapid changes of action dictated by conflicts of emotion.

Fielding: (*Dashing across the stage*) D'you see that! D'you see that! She's just told him the man's alive— And now he can't speak!

Gen. Stamburg: Colonel, is that what Miss McCreery said?

Brant: (*Without hesitation*) Nothing of the kind, sir—he's a contemptible liar!
(*Fielding strikes Brant in the face almost on the word. Brant seizes Fielding's arm before he can get it away and holds it.*)

Gen. Stamburg: (*Quickly on the blow*) Halt!—You forget yourselves! (*Brant instantly releases Fielding's arm.*) That man on the stretcher alive? Why the thing is impossible. . . .

Fielding: (*As he swings around*) Impossible—Ah—(*pointing to the stretcher*) Look at that!—look for yourself, General! Unless I'm greatly mistaken the man is *breathing!*

Gen. Stamburg: Surgeon—examine the body at once!
(*Fielding strides to the stretcher near c. and throws the covering from Hayne's head and breast and at once stoops over making hurried examination. Eunice, almost as Fielding throws back the blanket, glides quickly to the stretcher from up r. c. where she had been moving during last speeches, and stands on Fielding's right, very near to him, but bending over Hayne as if to see.*)

Eunice: (*In a sharp breathless whisper to Fielding as she is ap-*

parently looking at Hayne and as Fielding bends down with his hand at Hayne's heart) Oh, save us! Save us and I'll marry you! I will, I will! (*Fielding stops in his examination of Hayne—and listens*) I promise!—On my sacred word—whenever you say!—On my sacred word—that I'll never break! I will! (*She rises and stands back a few steps motionless—her eyes lowered—waiting*)
(*Fielding who has listened motionless while Eunice was whispering does not stir for an instant after she ceases.—Then he goes on with the examination for a moment, but his hand shakes as he puts it to Hayne's throat. He bends down and puts his ear to Hayne's body over the heart. Then he rises erect, and turns toward General Stamburg.*)

Fielding: (*Speaking with an effort*) General—I owe Colonel Brant—and this young lady—an apology. My suspicions were groundless. The man is dead.
(*Brant, whose eyes were lowered, slowly raises them and looks off front—realizing what has happened.*)

The last Act, in which Brant forces Fielding to release Eunice from her promise, is hardly up to the earlier ones. It has some charming love-making, however, between Susan and Beene.

Gillette's dramatization of *She*, the novel by Rider Haggard, need not detain us. No play based on such a novel could be important, and the play was apparently no better than its source.[1] *A Legal Wreck*, which began at the Madison Square Theatre, August 14, 1888, is laid mainly in a New England fishing village. It exists now in published form as a novelette, written by Gillette and based upon the play. In 1888 dramatizations of popular novels were plentiful, and it occurred to the management of the play that it would be helped by the publication of the book. Gillette wrote it in five and one-half weeks, and it appeared about one week before the production. Considering the circumstances, the novel is remarkably well done. The opening chapter, in which Gillette calls attention to the effects of the sea upon those who live near it, shows his power of observation. "Gap Harbor took gossip . . . with a chill-

[1] See Winter, *Life of Belasco*, I, 337–40.

ing calmness. And it was because the people, instead of being shut into a place where they were forced, for the excitement which the human system craves, to prey upon themselves, were neighbors with the ocean." The style is vivid, and while the conversations are brisk, as would naturally be the case, it is interesting to see how the plot is carried on by the revelation of the thoughts of the characters and by the descriptions furnished by their creator. Several stand out clearly. Captain Smith, a fine portrait of the retired seaman, has brought up tenderly the little girl Olive, left to him by her father, who in a fit of depression had cast himself into the sea. His son, "Ed," is a hulking, dissipated lout, whose passion for Olive leads him to attempt to secure her by having her abducted from a railroad train by the supposed agents of an insane asylum. Her salvation by Leverett, the hero; Ed Smith's attempts at revenge, and the recovery of Olive by her mother and sister, who has been, all unknowing, Olive's friend at college, are more in the conventional tone of melodrama. Yet a rereading of the novel, when the plot is fully known, shows that it is the manner of the telling which is its main attraction.

Gillette did not act in *A Legal Wreck*, in his dramatization of *Robert Elsmere* (1889) or in his farce comedy, *All the Comforts of Home* (1890), adapted from *Ein Toller Einfall*. This play deals with the adventures of Alfred Hastings, a young man whose uncle, Mr. Pettibone, leaves his residence in London in order to take his wife away from a supposed lover, Smythe, who is really in love with his daughter, Emily. Alfred is in financial difficulties and, together with the assistance of his man, Tom McDow, "who gits half," starts a lodging house in his uncle's handsome home. To this lodging house come various people, among them the Bender family, and Alfred falls in love with Evangeline Bender. The Pettibones come home unexpectedly and complicate matters, but, of course, everything ends satisfactorily. The play is clever but of no great significance. Alfred, however, is another example of the cool young man who meets circumstances adroitly.

A clever farce which went extremely well on the stage was *Mr. Wilkinson's Widows*, adapted by Gillette from *Feu Toupinel* by Alexandre Bisson. After a try-out at Washington, it opened at Proctor's Theatre, March 30, 1891.[1] The scene of the play is changed from Paris to Edinburgh. The central motive is that of the complications which arise from the bigamy of the late Mr. Wilkinson, who married two women, both of whom have remarried. His relicts, Mrs. Percival Perrin and Mrs. Henry F. Dickerson, meet, and on comparing notes, each believes that she is the legal wife, since they were both apparently married to Mr. Wilkinson on the same day. In Bisson's play, a wife and a mistress furnish the complications with more probability if less propriety. Another play of Bisson, *La Famille Pont-Biquet*, was the source of *Settled Out of Court*, a farce in three acts, produced at the Fifth Avenue Theatre, August 8, 1892.

After this period of adaptation, Gillette wrote a play with more original elements, *Too Much Johnson*, which was one of the most popular of his efforts, and in which he took the leading part of Augustus Billings. This character, the cool, unabashed center of overwhelming complications, was his own invention, and much of the plot was his. From *La Plantation Thomassin* of Maurice Ordonneau, a species of musical comedy, he took the idea of a tropical plantation, to which the characters go, and the confusion as to its ownership. Billings, who has been deceiving his wife by representing to her that his frequent absences have been due to his visits to his sugar plantation in Cuba, finds that she and her mother have decided to accompany him. He has barely time to secure staterooms when they arrive at the dock. On the same boat appears Mr. Leon Dathis, with whose wife Billings has been enjoying New York, and who is looking, with half a torn photograph, for his rival. There are also Mr. Francis Faddish, and his daughter, Leonora, whom he has contracted to marry Joseph Johnson,

---

[1] An English version, by Fred Hunter, under the title of *The Late Lamented*, was produced at the Court Theatre, London, May 6, 1891.

WILLIAM GILLETTE AS "CAPTAIN THORNE" IN *SECRET SERVICE*

the owner of the Columbia plantation in Cuba. Billings has been conducting his love affairs under the name of Johnson, because there are "about fifteen thousand in the directory," and the consequent complications when they arrive in Cuba and Johnson mistakes Mrs. Billings for the *fiancée* he is expecting, can be imagined. Johnson is so irascible that the confusion becomes hilarious and through it all Billings stalks unperturbed, finally escaping with his wife and mother-in-law, without their suspecting the real situation. Pure farce as the play is, that character remains in the memory as a real person.

Secret Service, Gillette's most significant play, was first produced as *The Secret Service* at the Broad Street Theatre in Philadelphia, May 13, 1895. While the usual statements concerning its original lack of success are exaggerated, it was in a revised form that it appeared in October, 1896, at the Garrick Theatre in New York, where it remained until March, 1897. Of even more importance, Gillette instead of Maurice Barrymore played the leading part. He has now so completely identified the rôle of Captain Thorne with his own personality that it is hard for those who have seen him play, to imagine anyone else in it. On May 15, 1897, Gillette began an engagement at the Adelphi Theatre in London, which terminated at the Comedy Theatre in August. After his return to America, William Terriss, Herbert Waring and other actors appeared in London and in the provincial theatres in the part of Captain Thorne. *Secret Service* was also produced in a version by Pierre Decourcelle at the Théâtre de la Renaissance in Paris, October 2, 1897.[1]

Secret Service is an admirably constructed play. Every action proceeds naturally without apparent effort on the part of the playwright. Unity is preserved, even that of time, for the first Act begins at eight o'clock, the second at nine, the third at ten and the fourth at eleven o'clock at night in Richmond, while the Union forces are attacking the city. Gillette has placed the scene well, for some of the incidents, which might

[1] *Plays of the Present,* 244–5.

otherwise seem impossible, are to be accounted for by the confusion natural to such a time. As in *Held by the Enemy*, he strikes a note of personal devotion to the Confederacy through the Varney family—Mrs. Varney with her cool, quiet repose of manner; Edith Varney, more intense and swayed by her love for "Captain Thorne"; and Wilfred Varney, the sixteen-year-old boy who is longing to go to the front where his father is fighting, while the older son, Howard, is lying wounded upstairs. They are all spirited people, and the sympathy of the audience goes out to them at once. It is not so keen, however, as the reaction when Lewis Dumont, the Northern spy, who has secured entrance to the city as "Captain Thorne" of the Confederate army, enters, for we feel instinctively that in addition to the personal liking we have for them all, his continued danger appeals to our interest in the preservation of the hero. Not a word is wasted and not an action. Edith has secured a commission for him as Major, attached to the Telegraph Service of the Confederate army, and the whole situation between them is revealed in their brief conversation, when after a few words in which he tells her he must leave Richmond that night, she begs him to stay and he bursts out with a passionate exclamation, "Ah, my dear one—how can I?" and then suddenly stops and recovering control of himself says, "No! You shan't have this against me, too." She tells him of the commission and he says quickly, decisively, "I won't take it, I couldn't take it, Miss Varney. . . . If you ever think of me again remember that I refused it." She leaves the room to get it, however, and he is about to avoid temptation by flight when he is stopped by the entrance of Caroline Mitford, a girl of sixteen, one of the most charming of all the creations of our stage. She and Wilfred Varney provide in their love affair the lighter side of the shield, and her efforts to help him so that she won't be "the only girl on Franklin Street that didn't have a—some one she was engaged to at the front," are so closely interwoven in the plot that she becomes a potent factor in it. But above all else, it is the absolute reality of the characters which is impressive. Without a bit of heroics, they all move under the shadow of danger, playing the game; even Benton Arrelsford, of the War Office, who is trying to prove Captain Thorne's real mission, is not overstressed. By the end of the first Act we seem to have known these people always, because in this play Gillette represented the indomitable spirit of the American gentleman and gentlewoman, intelligible to North and South alike, and the audience recognized that whatever happened to them, they were worth while. There is a dramatic heresy now current that "little souls" are just as well suited for the stage as great ones, but those who hold it will be burnt at the stake of oblivion. Edith Varney, forced by fate to submit her lover to the test of his fidelity to the Confederacy, and bound by her promise to Arrelsford to keep Thorne in her house until his brother, Henry Dumont, can be brought from Libby Prison to confront and expose him, goes to her task with the light words of apparent careless gaiety on her lips while her heart is almost breaking. A woman's frustrated love is sometimes tragic, sometimes merely pitiful, but love shot through with the agony of doubt in the truth of the lover, while the woman must use her power to bring the lover to the test that may prove him a traitor, is one of the most truly dramatic motives that can be conceived.

This motive is carried out in the second Act. Henry Dumont has allowed himself to be captured and has sent a message to his brother Lewis through old Jonas, the negro servant. This has been taken by Arrelsford from Jonas. It reads, "Attack to-night—Plan Three—Use Telegraph." Edith gives this to Lewis Dumont (Captain Thorne), and then Henry is brought into the room by the soldiers as though he were escaping. Arrelsford, who is concealed, hopes to convict Thorne in this way. But when the brothers meet, Thorne grapples with Henry, who shoots himself with his brother's revolver. Then as the lights flash up and everyone comes on, Thorne stands, with an easy swing of his arms replacing his revolver in his holster and saying quietly, "There's your prisoner, Corporal—look out for him."

Baffled in his efforts, Arrelsford makes one more attempt to prove to Edith that Thorne is a spy. The scene of the third Act is the War Department Telegraph Office. The atmosphere is again caught at once; the intensity of the struggle is underlined by the click of the instruments and by the rumors of imminent danger. Caroline comes to the office to send a telegram to Wilfred, who has gone to the front, and there is much pleasant comedy till Arrelsford arrives with orders to take charge. A clash between him and Caroline sends her off to bring General Randolph later, and Edith Varney and Arrelsford conceal themselves on the balcony outside the office. Then follows a scene of rapid action by which Thorne, who comes on with a forged order, clears the room of all the other operators and prepares to send the dispatch which will weaken the Confederate defense by withdrawing a division from an important point. Arrelsford, however, stops him by a shot from the balcony and calls for the guard. Then follows a sudden change of front. When the guard come, Thorne orders them instantly to arrest Arrelsford. With the instinct of the soldier to obey the man in uniform, they respond to Thorne's commands against Arrelsford's protests. Into the mêlée Caroline brings General Randolph, an irascible old officer, who combines a single-track military mind with a dislike of the secret service. With every fact and chance against him, Thorne proceeds quietly to send the order, despite Arrelsford's violent protests. Then when the men who have been sent away by his forged orders begin to come in and even General Randolph orders him to stop, Edith Varney appears with the commission which he has previously refused to accept and presents it to him.

This situation illustrates some profound laws of dramatic construction. Edith Varney has had a decision to make between her love of country and her love of Captain Thorne. She decides in favor of the human love and everyone in the audience approves her choice. As soon as the commission is given to

CHICAGO
FEBRUARY
1911

To William Gillette
with best wishes of
Charles Dana Gibson.

"CAPTAIN THORNE" SENDING THE MESSAGE IN *SECRET SERVICE*

him, the choice between patriotism and love is transferred to Thorne. He instantly glides to the telegraph instrument, to send the dispatch, and the audience follows his movements with equal approval. This apparent inconsistency is founded on the most primitive instincts of human nature. To the man, his duty to his country comes first, for he carries on the nation. To the woman, her love comes first, for she carries on the race. Then instantly a new element is introduced. Edith appeals to his honor. "I brought it," she says, "to save your life! I didn't think you'd use it—for anything else. Oh—you wouldn't!" Reinforced by this appeal, the love triumphs and he revokes the message and tears up the commission. And the audience approves, this time tumultuously.

If Gillette had ended the play here, he would have created a tragedy of uncommon power. But in the next act, by an improbable piece of clemency, Thorne is saved. The play becomes melodrama of a high order. On the stage the illusion of probability remains, because so deeply has the sympathy of the audience become involved in the success of the main motive of the play, the love of Thorne and Edith Varney, that it tolerates any device which will secure that success.

It is the fashion to classify as melodrama all plays in which the conclusions are not strictly logical and to treat them all as outside the province of art. One essential quality of melodrama, as I have explained elsewhere,[1] lies in its freedom, but like all products of art, it has its laws, and *Secret Service* obeys these perfectly. It is possible to point out the absurdity of the awarding of the commission, or of the details of the forged signature on the dispatch, but these are on the surface. *Secret Service* is founded on a proved law of the theatre, that the motives of self-preservation, love, patriotism, loyalty, and personal honor are the most universal in appeal. Many plays have succeeded with one of them—*Secret Service* has them all, now playing against each other, now joining forces, but al-

---

[1] *History of the American Drama from the Beginning to the Civil War*, p. 102. See also Chapter XVII in this history.

ways expressed through concrete characters who act as well as speak.

In 1898 Gillette turned from the intensity of *Secret Service* to the light comedy of *Because She Loved Him So,* adapted from *Jalouse* by Alexandre Bisson and Adolphe Leclerq, and first produced in New Haven, October 28, 1898. The play is a study of the effects of jealousy. Gertrude West, a young wife, is insanely jealous of her husband's supposed attentions to other women. They quarrel so frightfully in consequence that her parents, Mr. and Mrs. John Weatherby, who have never had a dispute in their lives, pretend to have fallen out in order to show their children the evil effects. They do this so realistically that Gertrude believes her mother has been deceived and nearly wrecks a friendship between her parents and Señora Gonzales, a charming tenant of John Weatherby. The action is rapid and amusing, and the play was a distinct success. The acting of J. E. Dodson as John Weatherby, the bride's father, was especially noteworthy, and the adaptation was made with Gillette's usual skill, for he succeeded in preserving the light touch of the original while omitting the unnecessary indelicacy.

There can be little doubt that it was the imperturbable personality of Sherlock Holmes which attracted Gillette's attention to his possibilities as a stage character. The detective whom Conan Doyle had modeled on Poe's Monsieur Dupin was well known and exactly suited Gillette's style of acting. In constructing the play, he took three characters from Doyle's stories, Sherlock Holmes, Dr. Watson and "Professor" Moriarty, the leader of the band of criminals, but the other eighteen were of his own creation, and the main plot is not found in Doyle's stories. The novelist, moreover, did not see the play until it was finished, and had no part in its construction.[1]

The plot turns upon the efforts of Sherlock Holmes to pro-

---

[1] Letter from Mr. Gillette, December 10, 1924. The publication in England of *Sherlock Holmes* as "By Arthur Conan Doyle and William Gillette" was unauthorized by the playwright.

cure certain letters and photographs which had been sent by a mysterious royal personage in Germany to a girl who had died some time before the play opened. Her sister, Alice Faulkner, is determined to punish the offender for his treatment of the dead woman. Alice Faulkner has fallen into the hands of a pair of precious rascals, James and Madge Larrabee, and Holmes, who visits their house and secures the papers by a clever trick, is so much impressed by Alice that he returns the papers to her and proceeds on a new tack, that of persuading her to deliver the papers herself to the representatives of his royal employer. The Larrabees call in Moriarty, who is anxious to circumvent Holmes, and then the audience is treated to a series of scenes in Holmes's own rooms, in Moriarty's "Gas Chamber" and in Dr. Watson's office, in which the detective balks with skill all the efforts of craft and violence, until he secures his purpose. Incidentally he wins Alice Faulkner, who gives up her scheme of revenge under the more alluring prospects of love. Naturally the play is not in the same category as *Secret Service*, for while the plot is skilfully constructed, Gillette was dealing with characters who are not and cannot be made real. Sherlock Holmes and Dr. Watson are faint copies of the brilliant creations of Poe, and it was only the superb acting of Gillette which carried the play into favor here and abroad.

In 1903 he departed from his policy of appearing in his own plays by taking the leading part in Barrie's *The Admirable Crichton*, but in 1905 reassumed his joint function of playwright and actor in *Clarice*. In this play, first produced at the Duke of York's Theatre, London, September 13, 1905, and during the season of 1906-7 in this country, Gillette probably made use of atmosphere and material which were the result of his earlier stay in North Carolina. At his home at Thousand Pines, in the western part of the state, he had regained his health and had written *Too Much Johnson*. *Clarice* is laid in a village in South Carolina in 1904, and most of the action takes place in the living room of Dr. Carrington. The atmosphere of refined comfort without ostentation is at once established by the furnishings of the room, and the characters, few in number, are woven into the background with his usual skill. Gillette took the old story of a man who has brought up a young girl, Clarice, only to find that he loves her, while he feels that he must hide his passion. The relations between Clarice and her guardian are delicately expressed, and the half-maternal care she takes of him is contrasted with the tender solicitude he feels for her. Over this idyllic situation hovers the guardian spirit of Clancy, the cook, who is as fine a picture of old-fashioned negro loyalty as Thomas Nelson Page or Hopkinson Smith ever drew. The close identification of Clarice with the doctor's life is revealed not only in the way she prescribes for one of his patients, but more definitely in her sketches that she is making for his book on plants, which is to be his great accomplishment.

But into this happy situation there comes the disturbing element that is inevitable in drama. There is a rival, of course, a younger man, Dr. Denbeigh, but he is not the moving force of what is almost a tragedy. To direct the countermotive Gillette provided one of the best-drawn characters in his gallery, Mrs. Trent, Clarice's aunt. Years before the play opens she had cared for Carrington and he had not responded, and while no word is said by her to indicate her continued resentment, the audience realizes that he is dealing with an implacable enemy, who will hesitate at nothing to injure him. Under the guise of fostering the love affair between Denbeigh and Clarice, she plays skillfully upon Carrington's dread of the incipient tuberculosis whose menace had broken up his early career and sent him to South Carolina. She is the feminine prototype of his favorite male character, the calm, clear-headed person who moves quietly and quickly among circumstances to her end. Her first plan, to persuade Clarice that Dr. Carrington approves of the match between her and Denbeigh, almost succeeds, for Carrington's generosity makes him an apparent party to it. But at the end of the first Act occurs one of those situations which Gillette has built up on the basis of his theory that action is more eloquent than words. Clarice has told him she will accept Denbeigh if he desires her to do so. But a natural circumstance leads her to leave the stage for a moment, and on her return she discovers him tenderly kissing the rose she had given him, and then plucking it to pieces. Without a word she glides from the stage to give Denbeigh his refusal, and returns to pledge her life to Carrington. This is the kind of scene which can either be sickening in its sentimentality or exquisite in its sentiment. In Gillette's hands it was the latter, but it also revealed the power of an action which could change the whole current of three people's lives.

Mrs. Trent is not daunted by apparent failure. She deftly insinuates into Denbeigh's mind the suggestion that he deceive Carrington into a belief that his condition is hopeless and she writes Carrington a note telling him that Clarice can remain with him only at the peril of her life. This note is brought to him at the end of the second Act, after a love scene between him and Clarice which is charming in its whimsical quality. The ending of this Act is a remarkable example of the sudden striking of terror into happiness. He begins to read it aloud under the impression that it is a letter of congratulation. The audience knows its contents and hears him falter, then sees him brace himself to turn the deadly missive into a harmless note of approval.

Car.: (*Calling out after her*) Nonsense, Clancy! (*He turns and looks down smiling at Clarice—who looks up in his face.*) Why, I know what it is!
(*He has the open letter and the envelope in his left hand, having just succeeded in getting the letter out. Clarice is silent, her head down again against his breast.*)
It's the answer to the note I sent her this afternoon telling her about you and me. (*She looks up into his face and he down into her eyes for a moment.*) You and me!—My dear, my dear— (*He turns again to the letter.*)
Listen, sweet—you'll like to hear this! Why, she's got to send us good wishes—whether she wishes 'em or not! Oh

yes, she has! There's nothing else to do! Let's come a little nearer the light! (*He moves up a little with her so that the lamp is near his left shoulder.*) There we are! Now listen! (*He holds the letter up in his left hand and reads it*) "Dear Dr. Carrington:—I'm afraid from what I hear that you changed your mind after I saw you this morning." (*He stops and looks down at her smiling. She looks up at him.*)
Changed my mind! Well, I should think I did! (*He continues to look at her tenderly for a moment—then turns to the letter again.*) "Now, sorry as I am to—" (*He stops suddenly and stands motionless looking at the letter. There is a slight pause and then he speaks*)
Wait a minute—I can't quite make out— (*Reads*) "Sorry as I am to—" Ha ha—this is odd, isn't it? (*Turning to her*) Of course she's sorry about something—we can understand that!
(*His eyes have glanced quickly down the sheet during the foregoing pauses.*)

Clarice: Why don't you read me the rest?

Car.: (*Quickly*) Yes—-yes—as soon as I—I was trying to—to get at it from the context. (*He turns back to the letter in his left hand.*) How far had I—

Clarice: She said she was sorry about something.

Car.: Oh yes—here we are! (*A fleeting glance toward her and back to letter again.*)
I told you she'd have to do it! (*Rather rapidly and as if reading from the letter*) "Sorry as I am that you were unable to see the wisdom of my plans, I have no doubt it will turn out for the best! I certainly hope so, and send my good wishes and congratulations . . . to you—you both!" (*He crumples the letter and envelope quickly in his left hand on the last word or close after it and crowds them hastily into the left hand pocket of his coat.*) There—you see! (*He holds her close in both arms.*)
Your Aunt Max is all right! (*Gently pressing her head down on his breast*) Your Aunt Max is all right!
(*He turns his head away to left front—his eyes down, and his face showing his dreadful anguish—while still holding her pressed close to him, and repeating mechanically—not knowing what he says*) Your Aunt Max is all right!

Powerful, too, is the climax of the third Act. Believing after Denbeigh's examination that his days are numbered, he declines to give Clarice that reason, for he knows she would pay no attention to it. He determines to make it impossible for her to remain with him, so he changes from the lover to the guardian and brusquely, almost violently, tells her that he has made a mistake; that she is interfering with his life work, even her amateurish sketches are a hindrance, and he harshly bids her prepare to go to Washington that night with her aunt. As he leaves the stage he calls Clancy to come help her mistress pack and then the scene closes.

> (*He turns and goes off unsteadily. Clarice makes an involuntary move toward him as he goes out but stops near the table and stands still. After a time she turns very slowly and goes toward the foot of the stairs. She stops there a moment without looking around. Then she slowly goes up the two or three steps to the landing, steadying herself by holding to the stair post with her right hand. She raises this hand to the post above her as she is starting at the first step. She goes up the stairway. When part way up she stops and turns her head a little, speaking to the front.*)
> Come, Clancy.
> (*She turns and goes up the stairway. Clancy, who has stood motionless, not looking at Clarice during the scene, turns and follows her up the stairs.*)

Judged by one standard, the play might have ended here in tragedy, and the last Act, containing his attempted suicide, his salvation by the unexpected return of Denbeigh and later of Clarice, can be conveniently called melodrama. But in reality it was quite probable that Carrington, facing the slow wasting of his life in utter loneliness, should decide to end it. It is equally probable that Denbeigh, who returns to inform Carrington that Clarice has refused to go with her aunt, should react to his discovery of Carrington's condition and, with a physician's instinct, save his life. It is also probable that Clarice should return, and that she times her arrival at the moment when her knowledge of the location of the antidote is essential, may be forgiven any dramatist. For the action in each case is determined by the character, and the characters in this play are among the most real that Gillette has drawn.

Gillette experimented in the next few years in the writing of one-act plays, among them *The Painful Predicament of Sherlock Holmes*, in which he appeared in 1905, and a rather vivid if improbable vaudeville sketch, *The Red Owl*, in 1907, laid at midnight in a house in the suburbs of New York. Better than the last is *Among Thieves*, a skillfully planned drama of situation, laid in Arizona. Gillette represents in this one-act play the lengths to which a criminal will go in loyalty to a man who has befriended him and also the eternal suspicion and watchfulness which are his only security.

In 1908 Gillette produced his translation of Henri Bernstein's *Samson*, which followed the original more closely than his other adaptations. He took the part of Maurice Brachard, who in order to revenge himself upon his wife's lover, pulls down in a day the great financial structure he has built up through years of effort, satisfied that he has wrecked his enemy. The part was created by Lucien Guitry in 1907 at the Théâtre de la Renaissance.

Gillette made an effort to employ new sources for his material in *Electricity*, which opened at the Park Theatre, Boston, September 26, 1910. It is a three-act comedy laid in New York City, and is concerned with the love affair between James Hollenden and Emeline Twimbly, the daughter of Duncan Twimbly, who is "at the head of a corrupt corporation." Emeline is a modern girl who declines to accept her lot in life as an idler and who is gently satirized by Gillette in her rather feeble efforts to secure employment. Hollenden, who belongs also to the inheritors of wealth, has fallen in love with her photographs which her brother Samuel has had in their joint rooms at college, and being warned by Sam that she will not be attracted to him unless he is a worker, Hollenden bribes Bill Brockway, who is wiring the Twimbly house, to let him take his place. The situation rapidly becomes farcical, and by 1910 the denunciation of corporate greed was no longer a fresh note. Yet there is some rather good characterization, especially of the Brockway family, and Emeline's call of ceremony on them when she believes herself to be engaged to Bill Brockway, is amusing comedy. *Electricity* in its published form is interesting reading even if its success on the stage was not great.

In his latest plays Gillette has returned to his favorite sphere, that of the character who is playing a difficult hand against a number of opponents, who are usually lawbreakers. *The Dream Maker*, produced in 1921 at the Empire Theatre, was founded on a short story by Howard E. Merton. The scene is laid in the cottage of well-to-do people in a summer resort near New York City, and the central character, Dr. Paul Clement, baffles a set of blackmailers who are preying upon a young matron, the daughter of a woman he had once loved. At times there was a flash of the earlier fire, but it was rather in the actor than in the playwright, for the pivotal situation, in which young Mrs. Bruce puts herself in their power through her midnight appointment with Geoffrey Cliffe, is unbelievable. In *Winnie and the Wolves*, based on short stories by Bertram Akey, and tried out at Philadelphia in May, 1923, the material was no more worthy and there was no such personality as Gillette to make the stage presentation significant.

Gillette's dramas may be classified most appropriately in three groups: the original plays, the dramatizations of fiction, and the adaptations from foreign sources.

Among his six dramatizations of fiction, *Esmeralda* and *Sherlock Holmes* were deservedly successful and in each he contributed his full share. Both his adaptations from the German, *The Private Secretary* and *All the Comforts of Home*, and his four plays taken from French sources, *Mr. Wilkinson's Widows*, *Settled Out of Court*, *Because She Loved Him So*, and *Samson*, were also distinctly well received. Like Augustin Daly and Belasco, Gillette worked from translations made by others, and, except in the case of *Samson*, he reshaped the material extensively. In *Samson* he kept the scene in Paris, in *Settled Out of Court* he transferred it to America, in *Mr. Wilkinson's Widows* he laid it in Edinburgh and in the others he placed it in England. In only two of the foreign adaptations did he play himself, *The Private Secretary* and *Samson*. Indeed, Gillette acted in only nine of his twenty full-length plays, *The Professor, The Private Secretary, Held by the Enemy, Too Much Johnson, Secret Service, Sherlock Holmes, Clarice, Samson* and *The Dream Maker*.

If Gillette has confined himself in his acting to the expression of a limited number of characters, it must not be forgotten that he has done so consciously and in accordance with his own theory of art.[1] Criticism is too prone to require an artist to accord with a preconceived standard to which he never attempted to suit his methods, and its real function is to ascertain what the playwright and actor have endeavored to accomplish. According to Gillette, "actors of recent times who have been universally acknowledged to be great have invariably been so because of their successful use of their own strong and compelling personalities in the rôles which they made famous. And when they undertook parts, as they occasionally did, unsuited to their personalities, they were great no longer and frequently quite the reverse."

The personality of William Gillette is so definite that it shines through every part in which the present writer has seen him. But he is not a one-part actor. It is not because Thomas Beene in *Held by the Enemy*, Augustus Billings in *Too Much Johnson*, Captain Thorne in *Secret Service*, and Sherlock Holmes are the same character that his performances are successful. They are quite different, as a matter of fact, and it is only because the compelling personality of the dramatist actor has so successfully infused them with his own nature that he has made of the group a dramatic unit. As characters the

[1] See his "The Illusion of the First Time in Acting," *Publications of Dramatic Museum of Columbia University*, 1915; also "Mr. William Gillette Surveys the Field," Supplement to *Harper's Weekly*, February 2, 1889.

Gen R. ~~Send it~~ Go on and send it!

[Thorne at once drops into seat at telegraph
instrument and begins to send rapidly]

Arrelsford [Seeing what is going on] [To Barracks] No no!! — It's ~~is~~ a —

Gen R. ~~Barracks~~ Silence!

[Pause] [Rapid click of telegraph instrument as Thorne sends. This holds barely four seconds.]

Arrelsford [Breaking in wildly] Do you know what he's
telling them.

Gen. R. ~~Send it~~ No! — Do you?

Arrelsford. ~~Yes that~~ Yes! — It's a damnable plot! He —

Gen. R. [To Thorne] Wait! [Takes copy of despatch from which
Thorne was sending.]
[Thorne stops telegraphing and stands waiting]

Gen. R. [Turns to Arrelsford] What was it?
What did he send just now?

Arrelsford [Repeating] ~~He told them to~~ withdraw
^ Marston's Division
from present position. ~~till~~

Gen R. That is perfectly correct!

Arrelsford ~~~~ Correct — by that despatch
— but that
despatch ^ is a forgery!

[Music swell slightly and down again]

General R [Looks at despatch] Nothing of the kind! — This is the Secretary's
signature!

Arrelsford He cut it off from a genuine order
— I saw him do it!... ~~~~ See if
the sheet isn't pasted on!

Thorne. It is, General — they often ~~~~ come that
way.

Arrelsford [Instant retort] He's a liar —
^ They never do!

[Thorne quick angry turn to
Arrelsford. Arrelsford glaring savagely
at him. Gen. R. eyeing them sharply.]
[Instant's Tableau as above]

A PAGE FROM THE ORIGINAL MANUSCRIPT OF *SECRET SERVICE*

A PAGE FROM THE ORIGINAL MANUSCRIPT OF SECRET SERVICE

playwright gave them variety; as an actor he gave them unity. These two qualities, the most essential in any product of art, have endowed them with a vitality in his hands which may set a limit to their stage life. For it would be a daring actor who would challenge Gillette's performance in *Secret Service* while the memory of stage generations is awake. Yet notwithstanding its creator's own words, it is a play to read as well as to see, for the spirit of a great epoch in our history is there set glowing against a background of heroic acts and impulses.

What makes this unity of accomplishment all the more significant is that it is based on a long experience during which Gillette saw the decline of the older school of acting, and the rise of the more repressed and delicate art of the theatre. He recognizes that an actor cannot be absolutely true to nature, but that he must constantly study, not simply to reproduce the words of the text, but rather to place himself in the mental and emotional position of the character, who is really only becoming aware of what he is to say, while the actor who represents him knows already just exactly what his lines are to be. Not only in what he says, but also in his actions, the actor must simulate that gradual or sudden birth of motor impulses whose handling or mishandling draws the line between success and failure.

Knowing how deeply their creator has pondered on these and other problems of the actor's art, the characters of Gillette the playwright take on an added significance. For the final judgment upon his position must rest, of course, upon the eight original plays, *The Professor, Held by the Enemy, Secret Service, A Legal Wreck, Ninety Days, Clarice, Electricity,* and *Too Much Johnson,* the last being so largely his creation that it must be included in this category. In these the types are by no means limited. The charm of naturalness not only in the characters he plays, but in the others he has created, like Caroline Mitford, Wilfred Varney, Mrs. Varney, Susan McCreery, Captain Smith, Gordon Hayne, Clarice, Judith Clancy, is that of intelligence. Intelligence, too, is

A HISTORY OF THE AMERICAN DRAMA

the basis of the distinct impression of restrained power for evil made by Mrs. Trent. They are not puppets: they do their own thinking and acting; and their thoughts and actions proceed as though Gillette, once having created them, allowed them to proceed on their own initiative. Of course this is only another way of saying that they are dramatic creations.

They are not parochial, and yet they are American. They are the embodiments of courage, chivalry, loyalty, self-sacrifice, patriotism—these are not the peculiar property of Americans—and yet they represent them in a way that is our own. For the European noblesse oblige they substitute that impelling motive of the responsibility which comes with the very disappearance of permanent caste, and they possess that poise which it is a cherished delusion of European criticism that we fail to possess. Perhaps it was this note of poise, of restraint and self-control, which accounted for Gillette's success in England. For while the British playwrights and British critics have never been overhospitable to our artistic products, everywhere the gentleman recognizes the gentleman.

NOTE TO REVISED EDITION

William Gillette died April 29, 1937.

CHAPTER X

AUGUSTUS THOMAS AND THE PICTURE OF AMERICAN LIFE

WHILE the seventies saw the early struggles of Howard and Harrigan in the East, of Herne and Belasco in the Far West, there was growing up in St. Louis, Missouri, a playwright who stands even more definitely than any of these for the drama of American life. It was the Middle West which produced Augustus Thomas, and the place and the period of his boyhood are similar to those out of which Mark Twain evolved. But while Mark Twain's instincts took him West, Thomas's broader interests made him at home in Alabama, in Arizona, in New York and in Washington. There can be no one play in which all the many facets of our national life may be reflected, but in his work there is the nearest approach to it. Lowell once said, "It is not enough to love one's country, one must be in love with it," and the pages of Thomas's fascinating autobiography reveal an American whose roots are deep in the soil, whose experiences have been native, and who combines a proper sense of patriotism with a broad toleration of all the elements of our national life. He has been a student of the best of the foreign drama, but he has imitated none of it, and his work has been singularly free from mannerisms or methods. He has simply depicted certain forms of native life, certain phases of modern American thought, with a sympathy and an art that have won him wide recognition.

Augustus Thomas was born in St. Louis, January 8, 1857. His father, Dr. Elihu B. Thomas, had served during the Mexican War on General Taylor's staff and raised a company of volunteers on the outbreak of the Civil War. But an old injury prevented his seeing active service, and in 1863 he

239

---

reopened the St. Charles Theatre in New Orleans to provid amusement for the Federal troops. Thomas grew up in democratic surroundings. The family fortunes were not ample, and his education was mainly a series of contacts with life. At the age of eleven, he became a page in the Missouri House of Representatives, and in 1870 went to Washington in a similar capacity. He was a keen, observant boy, and the regular education which circumstances interrupted was well replaced by a broadening intercourse with men and affairs. Here he met, at his uncle's table, E. L. Davenport, James E. Murdoch, and other actors of that generation, and his predilection for drama was strengthened.

In the fall of 1871 he was once more in St. Louis at high school, and at the age of fourteen he began his seven years' experience in the business of transportation with the St. Louis Transfer Company. Later he joined the St. Louis, Kansas City and Northern Railroad. He was also educating himself by wide reading, especially in English poetry.

In his *Print of My Remembrance* Thomas tells of his dramatic beginnings. His first full-length play, *Alone* (1875), was written for the Marion Place Dramatic Club of St. Louis. That Thomas is still a hearty advocate of the amateur dramatic society and of the Little Theatre is proved by these significant lines in his autobiography:

They [his readers] may infer that the money side of the return is of the lesser worth; that the big value is the self-expression obtained; that the debating society, the dramatic club, the singing school, the art class, the pursuits that invite brain to the finger tips, and to become articulate, are the interests that make life eloquent. They may even come to have opinions and to believe that the amount of self-expression encouraged and protected in any country is the measure of liberty in that country.

He was being trained as an actor, too, with this club, which was almost semi-professional. It was the transition period, when the traveling company was coming in, and he had opportunities to fill in as substitute professionally. He became, for

AUGUSTUS THOMAS

the moment, juvenile lead in the company of John W. Norton
and he saw the greatest actors of the day: Booth, Barrett,
Fechter and McCullough.

He gave up at this time, for family reasons, an opportunity
to study painting in Paris, and while it was a keen disappointment at that time, he now believes that the "rough and tumble
education" which he received from the world was of greater
value for the dramatist. He became a master workman in
the Knights of Labor and in 1876 was studying law in the
office of John P. Colby, father of Bainbridge Colby, now his
brother-in-law. But the lure of the theatre was stronger than
that of the law. He had joined the McCullough Club, an
amateur organization of St. Louis, of which he soon became
stage-manager and leading man. His performance of Rogers
in *Esmeralda* links him to the drama of Gillette and he also
was to make use of the dramatic quality of the fiction of Mrs.
Burnett. The story of *Editha's Burglar* in *St. Nicholas*
attracted the attention of Thomas and he dramatized it for
the club. Later it became his first play to be performed professionally. To the central idea, that of a little girl so charming a burglar that he failed to accomplish his purpose, Thomas
added the motive of paternal love by making the burglar the
father of the girl. Her stepfather, who has brought her up
after her mother's death, is devoted to her, and she believes
him to be her father. The anxiety of the child to save her supposed father from the dangers with which the name of burglar
is associated are very naturally expressed. The dramatic climax, in which Bill, her real father, tells her that his little girl
is dead, is also quite simply and effectively done. It is the
moral contrast, which has its perennial appeal on the stage.
But the progress of Thomas's art from *Editha's Burglar* to
The Witching Hour is apparent to any critic who turns the
pages of the manuscript of his first play, with its obvious introduction, its asides and the stilted language of Paul, the father,
much of which was altered during the extensive revisions which
the play underwent. Yet the secret of Thomas's art was

241

already expressed: the knowledge of what will appeal to human sympathies.

About 1880 he definitely abandoned the study of law and became the box-office man for Pope's Theatre in St. Louis. With *Editha's Burglar* and other attractions he organized the Dickson Sketch Club in 1883 and toured Minnesota, Iowa and Missouri towns, going as far south as New Orleans. During this New Orleans engagement Charles Frohman saw the performance of *Editha's Burglar* and arranged for its production by E. H. Sothern. This was the beginning of Thomas's relation to New York. It also led him to rewrite the play as a four-act drama called *The Burglar*, in which the past and future of the robber are woven around the one-act sketch.

Thomas advises would-be playwrights to do three things— read many and good plays, act professionally for a time, and report for a metropolitan newspaper. In 1885 he joined the staff of the St. Louis *Post-Dispatch*, and in his account of his experiences he pays eloquent tribute to the value of that training. During this time he wrote *A Man of the World*, as a newspaper sketch, a one-act play afterward produced at the Madison Square Theatre in 1889. The dialogue is refreshingly real; and very convincing is the way in which Captain Bradley saves a young woman from wrecking her happiness by the application of common sense to the solution of the eternal problem of readjustment to the conditions of early married life. Feeling that the newspaper work was only temporary, he refused flattering offers in Leavenworth, Kansas, and hoped for a New York opening. Yet when Sothern offered to put on *The Burglar* if Thomas would make changes which the playwright felt were inartistic, he refused.

Thomas came East in 1888 to act as manager for Julia Marlowe. He had in his trunk two full-length plays and five or six short ones, and he had a knowledge of theatrical business. He had produced four plays that he had written. But his managerial experience was short and it brought him back to St. Louis to act as advance agent for a mind reader, Wash-

ington Irving Bishop. Some experiences gained in this position led later to the writing of *The Witching Hour.* In June,
1889, his play, *The Burglar,* was produced in Boston with
Maurice Barrymore in the lead. It was successful there and
in New York, and was played for ten years. This led to a
long association with Barrymore, for whom he wrote *Reckless
Temple* (1890), a play based on a newspaper clipping which
told about two men who drew lots from a hat with the understanding that the man who drew the marked card was to
commit suicide.

Thomas has told us how inspiring to a young dramatist
was the association between playwrights and actors at the
Lambs Club and at other meeting places in New York. The
American playwright was coming into his own with the success of *Held by the Enemy, Shenandoah, The Midnight Bell*
and *Lord Chumley.* The Madison Square Theatre was becoming the theatrical center, rivaling the Union Square and
the Star Theatre as fashion was moving north.

In May, 1890, A. M. Palmer, the manager of the Madison
Square Theatre, offered Thomas the position as adaptor or
revisor of foreign plays, which had been occupied by Dion
Boucicault, thus again linking Thomas with the history of the
stage. At Palmer's request, he wrote a one-act play called *A
Constitutional Point,* for Agnes Booth, but it was not produced
until seventeen years later, when it became the germ of *The
Witching Hour.* Instead he produced a one-act play for
Agnes Booth, *Afterthoughts,* in which Thomas himself acted
during its Boston engagement. This may be considered his
period of probation. His next play established his reputation.

Alabama was written first as a one-act play, but realizing the
strength of the characters, Thomas developed a series of situations which have as their central motive the reunited country.
Colonel Preston represents the irreconcilable South, the man
who has driven his son away from him because of Harry Preston's sympathy with the North. Harry, who reappears as
"Captain Davenport," a railroad man, stands for the South-

erner who thinks nationally. Colonel Moberly is the type who stands midway between these extremes. He is chivalric, impetuous, but still is half-reconstructed. Squire Tucker is the type of white citizen whose horizon is quite limited, but who exists in much larger numbers than fiction or drama usually represents. Mrs. Page, Colonel Preston's niece, who had been engaged to Harry Preston but had broken the match because of their close relationship, is drawn as a charming widow and "Captain Davenport" wins her hand at last. The love story of youth, without which a play in the nineties could hardly have succeeded, was also introduced, beginning in the charming garden scene of the first Act. Thomas tells how this scene came to him in a dream. He had seen the city of Talladega some years before, and the picture of an old man and a young girl passing through the half-ruined gateposts of the old estate presented themselves to him.

The keynote of the play is struck in a speech of Captain Davenport:

I respect your feeling in the matter, Colonel Preston, but I can't help thinking that it is your personal view that blinds you. Things, sometimes, are too personal for a correct appreciation. The North and South were two sections when they were a fortnight's journey apart by stages and canals. But now we may see the sun rise in Pennsylvania, and can take supper the same day in Talladega. It is one country. Alabama sends its cotton to Massachusetts—some of it grown very near your graveyards. The garment you have on was woven twenty miles from Boston. Every summer Georgia puts her watermelons on the New York docks. Pennsylvania builds her furnaces at Birmingham. The North took some of your slaves away—yes—but one freight car is worth a hundred of them at transportation. Our resentment, Colonel Preston, is eighteen hundred years behind the sentiment of the day.

The difficulties which native playwrights have been required to surmount are well illustrated by the history of *Alabama*. A. M. Palmer accepted it but had no confidence in its drawing power and withdrew it from rehearsal. But after the failure of three English plays, Palmer ventured to produce *Alabama* on April 1, 1891, at the Madison Square Theatre. The play was an instant success and it not only relieved Thomas of the necessity of acting as an advance agent for Palmer's ventures but also enabled him to resign from his position as revisor of plays and proceed with his own work. *Alabama* won its critical and public approval through its directness and its human quality. Every sentence is brief, but telling, and there is a sense of form which never approaches fine writing but is definitely kept down to the proper level. When the play reached Louisville, Colonel Henry Watterson said publicly that *Alabama* had done more to reconcile the two sections of this country than his editorials had accomplished in twenty years.

Thomas, as was the custom in those days, wrote his plays with a definite actor or actress in mind. *For Money* (1891), which was begun as a serious play, became a farce because the public declined to take William H. Crane seriously. *Colonel Carter of Cartersville* (1892) was better adapted to E. M. Holland, who represented admirably Hopkinson Smith's Southern gentleman. *Surrender*, a Civil War play, although it ran for a month in Boston, beginning on November 21, 1892, was only moderately successful. *Surrender* is laid in or near Richmond during the last days of the Confederacy. The main incident, the attempt to free the Confederate prisoners at Johnson's Island in Lake Erie and attack New York, proved not to be sufficiently well known to make an instant appeal. There is a light touch which carries the play out of the category of *Shenandoah* and *Griffith Davenport*, and to the historian its chief interest lies in the real progress that was made in Thomas's art between *Surrender* and *The Copperhead*.

Thomas returned to the play of locality with *In Mizzoura*. Here he was at home and the characters are real. In his introduction to the published play Thomas tells how he built it up, beginning with the part of the sheriff for Nat Goodwin, and how his visit to the village of Bowling Green suggested the blacksmith, Jo Vernon, for the heroine's father, and the hired helper, Dave, who is one of the best-drawn characters and who, with Elizabeth, the younger daughter, makes up one of the three pairs of lovers. An express robbery gave Thomas the rival to the sheriff for Kate Vernon's affection and the incident of an older man providing the means of educating a girl until she grows above him gave the sheriff a sympathetic part. It is a well-worn motive in drama, but it usually appeals. Thomas provides the hero with a fortune through the discovery of a clay which, when fired, becomes hard as flint, and which was brought to the playwright's attention by a conductor on a Wabash train. A principle of playwriting is illustrated by Thomas's use of this clay. "If you use a property once," he says, "use it again and again if you can. It is a visual thing that binds together your stuff of speech like a dowel in a mission table." So he provided a climax for his second Act by an effective scene with a crippled dog whose wounded leg the sheriff has poulticed with his clay and to whom the sheriff turns when he has been discouraged by Kate's attitude toward him. *In Mizzoura* was first produced in Chicago on August 7, 1893, and came into New York in September. It was a success and became a stock piece.

Thomas was always interested in the relations of capital and labor and in their effect on politics. In 1894 the time seemed ripe for a dramatic treatment of the trusts and Thomas built up a play around a manufacturing company in which Courtland Crandall represented concretely the conservative and his son Van Buren represented the progressive elements in the governing board. When the play opened in Chicago on July 26, 1894, the strike of the Pullman operatives had begun, President Cleveland had interfered to keep the United States mail going, and the company rolled into Chicago between lines of burning freight cars. *New Blood* was a success in Chicago, but failed in New York. Thomas believed the failure was due to a surfeit of labor themes in the daily papers. Charles Frohman attributed it to the fact that the play was definitely a document on the side of labor, to which a New York audience would not respond.

Although it was not a popular success when produced in New York in 1895, Thomas's next play, *The Capitol*, is a masterly study of politics at Washington and financial and religious influences that are brought to bear upon them. Blake, a representative from Nebraska, has come to Washington with ambitions and a wife. Carroll, a railroad lobbyist, obtains a hold on Blake through the latter's desire to be Senator, and Carroll also makes love to Mrs. Blake, who repulses him. Garretson, a well-known author, and the Very Reverend Eustace Kennard are close friends, although holding very opposed religious views. Garretson is especially wrought up over the supposed influence of the Catholic Church on legislation. One form of this influence is represented concretely by Wetmore Boyd. He is a man of culture and of wide knowledge of European conditions who wishes to be an Ambassador. The Administration desires to have a representative at Rome who will be acceptable to the Vatican, and Boyd is offered the position. Garretson is vitally interested in helping the miners who are striking in Pennsylvania and North Carolina, and when Blake's resolution in Congress placing coal on the free list seems in danger, Garretson comes to Kennard to secure his assistance to block the railroad lobby that is trying to prevent the putting of coal on the free list. Kennard arranges through Boyd that certain financial interests shall call their loans to the railroad pool. This prevents the latter's gaining control of the road to Canada over which coal could be sent to break the monopoly. Boyd finally declines the Ambassadorship because he has been accused of obtaining it on account of his contributions to the party.

Thomas knew that economics and politics alone would not make drama. The personal motive is supplied by the relations of Father Kennard and Margaret Doane, who is the leader of the Royal Cross Society. Years before, when he was a rector of a small Episcopal church, they had been married. She was dissatisfied and had left him with her lover, Carroll, taking their daughter Agnes. Finding Carroll out, she had left him and as a penance had devoted herself to social work. Agnes had been brought up in ignorance of her parents and married Blake. The instinctive appeal of Agnes Blake to Kennard for protection without knowing him to be her father, the tragic intensity of the meeting of mother and daughter, the restraint and delicacy of the final parting of Kennard and Margaret, are characteristic of Thomas. He was dealing with forces that are real and powerful, and his knowledge of politics enabled him to portray the more subtle methods of control over legislation which in 1894 had not been revealed in drama. We are spared the usual flourish of money in large packages, and we are also spared the description of the sufferings of the strikers.

The most difficult theme in this play is the treatment of the Church. In order that his picture should be correct, the playwright submitted *The Capitol* to a prelate in Washington, and indeed no member of that Church should feel disturbed by the characterization of Father Kennard or Wetmore Boyd. Father Kennard is one of the few stage clergymen who seem real, and Wetmore Boyd is a representative of the cultivated Catholic who in this country seldom appears in general literature.

It is evident that at this period Thomas felt that he had written himself out. He was discouraged by the comparative failure of his two serious studies of American conditions, and the postponement of his carefully studied play on the youth of Washington, *Colonel George of Mount Vernon*. During the next two years he was marking time, rewriting earlier plays or dramatizing the published work of others, and it was not until he had refreshed himself with visits to new fields that he returned to significant original work.

In March, 1897, Thomas went to Arizona to collect material for a new play. How close was his observation, and how stimulating, are revealed both in his autobiography and in the play itself. For *Arizona* is reality—here is the West painted in primary colors, but with no exaggeration. From the moment the curtain rises on the courtyard of the Aravaipa Ranch, the conversation between Colonel Bonham and his father-in-law, Henry Canby, the owner of the ranch, reveals two types which govern the West of Arizona. Life has broadened Canby, who is one of the best-drawn figures in modern drama, but army tradition and discipline have narrowed Bonham. When the climax of the play arrives and Estrella, the Colonel's wife, is found in Lieutenant Denton's company late at night, and Denton's refusal to explain his presence leads to his enforced resignation from the army, the different ways in which Bonham and Canby react to the charge of theft, which Denton faces to save Estrella's honor, are in perfect keeping with their natures and their training. *Arizona* is not remarkable in its plot. The Colonel and the Colonel's lady and the two officers, one of whom is a cad and the other a gentleman, go back to *Shenandoah* and beyond it. Even a closer parallel to the climax of the play may be found in *The Galley Slave* and in Sardou's *Nos Bons Villageois*. But Thomas seems to have been inspired by real people whom he placed in well-tested dramatic situations, and he was not above substituting the Spanish War for an Indian uprising when events made it advisable. When one looks back on *Arizona*, however, it is not Estrella and her love affairs that one remembers. It is Bonita, her younger sister, Denton's sweetheart, who becomes the heroine. She was drawn from a real woman, and she has the freshness and the open-mindedness which do not prevent her from being alluring. Tony, the *vaquero*, is one of the most vivid of the characters. Captain Hodgman, whose attempted flight with Estrella has placed Denton in his false position, had seduced Lina, the daughter of Sergeant Kellar. When this fact is discovered, Kellar threatens to shoot Hodgman, but Tony, who loves Lina, wastes no time in threats. He shoots Hodgman on sight, and at the first opportunity departs on the swiftest horse on the ranch. It is the justice which the West understands, and Canby puts their standard in a few brief sentences, which Thomas took from the conversation of his prototype:

Canby: (*Pause*) Er—a—Captain Denton. (*Pause.*) You know I—er— (*Pause. Bonita goes to Canby, who puts an arm about her.*) We take a man on here and ask no questions. We know when he throws his saddle on his horse, whether he understands his business or not. He may be a minister backslidin', or a banker savin' his last lung, or a train robber on his vacation—we don't care. A good many of our most useful men have made their mistakes. All we care about now is, will they stand the gaff? Will they set sixty hours in the saddle, holdin' a herd that's tryin' to stampede all the time? Now, without makin' you any fine talk, you can give any-one of 'em the fifteen ball. I don't know whether it's some-thin' you learned in the school, or whether you just happened to pick the right kind of a grandfather, or what. But your equal has never been in this territory in my time.

It was a far cry from *Arizona* to *Oliver Goldsmith,* first pro-duced in Albany on November 30, 1899, and written for Stu-art Robson because he looked like Oliver Goldsmith. Thomas points out in his introduction to the printed play that the dramatist's failure in drawing a historical character is usually due to his attempt to cover "all the attractive incidents in a biography rather than to grasp formally and treat thoroughly the principal dramatic happening." The greatest event in Goldsmith's life was the production of *She Stoops to Conquer.* Thomas, therefore, made Goldsmith's conception and produc-tion of that play and the consequence of its success the mo-tives of his own drama. He placed the first Act in an English country house which Goldsmith mistakes for an inn, and he surrounded him with a group of which Samuel Johnson, Ed-mund Burke, David Garrick, James Boswell and Mary Horn-eck are the main figures. In the second Act *She Stoops to Conquer* is in rehearsal on the stage of the Covent Garden The-atre and there is a clever scene in which Garrick shows the rival company how to produce the play. In the last Act, laid in Goldsmith's garret, the struggle in his heart between his

Best wishes
Augustus Thomas

love for Mary and his feeling that he is not a fit husband provides the element of conflict, which is not indeed very convincing. Atmosphere rather than action is the salient quality of *Oliver Goldsmith*, but the picture of Eighteenth Century character and setting is thoroughly well done.

Although Thomas journeyed to the West again in search of material for his next play, *Colorado* was not a success, and he turned from the depiction of American life in its more significant phrases to the production of light comedy, bordering on farce. Indeed even before *Colorado* was produced, Thomas had built up from a real incident an amusing play, first called *Treadway of Yale*, but later rechristened *On the Quiet*. A young actor had allowed his marriage with a wealthy girl to be postponed until he had gone through college, at the stipulation of her family, who agreed to support him during his course at Harvard. When they had safely separated the lovers, they calmly notified the actor that the support was withdrawn. In *On the Quiet*, Bob Treadway and Agnes Colt are secretly married before he enters Yale, and the manner in which he meets all the complications of the situation until her brother apparently forces him into the marriage reminds one of the imperturbable heroes of Gillette.

For this type of comedy, it is essential that the circumstances should constantly threaten to engulf the hero, and Thomas showed a remarkable ability in making plausible situations which by their unusual quality render the position of the central character insecure. In *The Earl of Pawtucket* (1903), the idea of an English nobleman representing himself as an American in order to pursue a charming American woman, who is really the divorced wife of the man whose name he has taken, seems at first glance absurd. But it is just the stupidity, courage and good breeding so characteristic of the type of British gentleman the Earl represents which bring him safely through complications before which a more agile mind would have faltered. Thomas wrote the play for Lawrence D'Orsay, an English actor who had played in only minor parts, and against the judgment of a practical manager like Charles Frohman, he scored a popular success. In *The Other Girl* (1903), the attempted elopement of Catherine Fulton, a girl of refinement, with an engaging prize fighter, and the substitution of Estelle Kitteridge, who risks her own reputation and her ultimate happiness to save her friend from committing an act of folly, again seem far-fetched. But once more the art of the playwright presented a plausible series of situations, including the arrest of the prize fighter and his companion for running over the *fiancé* of Catherine Fulton. *Mrs. Leffingwell's Boots* (1905) is a clever portrayal of the havoc that may be made by an irresponsible young man who has been injured by a blow on the head and who yet remains at large. Dick Ainslie has preyed upon his friend Walter Corbin, forged his name, and by placing the boots of Mrs. Leffingwell at his door has brought upon him the jealousy of her husband and broken Corbin's engagement to Mabel Ainslie. But this serious side of the shield is kept as dark as possible while a series of amusing complications takes place at and after a dinner party during "the worst snowstorm since Conkling died." Dick is cured by osteopathy and the last sentence reveals the fact that Corbin had suffered all this obloquy patiently because his hand had accidentally struck the blow which made Dick abnormal.

Thomas knew that the essence of light comedy is relief. He therefore never let it descend into mere fooling, but there was always in the structure of the play some note of sincerity. The Earl of Pawtucket might have avoided some of his difficulties if he had not been so thoroughly a gentleman. Estelle Kitteridge could have cleared herself by a word had it not been for the gratitude she felt for benefits unforgot. Walter Corbin suffered silently until his accidental victim was restored to sanity. The central characters win over circumstances—that is comedy. But they also win and keep the sympathy of the audience. That is the reason for the response which these plays evoked at the time and which they still secure for the more permanent audience of the printed page.

Thomas has always been acutely aware of the period in which he worked. In the early nineties the clever stories of Richard Harding Davis and the equally clever illustrations of Charles Dana Gibson were establishing types of men and women which have now become conventional. Thomas dramatized *Soldiers of Fortune* (1902), a novelette out of which Davis had himself made a play, and he built up from the pictures of Gibson an entertaining comedy, *The Education of Mr. Pipp* (1905), in which the selfmade man, slight physically but with shrewd common sense, is led through England and France by his aggressive wife, accompanied by his daughters and their lovers. The best element in these adaptations was the conversation, which at least in the second case was largely of Thomas's invention. His resourcefulness is shown also by his quick turning of failure into success with *The Embassy Ball* in 1906. But his desire to work with more enduring material sent him back to a motive which had interested him for many years and which led to the writing of his most successful play.

In 1890 Thomas had written a one-act play for A. M. Palmer, called *A Constitutional Point*. It was not acted then, but after trying it out at the Lambs Club sixteen years later, Thomas was encouraged to build on it a four-act play. The first sketch dealt with telepathy, and grew out of his association in 1888 with Washington Irving Bishop. He pictured an elderly judge who had in his youth been in love with a girl who was fond of the odor of mignonette. Her daughter comes to plead with the judge to save her boy who is under sentence of death for murder. She hands him an old letter, written by him to her mother, who had kept it among her papers. The odor seems to the judge a symbol of the departed girl and he believes he has been in communion with her spirit. Bret Harte's *Newport Legend*, Thomas tells us, was the primary inspiration for this motive, which animates the second Act of *The Witching Hour*. But the playwright knew that this motive was not sufficient for a full-length play and he added to it the theme of hypnotism and the responsibility a person assumes who influences the mind of another. Clay Whipple, the boy whose mother has appealed to Justice Prentice, has a great fear of a cat's-eye and strikes and accidentally kills a man who annoys him with a pin containing such a stone. This takes place at the gambling establishment, in Louisville, of Jack Brookfield, a man who is above his business, and who has lost the chance to marry Clay's mother, Helen, through her dislike of his occupation. Brookfield has hypnotic power. Clay is convicted of murder, but the case is appealed on the ground that the trial has not been public, admission having been restricted to those favored by the district attorney, Hardmuth, Clay's disappointed rival in love. Justice Prentice at Helen's appeal orders a new trial. In an interview with Brookfield he shows the danger of the use of the hypnotic power. Brookfield asks him, "You mean it's bad for the man who tries it?" and the judge replies: "I mean that it constantly opens to the investigator new mental heights, higher planes—and every man, Mr. Brookfield, is ill in some manner who lives habitually on a lower level—than the light he sees."

Brookfield determines, however, to save Clay by this power. While the jury is deliberating, he publishes in the newspaper his accusation that Hardmuth has organized the plot by which a former governor had been murdered. He believes that the thousands who read this accusation will by the combined effect of their belief in it, so influence the minds of the jury against Hardmuth that his conduct of the case will react in favor of Clay and lead to the boy's acquittal. This proves true, and Hardmuth bursts into Brookfield's rooms intending to shoot him. Brookfield flashes a large drop light into his face and with the words, "You can't shoot—that gun—you can't even hold it," hypnotizes Hardmuth so that he drops the derringer in amazement. This scene, which was put on in fear and trembling, proved successful on the stage. That it does not represent accurately the process of hypnotism is of less importance than the fact of its apparent effect upon the audience. But Thomas does not leave the matter here. In the last Act he establishes the main motive of the play through Brookfield's journey across the state line with Hardmuth to save the latter from the consequences of the accusation. Brookfield gives Helen the reason:

Long before Scovill was killed, I thought he deserved killing and I thought it could be done just as it was done. . . . I never breathed a word to a living soul, but Hardmuth planned it exactly as I dreamed it, and by God, a guilty thought is almost as criminal as a guilty deed.

The part of Jack Brookfield was taken by John Mason, who gave a remarkable interpretation of the mingled lights and shades of the gentleman gambler's character. He is an outstanding figure, as is Justice Prentice, for both represent power and chivalry. It is essentially a man's play, for the women's parts are secondary in interest, though not negligible. Its greatest significance lies in its competent adaptation to drama of the theme of the occult, handled with discrimination, and never suffered to become too abstract.

The success of *The Witching Hour* and the belief that the public were interested in themes which savored of the less obvious phases of human influence and relationship, prompted Thomas to the writing of *The Harvest Moon*, first produced in October, 1909. Its theme was the sinister effect of suggestions of evil which are planted in the mind of a young girl by her aunt, one of those women who are never happy unless they control the actions of others. Dora Fullerton desires to become an actress, and her temperament makes her susceptible to the reception of such ideas. Her mother had gone to Paris to study and had finally been divorced from Professor Marshall Fullerton and married to M. Vavin, a French playwright. They had quarreled and Vavin in a fit of pique had told his wife that they were not legally married. When Dora is born Madame Vavin does not inform him and at her mother's death

Fullerton finds the baby and brings her up as his own. His sister, Cornelia, who feels that her brother's life has been ruined, plants in Dora's mind the belief that her mother was unreliable, impulsive and vain, and that she will inherit these qualities. Consequently she almost wrecks her own life when her family's opposition to the theatre and to her lover, a young playwright, calls for courage and decision. The visit of M. Vavin to this country and his delicate handling of the situation make the play. Vavin plants countersuggestions skilfully, and brings his daughter and her lover together in his apartment, using the subtle influence of colors in the production of moods. This scene, which was first tried out as a one-act play at the Lambs Club and has been recently revived with George Nash, the original creator of the part of Vavin, is remarkably effective, considering the difficulty of portraying such abstract themes on the stage. *The Harvest Moon* was an artistic rather than a popular success. The theme is too remote perhaps for general interest, and Thomas's evident care not to overstress the emotional relations of the central characters makes them less quick in their appeal.

Thomas carried over to his next original play, *As a Man Thinks*, produced in New York March 13, 1911, the idea of mental healing, but he incorporated it in a much more vivid and compelling personality, that of the liberal Jewish doctor, Samuel Seelig. As before, he tried the effect of a one-act play at The Lambs in which this doctor should cure a patient by driving out the ideas that were making him ill. As this sketch was well received he built up a play of four acts in which he added the theme that the trust of man in his wife's fidelity is the basic fact of our civilization, and he joined these themes through the character of Dr. Seelig, into a compact and vigorous drama. In it Thomas gave the answer to the sentimental discussion of the double standard of morality which is rampant in literature. Frank Clayton, a prosperous magazine proprietor, neglects his wife, who, in a moment of exasperation, visits the rooms of Benjamin De Lota, a Jew to whom

AUGUSTUS THOMAS

she had been engaged before she met Clayton. Clayton orders her to leave his house, but Dr. Seelig tells him their boy's life is in danger and Clayton leaves himself. In the next act, Dr. Seelig, in answer to Elinor's protest against the unfairness of the world's judgments, replies:

Seelig: Elinor. [*Pause.*] Do you hear that rattle of the railroad?
Elinor: Yes.
Seelig: All over this great land thousands of trains run every day starting and arriving in punctual agreement because this is *a woman's world*. The great steamships, dependable almost as the sun—a million factories in civilization—the countless looms and lathes of industry—the legions of labor that weave the riches of the world—all—all move by the mainspring of man's faith in woman—man's *faith*.
Elinor: I want *him* to have faith in me.
Seelig: This old world hangs together by love.
Mrs. Seelig: Not man's love for woman.
Seelig: No—nor woman's love for man, but by the love of both—for the children.
Elinor: Dick!
Seelig: Men work for the children because they believe the children are—their own—*believe*. Every mother *knows* she is the mother of her son or daughter. Let her be however wicked, no power on earth can shake that knowledge. Every father believes he is a father only by his faith in the woman. Let him be however virtuous, no power on earth can strengthen in him a conviction greater than that faith. There is a double standard of morality because upon the golden basis of woman's virtue rests the welfare of the world.

Clayton, maddened by the disclosure of Elinor's engagement to De Lota, of which he had been ignorant, doubts even that Dick is his son. He becomes ill through brooding over the matter and Dr. Seelig cures him of his delusion by a literal application of the teachings of Christ. "There is nothing so disappointing," Dr. Seelig says, "as a satisfied revenge." Without sentimentality, with just enough but not too much repression of emotion, Thomas reunites the family. No one who has had a child can see or read the last Act of *As a Man Thinks* without recognizing that the playwright has placed on the stage the inexorable truth, but represented it in the spirit of the Seer who modified the justice of the Old Law by the mercy of the New. As in *The Capitol*, the liberality with which Thomas views life enabled him to treat a difficult theme without offense, and his skill brought on the stage real people, who talk in brief, natural sentences, with not a word wasted. John Mason made a deep impression as Dr. Seelig and Chrystal Herne "*was* Mrs. Clayton," to quote the playwright's phrase.

It would seem that after a remarkably productive period, a dramatist must allow his creative powers to lie fallow or else it is likely that he will not produce work that is representative of his inventive powers at their best. Several of Thomas's plays from 1911 to 1917 were done in collaboration or were rewriting of other material like *Three of Hearts*. *Indian Summer* (1913) contains a sympathetic study of an artist in his forties, who wins the love of a girl because she learns to see beauty through his eyes. But the play does not hang together although the dialogue is crisp and telling. *Rio Grande*, produced first in Chicago in 1916, was laid on our borders during the trouble with Mexico, which entered into the play very little. The plot is reminiscent of *Arizona*, for it has to do with an illicit love affair between the Colonel's wife and a young officer. The difference lies in the real guilt of the lovers and the tragic suicide of the lieutenant, off the stage. But notwithstanding an eloquent plea of the Major's wife for forgiveness on the Colonel's part, because the experience will be of spiritual value to the young wife, the audience remained cold.

In *The Copperhead*, which opened at Hartford in January, 1918, Thomas triumphed over almost insuperable difficulties in order to produce the effect he desired. He took from a story by Frederic Landis, *The Glory of His Country*, the idea of a patriot serving his cause by pretending to be a sympathizer with the Confederacy, and thereby circumventing the movements of that body of Northern men who were organized to

AUGUSTUS THOMAS

obstruct the United States Government. Of course, a similar motive had occurred in *The Spy* and in Woodworth's *The Widow's Son*, and Thomas's treatment was free.

From the dramatic point of view, it is hard to keep an audience in ignorance of the spy's real character; indeed, Thomas does not attempt to do so. Milt Shanks, a farmer on an Illinois farm, is just a plain, apparently commonplace person. Yet Lincoln, who had been his neighbor, knows his man, and when the plays opens, Shanks is represented as a member of the "Knights of the Golden Circle" or "Copperheads," as they were called, from the insignia which they wore at the beginning of the struggle. The first two Acts are striking pictures of a little Illinois farming village at the outbreak of the war and at the fall of Vicksburg. It is a faithful portrayal of life which Thomas knew at first hand. Shanks brings upon himself the hatred of his neighbors, the intolerance which war always produces, and even his wife and son shrink from him. When Joey is killed at Vicksburg the boy leaves word with "Newt" Gillespie that his father is not to see him in his coffin, and the tragedy of the loneliness of the man is infinitely touching. Forty years later, Shanks is an old man, and under the stress of his fear that his granddaughter will lose her appointment at the school on account of his past, he breaks his silence in one of the most moving utterances of our stage. Thomas with a fine instinct represented the influence of Lincoln through the life mask of his face and hand. It seemed as though Lincoln were indeed present, so vividly did the words as spoken by Lionel Barrymore project his spirit into that commonplace room.

Shanks: Colonel, do you recollec' the time you druv me to the train in March o' sixty-one?
Hardy: Very well. You went to look at cattle.
Shanks: That's what I told you. I wuz called to Washington by Lincoln, an' two days later, at night, in his library—White House—he walked over to'erd a winder, and without turning round he says: "Milt—" Funny I remember a clock tickin'

259

on the mantelpiece—I sez: "Mr. President—" (*Pause.*) "Milt, how much do you love yer country?" (*Pause.*) "I cahilate I'd die fur it," I sez. "Thousands o' boys is a-cryin' to do that," he sez. Then he turned round. "Would you give up sumpin' more'n life?" "Try me," I sez. The President run his hands through his hair an' went on: "It means to be odious in the eyes of men and women—ter eat yer heart out—alone—fer yer can't tell yer wife—ner child—ner friend." "Go on," I sez. "The Southern sympathizers are organizing in our state—really worse than the soldiers. I want you ter jine them Knights o' the Golden Circle, the Copperheads—ter be one of them—their leader, if you kin. I need you, Milt. Yer country needs you." (*Pause.*) Hadn't been two minutes since he was laffin', but he lifted his hands, and it seemed we wuz the only folks in the world—and that clock—funny I remember that. (*Pause.*) "I'll do it," I sez. He tuk a little flag out o' his pocket—like as not this very one—put it on the table like I'm puttin' it. (*Pause.*) "As Chief Magistrate of the Nation, I'll muster you inter the Nation's service," he said. He took my hand and laid it where the blue is and all the stars, and put his hand over mine. Only open, of course—and said nuthin'—jes' looked in my eyes—an' looked—(*Pause.*) Well, I jined 'em. It was terrible, when I couldn't tell my boy—

The stress of war made the audiences more than usually responsive, but even when read in calmer moments, *The Copperhead* stirs the sense of national feeling. It is significant that of the five best plays of the Civil War, four should have a spy for a leading character, but unlike *Held by the Enemy*, *Secret Service* and *Griffith Davenport*, *The Copperhead* has no chivalric figure. He is individual, but he is also a type of the undistinguished American, the average man, who in times of national peril shows the potential devotion to his country which has led him to give his best without display. The patriotic hero has always been a favorite subject for drama, but as the race becomes more self-conscious his rôle becomes more difficult to establish to a sophisticated audience. It was a difficult task, also, to preserve any unity, with such an interval, and yet it is questionable whether the effect could have been secured without it. For as the old man goes on in his halting utterance, the sense of the forty years of spiritual exile in his native town makes his words poignant with the dignity that memory gives to sacrifice.

Since *The Copperhead* Thomas has not produced any very significant plays. *Speak of the Devil* (1920) is a melodrama, in which the love story of a returned war worker, Mildred Hanslow, and a French marquis whom she has nursed, turns from a promising beginning into a chaotic plot. *Nemesis* (1921) was a serious attempt to show the futility of the evidence based on the impression taken from the finger tips of a supposed criminal. Louis Jovaine, a sculptor, is in love with Marcia Kallan and her husband lays a trap for him. Kallan secures an impression of Jovaine's finger prints from some clay which he takes from the studio and he has rubber stamps made from these impressions. He then forces his wife to call Jovaine to their apartment and during the interval of waiting he kills Marcia and distributes the marks of her lover's fingers over the room and on the instrument with which he has killed her. Jovaine is convicted. The weakness of the play lies in the absence of anyone with whom the audience may sympathize. Interest is first directed toward the husband, but his cold-blooded action in laying the trap chills any feeling of compassion for him, and the playwright does not succeed in transferring it to the lover or the wife, who treats her marital obligations in too casual a fashion.

Still Waters, a propaganda play directed against the prohibition of liquor, attracted wide attention when it was performed at Washington, September 7, 1925, with Thomas taking the leading part, that of a Senator who votes for prohibition because his constituents desire it, but who promises himself to vote as he believes if he is elected again. It suffers from the defect of all propaganda plays and while the conversation is direct and telling, the character drawing does not rise to that of his great moments. In the character of Senator Clayborn, Thomas represented that intense love for personal liberty of action which has been characteristic of the man as well as the playwright.

Indeed, one may question whether this love of liberty, in the truly American sense, is not the controlling motive in the selection of themes by Augustus Thomas. The most obvious characterization of his work as a whole would be that he stands first, for the description of definite sections and of distinct phases of American life, as in *Alabama, Arizona* and *The Copperhead,* and second, for the reflection in drama of modes and problems of modern interest, such as the hypnotism and telepathy of *The Witching Hour,* the moral suggestion of *The Harvest Moon* and the double standard of morality in *As a Man Thinks.* These are certainly the backgrounds and the motives in which he has been most at home, and they prove conclusively the native quality of his talent.

But back of motive and scene there is always the theme and a more searching analysis of Thomas's work reveals a basic interest in those situations in which a human being becomes the center of a struggle between the intense desire for personal liberty and the circumstances which obstruct that desire in its fulfillment. The roots of all significant drama have, of course, lain in the struggle of the individual against fate or his surroundings. But the importance of Thomas's contribution lies in the distinctly American way he has treated that theme. Liberty is desirable, but in the European drama of revolt it is so desirable that everything else, from the family to the state, must go down before it. In Thomas's plays, as in the vast majority of American lives, the individual's liberty is precious, but the conflict for its preservation is constructive, not merely destructive. The prejudice of Colonel Preston, in *Alabama,* which had crushed two lives, had to break down before the wider liberty of the reunited country. The strict discipline of the army, impersonated in Colonel Bonham in *Arizona,* is contrasted with the free life of the ranch where natural standards permit Denton to defy an artificial code. In *The Capitol,* Father Kennard represents the use through the

Church of financial pressure to save the individual liberty of the new Senator and to prevent the tyranny of monopoly. Jack Brookfield, in *The Witching Hour*, has tasted the delights of individual liberty to the full. He has lost much in doing so, and he realizes, when the knowledge of his hypnotic power comes to him, that power brings responsibility with it and that his liberty has to be merged into a wider usefulness. It has been shown in the analysis of *As a Man Thinks* how the claims of woman to share the liberty of man in sex morality have been rendered abortive not by moral standards but by the justice of nature. More privilege, more responsibility, is the universal situation. In *The Copperhead*, Milt Shanks lays on the altar of his country's need the right even to his wife's love and to his son's respect. But whatever the characters give up in relinquishing individual freedom returns in the only final reward of human conduct, the consciousness of their own self-respect.

It is not necessary to insist that this basic theme is exclusively American, but it is expressed in any case by Augustus Thomas in a native fashion. It is certainly profoundly true to human nature as represented by the normal man and woman in the United States, and it may well be that the potential liberty of a republic leads definitely to a sense of constructive responsibility, just as the potential subjection of a monarchy leads to the celebration of personal revolt.

From the purely artistic point of view, Thomas's plays are decidedly uneven in merit, and yet his construction and dialogue are not different so much in kind as in degree of excellence. The plays in which the themes are largest, and the motives most significant, are constructed with the finest skill and are provided with well-rounded characters who speak that clear straightforward language which is so economical of the hearer's attention. When Thomas became too abstract or dealt with a theme almost too subtle for the theatre, as in *The Harvest Moon*, the brilliant dialogue could not save the play. When he descended to trivialities of plot or situation, as in *Speak of the Devil,* or labored in developing a theme not really interesting, as in *Nemesis,* the charm is of course not there. But in his best period, from *Arizona* to *The Copper-head,* he was the playwright to whom America turned with confidence for the drama that clothes significant ideas with power and restraint and the comedy that delights through kindly and adroit revelation of human frailty, and for that twenty years it did not turn in vain.

NOTE TO REVISED EDITION

Augustus Thomas died August 12, 1934 at the Clarkstown Country Club, near Nyack, New York State.

CHAPTER XI

CLYDE FITCH was the product of two very different American traditions. His father, William Goodwin Fitch, went from Hartford, Connecticut, with his regiment during the Civil War and found at Hagerstown, Maryland, his future wife, Alice Clark, whose family were loyal to the Union. The influence of his mother, who came of a race that loved beauty in costume and background, is strong in Clyde Fitch, but there is also a trace of the New England sense of ethical values in the author of *The Truth* and *The City*.

William Clyde Fitch was born at Elmira, New York, May 2, 1865, his early childhood being spent in Schenectady, where, like John Howard Payne, he organized and directed groups of children in productions of various kinds. Even in his school days at Hartford and at the Holderness School in New Hampshire, he showed that independence of public opinion which reveals character but which pays the tribute the tribe demands of those who are indifferent to the fetish of uniformity. Clyde Fitch's letters from his boarding school reveal, however, a fairly normal boy, learning Latin and Greek and French rather easily, taking part in sports when his slight physique permitted, and objecting strenuously to being considered "delicate." At Amherst College, which he entered in 1882, he pursued his self-determined course, wearing clothes which were the theme of campus comment but winning his recognized place as one of the leaders of the dramatic interests of Amherst. He not only acted such parts as Lydia Languish in *The Rivals* and Peggie Thrift in *The Country Girl*, but he directed Wycherley's play, painted scenery and designed costumes. His

265

facility in composition had already declared itself, for he composed an entire act for a college burlesque opera in an afternoon, and his letters reveal the love for the stage which was to become the great passion of his life. A constant contributor of social verse to his college magazine and the Class Poet of '86, his own taste led him toward literature as a career, but his father desired him to study architecture and disliked the stage.

Like Bronson Howard, Fitch went to New York in 1886 to conquer a position. While waiting for his opportunity, he made a living by tutoring, by readings, and by occasional short stories, and he was haunting the theatres. His first European visit came in 1888 and made a deep impression upon his instinctive love for the concretely beautiful. Here he wrote the first draft of *Frédérick Lemaître*.

At last his opportunity came. Richard Mansfield had, at the suggestion of William Winter, selected Beau Brummell, the Georgian dandy, as a fit character around whom a play could be written. Dithmar, the critic of the New York *Times*, suggested to Mansfield in November, 1889, that Clyde Fitch could write such a play and a contract was made by which Fitch was engaged to write for Mansfield on salary and royalty. To Fitch the character and the setting appealed strongly and he began work at once, reading first the play on Beau Brummell by Blanchard Jerrold, and the *Life of George Brummell*, by William Jesse, on which it had been based. Fitch received many suggestions from Mansfield, to whom naturally he deferred as to an older man and a successful actor who had himself written plays. From Jerrold's play, which is laid in Calais and Caen, he took the idea of Brummell's befriending a young *protégé* who desires to marry the daughter of a rich merchant. In *Beau Brummell* this motive is intensified by the substitution of his own nephew, and the attempt of Brummell to save himself by a rich marriage which he relinquishes for his nephew's sake. Other incidents, such as the appearance of the imaginary guests just before his death, are found in the older play and indicated in Jesse's biography.[1] Fitch followed the narrative less closely than Jerrold and laid the first three Acts in England, transferring the arrest of Brummell for debt to London, for the effective climax of the third Act.

How difficult became the task of writing a play for Mansfield is apparent in Fitch's letters, and the project was indeed for a time abandoned. But on May 19, 1890, *Beau Brummell* was performed at the Madison Square Theatre and made a profound impression upon the discriminating critics, even if others were unable to see even its more obvious merits. At the very beginning of his career Fitch was to meet that lack of understanding on the part of those who should have comprehended the delicacy and distinction of his art, but also from the outset there were minds capable of anticipating the calmer judgment of time.[2] For *Beau Brummell* has taken its secure place in dramatic literature. The episodic nature of its scenes, the preference of dialogue to action which disturbed the judgment of the early nineties, could not prevent the substantial success of this masterpiece of the comedy of manners. *Beau Brummell* is essentially a play built upon a striking personality, whose wit, polish, even whose heartlessness, made him "good theatre," while at just the right moment, Fitch lets the essentially heroic character of his creation shine through the mask of his personality and dominate the situation. This heroic quality was largely the creation of the playwright, for the real George Brummell was a gentleman who lived an apparently selfish life and died a miserable death in exile. The two qualities the playwright took from his original were courage and social ease. Such episodes as the cutting of Brummell by the Prince of Wales and the retort of Brummell—"Sherry, who's your fat friend?"—are traditional rather than historic. The climax of the second Act, in which Brummell, after defending Vincent, the city merchant, from the consequences of

---

[1] Jesse, Captain [William], *The Life of George Brummell*, 2v. London, 1844, II, 293–4.

[2] See the appreciative and penetrating critique by "Fileur" in *The Theatre Magazine*, VI (1890), 440–1, to which are appended reviews of a contradictory nature in the daily press.

his folly and drawing upon himself the anger of the Prince, says to the latter, "Wales, ring the bell," was chosen from among the anecdotes which Jesse [1] states are apocryphal. But the character as shown in Jesse's account grows in stature in the play, and the loyalty of Mortimer, the valet, contrasts sharply with the treachery of Isidore, Brummell's own valet. The loyalty of the servant is a fine dramatic motive, for it implies qualities in a master which do not appear on the surface, especially in such a hero as Brummell, to whom restraint is so essential.

Into the heated controversy over the authorship of the play which raged at the time of its production it is not necessary here to go. [2] Fitch's own words sum up the situation:

> The idea of a play on *Beau Brummell* is, I believe, Mr. William Winter's. The execution of that play—Mr. Winter claims it has been an execution in more senses than one—some of the business and the great bulk of the dialogue are mine. The artistic touch, some of the lines in the comedy (not the important ones), and the genius that has made it a success are Mr. Mansfield's.

To any student of Clyde Fitch's plays, his touch shows unmistakably in *Beau Brummell*. Among the talents of Fitch the three most prominent—the ability to visualize any place or period in terms of its social values, the power to incarnate virtues or vices in characters who are essentially dramatic, and the gift of writing clever dialogue—all these show in his first stage success. While no attempt was made at historical accuracy, for George IV and Sheridan were kept alive for years in order to attend Brummell's death scene, the vanity, the heartlessness, the cold calculating immorality of the age, which are typified in the person of George IV, live on the stage. Beau Brummell, who meets ruin without the flicker of an eyelid, was the first of those searching studies of men and women pos-

---

[1] I, 254–5.

[2] See Winter, William, *Life and Art of Richard Mansfield*, New York, 1910, I, 128–36; II, 63–88, 301–12, written with prejudice and containing obvious misstatements; *Clyde Fitch and His Letters*, esp. pp. 65–8, which contain Fitch's letter in the Boston *Evening Transcript*, April 13, 1891.

sessed by one absorbing trait, later to be joined by Becky Warder and Jinny Austin. The language of the characters is suited exactly to their parts, still a bit conventional, for *Beau Brummell* is essentially of the theatre. "Asides" are not infrequent and every other part was subordinated to the demands of the star. Mansfield was not an easy man to work for and even the ending had to be changed to suit his anticipation of popular judgment. Fitch wished to have the Beau die in his poverty. Mansfield insisted on a happy ending and suggested that the King be reconciled with Brummell. Fitch wrote, as a compromise, based partially on the older play, the scene in which the Beau's friends come back in his fancy and reappear in the flesh only at the time of his death.

If this did not furnish a happy ending it did provide a happy compromise, for in Mansfield's hands it was a fitting climax to an almost perfect union of playwright and actor. The part was exactly suited to Mansfield and he kept it in his répertoire until he left the stage. The relation between Fitch and Mansfield did not continue, although Mansfield more than once made overtures to him. Clyde Fitch, however, had secured his start.

His one-act plays, *Frédérick Lemaître* and *Betty's Finish,* were produced in Boston in December, 1890. Of these, *Frédérick Lemaître* is of especial interest for, although it was produced after *Beau Brummell*, it had been originally written in 1888 in Paris. It is a charming character study laid in that city in 1848. Lemaître is an actor who, in order to prove to Madeleine Fleury, a young stage-struck milliner, that she will never succeed, improvises a scene in which a young husband who has been abandoned by his wife acts the rôle of a broken-hearted man. Lemaître has hoped to charm her by his conduct, but the vividness of his portrayal sends her back to her own lover whom she thought of deserting for the stage. The characters are well conceived and the ability of Fitch to sense a period and portray a man who is establishing his purpose by indirect means is clearly shown. Fitch even used the real name of a French actor who long held a foremost position on the French stage.

Recognition came quickly from abroad, for Fitch was commissioned to write a play for Mrs. John Wood, to be produced at the Royal Court Theatre in 1891. *Pamela's Prodigy* is an amusing farce comedy, laid in London and on the sands of Margate about 1830. The dialogue is bright, but the play has no very great distinction. It was the first of his plays to be published and was charmingly illustrated by Virginia Gerson. Clyde Fitch was still primarily a man of letters. His novel, *A Wave of Life*, had appeared in 1891, but he wisely abandoned the field of fiction for one in which his talent could be more adequately shown.

A Modern Match, produced March 14, 1892, at the Union Square Theatre, was his first full-length play of modern social life. It is a study of the vain and selfish woman who leaves her husband at the moment of his financial ruin, and returning twelve years later is refused admittance to her daughter's wedding. The "asides," the artificial nature of the dialogue in certain portions, cannot conceal the cleverness of the playwright who covers with deft touches the thin plot and conventional situations by a mantle of interest. But the play is of most significance through its revelation of the advance Fitch made in the art of his later period. When Mr. and Mrs. Kendal produced *A Modern Match* in London, the scene and characters were Anglicized and it was renamed *Marriage, 1892*.

This early period of Fitch's work was distinctly one of experiment. His original work like *The Harvest* was tentative, being revived later in another form. *April Weather*, written for Sol Smith Russell, while it was a success in Chicago in 1893, failed later in New York.

Much more successful was *His Grace de Grammont* (1894), a charming comedy of manners of the court of Charles II, in which Otis Skinner [1] portrayed the gallant cavalier who dares

[1] See Skinner, Otis, *Footlights and Spotlights*, Chap. XIV.

the wrath of the King to win Mistress Hamilton, whom Charles desires to make his mistress. Maud Durbin, now Mrs. Skinner, played Mistress Hamilton. The sketchy plot is sufficient to carry the dialogue, but the play depended more upon the stage pictures than upon any reality in its depiction of character. Yet Fitch considered his portrait of Lady Castlemaine an important contribution, and there is something appealing in this discarded mistress of Charles who is trying to protect her unwilling rival from her royal lover.

Mistress Betty (1895), another romantic comedy of manners, was written for Modjeska and acted for a brief period, but the illness of the great actress closed the engagement. It was revived by Viola Allen in 1905 as *The Toast of the Town*. While the drama is reminiscent of *Nance Oldfield, Peg Woffington,* and all plays in which an actress simulates a part in order to convince a man she loves of her infidelity, nevertheless it has a charm and flavor of its own. Betty Singleton, who marries the Duke of Malmsbury, does so because she idealizes him; he marries her because she appeals to his vanity. She is the admired of everyone and he wishes to possess her. The consequent disillusionment of both and the tragedy that leaves her dying,[1] half crazed, in a little garret, are logical enough, but it is not the plot that is important. The characterization of the Eighteenth Century English patrician, with his or her cold-blooded attitude toward those less fortunately situated, is well done. The situations are built up cleverly, especially the farewell of Betty to the stage at the curtain of the first Act and the scene in which she pretends to love Lord Phillips, in order that the Duke will for his own happiness leave her, although her heart is breaking. The final curtain, in which she repeats while mad the speech of farewell she had given so gallantly in the first Act, is deeply moving. The conversation at times is in Fitch's best manner. The dialogue between the old man who tends Betty at the wretched lodging house to

---

[1] *Mistress Betty* ended with the death of the heroine. *The Toast of the Town* had a happy ending.

which she has retreated is worthy of him in his shrewdest moments, and provided Ferdinand Gottschalk with a part which made a profound impression upon the audience.

Meanwhile Fitch was constantly turning to the French drama for inspiration. He made a stage success with his adaptation of *Le Veglione* of Bisson and Carré under the title of *The Masked Ball* (1892) in which John Drew and Maude Adams were the stars. Its sole interest lies in the skill with which he preserved the French atmosphere of an amusing but very light farce-comedy. In this he kept the scene in France, but in *The Social Swim* (1893), based on Sardou's *La Maison Neuve*, the scene is transferred to New York City. It is a study of the young couple who leave their home expecting social progress and who meet disaster. When Daly had adapted this play in 1874 as *Folline*, he had kept the scene in France. *An American Duchess* (1893), from the French of Henri Lavedan, a satire on the shams of society and politics, proved a failure.

In *Bohemia* (1896), an adaptation of *La Vie de Bohème*, by Murger and Barrière, Fitch sacrificed the French atmosphere by keeping Mimi alive and preserving the proprieties to a degree that is absurd when dealing with such material. He varied the source of his adaptations by turning to the German of Ludwig Fulda and producing with Leo Ditrichstein *The Superfluous Husband* (1897), a well-constructed domestic drama of the Fulda type with some Fitch touches in the dialogue. The scene is transferred to New York where the conflict of husband and wife is set against an appropriate background.

Through these adaptations Fitch was learning his art and to a certain extent they bear evidence of being potboilers, to provide Fitch with the surroundings which his inherent love of beauty craved. His frank revelation in his letters of his reasons for writing *The Moth and the Flame*, a melodrama based on the earlier one-act play *The Harvest*, explains clearly why it is not of real significance. The party in the first Act with the head of the house lying dead upstairs, a suicide, is one of those effective contrasts which Fitch loved, but the rather lurid relations which develop later hurt the play. It proved a great popular success, however, and helped to establish Fitch in a position of independence in which he could work to please himself. This position was strengthened by the success of *Nathan Hale* (1898), the first of his plays based on American history. It was, however, not the history which carried the play into popular favor, but the human relations. Fitch follows correctly the main outlines of Hale's life up to his capture by the British, but the details of the council of war at which he volunteers are absurd and probability is cheerfully set at naught in order to heighten, through the refusal of all the other officers, the effect of his own sacrifice. The last days of Hale are still a matter of dispute and Fitch took advantage of this obscurity to invent certain episodes. The unconscious reaction of the audience to the fitness of things was shown by the failure of the third Act to appeal in its first form. Hale and Alice Adams, his sweetheart who has been brought by a trick of the British officer to the place of Hale's capture, are left apparently alone. Of course the officer is watching and everyone, including the audience and except Hale, suspects the ruse. Hale insists on embracing Alice and therefore discloses his identity. The audience, feeling instinctively that the business of a spy is to keep himself from discovery, did not respond to this outburst of emotion, and a change was made by which the discovery was brought about through Alice's negro servant. It was another illustration of the psychology of the auditor, who demands that the hero should not let his personal feeling conquer his patriotism, although the heroine may be permitted to do so. Fitch used effectively in the concluding scene the one dramatic episode in Hale's career, the traditional speech, "I only regret that I have but one life to lose for my country."

Fitch next departed from the scenes he knew, to write for Goodwin a Western melodrama, *The Cowboy and the Lady*, which succeeded in Philadelphia and on tour, but failed in

London, where Bret Harte[1] records his belief that Fitch was imitating him.   Midge, the central female character, is certainly a Bret Harte heroine, but in reality Fitch did not know the West except at second hand, and the play, while it has some vivid moments, is not of significance.   Fitch turned next to a field of which his knowledge was more sure.   His mother's family had lived in Hagerstown, Maryland, and he knew the Southern atmosphere.   The play of *Barbara Frietchie* (1899) opens on a charming scene in the evening, in which the boy and girl friendships of the central characters are seen ripening into love and are intensified by separation and the shadow of war.   Again it is the sense of personal and social relations of families who have known each other for generations that Fitch establishes best.   The war is only the background and history is violated cheerfully by making Barbara Frietchie a young girl who loves a Union officer, Captain Trumbull, and runs off to Hagerstown to marry him.   The love-making gave Julia Marlowe an opportunity of which she made the most, and the tragic scene on the balcony in which she is shot waving the Union flag while her lover lies dead in her room inside was very effective.   Fitch was vigorously criticized for falsification of history, and rather feebly defended himself on the grounds that Barbara Frietchie was ninety-six years of age and bedridden when Stonewall Jackson went through Fredericksburg. But Whittier's heroine, rightly or wrongly, had become established as the real Barbara and it was a dangerous experiment, since it distracted the attention of critics from the play itself. For while false to fact and legend, it is true to the spirit of the time from the social if not from the military point of view. It has not the vigor of *Secret Service* or the profound depth of *Griffith Davenport*, but it has a charm of its own, which helped largely in the success of its adaptation into the musical comedy, *My Maryland* (1927).

Fitch's adaptation of *Sapho* for Olga Nethersole, from the French of Alphonse Daudet and Adolphe Belot, is of interest

[1] *The Letters of Bret Harte*, p. 463.

chiefly as it reflects the change in taste between 1900 and our own day. The performance was stopped by the police on account of the scene in which Jean carries Sapho upstairs, an episode mild in comparison with what passes to-day without comment. It was in any case only an episode with him, for he was engaged in writing *The Climbers,* in which he entered upon his best period.

The Climbers is usually described as a satire upon New York society. If it were merely this it would not be of permanent worth. It is more truly a social comedy, depicting character and background realistically, and in truth every realistic picture of social life tends to satirize the elements of which it is composed. For men and women moving in social relations are not entirely natural, and the degrees of their repression provide a scale of effects which are fine material for a dramatist of the skill of Fitch in distinguishing lights and shades in social values. The first Act was a bit daring in 1900, and, running true to form, all the leading managers to whom it was offered refused the play. Yet Fitch knew better than they how effective it would be. It is laid in the home of Mrs. George Hunter, after she and her three daughters have returned from the funeral of their husband and father. The utter heartlessness of Mrs. Hunter and her youngest daughter, the finer nature of Blanche Sterling, the oldest daughter, who has married Richard Sterling, a weak but attractive man, are established by their reactions not only to the death of Hunter but to the fact of his having died a bankrupt. The manner in which wife and daughters attack and defend the dead husband and father, who, in order to meet the consequences of their extravagance, has gone down to ruin, is established with that almost uncanny knowledge of feminine nature Fitch possessed. But not only does Fitch reveal these characters; he creates another contrast, Ruth Hunter, the sister of the dead man, and in a few sentences makes one feel her essential superiority in breeding to her sister-in-law. He draws also, in Edward Warden, the reliable man, who has loved Blanche Sterling for years in silence, because she is his best friend's wife, and he has added two interesting types in Miss Godesby, the disillusioned woman, and Johnny Trotter, the climber who starts from the lowest social rung of them all. So much indeed did Ferdinand Gottschalk make of this part that Fitch developed it still further. No one but Fitch would have thought of the scene in which Miss Godesby and her friend bargain with Mrs. Hunter for her new Paris dresses, which now have become useless to the widow.

The theme of the play is perverted aspiration, for social standing, for money, even for happiness that is beyond the legitimate reach of the human being striving for it. But Fitch knew that such a theme alone would not carry a play, and he provided an appealing central motive in the love of Warden for Blanche Sterling, which watches over her and even her husband and becomes articulate only when Blanche reveals her own love for Warden. Then Warden turns to pursue his aspiration, illegitimate also, and his efforts to save Mrs. Sterling from disgrace and financial ruin hasten unintentionally Sterling's suicide. While this paves the way for happiness for Blanche and Warden, it is a perfectly natural solution for Sterling, who realizes too late that it is a cowardly act to avoid his responsibilities. The dialogue is extremely well done and, while there is not the unity of construction which came later, *The Climbers* is a masterly portrayal of human strength and human weakness. The strong characters are strong just in those qualities of courage, decision and unselfishness which kindle admiration, and the weak ones are tainted by a failing which, directed into a proper channel, might become legitimate ambition. They are consequently never uninteresting to the audience, for their motives always are comprehensible. *The Climbers* was well received in London, but the fact that royalty was not permitted to go to any play in which the theatre was in total darkness prevented complete success. Thus the powerful scene at the end of the second Act hurt its chances in England.

CLYDE FITCH

Captain Jinks of the Horse Marines (1901) is another period play, laid in the early seventies in New York City. The plot is thin and the character of the opera singer, Madame Trentoni, is idealized, but Fitch painted a real picture of the time and place, and the love story carried the play into great popular favor. *Captain Jinks* became a musical comedy in 1925. More significant was *Lovers' Lane* (1901), which had been written as early as 1894 and accepted by Sir George Alexander, but was not produced by him. It is a comedy laid in a small town in New York, the main theme being a contrast between the tolerant, lovable character of the minister, Thomas Singleton, and the intolerance and pettiness of his congregation. The psychology of the women of the rural community was as well known to Fitch as that of their sisters of the city, and his creation of Simplicity Johnson, the small girl whose jealousy of the woman the minister loves almost wrecks his happiness, proved again the fertility of his inventive power. Singleton is one of the few stage clergymen who seem real.

Clyde Fitch may be said to have reached the height of his popularity with the new century. Running to packed houses at the same time in New York were *The Climbers, Captain Jinks of the Horse Marines, Lovers' Lane* and *Barbara Frietchie*, plays of a varying order of merit and with widely different scenes. In the same prolific year of 1901, Beerbohm Tree produced his *Last of the Dandies*, a comedy of manners of the mid-Nineteenth Century, laid in London and Paris, with the central character of D'Orsay, a Victorian beau. *The Way of the World*, a melodrama of social life, laid in New York, was played by Elsie de Wolfe, with some success, though with little critical approval. The play is certainly not one of his best, but his inventive facility was shown in the introduction of the automobile in Central Park, as a means of bringing the characters together. For Annie Russell he wrote a play which was a departure from his usual manner. *The Girl and the Judge* was laid in "a Western state" and was based on an actual occurrence related by his friend Judge Galloway of Ohio.[1] The original incident was serio-comic, but the play is a study of a woman who is a kleptomaniac and of the power exercised over her by her daughter, who forces her to reveal her guilt. Fitch drew very well the characters of the Stanton family, the father who has been concealing his wife's shame but has taken to drink in consequence, and the girl who has unnatural responsibility thrust upon her, portrayed against the sinister background of the mother's vice. The judge, too, who must choose between his love for Winifred Stanton and his official duty, is adequately drawn and the dramatic sense of youth struggling against fate and human law for its right to happiness remains in the memory as the chief achievement of the play. Its production on December 4, 1901, marked the opening of the last play seen at the old Lyceum Theatre.

In justice to Fitch, it must be remembered that not all of these plays were written in 1901, and indeed it was not until November, 1902, that his next production occurred. *The Stubbornness of Geraldine* is one of that group which proceeded from the vivification of an emotion, in this case confidence, intensified by love. Geraldine Lang is an American girl with poise and standards. On the voyage home from Europe she meets Count Carlos Kinsey and they love each other. Circumstances bring him into disrepute. The continental custom of multiplying "Counts" by awarding the title to all the male members of a family leads to his being discredited by his brother's actions and even those who are nearest to Geraldine prove their affection by attempting to expose him. But all circumstances break in vain against her trust in the man she instinctively feels is honest and decent. As a matter of fact, Count Kinsey's reluctance to propose marriage to her until he had made good in his financial venture is overdrawn, but on the stage the American audiences found no difficulty in permitting the Hungarian noble to possess standards which would in reality have puzzled him. The very power of Geraldine's love

[1] *Letters of Fitch*, pp. 207–8.

CLYDE FITCH

seemed to have endowed him for the purposes of drama with qualities foreign to his real nature.

Fitch's methods of work are well illustrated in a letter written during the composition of this play.[1] "I feel very grateful to Bingham—so I got a very splendid play for her in Paris —— . . . and I have promised to do the version—it will take me perhaps three days." This play referred to was *The Frisky Mrs. Johnson* (1903), and the relative amount of effort expended upon it and one of the original plays indicates the reason for omitting any lengthy analysis, in nearly all cases, of his adaptations. He regretted indeed that he wrote such an adaptation as *The Bird in the Cage*, from the German of von Wildenbruch, but even in this absurd drama he could not help creating some interesting characters, and the Irish labor leader, played by Edward Harrigan, almost redeemed the play.

But there was no undue haste in the composition of the original plays, which were slowly matured and wrought out from the first conception to the last detail of stage setting. Eight years before *The Girl with the Green Eyes* was produced, in 1902, Fitch conceived the character of Jinny Austin, the woman who is possessed by the demon of jealousy. Here, as later in *The Truth*, he indicated that the fault was hereditary and wisely married her to a husband who was himself so incapable of jealousy that he could not sympathize with his wife's failing. He thus obtained a contrast from the start, and the very reticence of John Austin, born of his consideration for his wife's feelings, which prompts him to conceal her brother's secret marriage with Maggie the housemaid, contributes to feed her jealous suspicions. The invention of Fitch shows in the unusual scene in the Vatican, where the drama is all the more effective because the emotions aroused have to be repressed on account of the public character of the scene. The revelation which Ruth Chester makes to Austin that she and Geoffrey Tillman have been married comes like a blow to him, for he knows then that Geoffrey has committed bigamy

[1] *Letters*, p. 212.

and yet he has to conceal the fact from her and from Jinny. The instinct of the strong capable nature like Austin's is to take command of the situation, and Jinny's re-entrance into the art gallery at the moment when Ruth breaks down in her anxiety, precipitates the jealous feelings which have been held in check. The play proceeds logically to tragedy. After John has risked everything to conceal it, the disclosure of the bigamy is brought about in a powerful scene between Ruth Chester and Jinny, and John leaves his wife with the wreck of their happiness about her. She tries to commit suicide by turning on the gas and excluding the air, and the play would have been stronger if Fitch had ended it there. But probably in deference to the supposed desire on the part of the public for a happy ending, John Austin comes home in time to prevent Jinny's death.

In *Her Own Way* (1903) the most original character was that of Sam Coast, the millionaire who ruins the Carley family in order to force Georgiana Carley to marry him. Fitch proved in this play that he could draw masculine characters as well as feminine, and he portrayed admirably the conflict of wills, for Georgiana, fortified in her purpose by the right kind of love for Dick Coleman, wins eventually, while Sam Coast, whose passion is purely selfish, is helpless even with his money to back him. The opening scene at the children's party was one of those unusual stage pictures in which Fitch delighted.

Next came *Major André*, of which Fitch said, "It all lies closer to my heart, I think, than any other play."[1] Fitch made a careful study of the scene of André's capture but took liberties, as usual, with the historical details. He made André a sympathetic figure who departs on his mission with reluctance, largely because of the refusal of Sally Perkins, a Philadelphia girl, to marry him. Fitch established well the social atmosphere of New York City in 1780, the willingness of the American girls to flirt with the British officers but their real loyalty to their country. The dream of André on the night

---

[1] *Letters*, p. 251.

before his execution, in which he believes he sees Sally, is charmingly conceived. *Major André*, despite its fine qualities, ran only two weeks. Since Dunlap's *André* the same fate has overtaken the efforts of playwrights to vitalize the André story, and perhaps the knowledge that after all André went into the disgraceful episode with Arnold with his eyes open has prevented the success of the many efforts to place his personally attractive character on the stage. A comparison of the plays of Dunlap and Fitch will reveal the advance in skill of construction and natural quality of dialogue that has come with a century's experience. It will also reveal a certain sturdiness of character in the older play which is absent from Fitch's charming picture.

He had no time for regrets, for he was hard at work rehearsing *Glad of It*, which was produced in December, 1903, and was also a comparative failure. Yet there was something very real in the play, which took its characters through a department store, the stage of the Savoy Theatre and a boarding house in New Jersey. Fitch described it accurately when he said, "It is full of character types and subtleties of living instead of a story." The scenes and the minor characters are as real as any he has given us, and they drew an appreciative criticism from W. D. Howells, both in print and by personal letter. Howells was quite right when he said, "this is the way things happen, one after another, with only that loose allegiance to one another, that the facts of life have had hitherto to themselves, but that an artist had here recognized and recorded."[1] But *Glad of It* illustrated a stern law of the drama. Fidelity to life is not enough—the department store may be photographically reproduced, the stage rehearsal may be as funny as a perfect knowledge could make it, the boarding house may be absolutely true to such life, but unless these facts are fused into a coherent story, and unless important characters dominate the situations, there is no play. It was a sincere effort, however, and it was the occasion of a letter from Maude

[1] *Letters*, p. 258.

Adams to Fitch which is a remarkable analysis of his character
and the need it had of refreshment from even more vital sources
of inspiration than were provided by his usual experience.

I wish you could do some things that you'd hate to do. I wish
you could give over for a while your beloved Italy and your admired France and go to some place where the art is dead and life
is uppermost—common life. We live so much among people of
morbid tendencies, neuresthenics (I can't spell it), and the like—
that we begin to think they are real, and they are real of their
kind but it isn't a red blood kind.—You have been through a serious illness and a man doesn't recover from an illness like that in
a year, and while he's recovering he must be careful not to let himself drop back into an old environment of mind as well as of body.
Our illnesses are our vacations and we should use them to get
new turns of mind.—Don't get in a groove. Make yourself agree
with your critics for a time until you discover their secret—it is
a secret to them as well—they can't put in words the real thing
they criticize—they can't voice it—so you must discover it, but
when you've discovered it you'll find there will no longer be need
of it. Men of temperament, if they are very successful when they
are young, are in great danger. They either go to pieces or they
get two chances—and the second chance is usually better than the
first, if they are big men. It seems to me you're getting your
second chance.[1]

Seldom has an artist been better advised. What Fitch's
serious critics failed to understand was a certain overfineness
of perception which arose out of the very sensitiveness of his
impressions, and which led him to the study of feminine nature
because he found there a more fruitful field for his intuitive
talent. It cannot be said that Fitch followed the advice so
far as his work immediately following *Glad of It* is concerned,
for neither *The Coronet of a Duchess,* nor his two adaptations
from the French, *Granny* and *Cousin Billy,* marked any advance in his art. He drew in the first, however, a skillful picture of the Duke of Sundun, an English nobleman who marries
an American heiress, continues to keep his mistress, borrows
money from his wife to support "Pussy" Hawkins, and when

[1] *Letters,* pp. 256-7.

Milly demands a divorce, sells her freedom for cash. At the same time his manners remain impeccable and his steady adherence to his own peculiar standards of conduct make him more than a caricature. But the American characters were far inferior to those he drew later in *Her Great Match*, and the play was a definite failure. *Granny* was written to provide a star part for Mrs. Gilbert, then eighty-three years old. Fitch transferred the scene of *L'Aïeule* by Georges Michel to an American small town, with no local flavor. Granny first separates the husband of her dead daughter from his only son through her jealousy, and then secures the happiness of her grandson by providing him with a wife in the daughter of the woman she had traduced. There are some appealing scenes and Mrs. Gilbert made a personal success, but died suddenly while the play was on tour. In *Cousin Billy* he preserved the foreign scene for the first two acts, but he transformed one of Labiche's most striking characters to a caricature of a traveling American, possibly because the part was written to order for Francis Wilson.

The vital note is present, however, in *The Woman in the Case* (1905), a play of intense emotion, one of the finest types of melodrama our stage has known. The theme, the love of a wife for a husband, and the lengths to which she will go to save him from a false charge of murder, is made concrete in Margaret Rolfe, one of his most skillful characterizations. When her husband, Julian Rolfe, is accused of killing his friend, Philip Long, on account of his jealousy of Long's attachment to Claire Foster, whom Long was about to marry, Margaret wastes no time in natural feminine doubts of her husband's truth. She accepts his explanation that he had tried to save Long from a worthless woman, and she is contrasted with their attorney, Tompson, who is not in the beginning wholly convinced of Julian's innocence. At first glance it seems hardly likely that Margaret should give way so completely to her emotion at the end of the first Act when Julian is arrested, even trying to keep the police inspector off by force, and then should develop into the quiet intense woman of the next Act who plans to live with Claire Foster, to endure contact that she loathes, in order to worm out of Claire the evidence she needs to save her husband. But in reality it is just that intensity of her nature which justifies the great scene at the end of the third Act. Margaret has been living in the same apartment house with Claire for weeks; she has won her confidence by descending to her level of intrigue even to the assumption of an intimacy with Jimmy O'Neill, an old friend who helps her carry on the delusion. The supper scene in which Louis Klauffsky, a rich man who is keeping Claire, makes a fourth, is a masterly picture never overdone and carried naturally to a point where the men leave Margaret and Claire alone. Concealed in the next room, Tompson and an inspector listen while Margaret bit by bit draws out of Claire the description of Philip Long's suicide. Then when all is safely told she springs at Claire like a tigress and tells her who she is. The reaction is all the more powerful because of the earlier repression and all the more true because of Margaret's apparently hysterical outburst earlier in the play. Such intensity of action is usually called unnatural and "melodramatic." One is tempted to paraphrase and reply, "If this be melodrama, make the most of it." But as Fitch pointed out in his article "The Play and the Public," "One cannot live twenty-four hours in any of our cities without seeing vivid pictures of misery and happiness, vice and virtue, crime and innocence, poverty and wealth, in sharpest, loudest contrast— a daily life which is blood and iron mixed with soul and sentiment—melodrama of the ancients pure and simple." The danger of representing such intense scenes in which a woman lets her emotion control her is that in incompetent hands the scene becomes unpleasant through the shrillness of its interpretation. When Blanche Walsh played the part it was a triumph, and the success was repeated in other hands in Italy and in London. A reading of the scene will show how economical Fitch was in his demands upon the emotional reaction of his hearers. Not an unnecessary word is spoken by Margaret from the moment of her attack upon Claire until she falls unconscious on the floor. Yet she has in a few words epitomized the entire content of the character and she carries with every word the complete sympathy of the audience.

Perhaps the lightness and charm of *Her Great Match* (1905) came as a reaction from the intensity of *The Woman in the Case*. It is an international contrast in which the character of Jo Sheldon was written for Maxine Elliott, and the result was a popular success. Fitch placed against the background of a newly rich German family, who have lived some years in England, a love story between the Crown Prince Adolph of Eastphalia and Jo Sheldon, an American girl whose father is wealthy and whose stepmother is an accomplished scoundrel. His skill is shown in the opening act at a garden fête on the Botes estate, and our interest is excited by the picture of two young people charmingly in love with each other. One refreshing feature of the play is the omission of any sense of social hopelessness on the part of the American characters. The difficulties which threaten to prevent the match are official rather than social, and their solution through the relinquishment by the Prince of his right to reign is foreshadowed as soon as Jo makes clear to him that a morganatic marriage is out of the question. The few pointed words in which she draws a contrast between the basic conception of marriage in America and Germany reveals Fitch's complete understanding of his own country and of Europe. The play is better in characterization than his earlier international contrast, *The Stubbornness of Geraldine*, for not only are Jo and the Prince well drawn, but the whole Botes family are etched in skilfully, especially in the amusing scene on the morning after the party. Finally, as if for good measure, Fitch created in the Grand Duchess of Hohenstein, who is sent to break off the match but who becomes an ally, one of the most vivid characters in his plays, which the fine acting of Mathilde Cottrelly made memorable.

It was a busy period. The crisp melodrama of Western life, *Wolfville*, was adapted from a story by Alfred Henry Lewis; the reshaping of *Mistress Betty* into *The Toast of the Town* has already been described.

It is surprising at first glance that he did not make a success of his dramatization of Mrs. Wharton's novel *The House of Mirth* (1906). The theme of that story, the tragedy of a girl too fine to follow unquestioningly the rules of a selfish heartless social code and yet not strong enough to resist the appeal of its material luxury, was one to which Fitch certainly responded. That he felt the difficulties is evident, although none of the explanations he gives in his letters seems altogether convincing. For the story is really dramatic and the second scene of Act II, in Trenor's house, in which he follows the language of the book most closely, is the best in the play. That he saw the strength of the love story between Selden and Lily is to his credit, but the transfer of their exquisite scene of parting from Selden's rooms to the milliner's shop made any artistic ending difficult. In the novel, Lily goes to Selden through an uncontrollable impulse to see him once more before she takes the step, her marriage with Rosedale, which will separate them forever. Selden has nothing to say, for he has not yet recovered his belief in her, and since it is she who has taken the initiative, it is not necessary for him to say anything as yet. But in the play he is brought to the shop and then action on his part is demanded, and we are disappointed that he merely talks generalities. Again it is perhaps to Fitch's credit that he did not force a happy ending by attributing to Selden words and actions which are not in the novel, but it is surprising that the trained playwright could not see that the whole story is meaningless without the scene in Selden's rooms, for in it Mrs. Wharton lifted the novel to the lofty regions of feeling to which satire can never aspire. It is only fair, however, to add that Fitch made the dramatization after one refusal and under pressure, and it was probably his absorp-

Faithfully
Clyde Fitch

tion in his original work, about to rise to its climax, which prevented the successful treatment of the work of another.

The Truth, which opened in Cleveland in September, 1906, was not written hastily but grew up from the conception of the central character, Becky Warder, a woman who is a natural liar. She is marvelously drawn, never forced in her deceit, which seems instinctive rather than deliberate, and Fitch has cleverly revealed in the first Act how the ordinary prevarications of social and business intercourse have built up for her a mould of insincerity into which later her serious purposes run. She loves her husband devotedly, but she flirts with Lindon just the same, for she likes to be liked, and she indulges in philandering all the more recklessly because she feels so secure in her real love for Tom Warder. He is her opposite, and just as Fitch drew John Austin without the vice of jealousy, so Tom Warder is the sensible, true man who provides the necessary contrast to Becky. She keeps our interest better than Jinny Austin, for she is less selfish; even the deception she practices on Tom concerning the money she is sending her father springs from her generosity. All the characters, especially Eve Lindon, the jealous wife, and Lindon, her caddish husband, throw Becky into sympathetic relief, and the crowning achievement was the creation of her father. Roland explains her, for he too is a liar and yet he is not merely a repetition of her. He is as masculine in his weaknesses as she is feminine, but the selfishness of age in his character makes her own more generous impulses appealing, just as his shabby careless habits reflect her impeccable neatness and greater refinement. When Warder leaves her, broken by the discovery of her falsehoods, she flies to her father in Baltimore as her only refuge. Fitch prepares for their meeting by one of the most remarkable scenes in modern comedy, in which Roland baffles his landlady, Mrs. Crespigny, who has determined to marry him. He does this without offending her, for his material comfort is dependent upon her. Just as Becky's lies often spring from not wishing to hurt anyone's feelings, so Roland gently holds Mrs.

Crespigny at a safe distance. She is a striking picture of her type, vain, good-hearted, and longing to be a lady, just as he is the best picture of a frayed gentleman in American drama. When Becky comes to him he does not believe her, for he knows her too well, but she finally convinces him through her appeal to the memory of her mother, who had suffered from his weakness. This little scene might easily have been unbearably sentimental, but Fitch held it to utter simplicity. Nothing but the expression of Roland's face and his words to Mrs. Crespigny, "Mrs. Warder's changed her mind. She's stopping here to-night," tell the revolution in his mind between distrust and conviction.

Fitch does not force a reconciliation. Roland, true to form, wires Warder that Becky is dying and stages an elaborate deception upon his arrival, to which Becky only half agrees. Mrs. Crespigny, whose one hope of happiness depends upon their continued separation, reveals to Tom the plan and Tom, in disgust, is about to return to New York when Becky thrusts the temptation aside and tells the truth in time. Warder believes her, and when she cries out that he cannot forgive her, he replies with the elemental truth, "We don't love people because they are perfect . . . we love them because they are themselves."

The Truth marks the crest of Fitch's effort. Never before in his career did he create such vivid pictures of real people, never did he portray with such apparent simplicity the complicated motives of human conduct. Every sentence tells, every speech leads to the climax or the conclusion, yet the result is the apparently effortless product of genius. It is comedy, for it is based upon human weakness, but it is high comedy, for Tom, Becky, even Roland are spirited people and without the contrast of social values there could hardly have been a play.

This smoothness of action, the very clarity and directness of the play, misled the critics in this country who saw little of its real greatness when it opened its New York engagement on January 7, 1907, with Clara Bloodgood in the leading part. There was some belated appreciation, but it came too late to save the play, which was withdrawn after thirty-four performances. But on April 6, 1907, it was produced at the Comedy Theatre in London with Marie Tempest as Becky, who scored a notable triumph. Encouraged by this success, it was revived next season by Mrs. Bloodgood in America on tour, until in December she shot herself. In 1914, Grace George made a successful revival of the comedy.

The Truth gave Fitch an international reputation. In Italy, Germany, Russia, Hungary and Scandinavia, the success of the play was universal. As a contrast to the unsympathetic notices appearing in the American press, the appreciation of the German critics was especially pleasing.[1] Fitch was called before the curtain three times when he attended the performance at Hamburg, and he saw the play in Rome, Genoa and Stuttgart.

It is a grim commentary upon the state of criticism in New York that while *The Truth* was unappreciated, *The Straight Road*, which opened on the same evening, was warmly greeted. This is a melodrama, at times sensational, whose central character, Hester Street Moll, nearly ruins her own happiness in attempting to open the eyes of her benefactress to the real character of the latter's lover. While the play is not to be compared with *The Truth* in permanent value, the characters are very human, and if Fitch drew in high light the difficulties such a woman would experience in pursuing the "straight road," his defence might lie in the pertinent fact that such difficulties are real. And Fitch gave the language of Hester Street just as correctly as the conversation of the drawing-room. Certainly it was more convincing as a picture of life

---

[1] The criticisms of the Berlin papers, especially those in the *Börsen-Courier, Vorwärts, Lokal-Anzeiger* and *Post* for September 25, 1908, reveal the appreciation of the press. A quotation from *Vorwärts* will illustrate the tone of the criticisms:

"Eine mit Verstand, Geschmack und sicherem Bühnenblick durchgeführte Komödie, die sich von der flachen Harmlosigeit des deutschen Familien Lustspieltypus, wie von der Pikanterien und ausgeklügelten Verwechselungstricks des Pariser Schwankes in gleicher weise fernheit."

than *Her Sister* (1907), a domestic drama laid partly in a
clairvoyant palmist's establishment in Bond Street, London,
in which he collaborated with Cosmo Gordon-Lennox. *Toddles* (1906), an adaptation from Godferneaux and Bernard,
was an amusing but trifling farce-comedy in which Fitch kept
the foreign scene. There was more of his own quality in *Girls*
(1908), an adaptation from *Die Welt ohne Männer*, by Engel
and Horst. The picture of the three girls living in a studio in
New York, with the pressure of economic necessity stressed
just enough and their inevitable and natural desire for admiration breaking through their avowed hatred of men, is thoroughly characteristic.

Fitch felt that his name was appearing too frequently upon
playbills at this moment, so he did not acknowledge publicly
his share in the revision of *The Honor of the Family*, originally
translated by Paul Potter from *La Rabouilleuse*, a dramatization by Emile Fabre of Balzac's novel. This play was an
interesting example of collaboration. Potter's version was not
satisfactory to Charles Frohman, so he asked Fitch to rewrite
it. Then William Gillette suggested that Philippe Bridau
should enter not at the beginning of Act II but at the end of
Act I, and this change, which brings Bridau in with a flourish,
turned the character into comedy while the original play in
Paris presented him as a serious man of business. This play
provided Otis Skinner with one of the greatest successes of his
career.[1]

Notwithstanding illness and constant nervous fatigue, Fitch
continued to produce rapidly. Such a light farce comedy as
The Blue Mouse (1908), from the German, could have caused
little effort in writing, but *The Bachelor* (1909) was an original play with real characters and his usual attention to detail.
A Happy Marriage (1909) is even better, and merits more
consideration than several of the published dramas. It is unified and coherent in its structure and every character has reality. Without subplot or comic relief, it attacks the situation

[1] *Footlights and Spotlights*, p. 284.

in which a husband and wife find themselves faced with an ebb tide in their love. Frederick Thornton turns to business, Joan to another man. This is old, of course, but then Fitch draws with skill the other man's unwillingness to play the game except for the passing moment, and the struggle of Joan Thornton to keep her ideal of the man for whom she is willing to lose her husband's love. Thornton is no hero—but he is master of each situation as it arises, and the fine scene in the second Act when he finds his wife in Paul Mayne's rooms and pretends to be deceived by her explanations in order to protect her, is worthy of Fitch at his best. There is another scene, between Thornton and Granger, Mayne's partner, in which there is a remarkable picture of two men, the surface of whose conversation hides an effort to preserve an ideal of conduct to which neither outwardly aspires. Fitch almost spoils the scene by Thornton's offer of business to Granger as an offset to his firm's losses, but perhaps the strain was already showing.

Even while Fitch was apparently engrossed with adaptations and rehearsals, he was brooding over what he intended to be the best work of his career. *The City* was conceived in 1908 and finished in June 1909, just before he sailed on his last visit to Europe. It was not produced until after his death. Worn out by excessive labor and nervous tension, he did not rally from the operation for appendicitis which was the immediate cause of his death at Châlons-sur-Marne, September 4, 1909. But *The City* was produced by the cast he had selected, on December 21, 1909, and was received with acclaim as one of the strongest of his plays.

Its general theme is the influence of the city upon the family who come from a small town where they have been the leading people for generations. But Fitch knew that such a theme must be made concrete and he soon establishes as the central character George Rand, Jr., whose father, the "foremost citizen" dies at the end of the first Act, after confessing that Hannock, who has been blackmailing him, is really his son. George has high ambitions, political and social, wishes to be of service, but has the twisted morality which his father has bequeathed him, and it needs the terrible situation which develops to startle him into a realization of truth. The nomination for the governorship is his if his record is clear. But Cicely, his youngest sister, marries Hannock, whom George has made his private secretary, out of a feeling of responsibility for his father's sin. They return to the house and George endeavors to persuade Cicely to give Hannock up. She refuses and George has to tell Hannock that he is her brother. Hannock, who is a drug fiend, goes almost insane and when Cicely re-enters, rather than allow her to be separated from him, shoots her and then himself attempts suicide. George prevents him from killing himself, although Hannock threatens him with a revelation of some of the questionable deals which George has carried on, and with the family disgrace. Fitch has conceived probably the strongest temptation under which a man could be brought, for there is also the probability that Eleanor Voorhees, to whom George is betrothed, will give him up if his real character and actions are disclosed. But the fine qualities that are in George Rand hold fast to the one inexorable fact that he has no right to allow Hannock to escape the law. The curtain goes down on a climax of character, and the last Act, in which he declines the nomination and goes through the humiliation of confessing all his derelictions to the man who has been his model and his political sponsor, is a moral tonic. All seems to be lost to him but honor, but Eleanor remains faithful to him, an action in keeping with her nature as we have been allowed to see it.

It would seem as though the New England conscience of his father's family animated Fitch in his last play. *The City* is a grim drama, and Fitch did not allow the blame for the failure of the Rand family in winning the height of their aspirations to be laid at the city's door. He shows how the city brings out in a man or woman's nature the largest values that are there, for good or evil. If they bring to the city great qualities, they may win from her great recognition in return, but if they are weaklings, they will inevitably fail.

Fitch's adaptations from French and German were as a rule hastily done, from translations made for him, although he read French easily. Usually he treated the material freely. In his adaptations from the German the characters were made American and in *Girls* the play was largely his own. In the adaptations from the French, generalizations are not so easy. Where the original was well-known, as in *Bohemia* or *Sapho*, he preserved the French scene and characters, but in a majority of instances he made the atmosphere American, as in *Granny* or *The Social Swim*. The most lasting impression from a study of his foreign adaptations is that of the facility in imposing upon the work of other men the individuality of his own manner. His happiest results came when he treated the material with the greatest freedom.

In considering the work of Clyde Fitch as a whole, the first misconception that must be dispelled is that of excessive production. Disregarding his twenty-two adaptations of foreign plays and dramatizations of novels, there remain thirty-three original plays, for *The Moth and the Flame* and *The Toast of the Town* are revisions of earlier work. Thirty-three original plays in twenty years is not an extraordinary total; in fact it yields about the average of Shakespeare. While his adaptations took comparatively little effort, his original work was slowly developed in his mind and he came to its creation on paper with plan and even dialogue often fully conceived. It is true that he worked under pressure, but it is also true that to a man of his temperament pressure acted as a stimulant to creative effort.

A classification of Fitch's work at first seems to indicate an extensive variety in the selection of material and method of treatment. England, France and the United States in the Seventeenth, Eighteenth, Nineteenth and Twentieth Centuries; city life and rural life; the East, the Middle and the Far West, all have been treated with varying success. But as a matter of fact, with Clyde Fitch neither locality nor period was the prime inspiration, and any classification based upon them is confusing. He experimented with American history when the vogue of historical romance made it a popular motive; he ventured into unfamiliar scenes in the West, perhaps unwisely; his love of beauty made him luxuriate in the costumes and settings of an earlier day, but from *Beau Brummell* to *The City* the real inspiration of Clyde Fitch came from his unremitting study of men and women in their social and personal relations. In *Barbara Frietchie* or *Major André* the Civil War or the Revolution was the point of departure; what remains are the charming pictures of social life in Fredericksburg or in New York. George IV and Charles II are not historical figures in *Beau Brummell* or *His Grace de Grammont;* they are part of the social setting of more important characters. While Captain Jinks is redolent of the seventies, there is no historical figure; it is the force of social prejudice typified in Mrs. Jinks that almost wrecks the love story. And in *Lovers' Lane* the rural setting is only a means for satire upon the littleness of small-town life.

It was not satire, however, which makes Fitch's best work emerge more and more clearly from the plays of the period. Satire alone never keeps a play alive, and though Fitch could portray feminine weakness, selfishness and heartlessness as well as any playwright of his time, it was his steady refusal to limit his art to the satiric form which proved his essential strength.

Fitch will be finally remembered for his studies of human characters who are endowed with a shining virtue or possessed by one absorbing vice. Consciously or unconsciously, he was following the example of the writers of the medieval moralities, but his sense of the theatre clothed his abstractions with a concreteness that makes the characters living things. Beau Brummell is the incarnation of the phrase, "There are some things a gentleman cannot do." Practically all the characters in *The Climbers* are the representatives of ambition. Nathan Hale represents patriotism; Barbara Frietchie, love in conflict with patriotism; Geraldine Lang, trust; Jinny Austin, jealousy; Georgiana Carley, courage; Jo Sheldon, self-respect; Becky Warder, unreliability; Margaret Rolfe, wifely devotion; George Rand, Jr., ambition. This emotional content of the leading character gives a unity to the play which is, in some way, a measure of its merit, for *Beau Brummell, The Climbers, The Truth, The Girl with the Green Eyes,* and *The Woman in the Case,* in which the basic emotion stands out most clearly, are perhaps also the plays easiest to establish as permanent contributions to dramatic literature. Certainly the vividness of the emotion of the central character acts and reacts upon the others and they are brightened rather than dulled by its glow. The emotions are universal, too, recognizable to all humanity, which accounts for the international success of *The Truth* and *The Woman in the Case.*

But Clyde Fitch knew that unity is only one quality of high art. Variety is almost as essential, and his rich inventive faculty provided such delightful minor creations as Roland and Mrs. Crespigny in *The Truth,* Mortimer in *Beau Brummell,* the Grand Duchess in *Her Great Match,* or Johnny Trotter in *The Climbers.* It is to be noticed that the trained playwright never let these minor characters disturb the serenity of the star. They amplified or set off the main character for whom the play was written, and they fitted into a structure so compact that in the best plays it has taken on the inevitability of a result.

It is not necessary here to recapitulate the weaknesses which make any study of Fitch an exercise in discrimination. That such discrimination was not at his service to any large extent during his lifetime is a matter of regret, for he could have profited by it. He was keen for helpful criticism, as his letters show, but the criticism that depreciated *The Truth* and hailed *The Straight Road* as "a real play," on the same day, helped him little. For while others wrote historical plays and vivid melodrama, his contribution to our drama lies primarily in the portraiture of American men and women, prevented by their social inhibitions from frank expression of their complete natures, but presenting in the consequent struggle a drama quiet yet intense, so restrained in power that his own generation mistook its fineness for weakness. There has rarely been so complete a reversal of critical judgment, for he is now placed securely among the foremost writers of high comedy and his death at the height of his power is beginning to be looked upon as a tragedy in our dramatic history.

A HISTORY OF
THE AMERICAN DRAMA
VOLUME TWO
FROM WILLIAM VAUGHN MOODY
TO THE PRESENT DAY

CHAPTER XII

WILLIAM VAUGHN MOODY AND THE DRAMA OF REVOLT

IT WOULD be idle to emphasize unduly the change that came over the drama with the advent of the Twentieth Century, but it was real and significant. Daly died in 1899, Hoyt in 1900, Herne in 1901, and, while Howard wrote *Kate* in 1906 and Harrigan *Under Cover* in 1903, their important work belongs to the Nineteenth Century. Of those born after 1850, Gillette probably changed least in material and method. Belasco, with his singular capacity for adjustment, Thomas with his liberal receptivity to new ideas, and Fitch with his keen sense of social fluctuations, steadily developed, in power and achievement, during the first decade of the new century.

It is only natural that the turn of the century should stimulate creative artists to new endeavor. Human desire for change and experiment seizes such an occasion to express itself, and if the distinction between originality and mere difference of manner is often confused, there is beneath all the froth and eccentricity an undercurrent of hope and sincerity. Our drama shares with our lyric poetry and our fiction the quickening impulse of the new era, and if the strands of progress are not so easy to disentangle from the mesh of abortive effort, both in the drama and in the theatre, it is rather because of the excess of projects for their betterment than through lack of them.

Generalizations concerning the drama are always dangerous because of its dependence upon external conditions, and we are still so close to the times with which we are concerned that a perspective is difficult to establish. Moreover, the fruition of the new movement was delayed by unfortunate condi-

1

tions in the theatre, and even when it seemed to have become established, the early death of the playwright who was in a sense the pioneer deprived our dramatic literature of what would probably have been its chief ornament. The easiest method of procedure would be to present analyses of the individual dramatists and leave to the future the co-ordination of their work, but the historian of the drama cannot shirk the duty of classification. For, owing to the large number of playwrights who have produced a few plays of significance, the drama of the Twentieth Century must still be studied largely through its types and tendencies.

When we review the condition both of the drama and of the theatre in 1900, the outlook was certainly not encouraging. The establishment of international copyright in 1891, from which so much had been hoped, had not yet affected the situation to any great degree. The leading producers still looked abroad for material, though several object lessons had been taught them. Contemporary criticism, with a few honorable exceptions, while it preached encouragement to the American playwright theoretically, was rarely helpful in individual cases and was seldom discriminating. If the historian were to depend upon the newspaper of that day, unchecked by his own memory or by the saner judgment of the more careful reviews, the theatre and the drama were both apparently in ruins.

Of course this pessimism with regard to the theatre is chronic, and has not been limited to America. But certain of the discouraging features were the peculiar product of local conditions. The growth of the "syndicate," or the combination of theatrical interests formed in 1896, primarily to control the bookings on "the road," as the territory outside of New York City is still called, was harmful, as any monopoly is harmful. It placed the control of the theatre in the hands of those who were concerned chiefly with its commercial aspects, and it drove the actor-manager like Herne or Belasco to make terms or leave the stage. This syndicate in turn met successful rivalry, and competition was to a certain degree restored. But

it was still a difficult matter to put on a play unless the producing manager could secure the necessary bookings to ensure
a successful tour on the road after or before his run in New
York. This condition hurt the dramatist just as the warfare
of the two syndicates helped him to a certain extent by providing more opportunities. The playwrights who had been
hampered during the past by the necessity of writing to suit
a particular actor or actress, now had to share with these a
domination which was less personal but based its actions entirely upon a supposed public taste which was largely imaginary. Public opinion, too, was shocked by the fire in the Iroquois Theatre in Chicago, on December 30, 1903, in which 588
people lost their lives.

The very difficulties of the situation led to attempts at its
cure. While the critics were deploring the scarcity of good
plays, the exploiting of incompetent stars, the excess of theatres, the New Theatre in Chicago was established in 1906 and
the New Theatre in New York in 1909. These commendable
projects were both failures. The collapse of the latter has
been blamed upon the large size of the building, which forbade
the production that demands an intimate relation of the actor
and his audience. But an examination of the list of the plays
produced suggests another reason. The New Theatre in Chicago offered but one American play during its répertoire season, and that one, *The Spoilers*, while of no especial distinction,
was the only play that was financially successful. The New
Theatre in New York offered during its first season one American play, *The Nigger*. After all, the main function of the
theatre in America should be the encouragement of the American playwright, for the theatre is transitory, the drama permanent. Yet notwithstanding the failure of these two experiments, the discussion they evolved certainly was helpful in
calling attention to the serious necessity of intelligent support
of the stage. The inception of George Pierce Baker's course
in playwriting at Harvard in 1905 indicates the beginning of
an important movement in the colleges in the United States,

and the foundation of the Society of Dramatic Authors in 1906 was also significant.

It was in 1906, too, that signs of the new dramatic generation became apparent. A survey of the plays of the previous seasons presents a sharp contrast. When the century opened the vogue of dramatized novels was at its height. With leading actors and actresses like Crane, John Drew, Mary Mannering, Maude Adams and J. K. Hackett producing *David Harum*, *Richard Carvel*, *Janice Meredith*, *The Little Minister*, and *The Pride of Jennico*, the effect on the American playwright was not a happy one. Mansfield's production of *Monsieur Beaucaire* was somewhat more encouraging, for here Tarkington was both playwright and novelist. Outside of *Beaucaire*, however, the season of 1900-1 in New York was barren, except for *The Climbers, Captain Jinks* and *Du Barry*. In 1901-2 *The Stubbornness of Geraldine* and *The Darling of the Gods* were the leading plays, with Thomas's *Colorado* a failure, and his dramatization of *Soldiers of Fortune* revealing the trend of popular favor.

In 1903-4 the leading plays were Thomas's *The Other Girl*, Fitch's *Her Own Way*, and George Ade's *The County Chairman*. In 1904-5 they were Belasco and Long's *Adrea*, Fitch's *The Woman in the Case*, and McLellan's *Leah Kleschna;* in 1905-6, Fitch's *Her Great Match*, Klein's *The Lion and the Mouse*, Thomas's *De Lancey*, Royle's *The Squaw Man*, and Ade's *Just Out of College*. One has to include Klein's melodrama, of doubtful merit, and Ade's boisterous comedy of types to make even a passable showing. Then in 1906-7 came from the established playwrights Fitch's *The Truth* and *The Straight Road*, Gillette's *Clarice*, Belasco's *Rose of the Rancho*, and George Broadhurst's best play, *The Man of the Hour;* and even more significant, in Langdon Mitchell's *The New York Idea*, Moody's *The Great Divide*, MacKaye's *Jeanne D'Arc*, and Rachel Crothers's *The Three of Us*, we have the advance guard of the new drama. In one year we have about as many permanent additions to our dramatic literature as in the five years previous. In 1907-8 Thomas's *The Witching Hour*, Kennedy's *The Servant in the House*, Walter's *Paid in Full*, MacKaye's *Sappho and Phaon*, indicate if not so rich a list, at least some quite significant plays. In 1908-9 Sheldon's *Salvation Nell*, Walter's *The Easiest Way*, Tarkington's *The Man from Home*, MacKaye's *Mater*, continue the growing list of new playwrights. In 1909-10 Thomas's *The Harvest Moon*, Moody's *The Faith Healer*, Fitch's *The City*, Miss Peabody's *The Piper*, MacKaye's *Canterbury Pilgrims*, Sheldon's *The Nigger*, and Miss Crothers' *A Man's World*, revealed the serious attempt at a drama of sincerity.

One of the most salient characteristics of the new drama lay in its emphasis upon the individual's right to self-expression. Drama, of course, has always been concerned with the struggle of the individual against some opposing force, but there has been a progress, or at least a difference, in the forces selected as his antagonists. When Godfrey wrote his *Prince of Parthia* in 1759, his hero was a prince fighting against the tyranny of a paternal sovereign. In the period from the Revolution to 1850 the heroes of *Pelopidas*, *The Gladiator*, *The Bride of Genoa*, and *Sertorius* were battling against political tyranny. Even in 1835, Conrad saw the passing of this motive, and he made Jack Cade a leader of the peasants in their struggle for personal and economic rights. After the Civil War, the struggle between labor and capital naturally presented itself as a fit subject for dramatic treatment, and it is surprising, at first glance, that so few plays of importance were written in America upon this theme. Augustus Thomas would have been the natural leader in such a drama, but the failure of *New Blood* discouraged him. The subject is touched lightly in *The Capitol*, and novels like *The Pit* were dramatized, but the chief vogue of the capital and labor play seems to be in melodrama like Klein's *Daughters of Men* (1906), in which, curiously enough, the same solution for the problem is suggested as that offered by John Galsworthy three years later in *Strife*. Perhaps it was the general conviction that the labor unions might well be left to conduct the struggle with capital, and that it was a contest of organization with organization, in which the individual ran fairly even chances of being submerged. Labor and capital were already meeting upon equal terms, and, while in one way this should have provided stronger situations, yet it took away the possibility of sharp contrasts between opulence and misery, of which European drama makes use. Such scenes between the tyrannical employer and the cringing employees as are presented in Björnson's *Beyond Human Might* (1895) would have left American audiences cold. And as has already been suggested, the New York audiences, consisting largely of the well-to-do, were not especially sympathetic to the theme. When a sporadic play like *Kindling* (1911) appeared, it was saved by Chicago auditors and not by those of New York, and indeed the economic elements already seemed old-fashioned.

The individual having won his political rights in the first half of the Nineteenth Century and his economic status in the second half, became concerned toward the close of that century with the salvation of his personality from the dangers that lay in the increasing complexities of the social organization, in the standardization of life, in the prejudices and stupidities which prevent a full and free expression of each human soul. This feeling was worldwide, and took on a more virulent form on the continent of Europe than it did in America or even in England. Under the influence of Ibsen and Strindberg, European dramatists faced and revealed the cankers of life in their celebration of personal liberty, but our drama has followed them infrequently although it has been affected somewhat in its technique.

The drama of revolt in America took a different direction, less direct and obvious in the searching out of disease and degradation, but quite as profound in its own way. This is not the place to discuss relative values, but it must be recognized that great as the power of Ibsen and Strindberg may be, they present those facts of life which men must forget if life is to be noble or even endurable.

The American dramatists in general deal with the growth of spiritual life through the evolution of character. They have recognized that the preservation of character is much more important than the preservation of personality, of which indeed we are suffering at present from an excess. This motive runs through various phases in the first quarter of the new century, but one of its most striking manifestations is associated with the name of William Vaughn Moody.

Moody was born in Spencer, Indiana, July 8, 1869, his father coming from New York and being of English and French ancestry, as his mother was mingled English and German. Moody had to make his own way from the beginning and taught in public and private schools before he entered Harvard College in 1889. Completing the work for a degree in three years, he went as tutor to Europe and came in contact with German, Italian and Grecian influences. He returned to Harvard for two years as graduate student and instructor, and then became connected with the English Department at the University of Chicago, actively teaching until 1902 and preserving for some years thereafter a nominal connection. The authorities of the University wished to retain his services, but Moody had determined that his real work lay in lyric poetry and drama, and he resolutely maintained his independence. His scholarly publications show his interest in Milton and Bunyan, but his *History of English Literature* was written to provide means to support him while he was enriching his experiences with travel, in the West and abroad.

Moody's letters reveal his careful approach to his subjects and his absorption in his poetic work. While his first published drama, *The Masque of Judgment*, appeared in 1900, it had been begun in 1897. It has not been produced on the stage, but in the case of Moody his work must be considered in its entirety, for his dramas, in both verse and prose, represent a conception of life which is essentially dramatic. Indeed, two

7

of his verse dramas would have been performed except for accidental circumstances, and may be produced at any time. *The Masque of Judgment* celebrates the conflict between God and the creatures, good and evil, that he has created. This dramatic poem stretches from the Incarnation to the Day of Judgment, and in its personnel and background it is Miltonic and reveals Moody's close study of the Bible. Raphael is the protagonist, and through his conversation with Michael and Uriel the drama progresses in flexible verse, interspersed with exquisite lyric poetry in varying measures. Step by step, with what seems to Moody remorseless logic, he pursues the purpose of God in His creation and judgment of man until it ends in destruction. God to him is the creator not only of good but also of evil, and the Serpent typifies the evil that broods beneath, waiting for God's mistake. This mistake lies in God's failure to make the highest use of the individual will and desires of man, which He has planted in humanity, and for which He is responsible. To Moody the preservation of the individual's own dignity is all important. It is righteous in him to carry out those desires, physical and intellectual, which are part of his divinity, even if they lead him to rebellion against the Most High.

Michael represents the Hebraistic attitude that the lost were punished for their sins; Uriel urges that "the violence and the unclean acts were His," but Raphael answers:

> Snatch not
> From brows abased the crown of personal will
> Which made them noble, though it brought them down.

There is an insistence upon the doctrine of free will even at the cost of rebellion, or as Uriel says:

> Man's violence was earnest of his strength,
> His sin a heady overflow, dynamic
> Unto all lovely uses, to be curbed
> And sweetened, never broken with the rod!

8

Raphael is the representative of the angelic sympathy with humanity, and it was this phase of the work, the significance of human life, that Moody felt was most important. Raphael says in the third act:

> O heart of man, how I have loved thee!
> Hidden in sunlight what sweet hours were mine
> Of lover-like espial upon thine;
> Thrilled with thy shadowy fears, half guessing
> The hope that lit thy veins like wine,
> Musing why this was bane and that thy blessing,
> My angel-ichor moved by all that moved thee;
> Though oft the meanings of thy joy and woe
> Were hid, were hard to know;
> For deep beneath the clear crystalline waters
> That feed the hearts of Heaven's sons and daughters,
> The roots of thy life go.

There is Milton in the music of Moody's verse, but in the celebration of individual revolt, Moody has gone a step further than Milton. God is not to be considered as an all-powerful Deity, separate and distinct from His created servants. He is rather a compound of impulses, some high and some low, and in the working out of these impulses man is created and also the Serpent, the spirit of evil. God, failing to make use of all the forces of man, and punishing man for following out his impulses, is finally conquered by the Serpent. The Serpent himself is not left triumphant, however, for as Uriel remarks:

> Sorrow dies with the heart it feeds upon.

The Masque of Judgment, if taken by itself, would be misleading. The rebellion of man and the spirit of Evil were not, in Moody's conception, of supreme importance. To him the great theme of the projected trilogy was the unity of God and man. If one is destroyed, then so is the other, and Evil was to him rather a manifestation than an actual force. Christ, the supreme union of God and man, was the binding force of the trilogy, even though He does not appear in it. So the second verse drama, *The Fire Bringer* (1904), while it is laid in an earlier time, is spiritually a step forward. Its profound and noble treatment of the saviour of men cannot here be adequately discussed from the point of view of poetry, but it must be noted that as drama it marks a distinct advance over *The Masque of Judgment*, while in its purely lyrical quality it contains, especially in Pandora's songs, some of the finest utterances of Moody. The humanity grows even deeper, the structure grows more compact, the motives are more direct and the action becomes more concrete. It was intended for stage presentation, and plans were made to produce it at the New Theatre in Chicago, but it has not yet been performed. It is based on the story of Prometheus, and represents his struggle with the gods and his punishment by Zeus because he has scaled the heights of Olympus and brought back fire to Deukalion and Pyrrha, whom he had warned, in time, of the deluge. Again the supreme duty of rebellion is stressed.

The Death of Eve, the third member of the trilogy, was to have expressed the reconciliation of God and man through the woman who had apparently separated them. The first Act, which alone has been published, brings Eve back to Cain's city, which the arch-rebel rules in his declining strength, in order that she may lead him back with her to the place of her original sin. In the remaining portions of the drama, Adam in his broken age was to have followed her, and Eve, relieved of her long-borne burden, was to have seen in the love story of her descendants the solution of the eternal problem of the human race. Eve was to Moody the combination of God's creature and the foreshadowing of the Mother of God, and was the concrete expression of the impossibility of any separation of God and man. The fragment of *The Death of Eve*, which forms a unified act, was scheduled for production by Stuart Walker, representing the Poetry Society, in New York in February, 1924, but the performance had to be postponed. Of the verse dramas, it is clearly the best suited for stage production. The progress in unity and concreteness continues, and the limitation of the characters to human beings is a distinct advantage. Eve is the eternal mother. In Jubal's words:

> She saw Creation's morning; she will stay
> To watch the everlasting twilight fall.

But she becomes also the individual mother of Cain, the author of his sin as of his life, who takes upon herself his guilt.

As late as 1904, Moody wrote to Percy MacKaye that "I am heart and soul dedicated to the conviction that modern life can be presented on the stage in the poetic mediums and adequately presented only in that manner." But he was also deeply impressed by the importance of the practical considerations of the stage, and his association, beginning in 1898, with the men who were contributing to the theatre in New York probably shaped his decision to write in prose.

The actual composition of *The Great Divide* was the result, however, of an incident which was brought to his attention by Mrs. Moody. She had heard the story of a girl of her acquaintance who had gone with her brother to a cabin in the West, had been left alone and had been attacked by three men. She had appealed to one to save her from the others and had agreed to marry him. The marriage did not turn out successfully, and resulted in divorce. Moody became possessed with the dramatic possibilities of this theme and interrupted his other plans to write a play. *The Great Divide* was first produced by Miss Margaret Anglin under the title of *The Sabine Woman* at the Garrick Theatre, Chicago, April 12, 1906. On October 3 it was played by Henry Miller and Margaret Anglin at the Princess Theatre, New York, had a long run there and went on tour. In 1909 it was produced for a short time in London, with Edith Wynne Matthison in the part of Ruth Jordan, originally created by Miss Anglin.

The central theme of *The Great Divide* is the contrast between Ruth Jordan, the product of generations of New England ancestry, of inherited Puritan traditions and inhibitions, and Stephen Ghent, the man in the making, the freer spirit of the West, who is the master of his own impulses and is his own lawgiver. We shall fail to understand *The Great Divide* if we disregard Moody's verse dramas, for in Stephen Ghent, Moody transferred to prose and to contemporary America the ideal of personal independence which had its first flowering in *The Masque of Judgment* and *The Fire Bringer*. It is because Stephen Ghent is redolent of the soil that he made his popular appeal; but it is because he is the embodiment of a universal character that the play becomes a permanent addition to literature.

Moody had visited the Rocky Mountains with Hamlin Garland in 1901, and had spent some time in the Arizona desert in 1904. *The Great Divide*, however, was not inspired by Moody's interest in the West, which did not become keen until after his visit there in 1905, when he met the painter, Louis Aiken, who was living in a Hopi Village, and lived with him for a short time. Then he wandered out to a sheep ranch and spent a short time with the herders. These experiences are slightly reflected in *The Faith Healer*, but *The Great Divide* was prompted by his interest in a human story more than by the influence of locality. *The Great Divide* in fact had already been written before this visit, and yet its setting impresses one with its fidelity to the spirit of the West. The opening scene, in which Ruth, left alone in her brother's cabin, is attacked by three half-drunken men, is elemental in its swift development of character. Ruth has refused to marry Winthrop Newbury, her girlhood's friend, because he is "finished"; she longs for a more primitive mate, who has prospects of growth. When Stephen Ghent accepts her appeal to save her from the others at his own price, she instinctively responds to the call which his nature makes to hers. In the published play, revised by Moody in 1909, there is no mention of marriage in the first Act, and the drama gains in strength by the omission of any

WILLIAM VAUGHN MOODY

WILLIAM VAUGHN MOODY

discussion between them about the details of her bargain. He reads in her note to her brother what her own conception of their relation is to be, and that is enough for the present. There are several melodramatic touches in this scene, such as the kissing of her mother's photograph good-by, but it was a successful stage picture and was an original and fresh contrast between man and woman, for Ghent was a far cry from the heroes of *Wolfville* or *The Girl of the Golden West.*

The play develops as a contrast of character. Ghent rises materially and spiritually; Ruth tortures herself with the old Puritanic conscience, and fights even against happiness unless it proceeds, through discipline, to regeneration. Ghent simply cannot understand her refusal to accept their situation or her abandonment of him and return to her own people. He follows her to her home and, with the help of their new bond in the child that has been born to her, he makes his fight successfully against the portraits of her ancestors, for her heart fights for him.

Ghent: Ruth, it's these fellows are fooling you! It's they who keep your head set on the wages of sin, and all that rubbish. What have we got to do with suffering and sacrifice? That may be the law for some, and I've tried hard to see it as our law, and thought I had succeeded. But I haven't! Our law is joy, and selfishness; the curve of your shoulder and the light on your hair as you sit there says that as plain as preaching.—Does it gall you the way we came together? You asked me that night what brought me, and I told you whiskey, and sun, and the devil. Well, I tell you now I'm thankful on my knees for all three! Does it rankle in your mind that I took you when I could get you, by main strength and fraud? I guess most good women are taken that way, if they only knew it. Don't you want to be paid for? I guess every wife is paid for in some good coin or other. And as for you, I've paid for you not only with a trumpery chain, but with the heart in my breast, do you hear? That's one thing you can't throw back at me—the man you've made of me, the life and the meaning of life you've showed me the way to!

13

The Faith Healer was produced at the Century Theatre, March 15, 1909, in St. Louis, by Henry Miller, then in New York, January 19, 1910, and at Cambridge, Massachusetts, on January 24. It was not a popular success, but in some respects it is a finer play than *The Great Divide*, and its inherent dramatic qualities were apparent even in its recent revival in the moving pictures. While it followed *The Great Divide* on the stage, it was one of the earliest of Moody's conceptions. In 1895 he wrote to D. G. Mason, "I am losing sleep over a play dealing with a character and a situation which seem to me intensely significant and eloquent, that of Slatter, the 'New Mexico Messiah,' who has been doing things in Denver of late." At first he intended the drama to be in verse, but in 1899 he wrote the first draft, a play of about one hour in length, in prose. It was constantly in his mind, but the revision for the stage, even then not final, came in 1908, after the severe attack of typhoid fever which was the primary cause of his premature death in 1910.

Even before he heard of Slatter, Moody had conceived the idea of writing a play which should express the struggle between human love and the dedication to a mission. Moody's early feeling, as revealed in his lyric, "Road Hymn for the Start," is that a man should renounce his love and devote himself to the fulfillment of his mission. In a later mood he was inclined to have the hero renounce his mission in favor of love. But during the years in which *The Faith Healer* was slowly taking shape, it came to him that love and work could be facets of the same life, and one of the chief merits of the play lies in the way in which Moody, with delicate shades of understanding, showed that, by substituting for the selfishness of the personal claim the more impersonal and unselfish type of love, the hero could make a resolution of his problem which included every aspect of a man's life and aspiration. To have let the play run on to tragedy would have been not a more logical but a more obvious treatment.

He chose a faith healer for his hero because the choice

afforded him intense emotional conflicts, and he laid the scene in a farmhouse in the Middle West where he had grown to manhood and where such an emotional situation has not been infrequent. The wanderings of Ulrich Michaelis have led him to the household of Matthew Beeler, a well-drawn type of farmer, who keeps portraits of Darwin and Spencer on his walls, and whose skepticism yields with difficulty even when his wife, Mary, under Michaelis' treatment, walks for the first time in five years. This cure naturally forms the climax of action in the first Act, but Moody at once proceeds to a higher climax of character. As Mary Beeler, flushed with the hope that comes to her after five weary years, calls out to him that his hour has come and the crowd waiting outside for his ministration is ready, Michaelis falters, for his love for Rhoda, the young niece of Mary, seems to him to be an obstacle to his great mission. In the second Act, the external forces that oppose him are Dr. Littlefield, the modern physician, who represents the intolerant dogmatism of science, and the Reverend John Culpepper, the clergyman, who represents the age-long clerical opposition to the occult. Littlefield is no abstraction; he has been Rhoda's lover in earlier days, and their relations, rising from the past, make her feel that her love for Michaelis will be his destruction. He loses his grip upon his own self-trust, and as his confidence goes, his power to heal fails. Mary Beeler relapses to her former helplessness, and the little child who has been brought to him to heal fails to respond to his treatment. The curtain of the second Act falls on his broken-hearted cry of disillusionment. Then Rhoda tells him her story:

I thought that love had come to me. Girls are so eager for love. They snatch at the shadow of it. . . . I am not trying to plead for myself. . . . But I have told you the truth. I have set you free. I have given you back your mission.

But Michaelis does not accept this release. First he routs Littlefield, who returns with insolent proposals to Rhoda, then, as the power of his faith returns, the whole tone of the play rises to a high plane of spiritual hope. It is Easter morning; Mary Beeler feels the stir of some great beauty coming. She walks once more at Michaelis' command, and when Rhoda turns to Michaelis and tells him that she too is happy since she has delivered him from the influence that was hampering him, he replies:

> A little while ago you told me your life's bitter story. I tasted your struggle, went down with you into the depths of your anguish, and in those depths,—the miracle! . . . Out of those depths arose new-born happiness and new-risen hope. For in those star-lit depths of pain and grief, I had found at last true love. . . . You needed all the powers I had thrown away for your sake. You needed what the whole world needs —healing, healing, and as I rose to meet that need, the power that I had lost poured back into my soul.
>
> *Rhoda:* Oh, if I thought that could be!
> *Michaelis:* By the mystery that is man, and the mercy that is God, I say it is so.

The Faith Healer is the most significant of Moody's dramas because the theme is largest and the treatment most secure. More concrete than the verse dramas, it has a deeper imaginative quality than *The Great Divide*. One of his earliest conceptions, it was Moody's final plea for the dignity of human love and human faith. Its inherent nobility can best be appreciated when we compare it with the sordid treatment of a somewhat similar struggle in *Rain* or the inconsequential exposition of the faith healer in *The Miracle Man*. When we compare the play as published in 1909 in four acts with the revised version in three acts of 1910 we see how Moody relentlessly cut out the scene between Rhoda and Littlefield in which they wagered her future upon the success of Michaelis, and sacrificed apparent theatrical effectiveness for the higher climax of character. Had Moody written under the influence of the Scandinavian or Russian School, he would have produced tragedies which might have been faithful to fact, but Moody's dramas rise above isolated facts to the higher realism of universal truth. Moody's themes drew their inspiration from a soil in which their roots could still be watered by idealism, and his plays are as American as they are modern. Moreover, when we view his work from *The Masque of Judgment* to *The Faith Healer*, we see that, consciously or unconsciously, his inherent dramatic genius was finding its path to complete expression.

To one of Moody's classes at Radcliffe College in 1895 came a girl, Josephine Preston Peabody, as a special student. Born in Brooklyn, New York, May 30, 1874, she grew up passionately devoted to the drama, reading plays when she could not see them and determined, notwithstanding the enforced narrowness of her early life, to conquer experience. What Moody's encouragement meant to her is revealed in her diary at this time and later,[1] for he remained a constant critic of her work.

She had published verse and short stories even before going to Radcliffe College, and in 1897 began her verse tragedy *Marlowe.* Even her lyrics show a tendency to become colloquy or monologue; as she said herself, "very few of the poems stand still." Prevented by straitened circumstances from frequenting the theatre, she made little pasteboard pieces for her characters and even for the stage directions, and worked with this scenic laboratory, shifting and planning, so that she might clarify the action and situations in her dramas. Her first published play, *Fortune and Men's Eyes* (1900), is a one-act verse drama, whose main characters are Shakespeare and Mary Fytton. It is based upon reading, of course, rather than upon life, but there is real beauty in the conception of spiritual passion on Shakespeare's part. *Marlowe* (1901) is a decided improvement. It is a five-act tragedy, in nervous, flexible blank verse, with a clarity that is gripping. Marlowe is idealized, but perhaps Miss Peabody drew him as his poet's imagination

---

[1] See *Diary and Letters of Josephine Preston Peabody,* esp. pp. 57–8, 128, and 234: "Oct. 17, 1910. On this strange day two died: two lights went out—one old and one young—my two cherished lights, Will Vaughn Moody and dearest Julia Ward Howe."

made him for a few lofty hours, and that, after all, is all the world cares for in its dead poets. Alison, the girl whom he loves and whom he visits, with mixed motives, after her marriage, is well drawn also. Moody, in a very sympathetic criticism of the drama,[1] calls Marlowe "A woman's Marlowe." This judgment is correct, but there is an unusual insight in the playwright's understanding of Marlowe's infatuation for a lady of the Court and his love for Alison, existing at the same time. Her creation of Richard Bame, the unsuccessful lover of Alison, from "the name appended to the historical 'Note of Marlowe's Atheistical Opinions,' " till he becomes a man obsessed by the idea of revenge for a "small spite" and so gives rise to the climax of the last Act, is worthy of attention. For it allows her to close Marlowe's career with some dignity, in defiance of facts known to her or to be discovered later. The idea of having Marlowe quarrel with Bame on Alison's account and veil his quarrel by a pretence that it is over a courtesan, is drama even if it is not history. Miss Peabody sent *Marlowe* to Mansfield only to have it returned unopened, and it was produced by amateurs at the opening of the theatre at Agassiz House, Radcliffe College, in 1905.

Miss Peabody was a lecturer on poetry at Wellesley College from 1901 to 1903, but resigned as she felt that her teaching interfered with her writing. In 1906 she was married to Lionel Marks, of the Engineering Faculty at Harvard University. In May, 1905, her one-act play, *The Wings*, was published, but it was not performed until 1912 when it was put on at the Toy Theatre in Boston. *The Wings* is laid in Northumbria about 700 A.D., and is concerned with a struggle between Cerdic, a priest, and Edburga, King Ælfric's mistress, for power over the King. The verse has her usual distinction, but the play, like her other efforts, is of interest chiefly as leading up to her masterpiece.

Her verse drama, *The Piper*, written in 1907, at the first instance for Otis Skinner, but not produced by him on account

[1] *Some Letters of William Vaughn Moody*, pp. 142–3.

of other plans, won the Stratford Prize Competition of three hundred pounds in March 1910. This prize, offered for the best play with which to inaugurate the new Shakespeare Memorial Theatre at Stratford-on-Avon, was open to universal competition, and three hundred and fifteen manuscripts were submitted. Mrs. Marks went to Stratford for the first production of the play, July 26, 1910, with Frank Benson as the Piper. Its success was repeated when it was played at the New Theatre in New York, January 30, 1911, with Edith Wynne Matthison in the leading part. Notwithstanding her successful interpretation, the part was written for a man and should have been acted by one.

The Piper is a triumphant vindication of the belief that true poetry is the source of the finest drama, that verse is no bar to effective stage representation, and that a dramatic artist must be free to choose his subject from any time or place. It strikes the universal note, the note of love which triumphs over hatred, over revenge, over selfishness, over the powers of evil.

The story of the Pied Piper of Hamelin is familiar, and is essentially dramatic. But to the old legend Mrs. Marks added incident and character fused by poetic vision. With a few deft touches she sketches the crass burghers of the Middle Ages who have been freed from the plague by the Piper, a strolling player, to whom they feel they need not keep their word because he is a social outcast. She draws well the attitude of the bourgeoisie toward the theatre, and the directness of action and language strikes us at the first scene, for the blank verse is natural dialogue, broken easily into flexible rhythms. The children's own love of music leads them naturally to the Piper and suggests to him that he charm them away. His action, therefore, has the spontaneity which is the life of drama in action or word.

One of the elements of greatness in *The Piper* lies in its artistic economy of motive. Mrs. Marks knew the Middle Ages by instinct as well as assimilated study. She sketches in a few but vivid lines the century-old struggle between the power of Christianity and the power of the Devil—for to the Middle Ages charms and magic were the survivals of the old pagan worship, the old forces of pre-Christian, even pre-human life that must be conquered. Even the Piper is himself shaken by the power he wields—he charms the children to the old haunted "Hollow Hill" because he knows the burghers will not follow them there. When he finds out that as a sacrifice to bring back the children, the Burgomaster has been forced to give up his own daughter Barbara, and that the procession which is to lead her to a nunnery is to pass the lonely crossroads to Rudersheim, he charms the burghers, too, and makes them dance away to their own confusion while Barbara remains. The scene in which he releases Barbara from his charm so that his friend Michael may win her back to human love, is pure poetry. But the great climax of the drama comes at the end of the third Act, when Veronika, the mother of the little lame boy, Jan, scales the hills up to the lonely crossroads, where, under the figure of Christ, the "Lonely Man," she fights for the body and soul of her little boy. The Piper is the incarnation of the artist, who believes he is saving the children from becoming like their fathers, stolid, selfish souls—in cages all their lives. Earlier in the play he has stated his hatred of oppression: "I'll not have things in cages!" Perhaps the early struggles of the playwright herself found expression there. But when Veronika pleads with him, at first he is adamant, even when she tells him how, for her boy's sake, she has sold herself to her second husband, Kurt the Syndic:

> I meant, with my poor self, to buy him house
> And warmth, and softness for his little feet.
> Oh, then I knew not—when we sell our hearts,
> We buy us nothing.

In a passionate speech she tells him that her love will draw her son back to her, and she leaves the Piper alone. Then follows the magnificent struggle between the Piper and the ideal of Christ, between the spirit of hate and revenge and that of love and pardon, dramatic because it is a conflict between the soul of man and the power of God.

The Piper, alone, stands spell-bound, breathing hard, and looking after her. Then he turns his head and comes down, doggedly. Again he pauses. With a sudden sharp effort he turns, and crosses with passionate appeal to the shrine, his arm uplifted towards the carven Christ as if he warded off some accusation. His speech comes in a torrent.

Piper:

    I will not, no I will not, Lonely Man!
    I have them in my hand. I have them all—
    All—all! And I have lived unto this day.
    You understand. . . .

            (*He waits as if for some reply.*)
            You know what men they are.
    And what have they to do with such as these?
    Think of those old as death, in body and heart,
    Hugging their wretched hoardings, in cold fear
    Of moth and rust!—While these miraculous ones,
    Like golden creatures made of sunset-cloud,
    Go out forever,—every day, fade by
    With music and wild stars!—Ah, but You know.
    The hermit told me once, You loved them, too.
    But I know more than he, how You must love them:
    Their laughter, and their bubbling, skylark words
    To cool Your heart. Oh, listen, Lonely Man!—

        . . . .
    Oh, let me keep them! I will bring them to You,
    Still nights, and breathless mornings; they shall touch
    Your hands and feet with all their swarming hands,
    Like showering petals warm on furrowed ground,—
    All sweetness! They will make Thee whole again,
    With love. Thou wilt look up and smile on us!

        . . . .
    Why not? I know—the half—You will be saying.
    You will be thinking of Your Mother.—Ah,
    But she was different. She was not as they.
    She was more like . . . this one, the wife of Kurt!
    Of Kurt! No, no; ask me not this, not this!
    Here is some dawn of day for Hamelin,—now!
    'Tis hearts of men You want. Not mumbled prayers;

Not greed and carven tombs, not misers' candles;
No offerings, more, from men that feed on men;
Eternal psalms and endless cruelties! . . .
Even from now, there may be hearts in Hamelin,
Once stabbed awake!
>   (*He pleads, defends, excuses passionately; before his
>   will gives way, as the arrow flies from the bow-string.*)
>   —*I will not give them back!*
And Jan,—for Jan, that little one, that dearest
To Thee and me, hark,—he is wonderful.
Ask it not of me. Thou dost know I cannot!

. . . .

Look, Lonely Man! You shall have all of us
To wander the world over, where You stand
At all the crossways, and on lonely hills,—
Outside the churches, where the lost ones go!—
And the wayfaring men, and thieves and wolves
And lonely creatures, and the ones that sing!
We will show all men what we hear and see;
And we will make Thee lift Thy head, and smile.

. . . .

No, no, I cannot give them all! No, no.—
Why wilt Thou ask it?—Let me keep but one.
No, no, I will not. . . . .

. . . .
. . . . . . *Have Thy way.—I will!*

Notice that the soliloquy is natural here and, on the stage,
from the very first night, it stirred the audience profoundly.
The return of the children is brought about artistically, and
the Piper departs on his eternal quest.

In *The Wolf of Gubbio* (1913) Mrs. Marks dealt again
with the struggle between love and greed in the heart of man.
The medieval town, its people filled with their own importance
and selfish interests, forms a background to the splendid humility of Saint Francis of Assisi. He charms the Wolf of
Gubbio, long a terror to the village, until even the beast brings
back the baby he has intended to devour. Mrs. Marks' dramatic power created a scene of tender beauty in the last act,
when the woman who has been robbed and whose child has been

stolen, sits in the place of the Virgin in the Christmas spectacle, and the villagers bring her their best gifts while her heart is breaking. Mrs. Marks has interpreted well, too, the instinctive reaction to the influence of Saint Francis which turned the crass burghers of Gubbio, even if only for a time, into loving human beings. Neither *The Wolf of Gubbio,* nor her *Portrait of Mrs. W——* (1922), a charming play based on the love of Mary Wollstonecraft and William Godwin, has been acted, though both were written with stage presentation in mind. Mrs. Marks departed from her usual choice of literary or historical material to treat real life in her comedy, *The Chameleon* (1917), laid at the present day in a house out of town. The heroine, Honora Thorpe, continues to celebrate the individual's right to pursue her inclinations even if she breaks engagements, including that with the man she has promised to marry. Honora is a writer and so is the man she finally chooses, and there is some clever satire of temperamental instability and some charming love-making, even if the play does not soar to any such climax as *The Piper.* It reveals Mrs. Marks, however, as a skilful manipulator of the lighter shades of modern life. Mrs. Marks died December 4, 1922.

The New Theatre provided an opportunity for another play of high quality in *The Arrow Maker,* by Mary Austin, which was produced February 28, 1911. It is one of the very few dramas in which the American Indian is adequately portrayed, not the stage Indian of tradition, but the real red man, idealized a bit for the purpose, but characterized into life. The theme is the revolt of the Chisera, or medicine woman of the Paiute tribe, against the very sanctity which keeps her remote from human love and tribal interests. She is placed on a pedestal in order that she may commune with the gods, but when she finds that the man whom she loves and whom she has made the war leader of the tribe has deserted her for the daughter of the chief, she denounces him in very human fashion, and leads the tribe herself against their enemies. Edith Wynne

Matthison portrayed the Chisera with sympathy and distinction.

This note of repressed and insurgent desire for participation in life was expressed in Alice Brown's *Children of Earth,* a play with an interesting career. After the collapse of the New Theatre, its director, Winthrop Ames, offered a prize of $10,-000 for the best play to be submitted anonymously by an American. About seventeen hundred manuscripts were submitted. The jury of award, Augustus Thomas, Winthrop Ames and Adolph Klauber, gave the prize to *Children of Earth,* and the play was produced by Mr. Ames on January 12, 1915. It was not a stage success, although the characters are well drawn and there is drama in the central theme. Mary Ellen Barstow, a New England spinster, has been domineered over by her father and her brother Aaron, and when the former dies and the latter calmly informs her that she must live with him, she defies him and insists upon ordering her life at last. The lover of her youth returns, and she has built upon him an illusion of happiness which is shattered by the revelation of his meanness and cupidity. In despair she clutches at the offer of Peter Hale, whose wife Jane is a drunkard and a "Portygee," to elope with him. Then in a striking scene at morning in the woods, they see Jane, although she is heartbroken at their departure, going on to her daily tasks, and they decide to return. The play really ends here, and the fourth Act drags, even with Jane's brave effort to save their reputations. Miss Brown is a novelist rather than a playwright, although some of her one-act plays, like *Joint Owners in Spain,* have decided merit.

A play in which this note of individual protest is struck in a setting of an older fashion was the work of a young newspaper man of San Francisco, Charles Kenyon. *Kindling* opened in New York in December, 1911, failed to draw its public and was about to be withdrawn when it was saved by the efforts of a few fellow craftsmen who secured a new life for the play in Chicago. Through the efforts of the Drama League there it scored a success and went over the country.[1] The main theme is the right of everyone to have a fair start in life. Maggie Schultz is about to become a mother. She lives in terror of her child's future in the tenement district of New York, and in order to win their way to Wyoming and a healthier existence, she acts as a "fence" for a depraved thief who robs her own employers and benefactress. The economic background, however, is only incidental. What makes the play important is Maggie's remarkable plea, when she is discovered, for the right of her unborn child to have its chance. The vividness with which this scene lives in memory causes regret that Kenyon has produced nothing since of equal merit.

This group of dramatists does not by any means include all those who dealt with the revolt of the individual. They belong together in the history of our drama because they are nearly all men and women of letters who were brought into the theatre by the hope of achieving something fine and because they thought they saw a possibility in the quickening interest in the theatre which the new century seemed to inaugurate. It would be a mistake to ascribe the movement to any one institution, like the New Theatre, for, as a matter of fact, only two of the plays were produced there, but in a larger sense, the spirit of men like Winthrop Ames, its first director, or of actor-managers like Henry Miller, E. H. Sothern or Margaret Anglin was responsible for the creation of a new atmosphere in which better drama could flourish. Nevertheless, it must not be forgotten that the three leaders in the new movement, Moody, Miss Peabody and Percy MacKaye, had to fight hard to obtain a footing, and their inspiration came from an unconquerable desire to create. Their mutual encouragement grew into close friendship, which included two other poets, Edwin Arlington Robinson and Ridgeley Torrance, both of whom wrote plays intended for the stage. Four of them studied at Harvard, but only two met there, for while Moody and Mac-

[1] See introduction to the published play for an interesting account of its salvation, illuminating in its revelation of the theatrical situation in 1911.

Kaye were there for one year together, they did not meet, and it was only after MacKaye's return from Europe that the relationship began. Their work antedates by some years the establishment of Professor Baker's course in playwriting in 1905, and it would be an error to overstress the Harvard influence. But it is highly significant that some of the finest drama of the Twentieth Century should owe its birth to college men and women who, in spite of untoward circumstances, produced practical stage plays which are permanent contributions to dramatic literature.

CHAPTER XIII

Percy MacKaye and the Drama as Spectacle

ASSOCIATED with Moody not only in friendship and education, in the belief in the poetic drama, and, to a certain extent, in the drama of revolt, Percy MacKaye stands also for a quality of his own. This came to him from his father, Steele MacKaye, and while it has had different expressions, as we shall see, it may be epitomized as the desire to express dramatic ideas by means of large groups of actors, many of whom are but accessories to the main action, in short, the delight in the drama as a spectacle. This creation of emotion through mass and color and grouping has led to some striking achievements and has also placed a certain limitation upon his work, which will become apparent in a critical study.

Percy MacKaye comes from New England stock, mingled with Scottish ancestry on his father's side, and it may not be stretching a point too far to attribute his love of fantasy to his Celtic strain. His mother dramatized *Pride and Prejudice*, in a version long used in schools and colleges, and owing to his father's profession, Percy MacKaye grew up with the theatre. This association was interrupted by his stay at Harvard College, from which he graduated in 1897, some years before the "47 Workshop" of Professor Baker was established.

Before he entered Harvard he had written plays and had contributed choral songs to his father's drama of *Columbus*, which was to have been performed at the projected Spectatorium in Chicago in 1893. The years 1898-1900 were spent in Italy and Germany, where he studied at Leipsic, and four years of school teaching in New York followed. During all this time he was continuing his dramatic work, and among the

27

unproduced plays a prose drama, *The Bridge Builder*, was upon a sociological theme, thus allying him to the drama of revolt. He had been writing, then, for ten years before his play, *The Canterbury Pilgrims*, was accepted by E. H. Sothern in 1903. Although Sothern did not produce it, he offered the author another commission, and, abandoning teaching, MacKaye settled at Cornish, New Hampshire, to devote himself to play writing.

The only play from his journeyman period to be printed was begun at Harvard in 1896. It is of interest as showing his early inspiration from Shakespeare and for the preface which was written in 1910, the date of its publication. In *A Garland to Sylvia* the poet dramatist mingles with his own creations in the effort to save his heroine, with whom he has fallen in love, from the villain lover. It is boyish fancy, and the indirectness of approach which is MacKaye's besetting sin is already apparent. More important is the preface which reveals how deliberate was the movement with which he and Moody became associated and how he separated himself at the beginning from the purely commercial aspects of the theatre.

As this independence has frequently resulted in the postponement of production, MacKaye's dramatic work can be studied most profitably, not from the chronological point of view but from a classification based upon both the material and the method of treatment. His plays intended for the regular theatre fall into one group, which in its turn presents different aspects. In the second, fall the community plays and in the third, the operas. Of real interest also are his critical works upon the theatre, including his prefaces to the published dramas.

His plays written in regular form include his imaginative treatment of older literary material, usually in blank verse, *The Canterbury Pilgrims, Fenris the Wolf, Jeanne d'Arc, Sappho and Phaon, A Thousand Years Ago* and *The Scarecrow;* his satiric or serious discussions of themes of contemporary interest in *Mater, Anti-Matrimony, Tomorrow;* and his studies of provincial American life in *Yankee Fantasies, This Fine-Pretty World* and *Napoleon Crossing the Rockies*.

The Canterbury Pilgrims, written in 1902, though not produced by Sothern, was performed by the Coburn Players in 1909 and has proved one of the most popular of his plays. In 1917 it became the libretto of an opera with music by Reginald de Koven. In *The Canterbury Pilgrims* Chaucer travels with his characters, and conducts quite delicately a sentimental episode with the Prioress while being pursued by the Wife of Bath. Richard II saves him at the end of the play by ruling that the Wife may be married for the sixth time, but only to a miller, and the miller takes her cheerfully. Any attempt to test such a play by its characterization, except in the cases of the principal parts, is forbidden by the luxuriance of the *dramatis personæ*. The Wife of Bath is obviously the most vivid as she is the most vigorous, and on the stage she became the leading figure. What we remember is the spectacle, the moving figures, the poetic conception that visualizes the Fourteenth Century even if it idealizes it. MacKaye had a real knowledge of Chaucer's language and times, and his conception of the poet as feeling at once a spiritual passion for the Prioress and a more earthly leaning toward the Wife of Bath shows an understanding of the qualities that have kept Chaucer's narratives alive through the centuries.

Fenris the Wolf, written in 1904, has not been performed. Its conception is dramatic, however, for it is based on the eternal reaction between masculine passion and feminine purity, and it contains some of the best poetry MacKaye has written. Perhaps the setting is too remote and there is the usual indirectness of approach. Fenris, the wolf god, strives to win Freya, who is betrothed to Baldur, his brother. Odin decides that all four shall be transformed into human beings, and he becomes Ingimund, a priest. Fenris is changed to Egil, a huntsman; Baldur, to Arfi, a dwarf; and Freya, to Thordis, daughter of Ingimund. Egil is a werewolf and in his struggle upward to a finer conception of love for Thordis, her instinc-

tive response to the virility of his passion, his sweeping out of
his path all obstacles, even the life of Arfi his brother, and his
final height of sacrifice, MacKaye had a theme almost Titanic.
But the ending seems inconclusive and the machinery of the
gods' intervention interposes a barrier to our sympathy. Yet
lines like those of Thordis:

> A myriad loves the heart hath, but one mate.
> Once only may the cry of soul and body
> Be answered: the great need can be but once.

make us wish that MacKaye could always have written such
direct and coherent verse.

Jeanne d'Arc, while written in 1905, was the first of his
plays to be given professionally, being produced by Sothern
and Marlowe at the Lyric Theatre in Philadelphia, October 15,
1906. MacKaye has drawn Jeanne as a simple Norman peasant, the symbol of a faith that could arm a Latin race to a
supreme effort and a leader whom the descendants of a Celtic
clan could follow to the death. The two problems that confront a playwright who treats the Joan of Arc story are, how
to deal with the supernatural and how to provide a human
interest which the career of Joan does not afford. MacKaye
solved the first by bringing the voices into the play through
Jeanne, especially in the fine climax of the second Act. The
Dauphin is kneeling apparently at the feet of Jeanne; in
reality he is seeing mirrored in her face the vision of St.
Michael speaking through the stained glass figure of Charle-
magne, who hails his descendant as legitimate, thus removing
the doubt that clogged the actions of the Dauphin and paralyzed the loyalty of France. The human interest is strengthened by the character of D'Alençon, who loves Jeanne and
whose scepticism makes her faith more apparent. It is a good
touch to have his converted belief in her visions strengthen her
in her hour of doubt in the prison. The temporary discourage-
ment of Jeanne makes her more human, also, and D'Alençon
expresses a profound truth when he says:

Photo by Doris Ulmann

For there's no pang, 'mongst all our mortal hurts,
Sharp as the vivisection of a dream.

MacKaye went to the original documents for his historic
sources, and being in sympathy with medieval life and by nature
hospitable to mystical interpretations, without which Jeanne
d'Arc is unintelligible, he has given dramatic literature one of
the best representations of her character and career.   Jeanne
d'Arc has become in literature almost as much a source of
conflict as she was in real life, but there has seldom been so
effective a treatment, one so free from the intrusion of modern
theories or the distortion of personal bias, as that of MacKaye.
Its reception on the stage was a triumph for both playwright
and actors, and while Hauptmann's *Sunken Bell* and Sudermann's *John the Baptist* failed, the season was saved for Sothern and Marlowe by *Jeanne D'Arc*.[1]

Sappho and Phaon, though it held the stage only seven days
when it was produced in New York in 1907, is a powerful
tragedy, lofty in conception and faithful to the Greek spirit.
The tragedy proper tells the story of the love of Sappho for
Phaon, a slave, a love which brings him to disaster and urges
her to her fatal leap into the Ægean Sea.   Human characters
are brought into conflict with fate, typified by the gods, and if
this makes the play remote for the average playgoer, it simpli-
fies the action.   Phaon kills his little son in mistake for his
enemy; Thalassa, his wife, brings their baby, dead, into the
temple for sacrifice; and no explanation is required except the
anger of the gods.   There is fine drama in the conflict between
Thalassa and Sappho for the love of Phaon and the play builds
up well to Sappho's self-destruction.

MacKaye presented *Sappho and Phaon* through a Prologue
dealing with modern excavation at the site of Herculaneum,
and an Induction, which places Horace and Virgil among the
audience witnessing the tragedy, and paints with sympathy
the relations of playwright and actor in the Roman theatre of

[1] See Russell, C. E.   *Julia Marlowe, Her Life and Art*, pp. 416–20.

31

their day. These are interesting to read, and, while they seem to be foreign to the spirit of the modern theatre, they cannot be blamed for the failure of the play, for they were not included in the actual performance. Other causes, possibly Bertha Kalich's intonation, which was not reminiscent of Greek, were responsible. But it is significant that the stage picture received the highest praise, especially the final scene, as Sappho apostrophizes Aphrodite before her plunge into the blue water, with the sun rising above the mist and casting a rose-colored glow upon her. It was again MacKaye's sense of the pictorial, of his vision of the beautiful in form and color translated into terms of the theatre, which proved his mastery of one phase of his art.

The same impulse, the desire to experiment in a dramatic form, accounts for the charming romantic fantasy, *A Thousand Years Ago* (1913). The theme was suggested by an Eighteenth Century Italian comedy, *Turandotte*, by Carlo Gozzi, translated into German by Friedrich Schiller, based originally upon a romance from the *Thousand and One Tales*. But the old story of the prince in disguise, who guesses the riddle and wins the princess, is not the important element in MacKaye's drama. It is rather the framework, in which Capocomico and his vagabond players from Italy become involved in the suit of the Prince of Astrakhan, and apparently extemporize their lines. The student of the theatre was thereby given an opportunity to observe the methods of Carlo Gozzi, whose plays belonged to the Commedie dell' Arte Improvisata, and seem to have been composed by him in his war against the realistic work of Goldoni. In Italy they were acted by masked and semi-masked players who extemporized to a certain degree, after having their parts explained to them. This machinery is better interwoven into the structure of the drama than is usually the case with MacKaye. *A Thousand Years Ago* is also of some significance in the romantic revival referred to elsewhere.

The Scarecrow, MacKaye's most significant contribution to

the regular stage, belongs to his earlier period through its poetic conception and background of fantasy, and through its inspiration in literature. It was begun in 1903 and has been revised constantly, even after production.[1] Its central idea was taken from Hawthorne's story of "Feathertop," published first in 1852 and afterwards included in *Mosses from an Old Manse*. MacKaye has added to the number of persons in "Feathertop." He has made Dickon, the evil spirit, concrete as the tutor of the Scarecrow, who is masquerading as Lord Ravensbane, in order to win the hand of Rachel Merton, the niece of Justice Merton. MacKaye has amplified a hint in "Feathertop" of a guilty relation between Justice Merton and Goody Rickby, into the revenge of the witch upon her betrayer by the deception which convinces the Justice that the scarecrow is his son. But most important, he has made Lord Ravensbane a more heroic and therefore a more tragic character, and as he states in his preface, he has substituted the element of human sympathy for that of irony.

MacKaye uses satire effectively in his picture of the Justice and the dignitaries of Harvard College in the late Seventeenth Century, deceived, by the cleverness of Dickon, into believing the Scarecrow is Lord Ravensbane. Dickon is a good stage character and some of his lines, such as his reply to his pupil, for whom he has penned a poem to Rachel, "Indeed, my lord, I flatter myself that I have dictated some of the finest lines in literature," reveal MacKaye's verbal dexterity. But what raises *The Scarecrow* above the usual play of the period is the powerful employment of the fantastic, not remote as MacKaye too often makes it, but an active force in the drama, kindling the rather abstract creations of Hawthorne into life by the clash of witchcraft against witchcraft in the climax of the drama, the end of the third Act. Here again, he takes a suggestion of Hawthorne, but intensifies its dramatic quality. Ravensbane, who has fallen in love with Rachel Merton, sees

---

[1] "During and after its first production I altered it a good deal, resulting in the version as published in your *Representative American Plays*."—Letter from Mr. MacKaye, 1926.

in the magic glass of truth, which Goody Rickby has sold Rachel, the figure of a scarecrow. At first he thinks it is some evil thing that has frightened Rachel and he draws his sword and rushes at it. Then he realizes that it is his own image, and in the bitter moment of his realization the soul of a man is born in him and baptized with his despair. It is a fine climax of character and the play does not fall down in its conclusion, for, spurred on by his love for Rachel, he flings aside at the last his pipe which keeps him alive and dies in order to rid the woman whom he loves of his presence. But as Rachel says in her requiem, he died a man, and the tragedy of the defeated soul leaves us not with a sense of futility, but with the exaltation that comes when we have witnessed a struggle that has been worth while.

The Scarecrow was first produced by the Harvard Dramatic Club, December 8, 1909; was given professionally with Frank Reicher as the Scarecrow, during two seasons, beginning January 17, 1911, and was played by Muriel Pratt at the Theatre Royal in Bristol, November 30, 1914. It was translated into French as *L'Épouvantail*, by Charles Marie Garnier in 1910, and into German as *Die Vogelscheuche* by Walther Fischer, and was produced at the Deutsches Theater in Berlin in August, 1914, under the direction of Max Reinhardt. The disturbed conditions of the time soon brought the play to a close. This foreign appreciation of the play is due partly to the universal motive, for while the scene is laid in Massachusetts, the drama really takes place in the outer limits of the human soul.

MacKaye's three attempts at the treatment of contemporary themes are included in the years 1908 to 1912. *Mater*, a comedy based on modern politics, is the weakest of his plays. Cullen, the boss, is unlike any politician in real life, and Michael, the hero, is too much of an idealist for the son of a Senator.

Much more successful is his satire upon the effect of the dramas of Ibsen, Hauptmann and Shaw upon the younger generation. The first two acts of *Anti-Matrimony* contain some of the cleverest dialogue MacKaye has written, and the central situation is well conceived. Morris and Isabelle Grey have been married abroad, but in order to emancipate Morris's brother Elliott, and his wife Mildred, Isabelle's sister, the younger pair represent themselves, upon their arrival at the Grey homestead in Massachusetts, as unmarried. They are the apostles of freedom and the superman and anyone who has suffered from the pseudo-appreciation of the Scandinavian school of drama may have some delightful moments in reading the scenes in which Isabelle and Morris endeavor to educate their benighted relatives from the works of "the masters," which have been brought over in a suit-case. Mildred overhears a conversation between Isabelle and Morris which lets out their secret, and she and Elliott, by pretending that they are becoming emancipated and consequently by making love to their emancipators of the opposite sex, excite the jealousy of Isabelle and Morris and extort a confession of their respectability. While the play weakens toward the end, the directness of the language and the unity of structure are noteworthy and the tone of the play is like a breath of fresh air. It afforded Henrietta Crosman a congenial part in the rôle of Mildred.

This playful satire upon the absurdities which spring from the undigested influence of the continental dramatists, was more successful than MacKaye's serious attempt to treat one of their favorite themes. *Tomorrow*, which was given for a brief period at the Little Theatre in Philadelphia in 1913, dealt constructively with the problem of selection in matters of marriage, and was MacKaye's attempt at a positive treatment of a theme of which Ibsen in *Ghosts* and Brieux in *Damaged Goods* had furnished a negative aspect. If MacKaye failed to reach the standard set by Ibsen in the dramatic treatment of disease, he certainly excelled Brieux, for he at least wrote a play and not a tract. The idea of laying the scene in the garden of a botanist who has been studying the processes of grafting plants in order to develop similar processes among human beings was not a bad one, but there was too much discussion of eugenics and the type characters representing science and the church were not woven into the play with the skill that Moody showed in *The Faith Healer*.

MacKaye has well named his volume of one-act plays *Yankee Fantasies* (1912), for while the scene is native, there is no attempt at a realistic treatment of the material. The characters are types and those with which we are expected to sympathize appeal not on account of their fidelity to New England in racial characteristics, but rather because of their revolt from the dull routine of life or because of some alien strain in their blood. In *Chuck*, it is the kinship with the untamed animal that lends Abel his charm for Letty. In *The Antick*, the French blood in Julie, the "Canuck" girl, lures John Hale because of the unconscious inheritance from his own mother whom he believed to be of the New England stock, but whom he discovers was also of the proscribed race. This motive is essentially dramatic, and MacKaye might have made more of it. In *Gettysburg* the old soldier whose palsied legs come back to health at the sound of the martial music is a dramatic figure, for the intensification of memory until it produces a physical change provides adequate opportunity for acting. It seems a mistake, however, to have the soldier talk in blank verse. *Sam Average* has a larger theme, but one less suited to the theatre. During a scene in the War of 1812, in which two soldiers are preparing to desert, MacKaye symbolizes in the muffled figure that visits them the spirit of the average American who gives his best for the country he loves without outward expression but with quiet indomitable persistence. Again the conception is better than the execution, which is too abstract for the compass of a one-act play. These short dramas have had professional or semi-professional production, and yet they do not convince me that the one-act play is MacKaye's natural field. The necessary compression is alien to his whole habit of thought.

Along the same Appalachian Trail which harbors in New England the characters in the *Yankee Fantasies*, there lives, in

the Kentucky mountains, a primitive race which has already
been treated in fiction. In 1920 a Fellowship in Creative Literature was established for MacKaye at Miami University,
Ohio, near the Kentucky border, and he naturally seized the
opportunity to study at first hand what seemed fine material
for drama. The first fruit of his wandering and his sojourn
among these people beyond the "hundred-mile wall of Pine
Mountain" was the comedy, *This Fine-Pretty World*, performed at the Neighborhood Playhouse, New York, December
26, 1923.

In this play MacKaye has created a character. Beem Sprattling is a dreamer, called by his neighbors a "lie-swearer," who,
according to his own account, "follies the Oninvisible and the
Onbeheerd-of," combining with this imaginative quality a dishonest streak which has sent him to jail seventeen times. He is
quite willing, for a shoat, to testify that he has had illicit relations with Mag Maggot, whose husband wishes to divorce her
in order that he may marry a young girl. When their schemes
are defeated, in one of the most amusing court trials on our
stage, he declines to escape the penalty of his perjury, preferring jail, with its large leisure for dreaming, to the responsibilities of life. There is real comedy in character drawing
and in situation, touched with a well-restrained sentiment
which emerges in the silence of Beem Sprattling's wife, who
declines to testify against him because he is " her man," and
the chivalrous conduct of the judge who covers the courtroom
with his gun in her behalf, as a tribute to her spirit of devotion.
This Fine-Pretty World might have succeeded even better than
it did had it not been for MacKaye's very faithfulness to his
material. He became so charmed with the linguistic survivals
of Elizabethan English which he found unspoiled or quaintly
rearranged on the lips of the mountaineers, that for the first
fifteen minutes the audience was barely able to follow the play.
Dialect, after all, is in literature usually artificial, and on the
stage it is a dangerous experiment unless a compromise is

effected between the real speech of the people represented and the normal language of the theatre.

While *The Scarecrow* remains still his best play for the regular theatre, it is in the field of the "community drama" that MacKaye has probably done his most original work. From the early days of his association with his father, he has conceived of the drama as a social force, and the crusading spirit which has been an inspiration and also, at times, an interference with his artistic career, shows most clearly in his plays written for the community theatre. MacKaye is distinctly American in his conception of the community as a creative assisting force as well as an audience. To him the people are not "toilers," as they so frequently appear in the European folk drama; there is no class consciousness implied; they are united in a democratic art which does not need to assert equality, because its converse has not been suggested.

From 1905, when his Prologue to the *St. Gaudens Masque* was produced at Cornish, New Hampshire, he has been experimenting with the masque as a flexible form in the theatre. His *Canterbury Pilgrims* was given with fifteen hundred citizens of Gloucester, Massachusetts, in 1909, as *The Gloucester Pageant*, in honor of President Taft. *Sanctuary, a Bird Masque*, in which the conversion of a bird hunter is brought about by both symbolic and natural characters, was given first at Meriden, New Hampshire, September 12, 1913, in honor of President and Mrs. Wilson, to dedicate the bird sanctuary of the Meriden Bird Club. It has been repeated many times and has carried its message of humanity to a quarter of a million spectators. In 1914 he conceived and directed a civic masque concerned with the development of the city of Saint Louis from its foundation through the work of Spanish, French and English pioneers, including the conquest of gold. This masque had a real civic purpose apart from its artistic aim, and its importance as a union of social and artistic forces is rightly emphasized by MacKaye in the published play.

Caliban, by the Yellow Sands, a Community Masque of the

Art of the Theatre, was executed by MacKaye at the invitation of the committee which had in charge the celebration, in New York City, of the Tercentenary of Shakespeare's death. It was given on a great scale at the stadium of the College of the City of New York from May 25 to June 5, 1916, with about twenty-five hundred persons in the production, and with the help of artists like Joseph Urban and Robert Edmond Jones, and of organizations such as the Neighborhood Playhouse and the Washington Square Players. The music was by Arthur Farwell. It was truly a fine example of individual and community co-operation, and the result was magnificent. Mere size means nothing in itself, but there is a nobility in the unification of masses of human beings expressing one artistic conception of beauty, in celebration of a lofty theme. And for the creation and direction of *Caliban* the chief credit belongs to Percy MacKaye.

The inspiration of the masque was naturally some phase of Shakespeare's art. MacKaye chose to continue the theme of *The Tempest* and adapt it to a celebration of the art of which Shakespeare is the foremost exponent. Caliban is regenerated through two forces, his love for Miranda and his education by Prospero. According to MacKaye, "Caliban is that passionate child-curious part of us all, grovelling close to his aboriginal origins, yet groping up and staggering . . . toward that serener plane of pity and love, reason and disciplined will, where Miranda and Prospero commune with Ariel and his spirits."

On a raised stage, the great jaws of Setebos hold the form of Ariel imprisoned, while Caliban jeers at him. Then Miranda appears and Prospero frees Ariel and saves Miranda from Caliban's lust. But instead of spurning him as a brute, Prospero determines to educate him by a revelation of the progress of dramatic art. This is expressed in two ways. In the large central ground-circle, pageant groups represent typical dramatic spectacles of ancient Egypt, Greece and Rome, of medieval Germany, France, England, Spain and Italy. It is not too much to say that these spectacles were a revelation to modern eyes of the varying forms of dramatic creation, a protest against the canons of criticism that limit the art of the theatre by preconceived theories.

On an elevated inner stage there were enacted scenes from Shakespeare's plays. These were not so successful, for distance rendered them inaudible to nearly all the spectators, and they seemed less closely woven into the texture of the masque. But *Caliban* must be judged by its total effect, and, despite certain weaknesses which were inherent in any such production, the final picture of Caliban regenerated, rising from his stooping position to his height and calling to the spirit of Shakespeare for "More visions,—visions, Master," is unforgettable.

There is a distinction between the impression made upon a community through the effect of a masque upon its material progress and the impression made upon large groups of people by the masque which develops an artistic theme for an occasion of civic interest which has no local relation. Naturally, the universal has more quality of permanence than the particular, and that is why *Caliban* is of more significance than *Saint Louis*. *Saint Louis* could be given only in one time and place; *Caliban* could be given in any place in which Shakespeare's art is known, and indeed it was repeated in Boston with twice the personnel and before even larger crowds.

From the point of view of poetic expression, *The Evergreen Tree* (1917), a masque of Christmas, is one of MacKaye's most appealing productions. One after another, the persons connected with the Christmas story pass before the tree or are sheltered under it. Human interest is won by making Herod's slaughter of the children concrete in the story of the wounded peddler, Claus, and by a not too fanciful transition, he becomes the prototype of Santa Claus, the patron of the tree and of Christmas.

A drama which MacKaye classifies among his plays for the regular theatre, but which is also allied to his more spectacular dramas is *Washington, the Man Who Made Us,* first produced as a whole at the Belasco Theatre in Washington, before Congress and members of the Cabinet on February 22, 1920, with Walter Hampden as Washington. MacKaye calls it a "ballad play" and it is one of his brave attempts to develop a folk drama out of present-day conditions of the traditional theatre. *Saint Louis* and *Caliban* proceed symbolically. *Washington* deals with real events. So did the early chronicle plays, of course, but the progressive aspect of *Washington* is the attempt to develop a "participatory technique," both for indoors and for out-of-doors. By this is meant a technique which permits the performance of the play by a large number of actors who thereby express the spirit of the community producing the drama, and which allows also its production on a scale suited for the traditional theatre. MacKaye has expressed clearly the distinction between the two objects for which he strives:

The basic requirement of the Community Drama is expression—expression varied to its maximum to include expressional opportunity for the largest number of individual participants practicable.

The basic requirement of the commercial theatre is just the opposite—expression concentrated to its minimum, to include only the kind of expressional opportunity, within range of the fewest needful actors, and proportioned to their salaries for competence or reputation.

. . . .

For community necessities the play should have the maximum number of characters, with maximum opportunity for expression: for commercial necessities—the minimum of these.[1]

MacKaye tried to solve this problem by providing two forms of the play; one festal, with one hundred characters, and one in which the rôles may be taken by twenty-nine persons.

MacKaye has faced the usual difficulties of the chronicle play. He has attempted to portray Washington as a young

[1] Appendix to *Washington, the Man Who Made Us,* pp. 288–89.

man, at Mt. Vernon; in the conflict of the Revolution, and in his return to private life. He has conceived of him in his human and national relations. He has gone even farther and has represented him as a world figure, receiving the homage of the Allies. For such a drama, unity is almost impossible, but MacKaye endeavored to tie the episodes together by a series of ballads, based on old tunes traditional in New England or the Southern Appalachian Mountains. The words are at times traditional and sometimes original with MacKaye. The sole test of such an innovation is its success with an audience; but in reading, the ballads seem interruptions. Moreover, the whole play is not fused, and the very wealth of material, lofty in conception though it is, and based on a thorough study of Washington's character, defeats the purpose of the playwright. Perhaps, after all, the expert playwrights of the past, like Dunlap or Burnett, were wise in keeping Washington in the background. Certainly the many plays in which he figured as the chief character, and which have all perished, would seem to attest their wisdom. Washington is really too great a figure for the stage. He is too well-known in his actions, too little really understood in his nature. Having become a great national ideal, it is a mistake to depict him realistically. To paint him as an ideal character against a background of realistic scenes and characters is confusing.

MacKaye attempted another compromise by providing a chronicle play which could be produced either in its entirety or in separate episodes. This is a fatal compromise from the point of view of unity. But there are a number of the episodes that in themselves are quite effective. Indeed, the Valley Forge Episode, in Act III, was given in French by Jacques Copeau, at the Théâtre du Vieux Colombier in New York during the week of February 17, 1919, before the entire play was produced in Washington, while other actions have since been published for production as one-act plays.

The operas fall outside our province. *Rip Van Winkle*

(1919) is of interest, however, as a laudable attempt at an opera upon a native theme, in which words and music, the latter by Reginald de Koven, should both be the work of Americans. Rip is represented in his youth and a love motive is created by the invention of Peterkee, a child who later becomes his wife. There is a sympathetic interpretation of Rip Van Winkle as the representation of eternal youth, and the effect on the stage was charming within its limitations.

Not only in his play writing, but also in his critical essays, MacKaye has been a crusader for the gospel of democracy in the drama and for the development of the theatre as a force toward the kindling of a higher social consciousness. In *The Playhouse and the Play* (1909), *The Civic Theatre* (1912) and *Community Drama* (1917) he has argued for an endowed civic theatre as the only escape from the limitations which commercialism has set to the free exercise of the playwright's skill. He recognizes that a private business must pay, and he believes that managers will tend toward the production of the well-established forms of drama rather than toward the encouragement of original ideas. He shares, too, with Moody the revolt against the spirit of Puritanism in an eloquent passage:

But that same oblique-eyed spirit which broke the beautiful idols of fauns and Grecian deities, and smashed the images of stained-glass saints, long since looked upon the living images of the playhouse with suspicion, and shattered the earlier ideals of play and players with contempt. The iconoclast and the Puritan combined to close the doors of the playhouse as a public temple of the joy of life; and over its doors, suspended, they placed Satan, with Miltonian wings, to shed darkness on the drama, obscuring its religious function from the people. And so to-day, though the Puritan has departed and Satan has lost his anathema, and though the people once more flock back in multitudes to the playhouse, yet they no longer enter it as a public temple; new generations have forgotten that ever it was one, for they find it occupied by private merchants; and the joy of life which they view there is no longer dedicated to their common aspiration.[1]

[1] *The Playhouse and the Play*, p. 74.

It may well be that MacKaye's greatest service to the American drama will be that of inspiration. He grew up in the theatre and his knowledge of its history and technique is beyond question. His experiments in the traditional theatre, in the community out-of-door masque, as well as his constant writing upon the theatre, have undoubtedly helped to bring about the widespread revolt against the domination of the commercial standards in theatre and drama. From the beginning of his career he has stood resolutely, in the face of what must have been to a young man great temptation, against the lowering of his artistic ideals to the claims of personal vanity on the part of actors or managers who wished to alter his plays to suit themselves. For this courage and this devotion to his art there can be nothing but praise, and if for a long time he seemed a voice crying in the wilderness, he is entitled to the credit of the pioneer. Many of his dreams seem impossible of fulfillment, and the impracticability of some of them has obscured, perhaps, the essentially sound basis of others of more vital significance.

To a certain degree the result is the same with his dramas. With all his scrupulous care in the gathering of material to represent Greece, Italy or England of an older time, we feel that in the creation of atmosphere, life somehow has escaped. Nearly all his inspiration comes from history or literature—when he deals with real life, as in *Mater*, he has done his weakest work. With insight into the dramatic qualities of the characters of Chaucer or of Hawthorne, of historical personages like Joan of Arc, he has given us no character that is wholly his. This would not matter so much, for he has the best authority in the history of the drama for this appropriation, if we did not feel that the conception was greater than the execution. And so lofty has been his framework that mediocrity, even at times triviality in his language, jars more severely than it would in the work of a playwright less ambitious. Yet when his limitations have been mentioned, it is with regret. For the spiritual imagination that conceived the agony of the

Scarecrow, tortured with the birth pangs of a human soul, looked into the future of the drama of fantasy. And the visual power that conceived of *Caliban,* with its hundreds of actors moving harmoniously into a unity that brought the art of the theatre of the world into one great spectacle, looked far into the future of the theatre of the people.

Sympathetic as my interest is in this drama of the people, its nature forbids any treatment here, and I can only indicate its scope by a few illustrations which show the distinction between it and the traditional drama. The community drama, in fact, has not yet been defined, for it is still in an experimental stage. In its pure state it is a departure from the traditional theatre, for it is the expression by a group of people of a dramatic theme in which they are not merely repeating words written by one playwright, but are adding elements in action and characterization wrought out of their own interest in the occasion. In its extreme form the play should be composed by the group and directed by them; the costumes should be made, the setting devised and the lighting designed by the participants. This pure form of the community drama is far from being generally practicable and, as a matter of necessity, the community drama has had to be evolved by a few artists working harmoniously in their respective spheres. Most important is the force which directs the spectacle and ties together the various elements into unity. On account of the large scale on which some community plays are given, the question of acoustics is an insistent one, and in certain phases of the community drama pantomime has to be substituted for the spoken word. Music, as an accompaniment of pantomime, or of the word itself, is often a vital adjunct.

The most noteworthy of our masques or pageants have been inspired by a desire to celebrate a great historical personage or to preserve a picture of a period in our history. The *Mission Play,* which recreates the story of the founding of Christian civilization in the West, was produced for the first time April 29, 1912, at the Mission Play Theatre, San Gabriel, California, and has been given each season since then. The conception of the play was due to John Steven McGroarty (1862-   ), the historian of California. The *Mission Play* is especially interesting because it is centred, more than is usually the case, about a character, that of Fra Junipero Serra. The first Act reveals him in 1769 at San Diego, holding by his indomitable spirit the first settlement at San Gabriel which is just about to be abandoned when the relief ship arrives. The struggle of Fra Serra against the despair of starving men, against the unresponding Indians, against even the priests of his company who have begun to give up hope, makes fine drama. The second Act portrays the missions in their prime in 1784, and reveals Fra Serra's great love for California. The author rediscovered in 1923 the old Santo, a hymn which had not been sung for eighty years and which now forms part of the musical accompaniment of the drama. One of the most striking elements in the play is the part taken by descendants of the old Spanish and Mexican families who sing the songs and dance the dances of their forefathers. The third Act depicts the decay of the missions in 1847 after their seizure by the Mexican Government, and the play ends with the illumination of the cross that stands upon the hillside above Capistrano. It is estimated that over two million spectators have seen the *Mission Play* and it has become an institution of California, built up from her soil and with a wide social influence.

Another California production, *The Pilgrimage Play*, was first produced June 28, 1920, and each year it is presented nightly during the summer months, Sundays excepted, in the open air Pilgrimage Theatre set against the hills in the El Camino Real Canyon in Hollywood. *The Pilgrimage Play* was largely the work of the late Christine Wetherill Stevenson, of Philadelphia, who has accomplished a remarkable feat in transcribing the Biblical story of the earthly career of Jesus Christ as found in the Four Gospels, so as to reproduce the language of Christ without impairing the dramatic form. The basis of the play is the King James version of the English Bible, and there are only a few instances where the simpler language of other versions has been substituted. The play is presented in twelve episodes or scenes, with a prologue in which the coming of Jesus is heralded, and to which is added an epilogue of promise.

The first scene deals with the career of John the Baptist and the baptism of Jesus Christ. The second scene is in Samaria and the miracles are wrought. The third is at the court of Herod and dramatizes the incident of Salome. The fourth is the Transfiguration. The fifth is at the house of Martha in Bethany and deals with the resurrection of Lazarus. These scenes make up the first Act.

The second Act is laid in Jerusalem and proceeds with the dramatic incidents of Christ's Passion—the defiance of the authority of the Jews, the Last Supper, the Garden of Gethsemane, a trial scene before Caiaphas and again before Pilate, the scene at the tomb, and finally the brief scene of the Ascension. The setting was very well employed in the production of a dramatic atmosphere. While the Crucifixion was not represented on the stage, the three crosses on the distant hills were illuminated as the final touch of drama. The part of Jesus of Nazareth has been played by many well-known actors, including William Faversham, Henry Herbert, Reginald Pole, and Ernest Lawford. Reginald Pole has directed the production each season.

Far across the continent, a companion piece to the *Mission Play* was *The Pilgrim Spirit*, the pageant given in celebration of the Tercentenary of the landing of the Pilgrims at Plymouth in 1620. It was first produced July 13, 1921, and was repeated during the summer. The author and director was Professor George Pierce Baker and the participants included the people of Plymouth and the surrounding towns. After preliminary episodes describing the earlier attempts at settlement the persecution which drove the separatists out of England is portrayed in a number of scenes. Later episodes show the Pilgrims in Holland, the signing of the Mayflower Compact on shipboard, the landing, the struggles with the Indians, the disputes among the Colonists; and strike some notes of prophecy. The pageant was very effective and was more than a local undertaking since songs were written for it by Edwin Arlington Robinson, Josephine Preston Peabody and Robert Frost. It is significant that the three most striking pageants of the time, *The Mission Play, The Pilgrimage Play* and *The Pilgrim Spirit*, have all celebrated the power of faith and the triumph of the spirit even in apparent defeat.

Only a word can be said concerning the many masques and pageants produced by the colleges. Perhaps the most truly dramatic was the *Masque of American Drama*, produced by the Zelosophic and Philomathean Societies of the University of Pennsylvania in May, 1917, as part of the American Drama celebration, under the auspices of the Drama League of America. This came appropriately one hundred and fifty years after the production of the first American play, Thomas Godfrey's *The Prince of Parthia*. The *Masque* was inspired by MacKaye's *Caliban* and in a sense began where that finished. It represented the courtship of Drama by America, and the interruptions and discouragements, due to wars, commercialism and other impediments, of the development of the art of drama in this country, before its final triumph. The words of the *Masque* were written by Albert E. Trombly of the Faculty of Romance Languages, and the music by Reginald de Koven. Practically all the parts were taken by the students of the University. The symbolic characters acted on a front stage; the historical processions and dances took place in a middle ground and, on a rear stage, scenes from five American plays representing the progress of the art, were played in pantomime with musical accompaniment. The plays selected were Godfrey's *Prince of Parthia*, Bird's *Gladiator*, Boker's *Francesca da Rimini, Rip Van Winkle*, and MacKaye's *Scarecrow*. One effective episode was the representation of Thomas Godfrey explaining the meaning of his play to his fellows in the old College of Philadelphia.

These few instances of the community spectacle can only indicate the widespread possibilities of the art. But after all, it is not drama in the sense that the folk play as written in North Carolina [1] under Professor Koch's direction is drama. What separates the community play from the traditional drama most sharply is its lack of characterization. The progress of the drama has steadily been away from the play in which large room was needed for the display of turbulent emotion. The picture-frame stage has come with the intimate drama, with the play which appeals through slight gesture and pregnant sentences that make their insistent demand upon the quick appreciation of the audience. It has seemed to modern playwrights, as it has seemed to all the great dramatists of the past, that the word must carry with it its instant appeal, and that the most vital plays are those in which what the character says and does dominates both situation and background.

Community dramas have been written for a quarter of a century. Yet from them how many characters remain in our memories? Is not the reason that after all the discussion of the subject belongs in the history of the theatre, not in the history of the drama? For the theatre it is of great significance; for the drama that is to become a permanent literary inheritance it is still of interest mainly when it forms a portion of the work of a playwright who has proved himself in the regular form.

[1] See Chap. XXIII.

CHAPTER XIV

IT WAS only to be expected that the new spirit in drama would find its expression from the point of view of a woman. During the latter part of the Nineteenth Century, few women had followed the example of Mrs. Mowatt and Mrs. Howe, and those who did, like Marguerite Merington, the author of *Captain Lettarblair*, Madeleine Lucette Ryley, author of *An American Citizen*, or Martha Morton, who wrote a number of stage successes, including *A Bachelor's Romance*, need not detain us. They were usually romantic or farcical comedies and merely followed a mode of the time.

The work of Rachel Crothers, on the contrary, had from the beginning a quality of its own. Like Moody's, her plays have usually been a criticism of life, but unlike Moody she came to the drama not through the avenues of literature but through the definite training of the stage. She is, above all, a practical playwright, with a keen sense of what is theatrically effective. She directs her own plays and, with a feminine instinct for detail, presents a stage setting in which there is rarely a jarring note. Yet she has steadily declined to be merely entertaining, and in consequence her plays form a body of drama whose significance grows under inspection and whose unity of purpose becomes steadily more apparent.

Rachel Crothers was born in Bloomington, Illinois, in 1878. She is the daughter of Dr. Eli Kirk Crothers, a friend of Lincoln, who won the only lawsuit to which her father was a party, and Marie Louise DePew, who was the first woman physician in the central part of Illinois. Her grandfather, Elijah De Pew, was also a friend of Lincoln and promoted his Presidential

campaign. Against the traditions of her family, she developed a passion for the theatre as a child, and wrote and directed a play at the age of twelve. After graduating from the State Normal School in 1892, she began her training for the stage in Boston and in New York, principally at the Wheatcroft School, remaining as pupil and instructor for four years. She also filled three engagements on the professional stage, with Madame Rhea and others.

During her stay at the Wheatcroft School Miss Crothers began her creative work with the writing and directing of one-act plays, and her first work to be professionally performed was a one-act comedy, *The Rector*, presented at the Madison Square Theatre in 1902. This is a treatment, with real insight, of a young clergyman who marries a pretty but not very practical girl, instead of the wife selected for him by his congregation. Her first long play, *The Three of Us* (1906), was laid in a mining camp in Nevada. If it is not as profound a study of the contrasted Eastern and Western types as Moody gave us the same year in *The Great Divide*, it is a vivid and sympathetic presentation of a girl's character. Rhy MacChesney's determination to guide and protect her two younger brothers, even against their own ambitions and even at the risk of her own happiness, is appealing because it is carried out without heroics and because it celebrates the loyalty of thousands of women who, in the United States, play the dual rôle of sister and mother. But Rhy is not simply the self-immolating woman of European drama: she is also the head of the family and a woman of business. She is an active force, and when she has been put in a false position by giving her word to a clever schemer not to reveal certain information, she goes to his rooms at night and demands release from her promise. Much of the plot is conventional, it is true, but the characters are well drawn, and the preservation of the family of the MacChesneys kindles a responsive chord in anyone who sympathizes with youth fighting its battles against the world and its own inexperience.

The *Coming of Mrs. Patrick* (1907) and *Myself Bettina* (1908) showed no advance upon *The Three of Us*, but in her next play, *A Man's World* (1909), Miss Crothers produced one of the most significant dramas of the decade. With a few deft touches she establishes the atmosphere of an apartment house in lower New York. Around "Frank" Ware, a writer who is a woman of an independent but lovable nature, she places a well-drawn group of painters, writers and musicians, of whom Fritz Bahn, a violinist, Lione Brune, a singer, and Clara Oakes, a hapless miniature painter, are the most important. Frank Ware is bringing up "Kiddie," a boy of seven, whose mother had died in her house in Paris when the boy was born. Through her sympathy with this woman in her shame, Frank has become convinced that any scheme of things which permits the father of "Kiddie" to escape the consequences of his action is basically not fair, even if society has accepted the "double standard" of morality. So embittered is she that she fights against her growing love for Malcolm Gaskell, a vigorous personality who, unknown to himself and to her, is "Kiddie's" father. Miss Crothers's skill is shown in the way she makes every stroke count. In the second Act, laid in Clara's rooms, Lione, jealous of Fritz Bahn's love for Frank, points out in Clara's miniature of Kiddie his strong resemblance to Gaskell. It is a fine scene, in which is depicted the crystallization of rumor into suspicion. Moreover, Clara, the medium through which it is built up, is herself one of the best characters in the drama, and her outburst of grief at the failure of her pitiful exhibition and the uselessness of her life is truly pathetic, and made a deep impression on the stage.

Clara: No man has ever asked me to marry him. I've never had a beau—a real beau—in my life. I—I've always been superfluous and plain. Absolutely superfluous. I'm not necessary to one single human being. I'm just one of those everlasting women that the world is full of. There's nobody to take care of me and I'm simply not capable of taking care of myself. I've tried—God knows I've tried—and what is the use? What under Heaven do I get out of it? If I were a man—the most insignificant little runt of a man—I could persuade some woman to marry me—and could have a home and children and hustle for my living—and life would mean something. Oh, I can't bear it, Frank. I can't bear it! I often wish I were pretty and bad and could have my fling and die.

(*Sobbing she falls on the couch—huddled and helpless.*)

The height of the action comes in the third Act in two strong scenes. Lione tells Frank her belief in Gaskell's relation to Kiddie, and in the conversation of the two women Lione puts the conventional attitude clearly: "It's a man's world—that's the size of it. What's the use of knocking your head against things you can't change?" But Frank has a higher standard, and when Gaskell comes in to tell her he loves her, she questions him and finds he is really Kiddie's father. Skilfully Miss Crothers shifts the appeal from the general to the personal. Frank has been willing to love Gaskell without inquiring into his past. But when she finds out the truth she recoils.

Frank: Every time I've looked at Kiddie I've cursed the man who ruined his mother and branded him with disgrace.

Gaskell: Frank, stop!

Frank: I've loathed and despised that man, I tell you—and it's you. Before it was some one else—anyone—some one unknown, but now it's you—you—*you.*

(*She stops. They both turn with horror, as Kiddie, in his night clothes, stands watching them, a little wondering figure.*)

Frank refuses to marry him, for she cannot make him see that he has committed any crime. To him, Kiddie's mother was an incident, and he runs true to form, being too honest to pretend to a remorse he does not feel. Miss Crothers had the courage to end her play logically, for Frank had been in love with an ideal of Gaskell rather than with Gaskell himself. *A*

Man's World offers no solution for the situation it deplores, except the substitution of a career for a woman instead of the dependence upon marriage as her only resource. There is no railing at mankind, however, and it challenged Augustus Thomas' more profound analysis in his best play, *As a Man Thinks*, in which he definitely refers to *A Man's World*. It was not only her knowledge of feminine psychology that made the play important. When Fritz Bahn tells Lione, "Every woman keeps her own place in a man's heart," we realize that Miss Crothers knows both sides of the shield.

In *He and She*, first played on the road in 1911 and then produced in Boston as *The Herfords* in 1912, Miss Crothers dealt with a situation both modern and fundamental, the contest of husband and wife for supremacy and for the establishment of their respective spheres. Tom Herford and his wife Ann are both sculptors and have succeeded in keeping their professional and personal relations distinct until both enter an important competition. Her quick sympathy when she knows he has lost is sharply contrasted with his reaction when they learn a few moments later that Ann has won. He struggles bravely to rejoice with her, but he feels instinctively that her victory has brought about a crisis in their relations. Among the group gathered at their home to wait for the verdict, her father, his sister, and his assistant, Keith McKenzie, all show their disappointment, while the only one to rejoice is Ruth Creel, a representative of the girl who prefers her own career as an editor to the domination of the love of Keith. Then into this tense situation Millicent, the sixteen-year-old daughter of Tom and Ann, precipitates her love story with the chauffeur at her boarding school. This scene, in which Ann, with her heart full of the struggle between love and ambition, has to fight with all her skill to draw from Millicent the truth about her relations with the boy, is as quietly dramatic as anything Miss Crothers has done. Ann gives up her opportunity, although Tom tells her what will happen.

Tom: You're cut up now—but if you should give this thing up—there'll be times when you'd eat your heart out to be at work on it—when the artist in you will *yell* to be let out.

Ann: I know. I know. And I'll hate you because you're doing it—and I'll hate myself because I gave it up—and I'll almost —hate—her. I—I know. I know. You needn't tell me. Why, I've seen my men and women up there—their strong limbs stretched—their hair blown back. I've seen the crowd looking up—I've heard people say—"A woman did that" and my heart has almost burst with pride—not so much that *I* had done it—but for *all* women. And then the door opened—and Millicent came in. There isn't any choice, Tom—she's part of my body—part of my soul. Will you make my frieze, dear, will you?

Miss Crothers reveals so sympathetically the man's point of view—that he must be the breadwinner and the head of the family, that the play on the stage secures the sympathy for Tom rather than Ann. It was written for a woman star but, although it has been produced on four different occasions, the last time in 1920, with Miss Crothers acting the part of Ann, it has not been a popular success. Yet the dialogue is as fine as any she has written and her differentiation of the women like Ann and Ruth, as opposed to the domestic old-fashioned type like Daisy Herford, who frankly wants to be married, is complete. Perhaps the play is even yet ahead of its time, for the situation on which it is based does not occur as frequently as it undoubtedly will in the future. It was based, however, on an actual situation, in which the husband and wife were both skilled architects.

Ourselves (1913) is a powerful study of the responsibility which women of cultivation and refinement should assume for present moral conditions. Beatrice Barrington takes Molly from a reformatory into her own home and Molly develops an affair with Bob Barrington, Beatrice's brother. Molly delivers a curtain speech as she leaves the house of her benefactress:

Molly: I'm goin' fast enough. I didn't ask to come. Lord knows I didn't want to. I don't know what you call *good* and bad—the way you see it—all I want is to get out. You happen to find out one little thing and act like this when it's too late. Are you blind as bats? Don't you live in this world? Don't you know what is goin' on? If you feel like this about it, why don't you stop it? If this is the worst thing your men can do why do you let 'em? Why do you stand fer it and—and there wouldn't *be* any of us.

Young Wisdom (1914) is a comedy dealing with an attempt at a trial marriage and the triumph of convention. In the same year she showed her versatility by writing a charming romantic comedy, *The Heart of Paddy Whack*, laid in Ireland about 1790. While the plot was conventional, Miss Crothers revealed her understanding of the imaginative quality in the Irish peasant, especially in the character of the boy Michael. In *Old Lady 31* (1916) she took as a basis a novel by Louise Forsslund but enriched it by her additions. It is an appealing story of an old sea captain and his wife, who, through poor investments on his part, are brought to poverty. Rather than separate he secures admission to the Old Ladies' Home to which he has taken her and he becomes "Old Lady 31." The reaction of the women in the home, his rebellion and final capitulation and return, are dextrously managed to preserve the mellow fragrance of love in the twilight of two simple but gallant lives.

Miss Crothers's work was interrupted by her services as founder and president of the Stage Women's War Relief. But after a play, *Once Upon a Time*, hastily written for Chauncey Olcott and laid in a copper district in the Far West and in New York City, Miss Crothers wrote her striking comedy, *A Little Journey* (1918). It was not so much the unusual stage setting of the Pullman car, for that had been used before, but it was the natural way she made the various characters react to the situations. Julie Rutherford, a girl who has been brought up in luxury but is suddenly left with no alternative except a life with a distant brother who does not want her, loses her ticket and has to accept the help of Jim West, a

Western type, who is much more real than the conventional cowboy so long in possession of the stage. Their rapidly growing love story is set against an amusing background of the various types which throng a sleeping car. The contrast of the first Act, with the characters' instinctive distrust of each other, and the second Act, with its note of temporary intimacy, is wrought in the spirit of true comedy. Then comes the sudden crash of an accident, and the lights go out. The third Act, on the hill top, in which the real natures of the characters emerge under stress, is a fitting conclusion. They do not all become heroic by any means, but the transition in Julie's nature is at least possible, and the assumption of half the group that the blow on her head has injured her reason is one of Miss Crothers' sure touches. In fact, the very skill with which the minor characters are drawn threatens to dwarf the interest of the main action, and this dramatic danger became more apparent in *39 East* (1919), in which one remembers much more clearly the boarding-house types than one does the love story which is intended to be the central motive.

After twenty years of playwriting, Miss Crothers showed the flexibility of her talent by treating with freshness and fidelity the problems of conduct presented by the younger generation after the war. The picture of Teddy Gloucester and her friends in *Nice People* (1920) is accurate; we see vividly depicted the urge for pleasure at any cost and the shadow of boredom lurking over it all for the best of the group, while the others remain perfectly satisfied. The danger Teddy runs in her midnight escapade with Scottie Wilbur, both inflamed by liquor and passion, is indicated in a masterly scene in which the artistic reticence of the playwright scorns the details in which a Gorky or a Dreiser would have revelled. The polite unbelief of Teddy's friends in her story of the advent of Billy Wade and his midnight conversation with Teddy while Scottie lay in his drunken stupor on the couch, is also a clever touch. Miss Crothers does not make them all mere types—Eileen and Hallie are clearly differentiated; so are Trevor and Oliver.

The defect with *Nice People* is that we cannot quite believe in Teddy's reformation, and her determination to give up the life she has lived and spend her days in the open air with Billy Wade is hardly convincing.

Nice People was a popular success; *Everyday* (1921) was a failure, yet it was in some respects a more significant play. Miss Crothers laid the scene in the Middle West and depicted the rebellion of a girl who has been educated beyond the environment of her home and the tyranny of her father, who exercises a control over his wife almost beyond belief in this country. Yet the character of the mother, played by Minnie Dupree, remains one of Miss Crothers' best creations. At the end the daughter goes out of the front door and leaves her mother to face her husband's wrath.

Undeterred by her failure in *Everyday*, Miss Crothers produced her sympathetic exposition of the present day youth in *Mary the Third* (1923). She shows us Mary the First in 1870 taking her mate by the lure of physical attraction; then she pictures Mary the Second in 1897 being taken by the man who among her lovers is the most insistent. And then, bringing these two women into the play as grandmother and mother, she reveals Mary the Third in 1923, mistress of a vocabulary that conceals nothing and with a determination to know the theory and practice of marriage, before which conventions fly. The periodic scenes are not mere preludes; every appeal to propriety from the horrified grandmother's lips sends the audience back to the memory of her conduct on the sofa in 1870! And the despair of the children when they overhear their father and mother strip their married life of its illusions is really a dramatic theme, which Miss Crothers published first as a one-act play. When the curtain falls on this second Act it seems impossible for the family life to go on, but Miss Crothers shows that the irresistible pressure of habit will bring the parents together again and that Mary the Third will choose her mate just as her mother did, because he needs her most—or she thinks he does. Human nature makes the ending of *Mary the Third* probable, but to call it a happy ending is to misunderstand a few essentials.

In 1924 Miss Crothers turned from the celebration and scrutiny of irrepressible youth to a satire of the cult of adult self-expression. As usual she was concerned not so much with novelty of plot, for the framework of *Expressing Willie* was not new. Minnie Whitcomb, a music teacher who comes from the Middle West, is a simple, natural girl. So is Mrs. Smith, who invites Minnie to visit her in order to counteract the influence upon Willie Smith, her son, of a group of ultra-modern people who live on the outskirts of art and of fashion. Willie has made money in tooth paste and his new friends are quite willing to share his hospitality and pretend that he is one of them. Modest despite his success in business, he stands in awe of them. But his mother, penetrating beneath their pretence, and desperate in her efforts to circumvent them, especially the widow Frances Sylvester, who has marked Willie for her own, sends for Minnie as a last hope. Minnie herself falls under their spell at first, but her love for Willie reacts in an unexpected way. Visiting him in his bedroom at night, she begs him in terms of the new psychology to express his real self and win Frances, the symbol of all that is brilliant and desirable. When Frances herself arrives on the scene and Minnie takes refuge in the closet, it would seem as though Miss Crothers had deliberately chosen the most hopelessly ancient of devices to prove her originality. For the ensuing scene is high comedy and the artificial poseurs are routed by the alliance of a girl's unselfish love and a mother's shrewd wisdom, born of her devotion. Often have the love of a sweetheart and of a mother been pitted against each other on the stage. It remained for Miss Crothers to join them in a Holy Alliance against the powers of selfishness and pretence. The performances of Chrystal Herne as Minnie and Louise Closser Hale as Mrs. Smith were of a high order, but to Miss Crothers as playwright and director there rose from the critics who had been so often unaware of her achievement a veritable chorus of appreciation. How deft was her art can best be appreciated by a comparison of *Expressing Willie* with Booth Tarkington's *Country Cousin*.

In *A Lady's Virtue* (1925) Miss Crothers produced a human and natural play, but was hampered by her yielding to the demands of the two actresses for whom the play was written. Her real interest lay in the character of the eternal courtesan, Madame Sisson, and her entrance into the Halstead family was delightful. But the part of Sally Halstead, the rather silly wife who has invited her to visit them, demanded more extended treatment than the plot would bear, and in consequence the playwright, yoking her wagon to two stars, failed to write a convincing play.

The first and the most lasting impression that the work of Rachel Crothers leaves is that of the craftsman. So easy is the flow of her dialogue that it is often unappreciated by the school of critics who are looking constantly for the unusual and the peculiar. Writing for a quarter of a century, she has had few stage failures, and to another school of critics this almost unvarying success seems suspicious. It must, they argue, be because of her acceptance of standards which have sent other playwrights to the wall. But meanwhile Miss Crothers has gone steadily about her own task, and has used the real talent that is hers for the entertainment of those who seek the playhouse for that purpose. It is talent rather than genius which is her portion and she is abundantly conscious of the fact. But instead of railing at conditions she cannot change, she has unfolded a panorama of characters and scenes which are aimed at audiences of intelligence who desire, however, no oversubtlety of motive or expression. So determined has she been not to become a "literary person" that it is remarkable how well her plays like *A Man's World*, *He and She*, or *Nice People* read in print. Without inventive power of the highest order, she is a keen observer of life, especially in the concrete, and her plays are filled with minor characters who indeed at times, notably in *39 East*, attract attention more easily than the major ones.

RACHEL CROTHERS

Her view of life is sane and progressive. She has a keen hatred for injustice and in her early plays, like *A Man's World* and *Ourselves*, she conducted a crusade for a more equitable adjustment of the claims of woman. Of late her ardor in this direction has cooled, and she has turned her scrutiny upon the failings of her own sex. With this diminution in intensity has come a greater subtlety, and a growth from the domestic comedy of *A Man's World* to the social comedy of *Expressing Willie*. This ability to progress, to keep abreast of the fashions of the theatre and the conditions of life, reveals the flexibility and adaptability which are her most characteristic traits. But the quality that lifts her work above the mass of modern playwriting is epitomized in a sentence in *Nice People:* "The vital things of character don't belong to anybody's day— they're eternal and fundamental." She has steadily declined to take the superficial currents of opinion seriously and she has in consequence been called conventional and conservative. But in the final judgment of the discriminating she will have her reward.

CHAPTER XV

AS A consequence of the impossibility of treating in separate chapters all the playwrights of the Twentieth Century, one is forced into the search for categories which will not be artificial classifications, but will be of service in establishing the channels into which our play writing has run. So unsatisfactory are these categories that they may be used only with apology and must be flanked by definitions. Yet the term social comedy has some definiteness. We have found it to be the medium through which Bronson Howard and Clyde Fitch established their best effects, and their example, perhaps, led their successors to attempt a broader scope of theme and treatment than was permitted by the European comedy of manners. Social drama in America has a wider sphere than the drawing-room comedy of an older day, and, while it proceeds most frequently by means of satire, it is not limited to that mode of approach. Its prime essential lies in its employment of social inhibitions to accelerate or to prevent the actions of the characters. It takes place frequently in a house rather than in a home, and, while it is concerned often with the relations of husband and wife or parents and children, it is not limited by domestic ties as is the domestic drama. That at times it is so hard to distinguish it from the latter lies, perhaps, in the stronger bond of the domestic relations in the United States, where marriages are still based not so much on social convenience as on natural selection. As this becomes less often true, it is probable that our social drama will become more frequent.

It is obvious that the writer of this form of play must be equipped by breeding for the recognition of social values.

Most Sincerely Yours,

Langdon Mitchell

THE LATER SOCIAL COMEDY

Langdon Elwyn Mitchell was born in Philadelphia, February 17, 1862, the son of Dr. S. Weir Mitchell, the novelist and poet, and grew up in an atmosphere which sharpened his sense of social distinctions. Educated at St. Paul's School at Concord and by three years' stay abroad, he studied law at Harvard and Columbia Universities and was admitted to the bar in New York in 1886. But already he had published, in 1885, his *Sylvian and Other Poems, Sylvian* being a tragedy partly in verse, laid in Cordova in the Seventeenth Century. In 1892 occurred his marriage with Miss Marion Lea, who later created the part of Vida Phillimore in *The New York Idea.*

A writer of short stories as well as verse, Mitchell approached the stage with a quality which makes his work enduring. In 1899 he scored his first success in his dramatization of *Vanity Fair* under the title of *Becky Sharp.* Beginning September 12, 1899, it ran for two years in New York and on tour, and was revived by Mrs. Fiske ten years later. Its popularity prompted three other dramatic versions of the novel, one of which so closely resembled *Becky Sharp* that it was stopped by injunction. Mrs. Fiske was consummate in the part, and Mitchell wisely built up the play around the character. The Battle of Waterloo and the scene in which Rawdon Crawley finds Becky and Lord Steyne together remain in the memory most vividly, and the latter provided Maurice Barrymore with a splendid opportunity, of which he took full advantage. The adaptation of Weir Mitchell's *Adventures of François* (1900) was not a success. There were possibilities, however, in the play, and the scene in which the Paris waif and the Marquis keep the staircase from the rush of the Jacobin mob was a vivid stage picture.

Perhaps Mitchell's success with the material of the great social satirist showed him where his real strength lay. For, after an adaptation from the Yiddish of Jacob Gordin, *The Kreutzer Sonata* (1906), in which Bertha Kalich made a decided impression, Mitchell wrote his sterling comedy, *The New York Idea,* which was produced November 19, 1906, with a cast including Mrs. Fiske, Marion Lea, John Mason, George Arliss and Emily Stevens, and which has taken its place at the head of our social comedies. That Mitchell caught the spirit of the new century has been proved by the successful revival of the play by Grace George in 1915.

The title which indicates the theme, that of divorce, is in one sense a misnomer, for, as the playwright has acknowledged to me, the people are Philadelphians. Nowhere else could be found quite the same profound self-contentment and surety of standards as the Phillimores represent. Mitchell's skill, too, is revealed from the start in his delicate distinction between Judge Philip Phillimore, who has brushed aside some of the artificial code, and his mother and aunt who have built up their lives upon it. Grace, his younger sister, who is a bit rebellious against the prohibitions of the code, and Cousin William Sudley, the male snob, are also clearly differentiated. But, however different they may be, the tribal instinct, taken in with the air they breathe, unites them against Mrs. Cynthia Karslake, a divorcée, whom Philip is to marry. She has divorced John Karslake through impulse, but still loves him. Judge Phillimore has also divorced his wife, Vida, who is a perfect example of the refined vampire, and while it is difficult to believe in the contretemps which brings them all together in the first Act, such is Mitchell's brilliancy of dialogue that one forgives all the improbability for its sake. What lifts the dialogue above the average comedy of its time is its sincerity. It is never forced for the sake of the laugh. It springs out of the nature of the character and it helps the play on. Notice the approach to Karslake's character through the description of Cynthia:

Sudley: (*Always ready to think the worst*) We might put up with that. But you don't mean to tell me Philip has the— —the—the—assurance to marry a woman who has been divorced by—

Miss Heneage: Not at all. Cynthia Karslake divorced her husband.

Sudley: (*Gloomily, since he has less fault to find than he had expected*) She divorced him! Ah! (*He sips his tea.*)

Miss Heneage: The suit went by default. And, my dear William, there are many palliating circumstances. Cynthia was married to Karslake only seven months. There are no— (*glancing at Grace*) no hostages to Fortune! Ahem!

Sudley: (*Still unwilling to be pleased*) Ah! What sort of a young woman is she?

Grace: (*With the superiority of one who is not too popular*) Men admire her.

Miss Heneage: She's not conventional.

Mrs. Phillimore: (*Showing a faint sense of justice*) I am bound to say she has behaved discreetly ever since she arrived in this house.

Miss Heneage: Yes, Mary—but I sometimes suspect that she exercises a degree of self-control—

Sudley: (*Glad to have something against some one*) She claps on the lid, eh? And you think that perhaps some day she'll boil over? Well, of course, fifteen or twenty millions—but who's Karslake?

Grace: (*Very superciliously*) He owns Cynthia K. She's the famous mare.

Miss Heneage: He's Henry Karslake's son.

Sudley: (*Beginning to make the best of it*) Oh!—Henry!—Very respectable family. Although I remember his father served a term in the Senate. And so the wedding is to be to-morrow?

Into this reunion of divorcées there is introduced Sir Wilfrid Cates-Darby, an Englishman who reveals Mitchell's knowledge of that nation. He is not the caricature known to our stage, but the man who, while he speaks less readily than we do, acts often more quickly. With the characters established, Mitchell develops them in the striking scene in Vida's boudoir, in which, against the background of idle luxury, he reveals her, angling for John Karslake, who still loves Cynthia, and Sir Wilfrid, who has been attracted to both women and who solemnly proposes to Vida that she marry him in case Cynthia refuses. This element of farce is the one blot on the character drawing of the play, but we forget it on account of the strong scene which follows between Cynthia and John. Seldom have the relations between a divorced wife and husband who still care for each other been painted so adroitly. The rage into which Cynthia flies when she finds she has betrayed her emotion, her feminine twisting of the situation to her own advantage, and the curtain scene in which Sir Wilfrid and Cynthia depart for the races to try and see if she "has a whim" for him, show the daring of the dramatist, who carries his audience by the instinctive power of genius. If the second Act startles one, the third Act carries him away. It may be impossible to conceive in cold blood of the circumstances which bring them all together at the preparation for the wedding at ten o'clock at night, but, as the stage direction says, "as he [John Karslake] knows his coming to the ceremony on whatever pretext is a social outrage, he carries it off by assuming an air of its being the most natural thing in the world." Vida's flirtation with John "cuts both ways"—it attracts Sir Wilfrid and it raises Cynthia's jealousy. Then the play rises out of farce to utter sincerity, when John reveals to Cynthia her real feelings for him:

John: (*Quickly on her last word but speaking gravely*) Indeed! Will you? And *why* do you care what happens to me?
Cynthia: (*Startled by his tone*) I—I—ah—
John: (*Insistently and with a faint hope*) *Why* do you *care?*
Cynthia: I don't. Not in your sense—
John: How dare you then pretend—
Cynthia: I don't pretend.
John: (*Interrupting her; proud, serious and strong*) How dare you look me in the face with the eyes that I once kissed, and pretend the least regard for me? (*Cynthia recoils and looks away. Her own feelings are revealed to her clearly for the first time.*) I begin to understand our American women now. Fireflies—and the fire they gleam with is so cold that a midge couldn't warm his heart at it, let alone a man. You're not of the same race as a man! You married me for nothing, divorced me for nothing, because you *are* nothing!
Cynthia: (*Wounded to the heart*) Jack! What are you saying?
John: (*With unrestrained emotion*) What,—you feigning an in-

terest in me, feigning a lie—and in five minutes— (*Gesture indicating altar.*) Oh, you've taught me the trick of your sex —you're the woman who's not a woman!

Cynthia: (*Weakly*) You're saying terrible things to me.

John: (*Low and with intensity*) You haven't been divorced from me long enough to forget—what you should be ashamed to remember.

The curtain of this act, after Cynthia has fled, unable to go through with the wedding, is delightful. The choir boys have been placed ready to sing at a signal from Reverend Matthew Phillimore, and, mistaking his raised hands of protest, they burst into the hymn:

> "Enduring love—sweet end of strife!
> Oh, bless this happy man and wife!"

The last act is not so important, but John and Cynthia find their divorce was not legal, and Vida secures Sir Wilfrid.

The final impression of *The New York Idea* is one of rich invention, of consummate theatrical skill, and of a social knowledge so secure that it dares to go to the edge of farce or of the sentimental, knowing that it can return at any moment. The play is more than a mere satire on divorce. It is a celebration of the triumph of real love, about to make a mistake because of the pressure of social customs, and saved by the resurgence of human passion, aided by the spirited defiance of social law and by the skilful manipulation of social opportunities. Its universal quality has been proven by the critical success of *Jonathans Tochter*, under which title it was put on at Berlin, under Reinhardt's direction, in 1916, although the war prevented its receiving a fair hearing. It has also been translated into Danish, Swedish and Hungarian.

The wonder is that Mitchell never repeated his success. *The New Marriage*, which Mrs. Fiske produced in 1911, had clever dialogue but a plot almost farcical. It was a study of marriage, revolving around two couples, Wilmer and Agnes Bromley, high-strung, tired of the "dull, unceasing monogamy of daily existence," and Horace and Leona Byethorne, married flirts who become entangled in a cross flirtation. Although it had a brilliant first Act, the interest was not sustained, and the play was not successful on the stage. *Pendennis* (1916) was, however, much more fortunate. Mitchell built this dramatization of Thackeray's novel for John Drew, who interpreted the character of Major Pendennis admirably. The play is a series of scenes in which the Major presides over the love affairs of Arthur Pendennis, and the worldly-wise old officer and gentleman easily retained his interest as the leading character. *Pendennis* does not provide as rich an opportunity for the dramatist as *Vanity Fair*, and the play was not as successful as *Becky Sharp*, but it was a charming interpretation of Victorian life in England.

In the year of the production of *The New York Idea* Jesse Lynch Williams saw his first play on the professional stage. He was born in Stirling, Illinois, August 17, 1871, graduated from Princeton University in 1892 and became known first as a novelist and writer of short stories. Indeed it is only at intervals that Williams writes for the stage, for he works slowly, and the difficulties of production, commercial and otherwise, are obnoxious to him.[1]

The Stolen Story is not social drama: it is a play based on Williams' newspaper experiences. Billy Woods, the central character, is a real reporter, and the atmosphere of loyalty and the sense of the brotherhood of the craft which obtains in the offices of a great metropolitan newspaper is well caught. The climax of the play is gripping. Woods, having been discharged by his managing editor, and employed by a rival sheet, discovers a great "story" of political corruption which involves Senator Cunningham, the father of the girl he loves. To save the Senator, he has to appear in false colors even to her, and keyed up to a forgetfulness of everything but the one supreme goal, he forgets his discharge and returns to his desk

---

[1] See his interesting account of the production of *Why Marry?* in *Contemporary American Plays*, pp. 2–4.

at his old paper. The way in which the city editor senses the situation and keeps everyone, even the emissaries of the rival sheet, from breaking into Wood's absorbed writing of the "story," built up a masterly scene. The interest is professional rather than social, but the instinctive trust of the gentlewoman in the gentleman, which keeps Frances Cunningham true to Woods against all appearances, showed Williams' understanding of the finer shades of feeling. The *Stolen Story* was produced in Providence, in April, 1906, and after success there and in Chicago, went into New York in the autumn. Peculiar managerial stupidity seems alone to have prevented a long run. By a curious stroke of fate, the tour ended in Columbus, Ohio, where *Why Marry?* was born.

Why Marry? was published in 1914 as *And So They Were Married* and it was only after the comedy had been put on by amateurs that the commercial managers saw possibilities in one of the most successful plays of its day. It opened in Columbus, Ohio, November 1, 1917, with Nat Goodwin in the leading part of the lawyer and uncle who represents the voice of society in general. Goodwin's death while the play was in its second season had a disastrous effect on its history. It was awarded the first Pulitzer Prize for the best American play of the year 1917-8.

Why Marry? is not an attack upon marriage: it is a scrutiny of the institution. It begins by the capture of Rex Baker by Jean, who doesn't love him, but "who has been brought up to be married and nothing else." She is the younger sister-in-law of Lucy, mistress of a handsome house and John's wife, who is not so frank as Jean in the interview between the two women after Rex has gone. John is a successful business man "with plenty of ability but little perception," and he has invited to this week-end party his Uncle Everett, a judge who is a genial satirist of life; Cousin Theodore, a human clergyman; Ernest Hamilton, a scientist; and Helen, John's other sister, who demands a career and is assisting Ernest in his laboratory. Williams puts into the Judge's mouth a sweeping criticism of conditions:

Judge: It's all on a sliding scale, John. For keeping up the cost of living, you and old man Baker get—oh, so much. (*Stretches arms out full length.*) For saving the Constitution, I get, well, I get a good deal myself. (*Rises, hands three feet apart.*) For saving in wages and operating expenses, your superintendent gets—so much. (*Hands two feet apart.*) For saving human life, Ernest Hamilton gets— so much. (*Hands six inches apart.*) For saving immortal souls, Theodore gets—so much. (*Holds up two forefingers an inch apart.*) Now if anyone came along and saved the world—
Theodore: (*Interrupts*) They crucified Him.

Hamilton is a new kind of stage hero—as Helen describes him to her family, who are ardently discussing marriage:

Helen: Why, to me he's a perfect hero of romance!
John: (*Sneers*) Never even saw a battle—mollycoddle germ-killer.
Helen: The battle against yellow fever, John, down in Cuba. No drums to make him brave, no correspondents to make him famous—merely rolled up his sleeve and let an innocent-looking mosquito bite him, and then took notes on his symptoms till he became delirious. He happened to be among those who recovered. Four of the others died. (*She is betrayed into showing considerable feeling, after all.*)

Williams describes him in other terms:

(*Enter Ernest Hamilton, about thirty-five years old; although a highbrow, he looks like a pretty good fellow, and he is not in the least shy or embarrassed, being "well born and well bred." He talks very rapidly; does not take the trouble to despise conventions; merely views them with frank, scientific curiosity, tinged with amused contempt. He is startlingly honest.*)

As played by Shelley Hull, he can be seen in any scientific laboratory to-day. The struggle between the love of Helen

and Ernest and their belief that marriage is a handicap to a man of science provides the main conflict which is essential to drama. But in order to secure sympathy for their point of view, Williams draws a picture of another kind of marriage in the conversation between John and Lucy at breakfast, and her revolt, after years of suffering, is quite in keeping with her futile nature. Helen paints an ideal picture of life together without marriage, and Theodore remarks:

Theodore: But if you love him, my dear, marriage brings together those who love each other truly.
Helen: But those who love each other truly, don't need anything
to bring them together. The difficulty is to keep them apart.

As Helen tells them, first, that she has refused Ernest's pro-posal, second, that he knows nothing about her plan, they are horrified, and when he leaves her after she has refused to marry him, the tribe turn on her and tell her he despises her. But in the midst of this conversation Ernest returns. John demands why he went. He replies, "To protect her from myself." And when John continues, "Then why come back?" Ernest answers, "To protect her from you," and they depart together. The Judge brings them back and plans a family party for the announcement of the trip to Paris and, after a most amusing scene, he tricks them cleverly.

Judge: (*To Helen and Ernest, who are hand in hand*) Helen, you
know, because you've said it, that in the sight of God you
are taking this man to be your husband—
Helen: Why, of course. In the sight of God—I take Ernest to
be my husband, but—
Judge: And you, Ernest?
Ernest: Why, of course, in the sight of God—but—
Judge: (*Hand raised—august—authoritative*) Then, since you,
Helen, and you, Ernest, have made this solemn declaration before God, and in the presence of witnesses, I by the
authority vested in me by the laws of this state do now pronounce you man and wife.

Williams did not force a happy ending. As the Judge says:

Judge: (*To Ernest. Raising his hand. All are silent*) All you've
said of marriage is true. There is only one thing worse—
and that is what you tried to do. But bad as marriage is,
until we reform it, it is the best we have to offer you. What
are you going to do about it? (*Loud and laughing*) Separate and get divorced?

The problem is similar to that faced by Moody in *The Faith
Healer*, but Williams treats it in the spirit of comedy and yet
arrives at much the same conclusion. But the love of Helen
and Ernest is deeper than if they had not had the test through
which they have passed.

Why Marry? was a comedy of institutions. Williams called
his next play, *Why Not?* (1922), a "comedy of conventions," for, while marriage was the theme of the first, divorce is
the subject of the second. The plot was derived from the
author's own story, *Remating Time*. Leonard and Mary Chad-
wick find themselves butler and maid in the house of Bill and
Evadne Thompson, and the realization that both couples are
mismated and that they should rearrange their marital relations on the basis of earlier love which has been thwarted, provides a situation which Williams' skill keeps from being
farcical. The author's own description of the characters
reveals them better than any interpretation:

The two married couples in this play, although there is a
touch of phantasy in their behavior, are of a sort often met in
life, though seldom on the stage. Intellectually, they are neither
"low-brow" nor "high-brow"; socially, neither "low-life" nor
"high-life"—that is, they are not in the least smart, though they
doubtless would be classified as "Society people," if they got into
the newspapers. They are simple, gracious gentlefolk; too well-
born, well-bred and well-disposed toward one another and the
world to think much about intellectual or social "position." Nor
do they talk about "My Sense of Humor"—and thus demonstrate
how little they possess. Indeed, they are rather old-fashioned.
They even go to Church. Nevertheless they are all good.

The incongruity of this atmosphere helps to make the fun of

their fantastic predicament. For this is a comedy of Human Nature *versus* Human Institutions.

The situation in which Smith, a friendly lawyer, suggests official adultery as the only possible way of solving the difficulty is used by Williams to bombard the eccentricities of our divorce laws, with a dialogue so brilliant that the audience lost at times the subtlety in the frequency of epigram. He faces the complete situation by providing each pair with a child, but he provides no real solution. That, he has explained to me, is not his affair; he leaves that to the sociologist. To a French or Italian playwright, the satisfaction of passion would have been taken for granted as the great necessity. In America, the prime essential to be preserved is the individual's self-respect. Williams' great achievement lies in the way he strips conventions of their pretences and yet leaves life clothed in its precious illusions.

Lovely Lady (1925) is a comedy dealing with the relations of parents and children. The central character, Julia Dashiels, is a clever philanderer, who fascinates both Stanley Linton and his father, and really brings them together on a friendlier footing after their mutual discovery of her manipulations. Mrs. Linton, wife and mother, with much cleverness lets the situation work itself out. The conversation was on Williams' high level, but the play was a commercial failure for reasons hard to understand. The characterization in *Lovely Lady* was not so real as that in *Why Not?*, just as neither equaled in sharpness the drawing in *Why Marry?*. But the very object of Williams' art, his intense scrutiny of institutions, leads away from characterization. Divorce is satirized in *The New York Idea*, but what we remember first are the vivid personalities; the institution of divorce fades into the background. In *Why Not?* it is never forgotten and the characters are not as distinct. This does not imply that Williams' art is less fine than Mitchell's; the very subtlety of the former prevents him from creating such portraits. Perhaps life itself is growing less dependent upon character and more upon institutions, good and evil. But an historian of the drama cannot change his belief that the permanent test of drama is the creation of character.

The supreme difficulty of maintaining the tone of social comedy is illustrated best by the work of those who attempt it and fail to reach the standard set by Mitchell and Williams.

The failure of Albert E. Thomas (1872-1947) to achieve real distinction in this field is the more to be regretted since at times he has flashes of inspiration and since he is able to draw gentlemen and gentlewomen. His first play, *Her Husband's Wife* (1910), had as its theme the selection, by a woman who thinks she is ill, of a second wife for her husband. This plot is reminiscent of *Love in Tandem*, Augustin Daly's adaptation of *Vie à deux*, but it is worked out somewhat differently.

The Rainbow (1912), which, like *Her Husband's Wife*, was a popular success, is a clever social comedy in which the reconciliation of a husband and wife, who have been separated partly by misunderstanding and partly by the inability of the socially trained to express their real feelings, is brought about by their daughter. It is just the type of play which Bronson Howard introduced in *Young Mrs. Winthrop*, but the affection of Cynthia for her father is a solvent better suited to the theatre than the emotion awakened in the Winthrops over their child's grave. The tone is kept here better than in *Come Out of the Kitchen* (1916), *Just Suppose* (1920), or *Only 38* (1921). In *Just Suppose*, a romantic drama in which the Prince of Wales runs off and visits a Southern family, Thomas establishes quite well the poise with which Linda Lee Stafford meets the difficult situation caused by the mutual love of the Prince and herself. Then, apparently unable to trust the audience to use their intelligence, he introduces the preposterous scene between the British minister and Linda, in which the whole atmosphere is precipitated into farce.

The best play by Thomas, in which he collaborated with Clayton Hamilton, is *The Better Understanding*, acted with success in California by Henry Miller in May 1917, but not yet produced in the East. It is a serious study of the eternal triangle, but with more reality than is usually permitted in the theatre. When John Newton discovers that Philip Gibbs loves his wife, Grace, and intends to go away with her, and that he has lost her love through his immersion in his affairs, he determines to fight for her. So did John Rutherford in *The Wife* in 1887, but John Newton uses different weapons, for his conception of marriage is different. As he puts it, "A woman's love belongs to her husband only just so long as he deserves it and can keep it." Newton pretends that he is unaware of the name of the woman Philip loves and, in a masterly scene, he puts to Grace and Philip the case of the supposed husband who, though he has appeared to neglect his wife, really loves her. Like the people in *Why Not?*, they are all essentially decent, and Philip and Grace say good-by. There is still another step to be taken, however. John's pride has had its inevitable reaction and he cannot beg for the love in which he only half believes. Again there is verity in John's answer to his sister, Kate, "I hope you may never live to be pitied by some one you love. It's horrible." Grace lets him see how her love for Philip was the mature counterpart of that desire for love itself which is so much talked about in more youthful situations. It is a real impulse in many lives, however, and it is handled with distinction by the playwrights even to the curtain speech, in which Grace lets John see the difference between the love she had built up out of heartache and the love she really feels for him.

There have been sporadic successes in the field of social comedy, by playwrights whose work has been interrupted or who have gone into other fields. *A Woman's Way* (1909), by Thompson Buchanan (1877-1937), succeeded through its deft use of theatrical situations and its portraiture of Marion Stanton, a young wife who wins back her husband's regard by fighting for it against a more sophisticated rival. Buchanan made clever use of his newspaper experience, for, like A. E.

Thomas, he belongs to that group of college bred men who, about 1910, came into the theatre through the training of journalism. Of his later plays, *Civilian Clothes* (1919), while it reflected Buchanan's own war experience, and was a sincere attempt to show the snobbishness of the feminine attitude toward the men in and out of uniform, paid the penalty of its contemporary quality. After some time spent with the moving pictures, Buchanan returned in 1927 to the legitimate stage with *Sinner*, a study of a woman who, under the guise of perfect frankness and sincerity, gives herself to a married man before he secures his divorce, then marries him as a concession to her family, gives herself to her earlier lover in order to revenge herself upon her husband for his inattention, and calmly accepts his apology because he at last proves to her that she is first in his affections. The absurdity of this spectacle may have been due to Buchanan's association with a meretricious art, but its sole interest lies in the contrast between his earlier more sincere work and his response to the contemporary urge for sensation.

The Unchastened Woman (1915), by Louis Kaufman Anspacher (1878-1947), has attracted attention on account of its central character, Caroline Knollys, a woman of wealth who makes dextrous use of her social experience and moral unscrupulousness to gratify her sense of power over those near her. She is extremely well drawn, but the other characters are foils and types, and the relations of her husband and his mistress, upon which the plot turns, do not secure belief. The play was successful when first presented, but when revived in 1926 it made no distinct impression, possibly owing to the stress laid upon factory reform and the iniquity of the custom house.

One of the essential qualities of the comedy of manners is lightness of touch. The comedies of Clare Kummer possess this attribute almost to perfection. Of plot there is little. Miss Kummer imagines or perhaps hears of a large estate which is usually allowed to remain empty and straightway her fancy peoples it with "Annabelle Leigh, who has a husband somewhere" and a group of her friends, mostly artists and all insolvents, who fill gayly and irresponsibly positions from that of head cook down. There are two shares of stock which float through the play, but their main purpose is to provide a delightful satire upon modern psychological methods of discovering a thief by means of verbal suggestion. Wickham, the detective, is examining the servants:

Wickham: Now—I say the words "expectant—radical—Anthony Comstock—misanthrope." What word comes to you? (*sharp and quick*) Quick, the word!

Lottie: (*Sadly and slowly*) There's always something the matter with everyone that likes me— I have a brother in the asylum— I wish you could meet him. You remind me of him so much.

But what carried *Good Gracious, Annabelle* (1916) into high favor was the steady sparkle of the dialogue. It may be called comedy of manners because really all that remains in the memory is the complete suitability of the actions of these characters to any situation that occurs, and the skill, born of a sure knowledge of the weapons of social warfare, which carries Annabelle through her difficulties. The only form of drama to which it may be compared is the French *vaudeville*. But from the American vaudeville it is far removed, notwithstanding its superficial resemblance. It is true that question and answer follow each other with a rapidity that leaves one breathless, but there is only occasionally the obvious planting of the question for the mere sake of the reply which is so apparent in the work of Ade or Cohan. One minor situation in *A Successful Calamity* (1917) will illustrate this distinction. Henry Wilton, a wealthy merchant, pretends he is ruined in order to see what his young second wife and children will do about it. All rise to the occasion, and then Conners, the butler, apologetically offers his bankbook to his master. This situation, too well-worn for pathos, is given a new turn. Wilton, played by Gillette, asks with a courtesy all his own, "But are you sure you can spare it?" Conners hastens to reassure him. "Oh yes, sir. You see my sister's husband is dead, and she doesn't need my help any more, sir." To anyone who remembers this perennial situation, the reply comes with special point, but the important thing is that it comes out of that situation and is not merely a verbal explosion.

The very security of the social instincts of most of Clare Kummer's characters provides contrast to the unworldliness of others, such as the heroine of *Be Calm, Camilla* (1918). We are never quite sure whether Camilla, in her progress through cabaret and boarding house to the bliss of the hospital and Patterson's palatial lodge, is shielded by angels or by a sophistication too deep for tears. In *Rollo's Wild Oat* (1920) the gaiety becomes hilarious during the scenes which prepare for Rollo's playing Hamlet, but leads to a fiasco, when the telegram announcing his grandfather's dangerous illness sends Ophelia to him in the midst of the opening scene. The subtlest portions of the comedy, however, spring from the ever-present sense on Rollo's part that he is different from the professional actors, not artistically but socially. He can never step out of his part in life and, of course, can never be an actor.

Sometimes the plot becomes so tenuous that even the dialogue fails to hold it together. This was the case with *Pomeroy's Past* (1922), which had to be withdrawn after its tryout in Philadelphia but went on again in 1926. The attempt to provide Pomeroy Chilton with an illegitimate child, in order to make him attractive, was hardly successful.

In *The Mountain Man* (1920) Miss Kummer attempted a more serious study of the North Carolina mountaineers. But the effort only proved that her own earlier manner was her best, though the character of Aaron Winterfield, the son of a patrician and a mountain girl, is interesting in his revelation of the way in which the pride which was his father's bequest becomes his danger and also his salvation.

Some of the most interesting of our social dramas have been the work of playwrights who began in other fields. James Forbes (1871-1938), whose earlier work lay in the drama of domestic types, rose to a higher rank of achievement in *The Famous Mrs. Fair* (1919). This is a study of the effect upon a woman of the fame that she has acquired through her war work in France. She returns after an absence of four years to find her young daughter grown up, her son engaged to be married, and her husband being comforted by the widow next door. This play, which begins with comedy, rises at the end of the third Act to a very tense situation after Mrs. Fair finds out the relations that have been existing between her husband and Mrs. Brice. Then comes the announcement that Sylvia, her daughter, has run off with Dudley Gillette, Mrs. Fair's manager on her lecture tour. As Henry Miller, in the part of Jeffrey Fair, reached for the telephone to call police headquarters, one could see his face grow old. Another telling scene occurs in the third Act, when Sylvia outlines the situation to her father and mother as she sees it. Forbes continued to write social drama in *The Endless Chain* (1922), dealing with a real situation in the lives of people who come from smaller towns and try to make a social life in New York City. It was not successful, but it had some quietly effective scenes, and it was much more artistic than his earlier farces.

Among recent social drama of significance was *The Changelings* (1923), by Lee Wilson Dodd (1879–1933). Dodd is a poet with some claim to consideration on account of the finish of his verse. He has been writing for the stage since 1909, when *The Return of Eve* was played. But his farce comedies like *His Majesty Bunker Bean* (1916) and *Pals First* (1916) need not detain us. In *The Changelings* Dodd revealed through skilful representation of character that in real marriage there is no ending; in false marriage there was no beginning. Its success must be attributed partially to the remarkable cast, headed by Henry Miller and including Blanche Bates, Laura Hope Crews, and Ruth Chatterton. After three married couples, parents and children, have skirted the very edge of destruction, the powerful clutch of decency draws them back. It was refreshing to see an American play in which the four male characters represented an editor, a novelist, a publisher, and a college instructor as human beings.

Gilbert Emery, whose contribution to domestic drama is among the most important made by our playwrights, wrote in *Episode* (1925) a social comedy which treats the triangle in a very modern way. Its first title, *Saving Judy*, is probably the better one, for it reveals the ending, so hopeless yet so true to life. When Arnold Ryesdale finds that his wife Evelyn has been for a time the mistress of his friend Herbert Ballinger, his first instinct is revenge. Then gradually the futility of the position of the husband in our modern social organization is shown. With his emotional life in ruins, the pressure of the countless little things which social life brings up hourly press upon him. Judy Ballinger, Herbert's wife, is waiting for them at her place, where a party is going on. Already they are late and she is telephoning. What is he going to do about it? After revolt and refusal, he is left with no alternative. Shall he tell Judy the real reason? Why not save her, at least, from the agony he has suffered? So a combination of motives, the chivalry of an old friend and the powerful inertia of social custom, drag him off to dinner. Emery has the experience and the taste for social drama; he has the insight to treat life as a great comedy. It is not so easy to evaluate his share in *Love-in-a-Mist* (1926), which he and Amélie Rives (Princess Troubetskoy) wrote in collaboration, but while it is a charming comedy, it has not the significance of his other work. By the grim fate of drama, it succeeded while *Episode* failed.

Of the other playwrights who might claim consideration as writers of social drama, Booth Tarkington and Zoë Akins belong primarily under the category of romance. It is true that, considered superficially, *The Man From Home* (1907) and *The Country Cousin* (1917) seem to imply social contrasts, the first between American and English types, the second between those of the Middle West and New York. But, as we shall see, Tarkington's real interest lies in another direction. His nearest approach to a treatment of social contrasts for

themselves alone came in *Tweedles* (1923), which had for a
theme the essential snobbishness of everyone. The Castleburys,
who are supposed to represent Philadelphia patricians, and
the Tweedles, who have lived for generations in a New England
town, are both satirized. The scene in which Mr. and Mrs.
Castlebury come to the Tweedles' shop to inform the latter
that they cannot countenance their son's marriage with Win-
sora Tweedle on account of the difference in station, only to
find that Adam Tweedle believes they are acknowledging their
own deficiencies as "mere summer people," has some good moments. But the play failed, partly because of the atrocious
miscasting of the Castlebury family.

Among the newer generation, Philip Barry (1896-   ) is
the most promising. A graduate of Yale in 1919, he won the
Harvard Prize Play contest in 1922 with *You and I*, produced
in 1923. The conflict in this play lies between the claims of
love and the passion to create beauty, made concrete in the
persons of Maitland White and his son Roderick. In his
efforts to prove to Roderick that he should go abroad and
study architecture and not let his projected marriage with
Veronica Duane interfere, Maitland unconsciously reveals to
his wife that his desire to be a painter, which he had given up
in order to marry her, has remained hidden in his heart, never
quite forgotten. One fine scene in the play occurs when Nancy
Maitland watches her husband's face to see what his feelings
really are. She reads his secret and urges him to give up his
position and do the thing he loves. Another fine scene, reminiscent just a bit of Aldrich's poem *In an Atelier*, is laid in
Maitland's studio, in which he is painting Etta, the maid, who
has agreed to be a model. His efforts to make her feel like a
great lady, and her valiant struggles to become one, form one
of the most amusing bits of social comedy our stage has seen.

Barry draws skilfully the contrast between the way in which
Nancy cheerfully accepted Maitland's earlier sacrifice and the
manner of Veronica's refusal to allow Roderick to give up his
career. She persuades him that she does not love him, with a

brave imposture that clutches at our sympathies. The conclusion is not very logical, since Maitland invents a legacy to send Roderick to Paris with Veronica, though there is a good satiric touch in the purchase by Maitland's former employer of Etta's picture for a soap advertisement. But there is no question of Maitland's determination to give up his own dream for the sake of his son's, and the great promise of *You and I* lay in the skill with which Barry drew a picture of the comradeship, not always articulate, but rich with understanding, which exists in American families of tradition and breeding. Quiet recognition of responsibility, the making of grave decisions without display, the recognition of the rights of each individual, which are the touchstones of civilization, and by which we have passed from the tribe into beings of a social order, all these are revealed beneath a dialogue clever at times to brilliancy. There are many such fathers, mothers, sons and daughters in America, but they rarely come upon the stage.

At first glance *The Youngest* (1924) might seem to belong to domestic comedy, since it deals with the leading family of a town in New York State and is concerned with the revolt of the youngest son, who has been submerged by the tribal weight of stupidity and selfishness. But the Winslow family are the town institution, and Barry delightfully ridicules their social and economic assumptions. *The Youngest* had not quite the charm, however, of *You and I* or of *In a Garden* (1925). This is a clever, sophisticated social comedy, a bit remote from human interest and with a plot that is perhaps too intricate, but written with distinction and with a real insight into certain qualities of human nature. Adrian Terry, a playwright, and Lissa, his wife, have lived together for nine years happily. Roger Compton, a friend, suggests that Lissa has had an earlier romance with Norrie Bliss in a garden somewhere near Philadelphia. In order to test his wife's affection, Adrian decorates their living room to resemble the garden, of which he has secured photographs, and when Norrie and Lissa are left together the scene and the memories refresh their love and he begs her to go away with him. She has felt for some time that her life is too restricted and determined by her husband's theories, many of which she does not understand and none of which does she like, and she is about to go with Norrie. Then, in a scene after dinner on the same evening, she learns that the earlier romantic interview in the garden was in itself not "the one real thing" in her life but a more or less planned experiment by Norrie, suggested by an earlier remark of Compton's. In consequence she neither goes with her lover nor stays with her husband, but retires to think things over.

If *In a Garden* was too subtle for the public taste, *White Wings* (1926) baffled them, and despite general critical approval it failed to attract audiences. It is a satiric comedy in which the social contrasts have a deeper and yet a subtler implication. The family of Inches have been White Wings or street cleaning contractors for generations, as Archie Inch explains to Mary Todd while they are preparing to go home after a dance in the year 1895. The conversation is so natural that the implications are apparent more easily when the play is read. The horse has become to them a fetish, the symbol of all that is fine in life and they have become dependent upon him. Has the absurdity of family pride that has become stratified ever been put more effectively than in Archie's remark to Mary, whose father had been the furnace man of the Inches?

Archie: Grandfather,—but probably you've heard of him in connection with General Boocock's march upon Antietam?
Mary: I'm a little weak on the Civil War.
Archie: For the fact that a thousand horses rode two hundred miles without leaving a single clue, one man was responsible. And that was my grandfather.

The automobile, which is invented by Mary's father, is used as a symbol of progress which is to drive the horse out of existence. And there is a fine situation when the first automobile breaks down and has to be towed by old Joseph, a cab horse who provides some of the most delightful moments of the comedy.

Barry can put on the stage, too, the gallant defence of the Tory in Archie's refusal to give up the family employment as long as there is a horse left in town, even if he loses Mary's love. But love conquers, for Mary shoots the last horse, poor old Joseph, and takes Archie away in her car, teaching him to run it. Barry's dialogue is expressive as any now written. When Mary begs Archie to marry her he tells of the promise he has made to his mother on her death bed:

Mary: But the dead can't hold the living!
Archie: Oh—can't they!
Mary: A promise like that—
Archie: A promise is a promise.
Mary: Oh, my poor boy.
Archie: And I'll keep it. There's always some one who gets caught between the ages.

Very appealing is the final curtain, when poor old Mr. Inch, Archie's father, who has kept up the struggle to clean the streets until he is worn out, is forced to mount a garbage truck. Stung to the soul, he calls out shrilly, "Strawberries! Strawberries!" The sympathy of the hearer or reader is kept for the Inches by Barry's touch of fantasy which never obtrudes itself, but is at its best when it reveals the soul of a gentleman.

It is the usual commonplace to regret that we have produced no greater number of playwrights to follow the lead of Clyde Fitch in this form of drama. Blame has been laid on the conditions of our theatre, especially the mixed nature of audiences in New York, which make a social comedy less inviting a speculation than a more obvious form of drama. It is true that there is no longer a theatre like Daly's or Wallack's where a sure appeal was made to a public of taste and discrimination. But in the light of the popular success of *The New York Idea* and *Why Marry?* or of Arthur Richman's imitation of the former, *The Awful Truth*, this assumed unreadiness of the American audience may perhaps be overestimated. The truth really lies elsewhere. Fine social comedy is one of the most

difficult forms of art; that is the reason why we have so few specimens. It tolerates no crudities, which often carry the domestic drama; it rejects the violence of melodrama; it distrusts the color of romance.

One handicap, too, which our dramatists of social life have to encounter, is the element of time. A British or French playwright can by the very titles of his *dramatis personæ* prepare the audience for the atmosphere they are to expect. An American playwright must establish the social quality of his characters by their language and actions in the first few moments of the play. This is not an easy task, and his effect may be more easily ruined by a miscasting of parts than in any other form of drama. When all the handicaps are remembered, it is to be wondered, not that we have had so few, but that we have had the sterling examples we possess.

Note to Revised Edition

Langdon Mitchell died October 21, 1935. Jesse Lynch Williams died September 14, 1929, at Jordanville, New York.

CHAPTER XVI

THE significance of Edward Sheldon becomes most apparent in an effort to classify his work. He will not fit into any of the general categories into which the modern American drama runs, partly because of the variety of his plays but more especially because of the underlying unity of his purpose and of the individuality which marked him, up to the time of his illness, as one of the most promising playwrights of his time. In an interview given shortly after the production of *The Boss*, Sheldon remarked: "My next play will have beauty," and it was this recognition of the one supremely necessary quality of any art which accounts for his success.

Edward Brewster Sheldon was born in Chicago, February 4, 1886. Before he entered Harvard University he had written plays and he naturally took advantage of the opportunities offered by Professor Baker's courses. He graduated in 1907 and his first professional success came with the production by Mrs. Fiske of *Salvation Nell*, on November 12, 1908.

Salvation Nell was a remarkable play for a young man of twenty-two. The opening scene at the "Empire Bar" of Sid McGovern, with the stage divided by a partition that separated the "Ladies' Buffet" from the barroom, is as realistic a picture of slum life as can be imagined. Its likeness in setting to the first Act of *Anna Christie* is apparent, of course, but there is little similarity in the plot of the two plays. In fact, the effort of Sheldon was to establish the sordid atmosphere of the saloon in order that the rescue of Nell Sanders, by Lieutenant Maggie O'Sullivan of the Salvation Army, should form the emotional climax of the act. Nell is not the usual heroine: she is the mistress of Jim Platt, who lives on her earnings as a scullery maid in the saloon, and when he is arrested for his assault on Al McGovern and she is expelled from the saloon, she goes to the Salvation Army, not in any spirit of religious exaltation, but because the only other alternative, that offered by Mabel, of "Cloquette's," does not appeal to her. Nell's subsequent repulse of Jim when he returns from his ten years in jail, and her highly effective prayer in front of the tenements, which forms the climax of the play, gave Mrs. Fiske fine opportunities for emotional acting. It is perhaps unnecessary to point out flaws in *Salvation Nell;* they are obvious, but Sheldon showed in his first play an observation of life and a sense of the theatre that were undeniable.

The Nigger was selected as the only American play to be produced at the New Theatre in the season of 1909-10. The central motive, the discovery by Governor Philip Morrow, a young Southerner whose instincts are patrician and who has been elected to his office as an advocate of white supremacy in his state, that he is the grandson of a negro slave, is essentially dramatic. The disclosure is made effectively, for it comes through an attempt by his own cousin Noyes, the owner of a distillery, who has made Philip governor, to force him to veto a prohibition bill. Noyes has discovered a letter written years before by Belle, the octoroon slave, to Philip's grandfather, in which she says good-by before she is sold down the river by her master, in order that he may place their child, Philip's father, in the place of his own son, who has just died. One of Sheldon's qualities is his daring. This theme savors strongly of melodrama, but the letter of Belle is one of the finest bits of writing in our drama, and the intense tragedy of the scene is heightened by the introduction of Mammy Jinny, Belle's sister, who is still with the family and who has kept the secret for seventy years. The way she at first denies all knowledge of the substitution of Belle's child and her final outbreak when the reading of the letter brings back the memories of the past, are masterly. The reaction of Philip to the disclosure, his appeal to Grace, his *fiancée,* not to abandon him, her loathing and his tigerish clasp of her, were criticized by those who failed to see the profound understanding by the playwright of the effect of the slight negro taint in Philip when he realizes the black drop in his blood. Quite as natural was his determination to play straight, to defy Noyes, to tell his story to the crowd that has come to cheer him, and to show Grace, who has returned to bring him her love again, that there can be no marriage between them. Sheldon had the courage to deal with a large theme, to complete the tragedy logically, but to send Philip on to his bitter task of self-disclosure cheered by the knowledge that Grace still loves him and by the securing of his own self-respect. In the conversation which helps Philip to make his decision, Senator Long tells him: "Ye know, sonny, that's a way God has. He lets us tu'n the bad into good. Sometimes I think we oughtah thank Him mo' fo' that'n anythin' else." This may be the optimism of youth—it may be something far deeper—it is in any case not the flavor of Scandinavian pessimism.

Indeed, while one feels that Sheldon was acquainted with the dramatic literature of his period, its only influence upon him was in the selection of serious topics and a determination to approach them unshrinkingly. He was concerned with native themes, and his next play was a study of the political boss who is also a contractor and who has made a success by building up a modern feudal system, whose bases are the mutual loyalty of chieftain and follower. Michael Regan in *The Boss* (1911) is a well-drawn character. He is not a hero; he crushes those in his way without compunction; he is vulgar in his attempted trickery of the Archbishop; but his word is kept once it is given, and when Porky McCoy, his lieutenant, exceeds his instructions and throws a brick that almost kills Donald Griswold, Regan's brother-in-law and enemy, Regan quietly takes the blame upon himself. He does this just as inevitably as he expects Porky to obey his orders unquestioningly. In other words, he has the tribal instinct of the Celt, and he has also the Celtic reverence for womanly purity. His relations with Emily Griswold, the daughter of a wealthy family of contractors, who marries him to save her father from ruin, with the understanding that she is to be a wife in name only, are not so impossible as they seem at first glance. Sheldon has indicated with delicacy but with sufficient clarity the attraction which Regan's strength and virility have for Emily, and the old fable of Beauty and the Beast has a modern application in the growth of her love for him. As portrayed by Holbrook Blinn, the audiences sympathized with Regan for his courage and devotion to his own standards. Such scenes as that with the Archbishop, with its reminiscence of *Richelieu*, were absurd, but the memory of the unbeaten leader, deserted, he believes, even by his wife, but undaunted, is a vivid one, and his curtain cry on the second Act—"By Gawd, I'll beat 'em yet!" —as his fist crashes on the table, was good theatre and good drama.

While not on such a lofty plane as *The Nigger*, *The Boss* was even more compact and telling in its structure, and the dialogue more direct and crisp. Sheldon is supposed to have drawn Regan from a magazine article upon "Fingey Connors," a political leader, and it seemed as though he were tending in the direction of the group of melodramatic playwrights which grew up in the first decade of the new century and based its work upon contemporary events. But he turned aside to indulge his love of romance in *The Princess Zim-Zim* (1911), a love episode with the background of a side-show at Coney Island. Sheldon's sense of reality showed in the setting of the little stage and auditorium where Tessie Casey becomes three times each day the snake charmer, "Princess Zim-Zim." He depicted well, too, the reaction against a uselessly amusing life which sent Peter Milholland, the young millionaire, to seek adventure and the consequent romance that sprang up between him and Tessie. Peter's cry, "I'm twenty-four years old, I'm on the loose, and I'm looking for romance," strikes a responsive chord in our sympathies. She loves him with her whole being;

he loves her with only part of his nature, and the insistent call of his habits and the love for the woman of his own world take him back at last. There is a fine climax to the third Act in which Tessie, having just parted from Peter, rallies at the call of her professional duty and goes on the stage to do her part as usual. This note, incidentally, is the one element which lifted such a melodrama as *Broadway* for a moment to some distinction.

With a somewhat similar plot, and belonging to the same category of fine melodrama, his next play, *Egypt* (1912), was distinctly in an older fashion. A gypsy girl is taken from her tribe by her father, a rich man who, years before, had married a gypsy who had deserted him with her child. The struggle in Egypt's nature between the tendencies inherited from her father and from her mother provides some strong scenes, especially the climax of the third Act, when, on her wedding night, she runs off with Faro, the gypsy she really loves. But the play is one of Sheldon's weakest.

Much better was *The High Road* (1912), in which the study of the motives which determine politics is enriched by Sheldon's growing love of romance. The main interest in *The High Road* is not in the background. It is centered in the character of Mary Page, who begins life as a drudge on her father's farm near Albany and ends as the wife of the Governor, who is about to be elected President of the United States. The theme of the play is best expressed in her conversation with Alan Wilson, the young painter and connoisseur, who takes her from the farm and makes her his mistress.

Mary: (*Pointing*) Do you see where the moonlight hits the rocks on the top of that hill? It makes it look like a house all built o' gold! Now listen—! D'ye hear somethin'?
Alan: No—do you?
Mary: Oh yes. There's a sound o' music an' o' singin' voices comin' from that house o' gold! Wait! If you listen a little while you can imagine that too—
Alan: (*Looking at her*) Yes, yes, now I hear.
Mary: D'ye know why they be a-singin'—up there on the hilltop?

It's 'cause they're lookin' out over the whole wide world! Think o' the oceans an' the cities lyin' stretched out in the moonlight! Oh, think o' the towers an' the castles o' the kings! They see 'em all from up there— I guess they can see a million miles without no trouble at all—

Alan: Mamie, I've climbed those hills.

Mary: Oh yes!

Alan: (*Sits on stool L. of gate*) It's hard work, but I didn't care. I just pushed along and thought of the welcome waiting for me at the top.

Mary: (*She kneels before him*) An' what was it like when ye got there?

Alan: There was nothing but the plain, bare rocks.

Mary: Wasn't ye awful—disappointed?

Alan: Perhaps—just at first—but then right off I saw the golden house again.

Mary: Where?

Alan: Across the valley—on the hills beyond!—

Mary: An' ye forgot ye was tired an' started after it again!

Alan: Oh yes, one does.

Mary: An' when ye'd climbed up the next hill, it was just the same?

Alan: It always is.

Mary: An' no one's ever walked into that house an' sat close by a winder an' looked out over the whole wide world?

Alan: Not one. But each time that you climb a hill, it seems a little bigger and a little brighter. Each time the voices seem a little nearer—*some lucky ones* have even caught a few words of the song they sing!

It is a similar theme to that treated later by Eugene O'Neill in *Beyond the Horizon,* and its development in the second Act, when she leaves the luxurious apartment in which Alan has placed her, to find an outlet into a life of service, is inspired by Sheldon's sympathy with her unquenchable thirst for better things. Her cry, "Don't you believe that there are some beautiful things beyond just what we see and feel and hear?" puts the case clearly against the cult of mere luxury and beauty. The rest of the play, in which she fights her way out of the net of blackmail spread by the trust magnate who opposes her labors in behalf of the working girl, is not so effective. Sheldon drew accurately enough, however, the situation in which she meets the threat of public scandal by striking first. She is a great relief after the old type of "stage mistress," whose effort was to retain her lover, and, in her refusal to marry Alan because she does not love him, she is sister to Fanny Hawthorne of *Hindle Wakes*, played the same year. But her rejection of Alan's offer is not purely for her own freedom as Fanny's was: it is for an opportunity also to help others, and it makes her a nobler figure.

Sheldon's most conspicuous success on the stage was his period play *Romance*. It opened in New York on February 10, 1913, with Doris Keane as Madame Cavallini, and, after a long run in the United States, was produced in London, September 30, 1915, and ran for 1,128 performances. It was then played in Australia, New Zealand, South Africa, India, Egypt, Norway and Sweden, and was revived in London in 1926. Translated into French by Robert de Flers and François de Croisset, it was performed at the Théâtre de l'Athénée, in Paris, December 24, 1923.

Its world-wide acceptance was due to the universality of the theme, to the youthful daring which attempted to depict the passion of an American clergyman for an Italian opera singer, and to the sure theatrical instinct which carried Sheldon to success through pitfalls into which many a playwright would have fallen. He secured sympathy at once by the Prologue, in which the Bishop tells the story of his one great emotional adventure to his grandson, in order to keep him from marrying an actress. The story becomes the play and it is endowed with the fragrance with which the memory of youth surrounds romance. The scene shifts to the New York of 1867, and Sheldon's picture of the social standards of the time is as authentic as the Italian which Madame Margherita Cavallini pours out on her pet monkey or her waiting maid, Signora Vannucci. She attracts the Reverend Thomas Armstrong, Rector of St. Giles, at the party of Cornelius van Tuyl, as opposites often do attract each other. When Tom finds out

Edward Sheldon -

her past he can forgive her first slip when as a girl she was driven by ignorance and want to give herself. But when Van Tuyl, whose mistress she has been, lies like a true gentleman of romance to save her, she confesses her relations with him to Tom, and the imminence of her sin is too much for the man, if not for the clergyman. The great scene of the play takes place in her apartment at the Brevoort House after the opera. The atmosphere of her life, epitomized by her old attendant, Signora Vannucci, herself a picture of what Madame Cavallini may become, is all carefully prepared to make us feel that a separation is necessary between the lovers. There is a good scene between Van Tuyl and 'Rita, and then Tom breaks in, determined to save her soul. This is the weakest part of the play, but soon the man conquers again and he begs her to give herself to him just for that one night before she departs forever. The resulting appeal, from the good he has awakened in her to the better side of his nature, to leave her with the ideal she has built up of him, is one of those scenes which shows Sheldon's sure understanding of what the theatre means. It invited great success or flat failure, and it won the first. Through the Epilogue, in which the audience return to the Bishop's study, the impression of great passion remains with them, and the Bishop, with a whimsical smile, agrees to marry Harry to his actress and puts on the Victrola the old song which, in the Prologue, has stirred his memory.

It is easy to criticize *Romance* from the point of view of the drama of ideas, but it belongs not in that category but in the drama of emotions, where indeed the permanent masterpieces of the dramatic art belong. The characters are heightened, and the professional touches in Tom's conversation are at times absurd, but the impulse which leads him to make one mad clutch at romance before he settles down to the serenity of the clergyman's life with Susan van Tuyl, his proper mate, makes an appeal to old and young, to those who have a similar memory or to those who have missed it—in short, to nearly all human beings. 'Rita is herself at all times, with the consistency not only of the type, but also of a real woman, and she illustrates that moral contrast so often mentioned, which Bret Harte bequeathed to those who, like Sheldon, know how to make use of it.

In 1914 Sheldon made an unsuccessful attempt to dramatize Sudermann's novel of *Das Hohe Lied,* under the title of *The Song of Songs,* changing the scenes to New York City and Atlantic City. Sudermann had wisely decided that the scenes were too detached for dramatic treatment, and he was justified by Sheldon's adaptation.

In *The Garden of Paradise* (1914), however, Sheldon proved that he is a poet. It is not only the exquisite lyric grace of the songs, it is the imaginative power which turned the abstractions of Hans Andersen's story of *The Little Mermaid* into real characters. Swanhild, the mermaid who loves human life, becomes a woman, bartering her hopes of three centuries of the sea for a brief season of love and an immortal soul. She saves the King from the wreck and the static story becomes dynamic in Sheldon's vigorous picture of the race through the dark waters until she brings the King safe to the shore by the convent.

The ensuing scene, which is given in barest outline in the fairy story, develops into drama in the contrast of human love with the passion of Swanhild. The young girls chant a lyric that demands musical accompaniment:

> A voice in the wind that blows
> From the land beyond the sea
> Has sung to every rose
> The song it sings to me—
> To the white rose on my breast,
> To the butterflies and bees,
> To the little birds that nest
> Among the apple trees—
> "I bring you joy and sorrow,
> Rain and sunshine, everything,
> I shall have fled to-morrow—
> I am Love! I am Spring!"

The dark girl, who is really the Queen of the Southland, finds the young King, half drowned, and Swanhild has to watch while he wakes to find himself in the Queen's arms. She thinks he is a mere sailor: he thinks she is a poor girl—after an exquisite love scene under the shadow of the statue of the little god, they part.

Swanhild wins the charm from the Sea Witch which will turn her into a human being, but she must pay the price. If the King loves her and marries her all is well; if she fails, she must return to the Sea Witch to become a toad and to serve her forever. Sheldon deepens the horror of the original scene by his conception of the Sea Witch, who is just an ordinary fairy in Andersen, but here becomes a lovely though terrible monster, and he excites our sympathy by his creation of the mermaidens, turned into toads, who try to warn their sister of her coming fate. There are faint suggestions of the Three Witches of *Macbeth* in this scene, but on the whole, it is original, and it is one of the very best of its kind. The Little Mermaid had to sacrifice her tongue in the story, but Sheldon wisely restores it to her, for her dialogue with the King when she has turned herself into a woman is natural, yet touched delicately with the hopelessness and dignity of love that is not returned. The King longs for the girl he has seen on the island and yet, for state reasons, he agrees to marry the Queen of the Southland. She, too, has had her dreams and is about to fly from her approaching suitor, when Swanhild, out of her great love for the King, persuades the Queen to wait to see him. This scene vibrates with the contrast of dawning and fading hope, and is entirely of Sheldon's creation, as is the preceding one, in which Swanhild learns of the King's love for the dark maiden of his dreams. The bridal night scene is sumptuous in its splendor, and Swanhild guards them outside the tent. Her sisters come to offer her the knife with which to kill the King and thereby buy her freedom from the Witch. But she flings the knife into the sea and leaps after it, to meet her doom. As in the fable, however, her love and sacrifice have given her a soul, and the Witch is baffled while Swanhild mounts to her place in Heaven.

To the great loss of our dramatic literature, Edward Sheldon has suffered for some years from an illness which has allowed him to work only at intervals. Outside of adaptations which he has not acknowledged, he has worked with collaborators in at least two plays, and the difficulty of assigning his share in them is increased by his modest attitude toward his own work.

The Lonely Heart (1921) is the study of the kind of character Sheldon loves to draw, the emotional, charming artist, whose life is a constant struggle between the desire for pleasure and the aspiration for better things. With his usual courage in daring the close approach to the sentimental he presents us four scenes in the life of Patrick Alexander Trelawney. The first is laid in 1864 in his childhood, starved for lack of sympathy, when the vision of his dead young mother comes to comfort him at Christmas Eve. She reappears at each of the crises of his life, at college in 1860, in his artist's cabin in 1885, where he gives up his carefully planned plot to make a young girl his mistress, and finally in 1915 when, a broken old man, he sacrifices his claim to his one hold on life, his little grandson, and dies. The best scenes are the first and last, for no one could witness without sympathy the efforts of the sophisticated little grandson to take care of his drunken but still dignified guardian in their sordid surroundings.

Bewitched (1924), in which Sheldon collaborated with Sidney Howard, is pure romance. An American aviator, cruising about in France after the war, falls near the Château de Magny and partakes of the hospitality of the Marquis de Magny. He dreams, inspired by the tapestry upon the walls. In this vision he falls in love with Jeannette, the daughter of a sorcerer of medieval days, and escapes only after the most alluring temptations. The skill with which the authors establish the atmosphere of the sorcerer's house, and interpret the conflict between the aviator's love and his desire to return to his own world, made the play significant. There are flashes of insight in *Bewitched* which reveal the playwright who lifts romance above the level of incident to the heights of character. When Jeannette rebels against her father's opposition to her growing love, and denounces the vampire (really herself) who is destroying the young men that come into the forest, he demands to know how she has learned this. She replies, "When I saw Jimmy, I think I knew everything in the world." Or another remark, of Alice Lea, the girl Jimmie had loved— "Men remember what happened; women remember how it happened"—reveals the quality of the dialogue which in these two instances may be credited to either Sheldon or Howard. It had an imaginative quality which won critical approval, but it did not attract New York audiences, though it ran to capacity houses in Cleveland.

In 1926 a melodrama, *Lulu Belle*, was produced by Belasco and announced as by Edward Sheldon and Charles MacArthur. There was a sordidness about this drama of a negro harlot's progress which was unlike anything else in Sheldon's original plays, and for which it would be idle to try to fix the responsibility. There was, however, a power in the portrayal of the devouring passion of George Randall, the negro who leaves wife and family at the call of Lulu Belle, to follow her even to Paris and to kill her in the end, which savored somewhat of his manner. There were moments, too, in the scenes in front of the tenements and in the café, which showed that the author of *Salvation Nell* had not lost his sense of the picturesque quality that may be obtained from the massing of human beings in surroundings that permit the maximum of emotional expression. But while Salvation Nell rose from degradation through suffering to a spiritual height and carried her lover with her, Lulu Belle dragged hers down to the bottom into which she fell herself. More important, the sympathy of the audience was won for Nell: it was never with Lulu Belle and rarely with George Randall, and there was no exaltation in witnessing his struggles, for the object of his desire was beneath him.

In reviewing the work that is his alone, it would seem at first glance that Sheldon was merely experimenting in various forms. But from *Salvation Nell* to *The Garden of Paradise*, at least, there is a consistency not prohibitive of the freedom that belongs to any artist. He is the celebrator of the aspiration of those who strive to lift themselves out of circumstances or a mode of life to something higher, and his sympathy is always with them, even if they are doomed to disappointment from the beginning. Salvation Nell rises through awakened faith in God to a moral regeneration. Philip Morrow, thrown into the depths of racial degradation, climbs upon his agony to the achievement of a great tolerance for the race he had despised. Michael Regan wins the love of a woman who represents concretely the refinement and the purity he worshipped and which he knew he had missed. Mary Page not only leaves the farm in pursuit of a dream of beauty, but, when she finds that dream illusive, conquers her own past and grows in moral stature through her sacrifice. 'Rita Cavallini recognizes clearly the bliss she longs for in the love of Tom Armstrong, and just as resolutely puts it aside for a principle she has only just begun dimly to understand. Even *The Song of Songs* celebrated the longing for love that might exalt, and in *The Garden of Paradise* the desire of Swanhild passed the borders of the supernatural in her aspiration for human love, finer, even in its brevity, than the interminable contentment of the sea.

In this general attitude of sympathy with the aspiring soul, Sheldon points forward to Eugene O'Neill. But as in O'Neill the poet dominates the dramatist, so in Sheldon the playwright limits or at least defines the poet's power. That is why *The Garden of Paradise* is an advance upon *Salvation Nell* and why the fate that prevents the unhampered expression of Edward Sheldon's talent is so great a loss to the drama in America.

It would be a violation of confidence to record here the many instances in which Sheldon has been the unacknowledged collaborator with other playwrights or has adapted from other literature plays which have made wide popular appeal. On account of a modesty that must be respected this contribution cannot here be discussed. But if the truth were really known he would be more fully recognized not only as a playwright of originality but also as one who has inspired actors of prominence by providing them with plays which revealed to them and the public talents that otherwise might have been unsuspected. While our drama has been celebrated as the abode of "little people," it is the function of the historian to record and emphasize the ability which has never lost sight of the fact that in the theatre the touchstone of genius is the creation of power. Even in his failures, there was daring and mastery of all the resources of the theatre.

For Edward Sheldon is essentially a playwright. From his earliest youth he dramatized life, largely through his imagination. He has observed life carefully, it is true, and he has appreciated the aid which a realistic setting affords to a romantic theme. But on the whole he is best when he trusts to that imagination in the creation of beauty.

NOTE. Edward Sheldon died April 2, 1946.

CHAPTER XVII

THE HEIGHT OF MELODRAMA

THERE is nothing easier than to give a play a bad name and hang it. How often, after an evening in which a playwright has entertained, surprised and even thrilled us for a few moments, do we reward him by shamefacedly remarking to our semi-profound friends, "Oh, yes, it was an interesting play, but of course it was only a melodrama." It is partly the critical rage for classification that besets us. We think we know tragedy and comedy, but we do not know what to do with the vast body of plays which lie between these categories. We call them all melodrama, and then after an attempt to include *Fine Feathers* and *Rain* in the same category, perhaps the thought begins to dawn upon us that there is fine melodrama and poor melodrama. Tragedy exalts; comedy entertains. But there are times when we wish neither to have our souls exalted nor to have our weaknesses exposed. We wish to have our attention caught and held by interesting situations and capable dialogue, and we wish to have above all that element of intense suspense which is the heart and soul of melodrama. So we are willing to give the playwright freedom. He may play upon that profoundest impulse of our nature, the instinct of self-preservation, and the hero or heroine may be in danger all the time. We have progressed beyond the point when we demand a happy ending, but we do want the ending to be "satisfactory." The word is again quoted from Bronson Howard, who could write good melodrama when he chose to do so.

For melodrama has its own laws not so clearly felt but still real. When any artist deliberately frees himself from certain restrictions, he either takes on others or he observes faithfully the ones he preserves. We are willing to forgive the writer of melodrama if he heightens the sentiment or even exaggerates the passion. But not only must he make the ending satisfactory to us; he must also provide situations that are well knit together—the action must be sustained, and the illusion of probability must be preserved. For remember, it is an illusion. The older melodrama demanded neither probability nor possibility, but the new melodrama demands the first. The appeal of "soft music," brought in to lull our critical judgment to sleep, to rouse our emotions so that they would forgive absurdity, is no longer needed in the new art of melodrama. It is no longer satisfied with mere situations; it attempts character drawing and even concerns itself with the social problems of the day.

With such definition of the melodrama, we can be concerned only with its outstanding examples. During the Nineteenth Century melodrama of the poorer variety satisfied the demand which, since the advent of the moving picture, has been met by that institution.

The older melodrama which held the stage by reason of the sincerity of its portraiture of character as well as by the vividness of its situations is exemplified by *In Old Kentucky*, by Charles T. Dazey (1855-1938), a native of Illinois, who realized the possibilities of the Kentucky mountaineer in drama. Dazey knew Kentucky well. He was educated at the College of Arts in Lexington before he entered Harvard, where he was the class poet of 1881. He had the usual difficulties in obtaining an opportunity, until finally *In Old Kentucky* was produced by the stock company at the Grand Opera House in St. Paul, Minnesota, in June, 1893. The play was performed for twenty-seven consecutive seasons in New York or on the road. It was based on personal observation, and Walter Scott's contrasts of the highlander and lowlander suggested to Dazey a contrast between the mountaineer and the "blue grass people." The great success of *In Old Kentucky* was due not only to the plot, which is a skillful succession of fights and accusations of murder, culminating in a horse race. This race was suggested to Dazey by witnessing the actions of a Puritanical Kentucky woman who became wildly excited over a contest which she hoped would be won by her son's entry. Dazey made from her the character of Aunt Aleathea. But Madge, the mountain girl, is the central character, and the love story which develops between her and Frank Layson, a young patrician, ends in her riding his horse to win the race, the "Ashland Oaks," for him. That she runs the risk of losing his love by appearing in public in the riding breeches which the traditions of his class made it impossible for a gentlewoman to don, provides a striking climax for the third Act. But the secret of the combined appeal of *In Old Kentucky* was Dazey's picture of the intense loves and hates which the primitive life of the mountaineers made plausible. The emotion is heightened by the process of making it more simple, and the improbabilities lie in the grouping of incidents rather than in the incidents themselves. Dazey continued to write plays for James O'Neill, Goodwin, Crane, and other leading actors, but none of them need detain us.

The transition from the older melodramas to the new is illustrated best by the work of George Broadhurst (1866-   ). His early successes in farce-comedy like *What Happened to Jones* (1897) and *Why Smith Left Home* (1899), despite their wide appeal, did not content him, for in *The Last Chapter* (1899) he made an attempt to do more serious work. In 1906 came *The Man of the Hour*, a play of political conditions. Alwyn Bennett, a young man of apparently easy-going nature, is elected mayor of a large city by the organization which believes it can control him. He acts independently of the boss, Richard Horigan, who is in league with the capitalist who has financed the campaign. The usual methods of coercion and blackmail are tried in vain, and Alwyn wins in his fight against corruption. What made the play the best Broadhurst has done was the character drawing, not only of the young mayor, who drops his indifference when occasion for real effort arises, but even better, that of Phelan, the politician, by whose practical knowledge he circumvents the combination against him. Phelan is one of the few real politicians in the drama, and it may be that Broadhurst in his picture of the alliance between a man of education, independent through his fortune and position, and a practical politician, who is inspired by loyalty to his chief and animosity to his rival, has presented the only real solution for our political difficulties. Probably the strength and weakness of Broadhurst showed most clearly in *Bought and Paid For* (1911). The central theme, the marriage of a girl telephone operator to a rich self-made man, who drinks too much and who insists upon his marital rights, even breaking down the door of his wife's room as a climax to the second Act, was only mildly effective. It illustrated, however, one of the reasons why melodrama so often fails to respond to the test of permanent worth. The play was evidently built up for that scene, and an essentially improbable character of the wife was created to provide it. Plays of real value are not created for any one scene; they spring from the study of character. What saved the play and indeed turned it into a success, was the character of James Gilley, the brother of the wife, who is an amusing boaster and whose own keen interest in his return to prosperity brings about the reconciliation. This part, played by Frank Craven, is a type caricature, and illustrates again the quick response of this form of appeal. Indeed, the line between the melodrama and the comedy-type play is easily crossed.

Broadhurst's plays leave one with a sense of ability directed too constantly to the immediate return of the box office. Occasionally as in *The Price*, a sturdy melodrama, he leaves the heroine, who has secured her happiness at the cost of her employer's life, in a very insecure position, and paints a picture of wifely revenge which is powerful and perhaps original. The scene in which Ethel Bristol, knowing her own guilt, has to listen to Mrs. Dole read from her late husband's diary an account of his relations with Ethel, until she forces Ethel to a confession, is very effective. But the effect is heightened when Ethel reads the diary later and finds that Mrs. Dole has herself interpolated the passage that wrung out of her rival her avowal of guilt. In *The Law of the Land* (1914) after building up an appealing situation in which a wife who has been hounded into killing her husband, is saved from detection by the loyalty of her lover, her secretary, and her manservant, Broadhurst precipitates the play into farce by the action of the police inspector, who abandons the case apparently because he is the father of twins!

Of less merit than Broadhurst's plays, the melodramas written by Charles Klein (1867-1915) were among the most successful of the first decade of the new century. Born in England, he belongs to our dramatic history mainly by the fact that his plays were concerned frequently with themes of contemporary life in the United States. He had a theory of play writing which was higher than his practice.[1]

Practically all his plays seem written with the "big act" in mind. *The Lion and the Mouse* (1905) was prompted by his visit to the United States Senate. He drew in it the situation in which a girl, by becoming the private secretary of a magnate, saves her father, a judge of the Supreme Court, from certain financial interests that are attacking him. The scenes between Shirley Rossmore and Ryder have a certain power, but the characters are artificial. In *Daughters of Men* (1906) a capital and labor play, he points to the compromise suggested by Patrick McCarthy, the union leader, as the only way out. *The Third Degree* (1909) is based on the practice of the police in questioning criminals after arrest, and while realistic from

---

[1] "First comes the central idea of the play, then by a natural process the evolution of the characters needed for the exposition of the idea, then the sequence of events growing out of the conflict of the characters and last the unfolding of the story, consequent upon the conflict of temperaments. This is the natural order of development and that is one reason why melodramas are unnatural. The order of their development is to write the big act first and make everything else subservient. Mechanics receive first consideration and the characters are mere puppets bobbing about at the will of the monarch Mechanics."—*Theatre Magazine*, VI (1906), p. 159.

this point of view, is highly improbable and inconclusive. *The Gamblers* (1910) is a tense melodrama which deals with the conventional methods of finance that obtain on the stage. *The Next of Kin* (1909) strikes a lighter note, though the heroine is in danger of being sent to an insane asylum in order that her guardian may obtain her money. In *Maggie Pepper* (1911) he drew an extraordinary young woman, who at twenty-eight instructs her employers how to conduct a department store. These plays are all theatrically effective but they do not stand the test of analysis. His earlier sentimental successes like *The Music Master* (1904) are even less worthy of attention. The success of Broadhurst and Klein prompted others into the same field and all through the decade theatrical history is replete with the names of plays which made heroes or villains out of "captains of industry" or their opponents. Few of them survive, but the work of at least one man merits some scrutiny for he worked sincerely even if at times with unworthy material.

Eugene Walter (1874-1941) was born in Cleveland, Ohio, and had a varied experience in newspaper work in New York City, in the Middle West, and in Seattle. He also learned the theatrical business, "ranging," he says, "from minstrels and circuses to symphony orchestras and grand opera companies." He began writing with the new century, his *Serjeant James* being put on in Boston in 1902, and running for two weeks. But he first attracted attention with *The Undertow* (1907), a play of politics, railroads and newspaper life. Then came *Paid in Full* (1908), a study of the weakness of human nature in conflict with circumstances and with stronger natures. Joe Brooks, the clerk in the steamship company who steals money from his employer, Captain Williams, ostensibly to give his wife more comfort but really because he is a discontented weakling, is contrasted with Emma, who is the best character in the play. She is not the usual stage heroine, for she is a normal woman who dislikes housework but does it, and who, when her husband's defalcation is discovered, meets the situation effectively without heroics. Joe, driven into a corner by Williams' unexpected return, begs Emma to go to the captain and make terms. Full of contempt for him, Emma does so, expecting little, for the brutal character of Williams is well known. This scene made the fortune of the play. Captain Williams, instead of demanding the price which she anticipated, lets her husband resign with a clean slate and tells her he does so because he knows there are just two kinds of women, the good and the bad, and it is worth $19,000 to him to find out that she is the right kind. There is an essential falsity in this scene, for nothing in Captain Williams' character as portrayed earlier in the play warrants his action. But Walter was playing a sure card, for audiences like the moral contrast which the generosity of a hard man provides, and it does not need the author's statement that he drew the character from Jack London and Rudyard Kipling to recognize the touch of their ancestor, Bret Harte. That *Paid in Full* is a melodrama is shown by Walter's own analysis of it.[1]

Walter next wrote a successful melodrama of the Canadian woods, *The Wolf* (1908), in which he combined scenic realism, even to the reproduction of the howling of wolves from phonographic records taken in the Zoölogical Garden, with the excitement of a pursuit and a struggle in the dark between the lover and the villain. *The Easiest Way* (1908) has been hailed as a great example of realism and an epoch-making play. It is neither, but is rather a skilfully contrived melodrama, in which Walter had the courage to run the motive through to an unhappy ending, and the skill to preserve the suspense until that climax. He carefully presents us in the published play with an analysis of each of the characters up to the point at which they enter the drama. To anyone who has seen the play, these descriptions come as a surprise, for the three major

---

[1] *How to Write a Play*, Chaps. IV and V. "When the curtain descends on Williams, acknowledging gratification for performing a good deed, the result has been attained. There are a few broken threads to be tied together and that requires a short act . . . [but] . . . this act is essentially an anti-climax." In other words the play has been built up to one scene, and the characters have been motivated to its effect instead of determining it.

characters, Laura Murdock, Willard Brockton, and John Madison, do not conform to them. It would seem as though Walter, having built up a play out of situations, had then imagined the characters he would have liked to put in them. Or perhaps having had his original conception of the characters altered by the demands of production, he consoled himself by putting in print his implicit defense. Laura Murdock, the mistress of Willard Brockton, is the central character, and any claim the play may have to realism, stands or falls with her. As portrayed with skill by Frances Starr, she was essentially inconsistent, and the text of the play left the actress no alternative. The Laura of the first Act was refined and charming, giving up a prospect of luxury for a love for John Madison, which is to elevate and purify her. She keeps up her heroic and virtuous attitude nearly through the second Act, when the accumulated miseries of life in a second-rate boarding house in New York, and the schemes of Brockton, drive her back into his protection. She is weak enough not to keep up the struggle upon which she and Madison have agreed as a test of her fitness to marry him, when he shall make his fortune, and she is treacherous enough not even to send the letter which Brockton insists upon her writing to Madison when she returns to her earlier paramour. From this time on she runs true enough to the conception of her character as Walter outlines it in his introduction, and her final futile gesture toward suicide after Madison's return and discovery of her relapse, is also quite in keeping. But the heroic and spiritual Laura of Acts I and II is not the Laura of Acts III and IV, and the reason is not far to seek. If Walter had appeared on the stage and read his introduction, there would have been no play. The audience is led to sympathize with Laura because of her girlishness, her deep love for Madison, her apparent regeneration, and in real life Laura Murdock would not have had these qualities or been capable of this emotion. Walter has been clever enough to create a sentimental fallacy which for purposes of the theatre worked well, but to speak of the play as a forward step in realism is to misuse the word. It is the old theme of the moral contrast which Bret Harte used so often, but the keener eye of the master would have smiled at Laura. He drew harlots who were brave, who were generous, who could starve themselves to death, but he did not draw them as "girlish" and he did not permit any one of them to say to a colleague whose professional career had been uninterrupted, "I don't see how you dare show your face to a decent woman."[1] In short, he was not absurd. Brockton is more consistent, but his conscientious attitude toward Madison is also overstrained, considering the devices he uses to regain Laura. His entrance into her flat, in which he shows his relation to her by the possession of the latchkey, has been praised by those who have forgotten Pinero's *Iris* or Daly's still earlier adaptation of *Madeleine Morel*.

In *Fine Feathers* (1913) Walters almost rose out of melo-drama. This is a sincere treatment of the unsuccessful strug-gle of an individual against the temptations of modern life. These temptations in the case of Bob Reynolds are made con-crete in his wife, Jane, whose desire for fine clothes and whose response to the general urge of feminine competition lead him to dishonesty, disgrace and suicide. The offer of John Brand, the contractor, to bribe Bob, who is an inspecting chemist, to permit the substitution of an inferior grade of cement in the new bridge, is at first refused; then, when Jane enters into the conspiracy against his honor, he weakens and accepts the forty thousand dollars. Walter, unlike the older school of melo-drama, knows the modern methods of business, and he skil-fully draws the net around Bob. Brand leads him into specu-lation, sells him, through his broker, stock in a weak concern, and recoups himself for the money he has paid Bob. When the latter turns on him and announces his intention of confess-ing his share in the transaction, Brand again stops him by reminding him that Jane is an accessory before the fact and will go to jail also. Bob's character runs true to form. There is not enough steel in him to meet his crisis alone. He drinks

[1] *The Easiest Way,* Act II.

brandy to give himself courage and defies Brand—and Jane and he in a flash of mutual tenderness and understanding come to a realization of their common responsibility. Then, when it seems that possible happiness opens for them, the dam breaks on account of the weak cement and hundreds of lives are lost. Brand and Dick Meade, the friend who has been the concrete representative of a saner philosophy of life, urge them to run for Europe, but Bob has the combination of courage and weakness which takes him out of the situation with a bullet through his head. The suicide is logical and inevitable. *Fine Feathers* was Walter's last significant play. He made an attempt in *A Plain Woman* (1912) to dramatize a recent divorce suit in which a captain of industry forgot the wife who had helped him in his youth. But his skill was spent in adaptations of John Fox's stories of the mountaineers or in frank melodramas like *The Knife* (1917). Melodrama, after all, is his natural method.

The crest of the wave of melodrama which dramatized current events came about the end of the first decade. Naturally it was from the newspaper offices that playwrights were recruited. Usually their work has dropped below the level which requires our attention, but occasional plays at least need mention. Joseph Medill Patterson (1879-1946) and Harriet Ford drew a vivid, if exaggerated picture of a newspaper office and composing room in *The Fourth Estate* (1909). The background was more veracious than the leading character, a managing editor who commits suicide because he cannot carry to its finish his fight against corruption, a climax which was later changed to suit popular demand for a happy ending. In *Rebellion* (1911), Patterson illustrated the futility of religious discussion upon the stage. The audiences which watched Georgia Connor struggle to decide whether to divorce her drunken husband and remarry, in defiance of her belief as a Catholic, or to suffer while carrying out her marriage vow, remained generally cold, because to those who believed as she did, the elaborate arguments of Father Hervey left out the one supreme argument, while to those who were not Catholics, there seemed no problem at all. Probably the most powerful of the plays which attacked a form of religious belief was *Polygamy*, (1914) by Harvey O'Higgins and Harriet Ford. The difficulty of the individual who is caught in the net of Mormonism was skilfully drawn and the plight of the husband who is forced into infidelity against his will might have been even more tragic if a way out had not been found at the last moment.

The mechanics of melodrama were given a new turn in *On Trial* (1914), by Elmer Reizenstein (now Rice), a murder mystery which interrupted the progress of a court trial by enacting certain scenes which the witnesses have just started to describe. The result on the stage was certainly striking and the principle on which it was based has been adopted in several plays since that time. When *On Trial* was first produced, the prophecy was freely made that it would revolutionize play writing, but it has not done so. The "cutback" was of course suggested by the moving picture and the moving picture can produce the effect so much more easily than the play that dramatists have usually wisely left the field to their rival. Rice has not maintained his reputation as a playwright, and in *The Adding Machine* (1923) he descended into a sordid analysis of human life and an absurd description of heaven, couched in terms of exaggeration and so-called expressionism, which for a short time deceived some critics as to its importance.

Indeed while freedom has been one of the qualities of melodrama, it is not often that it attracts the pioneer in matters of form. It may introduce new devices like the noiseless pistol of *Within the Law*, but the authors of successful plays of this category usually rely on the well-established principles by which intensity of impression may be secured. The melodrama passed from a scrutiny of our economic and political institutions to an analysis of crime and its detection, and a deluge of "crook" plays ensued to which we need pay little attention. Indeed it never left this field, and occasionally, as in *Leah Kleschna* (1904) by C. M. S. McLellan, the character drawing

rose above the usual level. McLellan, who under the name of Hugh Morton had won popular success with *The Belle of New York*, attempted to portray sincerely the regeneration of a girl thief through the power of a man whom she loves, and if she is not altogether convincing, the play even yet bears reading better than many of its kind. Mrs. Fiske made a signal success in the part, both at home and abroad. The difficulties of the American playwright are reflected in the preface which records McLellan's protest against having to write a fifth Act to provide a happy ending when the play was complete at the end of the fourth.

Even the interminable succession of melodramas with a "gunman" as the hero achieve occasionally a character portrayal of some reality. Porter Emerson Browne's *The Bad Man* (1920) despite its improbabilities, caused a hearer to think, for in the action of Pancho Lopez, who applies to the usual triangle the quick methods of solution of a Mexican bandit, we may sense a reason for the continued misunderstanding of the two countries. When two races dislike each other for their virtues, it is almost a hopeless matter. *Seventh Heaven*, by Austin Strong (1922), a romantic melodrama laid in Paris, gave Helen Menken an opportunity for one of the most vivid scenes in the contemporary drama. The picture of Diane, animated by her love for Chico to a courage that enables her to defy the tyranny of years, was fine melodrama. One of the best of recent melodramas was *Twelve Miles Out* (1925), by William Anthony McGuire, for the character of Michael McCue, the modern pirate, was outstanding, and the purpose the author had in writing, the attack upon intolerance, is clear and yet not too evident.

At this moment the melodrama seems to be progressing not so much in the direction of probability as in that of rapidity. In *Broadway* (1926) and *Chicago* (1926) the tempo is keyed up to the intense rhythm of contemporary life. The picture of a night club in the former has photographic reality, of course, but the plot is as old as the French *mélodrame* of the

Eighteenth Century. The four stock figures, the heroine who is better than her surroundings, the hero, who has "honest intentions" toward her, the villain, who would delude her, and the detective, who circumvents the villain, are old friends. Even the one appealing note, that of the professional pride of the variety actors who "do their act" even if their hearts are breaking, has been anticipated by Sheldon and others. *Chicago* differed from *Broadway* in its satiric intent. The methods by which a murderess not only is saved from execution, but is made a heroine through the efforts of her attorney and the newspapers, are correct. There is a delightful touch at the end, when just as the acquitted murderess is posing for her picture, a shot is heard and all her admirers run off to pay court to the newest sensation!

But in the history of the drama, such plays are mere episodes, to be forgotten because they do not advance the art at all. The characters are not even as veracious as those of *In Old Kentucky;* they are only more active. They are as far from sounding the profounder realities of life as the daily newspaper from which they take their inspiration. Of all dramatic forms they fade most quickly, for they pay the price of their seizure of contemporary interest by certain oblivion.

CHAPTER XVIII

COMEDY TYPES AGAIN

PERHAPS the most persistent of the impulses that have made our drama continuous in its history, has been the effort to present types of character, whose primary purpose is the creation of laughter. From the two Jonathans in *The Contrast* and *The Forest Rose*, through the work of Harrigan and Hoyt, the tradition passed on unbroken to George Ade and George Cohan. Generally the type has tended to caricature, there has been an overemphasis upon certain qualities in the leading character, usually written for a star, and while the lessons Herne and Thomas taught our playwrights have not passed unnoticed, the species has never risen to the permanent worth of our social comedy, our serious domestic drama, or our romance. Yet because of its portrayal of American types and because of its great success in the theatre, it demands consideration.

When George Ade (1866-1944) began to write his comedies at the beginning of the Twentieth Century they were hailed as a new departure. But there is little really original in his choice of material or method of treatment. Ade has expressed his conception of play writing as an attempt to treat of American life "without slandering my own countrymen or holding them up to ridicule." [1] It is true that his satire is kindly rather than searching, but there are certainly ridiculous types in all his plays and the general effect is similar to that of Hoyt, who was undoubtedly his model. Ade has written at least seventeen plays, including musical comedies like *The Sultan of Sulu* (1902) and *The Sho-gun* (1904), and he continued his dra-

[1] "George Ade talks of his Stage Ideals," *Theatre Magazine*, IV (1904) 287-8.

matic work until 1914, but final judgment must rest upon the popular successes produced between 1903 and 1908.

The County Chairman (1903) is a study of the human politician in a small town in Indiana. The Honorable Jim Hackler, the county chairman, is the hero. As is usual with Ade, the minor characters establish the atmosphere of the town and provide rather obvious comedy. The plot is of no real significance. What carried the play was the character study of Jim Hackler, who represents the politician that dominates his town by his personality, and who, while believing in organization, has the saving grace of decency which marks him out from the herd. In *The College Widow* (1904) Ade presented a picture of Atwater College, evidently in the Middle West. All the types, from the president down to the waiters, are highly exaggerated and represent the most obvious features of college life. There is a trainer, a football coach, and a postgraduate tutor who is drawn after the stage professor of fifty years before, and the whole college atmosphere seems to be written from the point of view of an outsider. This is not due to ignorance on Ade's part, for he is a graduate of Purdue University and has been a trustee, but to the inherent weakness of the comedy of exaggeration. There is, indeed, some shrewd comment on modern athletics implicit in the conversation of the characters. The College Widow, Jane Witherspoon, the daughter of the president, is fairly well drawn, and Bill Bolton, the half-back hero, is not too heroic to be acceptable in comedy. But the play verges on farce all the time and any real interpretation of college life is nonexistent. What carried the play was the clever conversation and the continuous bustle.

Just Out of College (1905) is a satire on the college man who has nothing that is available from his education to sell in the business world. Edward Swinger, who has gone through college with a tennis racquet, tries to marry Caroline Pickering, the daughter of Septimus Pickering, who is in the pickle industry. Pickering loans him twenty thousand dollars, and Edward invests it in the pickle business without his prospective

114

father-in-law's knowledge, and of course makes money by it. The conversation is undoubtedly clever, but when it does not verge on slang, it is slang. *Father and the Boys* (1908) is laid in New York City; at a race course; and at the Eldorado Hotel near Goldfields, Nevada. It is a contrast between Lemuel Morewood, a wool broker, and his two sons, who let him see that they consider him a "back number." He tries to prove the contrary and succeeds. In it Crane had a congenial character part. It is difficult, and perhaps unnecessary, to tell the plot of one of Ade's plays, because the plot, after all, is not the important matter. What carried the plays was the snap of the dialogue, the hard, highly colored caricature, and an eternal optimism, with a shrewd comment on life. Ade also wrote a number of one-act plays, including *Marse Covington, The Mayor and the Manicure, Speaking to Father*, and *Nettie*, which partake of the same characteristics as the longer plays. In fact, *Speaking to Father* is a section of *Just Out of College*.

While the work of George M. Cohan (1878-1942) belongs to the same category as that of George Ade, there are certain differences, due to their training. Cohan, in his autobiography, reveals his limitations and also his genius for the theatre. If one feels that Ade was capable of better things than he accomplished, there is the impression that Cohan has developed his talent to its fullest extent. His education has been almost entirely in the theatre, and he has acquired a sense of what is theatrically effective, probably unexcelled, except by Belasco. He is more inclined to the melodrama than Ade, but the plays of both are based upon the principle of the variety show, the deliberate planting of the remark for the sake of the answer. There is an imaginative quality at times in Cohan's work to which Ade does not aspire, and there is an emotional element, shown in his work in music, which is seen for better or for worse in his plays.

It would be idle to chronicle his work completely. He has been on the stage since the age of nine, and his play writing began with vaudeville. He learned his art in the eighties and nineties and to those who saw *The Governor's Son* in 1901 and *American Born* in 1926 there was no essential difference in kind between the two, except that one was accompanied by music and the other was not. There is, however, a difference in degree of artistic effectiveness in Cohan's plays. *Forty-five Minutes From Broadway* (1906) is a farce, with an impossible plot, and the stage law of the eighties. In *Get-Rich-Quick Wallingford* (1910), however, he made out of the stories by George Randolph Chester, one of the most successful plays oɪ the day and a skillfully constructed piece of stage art. J. Rufus Wallingford, the adventurer who with his companion, "Blackie" Daw, makes a fortune out of covered carpet tacks and wakes up to find himself honest, typifies success at any price, and his wide appeal may be a criticism of the public that applauded him or it may be a criticism of the reality of the playwright and his fictional model. To be sure, the final curtain is brought down upon the reformed Wallingford's remark, "What a fool a man is for being a crook." But in any event the type play does not convince; and audiences are quite willing to be amused by dishonesty and even to applaud it, because they do not take it seriously. The student of stage technique may profit, however, by a consideration of the means by which Cohan secured his effects, especially in the first Act. Wallingford is kept off the stage until his picture, endowed by "Blackie" Daw with the quality of success, is mirrored in the consciousness of the leading citizens of Battlesburg, and his entry and the impression he makes upon his prospective victims are both based on an instinctive knowledge of human psychology.

In *Broadway Jones* (1912) there was expressed a sympathy for human joy and suffering that raised the play above the average of Cohan's work. The revelation to the young spendthrift that his responsibility for the business which had been left to him did not end with his mere decision to sell it, could not have been brought about so well if Cohan himself had not known the daily hazard of those whose margin of comfort is insecure. *Seven Keys to Baldpate* (1913) showed Cohan in one of his cleverest moods, though again he derived the idea from a story. One surprise follows another, until the audience, who have watched the wonderful collection of reporters, crooks and politicians and who believe they are in the secret, suddenly realize they have been tricked and that the whole thing is simply a story that Magee, a writer, has completed on a bet, at midnight. Everyone is a type and there is not a dull moment. There is a certain advance in characterization in *Hit the Trail Holliday* (1915) though it is so patently based on the career of "Billy Sunday" that it loses in part. The conception of a bartender taking the lead in a prohibition crusade is fundamentally comic.

The interest in *The Miracle Man* (1914) lay in the instinctive reaction of Cohan to the greater effect which a faith healer would exert on the audience if his influence were shown through the other characters and he were kept off the stage. In *Madeleine and the Movies* (1922) Cohan attempted to repeat the device of *Seven Keys to Baldpate* by having what is apparently a moving picture turn out to be a vision of a butler who is longing to act. But the play did not succeed notwithstanding that Cohan himself went into the cast to save it. This action, not limited to the play in question, reveals the essentially incomplete nature of his art as a playwright, which depends so much upon his personality as an actor that they are almost inseparable. They almost made *The Song and Dance Man* (1923) a play of permanent value. In the part of John Farrell or "Hap," Cohan rose almost above the type to an individual character. In this variety actor, who cherished the belief that he was the best "song and dance man" in the profession, there is a wistful fancy that remains after the gun play and the rest depart. Farrell was the incarnation of the experience of Cohan the actor, and the picture of a second-rate variety "performer," drawn by one of the most successful in the history of the theatre, with the sympathy that success has apparently left unkilled, was very appealing. Here Cohan was at home, while in *American Born* (1926) he was equally out of his element in an international contrast.

There is no final judgment as yet to be passed on Cohan's work, but in any such consideration, it must be remembered on the one hand that he has made his greatest successes by fashioning for the theatre material supplied by other hands and on the other that he has added something vital for the theatre in his treatment of that material.

James Forbes, a Canadian by birth, but a naturalized citizen since 1892, became a playwright after a long training in the theatre, as both actor and manager, and a varied newspaper experience. In *The Chorus Lady* (1906) and *The Show Shop* (1914) he drew situations with the background of the theatre, extremely effective on the stage, and couched in a witty dialogue which does not lose so much through the test of print as do his farce comedies of small town or suburban life, *The Travelling Salesman* (1908) and *The Commuters* (1910). There is a glamour about the stage pictures in *The Chorus Lady*, and a heroic sacrifice of one sister for another, strongly reminiscent of *One of Our Girls*, which gives it more permanent interest than the description of the "drummers" or the people in *The Commuters*, although the latter are more accurately painted. But all the characters are highly touched up, and to speak of any of them as veracious pictures of life is a mistake. Forbes did vastly superior work in the more difficult field of social drama in *The Famous Mrs. Fair*.[1]

That the type play is distinctly less a matter of writing than of acting is illustrated by the series of plays in which Winchell Smith (1871–1933) has collaborated with a number of playwrights who it may be presumed contributed the story while one of the most expert stage directors of to-day contributed that element which secures success upon the stage. But wherever the play is laid the interest lies in the caricature. The small-town types in *The Fortune Hunter* (1909), the doctor and nurse in *The Boomerang* (1916), the really delightful

[1] See Chapter XV.

board of trustees of a church in *Thank You* (1921), are farcical but interesting. The climax of absurdity was reached in *Turn to the Right* (1916) in which two crooks calmly marry into a respectable family with apparent general satisfaction. The height of Smith's success came with his association with the actor, Frank Bacon, in *Lightnin'*. Beginning August 26, 1918, this play ran for 1,291 consecutive performances, in New York, and it is significant that it broke the record held, for over twenty years, by Hoyt's *A Trip to Chinatown*. *Lightnin'* secured its success through the remarkable acting of Bacon in the type part of "Lightnin' Bill Jones," a lovable ne'er-do-well, who drinks more than is good for him and has a delightful gift of exaggeration. He is the lineal descendant of Rip Van Winkle and of Mink Jones in *A Temperance Town*, his resemblance to the first being emphasized by his noble forgiveness of his wife who has taken care of him, and by his refusal to sign a deed to their hotel, just as Rip had declined to sign the transfer of his property. The resemblance was completed by Bacon's modeling of his acting on that of Joseph Jefferson.

To the same school of writing belong the comedies of Frank Craven, who indeed acted in *Artie*, one of Ade's comparative failures. Craven is a very competent actor, and he has taken the leading parts in his own plays. Beginning in 1914 with *Too Many Cooks*, which dealt with suburban types and the interference of relatives-in-law, he scored his greatest success in *The First Year* (1920) which ran for seven hundred and forty performances in New York, and in which he represented the difficulties of a bride and groom in the necessary adjustments of married life. Each character, from the principals and the father and mother of the bride, down to an extraordinary negro servant, is a highly colored chromo, and the business methods of the purchasing agent of the railroad through which the fortune of the young pair is made, are so absurd as to be irritating. Yet the hilarity was continuous and Craven's play rose above the mass by the human touch which led thousands to remember their own difficulties in a similar period of life. There was a healthy tone in the depiction of the relations of father and son in *New Brooms* (1924), and in both this play and *Spite Corner* (1922) Craven appeared to be working out of the type play to a truer form of comedy. This he almost achieved in *Money From Home* (1927) a study of the girl who leaves her Pennsylvania Dutch home for an adventure in New York, and the young doctor, who after abandoning his profession to lead the life of a crook, resumes it by the instinctive response which an opportunity to save life offers him. Craven's art is evidently still in a formative state.

The type play naturally leads to the dramatization of current events, and this brings immediate attention and likewise emphasizes its temporary character. The automobile and the consequent extravagance of those who purchase it was satirized in a play, *Six Cylinder Love* (1921) by William Anthony McGuire, in which the character drawing was above the ordinary type casting in such plays. McGuire writes with a background of knowledge of the history of the drama, as evidenced by a thoughtful article on comedy recently published by him, and in such comedies as *I Wish I Was Rich* (1926) he gives evidence of ability which has not yet been fully expressed. The comic supplement is itself dramatized in *The Potters* (1923) by J. P. McEvoy, a graduate of Notre Dame University and a newspaper man. The efforts of "Pa" Potter, the head of a family of distinctly mediocre quality, to maintain his hold on life despite the pressure of his wife's desires, are set against a background of subways, lunch counters, Pullman cars, and back porches, which reflect observation of the surface of life.

The strength of the appeal of the type play, when written shrewdly and accurately timed, is illustrated by the career of *Abie's Irish Rose* which after a success in California began at the Fulton Theatre, New York, May 23, 1922, and was still running, after transfer to the Republic, in July, 1927. It is idle for the dramatic critic to dismiss such a play as unimportant. When any production on the stage, notwithstanding critical disapproval, makes such a continuous appeal, without salacious or spectacular elements, it behooves the historian to inquire into the reasons for the result. That it is the play which is responsible has been proved by the invariable success which has been met by each road company, no matter what the ability of the actors, none of whom have been of stellar rank. *Abie's Irish Rose* has succeeded because Anne Nichols has represented practically every form of love known to human beings. There is first, the love of a boy, Abraham Levy, and a girl, Rose-Mary Murphy, who have been married secretly, knowing the racial prejudice of their respective fathers. Next is the love of Solomon Levy and Patrick Murphy for their children; third, the love sanctified by memory, of the dead mothers of the young couple; and finally the love of the grandfathers for their twin grandchildren, through whom the reconciliation is brought about. There is thus secured an appeal to all ages and conditions, sharpened by the shrewdly conceived dialogue, which is based on the century-old principle of antithesis, and borrowed from the variety show. Miss Nichols wisely chose for the motive of prejudice the two races which probably feel most keenly any insult to their racial and religious instincts, and insults are hurled freely by Solomon Levy and Patrick Murphy at each other. Their sensitiveness makes for comedy, of course, but there is another element in *Abie's Irish Rose* which helped to secure its popular triumph. In 1922 the wave of intolerance which frequently comes after a war was sweeping over the country, and one of its forms was directed against the Jewish and the Irish Catholic elements in our population. Miss Nichols not only attacked this intolerance indirectly through her revelation of the absurdity of the fathers' prejudice, but she embodied in the characters of Father Whalen and Rabbi Samuels, through whom the reconciliation is effected, the opposite gospel of tolerance. Already the reaction against the germ of race hatred had set in, and if *Uncle Tom's Cabin* was a powerful weapon against slavery, *Abie's Irish Rose* has become important in our social history as a potent force toward sanity of feeling in the Republic.

In view of the fact that when *Lightnin'* had to relinquish the record of continuous performances on Broadway, it was to *Abie's Irish Rose* that it handed the popular laurel it had taken from *A Trip to Chinatown*, it is futile to treat the type play from the usual academic attitude. English audiences view them with favor, partly in the spirit of a visit to a museum, and some of the most eccentric productions, like *Potash and Perlmutter*, succeed even in Germany. But to speak of the type play as realistic, is a mistake. It is, in the true sense of the word, the exact opposite, idealistic, in method. The characters are overstressed for purposes of comedy and their very success is determined frequently, though not universally, by their exaggeration. Yet they are of the very life of the theatre; their glaring colors are a reflex of the paint and the tinsel. Perhaps because their authors know the theatre so well, they are not concerned with its changing fashions. They write in the accepted formulas which have stood the test for centuries. Occasionally, as in *Rip Van Winkle, Lightnin'* or *Abie's Irish Rose,* they strike with unusual skill some of the universal notes which awaken human sympathy and the historian can only observe and record their triumph. But he must also insist that they enclose life with the material and machinery of the stage; they do not bring life in its fullness into the drama. Their best function has been the training of playwrights who like George Kelly have begun in this category, and have progressed to more profound studies of human conduct.

NOTE TO REPRINTING OF REVISED EDITION

George M. Cohan died November 5, 1942. A moving picture, *Yankee Doodle Dandy,* had been made upon his life, and he had earlier received the Congressional Medal of Honor for his patriotic services.

CHAPTER XIX

The Romance of the Twentieth Century

D RAMATIC history does not pay attention to the calendar, and in the case of romance, is unlikely to be identified in its progress with any movements or tendencies of the day. Yet the production of *Madame Butterfly* in 1900 does seem to mark a departure from the older school of heroic drama. Its response to the spirit of the new century was to reveal itself more in form than in material and even here we shall, at times, see a reversion to the older type. After the work of Long and Belasco the new romance was to find in Edward Sheldon its chief exponent. And yet there were fields he did not touch.

The sincerity of treatment, the skillfulness of technique show in an interesting way in the work of Edwin Milton Royle (1862–1942) who belongs to an older generation, and who has written for the stage since 1892. Royle's first play, *Friends* (1892), is a melodrama of the nineties, based on his knowledge of the lives of struggling musicians, opera singers and writers. But his *Squaw Man* (1905), one of the most successful plays of its day, illustrates the change of manner even within itself. The first Act, laid in England, is conventional melodrama, whose only excuse is the transfer of Captain James Wynnegate from his ancestral halls, through an act of self-sacrifice, to the plains of Wyoming. Royle was justified in making his hero an Englishman since he provided a more distinct contrast with the cowboys and "bad men" of the West, but more important, he made the central situation, the marriage between Wynnegate or "Jim Carson" as he has become, and Nat-u-ritch, the squaw who saves his life, more probable than it would have been in the case of an American. What raised *The Squaw Man* above the level of the usual Western play is its fidelity to actual conditions. Once the romantic situation from the first Act is accepted, the realistic treatment of it during the rest of the play raises it out of melodrama. Royle determined to put the real Indian on the stage and he cast for the character of Baco White, the interpreter, a Ute Indian, through whom he secured an exact phonetic reproduction of the Ute dialect for the squaw Nat-u-ritch and her father, Tab-i-wana, the Peace Chief of the tribe, who was drawn from an Indian Royle had known during his stay in the West. But more important, he drew the Indian characters accurately. Nat-u-ritch never steps out of her position as the Indian squaw—indeed she speaks only half a dozen words, yet she carries on the play. Inarticulately she shoots the "bad man" who would have killed Carson; she kills herself just as simply when she sees that she stands between her husband's return to England and their son's future. The struggle in Captain Wynnegate's soul between his longing to return with his son to England and to Diana Kerhill, and his gratitude to Nat-u-ritch, instead of being given to the audience in a soliloquy, as in the old heroic play, is conveyed in a conversation with the British solicitor who brings "Jim Carson" the news that he is an Earl. No one who has had a child can fail to understand the art with which Royle built up the scene of parting between the father and his little boy. But after all, the Indians are the best drawn. Tab-i-wana, on hearing that his daughter has gone off into the hills, makes no protest against her husband's decision. "If she disobeys you, you beat her—if she disobeys again—kill her." She is merely a squaw. But at Jim's request, Tab-i-wana searches for her to tell her to keep away until the sheriff, who is looking for her, has disappeared. He brings back, however, the dead body of Nat-u-ritch, and the curtain goes down on the gaunt figure of the chief, with the limp body of his daughter lying across his arms, and with the new Lord Kervil and Lady Diana for the moment in the background of our interest. Royle allowed his audiences to exercise their imaginations and thus carry the play with them in their sympathies. *The Squaw Man* ran a year in London and, without permission, was played in Paris and Berlin.

Royle's work is varied and uneven. In 1907 he attempted in *The Struggle Everlasting* a modern morality play, written with sincerity and with some strong scenes. The characters are abstractions or types, and the struggle between Mind and Soul for the supremacy over Body is quite convincing. The third Act in which Body, a courtesan, is visited one after another by the lovers who have been ruined by her, made a vivid appeal on the stage, for Royle drew her victims, the pugilist, the banker, and the tragedian, with skill. The episode of the great actor coming to tell her how his mind has faltered through her influence, until he forgets his lines and the curtain is rung down on him forever is memorable. Her utter lack of sympathy for anyone who has failed is in perfect keeping with her character. If Royle had run through to the end with the same quality, he might have made one of the great plays of the time.

The Unwritten Law (1913) is a reversion in treatment to pure melodrama, with some understanding, however, of the power of hypnotism, but in *Launcelot and Elaine* (1921), a dramatization of Tennyson's poem, Royle endeavored sincerely and with some success to transfer the spirit of Elaine's tragic passion to the stage. He used many of Tennyson's lines, but added a good deal of his own composition. It is interesting to note in the reading of the manuscript, how the trained actor, who had spent his first two years in Edwin Booth's Company, deliberately took frequent liberties with the supposed normal blank-verse line of five stresses, and gave his characters lines of two, three or four stresses as the sense dictated. He probably realized that audiences cannot tell (and do not care) whether the presupposed line unit is preserved. To them the recurrence of the accented syllable at fairly even time intervals is sufficient, without uniform measurement. The verse gains in naturalness by this freedom, for the thought dictates the form instead of being forced into a metrical arrangement which is unfamiliar. The real difficulty with Elaine as a heroine lies in the lack of dramatic conflict in her story. There are opportunities for beautiful static scenes but that is all.

To the superficial observer, Booth Tarkington (1869-1946) may seem to belong to the writers of social drama. But as a playwright his material, even when it appears to be drawn from the life around him, is really born in his romantic fancy. His first play to reach the stage, *Monsieur Beaucaire* (1901), was a compound of his love of romance and his sense of social values, but it was the romantic flavor which, in the hands of Richard Mansfield, carried it into popular favor. The play, in which he collaborated with Evelyn G. Sutherland, has not the significance of the story from which it was derived. *Monsieur Beaucaire* lifted itself out of the vast number of historical novels which were published during the nineties, by its distinction of style and by the conception of the character of the French nobleman who after his adventure, doubly disguised, into the English society of the Eighteenth Century, left Lady Carlisle, who had failed to recognize his inherent nobility and returned to his own *milieu*. This note of the tragedy of disappointment was spoiled in the play by the happy ending, forced for the supposed taste of a public which would undoubtedly have accepted the logical conclusion of the story. American audiences were ready for tragedy as the success of *Nathan Hale* and *Barbara Frietchie* had proved. The play was a personal triumph for Mansfield, and as usual, all other parts were subordinated to his.

Although *The Man from Home* (1907) has been described as a realistic picture of the typical American, in contrast with European civilization, it is also purely romantic in its setting and in its conception of character. Daniel Voorhees Pike, the hero, who goes to Sorrento to look after his ward, Ethel Granger-Simpson, and who prevents her marriage with the

THE ROMANCE OF THE TWENTIETH CENTURY

son of a British peer, is the average American only in so far
as he lives near the center of population. He is a queer mixture of Colonel Manly and his servant, Jonathan, in our first
comedy, *The Contrast*, which was also a study of American
sincerity in contrast with British types. But how much more
accurately Royall Tyler drew the American in 1789 before
the stage convention of the type grew up and hardened into
caricature! Perhaps there are citizens of Indiana who are as
naïve and at the same time as shrewd as Pike, but while he is
not so absurd as the caricatures of British aristocracy, he is
quite incredible on the printed page. On the stage, however,
William Hodge made a success in the character, and Tarkington and H. L. Wilson, his collaborator, provided an amusing
if not important vehicle for him. Tarkington proceeded with
Cameo Kirby (1909), a romance of old slavery days, *Your
Humble Servant* (1909), in which Otis Skinner represented an
actor, Lafayette Towers, which gave him an opportunity to
depict the life on the road, and *Getting a Polish* (1910), in
which May Irvin played the part of a Western widow who goes
to Paris, presumably for culture. These, however, are not important. Inspired perhaps by a natural reaction against the
prosaic life of the small city, and with his horizon broadened
by his education at Princeton and his foreign travel, Tarkington has always had the urge to create the character of a human
being who represents beauty. Knowing Italy quite well, he
wrote for Otis Skinner a play, *Mr. Antonio* (1916), in which he
contrasted the character of a simple Italian organ grinder with
the selfishness of a small town in western Pennsylvania. There
was little structure in the play but Skinner's presentation was
highly successful. Tarkington has made several efforts to depict conditions as they are, but nearly always returns to the
province he knows best. The beginning of *The Country Cousin*
(1917), laid in Ohio, is quite faithful to life, but when he takes
the heroine to New York the unreality of the conditions among
which she is placed is apparent at once. *Clarence* (1919) was
satire of a searching kind, and the efforts of the young entomol-

ogist to straighten out the affairs of the family into which he is introduced were enlivened with a dialogue easily the most brilliant written by Tarkington. But the plot is farcical and even here the romance of adolescence, which in the characters of Bobby and Cora White found remarkable expression through the acting of Glenn Hunter and Helen Hayes, was one of the prime factors in the success. This was true also of *The Intimate Strangers* (1921) and the chance meeting of the hero and heroine in a railroad station at which they have to spend the night, is surely the romance which may be wrung out of familiar things. *Rose Briar* (1922) is even more frankly romantic, though Tarkington showed in it his uncanny knowledge of feminine nature, more adequately revealed in his fiction. That Tarkington is essentially a romanticist is shown clearly when he tries to build a play upon a capital and labor theme like *The Gibson Upright* (1919). The conversation between the owner of the factory and his employees takes place not in a business office, but in Tarkington's fancy. He is best in drama when he gives rein to that fancy, abandons effort to deal with ordinary conditions, and frankly takes his characters and situations into another time and place where he is freed from the limitations of accuracy. Then we have such a romance as *Beaucaire* or such one-act plays as *Beauty and the Jacobin* (1912) laid in the French Revolution, or *Bimbo the Pirate* (1926). Here he can let his imagination provide us with gallant men and beautiful women and "the ruffle's flutter and the flash of steel." Here he can indulge in his whimsical creation of delightful absurdities and occasionally, as in the characters of Clarence and of Bobby White, touch the routine of daily life with that spark of imagination which lifts *Clarence* far above the level of his usual attempts at reality. But we must not, in passing judgment upon Tarkington as a dramatist, allow ourselves to be confused by his excellence in depicting in his fiction certain phases of our life. As a novelist he thinks much more frequently in terms of real life. As a playwright he thinks in terms of the theatre and gives his characters not actual but theatrical life. He therefore just fails, usually, to produce work of permanent value. Part of this failure may be due to the obvious fact that as a novelist he is in absolute control of his material, while as a playwright he is not. But my final impression after seeing many of Tarkington's plays, is that he takes the playwright's function much less seriously than he takes that of the novelist. This attitude toward the theatre is reflected in his story *Harlequin and Columbine* and it may be the solution, after all, of the problem, disconcerting to the critic, who sees Tarkington approach artistic success so often and not quite reach the mark.

It is a well-known phenomenon of the drama that plays upon similar themes or of like categories appear together. Whether it be due to the success of one play and consequent imitation, or to a general tendency based upon elements foreign to the theatre, is not always easy to determine. Certainly at the end of the first decade, examples of romance, having been comparatively few, began to multiply. That the artistic success of *The Piper* or *The Scarecrow* in the season of 1910-11 was in any way responsible is unlikely, for the romance took a shape different from either. The great success of *Kismet* in London, before its production in December, 1911, in New York may have brought about the production of other exotic romances, but it must be remembered that Belasco, Long, Tarkington, Tully, Royle and Sheldon had kept alive the general interest in romance during the first decade, and Long, in particular, had revealed the possibilities of romance in the East.

Richard Walton Tully (1877-1945) who was born in California and graduated from the University of California in 1901, represents the romance in its choice of exotic themes, in deliberate departure from a realistic picture of familiar life and in a sumptuous use of scenery and lighting, to produce at times a symbolic background. His association with Belasco in *The Rose of the Rancho* (1906), taught him how to employ the accessories of the stage and his *Bird of Paradise* (1912) was a production of which the beauty at least may be unquestioned.

It is laid in Hawaii during the revolutionary days of the early nineties. The main and subsidiary themes, as stated by Tully, are "the disappearance of the so-called inferior races before the advancement of the Anglo-Saxon race," a study of the degeneracy and death which the higher race pays through any amalgamation with the lower, a plea for home missionary work as opposed to foreign, and "a dramatization of the well-known fact that though we dress, educate and polish the members of a lower race to the superficial religious and social equality with the Caucasians, at heart he is still the fetich-worshipping savage who will become atavistic in every moment of stress." This load of purpose would seem too heavy for a play to carry, but Tully has made it concrete by centering attention upon Luana, the Hawaiian girl who loves Paul Wilson, an American who has intended to go on to the leper settlement at Molokai and investigate the possibilities of cure, but who is kept on the island by his infatuation for Luana. Her character is remarkably well drawn. She is not merely a physically attractive savage; she is of the old royal stock of Hawaii, and the mingling of her primitive racial impulses, of her longing for union with a man of a higher race and of her passion of love, produces a character with which we are ready to sympathize. This sympathy is made keener by her final sacrifice to free her husband from the chains that are dragging him down, and her plunge into the mouth of the volcano which, according to the religion of her people, demands a human sacrifice, gives a touch of magnificence to the climax of the drama. Tully was as prodigal in his characters as in his scenery and as a contrast to Luana and Wilson he provided a vivid sketch of Dean, the American beach comber, who under the influence of Diana Larned redeems himself and seizes the opportunity Wilson has relinquished. The determination of Dean, drunken as he is, not to lose his white birthright through a native taint, is a good dramatic motive.

The influence of *Madame Butterfly* upon *The Bird of Paradise* is obvious, and the latter in its turn is important as one of the earliest plays to treat the life in the Pacific islands sympathetically, by a writer who had first-hand knowledge. The dances, the mystic ceremonies of the older cults are well managed as aids of romance, and the contrast of the incoming civilization of the United States is drawn sharply, in such characters as Captain Hatch, the sugar planter. *Omar the Tent-Maker* (1914), while sufficiently true to the traditional Persia of the time of Omar Khayyám, has not the interest of the plays which were based on Tully's actual experience. His imagination, powerful at times, needs the restraint of his own knowledge and *Omar*, with its love scenes, escapes, assassinations, trials and rescues, gives us no characters which remain with the vividness of those in *The Bird of Paradise*. In *The Flame* (1916) Tully laid the scene in Yucatan, and attempted another contrast of American civilization, this time with that of Mexico. The modern American types of consuls and oil and fruit prospectors are just as conventional as the Mexican generals and rebels, but Maya, the young guardian of the Treasure, who interposes as a protector over the fortunes of the Americans, gives occasion for scenes in which the beauty of the old Ritual of the Flame is contrasted with the terror of the Green Jungle where reigns Shantee, the priestess of the debasing rites of the Goat without Horns, of which the sacrifice of a white child is the center. Tully claims he is correct in his representation of these rites, and he certainly uses them effectively in the play. His employment of the tom-tom to intensify the feeling of terror in the whites of the approaching danger from the revolution, points forward to later plays. But on the stage the result was confusing and the introduction of too many themes and characters kept the audience bewildered.

One of the most original notes in romance was struck by a playwright who had begun in an earlier manner. George Cochrane Hazelton, Jr., after training on the stage with Booth and Barrett in 1890, wrote for Henrietta Crosman *Mistress Nell* (1900), one of the dramatic trifles of that period. In

1912, however, he collaborated with J. Harry Benrimo in *The Yellow Jacket*, in which the spirit of Chinese drama was preserved to a remarkable degree, while certain features like the Property Man were intentionally exaggerated and a chorus was introduced to make the play intelligible to American audiences. The theme of the play is a universal one. It shows first the love of a mother who kills herself that her little son may be preserved against the machinations of his father's second wife, and next the loyalty of the farmer and his wife, who bring up their young charge concealed from his enemies until the time comes to take his rightful place. Then it takes Wu Hoo Git, the hero, through many dangers, animated by his love for Plum Blossom and guided by the spirit of his mother, till he conquers his rival and half-brother and ascends his throne. The interest of the play on the stage lay in the clever use of the Chinese dramatic conventions for the creation of comedy. The nonchalant way in which the property man picked up a sword and presented it to Wu Hoo Git and then returned to his side of the stage and smoked until he was needed to bring a throne or a ladder for the spirit of Chee Moo, the mother, to ascend visibly to Heaven, kept the audience in good spirits, and the chorus, who explained everything carefully, preserved the delightful artificiality of the illusion. This artificiality permitted the quick passage from comedy to pathos and also allowed a *naïveté*, which was certainly not Chinese, to present the effect of a fairy tale. The printed play reveals a certain poetic conception and a satire which is probably the work of Hazelton, while to Benrimo the stage details were mainly due. Benrimo had been familiar with imitations of Chinese drama, for he acted in *The First Born* in 1897. *The Yellow Jacket* was a success, artistically and financially, but it probably affected our drama very little. It was a thing to be done once, but an imitation would have been impossible, for the very stage conventions were in a sense part of the individual play. When Benrimo and Harrison Rhodes collaborated in *The Willow Tree* (1917) they made no attempt to imitate *The Yellow*

Jacket, but wrought in a more usual fashion a fantasy of
Japanese romance, based on the old story of a wooden image
coming to life and the consequent love affair between herself
and a young Englishman who has purchased her. The note of
fantasy was unfortunately precipitated in the last act by the
departure of the Englishman to the war.

Edward Knoblock, the author of *Kismet*, presents in his
career an interesting result of theatrical conditions in the
United States. He was born in New York City in 1874 and
while an undergraduate at Harvard took an active part in
college theatricals in both English and French. Determined
to become a playwright, he was certain that the best way to
obtain a hearing in his own country was to win a place first
abroad,—so he has lived for the most part in London or on the
Continent. The history of his plays has perhaps justified
him, for several, if not all, of them have had their first performance abroad. He has lived to see conditions change,
but the nature of his dramatic work has been permanently affected by his foreign residence and by his modeling of his work
upon the Elizabethan dramatists. He has chosen themes that
are universal or perhaps better, cosmopolitan, in their scope
and he has constructed his plays so often in a series of scenes
that he has become almost identified with that form. His early
plays were largely the dramatization of fiction. One of these,
The Cottage in the Air (1909), was the second of the offerings
of the New Theatre, an adaptation of the novel, *The Princess
Priscilla's Fortnight*, by the author of *Elizabeth and Her
German Garden*. It was a trifle, delicate in treatment, concerning one of those princely episodes in disguise which were so
popular at that time. But no matter what the material or the
form of his plays may be, the original impulse is romantic.
Knoblock sometimes attracts attention by his central idea.
In *The Faun* (1911), for example, he introduced one of those
mythical persons into the house of a gentleman in England,
with satiric intent. In *Kismet*, which ran for many months in
London before it began its great popular success in New York

in December, 1911, Knoblock attempted to place the atmosphere of the Arabian nights on the modern stage. He was fortunate that in America Otis Skinner played the part of Hajj, the beggar, who conspires to kill the Caliph, finds in his prison cell his chief enemy whom he kills, drowns the Wasir, who would have possessed his daughter, and finally after the Caliph has taken his daughter as a wife, returns to his post on the steps of the mosque, asking for alms. It took all the charm of Skinner's personality to make the part convincing and the general effect was that of the play in which character has been so subordinated to situation that it soon fades from the memory. In fact the usual impression that we receive from Knoblock's plays is that he is so much interested in the theatrical effect of his situations that he really cares little about the development of character. There is somewhat more characterization in *Milestones* (1912), in which he collaborated with Arnold Bennett. The theatrical framework is probably Knoblock's. The central idea of representing the three generations of a British family, in 1860, in 1885 and in 1912, with the progressives of one period becoming conservatives of the next, is sufficiently obvious and affords opportunities for clever epigrams in which the hand of Bennett is clear. The manner in which love triumphs or fails was treated with sufficient universality to make the play successful in its day. But the difficulty with such satire lies in the danger that before the ink is dry the new generation will find its radicalism fading. The most elaborate attempt of Knoblock at the period play was *My Lady's Dress* (1914). In three acts, each of three scenes, he traces the manufacture, the trimming, and the making of the dress of an English gentlewoman, taking the characters into Italy, Holland and Russia and as far back as 1660. Through all the changes the physical resemblance to Anne, the modern heroine of the first scene, is preserved. The result is epic rather than dramatic, and each heroine who makes her sacrifice to contribute to the perfect result which Anne is to wear is with us too little to secure our interest. Knoblock failed to fuse the varying strands together by presenting Anne in the dress itself in some striking scene. There is a technical difficulty, too, about such a play. It must be hard for a leading actress to adapt herself to so many changes of personnel. To be sure the cast repeats in varying combinations, but still the reactions are dissimilar and that cumulative effect which a closely knit play provides is lacking, not only in the drama itself but in its process of interpretation.

Perhaps a sense of this led Knoblock, in *Marie Odile* (1915), toward a more unified form. But even the beauty of the Belasco production could not make the play believable. It is laid in 1870 when the Germans were invading Alsace, and Sister Marie Odile, a novice, left behind by the other nuns, believes Corporal Phillip Meissner is Saint Michael and when her baby is born is convinced it is the result of a miracle. The play, however, does not convince the audience of her belief because there is no establishment of the atmosphere in which, alone, miracles become credible on the stage. The mixture of supposedly realistic conversation on the part of the soldiers and later of the nuns, with the supernatural innocence of Sister Marie Odile left me cold, notwithstanding the acting of Frances Starr.

This lack of a convincing quality is apparent too in *Tiger! Tiger!* (1918) and *The Lullaby* (1923). The love story of an English gentleman and a crook simply does not persuade us of its reality and *The Lullaby*, while it portrays with some verisimilitude, the descent of a French peasant girl from respectability in 1860, to a den of infamy in Tunis in 1903, wearies one finally with the narrative of her misery. Knoblock is interesting mainly in his experiments in form. While he did not invent the period play or even treat for the first time the material of the East, he became one of the principal exponents of the exotic romance, and there can be little doubt of his influence upon other writers, like Zoë Akins, in such a play as *The Varying Shore*. But he is even more useful as an example of the difference between great and second-rate romance. John Luther Long before him, Sheldon in his own period and, of course, O'Neill after him, have shown the possibilities of the play in scenes separated by time, whether freed from the technical division into acts or not. But in each case an imaginative conception of great passion was fusing the scenes into unity. Knoblock with his keen sense for the theatre, and his love of beauty, has fancy but little imagination, and his characters are but thumbnail sketches, which the situations overshadow.

The play of a period without any definite historical background is found also in the work of Laurence Eyre, an actor who began his stage career in a revival of Boucicault's *The Jilt* in 1907 and who has represented in his plays the romance of sentiment with some real sense of the dramatic value of racial contrasts. *The Things That Count* (1913), a Christmas play, had a long run, and in 1915 he produced *Sazus Matazus*, an amusing comedy, with some characterization, and an accurate picture of the happy inconsequence of the negro. While statements concerning priority are always dangerous, it seems to be the first full-length play dealing entirely with negro characters to be produced professionally on the American stage. *Miss Nelly of N'Orleans* (1919), in which Mrs. Fiske played the part of a woman no longer young but not too old for romance, had some local color and a sense of the past striking into the present, with a broken love story to be renewed. In *The Merry Wives of Gotham* (1924) Eyre contrasted two sisters who had been separated as infants and had grown up, one in luxury and one in Shantytown in New York. The idea was not bad and Grace George and Laura Hope Crews gave splendid performances as the two sisters. But the audiences did not recognize Shantytown and the reality with which Harrigan had portrayed that region and its people was not present. The seventies had a somewhat better presentation in Arthur Richman's *Not So Long Ago* (1920), laid in New York City. Elsie Dover, a seamstress, who is engaged by the day to sew for Mrs. Ballard, builds up a purely imaginary love affair with the son

of the house, who is unaware of her existence.   The father demands an explanation and Billy Ballard visits the house with
the natural result.   It was not, however, the slender plot that
attracted the audiences but the clever dialogue and the lightness of the touch of the playwright who was to do such a different kind of work in *Ambush*.

During the early years of the century there came a natural
reaction against the deluge of plays which were made hastily
from the historical novels, frequently of dubious merit, whose
crest came about 1900.   The impulse to place historical characters on the stage never ceased, however, but when Long and
Belasco wrote *Adrea* in 1905, Long invented a country and an
atmosphere.   There was a real sense of history in MacKaye's
Jeanne d'Arc and *Sappho and Phaon,* and Mary Johnston in
The Goddess of Reason (1908) furnished Julia Marlowe a
play based on the French Revolution in which there is reflected
the spirit of that epoch.   This blank-verse play has some dramatic moments, especially in the last Act, but it secured a personal success for the actress rather than the playwright.

An individual quality, however, is to be found in the dramatization of historical characters in the work of Philip Moeller
(1880-   ), a Columbia man, whose education has also consisted of extensive foreign travel.   He was one of the pioneers
of the Washington Square Players and is now one of the directors of the Theatre Guild.   His first efforts were in the one-act
play, of which the best are *Helena's Husband* (1915), an
amusing travesty on the situation in the household of Menelaus
and Helen, and *Two Blind Beggars and One Less Blind*
(1915) a grim satire, laid in a ragpicker's cellar.   These were
produced during the formative period of the Washington
Square Players.   But in his first important play, *Madame
Sand* (1917), he proved himself a master of the sophisticated
romance of history.   Moeller thoroughly grasps his period not
only in its scenic accessories but also in the artistic essentials.
For example, in *Madame Sand* he carefully chooses the compositions of Chopin, which are to be played as gradual introduc-

tions to the love episode of the Polish composer and the heroine. The audience is to be placed in just the right mood and the *motif* is as clearly indicated as in grand opera. But the art conceals the art. Nothing is allowed to contest the supremacy of the central character. George Sand is present at all times, either concretely on the stage or by suggestion in the conversation of the other characters. Yet we never feel as we do in the obvious devices of many playwrights that we are being prepared for her entrance or exit. For she really is the center of all interest and it therefore becomes quite natural that the other creations of the dramatists should be thinking of her. Whether it be her three lovers, Alfred de Musset, Pagello the Italian doctor, and Frederic Chopin, or her enemies, like Madame de Musset, or Lucrezia Violente, who are endeavoring to save their sons or lovers from her, they are at all times vitally in contact with her or with her image. Even more skilfully portrayed, because less obviously necessary, are the men like Heinrich Heine, Franz Liszt, and Buloz, her editor and publisher, who know all her love affairs, see through her schemes, and yet remain her devoted friends. Their recognition of her genius, which places her in a class to them beyond ordinary law, their masculine attitude of toleration which forbids them to try to order her life, both flavored with a touch of gallantry though not of passion, feed delicately the demand of George Sand, the woman, for that sympathy which Moeller so deftly transfers through the minor characters to the audience. The historic characters make another contribution not so apparent. One of the most distressing qualities in smart comedy is the apparent planting of the epigram. But the epigrams, and they are many, come naturally from the lips of Heine, De Musset and Liszt. When Heine remarks: "Our enemies are the price we pay for fame"—and when Liszt says of the Italian doctor: "Why, all you had to do was to look at his perfect profile to realize his limitations," the playwright has defended himself in advance against the charge of artificiality. Even the choice of George Sand shows Moeller's sense of values. Her history is not well enough known to the average audience to make them critical, so he can take liberties with her career provided he creates a dramatic character. This he has done supremely well and he has made of her very inconstancy a consistent and unifying force. The three Acts deal with three love affairs, and in the hands of a lesser artist might have become merely episodic. But partly through the preservation of her personal background in the friends like Heine and Buloz, but more fundamentally through the co-ordinating motive of her remorseless demand as an artist that life should provide the novelist with experiences, the episodes fuse into a unity complete and satisfying.

Quite as effective was *Molière* (1919), in which Moeller took some liberties with history, but usually with success. There was a charming picture of the French playwright's method of work and of the devotion of his cook, who is his constant critic. The passion of the Marquise de Montespan, the mistress of Louis XIV, for Molière, leads her to plan a meeting between Armande, his young wife, and her lover De Luzon in Montespan's garden and she hopes by revealing to Molière the perfidy of his wife to bring him to her own arms. Then when he rejects her, and Louis enters unexpectedly there is a masterly scene in which the arrogance and suspicion of the King are met by the defiance of the playwright who gives up the favor of the court to return to the freer atmosphere in which his art can find its best expression. Through this scene, laid in France in the Seventeenth Century, rings the spirit of the independent theatre of America of the Twentieth, the universal challenge of the artist. The death of Molière, at the close of the performance of his *Le Malade imaginaire*, is a model for such scenes. Moeller has brought together the threads of the dramatic interest, the love of his work, the love of Armande, who returns to him, and even the favor of the King, who comes too late, into a situation whose restraint is telling. The tragedy meets the requirements—there is no depression, for we have assisted at the passing of a gallant soul who has been true to his own standards.

Sophie (1919) has not quite the distinction of *Madame Sand* or of *Molière*. The central character is not so significant, in the first place. But more important is the shift in the relative values of Moeller's impulses. In the two other plays, sophistication flavored the romance, which caught and held us. In *Sophie*, the romance has become merely the flavor of the sophistication, and the temptation to be brilliantly cynical captured him to the detriment of the drama. Yet *Sophie* is, even with this limitation, far above the usual play of its species. The temperamental nature of Sophie Arnould, the opera singer of the time of Louis XV, is extremely well drawn. The central situation, in which she assumes the position of mistress, in name only, to the Austrian Ambassador in Paris, accepting his support and giving him in return the social *éclat* attaching to the man who can win such an association with the greatest stage favorite of her time, is ripe for comedy. But it is so essentially heartless that the love story between herself and DeLauraguais cannot stir our sympathies. Moeller probably felt this, for he introduces another love story over which Sophie presides and for which she apparently sacrifices the Ambassador. The device of making the runaway daughter of the Chief of Police, a man who is her own worst enemy, the heroine of this other romance, which checkmates him and leaves Sophie in undisputed possession of DeLauraguais at midnight in the Ambassador's own house, is also clever. But cleverness alone, even when clothed in brilliant dialogue, is not enough. We do not really care for any of the characters. They are too cynical, too heartless, too sophisticated, for us to believe in them. They do not pronounce their epigrams, either, with the authority of the historical characters of the earlier plays, for they are all figments of the fancy. Yet the play makes delightful reading.

One of the most ambitious attempts at the historical play was the work of David Carb and Walter Prichard Eaton

(1878-   ). *Queen Victoria* (1923) was set in seven scenes, from her accession to the throne in 1837 to the sixtieth anniversary of that event in 1897. The production was sumptuous and the cast a fine one, but the audiences remained cold. The reasons for the comparative failure are significant as showing the limitations of this kind of play. In the first place, Queen Victoria was an epic, not a dramatic character. The scenes were unduly separated and it was impossible to find one actress who could impersonate the girl in 1837 and the old lady in 1897. Prince Albert, of whom much was made, is an almost forgotten figure to Americans. But the lack of any fusing emotion to bind the scenes together was the most apparent defect of the drama. Yet notwithstanding its limitations it remains to the historian, who happened to see it and John Drinkwater's *Robert E. Lee* on successive evenings, a much more effective drama than the latter. The American playwrights had taken the trouble to study the period of English history; the British playwright had not learned the language of American institutions.

A playwright who is representative of the sophisticated romance, without roots in history like Moeller, but concerned like him with the departure from real life into a world where romance is secured by a fanciful and satirical treatment of social relations, Zoë Akins (1886-   ) is an uncertain quality in the drama. She had some training in the Odeon Stock Company in St. Louis, and has written verse and fiction in addition to her plays, some of which remain unproduced and date from the early years of the Twentieth Century. She had been one of the pioneers in the establishment of the Juvenile Theatre in St. Louis about 1908, and here her *Magical City* was first performed; but her first real opportunity came when the *Magical City* was produced by the Washington Square Players in 1916. It is a one-act play in free verse, with the theme of the effect of the great city, New York, upon a girl, her "protector" and her young poet lover, who kills him. There are some fine lines, but the play is tainted by an artificial profundity, which has remained characteristic of Miss Akins. *Papa* (1916) is an example of the romance of sophistication. It is satire upon the heartlessness of charming people, though the charm lies mostly in the author's imagination. There is really no play, although there are occasional moments which permit clever acting, such as the group picture in which Doris, who has taken the responsibility for Chloe's child, hears the little girl's prayers in a sweetly devotional attitude while she holds a cigarette in her free hand. But there is neither fidelity to any life nor power in the imagination that lifts it above life. It is all superficial cleverness.

Miss Akins' first popular success came with the production of *Déclassée* (1919) in which Ethel Barrymore scored a personal success. While *Déclassée* is "good theatre," it is difficult to take it seriously. The decline of Lady Helen Haden from her secure position in England to a dubious one in America might be more convincing if Edith Wharton had not shown in *The House of Mirth* how a similar theme should be treated. The spectacle of a British Ambassador wasting time in a New York hotel in order that he might accidentally meet his old friend and socially rehabilitate her is almost as absurd as the death scene when Lady Helen runs out of the house and, having been hit by an automobile, takes fifteen graceful minutes to die. In *Daddy's Gone a-Hunting* (1921) Miss Akins made a brave struggle to be profound and original in her treatment of the situation in which a wife and husband find themselves mismated and are yet held together by a child. There is some reality in the character of Julien Fields, the artist who cares little about anything but his dreams of the great work he is to do and which he will never accomplish. Fields' refusal to take back his wife, whom his indifference has driven under the protection of another man, not because of his resentment but because of his selfishness, is a relief after the usual stage reconciliation, but the conclusion, with the heroine's smiling reply to the natural query as to her future conduct, "God knows," is rather inconclusive than profound. The preceding conversation too, between the wife, her lover and her husband is absurd, and when the death of the little daughter is announced, we recognize that Miss Akins is endeavoring to develop the contemporary unrest of spirit by means of the older sentimental devices of the theatre. Her real sphere lies in romance, not very significant but entertaining, such as *The Varying Shore* (1921). Here after revealing her heroine at Monte Carlo in her declining years, she took her back through the stages of her progress as a professional mistress, in 1870, in 1859 and in 1846. The remarkable acting of Elsie Ferguson almost made the character credible, for while it is hard to believe in her, she is frankly a romantic conception and humanity has often liked the generous, reckless harlot who sacrifices herself at certain crucial points in her career. The interesting feature of the play, however, was its method. Stung by some criticism, the direction reversed the scenes so as to follow the chronological order, and then happily replaced them as the playwright had written them. For the order of sympathy proceeded inversely to the order of time. The audience liked Julie Venable much more as a girl of sixteen, unwilling to be forced upon a reluctant young husband, than they did as a sophisticated woman of forty, and so it was best to lead up to the earlier period as a climax. In a sense, each act was a justification of her conduct in the preceding ones, and thus a certain probability was given to something improbable and fundamentally sentimental. Miss Akins's best play, *Greatness*, produced as *A Texas Nightingale* (1922) which had more character drawing in it than usual, failed because of atrocious miscasting. The opera singer Brasa Canava with her mixture of temperament, stupidity and practical sense, is very appealing, but the central situation, which reunites her to her second husband and their son, whose birth some delicacy, totally foreign to her nature, has led her to conceal, takes one back to the romantic novel of the eighteen-forties. There was not enough body to the plot to carry the central character, who had had four husbands, all of whom had been blighted by their union with her, although each one had helped her in his own way to the greatness which she had achieved. It is rather an epic theme than a dramatic one, but it has possibilities which were surely not realized in the play. Yet *Greatness* contains some of the best of Miss Akins' dialogue, and its failure was to be regretted. Still more quickly withdrawn was *A Royal Fandango*, a satirical romance laid in the Bay of Biscay. On the stage, it seemed to be a burlesque upon the romantic play of the type of Molnar's *Swan*, but it had no authority in its treatment of royalty and need not detain us. Nor need her recent adaptations from the French, like *First Love* (1926), although she did transfer to English the atmosphere of a boy and girl passion in the Latin Quarter.

The purely fanciful romance, although it has been revealed mainly in its coloring of the domestic drama or other forms, has nevertheless had some significant if sporadic examples, of which Sheldon's *The Garden of Paradise* remains supreme. In *The Poor Little Rich Girl* (1913) Eleanor Gates painted with sympathy and tenderness the longing of a little girl, whose mother and father were too busy to love her, for the simple natural life that is the right of every child. The originality of the play lay mainly in the transfer of the real characters such as her maid, her governess and teachers, the organ grinder, the policeman, and the doctor who is dining with her father and mother, into the dream which is caused by the overdose of the sleeping draught which Jane, the maid, has given her in order to be rid of her for the evening. The scenes in the Tell Tale Forest, in The Land of the Lights and around Robin Hood's Barn, mingle deftly the disordered fancies of a child's dream with the phrases, only half understood, which have made up the unreality of her life. Into this dream sound now and then through the character of the Doctor the echoes of the struggle that is being made to save Gwendolyn from the imminent danger of the drug. This note of suspicion is struck in just the right measure to keep our interest. It is difficult without extensive quotation to do justice to the tact with which

Miss Gates kept her symbolism under control. It is a pity that the author of *The Poor Little Rich Girl* did not continue in the same vein. While her next play, *We Are Seven* (1913), had some element of fancy, especially in the hopes of the heroine concerning her possible children, whom she is going to bring up in the proper way, it has not the appeal of her first effort. *Swat the Fly* is pure propaganda and is negligible.

One of the most original of the purely imaginative romances, which deserved a better fate, was *A Young Man's Fancy* (1919), by John T. McIntyre (1871-   ). The play is in prose but the conception is poetic. In fact the hero, Pickering, himself is a poet, and lives in the visions his imagination paints for him. While passing a shop window, he sees the figure of a girl who is used as a window dresser in a garden party scene and he falls in love with his ideal of her. The image has been made by a real artist and has been modeled after a girl, Mary Darling, in the employ of the establishment. We are taken from the street into the shop and then into the realm of Pickering's fancy, and he moves among his creations, who live, of course, only as long as his vision lasts. The love scenes between Pickering and Mary's image are among the best which our modern stage has given us, and the sense of impending fate which will separate him from the love and beauty of his own creation is heartrending in its restraint. The transfer from the dream to reality, in which the real Mary comes to Pickering, was done adequately, but was difficult to manage, especially under the conditions in which the drama was produced. The scenery, painted by Joseph Urban, practically killed the play, so strongly did it call attention to itself. It is a grim commentary upon the taste of the public that the actress who portrayed Mary for two weeks played for several years the leading part in such a drama as *Rain.*

It is not within the scope of this account to treat of the opera, but the work of Brian Hooker (1880-1946) rises above the standard of the libretto to that of dramatic poetry of real significance. *Mona* was awarded in 1911 the prize of ten thousand dollars, offered by the Metropolitan Opera Company, for the best American opera—the music being composed by Horatio Parker. It was produced at the Metropolitan Opera House, March 14, 1912, and four performances were given during the season 1911-12. Hooker, though he laid *Mona* in the first century in Britain, made no effort at historical accuracy. His theme is the conflict of love and patriotism in a woman's heart and the tragedy that ensues when she yields to the dream of conquest and empire and forgets her love. Gwynn, the son of the Roman governor, would have reconciled the Britons to their conquerors through his marriage with the legitimate princess of Britain—just how is not made clear—but she listens to the arguments of her kin and banishes Gwynn from her sight. There is a strong scene in the Cromlech or Druidic open-air temple when he pleads once more for the love that shall save them both, and the final scene, when after the defeat of the Britons, she kills Gwynn for what she believes to be his treachery, is also powerful. The inconsistencies inseparable from opera need not be emphasized and the lyrics with their structure based on Old English and not on Celtic rhythms may be excused, perhaps, on the ground that no audience would care about the matter. What makes *Mona* important is the sheer beauty of the conception of character and the distinction of the verse. Mona's speech at the last love scene in the Cromlech shows how Hooker had shaken off the Victorian tradition which persisted in writing narrative verse in drama:

Mona: There is a cloud over the moon—
    I cannot see thy face . . . Only thine arms
    Around me like strong sleep . . . Only thy voice—
    And all our children laughing in thine eyes . . !
    And it is good for me to put away
    Weariness, and the fever of high deeds,
    And the dry hunger . . . Now earth sinks and swims
    Falling, and the great river of joy flows down,—
    Inevitable, tender, luminous,—
    And whelms me, and I float under the moon
    Quietly, toward the foam-bright sea . . . Down, down,

Where the glimmering shores grow faint, and darkness
Buries the sky, and the stars drown, and the deep
Rises over me, and I dream . . .

The farewell of Mona to Gwynn over his dead body while his
father and the Roman soldiers stand ready to seize her, is so
far above the usual libretto of grand opera as to be of a different category.   A few lines will show its quality:

Mona:
                              I might have died
Yonder, and not known.
                              —See, how Earth holds up
Her freshness to the summer, and the light
Laughs over living green, and the birds are glad,
And the sweet blossoms brighten in the sun,
And all the bitter beauty of the day
Makes merry with my sorrow—And I go
To walk alive among dead hours, and see
Pitiless faces and the mirth of men
Whose eyes are evil, and be fawned upon
By strange hands . . . for I cannot even keep
My faith to him that died because of me,
Nor in a clean death lay my body down
Beside his body . . . I must bear my time,
Having done no good thing, remembering all—
And there will be so many other days,
So many other days . . .
                              Give me the sword—
It is mine . . .
              Dost thou think I can still fear?
I loved him . . . and I killed him . . .
                              Bear with me
A little.

Fairyland, which won a prize in the American Opera Association competition in 1915, is laid in the Thirteenth Century
in Central Europe, but as before, historical accuracy is not
preserved.   What is given is the romance of youth, the search
for adventure, the love that passes into Fairyland and returns
to real life at will.   It is written in the same varied and flexible

verse, and the lyrics are charming. Hooker proved again by his translation of *Cyrano de Bergerac* for Walter Hampden that he was a poet with a real sense of the stage, for a share of the great artistic success of that production belongs to him. His *White Bird* (1924), an attempt to place an operatic situation in the early Nineteenth Century in a rural district in central New York State, is dramatically not very effective.

The recent artistic success of the opera of *The King's Henchman* first produced at the Metropolitan Opera House, February 17, 1927, has recalled attention to the early work of Edna St. Vincent Millay, *Aria da Capo* (1919) and *The Lamp and the Bell* (1921), especially the latter, with its story of the deep affection of two girls for each other which survives even through disappointed love. Written for an anniversary of Vassar College, it translates into terms of medieval life the strong friendships made during undergraduate days, and is one more of the many links which have bound our drama from its beginning to the colleges.

But *The King's Henchman* far surpasses these plays in power. Viewed simply as a dramatic poem, even without the aid of the music of Deems Taylor, which helped to make it the artistic sensation of the season, it challenges admiration for the stark directness and simplicity with which it establishes character and atmosphere. It is laid in the Tenth Century, in the reign of King Eadgar, to whom history's significant silence pays a tribute. The story of Eadgar's sending of his foster brother Æthelwold, to woo for him Ælfrida, the daughter of the Thane of Devon, of the love that springs up between them, of Æthelwold's lying message to the King concerning her appearance, of the King's visit and the consequent tragedy are legendary romance. The power of *The King's Henchman* rises almost like a sea throughout the drama. The characters of the two men are drawn in the first Act, and the courtly savagery of the Saxon King's hall at Winchester is established by conversation in which Miss Millay has employed skilfully a vocabulary which is derived from English sources with almost too scrupulous an avoidance of words of Latin origin. After beginning with the Harper's chant in the Old English measures, she wisely avoids following them in her dramatic verse, though being a poet she cannot escape their influence, especially in the lyrics. These are magnificent, but while fine lyrics were to be expected from the author of *Renascence* the dramatic climaxes of the second and third Acts were not to be foreshadowed by anything she had done. The love scene when Æthelwold and Ælfrida meet in the forest on All Hallow's Eve pulses with the passion that rarely finds its way to the modern stage—one speech can hardly illustrate it:

Æthelwold: Oh, Godes Son!
> How wounding fair thou art!
> The sight of thee
> Is like a knife at the heart,
> Of thee the sight or the sound,
> The turn of thy head, thy speaking,
> Is like a thing found,
> To a man seeking.

But the play builds higher. When the two lovers have settled into the aftermath of passion, the King suddenly comes to Devon. Then Æthelwold tells Ælfrida of his deception and begs her for the sake of their love to keep her bower. But she appears in the splendor of her beauty to greet the King and Eadgar cries out in wonder at her charm and in grief at his betrayal by the man he loves best.

> Whose hand shall I take?
> Yea, for if thy tongue be forked, Æthelwold,
> Then from sea to sea my kingdom hisses!

Here Miss Millay leaves the original legend. According to William of Malmesbury,[1] on whose account all modern versions seem to depend, Æthelwold was killed by Eadgar. But for dramatic purposes, Miss Millay wisely has Æthelwold com-

[1] Book II, Chap. 8.

mit suicide. This transfers the sympathy to him and there is a splendid touch when Maccus, his friend, bids Ælfrida draw back from the body—

So.
I would not have thee foul this blood

and Eadgar bids her stay her weeping:

Eadgar: Have done, Ælfrida.
Thou hast not tears enow in thy narrow heart
To weep him worthily.
Wherefore have done.

Nor all of us here,
Nor all of England weeping,
Should weep his worth,
That was so young and blithe and bold,
Whom the thorn of a rose hath slain.

Wherefore let us hoard our tears for a little sorrow,
And weep not for Æthelwold at all.

Like *Mona, The King's Henchman* is a triumph of American art, dramatic and musical, universal in theme, free in treatment and distinguished in form.

The romance has taken on a verse form only sporadically and its form is less a matter of importance than its spirit. In 1920 the Poetry Society of America prepared a selected list of sixty-four dramas in verse which had been published since 1900.[1] Of these, which included the work of Moody, MacKaye and others already treated, more than half had been produced, though largely in the Little Theatres or by groups like the Provincetown Players.

Mrs. Jane Dransfield, who selected this list from over two hundred and fifty titles, has written one of the most widely performed verse dramas in *The Lost Pleiad* (1918), a dream fantasy laid in Greece. It was first produced at the Brooklyn Academy of Music and its frequent reproduction by Little Theatre groups is indicative of the need for drama of its kind.

[1] *The Library Journal,* XLV (1920), pp. 395–6.

At her instigation, a prize was offered by William Lindsey, through the Poetry Society of America, for the best play in verse. It was won in 1921 by Harry Lee with *Il Poverello*, later called *The Little Poor Man*, which was produced in 1925 and ran for several weeks. The central character is St. Francis of Assisi, in his progress from a youth of adventure through the serene dignity of humility and sacrifice, to his death. The human quality of St. Francis is stressed and the result is an attractive dramatic picture. The verse is rhythmical, but free in the number of stresses in each line; in fact like Royle's *Launcelot and Elaine* it is expressed in verse phrases rather than lines.

One of the hopeful indications of the vitality of the verse play and the growing popular appreciation of good things in the theatre was the success of *Caponsacchi*, the dramatization of Browning's *The Ring and the Book*, which ran practically all through the season of 1926-7. Originally suggested to Walter Hampden by Miss Rose A. Palmer as a fit subject for a play, it was put into dramatic form by his brother-in-law, Arthur Goodrich (1878-1941), who had been known as the author of such light theatrical fare as *So This Is London*. It was first produced in Indianapolis in 1923 as *The Ring of Truth*, and underwent considerable change before its performance in New York. Goodrich's task was no easy one. Browning's genius was dramatic and those who had the good fortune to see his *In a Balcony* performed by Otis Skinner, Mrs. Le Moyne and Miss Robson will not agree with the usual statement that all his plays are unsuited to the theatre. But he had not chosen to dramatize the theme of *The Ring and the Book*, which might have given Mr. Goodrich pause. The latter conceived, however, of the proper solution, to center the interest upon the priest, Caponsacchi, who has tried to save Pompilia, the wife of Count Guido Franceschini, from her devilish husband. The drama opens with the trial of Guido for the murder of his wife and her parents, and when Caponsacchi is asked to make his statement the ensuing scenes are a review or "flashback" of the events leading up to the murder. Then the play reverts to the courtroom until the Pope, who has been hidden behind the curtain, pronounces judgment upon Guido and blesses Caponsacchi. Walter Hampden's interpretation of the warrior-priest who conquered himself and dared public scandal to save a woman made desperate by cruelty and injustice, was memorable, and by a happy accident, Pompilia was played by Edith Barrett, the granddaughter of Laurence Barrett, the great exponent of the heroic drama. Goodrich provided Hampden with a heroic part, whose success disproved the distrust of the rhythmic drama. The reason the heroic drama is not often played is simply that there are few actors who are trained to interpret it. The real artistry of the dramatization can be appreciated, however, only when it is compared with Browning's poem. Mr. Goodrich, who had been a close student of Browning since his college career at Wesleyan, skillfully built up on a scaffold of Browning's verse a play which, so far as language is concerned, is largely his own. As was well said by Clayton Hamilton in his "afterword" to the published play, it is easy to parody Browning but to imitate him without parody "is a task that calls for special and peculiar delicacy."

While the romantic interest to be derived from the exotic or the historic or the fanciful has naturally been most frequently invoked by the playwright, there has been during this period a sincere attempt to treat the romance that can be developed out of familiar life. Perhaps the most consistent exponent of this species has been Edward Childs Carpenter (1872–   ), who began his dramatic work while financial editor of the Philadelphia *Inquirer*. It is true that he has departed from familiar life occasionally as in *The Barber of New Orleans* (1908), in which he lays the scene in New Orleans about 1804. In this romantic comedy he made use of the theme of mixed blood and shows the influence of *The Octoroon* and *The White Slave*. It won a prize offered by the New York *Globe* in 1908 and when produced with William Faversham as the Barber, Victor Jallot, made a charming impression. In *The Challenge* (1911) Carpenter sought the romance of the West and built up vigorous melodramatic comedy around the character of Alberta Bradley, the young owner of the Green Basin Ranch in Arizona. While Alberta is a stock figure, there are nevertheless some strong scenes, especially the one in which she attacks Douglas Quarrier, chief engineer of the Green Basin Land and Irrigation Company, and shows her real affection for him after he has conquered her. *The Tongues of Men* (1913) is a study of the contrast between the artistic and the clerical standards of life, with a rather obvious lesson of charity. But Carpenter has depicted a very real opera singer in Jane Bartlett.

Carpenter's most successful play, however, was *The Cinderella Man* (1916). Here he has taken the old fairy story and reversed the sexes. Anthony Quintard, a young poet and playwright who lives in a garret, is visited by Marjorie Caner, the daughter of a millionaire, who lives in the next house and who watches over him in a motherly fashion until the inevitable love story develops. It is easy to dismiss such a play as *The Cinderella Man* on the ground of its improbability. Audiences in this country, in England, and in other parts of the world were delighted by the play, and the secret of its success lies in the tender, wistful note which Carpenter succeeded in giving to the love story. There is no moment in the play when the audience does not earnestly desire that Marjorie Caner shall succeed, not only in winning Tony's love, but in revealing to him the depth of her own affection for him.

In *The Pipes of Pan* (1917) probably his best play, he has developed a very appealing theme, the incarnation of an ideal love of a man's youth, cherished through years, and crowned with the halo of illusion. Carpenter wisely chose a painter for his hero and frankly threw away actuality by the escapade which brings the revived Valentine after an all night's adventure to breakfast at the painter's studio. Wisely also he made the adventure an episode and so preserved the illusion for the rest of Redford's life. *The Pipes of Pan* gives Carpenter a right to serious consideration for the restraint with which he handled a situation that might have broken into erotic fragments, and for the delicacy with which he has touched the relations of the central characters.

In *Pot-Luck* (1921), Carpenter tried to draw out of small-town life a romance based upon Amy Jewell's marriage with a man whom she has met through a marriage bureau. There is some good characterization, but the play has not the interest of *The Cinderella Man* or of *The Pipes of Pan*. Nor has *Bab* (1920), founded upon a novel by Mary Roberts Rinehart, or *Connie Goes Home* (1923), founded on a story by Fannie Kilbourne, the interest of the original plays. *Bab* provided Helen Hayes with an appropriate part but the impression was chiefly that of stage dexterity.

The romance that is a revolt from the routine of familiar life, although it is based upon it, was the inspiration of *The Gypsy Trail* (1917) by Robert Housum (1886-   ), a Yale graduate and a newspaper man. He succeeded in translating into terms of modern life the longing for adventure which in the older drama was represented by the gypsy convention. What lifted *The Gypsy Trail* above the usual play upon this theme was the contrast of the two central characters, Frances Raymond and Michael Rudder. Frances is about to be engaged to Edward Andrews, who represents all that is solid and substantial. She welcomes Michael who appears in the guise of a newspaper man, as a way out into a freer life than she has known. But Michael, although he is very much attracted to her, sees in marriage a prison from which he revolts and he runs away in a borrowed car almost as soon as they have discovered they love each other. It seems a pity that Housum could not have closed his play on this note, but he brought Michael back a millionaire with a heavy load of respectability to recommend him, and turned the play into farce at the end. His other plays indeed are farce comedies, but there is a touch of fancy in *The Gypsy Trail*, and the scene in which Michael describes the wandering life he has led has a bit of poetry in it that is sincere.

The ethical romance has had as its principal exponent Charles Rann Kennedy (1871-   ), an Englishman who has become sufficiently identified with his adopted country to be considered here. His first work to attract serious attention, *The Servant in the House* (1908), was a study in human brotherhood. It was laid in England but the message was universal. The Bishop of Benares, India, comes into the house of his brother, the Vicar, disguised as a butler, Manson. Their other brother, who is a cleaner of drains, provides one aspect of the contrast, and their brother-in-law, the Bishop of Lancashire, the other. Manson is a Christlike figure and as played by Walter Hampden, made a profound impression. The significance of *The Servant in the House* as drama lay in the skilful way in which Kennedy kept his symbolism and ethical message in control. The language is natural and the searching criticism of hypocrisy and pretence is carried on in a convincing way, without the concreteness of the characters being lost. *The Winter Feast* (1908) also has a certain power, if somewhat unrestrained. This romance of the Eleventh Century in Iceland is hardly historical; it is a study of the evil effect of hate which, sprung from earlier love and friendship, brings death and destruction to the family of Thorkel. There are powerful scenes, such as that in which Swanhild, the little grand-daughter of Thorkel, tells her mother of the new love which has come to her, while her lover lies dead in the next room, having killed himself because he saw no alternative between the slaying of his own father and the breaking of his promise to Herdisa, Swanhild's mother, that he would avenge her upon her enemy. But the types are not so well controlled as in *The Servant in the House*. Kennedy's later writing has become steadily less dramatic and more ethical, until it passes out of our scrutiny. He has also been concerned with experiments in new forms, such as *The Terrible Meek* (1912), a daring attempt to interpret the Crucifixion in terms of modern pacifism. The stage is perfectly dark and voices are heard speaking in modern tones, those of a woman, whose son has been killed and of a captain and a soldier, who have executed him. At the end of their conversation the light comes on and they are seen to be in the costumes of the time of Christ, while the three gaunt crosses become visible. The difficulty with Kennedy's work is that he does not understand the difference between a shock and a thrill. After his first two plays he seemed anxious to preach by violence and lost the sense of what is capable of dramatic interpretation. Sincere as his later plays are, and they attack evil vigorously, they irritate by their disregard of artistic effect for the purpose of propaganda.

The romance of the supernatural has had in recent years little to rival *The Return of Peter Grimm*. But in 1923 *Children of the Moon*, by Martin Flavin, showed power of conception if not complete power of execution. Flavin was born in San Francisco, where *Children of the Moon* is laid. But the interest lies not so much in the setting as in the powerful study of the family insanity of the Athertons, based on old Judge Atherton's delusion that he can see life and beauty in the moon. Our stage has seldom witnessed a more tragic climax than that of the second Act when young Jane Atherton, the judge's grand-daughter, fights for her love and her reason against the malignant influence of her mother, who believes that the race should stop. The acting of Florence Johns in this part and the remarkable performance of Henrietta Crosman as Madame Atherton, representing the constant watchfulness of common sense over the fatal weakness of the family, will not soon be forgotten by those who had the good fortune to see them. This was the first long play of Martin Flavin to be performed, though several of his one-act plays had been produced. What appealed most in *Children of the Moon* was Flavin's ability to preserve the insanity as a lurking shadow, an impending doom, not a scientific phenomenon. His *Lady of the Rose* (1925) was not so well done. It is a dream play, in which John Meredith, a playwright, is pictured as living in communion with his ideal. His wife finds a play of her husband's with this motive, in "Maybury's Storehouse" and she plays the part without his permission and with tragic results. There was a poetic touch in *Lady of the Rose* which made its failure one to be regretted.

This survey of the romance after 1900 cannot, of course, be complete. For the species is more often than any other, perhaps, the work of those who produce one or two plays and then cease writing or producing. To this class belongs *Enter Madame* (1920) by Gilda Varesi and Dolly Byrne, a clever picture of a prima donna, who at the prospect of a divorce from her husband, wins him back from the clutches of an attractive widow who is waiting for him. Miss Varesi is supposed to have drawn the character from that of her own mother, but inasmuch as she had herself acted in *Romance*, the influence of Sheldon's play is probable. In fact I sense the influence of Edward Sheldon through most of this period, and if his unacknowledged work could be assigned to him, that influence would be made much more apparent.

What becomes clear, however, in any historical survey, is the ever-present demand for romance. Notwithstanding the critical suspicion of the departure from actuality, the theatre is temperamentally receptive to romance. For both the theatre and romance flourish because of the human desire for relief from the long stretches of existence through the few great moments or occasions in which we really live.

CHAPTER XX

CHANGING CONDITIONS OF THE THEATRE

THE impulse which had brought encouragement and power to the American playwright about the beginning of the century never lost its strength. But as in every art, there was an ebb as well as a flow and, as is usual just before a new creative period dawns, the criticism of the contemporary is tinged with dire prophecies of failure. By the end of the first decade, the rivalry of the moving picture had become definite, and by 1915 the obituary of the road company began to be preached. It would be idle to deny that the moving picture has been on the whole not only a rival for an audience, but also a training school for auditors who will demand dramatic fare, in the legitimate theatre, of a lower intellectual quality. It is easier to use one sense than two, and when one sees only, the reaction is more purely emotional, while when one both sees and hears, the appeal is to the intellect as well. The decline in the traveling company has been brought about by a variety of causes, notably the increase in railroad rates, the rivalry of the moving picture, the practice of sending incompetent second companies with good plays, caused in its turn partly by the disinclination of certain actors to leave New York City. The growth of a more intimate form of drama, suited to the newer playhouses in New York, raises another difficulty. In many of the smaller towns, the traveling company must play in a large theatre, built in the seventies or eighties, for performances of musical comedy. The psychology of the half-filled auditorium is a real factor in deterring companies from visiting towns where a smaller theatre would adequately house those who still would support the legitimate drama. The immediate result of these

158

developments was the acceleration about 1910 of the growth of the stock companies, which indeed had been in progress at least ten years before. These met the competition of the moving picture by a cheap scale of prices, and these still continue, though their fortunes have been fluctuating. But they contributed little to the creation of drama, for they contented themselves with the reproduction of Broadway successes, although they did present often the only opportunity for playgoers to see plays that were worth while.

While the second decade is too near us to trace the dramatic tendencies with surety, there are certain evidences of that constant reaction which, through the effort to counteract evils, brings about better things. The commercial spirit in the theatre, which has always existed, has been intensified by the growing emphasis laid on New York, as the road gradually failed. There were twenty theatres in New York in 1903. In 1927 there are eighty [1] offering legitimate drama. This really excessive competition and the high rent of the buildings has accentuated a condition which has long been detrimental to the production of first-class drama. The necessity of making an immediate appeal is no new phenomenon in the theatre—we have seen how *Shore Acres* was saved only by the contract which required a four weeks' run. But now a play may be doing a fair business and still if it fails to meet a comparatively high rental, it will be withdrawn. The most insidious result lies in the temptation to playwrights to sacrifice the inevitability of tragedy or the delicate shades of comedy in order to strike the more obvious chords to which success responds. The earlier conditions under which a play could find no opportunity in New York unless a road tour had been secured, have thus given place to another form of commercial tyranny.

Many of these unfortunate conditions became apparent at the end of the first decade, and there were other reasons which brought about a temporary depression in creative writing. Fitch died in 1909, Moody in 1910, both at the height of their

[1] These figures are given on the authority of the Editors of the *Theatre Magazine.*

creative powers. Thomas, Gillette and Belasco had done their best work by 1911, and while the average for the seasons of 1906-12, had been high, there is a decided falling off after that. To be sure, *Romance* and *The Yellow Jacket* came in 1912-13, *One Thousand Years Ago* and *Ourselves* in 1913-14, but *The Garden of Paradise* is the one play of the season of 1914-15, and *The Unchastened Woman* of the next, that are likely to be remembered, while in 1916-17 when the Pulitzer Prize was first announced, no award was made.

Yet just as this low point was reached, the forces that were to bring about regeneration were at work. If the conditions of the commercial theatre generally forbade experiment, play-houses in which opportunity for expressing original ideas in play writing, in scenic decoration, in production generally, began to be provided. It must not be forgotten that Winthrop Ames had founded the Little Theatre in 1913 and Holbrook Blinn had leased the Princess Theatre during the same year to put on plays, long and short, of the better type. But often these were of foreign make and so lie outside our province. In February, 1915, the Neighborhood Playhouse in Grand Street began its career, founded upon earlier settlement work and with a social purpose that became steadily more artistic. Under the devoted care of Helen Arthur, Agnes Morgan and Alice and Irene Lewisohn it became a potent force in providing plays of the right kind, and a background of training in many phases of theatrical work. Outside of one play each of Eugene O'Neill, Percy MacKaye, and Susan Glaspell, it confined itself, not entirely of its own volition, largely to the productions of foreign playwrights. Its main emphasis, too, was laid upon the production rather than the writing of plays. But the influence of the Neighborhood Playhouse was always upon the right side and it preserved a noncommercial attitude notwithstanding the dangers attendant upon popular success. The decision to close its doors in 1927 came as a blow to all those interested in our drama.

One week after the Neighborhood Playhouse gave its first

production, a group of young men and women, among whom Robert Edmond Jones, Philip Moeller, Edward Goodman, and Helen Westley were moving spirits, founded the Washington Square Players, and began to give at the Bandbox Theatre on Fifty-seventh Street, programs of one-act plays. Announcement was made that work by American authors was to be preferred and the record of the first season shows ten American to five foreign selections. This proportion became less pronounced as the Players proceeded at either the Bandbox or the Comedy Theatre. Their function in the encouragement of American playwrights was carried out in the production of the work of Philip Moeller, Alice Gerstenberg, Lewis Beach, Zoë Akins, Zona Gale, and others. The war stopped their activities in May, 1918, and when they reassembled with changes in personnel in 1919 as the Theatre Guild, the preference for foreign plays had become marked. The Theatre Guild has become less and less distinguishable from the commercial theatre. It has retained, however, to a certain degree its fondness for experiment, which has led it at times into queer places in the purlieus of dramatic art. But it is significant that its last substantial successes have been made with the plays of Sidney Howard. The plans now in operation of sending a road company of the Theatre Guild to tour not only the larger cities but also towns where a college or university may serve as a nucleus of interest, are another indication of a return to the support of the source from which our drama had its birth.

Much more important in the development of American play writing than the Neighborhood Playhouse or the Theatre Guild has been the organization known throughout various changes as the Provincetown Players. It sprang from the colony of artists at Provincetown, Massachusetts, in the summer of 1915, many of them coming from Greenwich Village, and the first plays were given on a porch. One of these, *Suppressed Desires*, by Susan Glaspell, has become a stand-by of the theatre. Robert Edmond Jones arranged the stage settings. In 1916 a fishing smack was remodeled, christened "The Wharf

Theatre," and with George Cram Cook as director, the group gave four programs of one-act plays. Among these were *Bound East for Cardiff* and *Thirst* by Eugene O'Neill, who became identified with the organization that gave him his first opportunity, and who acted the negro in *Thirst*. In the fall of 1916, with little money but great enthusiasm, the group rented 137 Macdougal Street, in the Village, and put on a series of nineteen one-act plays, including three by O'Neill. In 1918 they moved to 133 Macdougal Street, rebuilt a stable holding about two hundred, and despite the war, kept on producing. From the beginning the chief interest had been the playwright. According to the official list, printed by the Provincetown Theatre in 1925, the organization had produced ninety-three new plays by forty-seven playwrights, practically all American.[1] Among these were Edna St. Vincent Millay, Lewis Beach, and Edna Ferber. By 1920 they had graduated from the one-act play, and such notable productions as *The Emperor Jones, The Hairy Ape* and *Inheritors* were put on in 1920-2. After an interim of one season, Kenneth Macgowan, Eugene O'Neill and Robert Edmond Jones revived the organization and the character of the performances was somewhat changed. Revivals of older plays like Mrs. Mowatt's *Fashion* took place, but O'Neill's *All God's Chillun Got Wings* and *Desire Under the Elms* were the most significant productions. Although other changes came, consequent upon the leasing of the Greenwich Village Theatre by Macgowan, Jones and O'Neill, the character of the "Playwrights' Theatre" still remains. Hospitable to new ideas of stagecraft of which the dome of concrete is a testimonial, the great service to our drama has been the never faltering willingness to give an opportunity to untried playwrights whose work might otherwise not have found expression. In the season of 1926-7 the best example was the production of *In Abraham's Bosom* by Paul Green. Devotion to an ideal, with a disregard of merely com-

---

[1] For a glowing description of the origin of the movement, see Susan Glaspell, *The Road to the Temple*, chaps. 21, 22.

mercial success, an unconquerable youth, a passion for the theatre, animates every member of the staff, and gives to its business management, headed by M. Eleanor Fitzgerald, a quality of its own. The best way to estimate the significance of the Provincetown Playhouse, is to try to imagine what American playwriting would have been during the last decade without it.

One great service the independent theatres have rendered is the breaking down of the line between the professional and the amateur. The old scorn of the commercial manager for the amateur in general has suffered rude shocks, as he watched the successes of the independent theatres move to houses on Broadway and meet competition without apology. The amateur on the other hand has come to see the necessity for skilled direction, for drill and for strict attention to business. The real meaning, long obscured, of the word amateur, one who loves his art, has come into a new significance.

The decline of the road has been remedied to a certain degree by the rise of the art theatres with training schools for actors, by the establishment of "Little Theatres" and of college dramatic departments. While these have as yet produced in only a few rare cases a playwright of importance, they are raising standards of taste in some places, and in all cases are preserving the habit of theatregoing, in danger of disuse. In 1925 in the office of the Drama League of America, nineteen hundred Little Theatres were registered. There are probably three thousand such theatres, varying from the Little Theatre of Philadelphia, where "Plays and Players" owns a club house in the heart of the city, with professional director and an assured financial and social support, to the little country playhouse, with no equipment and only self-direction. But animating them all is the unquenchable love of the theatre, and their function in providing a market for the work of American playwrights is most important. Plays of merit which have been denied success in New York through accident or unfortunate circumstances have two chances of life—the stock company and the little theatre, where formerly they had only one. The programs of these amateur theatres is made up of lists furnished by the leading play publishers and the demand is so great that it may be said with truth that practically every play is now published in some form. An historian of the drama alone knows how radical a change has taken place in this regard over the condition existing twenty years ago. The encouragement to playwrights is beginning to be felt and while there will probably never be a time when the ambitious playwright will not turn first to the manager who can promise a production on Broadway, there is a second public waiting, of growing discrimination, for which the dramatist may also write.

The conferences on the American drama and theatre held at the Carnegie Institute of Technology in 1925 and at Yale University in 1927 revealed the nation wide interest in drama and brought to light certain aspects of the situation which are still in process of formation. One is the growing disinclination to take the verdict of New York City as final. Experience has shown that plays which have been called failures in New York can be put on successfully in Pasadena or Cleveland, with more sympathy and less dependence upon immediate box-office returns. There was evidence, too, of a realization that matters of production, which have engaged the attention of so many college departments and Little Theatre organizations are after all subsidiary to the creation of plays. Lee Simonson, the able scenic artist, has called attention to the fact that general rules in his art are really out of the question, for each play is its own designer. And even in the electric signs, flashing on the theatres, and in the advertisements, the growing recognition of the playwright is recorded.

CHAPTER XXI

EUGENE O'NEILL, POET AND MYSTIC

IT IS perhaps inevitable that when an original creative artist arises, a myth should speedily develop concerning him. It is even more inevitable when, as in the case of Eugene O'Neill, his influence extends beyond the limits of his own country and he becomes an international figure. When a playwright's work is produced in New York and Tokio, in Copenhagen and Bombay, in Prague and Manila, mistaken judgments naturally arise, caused in some cases by inability of the foreign producer to understand the meaning of the play. Perhaps the director of the Berlin production of *Anna Christie* may be pardoned some day for making Anna shoot herself. Gémier, who produced *The Emperor Jones* at the Odéon in Paris, sent a number of negroes across the stage between the scenes, to represent the chase after the Emperor. He was apparently unaware that one of the tragic elements in that play comes from the fact that the rhythmic tom-tom lures the Emperor back to the very spot at which he enters the forest, while the negroes simply wait for him to come!

It is perhaps unfair to expect foreign productions of an American dramatist to rival those in his own country, but surely his native land also has much to answer for in the growth of that "O'Neill myth" which obscures the real significance of his work. This myth is one result of the confusion of our standards of dramatic criticism, which discusses his work without apparently considering the possibility of his varying at times in his methods and often without any real understanding of the basic meaning of his art.

Like many other creative artists, he unconsciously chose the training that gave him his material. Eugene Gladstone O'Neill was born October 16, 1888, on Broadway, New York. He is the son of James O'Neill, the actor of romantic and heroic parts, like *Monte Cristo*, and the first seven years of his life were spent on tour in the larger towns all over the United States. His mother, Ella Quinlan O'Neill, accompanied his father on these tours, although she had, according to O'Neill, somewhat of an aversion for the atmosphere of the stage. That the mysticism of O'Neill came to him through her is beyond question. Six years were spent in residence at Catholic boarding schools, four years at Betts Academy, Stamford, Connecticut, and then one year at Princeton University with the class of 1910. He was suspended for an infraction of college discipline and did not return after the period had expired. A year was spent as secretary of a mail-order house; then to quote his own words,[1] "Discovering a chance to work off some of my latent romanticism I went to Spanish Honduras with a mining engineer on a prospecting expedition. At the end of eight months or so I caught the malarial fever so bad that I had to be sent home. Much hardship, little romance, no gold." After a few months as assistant manager of the *White Sister* Company, in which his father was acting with Viola Allen, the urge for the sea, strengthened by the reading of Conrad and Jack London, came upon him. So he sailed for Buenos Aires on a Norwegian barque and for sixty-five days was out of sight of land. That he mentions the last fact, years later, shows how the love of adventure which widened his horizon was not really derivative from books. It was in his blood. He worked in Buenos Aires during 1910 and 1911 with the Westinghouse Electric Company, the Swift Packing Company, the Singer Sewing Machine Company, just enough to maintain existence and also tended mules on a cattle boat taking a voyage from Buenos Aires to Durban, South Africa. Upon his return he was "on the beach for a considerable period in Buenos Aires,

---

[1] The facts of O'Neill's life are based on letters to the present writer, supplemented by Barrett Clark's accurate biography.

with no job, eating and place to sleep intermittent," until he shipped as an ordinary seaman on a British tramp steamer to New York. In that city he lived at "Jimmy, the Priest's," a resort on the water front, which he uses in *Anna Christie*. After a brief period he became an able seaman on the American line steamers *New York* and *Philadelphia*. This was his last experience on the sea, but the life of the forecastle had stamped itself indelibly upon him. Joining his father in New Orleans, he played a minor part in *Monte Cristo* on the Orpheum Circuit in the West. The tour ended with O'Neill in New London, the summer home of the family. He had grown to know New England through these summer experiences and he was now to add to his knowledge by becoming a reporter on the New London *Telegraph*, visiting police courts, among other assignments. Incipient tuberculosis sent him in December, 1912, to a sanitarium, Gaylord Farm, at Wallingford, Connecticut. Here he began to take account of his varied experiences, and to decide what he wished to do. His first encouragement to write had come from his chief on the *Telegraph*, but his enforced leisure gave him the time to think things out. Being discharged soon as not seriously affected, he began to write. To quote him again, "In that winter, 1913-14, I wrote eight one-act plays and two long plays. Of these *Bound East for Cardiff* is the only one worth remembering." He was reading much in these days, especially plays, and rebuilding his health. In 1914-15 he attended Professor Baker's class at Harvard, gaining there encouragement for the future, though the plays actually written while there are of no significance. The winter of 1915-16 was spent in and around Greenwich Village, New York, observing types among the curious medley, native and foreign, there. In the summer of 1916 he went to Provincetown, Massachusetts, and there he became associated with the Provincetown Players, who produced *Bound East for Cardiff* at the Wharf Theatre.

It was a fortunate combination of playwright and actors. O'Neill would, of course, have written plays if he had never met this group, but they encouraged him in an atmosphere of independence and they gave him an opportunity to experiment which the commercial theatre would probably have denied him. On the whole, he probably has given more to them than he received, but the result of the joint effort is a landmark in the history of our drama.

Of the early one-act plays which were published in 1914, *Thirst, The Web, Fog, Warnings,* and *Recklessness,* we are inclined to agree with O'Neill's repudiation, already quoted. They were apprentice work while he was feeling for a method. *Thirst* and *Fog* were produced by the Provincetown Players during the summers of 1916 and 1917. *Thirst* is laid on a raft in the South Seas, and has one good moment when a dancer goes mad with suffering. The best of these plays is *Warnings,* which deals with the struggle in the conscience of a wireless operator who is going deaf, between his duty to his work and his responsibility for his family. The remainder are of interest only because they are his early efforts. With *Bound East for Cardiff,* however, it is a different matter. This, the first of his plays to be produced, is also the first to be created of a series of one-act dramas in which he treated the life in the forecastle with an imaginative quality and a reality unsurpassed. In this play he created the characters of Yank, an American sailor who is dying of injuries received by a fall, and of Driscoll, an Irishman, who is his close friend and who watches with him in his dying moments while the others snore in their bunks. Yank tells him how he had dreamed of their living together on a farm and giving up the sea, and we see the inarticulate friendship of the two sailors who have been around the world, but have seen nothing of it. The agony is not drawn out when the inevitable death comes and there is no over sentimentality. But somehow, even the little touches like the slumber of the others, who leave the loyal friend and the dying man alone as he approaches his end without fear in the forecastle of a ship, reveal O'Neill's mastery of drama. Appropriately, too, the loyalty that comes to O'Neill's nature from his Irish ancestry and the moral courage of his American present are made concrete in Driscoll and in Yank. Having established these characters, O'Neill used them in other plays, which were produced in 1917 and 1918 by the Provincetown Players in New York. *The Long Voyage Home* is laid in a dive in London. Here O'Neill depicted the tragedy of Olson, the Swedish sailor, who, determining to keep sober, in order that he may return to his native land and settle on his mother's farm, is drugged by the proprietor, robbed and carried out to the horrors of a voyage around Cape Horn in the *Amindra*, notorious for the cruelty of her officers—"the worst ship that sails the sea." The pathos of the scene becomes almost unendurable as Olson describes in simple words his longing for home, when the audience knows the doom impending over him. In *The Moon of the Caribbees* there is a vivid picture of the rough side of life on a British ship, in a West Indian harbor, especially the drunkenness and the license which come with the visit of the negresses. Against this background is painted the figure of Smitty, the English sailor, whose soul revolts at the scene, but who drinks to forget the memories which the distant music wakens in him. *In the Zone*, while theatrically more effective, is less important than the others. Smitty is suspected of being a spy during the war, and the sailors, who are nervous over the prospect of submarines, believe he has a bomb concealed in his bunk. It is only a box containing letters from the girl whom he loved and for whom he could not give up the liquor that has been his undoing. When they seize him and rifle the box there is an interesting reaction, but that is all. Of the series, *Bound East for Cardiff* is the best and when the four were given together in one program under the title of *S. S. Glencairn*, at the Provincetown Playhouse in 1924, it was illuminating to see the cumulative effect of the characterizations as the plays progressed through *The Moon of the Caribbees*, *The Long Voyage Home*, *In the Zone* and *Bound East for Cardiff*. We grew to know the characters better as each play showed how true O'Neill had kept to his types. Driscoll,

Smitty, Olson and Yank were the most impressive, and the impulsive Irishman, the calmer Englishman, the phlegmatic Swede and the matter-of-fact American remain vividly in the memory. Those critics who speak of O'Neill as a writer of episodes were utterly confuted by the way the drama built up when the plays were put on together.

One of the best of the one-act plays, *Ile*, was produced by the Provincetown Players in 1917. This is a masterly study of the character of the captain of a whaler, revealing the iron determination which keeps him for two years in fruitless pursuit of the oil which his reputation demands he shall bring home. His wife who begs him to return, his men who threaten to mutiny, are put aside or quelled, and then, just as whales are sighted, his wife goes mad, from loneliness and the terrible effect of the ice. It is one of the earliest of the many modern plays which have dealt with the long-continued influence of climate upon human nature, and it is swift and powerful in the revelation of human reactions, when strained to the breaking point.

The other one-act plays need little comment. *Before Breakfast* (1916), which shows the influence of Strindberg, is a futile treatment of a man's suicide, off stage, driven to desperation by his wife's complaints. *The Rope* (1918) reveals the same influence, but has a theatrical situation which on account of its grim satire upon the futility of human meanness has a certain power. Luke Bentley returns to the farm to find the money he believes his half-crazy father has hidden. Out of bravado and to impress his sister and brother-in-law, Luke teaches his little step-niece, Mary, to skim a coin into the water. He then plots with his brother-in-law to rob his father, partly because old Abraham Bentley has hung a rope in the barn and told Luke to hang himself upon it. Mary swings on the rope and it gives way, pulling down with it the cherished hoard of gold pieces. Then she skips out to the cliff and skims them into the sea, while off stage Luke and his brother-in-law are plotting to torture the old man into revealing the hiding place of his hoard.   It is fortunate that O'Neill passed out of this stage.   All that he learned from writing this play or *The Dreamy Kid* (1919), a play of negro life, was a certain stage effectiveness, and the experience of working out results from unpromising material.   These early plays were studies for later productions of great value, like *The Emperor Jones* or *Desire Under the Elms*.   In fact the only other one-act play that needs to be mentioned, *Where the Cross is Made*, was written to help the Provincetown program in the fall of 1918, and forms part of the play *Gold*, conceived even in the first instance as a full-length play.

Stimulating as his association with the semi-professional group at the Playwrights' Theatre had been, it was time for O'Neill to progress from the one-act play to a larger form and to a strictly professional production.   The special matinée at the Morosco Theatre on February 2, 1920, marks a definite step in his career, for in *Beyond the Horizon* he challenged the attention of those who could recognize an original and powerful note in the drama.   Considered superficially, the love of two brothers for the same girl is an old story.   But that is not the central motive of *Beyond the Horizon*.   Robert Mayo is a dreamer, a poet, to whom the humdrum life of the farm is repellent.   He has visions of the adventures that lie beyond the limits one can see, and the opportunity of the voyage with his uncle comes as an answer to an unspoken prayer.   As a frail child, he has been comforted by the beauty that lies in the clouds, and he hears the voices of illusion calling him.   Across this dream come the homely things and the love of the two brothers, passing the usual, and then after they have said their inarticulate farewell, the wayward passion of Ruth Atkins strikes down the dream.   At the insistent clutch of her fancy, Robert, who, like all the family, had believed that Andy was her chosen mate, gives up his voyage and Andy takes his place. The scene in which their father, James Mayo, pours his wrath upon Andy's head for leaving the farm and in which the two brothers say good night with their friendship riveted rather than broken by the test it has undergone, is one of the finest revelations of human passion and restraint that the modern stage has seen.

The play proceeds through the inevitable results of the fatal mistake of Ruth. Robert is a failure as a farmer and his life becomes one long struggle against his wife's nagging, his mother-in-law's complaints and his own sense of inadequacy. His two consolations are his books and his little daughter. Ruth nourishes the hope of Andy's return and when Robert jestingly refers to Andy's letters which tell nothing of the places he has visited, the long-pent-up emotion bursts from her and she strips her soul of the restraint which has concealed her passion for her husband's brother. Upon his return, Andy tells Rob and Ruth separately that his passion for her was forgotten in a few months. To her it is the end of hope—to Rob, an added irritation—but Andy senses the situation and leaves them after only a day's visit. Five years later the tragedy has progressed naturally in terms of the daily routine of a decaying farm. Even after Mary's death, and with the fatal disease upon him, Rob keeps up his hope for the future. But when Andy brings the specialist who pronounces sentence, Rob breaks away from their care and they find him on the hillside watching the horizon he had never crossed. His last words strike the keynote of hope:

Robert: You mustn't feel sorry for me. Don't you see I'm happy at last—free—free!—freed from the farm—free to wander on and on—eternally! Look! Isn't it beautiful beyond the hills? I can hear the old voices calling me to come— (*Exultantly.*) And this time I'm going! It isn't the end. It's a free beginning—the start of my voyage! I've won to my trip—the right of release—beyond the horizon! Oh, you ought to be glad—glad—for my sake!

It was this exaltation of spirit which lifted *Beyond the Horizon* into greatness. O'Neill knows that the most precious gifts to humanity are the illusions that keep us alive, and he fulfills the most severe test of tragedy, which has come down to us from the Greeks, that it purifies us through our sympathy with suffering. He met another test, too. The characters all stand out, not as types, but as individuals, even the two mothers, different but alive, through whom he secures a few moments of the comedy that keeps the tragedy from becoming unendurable. He does not localize the farm, and while James Mayo seems of New England, the prevailing quality is simply that of native American stock.

Beyond the Horizon is written in three acts of two scenes each. He thus made a compromise between the accepted tradition and the freer form that he was to use later. But in any case, he made the form the servant to the dramatic conception and preserved the unity of motive. By a stupid stage direction, the last scene was omitted in the production, after the first performance, and the first scene of the last Act slightly changed. The real meaning of the play was thereby obscured and in the revival in 1926 it was apparent how integral a part of the drama is the last scene. But even with that handicap the play won the Pulitzer Prize and became, after its professional run ended in Chicago, a favorite of the Little Theatres. While O'Neill went onward to conquer new fields, *Beyond the Horizon* will always remain one of his finest plays. For in it he put his own longings for adventure, which led him to South Africa and South America, which took him into the hold of a steamer and the life "on the beach." When Robert Mayo says, "Supposing I was to tell you that it's just Beauty that's calling me, the beauty of the far off and unknown," it is O'Neill himself that is speaking.

Chris Christopherson (1920), his next play to be produced, was not a success, and was later rewritten as *Anna Christie*. In the meantime he had written *The Straw*, which had to wait for production until 1921 but which belongs to the same period of composition as *Beyond the Horizon*. In *The Straw* are reflected O'Neill's experiences in the sanitarium and in newspaper work, but just as Rob Mayo was not merely a copy of O'Neill, so Stephen Murray is not simply a self-picture. Starting with a vivid portrayal of the selfishness which manifests itself in Eileen Carmody's brutal father and cowardly lover when she has to leave home on account of tuberculosis of the lungs, he reveals the growth of love in Eileen for Stephen at the sanitarium, and her despair, bravely hidden at first when she finds it unreturned. *The Straw* is essentially an acting play. Those who saw it in its brief life at the Greenwich Village Theatre will never forget the scene at midnight on the road when Eileen tells Stephen she loves him, knowing that he has only friendship to give in return. Even stronger in its appeal was the final act in the isolation room, four months later, where Eileen lies, not knowing or caring that she is to be sent on to the hospital for the incurable. On one side of the stage her bed is placed and a door separates her from the main room. Stephen comes to see her and when the nurse begs him to make Eileen's last days happy by pretending he loves her, he agrees out of gratitude for the encouragement she had given him in his writing and for the love she had offered him. So far there was simply the chivalry of a stage convention. But O'Neill provided Otto Kruger and Margalo Gillmore with a great opportunity, of which they took advantage. As Stephen begins to tell her his story, the gallant lie grows before our eyes into truth. The beauty of her nature shining out of Eileen's eyes as the light of hope comes back to them, kindles the love in Stephen that flashes into passion. But as his love is born, there comes also the realization of her fatal illness and anxiety shudders into the sense of doom. She sees it and reads her sentence in the midst of her joy, and then Stephen rises quickly to the occasion and lies again, telling her that he had to come back because he has relapsed and they will go away together. When he leaves her, shuts the door of her sleeping porch and then first begs the nurse for encouragement and finally defies her to set a limit to the hope of human happiness, he seems to be not only Stephen Murray, but the incarnation of the unquenchable spark that carries on life itself. Once again, as in *Beyond the Horizon*, the tragedy ends with exaltation.

Two reworkings of earlier material, one a failure, one a great success, date from 1920, though they were not produced until 1921. O'Neill had conceived of *Gold* as a full-length drama, but he had written a one-act play, *Where the Cross Is Made*, for the Provincetown Players in 1918, and some of the characters reappear in the last act of *Gold*. In Captain Bartlett, the sailor who is obsessed by the idea that he has discovered a valuable chest of gold ornaments on a desert island in the Pacific, O'Neill drew a strong character. The action is sharper in the one-act play, but there is a powerful scene on the island, in the first act of *Gold*, which depicts the sufferings of the six men who are lost and the murder of two of them by the Kanaka with Bartlett's connivance. There was no character in *Gold*, however, in whom an audience could be vitally interested. Cupidity is death to heroism and while the relentless purpose of Captain Bartlett is a unifying force to the drama, he is not of sufficient importance to be an heroic figure. *Gold* lasted about ten nights when it was put on in June, 1921.

In *Anna Christie*, written in 1920, and produced in 1921, O'Neill worked over the material of *Chris*. In the earlier version the central character had been that of a Swedish sailor and he was carried over in part to the later play. While he remains in fact the best character in *Anna Christie*, he becomes second in importance to his daughter, and the play must be judged by the treatment of her character. The first act of *Anna Christie* is one of the most skilfully constructed scenes in all O'Neill's plays. His experiences in "Jimmy the Priest's" saloon blossom into the stark reality of "Johnny the Priest's," with the bar on one side of the stage separated by a partition from the back room, into which the "family entrance" opens. Chris Christopherson is a perfect portrait of a tough old seaman who has wasted his life and who has kept his daughter out on a farm in the West because he wishes to guard her against "dat ole davil, sea," upon which he blames all his misfortunes.

Just as he has finished building up an idyllic portrait of Anna, growing up in a state of pastoral innocence, largely for the benefit of Marthy, a drab whom he has been keeping on his coal barge, Anna enters the back room. Chris has gone out for a few minutes leaving Marthy alone, and when Anna enters, drops her suit case and says, "Gimme a whisky—ginger ale on the side," we have one of those sharp moments when reality crashes into a mental picture. The conversation between the two women is exposition of the highest order. When Marthy, irritated by Anna's tone, snaps out, "I got your number the minute you stepped in the door," Anna replies, "Ain't you smart! Well, I got yours, too, without no trouble. You're me, forty years from now."

The only criticism that may be leveled at the first Act is that O'Neill so clearly draws Anna's character that it is difficult for him to make us believe in her regeneration. It is, of course, natural that she should conceal her past from her father and that when Mat Burke, the giant Irish stoker, appears over the side of the coal barge out of the fog, she should like his sincere if possessive style of wooing. The second Act, in which Anna seems to be cleansed through the healing influence of the sea and the fog that blots out the past she hates, is one of O'Neill's touches of poetic symbolism that makes a strong appeal. If he had been able to preserve that note he might have made a greater play, but the sense of reality brought him back to the three characters as purely human and while their relations are developed naturally and their conversation is startlingly faithful to actual life, the play at the end is disappointing. Treated symbolically, we may believe in Anna's regeneration; treated realistically, we do not credit the retention of the inherent purity necessary to that regeneration. It is true that she is far superior to Laura Murdock in *The Easiest Way*. She does not take any lofty attitude—she is merely defiant of the two men who try to decide what is to become of her and while she feels that the cards of fate have been stacked against her from the beginning, she blames no one. O'Neill has himself explained that he felt such a woman could express herself only in terms of theatrical language she had learned from the novels and moving pictures with which she was familiar. She is honest in confessing her past when Burke wishes to marry her and the departure of the two men to get drunk as the only avenue open to them to forget the wreck her story has made of their lives is fine irony. So is their signing up, while drunk, upon the same ship for a long cruise. If Anna's character is not entirely defensible, the criticism that the play was forced into a happy ending is puerile. In a letter to the New York *Times* [1] O'Neill says:

Not even the most adversely prejudiced could call this a "happy ending." Meaning that I wish it understood as unhappy? Meaning nothing of the kind. Meaning what I have said before, that the play has no ending. Three characters have been revealed in all their intrinsic verity, under the acid test of a fateful crisis in their lives. They have solved this crisis for the moment as best they may, in accordance with the will that is in each of them. The curtain falls. Behind it their lives go on. But granting for the moment the absurdity that the ending is happy, why the objections to it raised on all sides? Have I not been told constantly that gloom is my failing, that I should see the brighter side, that I should grant my helpless human beings their one hundred per cent right to happiness? Well, in *Anna Christie*, haven't I? You claim I have and yet you will have none of it. You say it is unconvincing. Why? Is it, as I suspect, on moral grounds? Does the idea that two such "disreputable" folk as Anna and Burke are, as you think, going to be happy, disturb your sense of the proper fitness of things in this best of all possible worlds? Or is your reason, as I more than suspect, simply that you prefer the obvious to the inevitable? It would have been so obvious and easy—in the case of this play, conventional even—to have made my last Act a tragic one. It could have been done in ten different ways, any one of them superficially right. But looking deep into the hearts of my people, I saw it couldn't be done. It would not have been true. They were not that kind. They would act in just the silly, immature, compromising way that I have made them act; and I thought that they would appear to others as they do to me, a bit tragically humorous in their vacillating weakness. But evi-

[1] Dated December 12, 1921.

dently not. Evidently they are all happy—and unconvincing. No wonder! Their groping clutch at happiness is taken as a deadly finality.

But how about those sentimental ones to whom the Boy on the Burning Deck represents the last word in the heroic spirit our drama should strive to express—the American Œdipus Rex? Surely they must read something into my ending besides mere eternal happiness. But they don't. And yet there never was a more sentimental gesture of defiance at fate than that of Burke and Anna agreeing to wed.

Lastly, to those who think I deliberately distorted my last Act because a "happy ending" would be calculated to make the play more of a popular success I have only this to say: The sad truth is that you have precedents enough and to spare in the history of our drama for such a suspicion. But, on the other hand, you have every reason not to believe it of me.

O'Neill might have added, in his defence, that Matt Burke is just the kind of man who might help Anna in her upward struggle. He is the compound of two qualities which the Irish of his stamp possess—a worship of the purity of woman, and a superlative self-conceit. He believes he is the kind who can save her—perhaps he can—for it is of his kind, infinitely spiritualized, that the saints are made. If he fails, we may be sure that he will reproach her all their lives together.

Dates of production are less significant in O'Neill's case than dates of composition.[1] *The Emperor Jones* was produced before *Anna Christie*, by the Provincetown Players, November 1, 1920. But it marks a progress in O'Neill's art. In it he discarded any attempt at arrangement into acts, and dealt with the theme progressively in eight scenes. He also defied the old theatrical rule against monologue and created a moving and enthralling drama which is largely carried on by the utterances of one character. For this central character he chose no usual hero, but a negro Pullman car porter, who has had to leave the United States on account of his crimes, which include murder. The nature of this man is established

---

[1] See list of O'Neill's plays, arranged according to year of their composition; program of the Greenwich Village Theatre, 1925-6.

in the first scene, laid in the audience chamber of the "Emperor Jones," on a West Indian island, "not yet self-determined by white marines." The conversation between Jones, who has won his imperial dignity by his cleverness in imposing upon the natives, and a low-caste British trader, Smithers, is carried on in that natural manner of which O'Neill is a master. Instinctive dislike to both men comes first and then a gradual dawning of respect for the ability and courage of Jones, who, single-handed, holds the island in his grip. He has won his position by an unscrupulous employment of the devices he has learned "on de Pullman ca's listenin' to de white quality talk." To these he has added his own contribution, a skilful playing upon the superstitious fears of the negroes. He has taken advantage of the fact that when one of his enemies shot at him, the bullet missed fire, and he has told them that nothing but a silver bullet can kill him. When Smithers remarks that this is luck, Jones answers: "I got brains and I uses 'em quick. Dat ain't luck." But Smithers has news for him. His time has come; the negroes have deserted the Emperor. And then "from the distant hills comes the faint steady thump of a tom-tom, low and vibrating. It starts at a rate exactly corresponding to normal pulse beat—seventy-two to the minute—and continues at a gradually accelerating rate from this point uninterruptedly to the very end of the play." This device, not unknown to the theatre, has probably never elsewhere been used so effectively. It is a unifying force and it accentuates the needed mood in both character and audience, for it goes back to the primitive expression of emotion, the accentuated rhythm of the earliest race. Jones wins our admiration by his quick decision to leave and by his courage in going out by the front entrance. "De Emperor Jones leaves de way he comes, and dat black trash don't dare stop him." From the second to the seventh scene we watch the flight of the Emperor through the "brooding implacable silence" of the forest, on the other side of which lies safety and the gold he has deposited in the foreign bank. In each scene he encounters phantoms deepening in intensity and mystery and receding from the present into the prenatal stages of his being. In scene two, they are the "little formless fears" of his imagining. He dispels them with a shot from his revolver, loaded with five lead bullets and one of silver which he is keeping for himself if he is caught. In scene three he sees Jeff, the negro porter he had killed in a quarrel, and he talks to him, as he does to himself, in the natural monologue of a negro under the stress of emotion, until the shot dispels the vision again. In scene four, the murder of the white convict guard is re-enacted, and again the tension is increased. Tattered and worn, he stumbles, in the fifth scene, to a clearing, where he sees the vision of a slave auction in the fifties, and is himself sold as a slave. Then comes the apparition of the slave ship, with the negroes' slow rhythmic motion, like the roll of a vessel, which he is forced to join. The seventh scene takes him back to the Congo, to a dance of sacrifice and death, led by the Witch Doctor, who after raising the pitch of the scene to an almost unbearable note of intensity, summons the crocodile god from the river, and motions Jones to become the needed sacrifice. Jones has been hypnotized but he calls on the Lord and thinks of his one remaining silver bullet. He shoots the crocodile and falls on the ground.

For the last scene we return to the edge of the forest where Jones entered it. The negroes have simply waited for him, knowing he would make a circle in the woods. The tom-tom beats remorselessly and in the conversation between Lem, their leader, and Smithers, we learn that they have moulded silver bullets to break the charm. Four shots are heard and the body of the Emperor is brought in. Smithers has already pronounced his funeral oration: " 'E's a better man than the lot of you put together. I 'ates the sight of him but I'll say that for 'im."

It is a fine thing for an art when a creative master shatters conventions and thereby makes for freedom. O'Neill went back to a freer form, he defied the ordinary rules of technique, but he did not violate the fundamental laws of drama. He kept the unity of time; he violated the unity of place; but he substituted a higher unity—that of impression. *The Emperor Jones* is a drama of human fear; the emotion of terror is a binding force that fuses the scenes into an unforgettable picture of a human soul fighting against his own evil deeds, the cruel fate of his forefathers, the ignorance of centuries. Variety, too, is secured by the varying shades in the intensity of terror, and the originality of the whole conception of the play.

The Emperor Jones made O'Neill's position secure. After its run on Macdougal Street, it went uptown and was taken on tour. The chief rôle has been interpreted by negroes like Charles Gilpin and Paul Robeson and by white actors like Rutherford Mayne, in Dublin, and has never failed to impress an audience. For notwithstanding the crimes of the Emperor, there is something royal in his nature, something pitiful in his hopeless struggle against fate, which elicits our sympathy.

Diff'rent followed *Jones* at the Provincetown on December 27, 1920, but it was of far less significance. It is a study of the woman who, having had a high ideal of what her husband should be, finds that her betrothed sailor is like other sailors and declines to marry him. Then thirty years later, having been sexually starved, she throws herself at the head of a young soldier just returned from the Great War. Her lover of thirty years who has remained unmarried, sees his ideal crash and hangs himself. She goes down to the barn apparently to follow him. *Diff'rent*, of all the long plays, shows most clearly the influence of Strindberg, and it is the poorest. There is no one who excites our interest except for a few minutes in the first Act and the play can be looked upon only as an experiment whose result is distressing.

The First Man, although produced at the Neighborhood Playhouse March 4, 1922, is spoken of in a letter from O'Neill, dated February 5, as "one of the vintage of a year and a half ago." On the stage the play never had a chance. The newspapers harped upon a minor feature, the moaning of a mother in giving birth to a child, which as a matter of fact, was not stressed in the production, and the impression was created that the play was obscene. It is not one of O'Neill's best plays but it has some interesting rewards for the close student of his work. It is laid in a small New England city, and a vivid picture is given of the narrow-minded, suspicious natures of the Jayson family, whose sole concern in life is the preservation of their own importance. They are not merely types. As they come down from the generations of finer mettle, they swell into pomposity like John Jayson, or grow sharp in disappointment, like Lily. The most lovable is old Mrs. Davidson, the grand-aunt. Curtis Jayson, the only one who has gone out into a freer atmosphere, has become an anthropologist and is about to start on an expedition to find the first traces of mankind. He is absorbed in his work, and his wife, Martha, who helps him, is set against the background of the petty souls who turn on her with the tribal instinct of the insect. When she tells her husband that she is to have a child, he rebels, for he has grown to look upon her not as a mother but as his helpmate. This reluctance on his part is misinterpreted by his family as a doubt of the real parentage of the coming infant and they suspect an affair between Martha and Curtis' best friend, Biglow. Martha dies in childbirth and Curtis' dislike turns to hatred and he refuses to see his boy. But when he finds out what is in their minds, he rushes up to his son, brings him down and showing his scorn of their suspicions, gives the child to Mrs. Davidson, and departs.

The trouble with *The First Man* is that we do not believe in Curtis Jayson. The natural instinct of a father, the attitude taken by any human being toward his wife during confinement, cannot be so completely obliterated or even changed without removing our sympathy for the man. The rival claims of a profession and of love or family life may be a fit theme for dramatic treatment, but O'Neill pushed the contrast too far. It was a pity, for there is good writing in the framework, and a satirical comedy in the first Act rare in O'Neill's plays.

O'Neill is a conscious artist. In a letter of February 5, 1922, he speaks of *The Hairy Ape*, whose rehearsals he was attending, as "a much greater departure in form than *Jones*." It is not only in form that the progression has taken place. *The Hairy Ape* is symbolism. Yank, the stoker in an ocean liner, represents force, which if unguided, may wreck the world, but out of which all that is significant must grow. It is "a comedy of ancient and modern life" and in Yank we can see the primitive man,—"I kin make a bluff at talkin' and t'inkin' —a'most git away wit it—a'most!—and dat's where de joker comes in." To consider any of the scenes for themselves alone, from the forecastle and the stokehole, to the jail and the Zoological Garden, is to mistake the meaning of the play. O'Neill specifically states in the stage directions of the first scene, "The treatment of this scene, or of any other scene in the play, should by no means be naturalistic." He is showing the struggle of the primitive man upward and endeavoring to depict, in terms of modern institutions, the terrible struggle through which the race went, in beginning the processes of mental growth. It is akin to Moody's lyric of the polyp: "legs he will sprout, in spite of threats and jokes."

The stage pictures were something new in drama. The first scene, in the strokehole, crashed upon the auditor without apology. It was a carnival of force, expressed in terms of human beings, at first indistinguishable units in a chorus of international profanity. Then there emerged the dominant personality of Yank, the strongest man, who "belongs," who makes the ship go—emblem of the force that makes the world go on. He has no resentment at first for the rich or the idle; he scorns the cheap agitator, for Yank rejoices in his strength— even in the living hell of the stokehole he has solved the problem of humanity, to be content with his job. Against this background of tumult O'Neill then sounds, through the old Irish stoker, his marvelous requiem for the gallant old days of the sailing ships, beginning: "There was fine beautiful ships them days—fine strong men in them—men that was sons of the sea as if 'twas the mother that bore them." For him, Yank has only amused toleration. But into this content, which symbolizes stagnation, comes the divine discontent that causes progress. Mildred Douglas, the neurotic poser, the daughter of the owner of the steel trust, is also a symbol. Her look of horror when she sees Yank, cursing out his defiance to the engineer, stirs in Yank the desire for something of which he had not dreamed. She does not call him a "hairy ape," but Pat, the stoker, coins the phrase, which O'Neill, indeed, had used in *The Moon of the Caribbees*. Yank translates his discontent into terms of revenge upon her and what she symbolizes. But everywhere he is rebuffed; the symbolic procession on Fifth Avenue is hardly conscious of him, the I. W. W. rejects him, and when he seeks the gorilla, the real hairy ape, and frees him, in order that they may in friendly brotherhood seek the meaning of the power they possess, the gorilla crushes him to death. *The Hairy Ape* may be open to criticism on the score that since it is impossible in any case to represent the profanity adequately, it is unnecessary to stress it quite so much for the purposes of art. But the cumulative effect is that of tremendous power. There is no drama of futility here; it is the representation of profound forces, wrought by a thinker who has gone back to the primal strivings of the race.

Welded, written in 1923, is a study of the conflict between two souls whose power to torture each other is measured only in terms of their great mutual passion. The theme is dramatic, for in every marriage there comes the time when husband and wife struggle for the preservation of that identity which marriage naturally seems to threaten. The situation in *Welded* is rendered more intense by the fact that Michael Cape is a playwright and Eleanor is an actress who has interpreted his work. They are temperamental in the extreme and their union is haunted, against their own wills, by the ghosts of other relations before their marriage, although they believe themselves to be emancipated from such old-fashioned scruples. When the conflict comes to a head, each strives to hurt the other to the last degree. Eleanor goes to the man of whom Michael is most jealous, but he sees she does not love him and brings her back. Michael goes to a prostitute, but cannot bring himself to the actual commission of any breach of loyalty to Eleanor, and leaves the woman puzzled by his apparently insane behavior. In the actual performance this scene was the most effective one, possibly because the leading actress, who was playing Eleanor without any apparent understanding of the part, was not on the stage. The entire interpretation, in fact, was inadequate, yet even in the reading, the subtle interplay of emotion flashes almost too quickly. But there are fine moments in *Welded*. When after their return and apparent reconciliation the old struggle comes up again, Eleanor goes to the door to leave her husband. But *"she raises her hand and knocks on the door softly—then stops to listen. In a far-away voice she speaks. No. Never again, 'come out.' She opens the door and turns to Cape with a strange smile.* It opens inward, Michael." Both come to a realization that *"it is impossible that they should ever deny life, through each other, again."* But one is not certain that the fusion has been complete.

During the spring of 1924 there was produced at the Provincetown Theatre, a dramatization by O'Neill of *The Ancient Mariner*. While it was not a popular success, the experiment was interesting, for the dramatic qualities of Coleridge's poem were made evident. The Ancient Mariner waits outside the house in which the wedding is to take place and as the Wedding Guest approaches, he demands his attention and proceeds to tell him the story. The scenes are then portrayed on the back stage while the Mariner describes and narrates in front. Perhaps the most definite impression carried away from the rehearsal which I attended was O'Neill's knowledge of the sea, evidenced by his direction of the sailors, and the greater stage effect their actions produced after he had shown them how things were really done on shipboard.

The Fountain, while not produced until 1925, was written during 1921-2, and represents an experiment in romantic symbolism. In Juan Ponce de Leon, O'Neill has not attempted to follow an historical character. He has made of him a symbol of the search for the fountain of eternal youth, who will sacrifice even love for ambition and who is more concerned for the glory of Spain than for the faith which Columbus is desirous of planting in the New World. The second scene, on the deck of the flagship of Columbus on the last day of his second voyage, was a stirring spectacle. The struggle between the ideas of national glory and of the crusading spirit was kept concrete by the brief but telling clash between Ponce de Leon and Columbus. Then as the dawning vision of the New World bursts on the ship, all kneel, each with the cross that is the symbol of their faith: for Columbus, the cross of Christ; for Juan de Leon, the sword of Spain. In a brief scene, O'Neill dramatized the two forces that settled America, but the very excellence of the scene made it difficult to rise again to the same height of theatrical effectiveness.

There is, however, a definite growth in Juan's character as we see him twenty years later, governor of Porto Rico. He is disillusioned by the struggle to reconcile the warring elements. "I have fought small things so long that I am small," he tells Luis, the Dominican friar. And then Beatriz de Cordova comes to him, as his ward, the daughter of the dead woman who had loved him, with this message:

Beatriz: "Bring him tenderness," she said. "That will repay the debt I owe him for saving me for you."—She said these words were secrets to tell you alone. What did she mean, Don Juan?

O'Neill deftly combines in Juan's mind his search for the Fountain of Youth for its own sake with the hope of becoming young again in order that he may win the love of Beatriz. It is a good stroke, too, to make Nano, the Indian, guide the

Spaniards apparently for profit, but really for revenge. The vision of Juan at the fountain, where his expedition comes to ruin, is symbolic and poetically effective. The song which has been the *motif* of the play:

> Love is a flower
> Forever blooming,
> Life is a fountain
> Forever leaping
> Upward to catch the golden sunlight,
> Upward to reach the azure heaven.
> Failing, falling
> Ever returning,
> To kiss the earth that the flower may live

changes its note. He sees Beatriz and hears her voice:

> God is a flower
> Forever blooming,
> God is a fountain
> Forever flowing—

and he recognizes the real meaning of the Fountain of Eternal Life, "the Eternal Becoming which is Beauty."

The last scene is very human in the requiem it preaches over vanity. Juan has been saved and brought to Cuba. He is waiting for Beatriz to tell her how he had loved her and how it is all over for him. Then when she comes it is to bring with her another Don Juan, his nephew, and in a flash, Juan sees how it is between them. He smiles at them; then he says briefly, "You have stolen my last gesture," and dies in an ecstasy, having found the Fountain of Eternity. It is to be regretted that *The Fountain* did not have a longer life, for it revealed O'Neill's love of beauty, and it is written on a high poetic level. The production was fatally lacking in the casting of Juan, who was played by an actor extremely capable in domestic drama, but apparently incapable of expressing heroic parts.

To those who have failed to see O'Neill's underlying purpose, it would seem a far cry from *The Fountain* to *All God's Chillun Got Wings*, written in 1923 and produced in May, 1924, at the Provincetown Playhouse. In it and *Desire Under the Elms* he seemed to search for the most repellent themes and characters. Upon first reading *All God's Chillun* the reaction is unfavorable. The subject is forbidding. Literature has usually been content to represent the result of the mating of the white and the negro race as a tragic consequence to the next generation, but it has spared us the actual miscegenation. O'Neill has boldly set precedent at naught and even to those who approached the play with natural prejudice, the character of Jim Harris, as represented by Paul Robeson, gripped the sympathy on account of his hopeless striving for the unattainable. The mating of the negro with the white girl Ella Downey was not treated suggestively and the message, if there was any, seemed to be the hopelessness of amalgamation of the races. But the play was distinctly not propaganda. It was a tragedy of aspiration on Jim's part and Ella was only a concrete symbol of that aspiration. The tragedy was deepened because Jim chose some one who did not understand anything of his aspiration, who was spiritually beneath him, while she was racially above him. The white students who are his rivals in the Bar examination start on a higher level just as Ella does, and Jim's fine qualities cannot keep him on an equality with that level. All his strength is exhausted in simply reaching for it. The madness of Ella Downey, well portrayed on the stage, was conveyed by natural soliloquy. She was just the kind of person who would talk to herself under those circumstances. It was not like the old stage soliloquy, a device to give information to the audience. It was self-revelation.

Desire Under the Elms, written and produced in November, 1924, at the Greenwich Village Theatre, and after transfer uptown, continuing until October, 1925, has been one of the most provocative of discussion of O'Neill's plays. The unthinking saw in it a coarse discussion of lust; some inhabitants of New England resented it as a distortion of sectional character. O'Neill, of course, is not concerned with either of these aspects of the drama. Like *The Hairy Ape*, it is a study of human strength, misguided in its concrete results, but inevitable as a by-product of the development of power. When asked if he felt that he had represented New England fairly he replied with a smile, "I know the country pretty well, I grew up in it—and I reported the police news in a Connecticut town." But New England should not have been so sensitive about *Desire*, for O'Neill had no intention of reflecting on any section of the country. He writes about New England because he likes to write about what he knows, but his themes are really universal. The urge of the Spring, of the warm earth which every character in the play feels, which prompts Ephraim Cabot, at seventy-five, to take a third wife, which sends his two older sons to California, which inflames the passion of Abbie Cabot for the son of Ephraim's second marriage, and Eben Cabot's reciprocal desire for her, is not merely of New England; it is drawn from life. There is a hardness, in Ephraim's nature, akin to granite which lifts him into heroic size. In one sense, he is the Puritan, with the spirituality gone, but with the indomitable will to conquer the stony farm, to make it pay, to keep it, and even when he had had the prospect of easier living, to return to it because he liked a hard task. When the sheriff comes for Abbie after she has murdered the child she has borne to Eben, Ephraim tells her: "He'd ought t' been my son, Abbie. Ye'd ought t' loved me. I'm a man. If ye'd loved me, I'd never told no sheriff on ye no matter what ye did, if they was t' brile me alive."

The play radiates from him. Eben is a compound of his father's craving for possession of the farm and the softer nature his mother bequeathed to him. He and his brothers hate their father for his tyranny, but Ephraim has been the binding force of the family. The very animals know him best and he goes to sleep with them when the human beings seem unbearable.

There can be little doubt that Greek tragedy had its influence upon *Desire*. The horror of Abbie's murder of her child, in order that she may prove to Eben, by removing the only other heir to the farm, that she loves Eben best, causes us to shudder as we do at some of the situations in Greek drama, but there is not the self-torturing introspection that in the Scandinavian drama prefaces suicide or murder. If O'Neill does not succeed in endowing Abbie's action with the dignity of the Greek, it is because he has so thoroughly convinced us of the purely carnal nature of her passion. He has not succeeded in making her a great figure as he has made Ephraim. Eben also is not quite convincing, but the stage presentation of Eben was not even physically true to O'Neill's text, while Walter Huston gave as thoroughly satisfactory a performance in the part of Ephraim as he later failed to give, in *The Fountain*, a real picture of Don Juan. The stage setting of *Desire*, in which the four rooms of the house were shown in cross section, enabled two or three scenes to be enacted simultaneously. We could watch the dance going on below to celebrate the birth of an heir, while above Eben sat brooding and then joined Abbie in bending over the cradle of the son for whose advent Ephraim is rejoicing. The result is generally ironic, and it is not at all certain that the freedom thus secured compensates for the distracting influence of the stage setting.

With *The Great God Brown*, produced January 23, 1926, at the Greenwich Village Theatre, symbolism became triumphant. In the concrete play, there are four characters: Dion Anthony, an artist, Billy Brown, a successful architect and builder, Margaret Anthony, the wife of Dion, whom Billy has always loved, and Cybel, a prostitute. From the beginning of the play, at the dance after their graduation from school, Dion wears a mask, that of a handsome mocking sensualist, to conceal his real nature, too sensitive to stand the misunderstanding of the world. Margaret loves him as his mask reveals him, the poet and brilliant dreamer, and she, without ever understanding him, bears him children, mothers him and protects his reputation from the world. She even pretends to herself that he does not visit Cybel, the prostitute. She is loyal, as Dion says, to her vanity. Cybel sees Dion without his mask, she takes off hers in his presence, and their scenes together contain some of the most striking lines in the play—such as her words to him—"(*stroking his hair maternally*) You were born with ghosts in your eyes and you were brave enough to go looking into your own dark—and you got afraid." But even more powerful is the scene in which Dion reveals to Brown his inner nature: "I've been life's lover! I've fulfilled her will and if she's through with me now it's only because I was too weak to dominate her in turn. It isn't enough to be her creature, you've got to create her or she requests you to destroy yourself."

It is the cry of the creative artist again, and the bitter words with which Dion tells Brown how life has really passed him by though the world thinks him a success, are terrible in their truth. Then Dion dies, leaving Brown his mask. Brown takes it and Margaret thinks he is Dion. It is a revenge which no one but O'Neill would have conceived. The struggle between the dual natures in Brown now tears him in pieces as it has rended Dion. With one mask on he is Brown the successful architect, but hard pressed by the loss of Dion who has been the genius of the firm. With the other mask on he is Dion, "in paradise by proxy," pursued by God and by himself, till he can stand the torture no longer and welcomes the shot of the police who believe he is the murderer of Brown. Cybel comes to warn him of the pursuit and he dies in her arms. "I don't want justice," he begs; "I want love." "There is only love," she answers. And after Brown has died with the "Our Father, Who Art" upon his lips she bursts forth with the requiem:

Always spring comes again bearing life! Always again! Always, always forever again!—Spring again!—life again!—summer and fall and death and peace again!—(*with agonized sorrow*)—but always, always, love and conception and birth and pain again— spring bearing the intolerable chalice of life again!—(*then with agonized exultance*)—bearing the glorious, blazing crown of life again! (*She stands like an idol of Earth, her eyes staring out over the world.*)

It is this speech and the heartbroken cry of Margaret, "My lover, my husband and my boy!" that remain most vividly from the performance of the play. Notwithstanding the novelty of the masks, the audience quickly responded to their symbolism and the concrete tragedy, with its final note of exaltation, held the theatre spellbound for months.

As for the underlying meaning, it would be impertinent for anyone to substitute his interpretation for that of the author. O'Neill has given it as follows:

I realize that when a playwright takes to explaining he thereby automatically places himself "in the dock." But where an open-faced avowal by the play itself of the abstract theme underlying it is made impossible by the very nature of that hidden theme, then perhaps it is justifiable for the author to confess the mystical pattern which manifests itself as an overtone in *The Great God Brown*, dimly behind and beyond the words and actions of the characters.

I had hoped the names chosen for my people would give a strong hint of this. (An old scheme, admitted—Shakespeare and multitudes since.) Dion Anthony—Dionysus and St. Anthony—the creative pagan acceptance of life, fighting eternal war with the masochistic, life-denying spirit of Christianity as represented by St. Anthony—the whole struggle resulting in this modern day in mutual exhaustion—creative joy in life for life's sake frustrated, rendered abortive, distorted by morality from Pan into Satan, into a Mephistopheles mocking himself in order to feel alive; Christianity, once heroic in martyrs for its intense faith now pleading weakly for intense belief in anything, even Godhead itself. (In the play it is Cybele, the pagan Earth Mother, who makes the assertion with authority: "Our Father, Who Art!" to the dying Brown, as it is she who tries to inspire Dion Anthony with her certainty in life for its own sake.)

Margaret is my image of the modern direct descendant of the Marguerite of *Faust*—the eternal girl-woman with a virtuous simplicity of instinct, properly oblivious to everything but the means to her end of maintaining the race.

EUGENE O'NEILL, POET AND MYSTIC

Cybel is an incarnation of Cybele, the Earth Mother doomed to segregation as a pariah in a world of unnatural laws but patronized by her segregators who are thus themselves the first victims of their laws.

Brown is the visionless demi-god of our new materialistic myth—a Success—building his life of exterior things, inwardly empty and resourceless, an uncreative creature of superficial pre-ordained social grooves, a by-product forced aside into slack waters by the deep main current of life-desire.

Dion's mask of Pan which he puts on as a boy is not only a defense against the world for the supersensitive painter-poet underneath it but also an integral part of his character as the artist. The world is not only blind to the man beneath but it also sneers at and condemns the Pan-mask it sees. After that Dion's inner self retrogresses along the line of Christian resignation until it partakes of the nature of the Saint while at the same time the outer Pan is slowly transformed by his struggle with reality into Mephistopheles. It is as Mephistopheles he falls stricken at Brown's feet after having condemned Brown to destruction by willing him his mask, but, this mask falling off as he dies, it is the Saint who kisses Brown's feet in abject contrition and pleads as a little boy to a big brother to tell him a prayer.

Brown has always envied the creative life force in Dion—what he himself lacks. When he steals Dion's mask of Mephistopheles he thinks he is gaining the power to live creatively while in reality he is only stealing that creative power made self-destructive by complete frustration. This devil of mocking doubt makes short work of him. It enters him, rending him apart, torturing and transfiguring him until he is even forced to wear a mask of his Success, William A. Brown, before the world, as well as Dion's mask toward wife and children. Thus Billy Brown becomes not himself to anyone. And thus he partakes of Dion's anguish—more poignantly, for Dion had the Mother, Cybele—and in the end out of this anguish his soul is born, a tortured Christian soul such as the dying Dion's, begging for belief, and at the last finding it on the lips of Cybel.

And now for an explanation regarding this explanation. It was far from my idea in writing *Brown* that this background pattern of conflicting tides in the soul of Man should ever overshadow and thus throw out of proportion the living drama of the recognizable human beings, Dion, Brown, Margaret and Cybel. I meant it always to be mystically within and behind them, giving them a significance beyond themselves, forcing itself through them to expression in mysterious words, symbols, actions they do not themselves comprehend. And that is as clearly as I wish an audience to comprehend it. It is Mystery—the mystery any one man or woman can feel but not understand as the meaning of any event—or accident—in any life on earth. And it is this mystery I want to realize in the theatre. The solution, if there ever be any, will probably have to be produced in a test tube and turn out to be discouragingly undramatic.

Marco Millions, published in 1927, but written before *The Great God Brown,* is a satiric romance, simpler than the latter in its symbolism. In Marco Polo, O'Neill has taken the spirit of business enterprise, willing to run risks for the sake of great gain, and while giving it a tinge of splendor has shown the deadly blindness of its materialism. As usual, however, the lesson is submerged in the dramatic portrayal, and *Marco Millions* is a series of gorgeous, barbaric scenes, through which the arch-trader, Marco Polo, progresses from youth to middle age. The Prologue, in which the dead body of the Princess Kukachin is being brought back to Cathay for burial, lifts the play out of the usual into a realm where anything may happen. It seems quite natural in that vast Persian plain to have her lips move and give this message—"Say this, I loved and died. Now I am love, and live. And living, have forgotten. And loving, can forgive." The lashing of the human beings to the chariot, since the camels have failed, and the quick whirl of fate, by which the Captain forces the three merchants to take the places of the three peasants already driven to death, strikes just the right note of barbarism, of the utter disregard of human life, which tinges the satire with deeper irony. Ironic, too, is the love of Princess Kukachin for Marco Polo, which he does not return, because in him the eternal bourgeois respects her as a thing set apart. He is true to his own Venetian maiden, Donata, not physically but sentimentally, and it is not so much fidelity as limitation which bids him keep his faith. O'Neill succeeds in keeping our interest in his hero notwithstanding his crudity, his mercantile proclivities and his failure to respond to the beauty and mystery that surround him. For he has given him courage, fidelity to his word, and an innate sense of power to meet emergencies. If he is a rascal, he is, like the Emperor Jones, an able rascal, and he has the love of adventure which animated Robert Mayo in a different way. There is enough story, too, about an interesting hero and heroine to keep the sympathy of the reader or auditor.

But *Marco Millions* is more than a story of frustrated love and successful business. From the point of view of mere locality, O'Neill frees himself even more completely than in *The Fountain* from his own experience and establishes his right to be called a world dramatist. But in another sense he remains at home, for the setting is the human soul. He has shown again how futile is the attempt to limit genius by geography, for he has caught adequately for symbolic purposes the spirit of the East. Kukachin and Marco are the representatives of the two worlds, which fronted each other in the Thirteenth Century. The patrician princess, her father the Kaan, and the lesser characters, represent the East, infinitely longer in experience, distrusting through its very knowledge its own beliefs and seeking wisdom from a younger civilization, which gives it through its trading pioneers like Marco and his relative, only materialism. To O'Neill the poet, the East is a flower breaking after sleep through the sun-baked soil of centuries to ask refreshment from a new sky of inspiration and in return meeting only a hailstorm of efficiency and common sense. If *The Great Divide* represented a new philosophy of the conflict between the East and West in the United States, O'Neill has dramatized in a fresh and vital manner the age-long difference between the East and West of the world. Those who still speak of O'Neill as depressing, should read the noble scene in which Kublai Kaan mourns over the dead body of his beloved grandchild. Whether the form be prose or verse it throbs with rhythm:

Kublai: In silence—for one concentrated moment—be proud of life! Know in your heart that the living of life can be noble!

Know that the dying of death can be noble! Be exalted by life! Be inspired by death! Be humbly proud! Be proudly grateful! Be immortal because life is immortal. Contain the harmony of womb and grave within you! Possess life as a lover—then sleep requited in the arms of death! If you awake, love again! If you sleep on, rest in peace! Who knows which? What does it matter? It is nobler not to know!

Chronicler:

We lament the shortness of life. Life at its longest is brief enough.

Too brief for the wisdom of joy, too long for the knowledge of sorrow.

Sorrow becomes despair when death comes to the young, untimely.

As I write this, *Lazarus Laughed* has not been produced or published and out of respect for the confidence which has permitted me to read the manuscript, I can deal with it only in general terms, especially so far as its highly original technique is concerned. I regret this the more as I believe it to be the most truly poetic and the most highly imaginative of O'Neill's plays. It is symbolic and becomes the climax so far of that phase of his work which begins with *The Fountain* and proceeds through *Marco Millions* and *The Great God Brown*.

It is a daring and successful attempt to dramatize the life of Lazarus, after his return from the grave. He becomes the symbol of Love and Joy that conquer Death. His message, delivered in the most impressive moments of the drama, is "There is no Death." Laughter, one of the most distinctly human of attributes, which helps to distinguish us from the other animals, is made the keynote of Lazarus' passage from the gates of Death to his glorious martyrdom. He is revealed in a series of gorgeous scenes, conquering by the power of his personality the paganism of Greece and Rome, until the Empire, in the person of Tiberius, yields to his spell and grovels for a moment at his feet. In a mystical way, which cannot be revealed without extensive quotation, Lazarus conquers by the power of Love. He has looked once into the eyes of Christ

EUGENE O'NEILL, POET AND MYSTIC

and they have smiled at each other, for they know the secret. He carries the Spirit of Christ to a world not yet ready for it, and one of the best touches in the play is the way in which Lazarus recognizes how soon the human race forgets the lofty moments of its spiritual exaltation under the press of fear and selfishness.

Caligula is the symbol of this Fear, of the human dread of concrete Death. In the end he remains in possession of the scene, begging Lazarus to forgive him for the certain forgetfulness which is to come. As Lazarus says pregnantly to the crowd, "Cæsar is your fear of man. Laugh away your Cæsars."

But there is nothing mocking in the laughter of Lazarus. It wells up from the depths of his heart and it fills every heart that hears him with joy. A few words will show the rhythmic beauty of the message:

Lazarus: Listen! In the dark peace of the grave the man called Lazarus rested. He was still weak, as one who recovers from a long illness—for living he had believed his life a sad one! (*He laughs softly and softly they all echo his laughter.*) He lay dreaming to the croon of silence, feeling as the flow of blood in his own veins the past reenter the heart of God to be renewed by faith into the future. He thought: "Men call this Death"—for he had been dead only a little while and he remembered. Then, of a sudden, a strange gay laughter trembled from his heart as though his life, so long repressed in him by fear, had found at last its voice and a song for singing. "Men call this Death," it sang. "Men call Life Death and fear it. They hide from it in horror! Their lives are spent in hiding! They love their lives in hiding! They live their loves in fearing! Their fear becomes their living! Their hate becomes their loving! They worship Life as Death!"

Chorus of Followers: (*In a chanting echo*)
   Men call Life Death and fear it
   They hide from it in horror
   Their lives are spent in hiding
   They love their lives in hiding
   They live their loves in fearing

> Their fear becomes their living
> Their hate becomes their loving
> They worship Life as Death.

Lazarus: And here the song of Lazarus' life grew pitiful. "Men must learn to live," it mourned. "Before their fear invented Death, they knew, but now they have forgotten. They must be taught to laugh again!" And Lazarus answered "Yes." (*He now addresses the crowd—especially Caligula, directly, laughingly*) Thus sang his life to Lazarus while he lay dead! Man must learn to live by laughter! (*He laughs.*)

Chorus of Lazarus' Followers:
> Ha-ah-ah-ah!
> There is no Death!
> There is only Life!
> There is only laughter!
> Ha-ah-ah-ah!

Lazarus Laughed is not only lofty poetry; it is also fine drama. The mass effects are cumulative in intensity, until the magnificent climax in the banquet hall of Tiberius, where Lazarus, the symbol of the Spirit, achieves the mastery over the supreme power of Earth. Only O'Neill could have conceived that scene, in which the dead body of Miriam, the wife of Lazarus, comes for a moment back to consciousness, to bear witness that beyond Death there is Life. Left alone by her death, he wins the intense sympathy that always goes out to the character who faces singly with the weapons of the Spirit, touched by divine sanction, the sordid strength of human power. It seems as though O'Neill had reached at this climax a height that would make of all that was to come an anticlimax, but the last Act rises still into loftier regions, amid the flames of the Roman amphitheatre. It is as though O'Neill had gathered all the longing of a sick world for hope and faith and love and shown through the ancient story the way to eternal peace.

A writer is not always the best exponent of his own artistic purpose, but in a letter sent to me in 1925, O'Neill reveals his general philosophy of composition so forcibly that it must be quoted:

enough not for in me, but down to my own technique.
But where I got myself most neglected in just where
I set most store by myself — in a lot of a part who has
elsewhere with spoken word to evoke original rhythms of beauty
where beauty appeared not — "goin", "Ap", "Apr", "God", "Caliban", "Bruin"
etc. — and my new triumphant melody of tragedy in
a vein the truth sense as one can grasp it, in the most
ignoble, debased lives. And just here is where I am
a most confirmed mystic. For I'm always, always
trying to reinterpret life in terms of lives, never just-
lives in terms of character. I'm always actually conscious
of the force behind — (fate, God, our biological past creating
our present, whatever we call it — Mystery, certainly) —
and of the one eternal tragedy of Man in his glorious
self-destructive struggle to make the force express
him instead of being, in an arrival in self-obliteration in
And my profound conviction is that this is the
only significant worth writing about and that it is
possible — or can be — to develop a tragic expression

... of transfigured modern values and symbols ~~that~~ in the theatre which may to some degree bring home to members of a modern audience their ennobling identity with the tragic figures on the stage. Of course, this is very much of a dream, but where the theatre is concerned, one must have a dream, and the Greek dream in tragedy is the noblest ever!

All the above sounds a bit confused – it's just scribbled off – but I know it will accomplish its purpose of giving you some inkling of a lot I'd say if we could talk – as we surely must sometime.

In the meantime, if your article can't wait, you might send me some questions to be answered.

With all best wishes,

Sincerely, Eugene O'Neill.

FACSIMILE OF LETTER, SLIGHTLY REDUCED, FROM EUGENE O'NEILL, QUOTED ON PAGE 199

EUGENE O'NEILL, POET AND MYSTIC

It's not in me to pose much as a "misunderstood one," but it does seem discouragingly (that is, if one lacked a sense of ironic humor!) evident to me that most of my critics don't want to see what I'm trying to do or how I'm trying to do it, although I flatter myself that end and means are characteristic, individual and positive enough not to be mistaken for anyone's else, or for those of any "modern" or "pre-modern" school. To be called a "sordid realist" one day, a "grim pessimistic Naturalist" the next, a "lying Moral Romanticist" the next, etc. is quite perplexing—not to add the *Times* editorial that settled *Desire* once and for all by calling it a "Neo-Primitive," a Matisse of the drama, as it were! So I'm really longing to explain and try and convince some sympathetic ear that I've tried to make myself a melting pot for all these methods, seeing some virtues for my ends in each of them, and thereby, if there is enough real fire in me, boil down to my own technique. But where I feel myself most neglected is just where I set most store by myself—as a bit of a poet, who has labored with the spoken word to evolve original rhythms of beauty where beauty apparently isn't—*Jones, Ape, God's Chillun, Desire*, etc.—and to see the transfiguring nobility of tragedy, in as near the Greek sense as one can grasp it, in seemingly the most ignoble, debased lives. And just here is where I am a most confirmed mystic, too, for I'm always, always trying to interpret Life in terms of lives, never just lives in terms of character. I'm always acutely conscious of the Force behind—(Fate, God, our biological past creating our present, whatever one calls it—Mystery certainly)—and of the one eternal tragedy of Man in his glorious, self-destructive struggle to make the Force express him instead of being, as an animal is, an infinitesimal incident in its expression. And my profound conviction is that this is the only subject worth writing about and that it is possible—or can be—to develop a tragic expression in terms of transfigured modern values and symbols in the theatre which may to some degree bring home to members of a modern audience their ennobling identity with the tragic figures on the stage. Of course, this is very much of a dream, but where the theatre is concerned, one must have a dream, and the Greek dream in tragedy is the noblest ever!

If Eugene O'Neill is primarily a poet, he is a playwright, too, but he is a great dramatist because he is more than a dram-- atist. His own most distinct successes in the theatre, like *Anna Christie*, interest him least, and while the theatre is in

A HISTORY OF THE AMERICAN DRAMA

his blood, he will be finally estimated not by his stage devices, like the four-roomed cottage in *Desire Under the Elms*, but by his profound imaginative interpretation of aspiring humanity, struggling upward, even through sin and shame, toward the light.

O'Neill's art is progressive, within itself and as part of our dramatic history. To those who view our national art through diminishing glasses, he seems a radical departure from all before him. But to one who views it in its steady development he was to be expected. Essentially drama is a celebration of the individual in conflict with something—Fate, circumstance, moral and social law,—which hampers or crushes him. We have seen how during the Twentieth Century, political and economic rights having been secured, the dramatists, under the leadership of William Vaughn Moody, became concerned with the problem of the individual's right to self-expression, and the sanctity of rebellion was taught, even, as in *The Masque of Judgment*, to the overthrow of God himself.

Eugene O'Neill certainly marks the next step forward. The individual no longer rebels against God or Fate for the right to express himself. He demands something more. The Creative Force as part of its responsibility for the creation of the individual, must express him. O'Neill thus indicates the essential dignity of his art. Whatever his characters may attempt, success or failure means little, but the struggle was worth while. Misguided, blundering, *The Hairy Ape* was struggling for his place in creation, and the final words of the play, "And, perhaps, the Hairy Ape at last belongs," are clear. Ephraim Cabot in *Desire* talks to God as a taskmaster in whose very "hardness" he rejoices. The New Englander of Cabot's type gloried in an adversary worthy of his steel.

But the representation of the Force of life is not always so concrete as in *Desire*. In *The Great God Brown* it manifests itself in at least four of the main characters: Dion Anthony, the painter who represents the creative spirit of art; William Brown, the successful man of today; Margaret, the normal

200

woman; Cybel, the prostitute, all representing the eternal creative instinct in different phases. For O'Neill with all his symbolism never fails to create live people, and probably three-fourths of the audience of *The Great God Brown* were held by the human struggle without seeing the symbolism at all. They saw the tragedy in the dying words of Dion and of Brown, both begging for the belief which the paganism of one and the materialism of the other had crushed out of their lives. And this is really all O'Neill expected them to see. He did not propose any solution of this eternal problem, as he proposed no solution for *Anna Christie* or *The Hairy Ape*. Back of the human lives he treats he sees a force so infinitely greater than any character that man cannot estimate it, but can only feel, dimly or ecstatically, the power he can but vaguely interpret.

Lazarus Laughed marks a new step in O'Neill's interpretation of man's origin and destiny. He has already progressed in this drama even beyond the conception of the relations of God and man which he reveals in the letter I have quoted. There is less emphasis upon the struggle of man for the expression of his personality by the Divine Force; there is more emphasis laid upon the peace which comes to man as a merciful and bountiful gift from Death. But dying is not the mere release from weariness; it is the return to a full communion with Eternal Life. It is no mere Nirvana: the individual will is preserved. While there is peace, it is not that of forgetfulness. The divine necessity of remembering is stressed always, and the great tragedy of man is that he does not remember what might keep him noble. Man longs to know what is beyond, but does not realize that if he could remember what came before, he would solve the eternal riddle. There it is—"the glory and the dream."

For O'Neill is a mystic. Generations of Celtic ancestry flower in him, just as generations of the Puritan mystic flowered in Hawthorne and Emerson. In him the Celtic nature, with its intimate relations with the past, catches a gleam now and then of the dim regions where God brought into being a nobler form of life than had before existed. Because of this clutch of the primitive which the Celt as the oldest of the Indo-European races has guarded as its birthright, O'Neill goes down into the depths of human life to study apparently de-graded forms. His audiences gasp often, comprehend some-times, but always apprehend at least that a soul is speaking to them who has something important to say.

European and Asiatic audiences, even if they often mis-take his meaning, recognize, too, in some instances better than his own countrymen, the universal note in his work. It is this lack of the parochial that has carried his plays into critical favor on the Continent, and it is to the credit of the European at least that so little attempt has been made to "derive" him from Scandinavian sources. For while O'Neill is acquainted with drama that has preceded him, the mysticism of the Celt is not the mysticism of the Teuton. With the exception of *Diff'rent* indeed, his long plays all have a lift, an exaltation which is the touchstone of true tragedy. The drama of pessi-mism is not his province, for the Celt hears, even with the fingers of fate at his throat, a cry in his ears too vibrant for the other races to hear. We have seen how in the last act of *The Straw* O'Neill dramatized the insistent hold of hope in the human breast even in the face of death.

It is this Celtic ancestry which leads him to symbolism. The race in its painting, its poetry, its religion, thinks in symbols, knowing that mysticism has to be tied down to reality by some concrete expression. The procession on Fifth Avenue in *The Hairy Ape* bothered a great many. It appeared to them to be out of the picture of realistic life on which the rest of the play seemed to be based. To O'Neill it was only an experiment, differing not in kind but in degree, for the entire play was a symbolic picture of the struggle upwards of physical strength toward a spiritual growth.

One of the most interesting characteristics of O'Neill's work lies in his refusal to be neatly classified. *Beyond the Horizon*, his first long play to be produced, and *The Great God Brown* seem at first to be of a vastly different species. But in each, the hero, Robert Mayo or Dion Anthony, represents that protest of the artist against the limitations of ordinary life, and in each his marriage, while it satisfies one demand of his nature, sets one of those limits. Of course, like any true artist, O'Neill moves on. His first plays were written in the accepted mode. But what makes *Beyond the Horizon* still the best of his naturalistic plays is not only its sterling form, but also its flavor of the romance of aspiration.

He steadily declines to be limited in his theme or locality. His roots are in America, often in the New England where he has lived so long and which he understands so well. He can describe the decadent aristocracy of the small town in New England in *The First Man* as realistically as Mary Wilkins Freeman or Sarah Orne Jewett, but he is really not concerned with their limitations except as background. In *The Fountain* the elixir of eternal youth attracts him as a romantic theme, just as it attracted Hawthorne in *Doctor Grimshawe's Secret;* in *Marco Millions,* he took an old world wanderer for a hero; in *Lazarus Laughed* he passed beyond the gates of Death.

It is not only in his choice of such a theme as the water of eternal life that he resembles Hawthorne. In those striking passages in Emerson's *Journals* in which he describes Hawthorne's burial, the Concord philosopher tells us:

Clarke in the church said that Hawthorne had done more justice than any other to the shades of life, shown a sympathy with the crime in our nature, and like Jesus, was the friend of sinners.

Discussion raged at one time over the problem of the apparent contradiction between Hawthorne's retired life at Salem, Lenox or Concord and his deep knowledge of the effects of sin and even crime upon the consciences of his characters. No such problem occurs in the case of O'Neill. His wanderings in search of adventure and his experience as a reporter have both brought him into contact with the seamy side of human nature. But the important point does not lie in a discussion of their material. The significant fact remains that twice at least during our literary history a poet has used the medium of prose to reveal the beauty that lies in the human soul, even though it has gone through the crucible of temptation and sin, to fuse away the dross of life. To Hawthorne, Hester Prynne and Donatello were finer clay than if adultery and murder had not stained them, because through suffering they won a character not theirs before. Anna Christie, purified from her sordid past by the cleansing power of the "old davil, sea," Dion Anthony, hiding his longing to create under the mask of the sensualist, are expressions of the same sympathy with sinners. To Hawthorne's serene certainty of form O'Neill has not attained. O'Neill is working in a different medium, and has not even yet learned to avoid certain uglinesses of detail which are most apparent in *Diff'rent*, *The Hairy Ape*, and *Desire Under the Elms*.

These defects, however, are the result of misguided power, never of weakness or carelessness. Like Hawthorne again, O'Neill ruthlessly destroys his work if it is not up to his standard. Nineteen of his plays, many of which were in one act, have been sent to oblivion. Here again the romantic stories about his manuscripts being accidentally lost in an old trunk down in Washington Square are a part of the myth that is persistently being built up around him. There were no manuscripts left by him to such a chance, but he deliberately destroyed his less artistic efforts to keep him, as he humorously says, "out of temptation."

For O'Neill takes his art, but not himself, quite seriously. The O'Neill myth amuses him, for the sincere personality back of his plays has nothing of the theatre in his appearance or general outlook. He works in his own way—that is his right. Like anyone who does important work, he is intense in his concentration, and while the letters incorporated in this chapter are written in a clear and readable script, the manuscript of his plays is characteristic of the absorption of the artist in his work. The script begins in a fairly normal hand, then as it progresses, the writing becomes smaller and more crowded, until, as the mood grows more intense, it becomes almost illegible to the normal eye. Like all poets and mystics, he sees before him the supreme goal; the distractions of life and the opinions of men are apparently of not much significance, although O'Neill is not in any real sense a recluse. He lives in his home in Connecticut, a convenient place of escape, for work of the kind he is doing needs the quiet in which concentrated effort alone is possible. But he assumes none of the airs of the mystic, for the part is not assumed. It is only one of the phases of O'Neill's work which lifts him out of the parochial and leads him to the universal atmosphere in which great art flowers.

One group of our playwrights may go on painting amusing pictures which the comic supplement throws upon the screen of American life. That our audiences should crowd the theatres where such plays are produced is easily understood. But it is encouraging that when an artist like Eugene O'Neill resolutely sets his face against the picturing of the merely little things of life he should have won the wide recognition he already enjoys. He paints little souls and big souls, but he never consciously gives us the unimportant or the mean. We may not like all of his characters—we may even shudder at them—like the Emperor Jones himself, but O'Neill found in that thief and murderer a spark that distinguished him from all the natives of that imaginary island. We agree with the epitaph of Smithers: " 'E's a better man than the lot o' you put together."

O'Neill found that spark, of course, because he put it there. Even in the most degraded man, O'Neill recognizes the saving grace that comes from his divine origin. Nearly a century ago, Emerson called this universal brotherhood in us the creation of the Oversoul, the Life Force that animates everything, and founded on this conception his gospel of hope. O'Neill has dared to go further into the depths than Emerson or Hawthorne, for the Puritan had reactions of conservatism from which the Celt is free. But it is a pitiful stupidity of criticism that sees only the repellent in *All God's Chillun Got Wings* or *Desire Under the Elms.* I confess frankly that on reading the first I could see little beauty in it, but in the theatre I recog-- nized again the vision of the poet who saw more deeply than I. I felt, too, my academic objections to soliloquy on the stage go by the board, when I recognized that to these characters soliloquy was natural. But I have become accustomed to seeing theatrical rules broken with success by O'Neill because he prac- tically never breaks dramatic laws. It is a great thing for art when academic definitions are shattered by creative genius, and it is to be hoped he will go on shattering them. For he has become the concrete expression of the greatest principle in art, that of freedom, freedom to choose one's subject any- where, to treat it in any manner, provided always that the characters are great figures and the treatment is sincere.

It is, fortunately, too soon to pass any final judgment upon Eugene O'Neill, but it is high time to arrive at some perspec- tive concerning him. For he is, I think, passing through a phase of his development. His material has always been ro- mantic, whether it be chosen from the slums of New York or Xanadu in the Thirteenth Century. But he began with a treatment which is essentially realistic and in *Beyond the Horizon* he proved that there is no antithesis between romantic material and realistic treatment, but that the latter corrects and adjusts the imaginative processes of the first. With *The Hairy Ape* he passed into a stage of symbolic treatment which may have reached its height in *The Great God Brown* and *Laz- arus Laughed.* The danger here lies in the fact that romance and symbolism mix too easily, and the result may become con- fusion. But no matter what new phase in his development may come, there will be apparent still the poet, brooding and cre- ating, and the mystic, letting speak through him the Creative Force that lifts humanity from the beast that passes to the man who eternally aspires.

CHAPTER XXII

THE NEW REALISM OF CHARACTER

IT WOULD be a mistake to attribute to the Great War any of the changes which came in the drama about the beginning of the third decade of the new century. It is too early even to characterize those changes with finality and to ascertain their causes would naturally be more difficult. Yet the alterations in the standards of living and in moral and social judgments which came as a consequence of the disturbed mind of the world have been reflected in our drama. We suffered less change than Europe and our drama reflects in consequence less change. In life itself the chief results seem to be a natural reaction against the unity of purpose which war brings with it. There has come in consequence a confusion of standards, and on the part of the younger generation a scrutiny, pitiless in its rejection of authority and pitiful in its brave show of self-confidence, of institutions and laws, of manners and morals, in an effort to establish its own standards of life.

This searching scrutiny has resulted in drama in an examination of the institution of marriage, into the relations of parents and children, and the relations of the individual to society. These are of course no new themes; the novelty has come in the method of approach. There has too often been a mere sharpening of the tone and tempo, as in the melodrama, an underlining of the verbal expression, which is always a confession of weakness, for meaning and expression should be forcible enough to underline themselves.

Drama, of course, follows, not precedes, the progress of life. Conflicts, which are the life of drama, have often been in process

207

of settlement, while the tone of the plays which record these conflicts has still seemed daring. This is sometimes because human beings decline to recognize a social or moral change until long after it has occurred, and sometimes because the change has after all not been so fundamental as it at first appeared. Notwithstanding all the assaults upon marriage, for example, the institution will probably continue and if two people love each other and have children it will probably be happy—otherwise not. Attacks upon social or moral conventions seem more daring on the stage than they do in the novel, partly because in the theatre we feel compelled to observe with the traditions and standards of the herd, while in reading the novel, we judge entirely by our own standards.

The most significant tendency in the American drama since 1920 has been the attempt to deal sincerely with character. This realism of treatment may have arisen from the searching scrutiny of all human institutions to which allusion has already been made. But as yet generalizations are a bit dangerous. We have seen that the type play and the melodrama have not changed materially. The play of social life has progressed, but it is in the field of what is called for lack of a better name, domestic drama, that the most definite advance has been made. By domestic drama I mean the play that grows out of complications and conflicts among closely related people, drawn usually from a group not distinguished by acute social consciousness, but more concerned with the personal aspects of the struggle.

Two playwrights, both novelists, carry over into the third decade the drama of revolt, and link the impulse inspired directly by Moody to a newer technique. Zona Gale (1874-1938) won the Pulitzer Prize in 1921 with her dramatization of *Miss Lulu Bett*. Miss Lulu Bett, both in the story and the play, is the typical unmarried woman without a career beyond that of helping her married sister and enduring her brother-in-law's teasing. Her rebellion and her flight with her lover, who has concealed his earlier marriage in the belief that his wife is dead, give an opportunity for Lulu Bett to develop her character through her return to face the emptiness of her life and the taunts of her family. In the version first played, she departs to fight her battle alone, though with a new offer of marriage, one might say, on file. This ending was changed, to bring the first lover back, unmarried, and Miss Gale has published two third Acts, in the printed play, for her justification, or protest. Neither version is very impressive, but she has secured the humor which springs from a clever reproduction of dullness.

In *Mr. Pitt* (1924) Miss Gale made an attempt, not altogether successful, in the drama of futility. In adapting her novel of *Birth* for the stage she sharpened the lines of conduct materially, and made Mr. Pitt, the paper hanger, who longs to be something better and finer, a sympathetic character, well acted by Walter Huston, especially in the climax of the second Act, when he promises himself that he will break through the tangle of his life. The recognition of his inherent nobility by Rachel Arrowsmith, the gentlewoman, while his wife with her hopeless meanness of character never understands him, was also better expressed on the stage than in the novel.

Of more significance in the theatre, Susan Glaspell (1882-   ) and her husband, George Cram Cook, were perhaps the two driving forces in the inception of the Provincetown Players. Her *Suppressed Desires*, a one-act play which formed one of the two offerings on the first bill of that group, in the summer of 1915, is a delightful satire on the cult of self-expression. Through the trying period of establishment, her one-act plays formed with the work of O'Neill the most significant source of supply to the Provincetown Players. Among these the best perhaps is *Trifles*, a tense little scene in a farmhouse after the death of a man and the arrest of his wife on suspicion. Two women neighbors destroy the evidence which pointed to a motive, while the sheriff and county attorney are examining the premises. It is distinctly dramatic, and the effect of the personality of the absent wife is suggested by deft touches.

This representation of an absent woman through the conversation of others, may have led to the writing of Miss Glaspell's three-act play, *Bernice* (1919). While there is too much talk for the amount of action, nevertheless there is real power in the conception. The characters are the husband, the father, the best friend, and the servant of Bernice, with a note of contrast in her sister-in-law. Bernice has affected them all vitally and she has died suddenly, while her husband was away. He has been unfaithful to her and has not returned promptly to his home on his return from Europe. The character that impresses one most is that of Abbie, the servant who has been with Bernice since her birth. She never steps out of her place as a servant; she is laconic and tries to keep away from them all. This makes all the more striking her first revelation to Craig Norris, Bernice's husband, that Bernice had killed herself. The effect on Craig is to plunge him into remorse, yet he feels also a strange kind of joy, for it proves to him that Bernice loved him more deeply than he had ever suspected, and the veil that had separated him from her seems to have been lifted. He tells the secret to Margaret, her friend, alone and there is much talk between them concerning his trifling with life, which prepares the way, however, for Abbie's second revelation to Margaret that Bernice had not killed herself but had made Abbie promise to tell her husband that she had done so. Margaret is thrown into a terrible situation; she longs to tell Craig and yet when she sees that the lie has begun to work great changes for the better in him, that he feels that he must begin to be worthy of the love of the woman who had gone to her death because of her passion for him, she hesitates to enlighten him. And then she realizes that Bernice had sent this message to save him from the littleness of his life, knowing that only such a shock could work the miracle. *Bernice* is a play that lives in one's memory. It is too long drawn out but time is necessary for the character changes in Craig Norris, and Abbie's disclosures could not have been made except at intervals, granted her inarticulate guarded nature, shot through with devotion to her mistress. Abbie was played by Susan Glaspell at the Provincetown production.

In *The Inheritors* (1921) she produced another important play. It is a study of the way in which the liberals of one generation become the conservatives of the next. The theme had been treated by Bennett and Knoblock in *Milestones*, but Miss Glaspell gave to her play a distinctly American setting. Silas Morton, a pioneer in the Middle West, which Miss Glaspell knows well, founds in 1879 a college to carry on his liberal views, encouraged by his friend, Felix Fejevary, an exile from Hungary on account of his radical opinions. By 1920, the son of Count Fejevary has become intrenched in the responsibility and the conservatism of the Board of Trustees but the third generation of Mortons, represented by the granddaughter, has become definitely radical. One of the best touches is the attitude of the college professor, who is partly a sincere radical and partly anxious for martyrdom. The trouble with *The Inheritors* is its special pleading. It has held the stage, however, in this country and in England, and it represents Miss Glaspell's unquenchable love for freedom of speech.

Those who saw *The Verge*, as given by the Provincetown Players in 1921, witnessed an extraordinary play. It is a study of a neurotic woman who is going insane. She has a great desire to create new forms of life and is planting new flowers and developing new species. She is also experimenting with human souls in the shape of two men, friends of hers who are staying in the house. In the last act she kills one of these as a gift to him. Then she fires off a pistol and sings "Nearer, My God, to Thee" as the curtain goes down. Margaret Wycherly played the part of Claire in a very masterly way. She showed the gradual increase in violence of the symptoms of a woman in that condition, but the question remains, is the whole thing worth while? If there is one coherent idea in the play it is that only through violent suffering and wreckage of lives can any growth be attained. As this does not happen to be true the play fails by the test of verity. After all, Susan Glaspell and Zona Gale, keen as their love for the theatre may be, are more experimental than systematic in their work for it. This is shown clearly when we contrast their achievement with the plays of an expert craftsman, who devotes his entire attention to the theatre.

Among the new domestic dramas of character, *The Hero* (1921) by Gilbert Emery, is a model. The author, whose brilliant social comedy, *Episode*, has already been discussed, was born in Naples, New York, of New England ancestry. An Amherst graduate, he came into the theatre after writing short stories and verse, and after experiences of continental life both before and during the Great War, in which he held a commission as First Lieutenant. He has gained a thorough knowledge of the stage through his professional experience as an actor since his return from military service and *The Hero* is remarkable not only on account of its fidelity to the life of a small town, which Emery knows well, but also from its compact structure and its cumulative effect.

It is a study of the contrasted natures of two brothers, Andrew and Oswald Lane, and of their relations with Hester, Andrew's wife. Oswald has gone to France, leaving behind him a burden of broken pledges and of financial dishonesty, which Andrew has quietly assumed. When Oswald returns after the war, Emery shows skilfully how the prodigal hero, with a war cross, and a personal charm, fascinates his sister-in-law, and wins the passionate love of Marthe, a young Belgian refugee, who is living in Andrew's home. The war has changed Oswald little; he takes, whenever he can, what life gives him, and he has no sense of moral obligation. The one spark of good in him seems to be his response to the adoration of his little nephew, whom he teaches to build a camp fire and otherwise entertains. But he shows no disposition to take up any business and when Andrew hints, expostulates and finally explains clearly how limited his own resources are, the feminine psychology which turns his mother and wife against him for daring to deal harshly with a hero like Oswald is depicted with

Yours Sincerely
Gilbert Emery

the vividness of an etching. Oswald has his own standards, it is true, and when Hester shows him that she will be his for the asking, he implicitly declines her offer in a masterly scene, in which his cynical indifference to any interest but his own makes him brutal in his casual remark—"Hess—lemme give you a tip. You stick to your kid—he's hero enough for you." He gets her out of the room in order that he may steal the treasury of the church, for which Andrew is responsible, and thereby return to France to "his own kind of girl." Hester returns with a blanket for him and sees him take the money. Marthe, the Belgian girl, sees Hester in her turn and the curtain of the second Act comes down on a strong situation, in which only one word is spoken.

What made *The Hero* noteworthy in the theatre was its close hold on the principle of suspense. The third Act keeps one tense with a sense of brooding disaster, but the playwright has not, as is usual in domestic drama, **given away** his supreme moment in advance. When it comes it is woven out of the characters, prepared for carefully, but expressed swiftly and inevitably. Andrew returns in the morning upon a scene in which Hester is fighting to keep Oswald from leaving with the money. He defies her to stop him, threatening to expose her, and brutally leaving her Marthe as a legacy. Then when we seem to see the wrecks of a play before us, Emery lifts them into a climax. The fire bell rings as Andrew comes in and Hester and he rush out, fearing for the little boy, for Marthe has come in from her fruitless pursuit of Oswald with the one word "Kindergarten" on her lips. In a moment they re-enter with little Andy wrapped in Oswald's coat. The tragedy is unfolded in perfect simplicity:

Little Andy: I ain't hurted, mummy—not a bit. Uncle Oswal' come and got me. He found me. The fire got ev'rywhere, and Uncle Oswal' come. Where's Uncle Oswal'?
Hester: (*To her husband*) Tell me.
Andrew: He's gone.
Hester: Tell me.

Andrew: I don' know. The kindergarten. Andy lit a camp fire, he says, and it was all afire in no time, they say. Andy was missing and Oswald run in and got him. And then Oswald run back again, after another little boy, that's what they say—and the roof fell in on 'em. Oh, God—it's awful! Burned to death! That's his overcoat there on baby. And he's gone. And I was here a-talking and making jokes. It's awful.

Hester: (*A look of awe on her face*) Oh, Oswald could do that! Oh, thank God!

Then with our knowledge of Oswald's utter selfishness, we listen to Andrew's regret for the hard words he had used to him. Hester lies bravely with an improvised message of good-by from Oswald to his brother and then the play proceeds to its close:

Hester: Andrew, that money—the collection—the money you—
Andrew: Yes?
Hester: I gave it—to Oswald—to put it in the bank.
Andrew: Now? This morning?
Hester: Just now.
Andrew: (*Slowly, scarcely comprehending*) Then it's gone. It's burned. With him.
Hester: He took it—to put it in the bank.
Andrew: (*Sighing heavily, then squaring himself to meet the blow*) Then we'll have to make it up. That's all. We'll have to make it up—
Hester: Yes. We'll have to pay it. Oh, Andy, if you knew . . .
Andrew: 'Tain't your fault, Hester. Don't you worry. Natural enough for you to give it to him to put in the bank for you. Don't fret, honey, 'bout that.
Hester: Oh, Andy,—Andy! Why didn't I understand?
Andrew: Sh!— It's all right. Seems sometimes as though everything hits you all in a heap. . . . We'll get out of it somehow. . . . I'm so darn sorry for you, Hess. I know how you miss all the nice things that other girls have—
Hester: Andrew! Don't!
Andrew: Well, it's true—an' I don't blame you. Maybe I can borrow a little money somewhere. . . . Yes. It's tough, but it's got to be done.
Hester: I don't mind, Andrew. I'll help you. Oh, Andy—I'm so—so sorry.

Andrew: Why, of course. There doesn't anything matter much, dear, so long as I got you and the boy. Thank God for that!— Now I must go an' find ma. Poor ma! And then— go back there to—him—

Hester: (*Looking into his eyes with a new love born of her suffering and shame*) You are a good man, Andrew! Now I know! A good, *good* man.

Andrew: (*Humbly and simply taking her into his arms*) Me? I'm just old Andy, I am. But Os—Os was a hero.

The quotations cannot do justice to the art with which Emery drew three of the most living characters in modern drama. His vivid contrasts between the moral and physical hero, not types but real people, was rewarded by critical acclaim, but the keen analysis of the psychology of the returned soldier came perhaps too early for popular success. To his eternal credit, he refused to accede to managerial requests that he modify the ending by bringing Oswald back to marry Marthe, preferring to let the play pass from the stage into dramatic literature.

While *The Hero* had only a moderate run, *Tarnish*, (1923) Emery's next play, was a popular success. Though probably not on the whole as significant as *The Hero*, it is a worthy companion to it, for it is based on the universal motive of the triumph of love over circumstances, over doubt, and over human weakness. The central character is that of Letitia Tevis, a young girl whose strong yet delicate personality is set against a background of a complaining mother, a dissolute father, and a lover, Emmet Carr, whose past rises concretely in the person of Nettie Dark, the manicure girl, the active cause of what might have been a tragedy. Emery, of course, did not force a happy ending, but the stage directions of the printed version are an implicit defense of his final scene. Tishy has said good-by to Carr because she finds out that he, like all the rest, is tarnished. Then Mrs. Healey, the Irish charwoman, finds her in tears and comforts her.

Mrs. Healey: There's a lad on the stairs out there. . . . I don't know what you said to him, but if you love him, keep him, **for**

there's nothing worth the keeping in this world but love—
My God, they're a poor lot, the men, all of 'em, and dirty,
too—but the thing is, darlin', to get one that cleans easy.

The stage directions explain that Tishy forgives him because
of her love for him which will not let him go. No one who
saw the performance of Ann Harding can need any explanations. In this, her first part of importance, she won a place
for herself as an actress of distinction. The entire cast, in
fact, illustrated the high level of the acting of today. But,
after all, Emery provided them with a play based on the
old unities of time, of place, and of action, portraying a life
that is familiar to thousands of the inhabitants of New York
City by means of a conversation that preserved the necessary compromise between the language of literature and that
which is actually spoken by human beings. The play is a comedy in the sense that Balzac wrote comedy, but it rises above
the usual stage comedy because the material is not made sport
of, it is treated seriously. The sympathy of the audience goes
out completely to the high-hearted woman of twenty-three,
who squares herself to meet the blows of circumstance, quietly
and with dignity, and, to the onlooker, with infinite pathos.
But it is not only that Letitia Tevis exists—the important
thing is that she exists only in America.

While Arthur Richman (1886-1944) has written an attractive romance in *Not So Long Ago*, and a popular social comedy, *The Awful Truth*, his claim to consideration rests upon
a powerful domestic drama, *Ambush* (1921). The theme
of the play is put very forcibly by Mrs. Jennison, who tells
Walter Nichols, the central character, how the circumstances
of life lie in ambush to prevent him from living the upright,
decent life he desires. *Ambush* is laid in the home of a clerk
of moderate means, whose daughter brings him to shame
through her reckless love of pleasure and whose wife's tacit
support of her daughter's conduct leaves him helpless to meet
the situation. *Ambush* was terrible in its fidelity to the sordid
side of life, was well constructed and written with sincerity.

Richman has done nothing since that equals it in power. There was promise in the opening of *A Serpent's Tooth* (1922) but the play went to pieces in the last Act. To one auditor, it seemed as though some violence had been done to the original conception out of regard for the box office.

One of the most encouraging signs of the new spirit in the drama was the reform of Owen Davis (1874-   ), who having written over one hundred melodramas of a negligible quality, was prompted partly by the achievements of other native playwrights and partly by a study of Ibsen to write more sincere drama. Davis had graduated from Harvard in 1893 and having met with no response in his efforts to write tragedy in verse, turned his attention to playwriting as a business. In 1921 he wrote *The Detour* in which he tried to depict character rather than mere types, and while the play did not succeed financially, it was recognized by the discriminating as being among the best of the season's products. The theme of *The Detour* is the eternal quality of hope. Helen Hardy is the wife of a farmer on Long Island. Years before she had given up her dream of a career to marry her husband, who is land hungry, and she determines that her daughter Kate shall not make the same mistake. They have saved money enough to send Kate to an art school in New York, and then Steve, her father, demands that she give him the money to buy a lot which belongs to Tom Lane, Kate's lover. Helen defies her husband and decides to go to New York with Kate. This situation is developed by means of comedy and the dialogue is bright and direct. Helen's character is painted in these few words:

"I get so tired of sayin' nothin' but just exactly what's so and listenin' to folks that don't ever mean the least mite more'n they say, or the least mite less!"

A scene which reveals Davis's insight occurs when Steve Hardy and Lamont, a painter, are looking at Kate's work, not knowing that she overhears them:

Steve: I guess no man knows less about art, and such as that,
than I do, but it happened to be a bit of land around here she
painted, and I know land.

Dana: Your opinion should be of as much value then as my
own—what do you think of this yourself?

Steve: Somehow it seems to me it don't look like it ought—not
just like—I don't know—it's Tom Lane's twenty acres all
right—but it don't look just like it was alive somehow, does
it?

Dana: No.

Steve: It's grass but it ain't growing grass; there's the spring
wheat, but you can't somehow think of its ever ripening—
like wheat does.

Dana: No.

It is in such quiet moments as this that the course of a
life is changed. But in Kate's case it is not a tragedy; she
has been driven on more by her mother's desire than her own
ambition. She settles down with Tom contentedly while Helen
starts saving again for the grand-child who may come some
day. Even her husband's ridicule does not daunt her, for as
the curtain falls, "She is standing, her face glorified, looking
out into the future, her heart swelling with eternal hope." Her
husband has his land, her daughter and Tom have their love;
she has saved her power of dreaming.

Davis was discouraged by the reception of *The Detour*, but
decided that before he returned to the kind of play he could
market, he would write "one more good play." In consequence,
he undertook a study of the New England character, not the
conventional type, but the hard inarticulate survivals of long
struggle with the soil. Davis, who is descended from "generations of Northern Maine, small-town folk" to quote from his
introduction to *Ice Bound* (1923), knows his people well.
There is a certain similarity in the first Act of *Ice Bound* to
the first Act of *The First Man*, in the tribal conclave, but it
may be because both O'Neill and Davis know their people so
well. The Jordans, all waiting for their mother to die, turn
on Jane, the young cousin, who has tended their mother, and
then on Ben, the youngest and the prodigal. But they fawn

on Jane when they find she is left the property and she forces
Ben to work for her, for he is under indictment for arson and
has no option. Her reason for trying to reform him is revealed
in a masterly scene in which Jane reads to Judge Bradford,
who loves her, the letter Mrs. Jordan had left for her:

Jane: "My dear Jane, the doctor tells me I haven't long to live,
and so I'm doing this, the meanest thing I think I've ever
done to you. I'm leaving you the Jordan money. Since
my husband died there has been just one person I could get
to care about, that's Ben, who was my baby so long after
all the others had forgotten how to love me. And Ben's a
bad son, and a bad man. I can't leave him the money; he'd
squander it, and the Jordans' money came hard."

Judge: Poor woman! It was a bitter thing for her to have to
write like that.

Jane: "If squandering the money would bring him happiness, I'd
face all the Jordans in the other world and laugh at them,
but I know there's only just one chance to save my boy—
through a woman who will hold out her heart to him and let
him trample on it as he has on mine."

Judge: (*in sudden fear*) Jane!

Jane: "Who'd work, and pray, and live for him, until as age
comes on and maybe he gets a little tired, he'll turn to her.
And you're that woman, Jane! You've loved him ever since
you came to us. Although he doesn't even know it. The
Jordan name is his, the money's yours, and maybe there'll
be another life for you to guard. God knows it isn't much
I'm leaving you, but you can't refuse it, because you love
him, and when he knows the money's yours he will want to
marry you. I'm a wicked old woman. Maybe you'll learn
to forgive me as time goes on—it takes a long time to make
a Jordan."

There is little reformation of Ben; Jane marries him under
no illusions as to her permanent happiness, but simply because
she loves him. After all, no one ever loves anyone else for a
reason!

Davis was rewarded for his reformation by the Pulitzer
Prize, which was awarded to *Ice Bound*. It can hardly be said
with justice that his work since then has come up to that level.

He has written clever farces like *The Nervous Wreck*, murder mystery plays and a more ambitious attempt at a character study in *Gentle Grafters* (1926), a story of the girl who attempts to skirt the edge of danger, which a weak third Act disfigured. The desire of Davis to write drama that is worth while can hardly be questioned, but his very prolific habits are a handicap.

The progress from the type play to the character study is illustrated by the work of an interesting partnership in the drama. George S. Kaufman (1889-   ) and Marcus Cook Connelly (1890-   ), both born in Western Pennsylvania and both newspaper men, first attracted attention by their clever comedy *Dulcy* (1921). It was natural that they should dramatize the material of the newspaper and they selected a character created by Franklin P. Adams, then a columnist for the New York *Tribune*. *Dulcy* celebrated the stupid, well-meaning married woman, who almost wrecks her husband's prospects by her plans and revelations during the week-end party which has been given to secure them. The two playwrights recognized that dullness can be made entertaining, if it is constantly contrasted with cleverness, so they provided one of the best character parts in her young brother, and they aroused, in an inimitable scene, a responsive chord in all who have suffered from the recital of the plot of a moving picture.

To the Ladies (1922) is an improvement upon *Dulcy* because the types are less eccentric and the characters of Leonard and Elsie Beebe achieve reality. Elsie is the opposite of Dulcy; she is the guiding spirit of the household, saving her husband from the consequences of his stupidity or conceit and not only preserving his own self-respect, but also fighting hard for her own belief in him. Kaufman and Connelly recognized the truth that the most precious asset in our lives consists in our illusions, and Elsie Beebe won the hearts of her audiences and kept them. Her brave little speech at the end of the first Act when she talks to Mr. Kincaid, Leonard's employer, through Mrs. Kincaid, because she sees that Leonard has lost his chance to be invited to the great annual banquet of the Kincaid Piano Company, is her first high moment. Kincaid, who is a delightful picture of the self-important business man, has been deeply hurt by discovering that Leonard had borrowed money on his Kincaid Piano. He is about to leave, remarking that there is no reason why Elsie should explain the matter to him when she cries:

Oh, but there is! If I—if I could only make you understand! But, of course, you've never been poor—either of you—I mean— really poor—so that a few dollars actually mattered, and you had to be awful careful what you did with them. So that you had to plan weeks ahead . . . so much for each little thing, and if something came up that you hadn't counted on, and that just *had* to be paid, why, it meant doing without something that you— almost had to have to live. But you see—we've—done that— ever since we're married. And then, when it looks as though you've almost helped each other out of it—and the chance comes— oh, if I could only make you understand . . .

The play was praised highly for its satiric portrayal of the "public banquet," and it was amusing, but the climax was one in which character is wrought out of situation. Leonard has copied his speech out of a manual of speech making and is horrified to hear his rival, who is called just ahead of him, make the very same speech. He is paralyzed with stage fright and then Elsie rises—tells the table that he has suddenly been taken with laryngitis but that he has given her his notes and she will try to make his speech. He plays up to her and she gives them a human talk, skilfully touching Kincaid's weakness for approval, and makes the success of the evening. But what swept the audience was not only Helen Hayes' remarkable performance as Elsie; it was the quick response to the appeal of the young wife whose love had given her the inspiration that was to save them both. The light touch in *To the Ladies* concealed from many the really profound observation of life which gave birth to her, and the imagination that made her live. She has discovered that the wife who never lets her husband be discounted by the world achieves a glory for herself that is one of the actualities, and this study of young married life, treated with understanding, with sympathy and with reticence is worth many a bitter analysis of exceptional unhappiness. The authors placed in Elsie's mouth as many bright sayings as they had put stupid ones in *Dulcy*. Her words to Kincaid in the last Act—"Nearly every man that ever got any place, Mr. Kincaid, has been married, and that couldn't be just a coincidence"—are a contribution to philosophy.

Merton of the Movies (1922) is a dramatization of the story by Harry Leon Wilson and it would be difficult to assign the relative shares to the credit of the novelist, the playwrights and the actor, Glenn Hunter, in the delightful presentation on the stage. The figure of the movie-struck clerk whose sole value turns out to be his unconscious burlesque of the part he is trying to play sincerely, was certainly made to live. It was a popular success, but *The Deep Tangled Wildwood* (1923), a clever satire "upon the Winchell-Smith type of play" was a failure.

The capacity of the co-authors for satire was revealed, however, in a delightful dream play, *Beggar on Horseback* (1924). The idea of a play in which satire upon existing conditions is expressed in terms of dreams is not new, of course, but the immediate suggestion was made by Winthrop Ames, who derived the idea from reading *Hans Sonnenstössers Höllenfahrt* by Paul Apel. In order that the flavor of the satire should be native, the playwrights did not read the original German play [1] so any discussion of its effect is unnecessary. Indeed, one familiar with the work of Kaufman and Connelly hardly needs to be assured of their originality, for through all the vision of the musician, Neil McRae, who sees his future if he marries into the rich family of the Cadys, their unmistakable blend of humor steadily shines. In this dream, Mr. Cady, who manufactures "widgets," takes Neil into the business and Neil is

[1] Statement to the writer by Mr. Connelly.

tossed from one stenographer to another in the vain search for a pencil, in the clutches of the modern efficiency system that makes more impediments to progress by separating the individual from his job than the old decentralized business ever conceived. Even better is the scene of the four prison cells in which are working the greatest living novelist, poet, painter, and composer, the last being Neil himself. When the novelist stops a moment in his dictation the stenographer goes right on for he is dictating from his own last book! Neil is condemned to composing music for lines like

> You've broken my heart like you broke my heart
> So why should you break it again?

Then comes the most memorable line in the play. Neil in desperation tugs at his cell door and finds that it opens easily. "Why," he exclaims, "it was never locked!"

The dream is remarkably like a real dream; it has the peculiar assertion of verity, combined with the uncanny revelation of self-scrutiny and of the observation of others that is the experience of competent dreamers. The play is a fine expression of the resentment of the artist, the man who can do things that no one else can do, for the attitude of the Cadys and their like, whose ambition is to do everything just like other people and who are contemptuous of those who show originality. The title is a clever use of the phrase recorded by Robert Greene in his *Card of Fancie* in 1588: "Set a beggar on horseback, they say, and he will never alight."

Beggar on Horseback is the last collaboration, so far, of Kaufman and Connelly. There was no difference, but it was felt by both that it would be well for them to write separately for a time. The result has hardly been fortunate for the drama. Kaufman has written since then one original play, *The Butter and Egg Man* (1925). This is a clever farce, dealing with theatrical life, but while it was a financial success, it is hardly significant. It is in fact, a backward step, for it is a farce made up of hard caricature types, and depends entirely upon its situations. *Minick* (1924), which he wrote in collaboration with Edna Ferber, is a dramatization of the latter's short story, *Old Man Minick*. The collaborators have published in one volume the short story and the play, together with an amusing account of the way in which the dramatization was made. *Minick*, however, is not important. It is the product of careful observation of life, which runs, however, to caricature, and there is little charm in it, however much amusement it provided on the stage. *The Good Fellow* (1926) was also a collaboration and was a failure.

Connelly has written one original play alone, *The Wisdom Tooth* (1926). It is a charming comedy, with a note of fantasy. Bemis is just the average senior clerk. He has had ambitions when he was a boy, but they have been submerged by the hard knocks of the city and an inferiority complex. In his boarding house, Sally Field sees the spark in him and tries to bring it out. He sees also in a dream the boy he used to be and he is visited by his grand-parents, a delightfully conceived pair. Under their influence he braves his employer, to protest against injustice, and the way in which the boy of his visions goes with him concretely is very appealing. Of course even this interview turns out to be a dream and when he does call up his employer, he is promptly discharged. But he has Sally's appreciation and the consciousness of his own self-respect.

The Wisdom Tooth is of great interest, for it seems to settle the question as to which member of the original partnership contributed the imaginative quality that lifted *To the Ladies* and *Beggar on Horseback* into permanent value. There is hardly a spark of it in Kaufman's work done alone or in collaboration with others. And yet of the three other elements which made the success of the plays written together, he certainly contributed his share to the compact structure, the brilliant dialogue and the keen satire. Neither has written alone as fine a play as *To the Ladies* and it is to be hoped that they will once more bring together the nimble wit and the vivid fancy that made the union an unusual one in American play writing.

A playwright who has come definitely out of the theatre, George Kelly (1887-   ), made his début in juvenile parts in 1912, and his earlier work consisted of one-act plays, written for vaudeville. *Finders-Keepers* was the first of these; all of them have been acted with success. Probably the best are *The Flattering Word* and the first draft of *The Show-Off*. *The Flattering Word* portrayed, with keen satire, the conscious or subconscious belief in everyone's heart that he is a good actor, and the curiosity concerning the stage which possesses even those who denounce it.

Kelly's first long play to be produced, *The Torch-Bearers* (1922), is a delightful satire on the absurdities of those who use the Little Theatre as a social playground. It is laid in Philadelphia, where Kelly lives, and those who are acquainted with the intricacies, artistic and social, of amateur and semiprofessional ventures in that city, experienced an especial delight in its revelation of human vanity. The best character was Mrs. J. Duro Pampinelli, the professional exploiter of amateur theatricals, drawn from actual life, but universal enough to make an appeal anywhere. *The Torch-Bearers*, however, while the first two acts were brilliant, led to no real climax and is of interest now mainly as marking Kelly's transition from the one-act play to something more significant. It is a drama, too, of types rather than real characters, except in one or two cases. *The Show-Off* (1924) marked one step forward. It was built up from a one-act play which was already a success on the vaudeville stage when *The Torch-Bearers* was first produced. Kelly's skill was shown clearly to those who saw the play in its earlier and later forms. While the flavor of vaudeville still remains in the speeches that are obviously planted for the retort, there is no apparent padding in the structure; the character of Aubrey Piper was built up until he occupies the center of interest throughout a most amusing "transcript of life"—to quote from the program. The

scene is North Philadelphia; the family into which Aubrey
Piper marries is painted with unerring accuracy, especially
the mother, who sees through him and beyond, and whose
indignation at his boasting becomes all the more loquacious
because it really remains helplessly inarticulate. The ending
is weak; that any corporation would allow such a being as
Aubrey to extort twice the royalty they had already agreed to
give his young brother-in-law for his invention is incredible.
But through the verity of its character drawing, this play has
in it a human quality that redeems its plot. It is called a
comedy, but it was partly the subconscious tragedy of the ever
reaching for the unattainable which secured the slowly gathering sympathy of the audience for the boaster. Kelly recognized that one can allow all the other characters on the stage
to make fun of the hero, but if the heroine and the audience are
with him, the play succeeds.

Craig's Wife (1925) marked another step in Kelly's progress. *The Show-Off* was the product of acute observation;
Craig's Wife is observation fused by imagination. The types
have been still further rounded into characters, and there is a
deeper philosophy of life. Mrs. Craig is a powerful study of
the woman who attempts to dominate her entire household,
including her husband. Her desire is for authority and
through authority, security. Her god is her house, which
must be spotless although the heavens fall. For a time she
succeeds in excluding any interest that threatens her supremacy, but she is foiled partly by her husband's aunt and partly
by her own selfishness in allowing her husband to incur the
danger of an accusation of murder rather than betray her
own morbid curiosity. One by one, the inmates of her home
leave her, and the curtain descends upon her, left with her
cherished possessions, to the emptiness of her future life. In
a sense, it is the dramatization of the logical result of the feminine urge for domination, of whose opening wave *The Doll's
House* was one of the heralds. If Nora leaves her home, a

rebel, so do Mrs. Craig's subjects leave her. *Craig's Wife* was awarded the Pulitzer Prize in 1926.

The art which created *Craig's Wife* faltered a bit in *Daisy Mayme* (1926). The characters are true to life, and the two sisters who neglect Cliff Mettinger for months and arrive together when he is to return from Atlantic City with his niece, May, whose mother has recently died, are uncannily alive. But the central character, Daisy Mayme Plunkett, who accompanies Cliff and May for a visit, who senses the situation and routs one sister, converts the other into an ally and finally marries Cliff, was too blatant and breezy in the actual production quite to fit into the picture. After all, the rest of the characters, who live in a house a hundred years old, which is furnished with taste, are not barbarians if they are distinctly not smart. Just why Daisy Mayme could not have been made more effective by being somewhat subdued is a question that a little disturbs the admirer of Kelly's work. It seems as though the desire to raise a laugh, by broad strokes, has conquered the finer art which showed in *Craig's Wife*. Yet on reading the play the wistful longing on Daisy's part for a bit of romance which the matter-of-fact proposal of Cliff denies her, indicates that perhaps the actress may have been responsible for a lack of charm that the text at least permitted. But since Kelly directs his own plays, even that way out is problematical; and he might indeed reply that if Daisy Mayme were a gentlewoman, she would not be in the house at all! There was certainly no part which provided the opportunity of which Chrystal Herne took such splendid advantage in *Craig's Wife*. Kelly has still to learn that observation is not enough. But with the craftsmanship that is already his, with the apparent mastery of the devices of the theatre, his achievement will be limited only by the breadth of his vision and the power of his imagination.

While it is not so easy to characterize the work of Sidney Coe Howard (1891-1939), his development has been in the direction of the domestic character play. After graduation from the University of California in 1915 he took special courses with Professor Baker at Harvard, and has been engaged in editorial work on various magazines, since his return from the aviation service during the World War. This service is reflected in his share of *Bewitched*, already treated in the chapter on Sheldon's plays.

Howard began with romance, and his translations and adaptations such as *Sancho Panza* show his continued interest in the play which reflects the departure from the usual. *Swords* (1921) is a heroic play in a free blank verse, written for the ear and not the eye. The setting is the struggle between the Guelphs and Ghibellines but the playwright is concerned with this only as a colorful background to the central character, Fiamma, wife of Damiano, who is held as a hostage by Ugolino in his castle. The plot is at times absurd, and the play failed, but nevertheless it has some fine moments. The three men who love Fiamma—her husband, her jailer and Canetto, who betrays his master's trust for her and saves her from Ugolino, only to be killed by her inside her chamber door—are medieval, and Fiamma's momentary weakness before Canetto's passion is not badly indicated. *Swords* proved that Howard had imagination and a gift of expression.

With *They Knew What they Wanted* (1924) he showed that he had learned to write a compact play, to dare less and achieve more. To use his own expressive words, "I can get a kind of glamour around reality." He takes the Paolo and Francesca motive to California, and translates it, with modifications, into modern terms. Tony, an Italian wine grower of sixty, proposes marriage to Amy, a waitress whom he has admired at a distance. In order to win her he has sent, instead of his own photograph, one of Joe, a young American helper, whom he loves like a brother and who has written Tony's letters to her. When she arrives, she is shocked at her real husband and since Tony has been injured in his drive to the station to meet her, she gives herself to Joe that night. With the help of Pauline Lord's splendid interpretation, this incident was robbed somewhat of its sordidness. The subconscious power of expectant sexual gratification on Amy's part, made concrete by her recognition of Joe from his photograph, and the reaction from the resentment at the trick which has linked her to a man of Tony's years, were subtly portrayed by the actress who had played Anna Christie. Something fine in Amy and Joe's gratitude to Tony keep them from continuing the affair, and upon its discovery three months later Tony's action is also characteristic. At first he is about to kill Joe; then his love for Amy conquers and they decide to jog on together. One of the most interesting things about *They Knew What They Wanted* is the comparison it invites with Boker's *Francesca da Rimini*. To the audience, the ending is "satisfactory" in Bronson Howard's use of the word. We do not want Tony to be left alone and we do not want Amy, whatever her momentary impulse of passion, to go away with Joe. For we have been made to sympathize with all three of the leading characters; furthermore, their very limitations have made them unsuitable for tragedy. It was far different when Lanciotto, Paolo and Francesca played out their tragedy in Boker's great drama. They were lofty souls who could not go on with the stain of guilt upon them. But Tony and Amy can go on quite cheerfully. It is perhaps the difference between the Thirteenth and Twentieth Centuries. But the point is that both plays, the great tragedy and the fine domestic drama, ring true to their own standards. The play was one of the season's successes and won the Pulitzer Prize.

Lucky Sam McCarver (1925) failed, for reasons which are given in the preface to the published play, a dramatic document in which Howard reveals his ability to analyze his own weaknesses, together with an irrepressible youthfulness which is responsible for them—and also for much of the charm of his work. He attributes the failure of the play to its episodic character, to the fact that it is a biography of two characters, Sam McCarver, the proprietor of a night club on Second Avenue, and Carlotta Ashe, a woman of fashion who marries him because of the physical attraction he has for her, and partly because of his chivalric assumption of a murder which would have damaged her reputation if it had not been kept quiet through his influence. There are strong moments in the play and the two main characters are well portrayed. But a reading of the printed version reveals one difficulty. Howard has felt it necessary to explain by the stage directions, again and again, the emotions which the text may not make clear. Now the text of a play should not need so much explanation, and the necessity arises often from Howard's desire to make his dialogue so subtle that it is too elusive. He is depending upon the actor of course, but his own words in the preface show that he appraises the actor's part in the joint creation too highly, for he puts him above the dramatist.

A comparison with *The Boss,* in which a similar situation had been developed, reveals another weakness. So real is Sam McCarver that it is difficult to sympathize with him, and the last few minutes of the play in which he leaves Carlotta's dead body to go to a business appointment, while probably reflecting his character exactly, leave an audience in revolt. Sheldon knew his theatre better and he made Regan a more likable fellow without making him any less real. *Lucky Sam McCarver* failed, but it is an interesting piece of dramatic literature nevertheless. Its influence upon such recent successes as *Broadway* are clear, but the characters of *Broadway* are not of the same material as the characters of *Lucky Sam McCarver.*

There was a distinct advance in *Ned McCobb's Daughter* (1926) over the earlier plays. In Carrie McCobb, Howard epitomized one kind of New England character, the shrewd, courageous, honest woman who fights hard for her children's future, who forgives her worthless husband until she finds out that he has been unfaithful to her with her own housemaid, and who never wastes a moment in idle regrets. Her father, Captain McCobb, is of the race of New England sea captains that is now extinct. He has given up a fortune to protect

his good name and he has descended to the position of captain
of a ferryboat. But neither he nor his daughter sees any disgrace in her earning an honest living by her "Spa." What
alone is of importance is the preservation of their self-respect.
When the revelation comes that her husband, George Callahan,
has robbed the ferry company, Captain McCobb squares himself to meet the blow and raise the money to pay the sum that
will buy the silence of the company. He is willing to do anything that will keep his daughter and his grand-children from
disgrace. But when George, a worthless ex-convict from the
New York East Side, attempts to threaten him with the possibility of the Captain's being held as an accomplice, the fury
of the old man brings on the stroke that means death. His
daughter carries on, and meets, one after another, the disasters
in her way. With her father lying dead in the alcove of the
old McCobb parlor, she has not time for grief. When her
brother-in-law, Babe Callahan, who has "dropped in on them"
tries to comfort her she says:

> I'm all right. Thinkin' 'bout Pa's pleasant. I loved Pa. Only
> 'tain't thinkin', is it? What I was jest doin'. It's feelin'. . . .
> Seems like folks kin feel 'bout no end of things, but I don't reckon
> they think 'bout much 'cept money.

Babe Callahan is a well-drawn picture of a bootlegger operating on a large scale, who desires to use Carrie's barn as a
storehouse for liquor. His admiration for her courage, his
scorn for his weakling of a brother and his ruthless seizure of
the opportunity her need of money affords him, are vividly portrayed. He who at first has seemed to be a source of help,
turns out to be a menace to the lives of her children. But the
woman who has brushed aside the condolence of the lawyer
who has had to tell her of her desperate plight, with the words:
"The sooner we know the worst, the more time we hev t' think,"
foils the bootlegger by a clever trick. First she obtains an
extra thousand dollars by convincing him that she needs an
extension to her "Spa" to cover up the sudden appearance of
the crowd of bootleggers who will make life unbearable for

her. Then handing him her note for the amount of her debt to him, she calmly tells him the Federal agents are in the outer room and she gives him just enough time to escape. The friends she has planted in the outer restaurant answer cheerfully for the supposed agents and to Callahan's ears all Maine dialect sounds alike. He tears up the note, is frank in his admiration of her skill in thwarting him, and departs, leaving her in possession of the field. Notwithstanding the fine performance of Clare Eames as Carrie Callahan and a competent cast in general, the play reads even better than it acts, for the character contrasts have time to develop and every character rings true to life.

The Silver Cord (1926) while it has not an equal skill in the character drawing, stirs one more profoundly upon the stage, for it deals with a deeper stratum of human emotion, and it was not disturbed by the rattle of comedy, sometimes overstressed in *Ned McCobb's Daughter*. It is difficult to estimate what the effect of *The Silver Cord* might have been, had the central character, Mrs. Phelps, been interpreted by an actress of less skill than Laura Hope Crews. She brought out every shade in the character of a mother who loves her two sons with a passion that passes the maternal, which dominates their lives, breaks off the engagement of one and nearly wrecks the marriage of the other. Catlike, she prowls about the walls of their other affections which threaten to keep her out, weakening them by innuendo and undermining them by deft appeals to sympathy, until she is ready to pounce upon what is left of their love. There are some high points in *The Silver Cord*. The ending of Act II, Scene 1, when Hester, the *fiancée* of Robin, the younger son, breaks down under the strain of the broken engagement and warns Christina, the married daughter-in-law, that she must take her unborn baby away from "this awful house," is tense with unuttered terrors. And the final battle between Mrs. Phelps and Christina for David is even more intense. What stirs the audience is the way each woman fights. Mrs. Phelps draws a vivid picture of the things

she has given up for her sons, but she never steps out of the picture of Victorian motherhood. Christina, the modern girl scientist, strips the situation of reticence in language that startles us with its verity. Each in her way secures the sym-. pathy of her hearers, but Christina wins her husband, leaving Robin a prey to his mother-complex forever. The weakness of *The Silver Cord* lies in the characters of the sons. While the women are finely drawn, David and Robin are not worth fighting over, and the drama would be more significant if there were any real struggle in their minds or hearts. But they are merely confused. In drama a conflict is increased in value by the importance of the object of the battle. Yet the excellence of Howard's work is proved by the way we speculate about his characters. With a sense of the stage that is unusual, he affects to believe a play is less difficult to write than a story. Part of this is assumed, of course, but the prospect of his continued artistic success rests on the fact that he is first a sketcher of character, secondly a man of the theatre.

Like Howard, Maxwell Anderson (1888-   ) has made some contribution in literature outside of the theatre. He was born in western Pennsylvania but his youth was spent in North Dakota, where he studied at the State University, and later taught English at Leland Stanford University. After seven years of teaching, he became an editorial writer on The San Francisco *Bulletin*, the *New Republic*, the New York *Evening Globe* and later the New York *World*.

Anderson's first play to see the stage in New York City, *White Desert* (1923), was a somber tragedy of North Dakota, which failed, but which gave promise on account of its imaginative power. There are only five characters and the tragedy ensues through the loneliness of life upon the snowy plains on which Michael Kane, Sverre Peterson and their wives are driven in upon each other for company. Kane is insanely jealous of his wife, and while this is natural so far as her immediate relations with Sverre are concerned, his extortion of a confession from her as to her past emotions is not natural in the kind of

Irishman Michael Kane is supposed to be. Michael Kane might have a reverence for womanly purity that would lead him to demand a higher standard for her than for himself, but he would fight, not to destroy that purity, but to preserve it. His suspicions, translated into her mind and coming back to him after distortion, lead to the final catastrophe. He shoots her after her guilt with Sverre has been confessed and forgiven, for he cannot live with the prospect of another betrayal. *White Desert* showed the influence of the Scandinavian drama and is of interest chiefly as the beginning of Anderson's career.

In 1924 Anderson collaborated with Laurence Stallings in *What Price Glory.* Stallings, born in Georgia in 1894, and graduating from Wake Forest College in 1915, was in newspaper work until he enlisted in the United States Marine Corps in 1917. Rising to a captaincy, he was wounded at Belleau Wood, in June, 1918, and suffered an amputation of the leg. Returning to the United States he re-engaged in newspaper work and met Anderson on the staff of the *World.* Together they conceived of a new kind of war play, in which the unromantic, hard, daily grind of war would be represented. Wisely they chose for their leading characters two regular army men, Captain Flagg and Top Sergeant Quirk, and the spirit of the professional soldier, rare in our war plays, came as a novelty to the audiences, whose approval was unquestioned. Flagg and Quirk have nothing of the glamour of war, and they are not in it for a glorious adventure. They are in it to stay. They hate each other, for past rivalries and injuries, and their rivalry is made concrete by their passing passion for Charmaine, the daughter of a French tavern keeper. This thin plot carried the episodic scenes, and the philosophy of war from the point of view of a sergeant was explained with a profanity which was realistic but which since it could not do justice to the actual conditions, was perhaps unnecessarily violent for the purpose of art. Some of the play, like the episode of the General and his staff, was absurd, but the scene in the dugout cellar in a disputed town was masterly. The last scene threatened to end in violent melodrama, and then the playwrights saved the play by a touch of fine art. Flagg is worn out and drunk; but when the call to take the company in again comes, he responds with a curse. Then out of an inner room Quirk, wounded and flighty with fever, sallies. With a jest to Charmaine, their mutual mistress, he staggers out of the door. "Hey, Flagg," he calls, "wait for baby!" as the curtain falls. It was the note of quiet immediate response to duty, without display, that lifted *What Price Glory* out of melodrama into something higher.

Anderson and Stallings collaborated in two more plays, both of which failed at the Plymouth Theatre in 1925. *First Flight* is a romance of North Carolina in the last decade of the Eighteenth Century. The central character is Captain Andy Jackson, who represents the State of North Carolina, and has come down to "The Free State of Franklin" to prevent the separation of the western counties from the parent state. He fights two duels and acts generally as a romantic figure. The play has some merit as a picture of life at that time, undoubtedly fanciful, but without very much bombast. The character of Charity Clarkson is also not badly done. *The Buccaneer*, which is laid in Panama City in the 1600's, is a melodrama dealing with Captain Henry Morgan, a privateer, and Lady Elizabeth Neville. It is almost impossible to take the play seriously, as the language is stilted and the situations are improbable.

The collaborators parted company, but continued to produce dramatic work of a different kind. Stallings has been occupied with the moving pictures and has been successful in that field. He also wrote the book and lyrics for a striking opera, *Deep River* (1926), laid in New Orleans about 1830. The plot labors under the restrictions of opera but the performance was full of color and made an approach to life. The lyrics at times were very effective, especially in the scene in the voodoo den, where the music of Frank Harling combined with the words to establish a mood of terror.

Anderson produced in 1925 *Outside Looking In,* based on Jim Tully's autobiography, *Beggars of Life.* The scene shifts from a "hobo camp" in North Dakota, through a box car on a railroad to an abandoned "claim shack" in Montana, and the codes and standards of tramps were revealed in an entertaining if episodic manner. There was really no play, for the runaway romance of Little Red and Edna was not enough to build one on. Anderson did much better work in *Saturday's Children* (1927), and it is interesting to see him return to domestic drama after his excursions, either alone or with Stallings, into melodrama. The first Act of *Saturday's Children* is a remarkable picture of the methods by which a young man who is in love but intends to have his life adventure first, is led to propose marriage to a girl to whom marriage and life adventure are the same thing. The second Act, in which the young married pair quarrel, is reminiscent of *The First Year,* of course, but it is much more of a character study and there is a wistful searching for happiness, especially on the part of the wife, that is very appealing. Then after Anderson had separated them he apparently did not know what to do with them, for the device by which he brings about a reconciliation in the drab boarding house to which she has fled, is theatrical rather than dramatic. But there is a quiet restraint in *Saturday's Children,* a sympathy with human weakness rather than a caricature of it, which points to a growing surety in Anderson's art.

A playwright of some achievement, Lewis Beach, began with one-act dramas of which *The Clod,* produced by the Washington Square Players in 1916, had the merit of revealing the part little things play in important decisions. *A Square Peg* (1924) is a tragedy of the managing woman who drives all her family out of her life. Her husband becomes a suicide, her daughter runs away with a married man and her son enlists in the navy after a disgraceful affair. Beach is entitled to credit for the relentless treatment of the situation. The difficulty is that the people are not made important enough to render the tragedy significant. He was affected by the artistic delusion that it makes no difference what your material is, provided you let it develop logically. But no one in the audience really cared what became of the family. In his next play, *The Goose Hangs High* (1924), he had learned a lesson and he gave a much more human picture of a family in a small city in the Middle West, in which the relations of parents and children were treated with sympathy and understanding. The truth that parents care more for their children than their children care for them is brought out with fidelity to fact that is startling in its detail. But Beach had the good sense to show the reaction of the same children to the situation in which their father is placed by his honesty and the ending is just as true to nature as *The Square Peg* was, but it is vastly more interesting. In consequence, *The Goose Hangs High* succeeded. *Ann Vroome* is a return to tragedy and is sincere in its treatment of the dilemma in which many a woman is placed. But it has not the human quality of *The Goose Hangs High*.

Several playwrights of promise in this field of the domestic character drama have appeared sporadically. Leon Cunningham gave to the Equity Players in 1922 a fine tragedy in *Hospitality*, in which the central character was a mother who has been so busy working for her children that she has had no time to love them. Her death after she has saved her son from a marriage that would have eventually broken his life, left one with a feeling of exaltation, not depression. *Wild Birds* by Dan Totheroh, which was first produced by the University of California and then had a brief run in New York in 1925, is a tragedy of aspiration, thwarted by association with crass unseeing people, in the Middle West. There is an appeal in the pathetic love story of Mazie, an orphan, and Adam Larsen, a refugee from the Reform School, who elope and are brought back to the terrible farm of the Slags. Adam is beaten to death by John Slag and Mazie drowns herself in the well. While the situation is old the treatment is not shrill or wild, and the idea of having their emotions excited by the chanting and drumming of old Robert, the crazy man, is not bad. The play is a promise perhaps of better things.

Not so promising, but still worthy of recording, was *A Man's Man* (1925) by Patrick Kearney. This is a realistic drama of medium American life, with some real approach to fidelity. It is supposed to deal with the middle generation in America in its progress from rags to riches. Apparently the author wishes to show it on its ridiculous or pitiful side, and he succeeds. The character of Melville Tuttle, very well played by Dwight Frye, is representative of those young American men without much ability but with a great deal of conceit and ambition. He almost succeeds in making one like him at the end of the play, when he and his wife, having gone through all their trials and tribulations, plan a great future for their son who is to be, although they feel that themselves will not reach that future.

That it is a significant and a promising group of playwrights which this chapter chronicles, needs no emphasis. Nearly all of them are young, judged either by the calendar or by the more intangible but more accurate test of the spirit. They may be discouraged at times by unfortunate conditions but they love the theatre; they know it and they know life. Their danger is that in the effort to give a faithful picture of life they will be satisfied with the usual. But it is just because they have kept their sanity, because they have declined to be different just for the sake of difference, that their work shines in comparison with that other group, more noisy than important, who insist on breaking the mould of the drama in order to represent through its fragments, a symbolic picture of life. The shrill staccato of *Roger Bloomer*, of *Processional*, of *Pinwheel*, leads nowhere, despite the unquestioned sincerity of their writers. This is partly because their authors forget that there are two principles, old as the hills, which every product of art must possess, unity and variety, and that neither alone will suffice. Without the fusing power of imagination, mere violence arrives not at a new technique but only at a new form of confusion.

NOTE TO REPRINTING OF REVISED EDITION

Zona Gale died December 27, 1938, in Chicago.

Sidney Howard died August 23, 1939, in Tyringham, Mass. He was accidentally crushed to death by the tractor on his estate.

CHAPTER XXIII

THE DRAMA OF THE PROVINCES

ONE of the most significant tendencies in recent American play writing has been its search for material among primitive life, remote from the large centers of population. The impulse is a healthful one, for it is among these unsophisticated people that characters represent themselves freely and that strong passions and emotions may be represented without running into melodrama. Natives types, too, are to be found in these regions, and faults and virtues are therefore indigenous. It is obvious that if such provincial types are to be sought, they must be picturesque and provide contrast. The decadent primitives in northeastern Pennsylvania or in parts of New England, where the ambitious have departed, leaving a drab reminder of former virility, are not suitable fields. These have been found rather in the West or in the mountain regions of the Carolinas, of Georgia and Kentucky, where the climate and other circumstances have preserved the virility of the people.

Mrs. Burnett had seen the possibilities of this mountain race as early as 1881, when *Esmeralda* dramatized a contrast between them and the civilization of Europe. But while novelists have long made use of this material, the drama has turned to it only sporadically, until in very recent years. The credit for an interesting development, which was amateur in its inception, but which culminated in 1926-7 in the production of two plays on the professional stage in New York, is to be given to Professor Frederick H. Koch. In 1910 he founded the Dakota Playmakers at the University of North Dakota and produced there not only pageants like *The Pageant of the*

THE DRAMA OF THE PROVINCES

North West (1914) and *Shakespeare the Playmaker* (1916) but also stimulated the writing of plays growing out of the lives of the students who themselves acted in the dramas thus created. In 1918 he was attracted by the promise of the field of mountaineer life and began his work as Professor of Dramatic Literature at the University of North Carolina. Here he has developed something unique in playmaking, which has been imitated of course in other places. It differs essentially from the work of Professor Baker, of Harvard and Yale, whose stimulating courses attract students who are already playwrights in embryo, whose plays bear no relation in locale to Cambridge or New Haven and whose ambition is the professional theatre. At North Carolina the students are concerned with the material around them, drawn from a civilization that has remained homogeneous. The plays are community dramas in the proper sense—not pageants but plays with real characters and situations. More important, while they deal with the material of North Carolina, the best of them could be produced anywhere.

The Carolina Playmakers are not limited, in production, to Carolina. Their tours reach south to Georgia and north to Washington, in the Playmakers' omnibus, in which they also carry the scenery. Anyone who has traveled with them on their trips will not soon forget the enthusiasms, not only of their director, but of the entire group. They are truly taking the folk drama to the people. The limitations of such an organization are perhaps obvious. Undergraduates can never give performances of professional certainty and the Playmakers cannot with their shifting personnel develop into such artistry as the Provincetown Players or the Neighborhood Players. Their performances are therefore not so important as the plays that have been written for them, and, fortunately, two volumes of these one-act plays have been published.[1] They deal with superstitions still extant at least in tradition—such as

---

[1] In *Carolina Folk-Plays*, edited by F. L. Koch, 1922 and 1924. See COLLECTIONS.

the striking dramas of the supernatural *When Witches Ride* by Elizabeth (Lay) Green, or her vivid picture of the Eighteenth Century witchcraft in *Trista*. The romance of old traditions is given in *Off Nag's Head*, by Dougald MacMillan, which places on the stage the last moments of Theodosia Burr, daughter of Aaron Burr, victim of the land pirates who preyed on that coast in the early days. It soon becomes apparent that the best work has been done by Paul Green, whose *The Last of the Lowries* was produced in 1920. This one-act play, laid in 1874, deals with the visit to his home of an outlaw who pays the penalty for his desire to see his mother once more. These outlaws, the Lowrie gang, were a well-known band, partly Croatan Indian, who had resisted the conscription of the Confederate Government and had proceeded from defensive to offensive war. The last Lowrie was killed in 1874. Legend attributes the origin of the tribe to Sir Walter Raleigh's lost colony of 1590, who may indeed have been carried away by the Indians. Old Cumba Lowrie, who has lost her husband and two sons, and who waits for news that Henry and Steve will return, while in fact Steve is dead and Henry's captors are closing in upon him, is a strange and powerful figure. Suddenly the shot is heard, which tells her that the last Lowrie has been killed, and she meets the doom with dignity.

Cumba: Yes, it's better that-a-way, I reckon. An' I won't be livin' in hope and fear no mo', will I? And when the owls hoot through the swamp at night, and the whippoorwills sing in the thicket at dark, I won't have cause to think that's one o' my own a-givin' of 'is signals, an' tryin' to slip back to 'is ol' home, the only place he loves,—will I? An' I won't lie awake at night, thinkin' they're in danger . . . for He's done give 'em His peace at last.

Another striking one-act play, *The Scuffletown Outlaws* (1924), was built upon this outlaw band. The author, William Norment Cox, has lived from his boyhood near the settlement of the Lowries and his forefathers helped to exterminate them, one falling in the struggle. In the play, he acted Henry

A SCENE FROM *THE SCUFFLETOWN OUTLAWS*, A PLAY OF THE NORTH CAROLINA MOUNTAINEERS

Berry Lowrie, the chieftain. With a sense for contrasts, he brought in an outside influence, John Sanders, who has come among the outlaws to gain their confidence and then betray them to the law for the reward. But Sanders is so impressed by the tragic situation which fate and their own actions have brought on them, that he refuses at the last moment to carry out his bargain. Their suspicions have been aroused, however, and he is shot by Steve Lowrie, through the window of the house, after he had been allowed to escape.[1]

The tragedy of a "tenant-farm woman" is revealed in *Fixin's* by Paul and Erma Green, (1924). And in more than one of the plays the conditions wrought out of the limitation of opportunity which generations of separation from progressive civilization have brought about, are revealed with sympathy. Comedy is not neglected, either, but the comedies seem not to be so significant as the serious plays. One of the most successful comedies of courtship, *In Dixon's Kitchen*, has not been published, since much of the fun depends upon the stage business.

The test of the importance of such a movement as the Carolina Playmakers lies, of course, in the development of a creative dramatist. Paul Green seems to be such an artist. After his war service he returned to the University of North Carolina, where he is now a member of the Faculty of Philosophy. In his volume, *The Lord's Will and Other Carolina Plays* (1925), the most vivid are the romances of the earlier days— like *The Old Man of Edenton* and *Blackbeard*, the latter dealing with the pirate who first appeared in drama in Lemuel Sawyer's *Blackbeard* in 1824. There is a different charm in *The No 'Count Boy*, a negro comedy, which won the Belasco cup when produced by the players of the Dallas Little Theatre in New York in 1925. Here Green dramatized the philosophy of the attraction of the vagabond.

It was natural that Green should turn for sharper con-

---

[1] *The Scuffletown Outlaws* was published in *The Southwest Review*, XI (April 1926), pp. 179–204.

trasts to the negro, both because of the greater emotional possibilities, in a race that lives by feeling, and also because of the tragedies that come from the contact of white and black. The most significant of his one-act plays of negro life are to be found in the volume, *Lonesome Road* (1926). The preface, breathing deep sympathy for the lot of the negro, explains why Green can write so well about him. Of these plays perhaps the most powerful is the poignant tragedy of *White Dresses*. The symbol of the white dress sent by a white boy to Mary, the mulatto girl, as a farewell when she is being forced by her own white father and his, into a marriage with a negro, is remarkable in its restraint. A striking figure is Aunt Candace, the negress who burns up the white dress together with its faded yellowish prototype, sent nineteen years before to her sister, Mary's mother, by the man who is forcing his own daughter into marriage with a negro she loathes. The tragedy ends with the swiftness of fine art in Aunt Candace's acceptance of the inevitable, as she turns from the ashes of the two white dresses—"I knows yo' feelin's, chile, but you's gut to smother 'em in. You's gut to smother 'em in."

Two of the plays, *In Abraham's Bosom* and *Your Fiery Furnace*, deal with the tragedy of frustrated ambition on the part of a negro. These became portions of Green's play of seven scenes, *In Abraham's Bosom*, which created a profound impression when produced at the Provincetown Theatre in 1926, and won the Pulitzer Prize. While Green shows the apparent hopelessness of the effort of Abraham McCranie to help his race, the playwright is concerned not with propaganda, but with the tragedy of an individual. Abraham is the son of a white man, and his mixed blood is a symbol of the struggle going on between his intellectual gropings for higher things and his passionate nature which handicaps him through marriage with Goldie McAllister, and makes him also unfit to be a leader of men. His story runs logically through to disaster. Scoffed at by the whites and jeered at by his own race, he falls finally by the bullets of the avengers of his murder of his white half brother, who has been his evil genius. While too shrill at times and at others too wordy, the drama as a whole stirred the audience deeply, for it was the biography of a brave soul, defeated by circumstances and by his own limitations, with a spirit above his possible achievement. The colored characters were taken by negroes and the scenes in the turpentine woods in 1885 among the field hands, and later in the cabin of Abraham, were faithfully represented. One of the best-drawn characters was Muh Mack, Abraham's aunt, who represented the old unprogressive negress, and her comments on her nephew aided in the note of comedy which lightened the play at times.

Green returned in *The Field God* (1927) to the narrow life of the Southern white, not of the mountaineer, but of the farmer folk of eastern North Carolina. Hardy Gilchrist, the central character, is a study of a man of exceptional virility, linked to an ailing wife. He turns to youth in the person of Rhoda, his wife's niece, who loves him in return. Green establishes well the struggle of two vibrant natures against the deadly narrowness of the community that surrounds them. They are not sordid; they preserve their self-respect until one overpowering impulse bids them give way and brings on Mrs. Gilchrist's death. From this point the drama is too long drawn out. The suicide of Neill, Rhoda's suitor, shocks but does not stimulate us; the efforts of the preacher and his aids to save Hardy's soul are interminable and even the death of Rhoda's little child leaves us cold. Green has forgotten that on the stage too much misery makes an audience cease to believe in it. The ending which leaves Hardy and Rhoda in each other's arms, having rejected all gods but themselves, is curious rather than conclusive. There is a deep flavor in *The Field God* of the long stretches of North Carolina fields, unmarked by human habitation. But this after all is epic, not dramatic.

How much influence upon other playwrights the success of the Carolina Playmakers has had it is difficult to estimate.

But it is hardly probable that the appearance upon the New York stage of four plays of the mountaineers in one year (1923-4) could have been entirely accidental. The first of these to be produced, *Sun-Up*, was by Lula Vollmer, who was born in Keyser, North Carolina, and learned to know the mountaineers during her summer vacations among them. Miss Vollmer wrote plays as a girl and when she became the treasurer of the box office of the Theatre Guild at the Garrick Theatre, she had already written *Sun-Up*. It was suggested by a story she heard in May, 1918, of a Southern boy, who, upon arriving in camp, exclaimed, "Air this hyar France?" She dramatized this note of provincialism but as the play grew the central character became his mother, the widow Cagle, and in her became personified the hereditary opposition to that dread abstraction, the law, which had killed her husband, and insisted upon taking her boy from her, to fight in a quarrel too remote for her sympathy.

Her attitude was not a bit overstressed. It is well known that not only during the Civil War but even during the World War many of the mountaineers refused to serve in the army on the ground that they were not interested in the matter and it was not their war. But Miss Vollmer shows also in Rufe Cagle the feeling of the younger generation that the hills which had nourished them were worth fighting for. The marriage ceremony of Rufe and Emmy before he goes, the helplessness of the illiterate mother when the telegram comes announcing his death, her long vigil through the night, as she sits smoking by the fire and resumes her daily round in the morning light, are portrayed with utter simplicity. When she speaks it is in brief sentences. Her good-by is, "If ye fight, shoot to kill—" and then, "Well, take care o' yo'self"—and her philosophy of life is summed up in her words to the deserter who has sought shelter in her cabin, and whom she is protecting at the risk of her own life: "I ain't afeered and thar ain't no danger unless ye air afeered." *Sun-Up* was put on the stage at the Provincetown Theatre, May 24, 1923, by an independent group of producers, and after running a year, it went on tour. It had a triumphal reception in London and has been produced in Amsterdam. The performance of Lucille La Verne as the Widow Cagle was one of the achievements of modern acting.

Lula Vollmer's second play, *The Shame Woman* (1923), while more conventional in the form in which it was produced, is another tragedy. *Sun-Up* closed on a note of exaltation, in which a mother's love passed beyond the limits of life to commune for a moment with the spirit of the son she had lost. In *The Shame Woman* Lize Burns dies on the scaffold to keep from her own lifelong stain the adopted daughter who has been betrayed by her guardian's earlier seducer. Martha Case, the midwife, who represents the brooding figure of implacable fate, is as striking a creation as anything that the Russian stage has evolved. The play, as Miss Vollmer first wrote it, ended not in the jail but in the open air as the Shame Woman walked to the scaffold through the crowd who had come to scoff and who remained to pray. The gaunt figure of the midwife remained erect to the last; then the nobility of the woman at whom she had jeered brought even her to her knees. It is to be regretted that mere stage mechanics prevented the production of this scene.

The Dunce Boy (1925) is also laid in the North Carolina mountains. The central character is that of Tude Huckle, who is a half-wit, and yet has his emotional side developed beyond that of the normal human being. There is nothing morbid in the representation of abnormality, but the best character is that of his mother. She has nursed him and defended him against the cruelty of his father because she feels that the sawmill has entered into his pre-natal life in a strange and unwonted way, and that in a sense she was responsible for not insisting upon leaving a neighborhood in which she was unhappy. The sound of the saw runs through the play like the *motif* of an opera, and at the end, in a moment of intense exultation, caused by Rosie Pierce's kiss, Tude rushes out of the house and is caught and killed by the great saw. The other characters are background, and Miss Vollmer herself was not as much interested in them as she should have been. But there is an imaginative quality in *The Dunce Boy*, as in all of Miss Vollmer's plays, which distinguishes them from the usual domestic drama.

The comedy of the North Carolina mountaineers has been represented on the professional stage by two plays of Hatcher Hughes. Hughes has been a lecturer on the drama at Columbia and in 1921 had collaborated with Elmer Rice in a play for Mrs. Fiske, *Wake Up, Jonathan*. In the first of his mountain plays, *Hell-Bent Fer Heaven*, the central character, Rufe Pryor, is a curious mixture of religious cant and jealous passion, who in order to win the girl he desires, revives a slumbering feud between the Hunts and the Lowrys and nearly brings death and ruin upon them both. Hughes evolves this situation through a dialogue that is crisp and direct and holds the note of comedy by the uncanny hypocrisy of Rufe in contrast with the rough sincerity of the other characters. Hughes evidently knows his people. The hold that evangelical faith has over the women of both families, the unreasoning impulse of the feud, the triumph of common sense in the eighty-year-old grandfather, all were ably interpreted by a well-chosen cast. After all, it is the creation of character that is the acid test of drama, and Rufe Pryor will remain long in the memory as a human portrait, convincing and enduring. By a mistaken direction, the ending, delightfully ironic, which leaves Rufe imprisoned, in danger of the flood, and abandoned by his enlightened dupes to the mercy of a God with whom he has assumed such an intimate acquaintance, was changed to a rescue, and the play was weakened. It won the Pulitzer Prize, however, for the season of 1923-4.

Ruint (1925) is an amusing comedy laid in the North Carolina mountains. It has not as much significance as *Hell-Bent Fer Heaven*, because one can hardly believe that Mary Jane Horton would pretend to be ruined in order to obtain revenge upon her philandering suitor. In other words, the situation does not seem probable enough to excite either our intense sympathy or our sense of comedy. The best characters are the two mothers, Mrs. Horton and Mrs. Akins, who represent the conservative attitude, although not the attitude of the men of the family. The most insistent note struck in *Ruint* was that of the contentment of the mountain people with their own civilization, and their scorn of the city. When Mrs. Horton exclaims, "Think o' havin' to buy every mess o' gyarden truck that ye eat!" and Mrs. Akins replies, "La, that's nothin'! I've hyeard they even have to pay fer the water they drink," Mrs. Horton pronounces final judgment: "Well, all I got to say is that folks that's fool enough to live in sich a place 'tain't no matter fer 'em." After all, they have solved the problem of existence much after Thoreau's philosophy.

Percy MacKaye's *This Fine-Pretty World,* laid in the Kentucky mountains, has already been discussed. It is highly probable that other districts will be treated in drama, but the progress of civilization will push the frontier line further into the mountains and its social life will become less picturesque. The plays of the provinces may become therefore an episode in our dramatic history, but that episode is fruitful and significant.

NOTE. Frederick H. Koch died August 14, 1944.

CHAPTER XXIV

The New Decade, 1927–1936

THE record of the ten years that have elapsed since this
history was first written has been, I am happy to say,
a fulfillment of my critical judgments.   The living playwrights
I then treated are still the most significant forces in the drama,
especially that group which in 1927 were coming into prominence.   We have lost through death in this decade David
Belasco, Augustus Thomas, Langdon Mitchell, Jesse Lynch
Williams and Lee Wilson Dodd, to mention only the most important of the older playwrights.   But their work had already
been concluded.

Of the generation which began their playwriting in the first
decade of the twentieth century, Rachel Crothers has made the
most important contributions.   It is interesting to see the sharp
criticism of the double standard of morality which she uttered
in *A Man's World* in 1909 give place to the mellower philosophy
of *Let Us Be Gay* (1929), a delightful social comedy in which a
divorced wife recognizes the futility of that avenue of escape,
for her.   The character of Mrs. Boucicault, the dominating
elderly woman, was a real achievement.   Even better was *As
Husbands Go* (1931), a striking contrast between the American and the English conception of marriage, and an illustration of Miss Crothers' ability to use an old situation in a new
way.   When Charles Lingard, the American husband, finds
that his wife on her trip abroad has acquired an English lover,
he neither raves nor nobly abdicates in his rival's favor.   But
in a scene in which Miss Crothers made skilful use of the effect
of alcohol in removing British inhibitions, Lingard matches successfully his wits, his character and his love for his wife against

250

those of the man who is thinking mostly of himself, while Lingard is thinking mainly of his wife's happiness. Miss Crothers proceeds to prick the bubble of temporary infatuation with some of the brightest dialogue of her career. *When Ladies Meet* (1932) was another study of character in which the triangle consisted of two women, the wife and the mistress of a man who is by nature a philanderer. There was a remarkable scene in which the two women meet without knowing their common interest, but discuss an imaginary case which the mistress is using in her novel. Gradually the wife begins to suspect her, and the handling of the situation is deft and sure. It was just because they were both gentlewomen that the scene was so hard to write and so successful when played, and yet although Miss Crothers revealed her artistic purpose in the title, few if any of the contemporary reviews seemed to understand her achievement.

Among the other playwrights of the older generation, Percy MacKaye wrote and directed an ambitious folk masque, *Wakefield* (1932), at Washington, in celebration of the bicentennial anniversary of the first President. The masque revealed the growth of the spirit of freedom with Wakefield, the birth place of Washington, as a symbol. It was a brave attempt to represent the different folk elements in the United States and their contribution to freedom, in conflict with pestilence, war, poverty and other evils. But the audience seemed confused by the symbolism, and reacted only to the comedy and the folk songs. *Wakefield* was a sincere but not very successful effort which met the usual fate of any attempt to put Washington in person or in symbolism on the stage.

George Cohan varied the detective play with a clever comedy, *Confidential Service* (1932), in which the audience was told in the first act who committed the robbery. *Pigeons and People* (1933), was a fantasy reminiscent of *The Tavern*, but it gave Cohan an opportunity to play an apparently insane man with his usual skill. The play held audiences spellbound during a whole evening, for Cohan had imitated Philip Barry by having no intermission. Even if the ending is a trick, there was some fine ironic comment upon the inconsistencies and pretence of life. In *Dear Old Darling* (1936) Cohan returned to the detective play, cleverly written but not important.

Edward Sheldon, still handicapped by illness, has collaborated with Margaret Ayer Barnes in *Jenny* (1929), a light comedy, and *Dishonored Lady* (1930), a rather turgid melodrama. Jane Cowl made the first entertaining, and Katharine Cornell made the second glow for a few moments, but neither play was up to Sheldon's earlier standard.

The principal productions of Owen Davis were his dramatizations of *The Good Earth*, by Pearl Buck, in 1932 and of *Ethan Frome*, by Edith Wharton, in 1936. The first was an ambitious attempt to put on the stage something that was epic and not dramatic. Notwithstanding the remarkable acting of Nazimova as the Chinese wife, the play failed. *Ethan Frome* presented difficulties of another nature. There is comparatively little dialogue in the novel, and Davis and his son Donald, who collaborated with him, had to suffer comparison with the foremost novelist of the time. That they did this adequately, that they preserved the austerity of this great novel of New England character, and that they provided a vehicle which the fine acting of Raymond Massey, Pauline Lord and Ruth Gordon made memorable, proved that Owen Davis has not lost his cunning and that his son has promise of fine things to come.

Proceeding next to the work of those who began between 1910 and 1920, Eugene O'Neill has kept his unquestioned preeminence among American playwrights. When I discussed his contribution in 1927, *Lazarus Laughed* existed only in manuscript. It has not been produced in the East, but the performance at the Pasadena Theatre in 1928 proved that it had all the qualities which I saw in it in 1927, and which I need not further emphasize. But O'Neill's own explanation of its meaning in a letter to me in May, 1927 has unusual significance:

The fear of death is the root of all evil, the cause of all man's blundering unhappiness. Lazarus knows there is no death, there is only change. He is reborn without that fear. Therefore he is the first and only man who is able to laugh affirmatively. His laughter is a triumphant Yes to life in its entirety and its eternity. His laughter affirms God, it is too noble to desire personal immortality, it wills its own extinction, it gives its life for the sake of Eternal Life (patriotism carried to its logical ultimate). His laughter is the direct expression of joy in the Dionysian sense, the joy of a celebrant who is at the same time a sacrifice in the eternal process of change and growth and transmutation which is life, of which his life is an insignificant manifestation, soon to be reabsorbed. And life itself is the self-affirmative joyous laughter of God.

And still there are "dramatic critics" who speak of Eugene O'Neill as a pessimist and a writer of melodramas! They were baffled by *Strange Interlude* (1928), failing to see that the revelation of the actual thoughts of the characters to the audience while the other characters remained ignorant of them gave rise to a conflict between reality and unreality which was intensely dramatic. This device, however, could hardly be imitated successfully by other playwrights, although as a matter of fact it had been employed before. In drama the master who uses a stage device best makes it his own, but the importance of *Strange Interlude* did not lie merely in its technique. It links itself with *Lazarus Laughed* in one of the speeches of Nina Leeds: "Our lives are merely strange dark interludes in the electrical display of God the Father." O'Neill dramatized one of these interludes through a powerful study of the clutch of a woman upon five men who loved her. Each in his own way, her father, her two lovers, Marsden and Darrell, her husband, Sam Evans, and her son, Gordon, have their lives determined by her, just as hers is determined by her unfulfilled passion for the dead aviator whom her father had prevented her from marrying. Each of these men fulfils only in part the functions Gordon Shaw might have satisfied completely—that is her tragedy. Her father dies broken hearted, her son finally escapes her, her husband dies in ignorance of the fact that she has never loved him. Charley Marsden, who is a friend rather than a lover, wins her in the end. Tragedy seizes most bitterly upon Dr. Darrell, who has come nearest to possessing her, and one of the most poignant scenes was that in which she prevented him from letting their son know that Darrell is his father. *Strange Interlude* is not "a pleasant play"—it is not intended to be, but if it is understood, certain phases of it, like Nina's promiscuity and her intense selfishness, which at first tend to weaken our sympathy for her, become part of a picture which is symbolic.

That the use of the new form of "asides" was not the cause of the success of *Strange Interlude* was proved by the failure of *Dynamo* (1929) in which the same device was used. *Dynamo* was an attempt to dramatize the struggle in a boy's soul between his inherited Evangelical beliefs and the worship of electricity, out of which he has fashioned a new god. But the conflict is not established in terms that vitally interest a reader or a hearer. The characters remain abstractions, especially the central figure of the boy. It was a dramatic mistake also to make the climax of the first Act his challenge of God to strike him dead, when it had already been indicated in the play how absurd such a challenge is. The final climax, when Reuben prays to the dynamo for the knowledge of truth and dies by its current, cannot be made credible through such a character. The various elements of the conflict, including his purely physical passion for a neighbor's daughter, never really come to grips, largely because he is not made sufficiently interesting for the struggle to seem important.

To make amends, O'Neill gave us one of the greatest of his plays. "For many years," he states in the Introduction to *Mourning Becomes Electra* (1931) [1] "the idea of using one of the old legend plots of Greek tragedy as a basis for a modern psychological drama had occurred to me. Would it be possible to achieve a modern psychological approximation of the Greek sense of fate which would seem credible to a present-day audience and at the same time prove emotionally affecting? The

[1] *Wilderness Edition,* II, xiii.

Electra story, with its complex human inter-relationships and its chain of fated crime and retribution, seemed best suited in its scope and in its implications to this purpose."

There has been much speculation concerning the relative influence of the dramas of Aeschylus, Sophocles and Euripides upon *Mourning Becomes Electra.* O'Neill's own statement, in reply to my inquiry, is definite:

> The Trilogy of Aeschylus was what I had in mind. As for individual characters, I did not consciously follow any one of the Greek dramatists. On the contrary, I tried my best to forget all about their differing Electras, etc. All I wanted to borrow was the theme-pattern of Aeschylus (and the old legends) and to reinterpret it in modern psychological terms with Fate and the Furies working from within the individual soul.

Mourning Becomes Electra was the product of two years of hard work, being rewritten completely twice and even then revised.

O'Neill laid the play in the Civil War period because it gained perspective, and the choice of the New England scene was fortunate, for it gave him the opportunity to draw with his usual skill the hardness and repression of one kind of New England character. The play is a trilogy, and the original intention had been to perform it on three successive evenings. But although like *Strange Interlude* it was begun in the afternoon and an intermission of one hour was allowed for dinner between *Homecoming* and *The Hunted*, while another fifteen minutes elapsed before the third member of the trilogy, *The Haunted* was played, the complete unity of impression was preserved.

The play is a profound study of the tragic relations of the Mannons, a family of strong passions, proud of its traditions. The passionate love of Lavinia for her father, the hatred of her mother Christine for her husband, and Christine's illicit passion for Adam Brant, which leads to her murder of General Mannon on the night of his return from the Civil War, make up *Homecoming*. From this point, Lavinia dominates the play. It is she who leads her brother Orin to kill Brant, and it is she who drives her mother and Orin to suicide. Then judging herself as she had judged the others, she shuts herself in the Mannon house, to be a prey to the ghosts which will haunt her until her death.

In *Mourning Becomes Electra*, O'Neill indicated an avenue for new playwrights to follow. Taking a great plot from the Greeks, he made it in terms of American life a new thing. There are, after all, only a few great plots; instead of avoiding them and writing about nothing, as is so often done today in both drama and fiction, why not frankly take an old one and, by calling attention to the source, disarm criticism? The chorus of the Greeks becomes the gossiping villagers of a New England town. The cry of "Justice" that comes from Lavinia's lips is a reflection of Electra's words in Euripides' drama, and Seth, a remarkable portrait of a New England servant, is drawn from the "Old Man" who recognizes Orestes and helps Electra, and who is bound up with the fortunes of the house.

But there is no dependence upon outside forces as in the Greek. No gods come down to straighten things out or hold out promise of pardon to Orin or Lavinia. They are human beings facing the consequences of their own acts, in this world and the next. The essentially American nature of the play is shown in the relentless drive of the morality, the sense of duty to oneself as well as to the family, the renouncing of love, on Lavinia's part for the sake of duty. While Electra mourns for her own unmated state, Lavinia has little self-pity. The criticism of war for its futility, not the criticism of the pacifist— there is too much of the Celt in O'Neill for him to be that—but the arraignment of war for its confusion of values in the individual's outlook on life—this is American. For Americans generally look upon war not as a career, but as an interruption to a career, necessary at times, but something to be forgotten as soon as possible. As Orin says, "I had a queer feeling that war meant murdering the same man over and over, and that in the end I would discover the man was myself."

Much more than in *Strange Interlude* we have an intense

sympathy for several of the characters. Lavinia first, for the steel of her nature, for the way she nerves herself to secure justice upon the erring, for her very moments of weakness in which the young girl in her begs for direction from her dead father, or the appeal at the end of the play to him to tell her that she has guarded well the family honor. She is not all steel; she has loved Adam and crushed her love within her. She hates her mother for taking her lover away from her, and she has that mixture of motives for her actions which keeps her human. Yet O'Neill has given to her, in her quality of being animated by a fate stronger than herself, a dignity which makes her ending not pathetic, but tragic. O'Neill knows that from the days of the Greeks onward, no audience refuses its sympathy (in the Greek sense, at least) to a murderer, or to the inciter to murder. Treachery it does not like, or lying or stealing, but murder it will forgive, for the audience knows, subconsciously at least, that a murderer will be punished by his own conscience or his fear of discovery. For a murderer strikes at a great principle, the human being's intense love of life, the motive of self-preservation, and that gives to his action an importance unknown to the movements of a thief. Alice Brady's performance of Lavinia was superb. As Lavinia turned into the empty Mannon house, a sacrifice to her mistaken but lofty sense of duty to keep the secret of the family disgrace from all eyes, those who were privileged to see her knew they were present at one of the supreme moments in the history of the theatre of the world.

Sympathy for Christine is not so unqualified. Admirably played by Nazimova, whose foreign accent deftly separated her from the Mannon family, she is ruthless in pursuing her passion for Brant, but weak at times before the moral strength of Lavinia. Christine is not a lofty figure—she is more like the Clytemnestra of Euripides than the Clytemnestra of Aeschylus or of Sophocles. The reason lies partly in the unavoidable change in the plot. In Greek tragedy Clytemnestra has a powerful motive for her hatred of Agamemnon, in his sacrifice of their daughter, Iphigenia. O'Neill substituted for this motive,

Christine's disgust at the implied brutality of her husband on their wedding night. But nothing in Ezra Mannon's character as he appears in *Homecoming* indicates a brutal nature; indeed his appeal to his wife to break down the walls between them is the cry of a proud and sensitive man overcoming a reluctance to disclose a feeling deeper than he can express. Christine is drawn, too, as a sensuous woman with no instinctive repulsion to passion. But this contradiction is perhaps the one flaw in the plot. Orin is a masterly picture of a man torn between love and duty, and too weak to resist the dominance of a stronger nature. Even Adam Brant elicits sympathy for his recognition of his unfitness longer to command his vessel or to rule the sea. O'Neill showed in this character that he had not forgotten the hold the sea has on those who love it.

Mourning Becomes Electra is not simply a trilogy. It is a landmark in the history of American drama, for in it one of our playwrights matched his strength with the Greeks and rose from the test triumphant.

O'Neill's own comments upon his plays are so illuminating that I quote from a letter of February 10, 1932, in which the modesty of our foremost playwright is revealed:

Much gratitude for your flattering appreciation of *Mourning Becomes Electra!* I only hope it is as worthy as you think it. I am very satisfied with it—(taken all around it *is* my best, I think)— but at the same time, deeply dissatisfied. It needed great language to lift it beyond itself. I haven't got that. And, by way of self-consolation, I don't think, from the evidence of all that is being written today, that great language is possible for anyone living in the discordant, broken, faithless rhythm of our time. The best one can do is to be pathetically eloquent by one's moving, dramatic inarticulations!

Those who had not seen the first Act of *The First Man* were surprised when O'Neill wrote *Ah, Wilderness!* (1933). It is a human, tender, compelling comedy of recollection, laid in a small town in Connecticut in 1906. The central character is that of the father of a family, the editor of the town's paper, who faces his responsibilities with a wisdom and a tolerance which made him a striking figure. His sympathy with his son who is undergoing the distress of adolescent love, and who is reading what seems to his mother and to other reactionaries very dangerous literature, such as *The Rubáiyát of Omar Khayyám*, is expressed through the comedy of the liberal mind, who refuses to see evil where there is no evil. The climax of the drama comes when Nat Miller, hearing that his boy has been in a disorderly house, works himself up to a dreaded interview in which he is to tell his son "the facts of life" and advise him concerning the steps necessary to secure immunity from the consequences of relations with prostitutes. The scene is humorous, but out of the humor there rises the fine nature of a man, himself fastidious and loath to invade the privacy of his son's feelings, who finds to his great relief that his son is too much like himself to make any further discourse necessary. George Cohan made a great success in the role of Nat Miller, and Will Rogers played the part with apparently equal acclaim in San Francisco.

Days Without End (1934) was a profound study of the conflict in a man's nature between his finer spiritual qualities and a cynical superstructure based upon "Atheism wedded to Socialism . . . living in free love with Anarchism, with a curse by Nietzsche to bless the union." These two aspects of John Loving were represented on the stage by two actors, one the living "John" and the other, "Loving," a masked figure dressed like him, who is invisible to the other characters but who is heard by them, expressing ideas which reflect the bitter quality of disillusion. This dualism was quite effective, for O'Neill permitted "Loving" to say only such things as could be caught up by "John" in his conversation and either smoothed over or retracted. John's earlier life, especially his boyhood when he had lost his faith as a Roman Catholic because he had prayed to God to preserve his parents and had not been answered, is brought out through his conversation with his uncle, Father Baird, an extremely well drawn character. John's liaison with his friend's wife, his remorse, his own wife's illness and his final repentance at the foot of the Cross in a neighboring church are skilfully interwoven with a novel he is writing in which he is representing his own problem. The solution comes when the evil spirit dies, defeated, in the church, and John Loving is no longer a duality but once more himself. Again O'Neill celebrated the triumph of individual integrity, the basic problem with which Poe, Hawthorne and Moody were so deeply concerned. The return to the faith of his youth brings John Loving peace because it restores him to the complete control of his being, undisturbed by ill-digested excursions into negations in which he finds no resting place, or into illicit sexual adventures in which he has no real pleasure. It is worth noting that *Days Without End*, notwithstanding the fine production given it by the Theatre Guild, received only mild acclaim in New York, while its reception at the Abbey Theatre in Dublin in April, 1934 was enthusiastic.[1] It is significant that *Days Without End* closes with the words "Life laughs with God's love again. Life laughs with love," whose similarity to the chorus of *Lazarus Laughed* is evident. O'Neill is still experimenting with methods of expression, but his basic philosophy of life, an open eyed, searching, liberal scrutiny of human nature, too keen to be merely optimistic, too broad to be merely pessimistic, remains the same. There is a progress in his symbolism, for the masks in *Mourning Becomes Electra* are not external but are integral elements in the expression of the faces of the characters. The concrete mask of John Loving is used more skilfully than those in *The Great God Brown*, and the dualism in *Days Without End* needs no such elaborate explanation as that of the earlier play. O'Neill is still the poet and the mystic, speaking clearly to those who approach his work without preconceived theories and are not restrained by an urge for classification to welcome the variety which gave us *Strange Interlude, Mourning Becomes Electra, Ah, Wilderness!* and *Days Without End* within a period of six years.

[1] Dublin letter to *New York Times,* April 23, 1934.

THE NEW DECADE, 1927–1936

Associated with O'Neill in the early days of the Provincetown Playhouse, Susan Glaspell had turned from the drama to fiction. In 1930 she returned to the stage with *Alison's House*, in which the mooted question of the right of the members of the family of a dead poet to keep from the public her self-revelations was probably prompted by the revived interest in Emily Dickinson. Miss Glaspell combined with this theme the contrast between the way the older and the newer generations of women faced the problem of accepting the love of a man already married, and the result was an interesting play which won the Pulitzer Prize for the year. While there are strong situations in *The Comic Artist* (1933) it was not clear in its conclusion. The best element in it was the picture of the havoc wrought in two men's lives by the grip of two selfish women.

Among the other playwrights who began their work in the second decade of the twentieth century, Zoë Akins has continued at intervals to produce in the romantic vein. Her most important play was the dramatization of Edith Wharton's novelette, *The Old Maid* (1935). This profound study of the conflict between the real and the adopted mother of an illegitimate child for the girl's love, provided fine material for a play, and Miss Akins made adroit use of it. She emphasized the love Mrs. Delia Ralston had felt for the girl's father and her jealousy of her cousin, whose life had been wrecked by her illicit passion but who had had at least a few months of rapture. Mrs. Wharton had kept this love in the background. But Miss Akins preserved the tragic note of the penalty which all pay personally or vicariously when they try to arrange the lives of others. *The Old Maid* won the Pulitzer Prize, for the year. *O Evening Star* (1935) was a romantic picture of a famous actress who has lost her hold on the public and then makes a success at Hollywood. It had good scenes, especially that presenting the hopes and fears of a group waiting outside the gates of a motion picture studio early in the morning. But after a fairly successful tryout in Philadelphia, it failed in New York. Clare

Kummer after a long silence returned with a very amusing farce comedy, *Her Master's Voice* (1933), but her production has been intermittent.

Elmer Rice has probably caused more differences of critical opinion than any other playwright who began before 1920. His best play, *Street Scene* (1929), gained its main interest from the stage device which presented the front of a tenement house in New York. The constant flow of life, comic or tragic, was impressive, and the character types stood out sharply against the background. But they are still all types, and the essentially melodramatic nature of *Street Scene* is apparent when it is realized how Rice has built it all up for the "big scene" of the murder of Anna Maurrant by her husband. The character nearest to reality was the daughter, Rose Maurrant, and Rice is entitled to credit for his depiction of a girl with just that amount of refinement and ambition which her parentage and surroundings would permit. *Street Scene* won the Pulitzer Prize. *The Subway* (1929), a play written earlier, told the unhappy fate of a filing clerk who throws herself in the way of a subway train. Again Rice is to be credited with the effort to make her a personality instead of a figure of economic protest. But he forgot that while recognition is a function audiences like to exercise, it is recognition of something they wish to remember rather than something like the subway which they want to forget. Rice next tried the European scene with an amusing but not very important comedy, *See Naples and Die* (1929), and *The Left Bank* (1931), a more serious study of the expatriated American writer who cannot bear to live in America. His wife, however, returns to this country and he stays in company with his wife's niece, which does not, of course, settle the main question. *Counsellor-at-Law* (1931) was a dramatization of the old fable of Beauty and the Beast, but the weakness lay in the improbability of the marriage between the able Jewish lawyer and the woman of fashion who departs with her lover at the end of the play. Cora Simon shows none of the qualities which made Emily Griswold's similar action in *The Boss* at least plausible.

The plot of *Counsellor-at-Law* is constantly interrupted by minor actions which have nothing to do with the main story, and Rice seems to have been inspired by subconscious race irritation against the 100% American, for all his foreign types are noble and his native citizens rotten at heart.

Elmer Rice went over completely into propaganda with *We, the People* (1933) in which it is hard to doubt his sincerity in his effort to evoke sympathy for the poor both in the city and on the farm.   But the financial magnates are absurd, and also the college president.   Some day a playwright will draw a real college president, but the day is not yet.   Rice does not understand either, in this play or in *Judgment Day* (1934), a melodrama concerned with the trial of three revolutionists in a European country, that if you make oppression so brutal and above all so stupid, audiences cease to believe in it.   *Between Two Worlds* (1934) was concerned with a number of types on an ocean liner, who drink a good deal but never become individualized.   To a critic, Rice is one of the most irritating of playwrights.   Judging from his introduction to *Two Plays*, he understands the handicaps of a dramatist completely and has the desire to write for the highest standards which the circumstances of the theatre will permit.   But the trouble is that he has not done this.   Instead of defying these conditions, like O'Neill, and trusting that there is an audience somewhere for the best, he has given us a long series of plays most of which are melodramas, and out of which not one single memorable character emerges. He has renounced the theatre more than once, either because he objected to the critical treatment his plays received, or because the government under which he was producing differed from him on a matter of good taste.   I am under no illusions concerning the calibre of the dramatic critics in New York, but they treated Rice on the whole quite fairly.   The truth is he seems to have almost a persecution mania, and demands that his theatrical devices, at times quite clever, should be taken seriously as important steps in the progress of the drama.   His *Not For Children* (1935), an involved satire upon nearly everything, explains the reason for his comparative failure as a playwright. He loves to talk about the drama, but he really is not a creative artist. He can build a shell around an idea, but he cannot imbue it with life.

Among the many plays Martin Flavin has written since 1927, there were some successful light comedies like *Service for Two* (1926) or *Broken Dishes* (1929), but the most important was his grim tragedy of prison life, *The Criminal Code* (1929). This was a profound study of the psychology of the condemned, of the power of the code of honor established by them for their own protection, and of the methods of a warden who understands them. Flavin had the dramatic sense to prefer a logical to a happy ending. *Cross Roads* (1929) was one of the few college plays which seemed real on the stage, and *Amaco* (1933) was a thoughtful, sincere dramatization of the rise of the machine and its effect upon the workers. Burke, who starts as an operative at a machine and rises until he becomes president of the concern, tries to build up through the sense of loyalty which has enabled him to rise, an organization which will solve the labor problem. He is defeated partly by the controlling bankers and partly by the mob, but he points to the only real solution. *Spindrift* (1930), a drama of futility, does not seem to me important. Flavin's work is as uneven as it is varied. *Tapestry in Gray* (1935) is a powerful study of the effect upon two men, both physicians, of the woman whom they love. It was developed in a series of forty-six scenes, like a moving picture, in which Iris and Stephen tell another specialist, Dr. Marius, about their past life during and after the war. Meanwhile Erik, the husband of Iris, has killed himself and unknown to them is in the morgue. Iris, whose life has been filled with a great desire to *be* something, but has lived only in Erik until she ruins him by her very insistence upon his professional preëminence, is a very real figure. So, too, is Erik, and his self-confidence which, fed by her demands, leads him to operate with fatal results upon their little son, is admirably pictured. Iris finally achieves some real existence when she sends Stephen away from her to fulfill his mission as a great investigator in China, even although she and Stephen find they love each other. While the play failed after three weeks, it has a real significance as a character study. It is also interesting because it carried to the extreme the transfer of a moving picture technique to the stage, and indicated the limitations of such experiment.

Outside of the work of Eugene O'Neill, the most significant plays have been written by men who began to produce in the early twenties. The oldest of that generation, George Kelly, has for a time ceased to write for the theatre. Yet his three plays produced during this new decade revealed a broadening of his interest and a firmer grasp upon his art. *Behold the Bridegroom* (1927) was a character study of a sophisticated girl, who after many experiences, meets the right kind of man and has the honesty to realize that she has not those qualities within her that would make her worthy to be his wife. Kelly had the courage to keep the situation clear of sentimentality. The "bridegroom" did not love her and, given the two characters, the tragedy was inevitable. Perhaps the treatment was too subtle for the stage; it certainly was for the newspaper critics who judged the play as a study of social life while it really was a drama of character. *Maggie the Magnificent* (1929) was a thoughtful representation of the career of a girl who has inherited from her artist father the love of beauty, while her mother is a vulgarian who, while loving Maggie deeply, makes life impossible for her. The ruthless determination of Maggie to break away, and the consequent struggle between her mother and herself, illustrated Kelly's ability to represent the way life goes on, even under stress. *Philip Goes Forth* (1931) was a satire upon the young man who determines to be a playwright when he really only desires to express his own individuality and gain some publicity. The weakness of this play lay in the fact that while the situation was a real one, it did not affect a large number of people. The comparatively unsuccessful career of these plays is probably the reason for Kelly's withdrawal, which it is to be hoped is only temporary.

Although Maxwell Anderson's *Sea Wife* has not been published and has not yet had a professional production, it was written in 1924. *Sea Wife* is a highly imaginative drama with splendid passages in verse. Taking from Matthew Arnold's *Forsaken Merman* the theme of the woman who has deserted her own race for a time and lived in the sea where she has borne children to the sea king, Anderson has built up a stark tragedy upon the lives and customs of a small island off the coast of Maine. In Arnold's poem, the sea king is a tragic figure, deserted by his human wife. But in *Sea Wife*, Margaret is the center of interest, and the dramatic conflict lies not only between her and the brutal, half savage men who try to brand her as a witch with a hot iron, but also within her soul between the love for her husband and her longing for the two children she believes she has had by the sea king. Anderson skilfully permits a possible explanation for the supernatural. Margaret may be mad, and the two children that are seen lying dead on the beach may be those of another pair whose guilty flight has been used effectively in the climax of the play. The atmosphere of the island, which might well have been the curious place off the Maine coast which until recent years belonged to no legal jurisdiction, is portrayed admirably, and Margaret's answer to the summons of her sea mate is a superb example of tragedy.

Anderson's *Gods of the Lightning* (1928) written with Harold Hickerson, obviously based upon the Sacco-Vanzetti Case, was a grim, powerful plea for justice, in which the characters are not all individualized. While the sympathy of the playwright was obviously with the radical group, they are not all idealists by any means. The best character was Suvorin, the proprietor of a restaurant, who is by no means an idealist, and whose earlier criminal record helps precipitate the tragedy. The clearest impression is that of the stupidity of the authorities in dealing with the situation. *Gypsy* (1929) was the tragedy of a girl who passed from one man to another and was unable to fix her affection upon any one. Her suicide was logical and inevitable, but the play lacked action, especially in the second Act. Fortunately Anderson next turned to the creation of historical figures and rose to his unquestioned position in the front rank of living playwrights. In *Elizabeth the Queen* (1930) he drew a stirring picture of the conflict between Elizabeth's love for Essex and her desire to rule alone. He transferred to the stage the ambition, the cruelty and the sensuous passion, the keen sense for reality and the royal dominance, which make the daughter of Henry VIII and Anne Boleyn such an arresting figure. The Earl of Essex, who is ambitious to be king of England and who considers that his own blood is quite as good as the Tudors or the Boleyns, is almost as well drawn. Anderson wrote the play in a blank verse singularly well adapted for the stage. He did not imitate the conventional measure, but keeping the spirit of the older verse rather than its pattern, he wrote a flexible line, preserving the four stress beat, but breaking up the lines to suit the thought. In other words, knowing the history of English poetry, he made the thought rule the verse. The curtain speeches of Act II when Elizabeth has tricked Essex into dismissing his guard illustrate this:

Eliz.: I have ruled England a long time, my Essex.
And I have found that he who would rule must be
Quite friendless, without mercy, without love.
Arrest Lord Essex!
Arrest Lord Essex! Take him to the Tower
And keep him safe.
Essex: Is this a jest?
Eliz.: I never
Jest when I play for kingdoms, my lord of Essex.
Essex: I trusted you.
Eliz.: I trusted you,
And learned from you that no one can be trusted.
I will remember that.
Essex: Lest that should be all
You ever have to remember, Your Majesty,
Take care what you do.
Eliz.: I shall take care.

It will be a long while before we forget Lynn Fontanne's magnificent portrayal of Elizabeth.

Night over Taos (1932), a romantic tragedy laid in New Mexico in 1847, was vivid in its pictures of the dying ideals of imperialistic Spain. There was too much discussion, however, about the social and political conditions and too many minor characters, and the play failed. Anderson's disgust at political corruption next led him to the writing of *Both Your Houses* (1933), a direct and stinging arraignment of the methods by which appropriations are lobbied through Congress. The hero, a young reformer, is well drawn, and the mixed motives of the Chairman of the Appropriations Committee who has been in control for years, as well as the methods by which the old hands trick the reformer, are real enough. The usual trouble with political plays showed in *Both Your Houses*. The very title revealed Anderson's purpose to keep out any conflict between the two great parties. Without raising the question of the relative merits of these parties, this avoidance of party names gives a vagueness and a lack of conflict to a play. The Committee meetings seem to be confined to the majority members, yet if this be true the title is meaningless. Some day a playwright will have the courage to write a drama which will make use of the real difference between the two parties, and if reformers are kept out of it in consequence, perhaps the play will not suffer. By an ironic chance, *Both Your Houses* won the Pulitzer Prize, while a much better play by Anderson during the next season received the recommendation of the committee and yet was not awarded the prize by the board of the Pulitzer Foundation.

Mary of Scotland (1933) is also better than *Elizabeth*. Elizabeth is not as dramatic a figure as Mary because her history does not offer so many contrasts. But in *Mary of Scotland*, all the dice are loaded against Mary and from the moment she lands at night, almost friendless, on the bleak shore of her kingdom she has the sympathy of the audience. Knowing his art well, Mr. Anderson has made the three great forces opposed to Mary—the power of Elizabeth, religious intolerance and the rule of the oligarchy of the Scottish lords—as concrete as possible. John Knox attacks her as soon as she lands; her half-brother, Murray, begins at once to encircle her with the conspiracy that is to ruin her, and, by deft interludes, the sinister power of Elizabeth brings on her doom. Mary has tried to rule by her charm and her desire to tolerate all forms of belief; Elizabeth, who is more clever as well as more unscrupulous, illustrates the struggle between a keen mind and a warm heart, in which the mind, of course, wins. Anderson took liberties with history. Bothwell, one of the few friends of Mary, is idealized, but there were good precedents in Swinburne's play. For the last powerful Act, Anderson had to draw on his imagination, for Mary and Elizabeth never met, after Mary fled to England. But the playwright had to bring them together and, so far as I could see, no one in the audience knew or cared about the facts, for the basic truth was there. If Mary had met her rival, something like that scene would have happened. *Mary of Scotland* is a great play, also, because the conflict between Mary Stuart and her enemies represents an eternal struggle between the idea of personal rule by one responsible individual, and the government by a less responsible and more impersonal group, whether they be a council of nobles or a parliament, a struggle which brought not only Mary but also her grandson, Charles I, to the block. It is a struggle which is perennial no matter what the ruler may be called. From the dramatist's point of view, the individual fighting against odds is a fine subject, for an audience likes a gallant, losing fight, and has a subconscious feeling that the rule of an oligarchy is the most dangerous form of tyranny.

The verse of *Mary of Scotland* is one of its chief assets. In the poignant love scenes between Mary and Bothwell, the flexibility and power are clear:

Mary: Yes. You are man enough.
It's dangerous to be honest with you, my Bothwell,
But honest I'll be. Since I've been woman grown

> There's been no man save you but I could take
> His hand steadily in mine, and look in his eyes
> Steadily, too, and feel in myself more power
> Than I felt in him.   All but yourself.   There is aching
> Fire between us, fire that could take deep hold
> And burn down all the marches of the west
> And make us great or slay us.   Yet it's not to be
>   trusted.
> Our minds are not the same.   If I gave my hand
> To you, I should be pledged to rule by wrath
> And violence, to take without denial,
> And mount on others' ruin.   That's your way
> And it's not mine.

Bothwell: You'll find no better way.
> There's no other way for this nation of churls and
>   cravens.

Mary: I have been queen of France—a child-queen and fool-
>   ish—
> But one thing I did learn, that to rule gently
> Is to rule wisely.   The knives you turn on your people
> You must sometime take in your breast.

Bothwell: You know not Scotland.
> Here you strike first or die.

The acting of Helen Hayes as Mary and of Philip Merivale as Bothwell was memorable.   Merivale, however, could not make the character of Washington in *Valley Forge* (1934) a theatrical success.   Anderson's conception of Washington was, in most respects, correct.   Once more he drew a great individual in conflict with an oligarchy, that is, with the ineptitude, corruption and even treachery of the Continental Congress, and he understood the real animus of the Conway Cabal.   But Washington would never have thrown a member of Congress out of the room by his neck, and he would never have decided to continue the war through the arguments of the soldiers.   I have given earlier the reasons why Washington is not a good subject for a play, but the effort was a fine one even if it was not a popular success.

The superiority of the universal over the particular for dramatic purposes was illustrated by the contrast between *Win-*

terset (1935) and *Gods of the Lightning*. The flavor of propaganda was absent from *Winterset*, for while the central motive was the devotion of a boy whose father had been unjustly convicted of murder, the audience was not disturbed by the controversy concerning a doubtful case, and could enjoy the lofty poetry and could sympathize fully with the son who gave his life in an effort to clear his father's name. The atmosphere of *Winterset*, laid in a dark street under the shadow of a mighty bridge near the river in New York, was heavy with fate. Through this figure of the youthful son of Romagna, Anderson uttered a protest against two powerful agents of injustice, made concrete in the persons of Trock, the chief of the murder gang, and Judge Gaunt, who had presided at Romagna's trial and whose conscience has driven him insane. Anderson has expressed his philosophy of composition in the introduction to *Winterset*. He believes that audiences are ready for plays "which will take up again the consideration of man's place and destiny in prophetic rather than prosaic terms." He may be an optimist, but in any event he has helped to bring back the spell of splendor into the American theatre. Like O'Neill, he has had the courage to face comparison with the highest standards, for the resemblance of the central motive of *Winterset* to that of *Hamlet* is evident. But Anderson proved not only that the fidelity of a son to his father's memory may be expressed in modern terms with a new meaning, but also that poetry may interpret modern life without apology, if the playwright is a poet of eminence.

After an unsuccessful attempt at dramatizing the career of an evangelist in *Salvation* (1928), in which he collaborated with Charles MacArthur, Sidney Howard discussed the marriage problem in *Half Gods* (1929). While there was some clever satire on psychoanalysts who lead women to think too much about themselves, the play was inconclusive, for the husband's solution by knocking his wife down did not seem to appeal to critical or public taste. After these two failures, Howard fashioned one of the most successful comedies of the decade from

Prenez Garde à la Peinture by René Fauchois, which had been acted at the Théâtre des Mathurins in Paris in February, 1932. In *The Late Christopher Bean* (1932), Howard followed the main plot, which is a delightful satire upon a family in a small provincial town, who had once known a young painter, and had deemed him worthless. The only person who had understood him was the house-maid, and in adapting the play, Howard made this the leading part for Pauline Lord. After the painter's death, he becomes famous, and the art critic and dealers who visit the family are delightful figures, especially the forger of pictures who enters into a deal with the doctor, the head of the family, to create a number of "Mavriers" in the French, or "Christopher Beans" in English, to which the doctor will certify. Howard changed the ending by having "Abby," the maid, disclose that she is the wife of the painter, thus giving her the pictures. This is an improvement, because in the French, the doctor who is selfish and dishonest is left with the property, which is irritating rather than inevitable. The skill of Howard is shown by the way in which, through comparatively few changes, he transforms the scene to a provincial New England town, and no suspicion would enter the head of a spectator that he was seeing an adaptation from the French if the program did not inform him. Perhaps after all, provincials are the same the world over. Indeed it is possible that Fauchois may have taken a hint from Mark Twain's story "Is He Living or Is He Dead," in which a group of French painters make François Millet famous by pretending he has died! The contrast of the artist with provincial limitations was the basis for Howard's *Alien Corn* (1933). Here the atmosphere is that of a small college in the Middle West, and the struggle of Elsa Brandt, the pianist, against it made an appealing if a bit inconclusive play, which owed its interest largely to the playing of Katharine Cornell.

Howard's adaptation of Sinclair Lewis's *Dodsworth* (1934) was an unusually interesting occurrence in the American theatre. Fortunately the playwright and the novelist have contributed forewords which make very clear how much better a playwright

Howard is than Lewis is a novelist. Howard not only has omitted much of the tiresome detail which cluttered the novel, but he has added some remarkably fine scenes, which are not in the novel at all. He took the character, of course, the American business man who sells his automobile factory and tries to satisfy his wife's desire for European travel and social life. But if one compares, for example, the thirty-eight pages of the novel for which have been substituted nine pages of Act III, Scene 2, he will notice that the language is practically all Howard's, and that the wanderings of Dodsworth over Europe have been condensed into one brief scene. Moreover, the description of his infidelity to his wife has been entirely omitted and is shown conclusively to be quite unnecessary in the development of the situation. Even more striking is the creation of that marvelous third scene of Act III, between the Baroness and Fran Dodsworth which the acting of Madame Ouspenskaya made unforgettable. In the novel, Fran's letter tells Dodsworth that "Kurt's mother was pretty rude to me" and "wailed at Kurt and ignored me." In the play it is the perfect courtesy of the patrician which defeats the selfish woman by sending Kurt from the room and then saying quietly:

Baroness: Rich or poor, Kurt should have children to carry on the name. Could you give them to him?
Fran: What makes you think I couldn't?
Baroness: I am so much older than you, my dear! You will forgive me if I observe that you are older than Kurt.
Fran: Children or no children, Kurt loves me and I love him, Baroness! So why shouldn't we do without your permission and marry anyway and take our happiness!
Baroness: I do not know what power you have over Kurt. I should think of my own happiness, if I were you.
Fran: I am thinking of that!
Baroness: (*leaning forward and speaking with grave deliberation*) Have you thought how little happiness there can be for the old wife of a young husband?

In short, Howard made a new creation out of *Dodsworth*, and to those who saw the production with Walter Huston in the title role, it will be the play and the actor who will remain to them and not the novel.

Howard's most important contribution during the decade was *Yellow Jack* (1934), not only because it was a fine play, but because it suggests a new way in which the old motives of self-preservation and heroism may be established. *Yellow Jack* is a dramatization of those quietly heroic moments in which science achieves its victories. Most of the action is laid in Cuba in 1900 when the Walter Reed Commission was trying to discover the source of yellow fever. Howard made the struggle concrete through characters like Dr. Finlay, who first suggests the mosquito, or like Carroll and Lazear, members of the Commission who inoculate themselves with the poison of the mosquito carrier, and through the volunteers among the privates, who also furnish some good comedy. The conflict is not only between science and disease, it is also between science and the single track mind of the army, who in the person of Colonel Tory almost blocks the progress of discovery. The death of Lazear is one of the most thrilling moments of modern drama:

Gorgas: He's getting weaker.
Finlay: No, Major Gorgas! The stuff of courage doesn't grow weaker. It grows stronger. Stronger and brighter! Until it blinds us! But we do see its flaming sword cut through the veil!
Gorgas: What veil?
Finlay: (*Pointing*) Out there, where knowledge hides!

Yellow Jack was not a popular success, but it deserved to be. Perhaps the prologue and epilogue which dealt with later developments in London and South Africa destroyed the unity which was so essential. To secure this unity the play was performed without interruption. Howard, taking the central idea from Paul de Kruif's *Microbe Hunters*, resolutely kept the play strictly to the matter in hand, and permitted no "love interest" or other episodes to interrupt the quiet progress of a great idea across the stage.

The difference between what is proper dramatic material and

what is not, was illustrated by Howard's next play, *Gather Ye Rosebuds* (1934), based on the attempt of two characters, one drawn from Insull and one from Dillinger, to teach the Greeks how to run their finances. It died after tryouts in Philadelphia and Washington. His adaptation from the French, *Ode to Liberty* (1935), was clever but had such a light plot even for farce that it hardly needs discussion. Howard's adaptation of Humphrey Cobb's novel *Paths of Glory* (1935), while a failure on the stage, affords an excellent opportunity to test the principles of adaptation and the dramatic values of a peace play. Howard has a singularly acute critical sense and his Foreword to the printed play is more interesting than the play itself. He calls attention to the unfortunate "compromise between the literal and the abstract" in this play, and adds the trenchant sentence "Suggestive scenery will never again suggest anything to me but stage hands pulling objects which have no meaning." If all those who love the theatre would join Sidney Howard in his protest against the tyranny of scenery, one way of escape from the evils of the theatre might be opened. *Paths of Glory* really was not a play at all, but a series of scenes, cluttered with characters who rarely became individuals, and even in the theatre looked so much alike that the audience began to recognize them only when they were whisked off the stage. There was also too much of the novel and not enough of the playwright, for Howard did not make of the play a new thing as he had done in *Dodsworth*. This was the basic trouble, since *Paths of Glory* is an irritating rather than a tragic novel. Indignation is directed not at war, but at an individual general, and there is no lift at the end of *Paths of Glory* as there was at the curtain of *What Price Glory* by Anderson and Stallings. *Paths of Glory* ends with the collapse into cowardice or brutality or cynicism of three men who have been the bravest of the regiment. *What Price Glory* ended on the note of the return to duty of two men, worn out with fatigue, because of their innate courage. The last is good theatre; the first is not.

Philip Barry has continued to write the most brilliant social comedy of the decade and at times the most profound studies of modern character. After a brave but unsuccessful attempt to dramatize the career of John the Baptist under the title *John* (1927), he wrote *Paris Bound* (1927), a sincere defence of the institution of marriage, conveyed through delicious comedy. Barry starts out his young people, Jim and Mary Hutton, with every advantage, and when, six years later Mary discovers that Noel Farley, who loves Jim, has captured him while he was abroad alone, she decides to divorce him. The argument against divorce has never been put better than in the pleading of Jim's father, who has himself been divorced, that Mary will not wreck the lives of his son, of herself and of their children because of one marital dereliction. As he says: "I don't mean to belittle sex. It holds a high and dishonored place among other forms of intoxication. But love is something else again, and marriage is still another thing. . . ." In the real marriage a spiritual relationship is established that is far more important than the physical union. So when she insists upon divorcing Jim, his father turns upon her with the charge that it is she who is placing their physical relationship above every other phase of their union. The play is no plea for the extenuation of adultery; it is an argument for the permanence of the family as opposed to the individual. This appeal is never sentimentalized. The children are kept off the stage but they are in the background, and it is they, together with Jim's charm when he returns and his trust in Mary when he meets her with the young musician with whom she has been flirting, that carries them both back to safety. One of the delightful minor characters in *Paris Bound* was acted by Hope Williams, and for her Barry wrote *Holiday* (1928). Linda Seton is an unusual occurrence in a stodgy family of wealth, and she alone understands the young lawyer, who is engaged to her sister, but who wishes to have some leisure to enjoy life while he is young instead of waiting until a fortune is accumulated but the capacity for enjoyment is gone. As soon as Linda and Johnny Case meet, they see they are kindred spirits, and their dialogue becomes that distinguished persiflage which Philip Barry alone knows how to write.

In 1930 Barry's *Hotel Universe* marked the high point so far of his career. To understand *Hotel Universe* does not require a painful mental effort, as some of the reviews seemed to indicate. It is, to be sure, a play for people of brains and breeding, but Barry never forgets that drama proceeds not primarily through ideas but rather through emotions. Indeed, my one criticism of the play lies in the fact that our sympathies are so strongly enlisted in the joys and sorrows of the characters that there is a certain strain after two hours from the very intensity of our interest.

Now what is the reason some auditors were puzzled by *Hotel Universe?* I fancy it is because, having been fed on trivialities in our modern drama, they did not expect to find something important proceeding on the stage. "Facts of life" in a flat in Harlem or in an English country-house, facts so obvious that they cannot fail to amuse or terrify, have been fed to us so long that when Barry or O'Neill give us fundamental *truths* made up of the fusion of a number of facts, we gasp a bit. In *Hotel Universe* Barry is dramatizing the significant truth that the most important element in our lives, for good or evil, is some illusion we are cherishing. A group of friends are gathered on a terrace of a house in the south of France, near Toulon. They represent various types, but they are not merely types, they are real people. Ann Field, the hostess, has rented this house to take care of her father, Stephen Field, who is supposed to be slightly abnormal. Pat Farley, whom she loves, is the rich son of a stock that has been important for some time. Tom Ames, also wealthy, has been a publisher, but has stopped publishing about life in order to live himself. His wife, Hope, is a fairly normal mother and wife. Lily Malone is an actress. Norman Rose is a great Jewish financier. Alice Kendall is "twenty-six, very smart and rather pretty." In a few swift moments we realize that every one has some worry which he is concealing or else has no real interest in life and is bored by it. For relief the characters do the things human beings would naturally do—amuse the crowd by making fun of each other, hurt each other deliberately, wounding their best friends as they strike back at something they do not understand. Through the atmosphere of the house, but more concretely through the influence of Stephen Field, Ann's father, who enters midway in the play, the characters begin to reveal their inner selves to him or to each other. Stephen is very wise, for he has learned what a great playwright said many years ago—

> There are more things in heaven and earth, Horatio,
> Than are dreamt of in our philosophy.

Stephen sees that Pat Farley is contemplating suicide by dropping off a mountain and checks him. Pat wins through to health by telling for the first time to any one the thing that is gnawing at him, his betrayal and abandonment of a girl who had loved him. He had refused to tell Ann what is troubling him, but he does so under the spell of a belief that he is going back to the past and telling his mother about Mary's suicide. Delicately the maternal element in Ann Field's love for him is translated into the spell which finally releases him from his obsession of guilt.

Alice Kendall's passion for Norman Rose, revealed in her sleep walking, is powerful, realistic, and somehow not quite so satisfying. But it leads to some magnificent lines:

Stephen: Sleep has freed her from time and space. One day sleep's sister will free her further. We are not so much slaves of time as we think ourselves—in my opinion time is something of a humbug like most man-made inventions—it has one decent function; to heal, and when it does not do that . . . Yes, it does bewilder one at first. I know. I too used to believe life had one aspect only. I was so sure that sleep and dreaming was—well, sleep and dreaming. And of course I knew that with death it was all over—

Pat: (*Coming across to table*) Well?

Stephen: Well, now I know I was mistaken.

Pat: How?

Stephen: I have found out a simple thing: that in existence there are *three* estates. There is this life of chairs and tables, of getting up and sitting down. There is the life one lives in one's imagining, in which one wishes, dreams, remembers. There is the life past death, which in itself contains the others. The three estates are one. We dwell now in this one, now in that—but in whichever we may be, breezes from the others still blow upon us.

Stephen helps them one by one. Ann, who has given always —to Pat, to her father—needs no destruction of illusions, for she has built her life up not on her own self-absorption but upon the happiness of others. But no moral is drawn from her by Barry. He is too much of an artist for that. After the rest are gone, and Stephen has had his stroke, which carries him off, he sits there concealed by his great chair, while Pat and Ann plan their future in the presence of death. How simply it ends:

Pat: I want to make love to you for years. Oh it's a life, Ann.

Ann: I know dear—don't I know. Thank you, Father.

Pat: Yes—thanks. (*Cock crows.*) What's that? What time is it?

Ann: Hush, darling, never mind. It's just an old white rooster— one of Father's pets, his clock he calls him.

Pat: It must be dawn somewhere.

Ann: But of course dear—always!

Pat: "Wherever there is an end" he said—

Ann: "From it the beginning springs." (*She turns to Stephen— her hand drops. She walks a step toward Stephen as the curtain falls.*)

The completely unified form of *Hotel Universe* which was the first of the contemporary plays to be performed without the curtain falling, was justified by its success. The atmosphere in which strange things may happen is built up too carefully to be destroyed even for a moment. Like all theatrical experiments, its importance rests not upon its novelty, but upon its aid in interpreting the thought and the tone of the play.

Tomorrow and Tomorrow (1931) was a worthy successor to *Hotel Universe.* Taking a suggestion from the Fourth Book of Kings II, in the Bible, he drew a woman, married but childless, whose longing to create makes her give herself to a visitor, a distinguished biologist whom she loves, and by whom she has a child. Her husband believes the boy his own and builds his life upon his pride in his family. When the boy some years later is injured and Mrs. Redman summons his real father, who is ignorant of his parenthood, to save the boy's life, there comes one of those climaxes that show Barry's deep understanding of the fundamental realities of life. Quietly Eve Redman realizes that even great passion may have its moment and pass on, while the acceptance of responsibility demands an even greater sacrifice for others. It is her power of imagination which shows her what the "tomorrow and tomorrow" of her husband would be without her and the boy, and it is not the least of Barry's qualities that permits him to endow his characters with an imagination which seems to be their own spiritual property. In *Tomorrow and Tomorrow* Barry again showed his ability to draw Americans in a situation where a European dramatist would paint the satisfaction of passion as sacred, while the American playwright knows that self-respect and generosity of soul establish character more surely than desertion of duty and satisfaction of passion.

In his next study of the married relation, *The Animal Kingdom* (1932), Barry's belief that marriage is a union of spiritual and intellectual equals who are bound by like tastes and by what they give to each other quite as much as by any physical relation, is still apparent. But in this play, Tom Collier has made a mistake in the woman he marries and his former mistress is his real wife, to whom he ultimately returns. The play becomes rather a struggle on his part for the preservation of his individual integrity, than a study of marriage. Indeed the weakness of it lies in the fact that there is no very good reason why he should not have married the right woman in the first place, and the more clearly the play reveals their deep and tender understanding, the less credible the initial situation becomes.

But on the stage, the acting of Leslie Howard made it seem credible.

The Joyous Season (1934) appeared to be beyond the comprehension of the critics, but its central motive is really quite clear. It is a study of a family in Boston, coming from Irish stock, which has won its way to a position of standing, but whose members are each limited by the solidarity of the clan or by their own inhibitions. The eldest sister, Christina, the Mother Superior of an order of nuns, has not seen the family for some years. She visits them at Christmas time and through her tact and understanding helps them to break through the barrier that stands in the way of their happiness. She leaves them, not with their problems all solved, but with something planted in them that will help to solve these problems. It is her Christmas gift to them. There are many fine passages in *The Joyous Season,* such as Christina's remark to Terry: "You see I believe faith to be of first importance. I believe it is the soul's adventure out of sight of land."

It seems a pity that there are few critics to appreciate and no audiences to support such a deeply moving play as *Bright Star* (1935) which lasted just five nights. It is the tragedy of an egotist, Quin Hanna, with "too much head and too little heart" who marries a rich girl, Hope Blake. She is deeply in love with him, but he has within himself no capacity for love. The first act in which, through conversation with his two best friends, Sam and Kate, he realizes what he is facing not only for Hope but for himself and yet cannot bring himself to tell her because of the truly exquisite expression of her love for him, is one of the finest instances of dramatic exposition I know. Hope's willingness to risk all, though she too senses his isolation, is natural, and her absorption in him of course becomes possession, which helps to bring on the tragedy. One of the best elements in the play is the picture of the political and social idealist who, in the midst of his broad schemes for the betterment of the New England town, is a failure in the personal relation with the one who loves him best. As the play approaches its catastrophe, when, after the loss of their child before it was born, Quin decides to go away alone, Barry skilfully deepens our sympathy for both of them. Quin pronounces his own doom to Kate: "I've found out a funny thing—you have to have a heart to love, all right. But you don't need one to suffer. The inability to love is just about the finest torture there is." And Hope tells him: "I don't have to be spared things. You see my love for you has changed a little—it doesn't even need your presence any more. It can live on empty air." It is because of their spiritual importance that the wreck of this marriage leaves one at the end of the play with a pity that is almost unbearable, but it is a tribute to Barry's insight into the ways of grief.

Marc Connelly has given us only three plays during the new decade, but one of them, *The Green Pastures* (1930), is among the outstanding contributions of the period. It is a remarkable expression of the negro's idea of the creation, the deluge and the history of the world up to the time of Christ. The supreme difficulty was, of course, the representation of "de Lawd." How this was solved through the superb acting of Richard Harrison, a negro, whose native dignity gave the character exactly the right tone, is now theatrical history. But the play has also been presented abroad at Stockholm, for example, with great success. *The Green Pastures* was suggested by a humorous book, *Ol' Man Adam an' His Chillun* by Roark Bradford (1928). But Connelly visited Louisiana in company with Bradford to study the phases of the life he has represented. The skill with which Connelly created the play can best be appreciated when it is compared with the sketches. Some of the most effective scenes are original. The framework of the preacher who tells the children the story is new; the Lord's "private office" where he interviews Gabriel is Connelly's invention. The way in which he changed the expression to lift the sentiment to a higher plane is illustrated by the scene of the ascension of Moses. In the original it is an amusing paragraph. But in *The Green Pastures* it is a remarkable scene of

the marching Israelites approaching Jericho, of Moses' blindness and his sudden fear:

God: What's de matter?
Moses: We cain't be doin' dis!
God: Co'se we kin!
Moses: But I fo'got! I fo'got about Joshua and de fightin' men!
God: How about 'em?
Moses: Dey're marchin' on Jericho. I tol' 'em to march aroun' de
    walls and den de Lawd would be dere to tell 'em what to do.
God: Dat's all right. He's dere.
Moses: Den who's helpin' me up de hill?
God: Yo' faith, yo' God.
Moses: And is you over dere helpin' dem too, Lawd? Is you goin'
    to tell dem poor chillun what to do?
God: Co'se I is. Listen, Moses. I'll show you how I'm helpin'
    dem.
    (*From the distance comes the blast of the rams' horns, the
    sound of crumbling walls, a roar, and a moment's silence. The
    choir begins "Joshua Fit De Battle of Jericho" and continues
    through the rest of the scene.*)

One of the finest scenes is that in which Hezdrel, the Hebrew
leader, talks with God before he makes his last stand before
Herod:

Hezdrel: Oh, dat ol' God dat walked de earth in de shape of a man.
    I guess he lived wid man so much dat all he seen was de sins in
    man. Dat's what made him de God of wrath and vengeance.
    Co'se he made Hosea. An' Hosea never would a found what
    mercy was unless dere was a little of it in God, too. Anyway,
    he ain't a fearsome God no mo'. Hosea showed us dat.
God: How you s'pose Hosea found dat mercy?
Hezdrel: De only way he could find it. De only way I found it.
    De only way anyone kin find it.
God: How's dat?
Hezdrel: Through sufferin'.

Hezdrel is not in Bradford's book but, more important, he
is not in the Bible. Yet few if any of the auditors of the play
seemed to suspect that he was Connelly's creation. To project

the imagination of a race into the relations of God and man, to dare the seemingly impossible and achieve success, might teach other playwrights that the negro, in his wistful, exalted and emotional phases, is much better suited to the stage than when he is being exploited as the symbol of a struggle for racial equality.

In *The Farmer Takes a Wife* (1934) Connelly took the atmosphere of the Erie Canal in the fifties and some of the characters from a novel *Rome Haul* by W. D. Edmonds. Since the novel concerned people who were constantly moving there were many changes necessary, and the climax of the novel, the fight between Dan Harrow and the bully, took place off stage. The nature of the heroine, Molly Larkin, and her devotion to the Canal, which separated her from Dan when he returned to farming, was changed also to make their union possible in the play. What came out of *The Farmer Takes a Wife*, therefore, was mainly an authentic picture of a past era, portrayed with humorous touches that set off the glamour. What was lacking was the conflict of character which made the novel interesting.

George Kaufman has continued to shape the material, usually in collaboration, of satiric comedy. His own contribution is not easy to evaluate, for in addition to a wit which has individual quality, he possesses a remarkable sense of the dramatic as well as of the theatrical. This knowledge of the stage shone in *The Royal Family* (1927) written with Edna Ferber. It is a glowing reproduction of the lure which the theatre has for the members of the Cavendish family, which results in a temperamental life, furious at times in its inconsequence. It was a delightful evening in the theatre, especially noteworthy through the performance of Haidee Wright as Fanny Cavendish, the trouper of the old days. *June Moon* (1929) was amusing but not important, and *Once in a Lifetime* (1930), a blistering satire upon the absurdities of Hollywood, written with Moss Hart before either of the authors had been there, did not reach quite to the level of the succeeding plays. In *Of Thee I Sing* (1932) Kaufman approached the standard of W. S. Gilbert in the use of political material for satire, without offence, but with penetration and a shrewd estimate of the stupidity, banality and falsity of much of our party manipulation. There is much more plot than is usual in a musical comedy, and it is coherent. Writers of this vein of satire will have to go far before they can equal the spectacle of the Vice-President presiding over the Senate during the impeachment of the President. The widely different fortunes of *Of Thee I Sing* and its sequel *Let 'Em Eat Cake* (1933) illustrate a dramatic law. The satire of the first of these bit deeply into the Toryism and lack of a constructive policy of the years preceding 1932, and came just at the right time. The sequel satirized an imaginary political revolution which bore no relation to the actual situation. Dramatic satire must have reality as a basis and above all it must be concrete.

Between these musical plays, Kaufman collaborated with Edna Ferber in a powerful social satire, *Dinner at Eight* (1932). It deals with the fortunes of various people who have been invited to dine with a social climber to meet two members of the British nobility, culminating in the death of one guest, the fatal disease of her husband and her daughter's danger, all of which seem to her of no moment compared to the calm breaking of the engagement by Lady Ferncliff. *The Dark Tower* (1933) with Alexander Woollcott was too reminiscent of *Trilby* to seem important. But in *Merrily We Roll Along* (1934) George Kaufman and Moss Hart progressed from the amusing burlesque of Hollywood to the searching drama of a playwright's spiritual disintegration. The trouble with most satires of modern life is that they are too abstract and general, but here we are never allowed to forget the three central characters. Niles, the playwright, is caught by the lure of success and by the clutch of a woman unworthy of him and writes plays that bring him merely money but no satisfaction. Crale, the painter, keeps his own standards. Julia, the novelist, cannot fight it out, because of her love for Niles, and drinks herself to disgrace. This friendship between two men and one woman is as real as life itself. The retrogressive method of the play, by which the scenes begin in 1934 and go back to 1916, was eminently successful. It is, of course, not new, the closest parallel being Zoë Akins' *Varying Shore*, but it is carried out in a much more telling way, without sentimentality. Every young playwright should see or read the scene between Niles and Crale in which the latter begs his friend to go back to his earlier high standard. The last scene, laid in the college chapel where Niles is giving his valedictory, full of ideals, is terrific in its irony, for the audience has seen the crash of these lofty aspirations. This play illustrates a principle which is often forgotten, that theatrical rules may easily be broken, while dramatic laws remain constant. It has been a theatrical rule that plays must proceed chronologically, but *Merrily We Roll Along* disproves this assertion. At the same time the dramatic law of which it is an evidence still holds good. An audience loves to know something that the characters do not know. The audiences of *Merrily We Roll Along* are in possession of the future, and it adds tremendously to their appreciation of the past. If the play proceeded chronologically, they would know only as much as the characters know. It is the same dramatic law as that which O'Neill made use of in *Strange Interlude*, though the theatrical device is quite different.

In *First Lady* (1935), written with Katharine Dayton, Kaufman returned to political satire. Around the leading character, supposed to be drawn from Mrs. Longworth, revolve the interrelations of social and political life in Washington. The ambitions of Lucy Wayne who wants her husband, the Secretary of State, to become President, were drawn skilfully and while most of the characters were types, as a group they presented a fine illusion of veracity.

In the drama of the provinces, Paul Green has remained one of the most significant figures. *The House of Connelly* (1931) was a vivid contrast between the decaying forces of a southern family whose earlier virility had run to seed, and the vigor of a generation of tenant farmers who have lived closest to the soil. There were some extremely well drawn characters, especially Will Connelly, the son, Uncle Bob and Mrs. Connelly of the older generation, and Pansy, the daughter of the tenant, who first tricks Will into marrying her and then ends by loving and saving him. *Potter's Field*, published with *The House of Connelly*, was not produced professionally until April, 1934.   Then after revision it appeared on the New York stage as *Roll, Sweet Chariot*.   Here is negro life as it really is, sordid in its details, but with a lift at the end.   The casual moral relations of the negro, his animal nature, his living for the moment only, are shown clearly.   The symbolism is not completely worked in, but the slow, impassive march of the convict gang working on the new road that runs over the spot where the characters formerly lived, is impressive.   In *Tread the Green Grass*, symbolism became triumphant.   It is according to Green the tragedy of a sensitive soul driven mad by her environment, but Tina's adventure with a young faun-like creature leaves one confused, at least in reading.   Owing to the circumstances of production, I have not seen Green's plays since *The House of Connelly*. Several have been produced at Chapel Hill at the Playmakers' Theatre, the last, *The Enchanted Maze* (1935), being a sweeping criticism of college education.   I have read only the last scene, in manuscript, and while I recognize the sincerity of the disappointed aspirations of the young seeker after inspiration, there seems to be a solution of the matter which has not occurred to Green.   But that is a matter of practical education and not of drama.   Green's symphonic plays with musical accompaniment indicate an avenue in which drama may develop a rich variety of effects.   That they have so far not captured or held the attention of audiences in the professional theatre, is no evidence that they will not eventually do so.   For Green has imagination and artistry.   His danger is a slight tendency toward propaganda, but usually he keeps free of this pitfall.

Lula Vollmer's two plays of the South have not come up to the high level of *Sun-Up* or *The Shame Woman*.   *Trigger* (1927) was a play about a girl who was a curious mixture of religious enthusiasm, superstition, bad manners and human affection. *Sentinels* (1931) was primarily a study in the loyalty of an old negress to the family to which she belongs.   There were good characters, and "Mallie," while not a success in New York, was much more appreciated when Lucille LaVerne played the part in the West. The defect of the play lay in the elaborate exposition for a final situation which in itself was not satisfactory.

The excellence of these plays can best be appreciated when they are compared with such a production as *Tobacco Road* (1933) dramatized by Jack Kirkland from Erskine Caldwell's novel. This play marks probably the depths of degradation into which the drama may descend. It is not only the dialogue in which indecency, profanity and blasphemy contend for first place, but the essential lack of any significance in the characters or situations. There may be people in Georgia as low in the scale of humanity as the Lesters, but they could only be legitimate material for drama if they were used as a background out of which something tragic might be evolved. Joel Chandler Harris showed in his short story "Azalia" how they might be used artistically. But Jeeter Lester, who sells one daughter for seven dollars, sends another to act as a prostitute and treats his mother's death in the fields as a mere incident, cannot be made appealing because he presents no contrast to his background. Even the acting of Henry Hull, who bravely attempted to capitalize Jeeter's disinclination to leave his farm could not lift the play out of dullness. The long run of *Tobacco Road* must be attributed to the existence of a certain type of mind which loves to be shocked, and is amused by cheap cynicism and the spectacle of humanity in disgrace.

The new decade has witnessed an increasing interest in the negro as a dramatic theme. Among the best results of this interest was *Porgy* (1927), a dramatization by Dorothy and Dubose Heyward of the latter's novel. Mrs. Heyward had won a prize at Harvard with her *Nancy Ann* (1924) and the combination of her talent and that of her husband created a remarkable picture of negro life in Catfish Row in Charleston. The effect upon Porgy, the cripple, of the appeal of Bess, the prostitute, to his protection, the temporary regeneration of Bess, her relapse and flight and Porgy's departure in search of her, are told through a series of scenes in which the humor lightens tragedy and the solidarity of the negro race when menaced by "white man's law" was finely revealed. Encouraged by the success of the spirituals, the Theatre Guild revived the play as a folk opera, *Porgy and Bess* (1935). As entertainment the opera was a great success. But as drama, it illustrated the artificiality of opera. In the original play, there was a powerful scene in which Crown, the gigantic negro, comes in search of Bess, and Porgy, lying in wait behind his window shutter, suddenly clutches Crown by the neck in his powerful grip and chokes him to death. It was good drama because it seized the one moment when the cripple was on even terms with his rival, and it made use of that provision of nature which frequently endows a man whose legs are crippled with super power in his arms. But in the opera, it was deemed necessary to have the singer representing Porgy take the center of the stage, so he stabbed Crown and then pursued him to the central position, losing thereby the best situation in the play. Dubose Heyward in the meantime had written *Brass Ankle* (1931), a tragedy of miscegenation, when Ruth Leamer, the granddaughter of a "Brass Ankle," a race in which white, Indian and negro blood is mingled, gives birth to a negro boy. Her terror, for she is ignorant of the taint, and her husband's horror of the child, are heightened by the fact that their eldest child, June, is perfectly white. To save June Ruth calls in her neighbors and tells them that the boy is the son of a negro who had been in their employ. Her husband kills her and the baby. The tragedy is almost unbearable, but it is powerful for it represents human beings in the grip of something they cannot fight. Heyward was on a surer artistic path in *Porgy* than in *Brass Ankle*.

One of the most thrilling of spectacles belonged to the same impulse as *Porgy*. *Run, Little Chillun* (1933) by Hall Johnson, was of especial significance because it was written by a negro and produced by an all-negro cast. The contrast between the emotional religion of a Baptist negro church and the survival of primitive elements of pagan origin was made concrete in the person of the young preacher, and his wife and his mistress. The final scene in which the pagan chant of the "New Pilgrims" becomes an integral part of the triumphant revival hymn of the Baptist congregation will not be forgotten by those who heard it. *Run, Little Chillun* points clearly to the future of the negro play because Johnson, instead of repeating the theme of conflict between whites and negroes which negro novelists and playwrights have been dwelling upon too long, dealt like Paul Green with a conflict within the race itself.

The West has produced some interesting plays of locality, but none to equal the work of Green or Heyward in the South. Lynn Riggs, of Oklahoma, has written some of the most entertaining and some of the most absurd plays of the decade. When he is content with comedy as in *Green Grow the Lilacs* (1930) or *Roadside* (1930) or *Russet Mantle* (1936) he can write amusing dialogue and create such delightful characters as Curly McClain and Aunt Ellen Murphy in the first, or even better, Effie Rowley and Susanna Kincaid in the last. They are all caricatures, of course, but in her helpless inability to control her promiscuous daughter, Mrs. Rowley was a sheer joy to the eye and ear. But when Riggs began to be serious in *Russet Mantle*, he became confused and his tragedies of futility like *Big Lake* (1927) and *Sump'n Like Wings* (1928) do not stir us. The heroine of *Sump'n Like Wings* escapes from the deadly hotel life not into anything worth while, but only into the world of her own desires, which are entirely selfish. They lead her not upward but within. Like many others, Riggs does not understand the difference between enlarging one's soul to take in a finer and broader world, and narrowing the world to make it fit into a narrow soul. Great plays are written about the first process, little ones about the second. There is more interest in "Jodie" Harman of *A Lantern to See By* (1928) because he is a finer character, but even he inspires only a languid attention.

Dan Totheroh, another Western playwright of whom I have

already spoken in an earlier chapter, dramatized the pioneer days in *Distant Drums* (1932) with moderate success. But his best play, *Moor Born* (1934) was not laid in the West, but in the bleak Yorkshire of the Brontë family. The sacrifice of the sisters for their weak and dissolute brother is joined in highly dramatic scenes with their discovery of their common talents. The practical qualities of Charlotte, the gentle nature of Anne and the passionate quality of Emily's genius are developed in a sombre but powerful play, profoundly stirring.

Among the other playwrights of Western provincial life, Virgil Geddes has at times a directness of dialogue which is encouraging. But in *The Earth Between* (1929), a study of the unnatural love of a father for a daughter, he seemed to be reaching for something he hardly secured.

Among the playwrights who began to produce during the decade 1927–1936, Samuel Nathaniel Behrman has made perhaps the most considerable contribution. After some collaborations which he apparently wishes to disregard, *The Second Man* (1927) was produced by the Theatre Guild. It was a clever comedy of manners, inspired, he says, by a letter of Lord Leighton, the British painter: "There is always that other strange second man in me, calm, critical, observant, unmoved, blasé, odious." The dual character of Clark Storey, a writer, is admirably brought out through the two women who love him, one a rich widow, the other a young girl. Mrs. Frayne wins because she is aware of both sides of his nature: Monica loses him because she is shocked when he reveals his clear sighted vision of their future, if he marries a poor girl. The dialogue is kept on a level of epigram without forcing it. Behrman stated his philosophy of composition in this play:

Storey: Why is a book about unhappy dirty people better than one about gay and comfortable ones?
Monica: But life isn't gay or—comfortable.
Storey: (Seriously) Life is sad. I know it's sad. But I think it's gallant to pretend that it isn't.

Such a philosophy limits a dramatist, of course, but since Behrman is one of the few successful writers of social comedy, it is perhaps fortunate that he chose to write in this manner.

His next play, *Serena Blandish* (1929), was a dramatization of the novel by "A Lady of Quality," since announced as Enid Bagnold. It has not the importance of his original work, for he uses at times the language of his model, which is a brittle, artificial story of a girl who is too generous with her favors, and, having no money, is forced to marry a half breed Indian from Nicaragua. Behrman provided a white husband for her and made other changes, but kept the atmosphere of the utter heartlessness of those who are secure and the helplessness of a girl in her struggle against the financial basis of caste in England.

Meteor (1929) was of more moment than either of the preceding plays. The character of Raphael Lord, who proceeds ruthlessly to carve out his own career without thought of others, was inspired by Napoleon, but became a remarkable symbol of the age when financial success was the only measure of greatness, and the United States was riding to its inevitable disaster. Behrman was instinctively right in permitting Lord apparently to triumph over his enemies, for there would have been little satisfaction to an audience to have the rival financiers, who were even worse than he, win out. Lord's tragedy is a personal one for his wife leaves him because she no longer is able to bear his disregard of her individual rights. *Meteor* is not a comedy of manners, but the dialogue is at times brilliant and the clash of character and of ideals is concrete.

Brief Moment (1931) was disappointing. The central motive—that of a man of wealth and assured position marrying a cabaret singer who had already been the mistress of more than one man, was reminiscent of *The Second Mrs. Tanqueray*. There was no significant treatment of the social atmosphere, and the characters seemed types rather than the real people Behrman usually draws. It would have been more logical as a tragedy, for the two chief characters have no real community of interest

The cast, too, was not distinguished. *Biography* (1932) was a delightful comedy with a conflict of the liberal, the Tory and the radical qualities of the chief characters. Marion Froude, a painter, represents the liberal, who has even forgotten her first lover until he returns to her, a solemn success, and who refuses to marry the young radical because she sees clearly that her easy going indifference to right or wrong will kill that in him which she loves. The hold she has upon her lovers, and the way they give her as an artist the tolerance in matters of morality they usually keep for themselves and their men friends, are both cleverly established. *Love Story* (1933) which died after a brief tryout in Philadelphia, seemed like an early play revived, for the characters had difficulty in leaving the stage gracefully. It was a domestic tragedy, which committed the mistake of having the principal male character kept off the scene until the last act.

Rain from Heaven (1934) began, Behrman tells us, in the repudiation by Gerhart Hauptmann of Alfred Kerr, the critic who had been a devoted disciple, but whom Hauptmann cast off because he did not subscribe to the nationalistic and Fascist wave in Germany. Out of this incident Behrman created Hugo Willens, a German critic who finds himself in the house of Lady Wyngate in England, after having been put in a concentration camp in Germany for his satire, "An Oriental Fantasy," in which he describes the last Jew on earth and how he is saved so that the Nazis will still have a program. There are a number of guests at Lady Wyngate's, and they vary from the extreme Toryism of an American magnate to the rather indiscriminate liberalism of Lady Wyngate. The play is clever, but it leaves every one in the air. Hugo goes back to Germany to fight for his cause. He is one-eighth Jew and he seems to think he owes it to that inheritance to fight for it, just how is not indicated. Behrman probably intended to show that racial streaks and social convictions in the broad sense are more powerful than love. They may be in certain cases, but these cases are not the best ones for the theatre. Several of the characters in *Rain from Heaven* seem to have been intended for more important parts in the drama, but they simply fade out of the picture, leaving Lady Wyngate and her young American lover both shut in behind their little fences. There was more clarity in *End of Summer* (1936), a charming social comedy laid at a summer home in Maine. Behrman had here no thesis to prove except perhaps that the mere possession of wealth is no certainty of happiness, it all depends upon the use that is made of it. This is a motive of sufficient universality to permit the clever dialogue and the fine characterization to have their own way. There is a brilliant portrait of a psychiatrist, remarkably interpreted by Osgood Perkins, bitter with his upward struggle, through whom Behrman brings the motives of his other characters to light. Behrman is better in social drama in its more limited sense where his command of epigram is more relatively important. His strength lies here and not in the invention of situations or stories. It is not to be forgotten, also, that his characters even as people of breeding have less reality than Barry's. His theory that literature is as good a source as life for drama may possibly account for this artificial quality.

The new decade witnessed a compelling play of the supernatural in *Berkeley Square* by John L. Balderston and J. C. Squire. Balderston, a Philadelphian who has for some years been resident in London, framed from *The Sense of the Past*, an unfinished novel of Henry James, a romance in which the power of human love to defy time, and triumph for a brief interval, leaving an indelible mark upon the lives of a man of the twentieth and a woman of the eighteenth centuries, was established with a delicacy and a distinction not exceeded in modern drama. It is of great interest to see how Henry James, whose ambition to write successful plays was never fulfilled, provided Balderston with a theme which grew into one of the most successful as well as one of the most artistic of dramas. Balderston took from the novel the central idea of the return of Peter Standish, a young American visiting London to examine his inheritance, and, through his great love for the past, exchanging bodies with his own ancestor who had in a similar fashion re-visited his ancestral home. Balderston changed the time from 1820 to 1784, and developed Peter's love for Helen Pettigrew, whom he had barely met, in the fragment of the novel, under another name. The change to the eighteenth century was an improvement; it gave the playwright his opportunity to depict the sordidness and cruelty of that time which made clear to Peter Standish the impossibility of his remaining there even with the love that has become precious to him. To an American of the twentieth century a land and time in which women are burned and flogged openly in the public square is not a possible home. What he has loved in the past have been the survivals of its art and of the ordered beauty of its architecture. The conflict in Peter's soul is worthy of a great conception, the tragedy of a man who realizes that the one woman in the past who loves and understands him is lost to him forever. The human being, hemmed in by events of the past which he knows he cannot change, is an original creation; and the ending of the play, which leaves Peter Standish an exile from two centuries, is Balderston's own. From the notes which James left, it is evident that his hero was to marry the American girl of the twentieth century. But Peter's simple reading of the inscription upon Helen's grave which tells the audience that she died in 1787, three years after their meeting, is much more effective. The play had been performed in London in 1926, but was extensively revised in 1929 and Leslie Howard played Peter Standish in London before he brought it to New York. The part suited him admirably and he took full advantage of the exquisite spiritual and poetic values of a play that is as truly a piece of literature as the novel that inspired it. Balderston's other plays show his flair for the strange, but outside of *Dracula* (1927), a dramatization of Bram Stoker's novel, they have not been successful on the stage. But to have written *Berkeley Square* establishes him as a playwright of major importance.

Robert E. Sherwood has contributed several amusing comedies. *The Road to Rome* (1927) was a travesty upon Hannibal's career, with some rather obvious vulgarity in which fine actors like Philip Merivale and Jane Cowl seemed out of place. *The Love Nest* (1927), based on a story by Ring Lardner, was simply dull. In *Waterloo Bridge* (1929) Sherwood made an attempt at a serious play. The old situation of a street walker who will not permit the simple hearted youth to marry her was given a new setting. Such a play needs a fine presentation to make it credible, and the cast I saw was not well selected. In Berlin, however, where it was given in 1931, the acting of Grete Mosheim seems to have produced a profound impression, and Sherwood must have the credit for providing the material with which she made it. *Reunion in Vienna* (1931) was a romantic trifle with some keen satire on the psychoanalyst. Sherwood was extremely fortunate in securing Leslie Howard for the hero of *The Petrified Forest* (1935). Howard almost made credible the figure of the poet who wanders into a gas station in the West, and falls in love with the daughter of the proprietor, a girl who is as unlikely a mortal for this poet to love as can well be imagined. The climax of absurdity is reached by the advent of a gang headed by a cold blooded person who alone is able to appreciate the noble action of the poet in begging the gangster to shoot him in order that his life insurance may be paid to the young woman! The confused critical standards of today need no better example than the praise accorded to this play. If it had frankly been a burlesque, it would have at least been amusing. But in the endowing of a murderer, who does not even care about the lives of his own men, with an imaginative reach to which he would of course be a stranger, there was a deliberate falsity of tone which is hard to forgive.

One definite development of the new decade has been the growth of the propaganda play. It has dealt with war, with capital punishment, labor troubles, social oppression and kindred matters. Inevitably the element of propaganda has hurt the dramatic values, however sincere the playwrights may be. If we compare Martin Flavin's *Criminal Code* with John Wexley's *The Last Mile* (1930), the difference is at once apparent.

Flavin presents both sides of the question, Wexley only one side. Consequently the first is a stark tragedy, the second a sentimentalized argument against capital punishment, in which "Killer Mears" is made a hero.   The sympathy in *The Criminal Code* is secured by a dramatic presentation, never overstressed, of a human soul caught in the meshes of fate.   Wexley plays on the nerve of sympathy till it snaps and we no longer care what becomes of the occupants of the death cells.   The result is much the same in Wexley's *They Shall Not Die* (1934), a play based on the Scottsboro trial.   Wexley has yet to learn that facts are not what matters; it is the impression of truth.   But the great defect of the play lay in the lack of an individual character in which the injustice is centered.   The negroes who are unjustly convicted are not individualized and though an attempt is made to center attention upon the lawyer for the defence, it is not easy to transfer sympathy on the stage, for the attorney is not in danger.

There was a recognition of this dramatic law in *Stevedore* (1934) by George Sklar and Paul Peters, a play dealing with the persecution of negroes in New Orleans.   The racial intolerance is individualized in Lannie Thompson, a negro who is trying to secure admission of negroes into a white union, and his death is the high spot of the play.   The defect of *Stevedore* lies in the exaggeration and the appeal of race prejudice of another kind.   Every negro is a perfect example of justice and charity.   Every white man but one is unjust and brutal.   Consequently, a white audience declines to believe in the play.   On the other hand, it became in the theatre a call to arouse race animosity and the attitude of the negroes in the audience raised a question not of dramatic merit, but of the use of the stage to make even more difficult of solution a social problem that demands calm judgment and breadth of vision.

Let Freedom Ring (1935) by Albert Bein is a better play than *Stevedore* because it has more restraint and because it derives from the novel on which it is based the theme of the North Carolina mountaineer bringing into a mill town the traits of courage and independence which have been instilled into them by generations of living in the hills. The mob of strikers is wisely kept off stage and the most interesting dramatic conflict takes place in the character of John McClure when he has to make his choice between his future in the mill, where his skill has won him rapid promotion, and his devotion to his own clan. Rightly he is made a descendant of a Scottish race and the clan loyalty proves the strongest. The death of his brother, Kirk, the strike leader, is also used effectively as a means of unifying the workers. Bein's heroes are not wordy radicals; they are men who deplore violence and hope to win by solidarity. His weakest characters are the mill owners and officers. Here Flavin's *Amaco* could have taught him some lessons.

The propaganda for peace has found its most vigorous advocate in Reginald Lawrence. His *Men Must Fight* (1931) dealing with the inevitability of war illustrated the futility of argument on the stage, for the pacifist discussion of the first Act is speedily forgotten when the real action is begun. It was a sincere play and his *If This Be Treason* (1935), written with John Haynes Holmes, showed what a President of the United States could accomplish if he determined to prevent war. The last Act in which the President went to Japan to appeal to the people was absurd, but the earlier acts in which he withstands the jingoism of the army, the navy and the politicians, had some very good scenes. Yet with all the evils of war, there has never been a peace play that has had such moments as those which *Secret Service* or *Journey's End* gave to the theatre. In these plays Gillette and Sheriff never permitted their theme to submerge their characters, and it is this exaltation of the theme over the central motive which keeps the propaganda play in a lower rank. When social or economic questions are treated by a playwright of high rank they are naturally kept in the background and the personal tragedy remains uppermost.

The question naturally arises in such a survey as this,—is there a group of playwrights who are beginning their careers and who have the promise which led me to select Barry, Anderson, Kaufman, Connelly, Howard and Kelly in 1927 as the new dramatists who would rise to the front rank? I am hopeful but not yet convinced.

Sidney Kingsley in *Men in White* (1933) made an effective play out of the way in which a physician rises to emergencies and in spite of an emotional conflict proceeds instinctively with his duty. The scene in the dissecting room was powerful quite as much by its timing and its reticence as through its touch of melodrama. Kingsley's *Dead End* (1935) was a realistic picture of the shifting currents that pass through an alley in which a gang of boys are growing up with the standards which will make them fit candidates for gangdom on a large scale. Babyface Martin, a real gangster, returns to his early haunts and ends his life at the hands of Federal police. Without becoming a propaganda play, *Dead End* states a broad social problem and the scene in which Martin instructs the boys in the methods by which they will defeat their rivals is noteworthy. The thin partition which divides rich and poor is represented by the close neighborhood of the apartment house and the alley. The gangster is not made an absurdly sentimentalized figure as in *The Petrified Forest;* he is pictured as he is, cruel, mean and treacherous.

Emmet Lavery's *The First Legion* (1934) was a remarkable first play. Without a woman in the cast, and with the scene limited to a Jesuit House, he built up a series of dramatic conflicts out of which emerged distinct characters who represented loyalty, doubt, scepticism, and the final triumph of faith. As in all plays of high rank, the struggle is within the human soul and the position in which a young priest is placed by the order of his superior to act as advocate of a miracle in which he does not believe, and which, he has learned, under the seal of confession, has been certified to by a sceptical physician in order to embarrass the Jesuits, is about as tragic as can be imagined. But the final scene of the play in which a crippled boy is cured by his faith in this supposed miracle was one of the most thrilling I have seen in the theatre, especially when Frankie Thomas played the part.

There have been some charming comedies of recollection, such as James Hagan's *One Sunday Afternoon* (1933) or *Remember the Day* (1935) by Philo Higley and Philip Dunning. The comedy of domestic life touched by the tragedy of parental tyranny had an excellent example in Rose Franken's *Another Language* (1932). To the same species, but less important, were Clifford Odets' *Awake and Sing* (1935) and *Paradise Lost* (1935). The critical acclaim which hailed Odets as a "major playwright" is one of the most amusing episodes in the recent theatre. The queer mixture of *Another Language* and *Storm Song* which was called *Awake and Sing* was concerned with characters which are not of the slightest importance spiritually or intellectually, and they neither awake nor sing. Even the skilful production of the Group Theatre could not torture aspiration out of a situation in which a young married woman elopes with a brutal, callous man who is really "the father of her child." It was interesting to see how the calmer critics began to hedge when *Paradise Lost*, a confused domestic melodrama, was produced. This picture of the decay of a lower middle class family was incredibly naïve in its thinking and dull in its action.

It was irritating, also, but for a very different reason, to see the critical and popular reaction to *The Children's Hour* (1935). Lillian Hellman is a much more talented playwright than Clifford Odets, and when she finds a theme worthy of her, she may make important contributions. For she revealed in her study of this intolerable child, who wrecks a school by her slander of the two women principals, a mastery of exposition that was striking. But having established the situation, she did not know what to do with it, and the play went to pieces in the last Act. In real life, the doctor whose fiancée has been attacked would have insisted upon immediate marriage which would have put an end to the scandal. Then there would have been no play, of course, but as a matter of fact, there is no conclusive play as it is.   Much more moving was the study of the effects upon a boy of his parent's divorce in *Wednesday's Child* (1934) by Leopold Atlas.   The boy's horror at his mother's infidelity, his dislike of his father's second choice and above all his pluck in facing the future after he realizes that each parent is relieved when he goes to boarding school and permits them to live their own lives, owed something to the talent of the young actor who made *The First Legion* and *Remember the Day* impressive.   But the character after all was there, and the sympathy of the audience was with him.

It is perhaps obvious that none of the very recent arrivals rank with the group that began in the early twenties.   Of the playwrights whose work I have discussed for the first time in this survey of the decade, 1927–1936, Behrman, Heyward, Riggs, Kingsley, Lavery, Bein, Mrs. Franken and Miss Hellman seem most promising.   New avenues have been opened by the older group, like the heroic qualities of science, or older avenues like the recreation of historical figures, which the newer playwrights might notice.   The main difficulty today lies not in the rivalry of the moving picture, or the subtler danger that inspires the writing of plays in imitation of the picture technique.   It lies in the fact that most of our playwrights write about trivial things, or draw trivial people.   If there has ever been a dangerous heresy in fiction or drama, it is the heresy of little souls.   According to this theory, it makes no difference what one writes about provided we are given a photograph of something.   But in reality it makes all the difference in the world.

The most encouraging aspect of the American drama lies in its perennial vitality, which this record has indicated.   In spite of all the discouraging aspects of the theatre, from the demands of stage unions to the quieter racketeering of the owners or lessees of theatres when a hit comes in, the drama will go on. There is still a place on our stage for the poet, whether his medium be in verse or prose.   He may go out of fashion for a time, but it is the man of imagination who writes drama that lasts. Keenness of observation is not enough; skill in expression is not enough; courage to enter the dark places of the soul is not enough—the dramatist must have the power to draw from any worthy material, beauty and truth, by the force of that imagination which placed them there, and to speak to us through his characters in the language which the heart understands and remembers. It is because I believe there are more playwrights today in America who answer this description than in any other country in the world, that I need make no prophecy concerning the future, but may bring this record to a close.

NOTE TO REPRINTING OF REVISED EDITION

Dubose Heyward died June 16, 1940, in Tryon, North Carolina.

GENERAL BIBLIOGRAPHY
AND
LIST OF AMERICAN PLAYS
1860–1936

BIBLIOGRAPHY

THE Bibliography and Play List follow the general plan of my Bibliography of the Early Drama in the *Cambridge History of American Literature*, rather than that of the Bibliography of *The History of the American Drama from the Beginning to the Civil War*. The great number of articles, mostly of a fugitive nature, demands that the Bibliography shall be selective, and forbids the extensive critical comments of the earlier volume, where the historical perspective was more definite. In the modern period the individual dramatist is better known to students and readers and therefore instead of separating the individual bibliographies and lists of plays it seemed best to bring all the information concerning a playwright together in one place.

HISTORY AND CRITICISM
OF THE AMERICAN DRAMA AND STAGE SINCE 1860

BIOGRAPHIES of playwrights are included here only when they present a general picture of the drama of their time. Works referring to the whole field are ordinarily not repeated under the individual bibliographies. The place of publication, when not mentioned, is New York.

"American Playwrights on the American Drama." *Harper's Weekly,* Supplement, Feb. 2, 1889.

ANDREWS, CHARLTON, *The Drama To-day.* Philadelphia, 1913.

ARCHER, WILLIAM, "The Development of American Drama," *Harper's Magazine,* CXLII (1920) 75–86.

Art of Playwriting, The. Lectures delivered at the University of Pennsylvania, by Jesse Lynch Williams, Langdon Mitchell, Lord Dunsany, Gilbert Emery, and Rachel Crothers. Phila., 1928.

ARNOLD, ALFRED G., *The Little Country Theater.* 1922.

BOUCICAULT, DION, "The Future of American Drama." *Arena*, Nov., 1890, 641–52.

BRICKER, HERSCHEL L., *Our Theatre Today.* 1936.

BROWN, JOHN MASON, *The Modern Theatre in Revolt.* 1929.

BROWN, JOHN MASON, *The American Theatre as It Is To-day.* 1930.

BROWN, T. A., *A History of the New York Stage.* From the First Performance in 1732 to 1901. 3 Vols. 1903.

BURLEIGH, LOUISE, *The Community Theatre.* In Theory and Practice. Boston, 1917.

BURTON, RICHARD, *The New American Drama.* 1913.

CHENEY, SHELDON, *The New Movement in the Theatre.* 1914.

CHENEY, SHELDON, *The Open Air Theatre.* 1918.

CHENEY, SHELDON, *The Art Theater.* 1917; rev. 1925.

CLAPP, HENRY AUSTIN, *Reminiscences of a Dramatic Critic.* Boston, 1902.

CLARK, BARRETT H., *The British and American Drama of To-day.* 1915.

CLARK, BARRETT H., *A Study of the Modern Drama.* 1925; rev. 1928.

CLARK, BARRETT H., *An Hour of American Drama.* Phila., 1930.

CRAWFORD, MARY C., *The Romance of the American Theatre.* Boston, 1913; rev. 1925.

DALY, JOSEPH FRANCIS, *The Life of Augustin Daly.* 1917.

DE GOVEIA, C. J., *The Community Playhouse.* 1923.

DICKINSON, THOMAS H., *The Case of American Drama.* Boston, 1915.

DICKINSON, THOMAS H., *The Insurgent Theatre.* 1917.

DICKINSON, THOMAS H., *Playwrights of the New American Theater.* 1924.

DRUMMOND, A. M., *Plays for the Country Theatre.* Cornell Extension Bulletin, No. 53. Ithaca, N. Y., June, 1922.

EATON, WALTER PRICHARD, *The American Stage of To-day.* Boston. c. 1908.

EATON, WALTER PRICHARD, *At the New Theatre and Others.* Boston. c. 1910.

EATON, WALTER PRICHARD, *Plays and Players: Leaves From a Critic's Scrapbook.* Cincinnati, 1916.

EATON, WALTER PRICHARD, *The Actor's Heritage.* Boston, c. 1924.

EATON, WALTER PRICHARD, *The Drama in English.* 1930.

EDWARDS, THOMAS R., "The Evolution of Play Publishing." *The Drama*, XV (March, 1925) 121–122.

BIBLIOGRAPHY AND PLAY LIST

HALSEY, ABIGAIL F., *The Historical Pageant in the Rural Community.* Cornell Extension Bulletin, No. 54, Ithaca, N. Y., June 1922.

HAMILTON, CLAYTON, *The Theory of the Theatre.* 1910.

HAMILTON, CLAYTON, *Studies in Stagecraft.* 1914.

HAMILTON, CLAYTON, *Problems of the Playwright.* 1917.

HAMILTON, CLAYTON, *Seen on the Stage.* 1920.

HAMILTON, CLAYTON, *Conversations on the Contemporary Drama.* 1924.

HAMILTON, CLAYTON, *So You're Writing a Play.* 1935.

HAPGOOD, NORMAN, *The Stage in America, 1897–1900.* 1901.

HENDERSON, ARCHIBALD, *The Changing Drama.* 1914.

HORNBLOW, ARTHUR, *A History of the Theatre in America from Its Beginning to the Present Time.* 2 Vols. Philadelphia, 1919.

HUGHES, GLENN, *The Story of the Theatre.* 1928.

HUTTON, LAURENCE, *Plays and Players.* 1875.

HUTTON, LAURENCE, *Curiosities of the American Stage.* 1891.

LEWISOHN, LUDWIG, *The Drama and the Stage.* 1922.

MACGOWAN, KENNETH AND JONES, ROBERT EDMUND, *The Theatre of To-morrow.* 1921.

MACKAYE, PERCY, *The Playhouse and the Play.* 1909.

MACKAYE, PERCY, *The Civic Theatre.* 1912.

MACKAYE, PERCY, *Epoch. The Life of Steele MacKaye.* 2 Vols. 1927.

MALEVINSKY, M. L., *The Science of Playwriting.* 1925.

MANTLE, BURNS, *American Playwrights of Today.* 1929.

MATTHEWS, BRANDER. "The American on the Stage," *Scribner's Monthly,* XVIII (July, 1879), 321–33.

MATTHEWS, BRANDER, *The Development of the Drama.* 1904.

MATTHEWS, BRANDER, *Inquiries and Opinions.* 1907.

MATTHEWS, BRANDER, *The American of the Future and Other Essays.* 1909.

MATTHEWS, BRANDER, *A Study of the Drama.* Boston, 1910.

MATTHEWS, BRANDER, *A Book About the Theater.* 1916.

MATTHEWS, BRANDER, *Principles of Playmaking.* 1919.

MATTHEWS, BRANDER, *Playwrights on Playmaking.* 1923.

MATTHEWS, BRANDER, *Rip Van Winkle Goes to the Play, and Other Essays on Plays and Players.* 1926.

MAYORGA, MARGARET, *A Short History of the American Drama.* 1932.

MODERWELL, HIRAM K., *The Theatre of To-day.* 1914.

A HISTORY OF THE AMERICAN DRAMA

Moses, Montrose J., "The Drama, 1860–1918," *The Cambridge History of American Literature,* III, 266–298. Bibliography in IV, 760–774. 1921.

Moses, Montrose J., *The American Dramatist.* Boston, 1911; rev. 1925.

Moses, Montrose J., and Brown, J. M., *The American Theatre as Seen by Its Critics.* 1934.

Odell, George C. D., *Annals of the New York Stage,* Vol. VII–Vol. XIV (1857–1891). 1931–1945. (Succeeding vols. will also deal with this period.)

Peirce, James Harry, *The Magazine and the Drama.* Dunlap Society Publications, Series 2, Vol. II. 1896.

Phelps, H. P., *Players of a Century. A Record of the Albany Stage. Including Notices of Prominent Actors who have appeared in America.* Albany, 1880; repr. 1890.

Phelps, William Lyon, *The Twentieth Century Theatre.* 1920.

Plessow, Gustav L., *Das Amerikanische Kurzschauspiel zwischen 1910 und 1930.* Halle, 1933.

Quinn, Arthur H., "The Significance of Recent American Drama," *Scribner's Magazine,* LXXII (July, 1922), 97–108. Reprinted in *Contemporary American Plays.*

Quinn, Arthur H., "The Real Hope for the American Theater," *Scribner's Magazine,* XCVII (Jan., 1935), 30–36.

Ruhl, Arthur, *Second Nights.* 1914.

Sayler, Oliver M., *Our American Theatre.* 1923.

Shipman, Louis Evan, *The True Adventures of a Play.* 1914.

Skinner, Richard Dana, *Our Changing Theatre.* 1931.

Stevens, Thomas Wood, *The Theatre from Athens to Broadway.* 1932.

Strang, L. C., *Players and Plays of the Last Quarter Century.* 2 Vols. Boston, c. 1902.

Stuart, Donald Clive, *The Development of Dramatic Art.* 1928.

Thomas, Augustus, *The Print of My Remembrance.* 1922.

Tompkins, Eugene, and Kilby, Quincy, *The History of the Boston Theatre.* Boston, 1908.

Towse, John R., *Sixty Years of the Theatre.* 1916.

Willard, G. O., *History of the Providence Stage.* Providence, 1891.

BIBLIOGRAPHY AND PLAY LIST

WINTER, WILLIAM, *The Wallet of Time, Containing Personal, Biographical, and Critical Reminiscence of the American Theatre.* 2 Vols. 1913.

YOUNG, STARK, *The Flower in Drama.* 1923.

BIBLIOGRAPHIES AND LISTS OF PLAYS

ADAMS, W. DAVENPORT, *A Dictionary of the Drama.* Philadelphia, 1904. [Vol. I. A–G.]

BAKER, BLANCH M., *Dramatic Bibliography.* 1933.

CARSON, LIONEL, ED., *The Stage Year Book,* from 1908: after 1909 gives American plays. London, 1908–

Catalogue of the Dramas and Dramatic Poems contained in the Public Library of Cincinnati. Cincinnati, 1879.

CLAPP, J. B. and EDGETT, E. F., *Plays of the Present.* Dunlap Society Publications, Ser. 2, extra Vol. 1902.

CLARENCE, REGINALD, *The Stage Cyclopedia.* London, 1909. [For English performances of American plays.]

Dramatic Compositions Copyrighted in the United States, 1870– [Issued by the Copyright Office, Library of Congress, Washington, D. C. This is most helpful and appears annually.]

FAXON, FREDERICK W., *The Dramatic Index.* Boston. From 1909 has been published annually as Part 2 of *The Annual Magazine Subject Index.*

FAXON, FREDERICK W., Editor, *The Bulletin of Bibliography and Dramatic Index.* Published quarterly. Boston.

HASKELL, DANIEL C., *A List of American Dramas in the New York Public Library.* Revised January, 1916, from *Bulletin* of October, 1915.

MANTLE, BURNS, *Best Plays* [of the year]. Annually published since 1919. [Especially useful for statistics and casts of plays.]

MANTLE, BURNS, *Best Plays of 1909–1919.* 1933. [Very useful.]

RODEN, R. F., *Later American Plays, 1831–1900.* Dunlap Society Publications, Ser. 2, Vol. XII. 1900.

SHAY, FRANK, *A Guide to Longer Plays.* A List of Fifteen Hundred Plays for Little Theatres, Professional and Stock Companies, etc. 1925.

BIOGRAPHIES OF ACTORS AND MANAGERS AND SIMILAR WORKS GIVING INFORMATION CONCERNING THE DRAMA

BARRETT, LAWRENCE, *Charlotte Cushman, a Lecture.* Dunlap Society Publications, Ser. 1, Vol. IX. 1889.

BARRYMORE, JOHN, *Confessions of an Actor.* Indianapolis, 1926.

CLAPP, J. B. and EDGETT, E. F., *Players of the Present.* Dunlap Society Publications, Ser. 2, Vols. IX, XI, XIII. 1899–1901.

CLARKE, JOSEPH I. C., *My Life and Memories.* 1925.

CREAHAN, JOHN, *Life of Laura Keene.* Philadelphia, 1897.

The Diary of a Daly Débutante [Dora Knowlton]. 1910.

DITHMAR, EDWARD A., *John Drew.* c. 1900.

DREW, JOHN, *My Years on the Stage.* 1922.

Autobiographical Sketch of Mrs. John Drew. 1899.

EATON, WALTER PRICHARD, *The Theatre Guild.* 1929.

The Memories of Rose Eytinge. 1905.

FORD, JAMES L., *Forty Odd Years in the Literary Shop.* 1921.

FROHMAN, DANIEL, *Memories of a Manager.* 1911.

FROHMAN, DANIEL, and MARCOSSON, ISAAC F., *Charles Frohman.* 1916.

FROHMAN, DANIEL, *Daniel Frohman Presents.* 1935.

GILBERT, MRS. ANNE H., *Stage Reminiscences.* Edited by C. M. Martin. 1901.

GOLDEN, JOHN, and SHORE, VIOLA B., *Stage Struck John Golden.* 1931.

GROSSMAN, EDWINA BOOTH, *Edwin Booth, Recollections by His Daughter.* 1902.

HANAU, STELLA, and DEUTSCH, HELEN, *The Provincetown.* 1931.

HUTTON, LAURENCE, *Edwin Booth.* 1893.

ISMAN, FELIX, *Weber and Fields.* 1924.

LEGALLIENNE, EVA, *At 33.* 1933.

The Autobiography of Joseph Jefferson. 1890.

LEAVITT, M. B., *Fifty Years of Theatrical Management.* 1912.

MAEDER, CLARA FISHER, *Autobiography.* Ed. by Douglas Taylor. Dunlap Society Publications, Ser. 2, Vol. III. 1897.

MARBURY, ELIZABETH, *My Crystal Ball.* 1923.

BIBLIOGRAPHY AND PLAY LIST

MATTHEWS, BRANDER, and HUTTON, LAURENCE, *Actors and Actresses of Great Britain and the United States from the Days of David Garrick to the Present Time.* 1886.

MORRIS, CLARA, *Life on the Stage. My Personal Experiences and Recollections.* 1902.

MOSES, M. J., *Famous Actor-Families in America.* c. 1906.

MURDOCH, JAMES E., *The Stage, or Recollections of Actors and Acting from an Experience of Fifty Years.* Philadelphia, 1880.

REED, JOSEPH VERNER, *The Curtain Falls.* 1935.

ROURKE, CONSTANCE M., *Troupers of the Gold Coast; or, The Rise of Lotta Crabtree.* 1928.

RUSSELL, CHARLES E., *Julia Marlowe, her Life and Art.* 1926.

RYAN, KATE, *Old Boston Museum Days.* Boston, 1915.

SIMONSON, LEE, *The Stage is Set.* 1932.

SKINNER, OTIS, *Footlights and Spotlights.* Indianapolis, 1924.

SKINNER, R. DANA, *Our Changing Theatre.* 1931.

SOTHERN, EDWARD H., *The Melancholy Tale of Me. My Remembrances.* 1916.

STODDART, J. H., *Recollections of a Player.* 1902.

STRANG, LEWIS C., *Famous Actors of To-day in America.* Boston, 1900.

TYLER, GEORGE C., (in collaboration with J. C. Furnas), *Whatever Goes Up.* 1934.

WALLACK, LESTER, *Memories of Fifty Years.* 1889.

WHIFFEN, MRS. THOMAS, *Keeping Off the Shelf.* 1929.

Francis Wilson's Life of Himself. Boston, 1924.

WILSTACH, PAUL, *Richard Mansfield, the Man and the Actor.* 1909.

WINTER, WILLIAM, *The Jeffersons.* Boston, 1881.

WINTER, WILLIAM, *A Sketch of the Life of John Gilbert.* Dunlap Society Publications, Ser. 1, Vol. II. 1890.

WINTER, WILLIAM, *Ada Rehan, A Study.* 2 Vols. 1891.

WINTER, WILLIAM, *Other Days; Being Chronicles and Memories of the Stage.* 1908.

WINTER, WILLIAM, *Life and Art of Richard Mansfield.* 2 Vols. 1910.

WINTER, WILLIAM, *Vagrant Memories.* 1915.

WINTER, WILLIAM, *The Life of David Belasco.* 2 Vols. 1918.

WITTKE, CARL, *Tambo and Bones—A History of the Minstrel Stage.* 1931.

WOOLLCOTT, ALEXANDER, *Mrs. Fiske. Her Views on Actors, Acting and the Problems of Production.* 1917.

A HISTORY OF THE AMERICAN DRAMA

COLLECTIONS OF AMERICAN PLAYS

IN THE ORDER OF PUBLICATION

REPRESENTATIVE AMERICAN PLAYS. Edited by Arthur Hobson Quinn. The Century Company, 1917. (Revised edition, 1938.) Contains twenty-nine plays. Plays of this period are: Steele Mac-Kaye's *Hazel Kirke;* Howard's *Shenandoah;* Herne's *Margaret Fleming;* Gillette's *Secret Service; Madame Butterfly,* by Belasco and Long; Fitch's *The Girl with the Green Eyes;* Mitchell's *The New York Idea;* Thomas's *The Witching Hour;* Moody's *The Faith Healer;* Percy MacKaye's *The Scarecrow;* Sheldon's *The Boss;* Miss Crothers' *He and She;* O'Neill's *Beyond the Horizon;* Miss Vollmer's *Sun-Up;* Sidney Howard's *The Silver Cord;* Barry's *Paris Bound;* Anderson's *Winterset.*

REPRESENTATIVE ONE-ACT PLAYS BY AMERICAN AUTHORS. Edited by Margaret G. Mayorga. Little, Brown & Co., 1919. Contains twenty-four one-act plays.

MODERN AMERICAN PLAYS. Edited by George Pierce Baker. Harcourt, Brace & Howe, 1920. Contains Thomas's *As A Man Thinks;* Belasco's *The Return of Peter Grimm;* Edward Sheldon's *Romance;* Anspacher's *The Unchastened Woman;* and Massey's *Plots and Playwrights.*

REPRESENTATIVE PLAYS BY AMERICAN DRAMATISTS. Edited by Montrose J. Moses. E. P. Dutton & Co., Vol. III, 1921. Plays of this period are: MacKaye's *Paul Kauvar;* Howard's *Shenandoah;* Thomas's *In Mizzoura;* Fitch's *The Moth and the Flame;* Mitchell's *The New York Idea;* Walter's *The Easiest Way;* and Belasco's *The Return of Peter Grimm.*

TWENTY CONTEMPORARY ONE-ACT PLAYS (American). Edited by Frank Shay. 1921 (Revised edition, 1922).

LONGER PLAYS BY MODERN AUTHORS (American). Edited by Helen L. Cohen. Harcourt & Brace, 1922. Contains Fitch's *Beau Brummell;* Thomas's *The Copperhead;* Kaufman and Connelly's *Dulcy;* and Tarkington's *The Intimate Strangers.*

CONTEMPORARY AMERICAN PLAYS. Edited by Arthur Hobson Quinn. Charles Scribner's Sons, 1923. Contains: Jesse Lynch Williams' *Why Marry?;* Eugene O'Neill's *The Emperor Jones;* Rachel

312

BIBLIOGRAPHY AND PLAY LIST

Crothers' *Nice People;* Gilbert Emery's *The Hero; To The Ladies!* by George S. Kaufman and Marc Connelly.

ONE-ACT PLAYS FOR STAGE AND STUDY. [Chiefly American.] Samuel French. First Series, 1924; Second Series, 1925; Third Series, 1927; Eighth Series, 1934.

REPRESENTATIVE AMERICAN DRAMAS. NATIONAL AND LOCAL. Edited by Montrose J. Moses. Little, Brown & Co., 1925. Contains: Charles H. Hoyt's *A Texas Steer;* David Belasco's *The Girl of the Golden West;* Augustus Thomas's *The Witching Hour;* Clyde Fitch's *The City;* Percy MacKaye's *The Scarecrow;* Josephine Preston Peabody's *The Piper;* Harry James Smith's *Mrs. Bumpstead-Leigh; It Pays to Advertise* by Roi Cooper Megrue and Walter Hackett; James Forbes' *The Famous Mrs. Fair;* Eugene O'Neill's *The Emperor Jones;* Rachel Crothers' *Nice People;* Owen Davis's *The Detour; Dulcy* by George S. Kaufman and Marc Connelly; Elmer L. Rice's *The Adding Machine;* George Kelly's *The Show-Off.*

PLAYS OF NEGRO LIFE. Edited by Locke, Alain, and Gregory, Montgomery. 1927.

REPRESENTATIVE MODERN PLAYS. Edited by Richard A. Cordell. 1930. Contains six plays by American playwrights: Fitch's *The Climbers;* George Ade's *The College Widow;* Miss Crothers' *Expressing Willie;* Hatcher Hughes's *Hell Bent for Heaven; Beggar on Horseback,* by Kaufman and Connelly; O'Neill's *Diff'rent.*

MODERN AMERICAN AND BRITISH PLAYS. Edited by S. M. Tucker. 1931. Contains eleven plays by American playwrights: Paul Green's *The Field God;* O'Neill's *The Great God Brown;* Emery's *The Hero;* Barry's *In a Garden;* Miss Millay's *The King's Henchman;* Moeller's *Madame Sand;* Miss Crothers' *Mary the Third;* Anderson's *Saturday's Children;* Sidney Howard's *The Silver Cord;* Miss Vollmer's *Sun-Up; To the Ladies,* by Kaufman and Connelly.

TWENTIETH CENTURY PLAYS, AMERICAN. Edited by Richard A. Cordell and Frank Chandler, 1934. Contains *What Price Glory,* by Maxwell Anderson and Laurence Stallings; O'Neill's *Marco Millions;* Elmer Rice's *Street Scene;* Marc Connelly's *The Green Pastures;* Rachel Crothers' *As Husbands Go.*

PLAYS FOR THE COLLEGE THEATRE. Edited by Garrett H. Leverton. 1933. Contains ten plays by American playwrights: Dion Boucicault's *Belle Lamar;* Winthrop Ames's *A Kiss in Xanadu;* Alfred

Kreymborg's *Lima Beans;* Kaufman's *Butter and Egg Man;
Houseparty,* by Britton and Hargrave; O'Neill's *The Moon of the
Caribbees;* Strong's *The Drums of Oude;* Paul Green's *The Lord's
Will;* Lynn Riggs' *Green Grow the Lilacs;* Barry's *Hotel Uni-
verse;* Frank Elser's *Low Bridge.*

AMERICAN PLAYS. Edited by Allan Gates Halline. 1935. Contains
seventeen plays. Plays of this period are: Daly's *Horizon;*
Joaquin Miller's *The Danites in the Sierras;* Bronson Howard's
The Henrietta; Mitchell's *The New York Idea;* Moeller's *Madame
Sand;* Barry's *You and I;* Owen Davis's *Icebound;* O'Neill's *The
Great God Brown;* Paul Green's *The Field God.*

AMERICA'S LOST PLAYS. Edited by Barrett H. Clark. Princeton, 1941.
For detailed list, see pp. 403–404. Plays published in this series
have "A.L.P." after title or date of production.

Among many collections of One-Act Plays the following will represent the amateur and semi-professional drama.

PROVINCETOWN PLAYS. Edited by FRANK SHAY. 6 Vols. 1916–18.

PLAYS OF THE 47 WORK SHOP. Edited by George P. Baker. Vols.
I–IV. 1918–25.

GROVE PLAYS OF THE BOHEMIAN CLUB. Edited by Porter Garnett.
3 Vols. San Francisco, 1918.

CAROLINA FOLK-PLAYS. Edited by Frederick H. Koch, 1922; Second
Series, 1924. Third Series, 1928. Fourth Series, 1931.

CRICK BOTTOM PLAYS. Edited by E. P. Conkle. 1930.

YALE ONE-ACT PLAYS. Edited by George P. Baker. 1930.

CORNELL UNIVERSITY PLAYS. Edited by Alexander M. Drummond.
1932.

PLAY LIST

INDIVIDUAL AUTHORS

In this list are included only playwrights whose work has been treated
or referred to in the text. It is obviously impossible to list completely
the plays of American authorship during this period, but I believe I
have omitted no playwright of real significance.

Under each playwright's name are listed his plays, in the order of
their performance. Where it seemed appropriate I have presented a

complete list of the playwright's work. Owing in some cases to the mass of material, in others to the system of trying out a play on the road, it was impracticable to make every list complete. In such cases I have presented a representative list of plays.

With each play is given the date of publication and the place and date of first production. Anyone familiar with the circumstances of production in America will recognize that errors are inevitable, and I have never hesitated to give information in one case because it was not available in every instance. For example, London performances were of interest when American playwrighting was becoming established. Today such performances are of much less significance. I have applied the same principle in giving the sources of the plays.

The material of this bibliography presents difficulties of a special kind. From 1860 to 1900 many plays remained unpublished, owing to insufficient copyright protection. But any attempt to distinguish between extant and non-extant plays, as I did in my earlier *History,* would be fruitless, since it is reasonably certain that nearly all these plays exist in some form. For this reason, the word "MS." has been added only in those cases in which I have actually identified the manuscript. Many plays have been issued without any date, and the printed copyright date may indicate either the date of actual publication or merely the year in which application for copyright as a dramatic composition was filed at Washington. It may even indicate the year in which a novel was made out of the play. With the help of the publishers and of the useful list of Dramatic Compositions, published by the Copyright Office and of the cards issued by the Library of Congress, this tangle has been solved so far as practicable.

Where place of publication or of performance is omitted, "New York" is to be understood.

I shall welcome heartily any corrections, in order that the facts may be finally established.

An asterisk (*) indicates a one-act play. No attempt has been made to give a complete list of one-act plays.

ABBOTT, GEORGE

THE FALL GUY. With James Gleason. 1928. (Eltinge Theatre, March 10, 1925)

A HOLY TERROR. With Winchell Smith. 1926. (Cohan Theatre, Sept. 28, 1925)

A HISTORY OF THE AMERICAN DRAMA

BROADWAY. With Philip Dunning. 1926. (Broadhurst Theatre, Sept. 16, 1926)

LOVE 'EM AND LEAVE 'EM. With J. V. A. Weaver. 1926. (Sam H. Harris Theatre, Feb. 3, 1926)

FOUR WALLS. With Dana Burnett. c. 1928. (John Golden Theatre, Sept. 19, 1922)

COQUETTE. With Ann P. Bridgers. 1928. (Adelphi Theatre, Phila. Oct. 18, 1927; Maxine Elliott Theatre, Nov. 8, 1927)

RINGSIDE. With Edward E. Paramore, Jr. and Hyatt Daab. (Broadhurst Theatre, Apr. 29, 1928)

THOSE WE LOVE. With S. K. Lauren. (John Golden Theatre, Feb. 19, 1930)

LILY TURNER. With Philip Dunning. (Morosco Theatre, Sept. 19, 1932)

HEAT LIGHTNING. With Leon Abrams. (Booth Theatre, Sept. 15, 1933)

LADIES MONEY (previously written by Lawrence Hazard & Richard Flournoy). (Ethel Barrymore Theatre, Nov. 1, 1934)

THREE MEN ON A HORSE. With John Cecil Holm. 1935. (The Playhouse, Jan. 30, 1935)

ADE, GEORGE

THE SULTAN OF SULU. 1903. (Studebaker Theatre, Chicago, March 11, 1902)

PEGGY FROM PARIS. (Wallack's Theatre, Sept. 10, 1903)

THE COUNTY CHAIRMAN. c. 1924. (Wallack's Theatre, Nov. 24, 1903)

THE COLLEGE WIDOW. c. 1924. (Garden Theatre, Sept. 20, 1904)

THE SHO-GUN. (Wallack's Theatre, Oct. 10, 1904)

THE BAD SAMARITAN. (Garden Theatre, Sept. 12, 1905)

JUST OUT OF COLLEGE. c. 1924. (Lyceum Theatre, Sept. 27, 1905)

ARTIE. (Garrick Theatre, Oct. 28, 1907)

FATHER AND THE BOYS. c. 1924. (Empire Theatre, March 2, 1908)

THE FAIR CO-ED. (Knickerbocker Theatre, Feb. 1, 1909)

* MARSE COVINGTON. c. 1923.

BIBLIOGRAPHY AND PLAY LIST

* NETTIE. c. 1924. (Princess Theatre, Nov. 24, 1914)
* SPEAKING TO FATHER. c. 1923. [Abridged form of JUST OUT
  OF COLLEGE]
* THE MAYOR AND THE MANICURE. c. 1923.
THE WILLING PERFORMER. *Country Gentleman,* Phila., 1928.

AKINS, ZOË

* THE MAGICAL CITY. *Forum,* May, 1916. (Comedy Theatre,
  March 20, 1916)
PAPA. 1913. (Little Theatre, Los Angeles, Calif., Nov. 16, 1916;
  Little Theatre, N. Y., April 10, 1919)
DÉCLASSÉE. 1923. (Empire Theatre, Oct. 6, 1919)
FOOT-LOOSE. Adap. of FORGET-ME-NOT by H. C. Merivale and
  F. C. Groves. (Greenwich Village Theatre, May 10, 1920)
DADDY'S GONE A-HUNTING. 1923. (Plymouth Theatre, Aug.
  31, 1921)
THE VARYING SHORE. (Hudson Theatre, Dec. 5, 1921)
GREATNESS. 1923. (As THE TEXAS NIGHTINGALE, Empire
  Theatre, Nov. 20, 1922)
A ROYAL FANDANGO. (Plymouth Theatre, Nov. 12, 1923)
* SUCH A CHARMING YOUNG MAN. In *One-Act Plays for Stage
  and Study.* 1924. Also separately, 1933.
PARDON MY GLOVE. (Lyceum, Rochester, May 17, 1926)
FIRST LOVE. Adap. of PILE OU FACE by Louis Verneuil. (Broad
  St. Theatre, Phila., Sept. 13, 1926)
THOU DESPERATE PILOT. (Werba's Theatre, Brooklyn, Feb. 28,
  1927)
THE FURIES. (Shubert Theatre, March 7, 1928)
THE LOVE DUEL. Adap. from play by Lili Hatvany. (Ethel
  Barrymore Theatre, April 15, 1929)
THE GREEKS HAD A WORD FOR IT. (Sam H. Harris Theatre,
  Sept. 25, 1930)
THE OLD MAID. 1935. (Empire Theatre, Jan. 7, 1935)
O EVENING STAR. (Chestnut St. Theatre, Phila., Dec. 25, 1935;
  Empire Theatre, Jan. 6, 1936)

ALDRICH, THOMAS BAILEY

MERCEDES. Boston, 1884. (Palmer's Theatre, May 1, 1893)
JUDITH OF BETHULÎA. Boston, 1904. (Tremont Theatre, Boston, Oct. 13, 1904; Daly's Theatre, Dec. 5, 1904)

Biographical and Critical

Aldrich, Mrs. Thomas Bailey, *Crowding Memories.*   Boston, 1920.

ANDERSON, MAXWELL

WHITE DESERT.   (Princess Theatre, Oct. 18, 1923)

WHAT PRICE GLORY.   With Laurence Stallings.   In *Three American Plays.*   1926.   (Plymouth Theatre, Sept. 3, 1924)

FIRST FLIGHT.   With Laurence Stallings.   In *Three American Plays,* 1926.   (Plymouth Theatre, Sept. 17, 1925)

OUTSIDE LOOKING IN.   1929.   (Greenwich Village Theatre, September 7, 1925)

THE BUCCANEER.   With Laurence Stallings.   In *Three American Plays,* 1926.   (Plymouth Theatre, Oct. 2, 1925)

SATURDAY'S CHILDREN.   1927.   (Booth Theatre, Jan. 26, 1927)

GODS OF THE LIGHTNING.   With Harold Hickerson.   1928.   (In same volume with OUTSIDE LOOKING IN, Little Theatre, Oct. 29, 1928)

GYPSY.   (Klaw Theatre, Jan. 14, 1929)

ELIZABETH THE QUEEN.   1930.   (Garrick Theatre, Phila., Sept. 29, 1930; Guild Theatre, Nov. 3, 1930)

NIGHT OVER TAOS.   1932.   (Forty-Eighth Street Theatre, March 9, 1932)

SEA WIFE.   MS.   (University of Minnesota, Minneapolis, Dec. 6, 1932)

BOTH YOUR HOUSES.   1933.   (Royale, March 6, 1933)

MARY OF SCOTLAND.   1934.   (Alvin Theatre, Nov. 27, 1933)

VALLEY FORGE.   Washington.   1934.   (Pittsburgh Guild Theatre, Dec. 10, 1934)

WINTERSET.   1935.   (Martin Beck Theatre, Sept. 25, 1935)

Biographical and Critical

Clark, Barrett H., *Maxwell Anderson, The Man and His Plays.* 1933.

ANSPACHER, LOUIS KAUFMAN

THE EMBARRASSMENT OF RICHES.   (Wallack's Theatre, May 14, 1906)

TRISTAN AND ISOLDE.   1914.

BIBLIOGRAPHY AND PLAY LIST

OUR CHILDREN. 1932. (New Haven, Sept. 6, 1915)

THE UNCHASTENED WOMAN. 1916. (Thirty-ninth St. Theatre, Oct. 9, 1915)

THE RHAPSODY. (Cort Theatre, Sept. 15, 1930)

ARMSTRONG, PAUL

THE HEIR TO THE HOORAH. (Hudson Theatre, Apr. 10, 1905)

SALOMY JANE. Dram. of Bret Harte's story. (Liberty Theatre, Jan. 19, 1907)

ALIAS JIMMY VALENTINE. Dram. of A RETRIEVED REFORMATION, by O. Henry. (Studebaker Theatre, Chicago, Dec. 25, 1909)

THE DEEP PURPLE. (Shubert's Theatre, Rochester, Sept. 26, 1910)

GOING SOME. With Rex Beach. 1923.

ARTHUR, JOSEPH

THE STILL ALARM. (Fourteenth St. Theatre, Aug. 30, 1887)

BLUE JEANS. (Fourteenth St. Theatre, Oct. 6, 1890)

THE CHERRY PICKERS. (Fourteenth St. Theatre, Oct. 12, 1896)

THE LOST RIVER. (Fourteenth St. Theatre, Oct. 3, 1900)

ATLAS, LEOPOLD

WEDNESDAY'S CHILD. 1934. (Longacre Theatre, Jan. 16, 1934)

HOUSE WE LIVE IN. 1934. (In volume with WEDNESDAY'S CHILD)

AUSTIN, MARY

THE ARROW MAKER. 1911. (New Theatre, Feb. 27, 1911)

FIRE. In the Play Book. Madison, Wis. 1914.

BACON, FRANK

LIGHTNIN'. With Winchell Smith. c. 1918. (Gaiety Theatre, Aug. 26, 1918)

FIVE O'CLOCK. (Fulton Theatre, Oct. 13, 1919)

BAKER, GEORGE PIERCE

THE PILGRIM SPIRIT. Boston. c. 1921. (Plymouth, Mass., July 13, 1921)

BALDERSTON, JOHN

THE GENIUS OF THE MARNE. 1919.

* A MORALITY FOR THE LEISURE CLASS. 1924.

DRACULA. With Hamilton Deane. (From Bram Stoker's novel, DRACULA) 1933. (Fulton Theatre, Oct. 5, 1927)

BERKELEY SQUARE. With J. C. Squire. Adaptation of novel THE SENSE OF THE PAST, by Henry James. London, 1928. N. Y.

1929. (St. Martin's Theatre, London, October, 1926; Lyceum Theatre, Nov. 4, 1929)

RED PLANET. With J. E. Hoare. (Cort Theatre, Dec. 16, 1932)

BARNARD, CHARLES

THE COUNTY FAIR. With Neil Burgess. Priv. Printed. 1889. Also French, 1922. (Proctor's Twenty-third St. Theatre, March 5, 1889)

BARRY, PHILIP

A PUNCH FOR JUDY. MS. (Harvard, 1921)

YOU AND I. 1925. (Belmont Theatre, Feb. 19, 1923)

THE YOUNGEST. 1925. (Gaiety Theatre, Dec. 22, 1924)

IN A GARDEN. 1926. (Plymouth Theatre, Nov. 16, 1925)

WHITE WINGS. 1927. (Booth Theatre, Oct. 15, 1926)

JOHN. 1929. (Klaw Theatre, Nov. 2, 1927)

PARIS BOUND. 1929. (Broad St. Theatre, Newark, Dec. 20, 1927, as THE WEDDING. Music Box Theatre, Dec. 27, 1927, as PARIS BOUND)

COCK ROBIN. With Elmer Rice. 1929. (Forty-eighth Street Theatre, Jan. 12, 1928)

HOLIDAY. 1929. (Plymouth Theatre, Nov. 26, 1928)

HOTEL UNIVERSE. 1930. (Martin Beck Theatre, Apr. 14, 1930)

TOMORROW AND TOMORROW. 1931. (Henry Miller Theatre, Jan. 13, 1931)

THE ANIMAL KINGDOM. 1932. (Broadhurst Theatre, Jan. 12, 1932)

THE JOYOUS SEASON. 1934. (Belasco Theatre, Jan. 29, 1934)

BRIGHT STAR. (Empire Theatre, Oct. 15, 1935)

THE WILD HARPS PLAYING. First Act in *Yale Literary Magazine,* Feb. 22, 1936.

BEACH, LEWIS

FOUR ONE ACT PLAYS. 1921. Includes THE CLOD.

A SQUARE PEG. Boston, 1924. (Punch and Judy Theatre, Jan. 27, 1923)

THE GOOSE HANGS HIGH. Boston, 1924. (Bijou Theatre, Jan. 29, 1924)

ANN VROOME. Boston, 1924. (Garrick Theatre, Phila., July 21, 1930)

MERRY ANDREW. 1930. (Henry Miller Theatre, Jan. 21, 1929)

THE CLOD. 1934.

BIBLIOGRAPHY AND PLAY LIST

BEHRMAN, SAMUEL NATHANIEL

LOVE IS LIKE THAT. With J. Kenyon Nicholson. (Cort Theatre, Apr. 18, 1927)

THE SECOND MAN. 1927. Also in *Three Plays,* 1934. (Guild Theatre, Apr. 11, 1927)

METEOR. 1930. Also in *Three Plays,* 1934. (Hollis St. Theatre, Boston, Dec. 2, 1929; Guild Theatre, Dec. 23, 1929)

SERENA BLANDISH. Dram. of novel of same name by "A Lady of Quality." In *Three Plays,* 1934. (Morosco Theatre, Jan. 23, 1929)

BRIEF MOMENT. 1931. (Belasco Theatre, Nov. 9, 1931)

BIOGRAPHY. 1933. (Guild Theatre, Dec. 12, 1932)

LOVE STORY. (Walnut Street Theatre, Phila., Dec. 13, 1933)

RAIN FROM HEAVEN. 1935. (John Golden Theatre, Dec. 24, 1934)

END OF SUMMER. 1936. (Bushnell Memorial Theatre, Hartford, Conn., Jan. 30, 1936; Guild Theatre, Feb. 17, 1936)

BEIN, ALBERT

LITTLE OL' BOY. 1935. (Playhouse Theatre, April 24, 1933)

LET FREEDOM RING. Dram. of TO MAKE MY BREAD, by Grace Lumpkin. 1936. (Broadhurst Theatre, Nov. 6, 1935)

BELASCO, DAVID

Six Plays. Boston, 1928.

MADAME BUTTERFLY, DU BARRY, THE DARLING OF THE GODS, ADREA, THE GIRL OF THE GOLDEN WEST, THE RETURN OF PETER GRIMM.

The following plays were produced in California before 1872: JIM BLACK; OR, THE REGULATOR'S REVENGE, THE ROLL OF THE DRUM, SPIRITLAND, THE SIGNING OF THE DECLARATION OF INDEPENDENCE, THE HANGING OF NATHAN HALE, THE DYING BOY'S LAST CHRISTMAS, ADAM AND EVE IN THE GARDEN OF EDEN, THE BUTCHER'S REVENGE; OR, THE SEVEN BUCKETS OF BLOOD, AN ANGEL IN HELL, THE BRONZE STATUE, ALADDIN AND THE WONDERFUL LAMP.

SYLVIA'S LOVERS. (Piper's Opera House, Virginia City, 1875?)

THE DOLL MASTER. (Sacramento Theatre, Sacramento, 1874–5?)

THE CREOLE. Adap. of ARTICLE 47. (California, 1876–7; Union Square Theatre, Jan. 17, 1881)

THE HAUNTED HOUSE. (Egyptian Hall, San Francisco, Feb. 16, 1877)

THE MYSTERIOUS INN. (Egyptian Hall, San Francisco, Feb. 16, 1877)

A STORM OF THOUGHTS. (Egyptian Hall, San Francisco, Feb. 17, 1877)

THE PERSECUTED TRAVELLER. (Egyptian Hall, San Francisco, Feb. 17, 1877)

OUR MYSTERIOUS BOARDING HOUSE. (Egyptian Hall, San Francisco, Feb. 20, 1877)

THE PRODIGAL'S RETURN. (Egyptian Hall, San Francisco, April 2, 1877)

WINE, WOMEN AND CARDS. (Egyptian Hall, San Francisco, Feb.–May, 1877)

THE CHRISTMAS NIGHTS; OR, THE CONVICT'S RETURN. (Egyptian Hall, San Francisco, Feb.–May, 1877)

OLIVIA. Drama of THE VICAR OF WAKEFIELD. (Baldwin Theatre, San Francisco, Sept. 2, 1878)

NOT GUILTY. Adap. of Watts Phillips's play of same name. (Baldwin Theatre, San Francisco, Dec. 25, 1878)

WITHIN AN INCH OF HIS LIFE. With James A. Herne. Dram. of story by Gaboriau. (Grand Opera House, San Francisco, Feb. 17, 1879)

THE MILLIONAIRE'S DAUGHTER. Based on THE BANKER'S DAUGHTER. (Baldwin Theatre, San Francisco, May 19, 1879)

MARRIAGE BY MOONLIGHT, afterwards HAP-HAZARD. With James A. Herne. MS. Adap. of Watts Phillips's CAMILLA'S HUSBAND. (Baldwin Theatre, San Francisco, June 30, 1879)

DRINK. Dram. of Zola's novel, L'ASSOMMOIR. (Baldwin Theatre, San Francisco, July 15, 1879)

HEARTS OF OAK. With James A. Herne. MS. (As CHUMS, Baldwin Theatre, San Francisco, Sept. 9, 1879; as HEARTS OF OAK, Hamlin's Theatre, Chicago, Nov. 17, 1879)

PAUL ARNIFF; OR, THE LOVE OF A SERF. (Baldwin Theatre, San Francisco, July 19, 1880)

TRUE TO THE CORE. Adap. of T. P. Cooke's play of same name. (Baldwin Theatre, San Francisco, Aug. 30, 1880)

THE EVICTION. (Baldwin Theatre, San Francisco, Jan. 10, 1881)

LA BELLE RUSSE. Adap. of FORGET-ME-NOT by Merivale and

322

Grove and NEW MAGDALEN by Wilkie Collins. A.L.P. (Baldwin Theatre, San Francisco, July 18, 1881; Wallack's Theatre, May 8, 1882; Pavilion Theatre, London, April 17, 1886)

THE STRANGLERS OF PARIS. Dram. of LES ETRANGLEURS DE PARIS, by Adolphe Belot. A.L.P. (Baldwin Theatre, San Francisco, Aug. 15, 1881; Park Theatre, Nov. 12, 1883)

THE LONE PINE. (Sacramento Theatre, Sacramento, before 1882)

THE CURSE OF CAIN. With Peter Robertson. (Baldwin Theatre, San Francisco, March 7, 1882)

AMERICAN BORN. Adap. from BRITISH BORN by Paul Merritt and Henry Pettitt. (Baldwin Theatre, San Francisco, July 10, 1882)

MAY BLOSSOM. c. 1882. (Madison Square Theatre, April 12, 1884)

VALERIE. Adap. of Sardou's FERNANDE. (Wallack's Theatre, Feb. 15, 1886)

THE HIGHEST BIDDER. Adap. of TRADE by J. M. Morton and R. Reece. (Lyceum Theatre, May 3, 1887)

PAWN TICKET No. 210. With Clay M. Greene. (McVicker's Theatre, Chicago, Sept. 12, 1887)

THE WIFE. With Henry C. DeMille. A.L.P. (Lyceum Theatre, Nov. 1, 1887; as THE SENATOR'S WIFE, Theatre Royal, Manchester, Sept. 30, 1892)

LORD CHUMLEY. With Henry C. DeMille. A.L.P. (Lyceum Theatre, Aug. 21, 1888)

THE CHARITY BALL. With Henry C. DeMille. A.L.P. (Lyceum Theatre, Nov. 19, 1889)

MEN AND WOMEN. With Henry C. DeMille. A.L.P. (Proctor's Twenty-third St. Theatre, Oct. 21, 1890; Opera Comique, London, March 5, 1893)

MISS HELYETT. Adap. from the French of Maxime Boucheron. (Star Theatre, Nov. 3, 1891)

THE GIRL I LEFT BEHIND ME. With Franklyn Fyles. A.L.P. (Empire Theatre, Jan. 25, 1893; Sadler's Wells Theatre, London, Jan. 6, 1893)

THE YOUNGER SON. Adap. of SCHLIMME SAAT, by O. Vischer. (Empire Theatre, Oct. 24, 1893)

THE HEART OF MARYLAND. A.L.P. (Grand Opera House, Wash-

A HISTORY OF THE AMERICAN DRAMA

ington, D. C., Oct. 9, 1895; Herald Square Theatre, Oct. 22, 1895)

UNDER THE POLAR STAR. With Clay M. Greene. (Academy of Music, Aug. 20, 1896; earlier form in California, 1875–8)

ZAZA. From the French of Pierre Berton and Charles Simon. (Lafayette Opera House, Washington, D. C., Dec. 25, 1898; Garrick Theatre, Jan. 9, 1899)

NAUGHTY ANTHONY. MS. (Columbia Theatre, Washington, D. C., Dec. 25, 1899; Herald Square Theatre, Jan. 8, 1900)

MADAME BUTTERFLY. With John Luther Long, from story by Long. In Quinn's *Representative American Plays.* 1917. Also in *Six Plays.* 1928. (Herald Square Theatre, March 5, 1900; Duke of York's Theatre, London, April 28, 1900)

DU BARRY. 1928. (New National Theatre, Washington, D. C., Dec. 12, 1901; Criterion Theatre, Dec. 25, 1901)

THE DARLING OF THE GODS. With John Luther Long. 1928. (New National Theatre, Washington, D. C., Nov. 17, 1902; Belasco Theatre, now Republic, Dec. 3, 1902; Theater des Westens, Berlin, May, 1903; His Majesty's Theatre, London, Dec. 28, 1903)

SWEET KITTY BELLAIRS. Adap. of THE BATH COMEDY by A. and E. Castle. (Lafayette Opera House, Washington, D. C., Nov. 23, 1903; Belasco Theatre, now Republic, Dec. 12, 1903; Haymarket Theatre, London, Oct. 5, 1907)

ADREA. With John Luther Long. 1928. (Convention Hall, Washington, D. C., Dec. 26, 1904; Belasco Theatre, now Republic, Jan. 11, 1905)

THE GIRL OF THE GOLDEN WEST. In Moses's *Representative American Dramas.* Also in *Six Plays.* 1928. (Belasco Theatre, Pittsburgh, Oct. 3, 1905; Belasco Theatre, now Republic, Nov. 14, 1905)

THE ROSE OF THE RANCHO. With Richard Walton Tully. MS. (Majestic Theatre, Boston, Nov. 12, 1906; Belasco Theatre, now Republic, Nov. 27, 1906)

A GRAND ARMY MAN. With Pauline Phelps and Marion Short. (Hyperion Theatre, New Haven, Sept. 23, 1907; Stuyvesant Theatre, now Belasco, Oct. 16, 1907)

THE LILY. From the French of Pierre Wolff and Gaston Leroux. (Belasco Theatre, Washington, D. C., Dec. 6, 1909; Stuyvesant Theatre, now Belasco, Dec. 23, 1909; Kingsway Theatre, London, Feb. 23, 1911)

THE RETURN OF PETER GRIMM. In Baker's *Modern American Plays*. Also in *Six Plays*. 1928. (Hollis Street Theatre, Boston, Jan. 2, 1911; Belasco Theatre, Oct. 17, 1911)

THE GOVERNOR'S LADY. With Alice Bradley. (Broad Street Theatre, Phila., April 29, 1912; Republic Theatre, Sept. 9, 1912)

THE SECRET. From the French of Henri Bernstein. (Belasco Theatre, Dec. 23, 1913)

VAN DER DECKEN. (The Playhouse, Wilmington, Del., Dec. 12, 1915)

THE SON DAUGHTER. With George Scarborough. (Ford's Opera House, Baltimore, Nov. 4, 1919; Belasco Theatre, Nov. 19, 1919)

KIKI. Adap. of KIKI by André Picard. (Apollo Theatre, Atlantic City, N. J., July 25, 1921; Belasco Theatre, Nov. 29, 1921)

THE COMEDIAN. Adap. from the French of Sacha Guitry. (Playhouse, Wilmington, Del., Jan. 26, 1923; Lyceum Theatre, March 13, 1923)

LAUGH, CLOWN, LAUGH. Adap. by Belasco and Tom Cushing of RIDI PAGLIACCIO, by Fausto Martini. MS. (Lyceum Theatre, Rochester, Oct. 18, 1923; Belasco Theatre, Nov. 28, 1923)

FANNY. With Willard Mack. (Lyceum Theatre, Sept. 21, 1926)

MIMI. Adap. from THE RED MILL, by Ferenc Molnar. (Belasco Theatre, Dec. 12, 1928)

Biographical and Critical

Belasco, David, *The Theatre Through the Stage Door*. Ed. by L. V. DeFoe. 1919.

Belasco, David, *A Souvenir of Shakespeare's The Merchant of Venice, as presented by David Belasco, at the Lyceum Theatre, Dec. 21, 1922*. Priv. printed, 1923.

Belasco, David, *Plays Produced under the Stage Direction of David Belasco*. Priv. printed, 1925.

Winter, William, *The Life of David Belasco*. 2 Vols. 1918. [This is the standard biography. Belasco's "My Life Story,"

printed in *Hearst's Magazine,* beginning March, 1914, and
not published in book form, is interesting but inaccurate.]

Dransfield, Jane, "Behind the Scenes with Belasco," *Theatre
Magazine.* XXXV (April, 1922), 228–230; 260.

Huneker, James G., "David Belasco," *The Outlook,* CXXVII
(March 16, 1921), 418–422.

Reichert, Edwin Tyson, "Dr. Jekyll and Mr. Hyde and The Case
of Becky as staged by Mr. David Belasco." *Public Lectures
of the University of Pennsylvania,* Phila., 1915.

BENRIMO, J. HARRY

The Yellow Jacket. With G. C. Hazelton, q.v.

The Willow Tree. With Harrison Rhodes. 1931. (Cohan
and Harris Theatre, March 6, 1917)

BROADHURST, GEORGE

The Speculator. (Fifth Avenue Theatre, April 18, 1896)

What Happened to Jones. c. 1910. (Manhattan Theatre, Aug.
30, 1897)

The Wrong Mr. Wright. c. 1918. (Bijou Theatre, Sept. 6,
1897)

The Last Chapter. (Garden Theatre, March 6, 1899)

Why Smith Left Home. c. 1912. (Chestnut St. Theatre,
Phila., Oct. 10, 1898; Hoyt's Theatre, Sept. 2, 1899)

The House That Jack Built. (Hoyt's Theatre, Dec. 24, 1900)

An American Lord. With C. T. Dazey. (Hudson Theatre,
April 23, 1906)

The Man of the Hour. c. 1916. (Savoy Theatre, Dec. 4,
1906)

The Mills of the God. (Astor Theatre, March 4, 1907)

The Easterner. (Garrick Theatre, March 2, 1908)

Wildfire. With George V. Hobart. (Liberty Theatre, Sept. 7,
1908)

The Dollar Mark. (Wallack's Theatre, Aug. 23, 1909)

Bought and Paid For. c. 1916. (Playhouse, Sept. 26, 1911)

The Price. MS. (Hudson Theatre, Nov. 1, 1911)

To-Day. Adap. from Yiddish of A. S. Schomer. (Forty-eighth
St. Theatre, Oct. 6, 1913)

The Law of the Land. (Harmanus Bleecker Hall, Albany,
Sept. 21, 1914; Forty-eighth St. Theatre, Sept. 30, 1914)

BROWN, ALICE
> CHILDREN OF EARTH. 1915. (Booth Theatre, Jan. 12, 1915)
> *One-act Plays.* 1921.
> CHARLES LAMB. 1924.

BROWNE, PORTER EMERSON
> A FOOL THERE WAS. (Liberty Theatre, March 24, 1909)
> THE BAD MAN. c. 1926. (Comedy Theatre, Aug. 30, 1920)

BUCHANAN, THOMPSON
> A WOMAN'S WAY. 1915. (Davidson Theatre, Milwaukee, Jan.
> 7, 1909; Hackett Theatre, Feb. 22, 1909)
> THE CUB. (Comedy Theatre, Nov. 1, 1910)
> LIFE. (Manhattan Opera House, Oct. 24, 1914)
> CIVILIAN CLOTHES. c. 1920. (Morosco Theatre, Sept, 12, 1919)
> THE SPORTING THING TO DO. (Ritz Theatre, Feb. 19, 1923)
> SINNER. (Klaw Theatre, Feb. 7, 1927)
> AS GOOD AS NEW. (Times Square Theatre, Nov. 3, 1930)

BURGESS, NEIL
> THE COUNTY FAIR. With Charles Barnard, q. v.

BURNETT, FRANCES HODGSON
> ESMERALDA. With William Gillette, q.v.
> LITTLE LORD FAUNTLEROY. Dram. of novel of same name. 1889.
> (Terry's Theatre, London, May 14, 1888; Boston Museum,
> Sept. 10, 1888)
> THE FIRST GENTLEMAN OF EUROPE. With George Fleming.
> (Lyceum Theatre, Jan. 25, 1897)
> A LADY OF QUALITY. With Stephen Townsend. Dram. novel of
> same name. (Wallack's Theatre, Nov. 1, 1897)
> THE PRETTY SISTER OF JOSÉ. Dram. novel of same name. (Em-
> pire Theatre, Nov. 10, 1903)
> THE DAWN OF A TO-MORROW. (Academy of Music, Norfolk, Va.,
> Dec. 18, 1908; Lyceum Theatre, Jan. 25, 1909)
> THE LITTLE PRINCESS. 1911. (Avenue Theatre, London, Sept.
> 18, 1902; as A LITTLE UNFAIRY PRINCESS; Criterion Theatre,
> Jan. 14, 1903, as THE LITTLE PRINCESS)
> THE RACKETTY PACKETTY HOUSE. N. Y., 1927.

CALHOUN, ALFRED ROCHEFORT
> THE COLOR GUARD. Pittsburgh, 1870. (California Theatre, San
> Francisco, Sept. 22, 1879. Prob. not first)

CAMPBELL, BARTLEY

THROUGH FIRE. (Pittsburgh Opera House, Dec. 25, 1871)

PERIL; OR, LOVE AT LONG BRANCH. A.L.P. (Chestnut St. Theatre, Phila., Feb. 12, 1872; Union Square Theatre, June 22, 1874)

FATE. (Hooley's Theatre, Chicago, 1872–3; Wallack's Theatre, June, 1874; Gaiety Theatre, Glasgow, Feb. 21, 1876; Gaiety Theatre, London, Aug. 6, 1884)

RISKS; OR, INSURE YOUR LIFE. (Hooley's Theatre, Chicago, May 5, 1873; Park Theatre, Jan. 14, 1878)

THE VIRGINIAN. A.L.P. (Hooley's Theatre, Chicago, Oct. 26, 1874; St. James's Theatre, London, Nov. 20, 1876)

GRANA UAILE. (Academy of Music, Chicago, Feb. 1, 1875)

BULLS AND BEARS. Adap. of ULTIMO, by Gustav von Moser. (Maguire's Opera House, San Francisco, June 7, 1875)

ON THE RHINE. (Maguire's Opera House, San Francisco, May 31, 1875)

A HEROINE IN RAGS. (Euclid Ave. Opera House, Cleveland, March 28, 1877)

HEARTS. (Hooley's Theatre, Chicago, Oct. 20, 1873)

HOW WOMEN LOVE; OR, THE HEART OF THE SIERRAS. (Arch St. Theatre, Phila., May 21, 1877) Rewritten as THE VIGILANTES.

MY FOOLISH WIFE. (Chestnut St. Theatre, Phila., Oct. 15, 1877)

STRUCK OIL. (Arch St. Theatre, Phila., Oct. 29, 1877)

CLIO. (McVicker's Theatre, Chicago, 1878; Elephant and Camel Theatre, London, Aug. 14, 1885 [copyright]; Niblo's Garden, Aug. 17, 1885)

MY PARTNER. A.L.P. (Union Square Theatre, Sept. 16, 1879; Olympic Theatre, London, April 10, 1884; Residenz Theater, Berlin, Sept. 15, 1884)

THE GALLEY SLAVE. A.L.P. (Chestnut St. Theatre, Phila., Sept. 29, 1879; Theatre Royal, Hull, England, Nov. 22, 1880; Grand Theatre, London, Feb. 8, 1886)

FAIRFAX. A.L.P. (Park Theatre, Boston, Dec. 8, 1879; Park Theatre, Dec. 29, 1879)

MATRIMONY. Revision of PERIL. (Standard Theatre, Dec. 6, 1880)

MY GERALDINE. (Standard Theatre, Dec. 21, 1880)

THE WHITE SLAVE. A.L.P. (Haverley's Theatre, April 3, 1882; Grand Theatre, London, Aug. 18, 1884)

FRIEND AND FOE. Revision of ON THE RHINE. (Windsor Theatre, Oct. 16, 1882)

SIBERIA. MS. (California Theatre, San Francisco, Nov. 28, 1882; Haverley's Fourteenth St. Theatre, Feb. 26, 1883; Princess's Theatre, London, Dec. 14, 1887)

SEPARATION. MS. (Union Square Theatre, Jan. 28, 1884)

PAQUITA. (Bartley Campbell's Fourteenth St. Theatre, Aug. 31, 1885)

Biographical and Critical

M[ontgomery], G. E., "Bartley Campbell," *The Theatre,* I(1886), 348–9.

CARB, DAVID

THE VOICE OF THE PEOPLE. Boston, 1912.

QUEEN VICTORIA. With W. P. Eaton. c. 1923. (Forty-eighth St. Theatre, Nov. 15, 1923)

LONG AGO LADIES. Boston, 1934.

CARLETON, HENRY GUY

MEMNON. Priv. printed, Chicago, 1881.

VICTOR DURAND. MS. (Wallack's Theatre, Dec. 18, 1884)

YE EARLIE TROUBLE. (Proctor's Theatre, Sept. 10, 1892)

THE LION'S MOUTH. (Grand Opera House, Phila., 1891; Star Theatre, Sept. 11, 1892)

A GILDED FOOL. (Miner's Fifth Avenue Theatre, Nov. 7, 1892)

THE BUTTERFLIES. 1894. (Palmer's Theatre, Feb. 5, 1894)

LEM KETTLE. (Bijou Theatre, Sept. 24, 1894)

THAT IMPRUDENT YOUNG COUPLE. (Empire Theatre, Sept. 23, 1895)

AMBITION. (Miner's Fifth Ave. Theatre, Oct. 22, 1895)

COLINETTE. Adap. from French of Lenôtre and Martin. (Knickerbocker Theatre, April 10, 1899)

CARPENTER, EDWARD CHILDS

THE DRAGON FLY. With John Luther Long. (Garrick Theatre, Phila., 1905)

CAPTAIN COURTESY. (Belasco Theatre, Los Angeles, 1906)

THE BARBER OF NEW ORLEANS. Priv. printed. (Garrick Theatre, Chicago, Oct. 19, 1908; Daly's Theatre, Jan. 5, 1909)

THE CHALLENGE. (Parson's Theatre, Hartford, Conn., Oct. 26, 1911)

THE TONGUES OF MEN. c. 1926. (English's Theatre, Indianapolis, Oct. 27, 1913; Harris Theatre, Nov. 10, 1913)

THE CINDERELLA MAN, c. 1915. (Hudson Theatre, Jan. 17, 1916; Queen's Theatre, London, 1919)

THE PIPES OF PAN. c. 1926. (Hudson Theatre, Nov. 6, 1917)

THREE BEARS. c. 1926. (Empire Theatre, Nov. 13, 1917)

BAB. Dram. novel by Mary R. Rinehart. c. 1919. (Hollis St. Theatre, Boston, Feb. 16, 1920; Park Theatre, Oct. 18, 1920)

POT LUCK. MS. (Comedy Theatre, Sept. 29, 1921)

CONNIE GOES HOME. 1934. (Forty-ninth St. Theatre, Sept. 6, 1923)

WHEN YOUR SHIP COMES IN. 1927.

THE BACHELOR FATHER. 1932. (Belasco Theatre, Feb. 28, 1928)

DUMB AS A FOX. 1928.

WHISTLING IN THE DARK. With Laurence Gross. (Ethel Barrymore Theatre, Jan. 19, 1932)

ORDER PLEASE. (Playhouse Theatre, Oct. 9, 1934)

ROMEO AND—JANE. 1927.

THE LEOPARD LADY. 1928.

CHURCHILL, WINSTON

THE TITLE MART. 1905. (Madison Square Theatre, Feb. 19, 1906)

DR. JONATHAN. 1919.

THE CRISIS. c. 1927.

COHAN, GEORGE M.

THE GOVERNOR'S SON. (Savoy Theatre, Feb. 25, 1901)

RUNNING FOR OFFICE. (Fourteenth St. Theatre, April 27, 1903)

LITTLE JOHNNY JONES. (Liberty Theatre, Nov. 7, 1904)

FORTY-FIVE MINUTES FROM BROADWAY. MS. (New Amsterdam Theatre, Jan. 1, 1906)

GEORGE WASHINGTON, JR. (Herald Square Theatre, Feb. 12, 1906)

POPULARITY. (Wallack's Theatre, Oct. 1, 1906)

FIFTY MILES FROM BOSTON. (Garrick Theatre, Feb. 3, 1907)

THE TALK OF NEW YORK. (Knickerbocker Theatre, Dec. 3, 1907)

THE YANKEE PRINCE. (Knickerbocker Theatre, April 20, 1908)

THE AMERICAN IDEA. (New York Theatre, Oct. 5, 1908)

GET RICH QUICK WALLINGFORD. Dram. of story by George Randolph Chester, MS. (Gaiety Theatre, Sept. 19, 1910; Queen's Theatre, London, Jan. 19, 1913)

THE LITTLE MILLIONAIRE. (Cohan Theatre, Sept. 22, 1911)

BROADWAY JONES. c. 1923. (Parson's Theatre, Hartford, Conn., Sept. 16, 1912; Cohan Theatre, Sept. 23, 1912)

SEVEN KEYS TO BALDPATE. Priv. printed, 1914. Also regular ed. n. d. Dram. of story by Earl Biggers. (Astor Theatre, Sept. 22, 1913)

THE MIRACLE MAN. Dram. of story by Frank L. Packard. (Astor Theatre, Sept. 21, 1914)

HIT THE TRAIL HOLLIDAY. Priv. printed, 1916. (Astor Theatre, Sept. 13, 1915)

THE TAVERN. 1933. With Cora D. Gannt, from her novel, THE CHOICE OF A SUPERMAN. (Cohan Theatre, Sept. 27, 1920)

A PRINCE THERE WAS. Dram. of ENCHANTED HEARTS by Darragh Aldrich, 1927. (Apollo Theatre, Atlantic City, N. J., Oct. 31, 1918; Cohan Theatre, Dec. 24, 1918)

MADELEINE AND THE MOVIES. (Gaiety Theatre, March 6, 1922)

THE SONG AND DANCE MAN. (Garrick Theatre, Phila., Nov. 19, 1923; Hudson Theatre, Dec. 31, 1923)

AMERICAN BORN. (Hudson Theatre, Oct. 5, 1925)

THE HOME-TOWNERS. (Chicago, 1926; Hudson Theatre, Aug. 23, 1926)

BABY CYCLONE. 1929. (Henry Miller Theatre, Sept. 12, 1927)

MERRY MALONES. (Erlanger's Theatre, Sept. 26, 1927)

WHISPERING FRIENDS. (Hudson Theatre, February 20, 1928)

BILLIE. Musicalization of BROADWAY JONES. (Erlanger's Theatre, Oct. 1, 1928)

GAMBLING. (Garrick Theatre, Philadelphia, May 13, 1929)

A WELL KNOWN WOMAN. (Broad St. Theatre, Phila., Sept. 29, 1930)

CONFIDENTIAL SERVICE. (Broad St. Theatre, Phila., March 28, 1932)

FRIENDSHIP. (Fulton Theatre, Aug. 31, 1931)

PIGEONS AND PEOPLE. c. 1932. (Sam H. Harris Theatre, Jan. 16, 1933)

DEAR OLD DARLING. (Nixon Theatre, Pittsburgh, Dec. 30, 1935; Alvin Theatre, March 2, 1936)

Biographical and Critical

Cohan, George M., *Twenty Years on Broadway and the Years It Took to Get There.* c. 1925.

Anon. "Get Rich Quick Wallingford. A Racy Satire of American Commercialism." *Current Literature, LI* (Aug., 1911), 185–191.

CONNELLY, MARC[US COOK]

DULCY. With G. S. Kaufman, q. v.

TO THE LADIES. With G. S. Kaufman, q. v.

MERTON OF THE MOVIES. With G. S. Kaufman, q. v.

THE DEEP TANGLED WILDWOOD. With G. S. Kaufman, q. v.

BEGGAR ON HORSEBACK. With G. S. Kaufman, q. v.

THE WISDOM TOOTH. 1926. (Little Theatre, Feb. 15, 1926)

THE WILD MAN OF BORNEO. With Herman J. Mankiewiez. (Bijou Theatre, Sept. 13, 1927)

THE GREEN PASTURES. 1930. (Mansfield Theatre, Feb. 26, 1930)

THE FARMER TAKES A WIFE. With Frank B. Elser. Based on ROME HAUL, a novel by Walter D. Edmonds. (National Theatre, Washington, Oct. 8, 1934; Forty-sixth St. Theatre, Oct. 30, 1934)

CRAVEN, FRANK

TOO MANY COOKS. c. 1927. (Thirty-ninth St. Theatre, Feb. 24, 1914)

THIS WAY OUT. (Cohan Theatre, Aug. 30, 1917)

THE FIRST YEAR. 1921. Rev. 1928. (Ford's Opera House, Baltimore, Oct. 11, 1920; Little Theatre, Oct. 20, 1920)

SPITE CORNER. c. 1923. (Little Theatre, Sept. 25, 1922)

NEW BROOMS. 1925. (Fulton Theatre, Nov. 17, 1924)

THE 19TH HOLE. 1930. (George M. Cohan Theatre, Oct. 11, 1927)

THAT'S GRATITUDE. 1931. (John Golden Theatre, Sept. 11, 1930)

BIBLIOGRAPHY AND PLAY LIST

CRAWFORD, FRANCIS MARION

Dr. Claudius. With Harry St. Maur. (Fifth Ave. Theatre, Feb. 1, 1897)

In the Palace of the King. With Lorimer Stoddard. Printed in abstract, 1909. (Republic Theatre, Dec. 31, 1901)

Francesca da Rimini. London, 1902.

The White Sister. With Walter Hackett. 1937. (Daly's Theatre, Sept. 27, 1909)

CROTHERS, RACHEL

* Criss-Cross. 1904.

* The Rector. c. 1905. (Madison Square Theatre, April 3, 1902)

The Three of Us. c. 1916. (Madison Square Theatre, Oct. 17, 1906)

The Coming of Mrs. Patrick. (Madison Square Theatre, Nov. 6, 1907)

Myself Bettina. (Powers Theatre, Chicago, Jan. 1908; Daly's Theatre, Oct. 5, 1908)

* Katy Did. In *The Smart Set*. Jan., 1909.

* Mrs. Molly. In *The Smart Set*. March, 1909.

A Man's World. Boston, 1915. (National Theatre, Washington, D. C., Oct. 18, 1909; Comedy Theatre, Feb. 8, 1910)

He and She. In Quinn's *Representative American Plays*. (Poughkeepsie, 1911; Plymouth Theatre, Boston, Feb. 5, 1912, as The Herfords; Little Theatre, Feb. 12, 1920 as He and She)

Ourselves. MS. (Lyric Theatre, Nov. 13, 1913)

Young Wisdom. (Criterion Theatre, Jan. 5, 1914)

The Heart of Paddy Whack. c. 1925. (Baltimore, Oct. 5, 1914; Grand Opera House, Nov. 26, 1914)

Old Lady 31. 1923. (Schenectady, N. Y., Sept. 4, 1916; Thirty-ninth St. Theatre, Oct. 30, 1916)

Mother Carey's Chickens. With Kate Douglas Wiggin. (Cort Theatre, Sept. 25, 1917)

Once Upon a Time. c. 1925. (Atlantic City, N. J., Oct., 1917; Fulton Theatre, April 15, 1918)

A Little Journey. 1923. (Little Theatre, Dec. 26, 1918)

39 East. 1924. (Broadhurst Theatre, March 31, 1919)

Nice People. In Quinn's *Contemporary American Plays*. (Atlantic City, N. J., Dec. 26, 1920; Klaw Theatre, March 2, 1921)

EVERYDAY. 1930. (Atlantic City, N. J., Oct. 27, 1921; Bijou Theatre, Nov. 16, 1921)

MARY THE THIRD. 1923. (Thirty-ninth St. Theatre, Feb. 5, 1923)

EXPRESSING WILLIE. 1924. (Forty-eighth St. Theatre, April 16, 1924)

A LADY'S VIRTUE. (Selwyn Theatre, Chicago, Oct., 1925; Bijou Theatre, Nov. 23, 1925)

Six One-act Plays. Boston, 1925. Contains THE IMPORTANCE OF BEING CLOTHED, THE IMPORTANCE OF BEING NICE, THE IMPORTANCE OF BEING MARRIED, THE IMPORTANCE OF BEING A WOMAN, WHAT THEY THINK, and PEGGY.

VENUS. (Masque Theatre, Dec. 26, 1927)

LET US BE GAY. 1929. (Little Theatre, Feb. 21, 1929)

AS HUSBANDS GO. 1931. (John Golden Theatre, March 5, 1931)

CAUGHT WET. 1932. (John Golden Theatre, Nov. 4, 1931)

WHEN LADIES MEET. 1932. (Royale Theatre, Oct. 6, 1932)

CUNNINGHAM, LEON

HOSPITALITY. (Forty-eighth St. Theatre, Nov. 13, 1922)

DALY, AUGUSTIN

In the following list of plays written or adapted by Daly, manuscripts are indicated only when no printed copies exist. MSS. are in possession of Samuel French.

LEAH THE FORSAKEN. Adap. of DEBORAH by S. H. von Mosenthal, New York, n. d. (Howard Athenæum, Boston, Dec. 8, 1862; Niblo's Garden, Jan. 19, 1863; Adelphi Theatre, London, Oct. 1, 1863)

TAMING A BUTTERFLY. Adap. of LE PAPILLON by Sardou. Priv. printed, n. d. (Olympic Theatre, Feb. 25, 1864)

LORLIE'S WEDDING. Adap. of DORF UND STADT by Charlotte B. Pfeiffer. MS. (Winter Garden, March 28, 1864)

JUDITH. With Paul Nicholson. MS. (Winter Garden, April 8, 1864)

THE SORCERESS. Adap. of LA SORCIÈRE. (Winter Garden, April 26, 1864)

GRIFFITH GAUNT; OR, JEALOUSY. 1868. Dram. novel by Charles Reade. (New York Theatre, Nov. 7, 1866)

BIBLIOGRAPHY AND PLAY LIST

Hazardous Ground. Adap. of Nos Bons Villageois by Sardou. 1868. (Conway's Park Theatre, Brooklyn, March, 1867?)

Under the Gaslight. 1867. (New York Theatre, August 12, 1867; Pavilion Theatre, London, July 20, 1868; adapted as London by Gaslight at Sadler's Wells Theatre, London, Sept. 19, 1868)

A Legend of Norwood; or, Village Life in New England. Dram. of novel by Henry Ward Beecher. Priv. printed, 1867. (New York Theatre, Nov. 11, 1867)

Pickwick Papers. Dram. of novel by Dickens. Auto. MS. (New York Theatre, Jan. 22, 1868)

A Flash of Lightning. Priv. printed, 1885. (Broadway Theatre, June 10, 1868; Grecian Theatre, London, Nov. 21, 1870)

The Red Scarf. MS. (Conway's Park Theatre, Brooklyn, Oct. 12, 1868; Bowery Theatre, Nov. 1868)

Sanya; or, The Red Ribbon. 1869? [Probably the play in MS. as Rhoda]

Come Here; or, The Débutante's Test. MS. 1870. [Prepared for Janauschek's English performance]

Frou-Frou. Adap. from Henri Meilhac and Ludovic Halévy. c. 1870. (Fifth Ave. Theatre, Feb. 15, 1870)

Man and Wife. Dram. of novel by Wilkie Collins. A.L.P. (Fifth Ave. Theatre, Sept. 13, 1870)

Horizon. Priv. printed, 1885. In Halline's *American Plays.* 1935. (Olympic Theatre, March 21, 1871)

No Name. Dram. of novel by Wilkie Collins. (Fifth Ave. Theatre, June 7, 1871)

Delmonico's; or, Larks up the Hudson. Revision of Taming a Butterfly. MS. (Fifth Ave. Theatre, June 20, 1871)

Divorce. Priv. printed, 1884. A.L.P. (Fifth Ave. Theatre, Sept. 5, 1871; Theatre Royal, Edinburgh, Dec. 12, 1881)

Article 47. Adap. of L'Article 47 by Adolphe Belot. MS. (Fifth Ave. Theatre, April 2, 1872)

King Carrot. Adap. of Le Roi Carotte by Sardou. Auto. MS. (Grand Opera House, Aug. 26, 1872)

Alixe. Adap. of La Comtesse de Somerive by Baroness de

A HISTORY OF THE AMERICAN DRAMA

Prevois and Théodore Barrière. Auto. MS. (Daly's Fifth Ave. Theatre, Jan. 21, 1873)

ROUGHING IT. MS. (Grand Opera House, Feb. 18, 1873)

MADELEINE MOREL. Adap. from German of S. H. von Mosenthal. Priv. printed, 1884. (Daly's Fifth Ave. Theatre, May 20, 1873)

OUR CITY. (Bowery Theatre, Nov. 17, 1873)

ROUND THE CLOCK. Adap., in part, of LA TOUR DU CADRAN, by Hector Crimieux and Henri Bocage. MS. (Grand Opera House, Nov. 25, 1872)

FOLLINE. Adap. of LA MAISON NEUVE by Sardou. Auto. MS. (New Fifth Ave. Theatre, Jan. 27, 1874)

MONSIEUR ALPHONSE. Adap. from Alexandre Dumas, fils. Priv. printed, 1886. (New Fifth Ave. Theatre, April 25, 1874)

WHAT SHOULD SHE DO? OR, JEALOUSY. Adap. of GERMAINE by Edmond About. Auto. MS. (New Fifth Ave. Theatre, Aug. 25, 1874)

THE TWO WIDOWS. Adap. of LES DEUX VEUVES by Felicien Mallefille. Auto. MS. (New Fifth Ave. Theatre, Oct. 10, 1874)

YORICK. Adap. of UN DRAMA NUEVO by Manuel Tamayo y Baus (Estabanez). Auto. MS. (New Fifth Ave. Theatre, Dec. 5, 1874)

THE BIG BONANZA. Adap. of ULTIMO by Gustav von Moser. Priv. printed, 1884. A.L.P. (New Fifth Ave. Theatre, Feb. 17, 1875)

PIQUE. Priv. printed, 1884. A.L.P. (New Fifth Ave. Theatre, Dec. 14, 1875; as ONLY A WOMAN, Brighton Theatre Royal, Oct. 16, 1882; as HER OWN ENEMY, Gaiety Theatre, London, March 26, 1884)

LIFE. Adap. of LE PROCÈS VEAURADIEUX. MS. (New Fifth Ave. Theatre, Sept. 27, 1876)

THE AMERICAN. Adap. of L'ETRANGÈRE by Dumas, fils. Auto. MS. (New Fifth Ave. Theatre, Dec. 20, 1876)

LEMONS. Adap. of CITRONEN by Julius Rosen. Priv. printed, 1877. (New Fifth Ave. Theatre, Jan. 15, 1877)

BLUE GLASS. Adap. of EPIDEMIC by Schweitzer. MS. (New Fifth Ave. Theatre, March 12, 1877)

THE PRINCESS ROYAL. Adap. of L'OFFICIER DE FORTUNE by

Jules Adenis and Jules Rostaing. Auto. MS. (New Fifth Ave. Theatre, March 31, 1877)

VESTA. Adap. of ROME VAINCUE by Alexandre Parodi. Auto. MS. (New Fifth Ave. Theatre, May 28, 1877)

THE DARK CITY. Auto. MS. (New Fifth Ave. Theatre, Sept. 10, 1877)

* LOVE'S YOUNG DREAM. "From the French." Priv. printed, n. d. (Daly's Theatre, Sept. 18, 1879)

AN ARABIAN NIGHT; OR, HAROUN AL RASCHID AND HIS MOTHER-IN-LAW. Adap. of HARUM AL RASCHID by Gustav von Moser. Priv. printed, n. d. (Daly's Theatre, Nov. 29, 1879)

THE ROYAL MIDDY. With Fred Williams. Adap. of DER SEE-KADETT by Richard Genée. MS. (Daly's Theatre, Jan. 29, 1880)

THE WAY WE LIVE. Adap. of DIE WOHLTHÄTIGEN FRAUEN by A. L'Arronge. MS. (Daly's Theatre, April 10, 1880)

TIOTE. With Fred Williams. Adap. of LA PETIOTE by Maurice Drach. Auto. MS. (Daly's Theatre, Aug. 18, 1880)

NEEDLES AND PINS. Adap. of STARKE MITTELN by Julius Rosen; Priv. printed, 1884. (Daly's Theatre, Nov. 9, 1880; Crystal Palace, London, Aug. 12, 1884)

ZANINA; OR, THE ROVER OF CAMBAYE. Adap. of NISIDA by R. Genée. MS. (Daly's Theatre, Jan. 18, 1881)

ROYAL YOUTH. Adap. of LA JEUNESSE DE LOUIS XIV by Dumas père. MS. Partly auto. (Daly's Theatre, Oct. 22, 1881)

THE PASSING REGIMENT. Adap. of KRIEG IM FRIEDEN by G. von Moser and F. von Schönthan. Priv. printed, 1884. (Daly's Theatre, Nov. 10, 1881)

ODETTE. Adap. from Sardou. Auto. MS. (Daly's Theatre, Feb. 6, 1882)

OUR ENGLISH FRIEND. Adap. of REIF VON REIFLINGEN by G. von Moser. Priv. printed, 1884. (Daly's Theatre, Nov. 25, 1882)

SERGE PANINE. Adap. from Georges Ohnet. Auto. MS. (Daly's Theatre, Feb. 1, 1883)

SEVEN-TWENTY-EIGHT; OR, CASTING THE BOOMERANG. Adap. of DER SCHWABENSTREICH by Franz von Schönthan. Priv. printed, 1886; also pub. New York, n. d. (Daly's Theatre, Feb. 24, 1883)

A HISTORY OF THE AMERICAN DRAMA

Dollars and Sense; or, The Heedless Ones. Adap. of Die Sorglosen by Adolph L'Arronge. Priv. printed, 1885. (Daly's Theatre, Oct. 2, 1883)

Red Letter Nights. Adap. of Ein Gemachter Mann. By Jacobson. MS. (Daly's Theatre, March 12, 1884)

A Wooden Spoon; or, Perdita's Penates. Adap. of Roderick Heller by F. von Schönthan. Auto. MS. (Daly's Theatre, Oct. 7, 1884)

Love on Crutches. Adap. of Ihre Ideale by Heinrich Stopitzer. Priv. printed, 1884. (Daly's Theatre, Nov. 25, 1884)

* A Woman's Wont. Adap. of Gott sei Dank, der Tisch ist Gedeckt from Dieu Merci, le couvert est mis, by Leon Gozlan. (Chestnut St. Opera House, Phila., May 2, 1884)

A Night Off; or, A Page from Balzac. Adap. of Der Raub der Sabinerinnen by Franz and Paul von Schönthan. c. 1897. (Daly's Theatre, March 4, 1885)

Living for Show. From the German. Auto. MS. (Boston Museum, Dec. 7, 1885)

Denise. Adap. from Dumas, fils. Auto. MS. (Daly's Theatre, April 21, 1885)

* A Wet Blanket. Adap. from French of Bilhaud and Levy. Priv. printed, n. d. (Daly's Theatre, Feb. 13, 1886)

* A Sudden Shower. From the French of Beissier. Priv. printed, n. d. (Daly's Theatre, Feb. 18, 1886)

Nancy and Company. Adap. of Halbe Dichter by Julius Rosen. Priv. printed, 1884. (Daly's Theatre, Feb. 24, 1886)

After Business Hours. From German of Oscar Blumenthal. Priv. printed, 1886. (Daly's Theatre, Oct. 5, 1886)

Love in Harness. Adap. of Bonheur Conjugal by Albin Valabrégue. Priv. printed, 1887. (Daly's Theatre, Nov. 16, 1886)

The Railroad of Love. Adap. of Goldfische by F. von Schönthan and G. Kadelburg. Priv. printed, 1887. (Daly's Theatre, Nov. 1, 1887)

The Lottery of Love. Adap. of Les Surprises du divorce by Alexandre Bisson and Antony Mars. Priv. printed, 1889. Daly's Theatre, Oct. 9, 1888)

Undercurrent. Auto. MS. (Niblo's Garden, Nov. 13, 1888)

BIBLIOGRAPHY AND PLAY LIST

AN INTERNATIONAL MATCH. Adap. of CORNELIUS VOSS by Franz von Schönthan. Priv. printed, 1890. (Daly's Theatre, Feb. 5, 1889)

SAMSON AND DELILAH. Adap. of UN CONCEIL JUDICIARE by A. Bisson and J. Moineaux. Auto. MS. (Daly's Theatre, March 28, 1889)

THE GOLDEN WIDOW. Adap. of LA MARQUISE, by Sardou. Auto. MS. (Daly's Theatre, Oct. 2, 1889)

THE GREAT UNKNOWN. Adap. of DIE BERÜHMTE FRAU by F. von Schönthan and G. Kadelburg. Priv. printed, 1890. (Daly's Theatre, Oct. 22, 1889)

THE LAST WORD. Adap. of DAS LETZTE WORT by F. von Schönthan. Priv. printed, 1891. (Daly's Theatre, Oct. 28, 1890)

LOVE IN TANDEM. Adap. of VIE À DEUX by Henri Bocage and Charles de Courcy. Priv. printed. (Daly's Theatre, Feb. 9, 1892)

LITTLE MISS MILLION. Adap. of DAS ZWEITE GESICHT by Oscar Blumenthal. Priv. printed, 1893. (Daly's Theatre, Oct. 6, 1892)

A TEST CASE. Adap. of GROSSTADTLUFT by O. Blumenthal and G. Kadelburg. Priv. printed, 1893. (Daly's Theatre, Nov. 10, 1892)

A BUNDLE OF LIES. Adap. of DER HÖCHSTE TRUMPF by Carl Laufs and Wilhelm Jacoby. MS. (Daly's Theatre, March 28, 1895)

THE TRANSIT OF LEO. Adap. of DAS SCHÖSSKIND by Köhler and Blumenthal. MS. With auto. Alterations. (Daly's Theatre, Dec. 10, 1895)

THE COUNTESS GUCKI. From German of F. von Schönthan. Priv. printed, 1895. (Daly's Theatre, Jan. 28, 1896)

The following plays exist in autograph manuscript or typewritten copies with "by Augustin Daly" on the title page. They are not mentioned in the life of Daly and have probably not been performed:

AFTER THE WEDDING; OR, A GRAIN OF SAND. From the German of Heineman. Auto. MS.

THE BRIDE OF THE WHIRLWIND. Auto. MS.

A DROP OF POISON. From the German of Oscar Blumenthal.

GRANDMAMA. From the French of Edou[a]rd Cadol.

A HISTORY OF THE AMERICAN DRAMA

THE GREEN EYED MONSTER. From the German of Misch and Jacoby.

HONOR. With Jerome K. Jerome. Adap. of DIE EHRE by Hermann Sudermann.

THE KING'S GUARDSMAN. From the French.

A LIMITED LIABILITY; OR, THE LAW OF THE HEART.

LOVE IN A MASK: OUR PRETTY GRANDMOTHERS; OR, SEVENTY YEARS AGO.

AN OLD FASHIONED MARRIAGE. Auto. MS.

ROSE MICHEL.

TEMPERS AND TEMPESTS; OR, EXTREMES TOUCH. From the German of Clement Lithou.

THE TEST ARROW.

TRICKS.

WAR IN PEACE. From the German of Gustav Kadelburg. Auto. MS.

Biographical and Critical

Daly, Augustin, "The American Dramatist," *North American Review*, CXLII (May, 1886), 485–492.

"Mr. Augustin Daly's Views," *Harper's Weekly*, Supplement, Feb. 2, 1889.

Daly, Augustin, *Woffington, a Tribute to the Actress and the Woman*. 1888.

Daly, Joseph Francis, *The Life of Augustin Daly*. 1917. [The authoritative biography]

Dithmar, E. A., *Memories of Daly's Theatres*. Priv. printed, 1896.

"An American School of Dramatic Art": (a) "A Critical Review of Daly's Theatre," by J. R. Towse; (b) "The Inside Workings of the Theatre," by George P. Lathrop, *Century Magazine*, June, 1898.

DAVIS, OWEN

THROUGH THE BREAKERS. (Star Theatre, Oct. 9, 1899)

AT YALE. c. 1906. (Kansas City, Sept., 1907)

CUPID AT VASSAR. c. 1907. (Hartford, Conn., 1911)

AN OLD SWEETHEART OF MINE. c. 1911. (Richmond, Va., 1911)

THE FAMILY CUPBOARD. 1914. (Playhouse, Aug. 21, 1913)

SINNERS. MS. (Playhouse, Jan. 7, 1915)

340

BIBLIOGRAPHY AND PLAY LIST

ROBIN HOOD; OR, THE MERRY OUTLAWS OF SHERWOOD FOREST. c. 1923. (By Frank Lee Short Players, St. Louis, Mo., 1915)

THE DETOUR. Boston, 1922. (Astor Theatre, Aug. 23, 1921)

ICEBOUND. Boston, 1923. (Harris Theatre, Feb. 21, 1923)

HOME FIRES. (Thirty-ninth St. Theatre, Aug. 20, 1923)

THE NERVOUS WRECK. Dram. novel by E. J. Rath. c. 1926. (Harris Theatre, Oct. 9, 1923)

THE HAUNTED HOUSE. 1926. (Cohan Theatre, Sept. 2, 1924)

EASY COME, EASY GO. 1926. (Cohan Theatre, Oct. 26, 1925)

GENTLE GRAFTERS. (Broad St. Theatre, Phila., Oct. 18, 1926)

THE DONOVAN AFFAIR. 1930. (Fulton Theatre, Aug. 30, 1926)

SANDLEWOOD. (Gaiety Theatre, Sept. 22, 1926)

THE TRIUMPHANT BACHELOR. (Biltmore Theatre, Sept. 15, 1927)

CARRY ON. (Masque Theatre, Jan. 23, 1928)

TO-NIGHT AT TWELVE. (Hudson Theatre, Nov. 13, 1928)

THE NINTH GUEST. 1932. (Eltinge Theatre, Aug. 25, 1930)

JUST TO REMIND YOU. 1931. (Broadhurst Theatre, Sept. 7, 1931)

THE GOOD EARTH. With Donald Davis. Adap. of novel by Pearl Buck. (Chestnut St. Opera House, Phila., Sept. 19, 1932; Guild Theatre, Oct. 17, 1932)

A SATURDAY NIGHT. (Playhouse, Feb. 28, 1933)

JEZEBEL. (Ethel Barrymore Theatre, Dec. 19, 1933)

TOO MANY BOATS. Adap. of novel by Charles Clifford. (Playhouse, Sept. 11, 1934)

SPRING FRESHET. (Plymouth Theatre, Oct. 4, 1934)

ETHAN FROME. With Donald Davis. Adap. of novel by Edith Wharton. (Garrick Theatre, Phila., Jan. 6, 1936; National Theatre, Jan. 21, 1936)

Biographical

Davis, Owen, *I'd Like to Do It Again.* 1931.

DAVIS, RICHARD HARDING

* THE OTHER WOMAN. Dram. of story by author. (Hermann's Theatre, March 23, 1893)

* THE DISREPUTABLE MR. REAGAN. Dram. of story by author. (Broad St. Theatre, Phila., March 7, 1895)

A HISTORY OF THE AMERICAN DRAMA

SOLDIERS OF FORTUNE. Dram. of novel by author. Stage version by Augustus Thomas, q.v.

THE TAMING OF HELEN. Dram. of THE LION AND THE UNICORN, by author. (Princess Theatre, Toronto, Ontario, Jan. 5, 1903; Savoy Theatre, March 30, 1903)

RANSON'S FOLLY. Dram. of novel by author. (Providence Opera House, Providence, R. I., Jan. 11, 1904; Hudson Theatre, Jan. 18, 1904)

THE DICTATOR. 1911. (Criterion Theatre, April 4, 1904; Comedy Theatre, London, May 3, 1905)

THE GALLOPER. 1909. (Plainfield, N. J., Dec. 16, 1905; Garden Theatre, Jan. 22, 1906)

* MISS CIVILIZATION. 1920. Dram. of story by James Harvey Smith. (Broadway Theatre, Jan. 26, 1906)

THE YANKEE TOURIST. Musical comedy based on THE GAL-LOPER. (Astor Theatre, Aug. 12, 1907)

VERA, THE MEDIUM. Dram. of novel by author. (Harmanus Bleecker Hall, Albany, Nov. 2, 1908)

THE SEVENTH DAUGHTER. Based on novel, VERA, THE MEDIUM, by author. (Colonial Theatre, Cleveland, Ohio, Nov. 10, 1910)

* BLACKMAIL. (B. F. Keith's Union Square Theatre, March 17, 1913)

WHO'S WHO. (Hyperion Theatre, New Haven, Aug. 28, 1913; Criterion Theatre, Sept. 11, 1913)

* PEACE MANOEUVRES. 1914. (By amateurs)

* THE ZONE POLICE. 1914. (By amateurs)

THE TRAP. Revision of BLACKMAIL. With Jules Eckert Goodman. (Majestic Theatre, Boston, Sept., 1914; Booth Theatre, Feb. 19, 1915)

Biographical and Critical

Quinby, Henry Cole, *Richard Harding Davis, a Bibliography.* c. 1924.

Downey, Fairfax, *Richard Harding Davis, His Day.* 1933.

DAZEY, CHARLES TURNER

IN OLD KENTUCKY. Priv. printed, 1894. (Grand Opera House, St. Paul, Minn., June, 1893; People's Theatre, Sept. 11, 1893)

342

BIBLIOGRAPHY AND PLAY LIST

DE MILLE, HENRY C.

JOHN DELMER'S DAUGHTERS. Priv. printed, c. 1883. (Madison Square Theatre, Dec. 10, 1883)

THE MAIN LINE; OR, RAWSON'S Y. With Charles Barnard. A. L. P. (Lyceum Theatre, Sept. 18, 1886)

THE WIFE. With David Belasco, q.v.

LORD CHUMLEY. With David Belasco, q.v.

THE CHARITY BALL. With David Belasco, q.v.

MEN AND WOMEN. With David Belasco, q.v.

THE LOST PARADISE. Adap. of DAS VERLORENE PARADIES, by Ludwig Fulda. c. 1897. (Proctor's Twenty-third St. Theatre, Nov. 16, 1891)

DE MILLE, WILLIAM C.

STRONGHEART. c. 1909. (Hudson Theatre, Jan. 30, 1905)

THE GENIUS. With Cecil B. De Mille. (Bijou Theatre, Oct. 1, 1906)

CLASSMATES. With Margaret Turnbull. (Hudson Theatre, Aug. 29, 1907)

THE WARRENS OF VIRGINIA. A.L.P. (Lyric Theatre, Phila., Nov. 18, 1907; Belasco Theatre, Dec. 3, 1907)

THE ROYAL MOUNTED. With Cecil B. De Mille. (Garrick Theatre, April 6, 1908)

THE WOMAN. (New National Theatre, Washington, D. C., April 17, 1911; Republic Theatre, Sept. 19, 1911)

* FOOD. c. 1914. (Princess Theatre, April 14, 1913)

* IN 1999. c. 1914.

DE WALDEN, T. B.

SAM. (Broadway Theatre, Oct. 9, 1865)

BRITISH NEUTRALITY. (Olympic Theatre, July 1, 1869)

KIT, THE ARKANSAS TRAVELLER. With Edward Spencer. (Boston Theatre, Feb. 14, 1870)

THE BARONESS. (Fifth Ave. Theatre, Dec. 12, 1872)

DICKINSON, ANNA

AN AMERICAN GIRL. MS. (Haverley's Fifth Ave. Theatre, Sept. 20, 1880)

DODD, LEE WILSON

THE RETURN OF EVE. (Herald Square Theatre, March 17, 1909)

HIS MAJESTY BUNKER BEAN. Dram. of novel by H. L. Wilson. c. 1922. (Astor Theatre, Oct. 2, 1916)

A HISTORY OF THE AMERICAN DRAMA

PALS FIRST. Dram. of PALS FIRST by F. P. Elliott. c. 1925. (Hartford, Conn., Dec. 27, 1916; Fulton Theatre, Feb. 26, 1917)

THE CHANGELINGS. 1924. (Broad St. Theatre, Phila., April 16, 1923; Henry Miller Theatre, Sept. 17, 1923)

A STRONG MAN'S HOUSE. (Ambassador Theatre, Sept. 16, 1929)

DRANSFIELD, JANE

THE LOST PLEIAD. 1918. (Academy of Music, Brooklyn. By amateurs)

DUNNING, PHILIP

BROADWAY. With George Abbott. 1926. (Broadhurst Theatre, Sept. 16, 1926)

REMEMBER THE DAY. With Philo Higley. (National Theatre, Sept. 25, 1935)

EATON, WALTER PRICHARD

QUEEN VICTORIA. With David Carb. c. 1923. (Forty-eighth St. Theatre, Nov. 15, 1923)

EMERY, GILBERT

THE HERO. In Quinn's *Contemporary American Plays*. (Long-acre Theatre, March 14, 1921; Belmont Theatre, Sept., 1921)

QUEED. Dram. of novel by H. S. Harrison. (Main St. Theatre, Long Branch, N. J., July 4, 1921)

TARNISH. c. 1924. (Belmont Theatre, Oct. 1, 1923)

* THANK YOU, DOCTOR. 1924. (In vaudeville)

EPISODE. MS. (Bijou Theatre, Feb. 4, 1925)

LOVE-IN-A-MIST. With Amelie Rives (Princess Troubetzkoy). c. 1926. (Gaiety Theatre, April 12, 1926)

* THE PERSIAN POPPY. Summit, N. J., c. 1926.

THE HANDKERCHIEF. (Atlantic City, N. J., June 6, 1927)

HOUSEWARMING. (Charles Hopkins Theatre, April 7, 1932)

FAR-AWAY HORSES. With Michael Birmingham. (Martin Beck Theatre, March 21, 1933)

EYRE, LAURENCE

THE THINGS THAT COUNT. 1930. (Maxine Elliott Theatre, Dec. 8, 1913)

SAZUS MATAZUS. MS. (Atlantic City, N. J., June, 1915)

MISS NELLY OF N'ORLEANS. 1930. (Ford's Theatre, Baltimore, June 6, 1919; Henry Miller Theatre, Feb. 4, 1919)

BIBLIOGRAPHY AND PLAY LIST

THE MERRY WIVES OF GOTHAM. 1930. (Henry Miller Theatre, as FANSHASTICS, Jan. 16, 1924)

GALA NIGHT. (Erlanger's Theatre, Feb. 25, 1930)

MAYFAIR. (Belmont Theatre, March 17, 1930)

FAWCETT, EDGAR

A FALSE FRIEND. (Union Square Theatre, June 21, 1880)

OUR FIRST FAMILIES. MS. (Daly's Theatre, Sept. 23, 1880)

AMERICANS ABROAD. MS. (Daly's Theatre, Oct. 5, 1881)

THE BUNTLING BALL. 1884.

THE NEW KING ARTHUR. 1885.

THE EARL. (Hollis St. Theatre, Boston, Mass., April 11, 1887)

FITCH, CLYDE

Plays. Memorial Edition. Edited by Montrose J. Moses and Virginia Gerson. Boston, 1915.

Vol. I. BEAU BRUMMELL; LOVER'S LANE; NATHAN HALE.

Vol. II. BARBARA FRIETCHIE; CAPTAIN JINKS OF THE HORSE MARINES; THE CLIMBERS.

Vol. III. THE STUBBORNNESS OF GERALDINE; THE GIRL WITH THE GREEN EYES; HER OWN WAY.

Vol. IV. THE WOMAN IN THE CASE; THE TRUTH; THE CITY.

BEAU BRUMMELL. 1908. (Madison Square Theatre, May 19, 1890.

* FRÉDÉRICK LEMAÎTRE. MS. (Tremont Theatre, Boston, Dec. 1, 1890; Daly's Theatre, April 22, 1891)

* BETTY'S FINISH. (Boston Museum, Dec. 29, 1890)

PAMELA'S PRODIGY. 1893. (Royal Court Theatre, London, Oct. 21, 1891)

A MODERN MATCH. MS. (Union Square Theatre, March 14, 1892; Royalty Theatre, London, as MARRIAGE 1892, Oct. 28, 1892)

THE MASKED BALL. Adap. of LE VEGLIONE, by Alexandre Bisson and Albert Carré. MS. (Palmer's Theatre, Oct. 3, 1892; Criterion Theatre, London, Jan. 6, 1900)

THE SOCIAL SWIM. Adap. of LA MAISON NEUVE, by Victorien Sardou. MS. (Alvin Theatre, Pittsburgh, Jan. 12, 1893; Harlem Opera House, Sept. 22, 1893)

* THE HARVEST. (Fifth Ave. Theatre, Jan. 25, 1893) Revised as THE MOTH AND THE FLAME, q.v.

345

A HISTORY OF THE AMERICAN DRAMA

APRIL WEATHER. (Chicago Opera House, May 29, 1893; Daly's Theatre, Nov. 13, 1893)

A SHATTERED IDOL. Adap. of PÈRE GORIOT by Balzac. (Globe Theatre, St. Paul, July 30, 1893)

AN AMERICAN DUCHESS. Adap. of LE PRINCE D'AUREC, by Henri Lavedan. (Lyceum Theatre, Nov. 20, 1893)

MRS. GRUNDY, JR. Adap. from the French. (1893)

HIS GRACE DE GRAMMONT. MS. (Rockford, Ill., Sept. 22, 1894; Grand Opera House, Chicago, Sept. 24, 1894)

GOSSIP. With Leo Ditrichstein. Adap. from the French of Jules Claretie. (Palmer's Theatre, March 11, 1895; Grand Theatre, London, June 3, 1895)

MISTRESS BETTY. (Garrick Theatre, Oct. 15, 1895) Revived as THE TOAST OF THE TOWN, q.v.

BOHEMIA. Adap. of LA VIE DE BOHÈME by Théodore Barrière and Henri Murger. MS. (Empire Theatre, March 9, 1896)

THE LIAR. Adap. from the French of Alexandre Bisson. (Walnut St. Theatre, Phila., April 3, 1896; Hoyt's Theatre, Sept. 2, 1896)

THE SUPERFLUOUS HUSBAND. With Leo Ditrichstein. Adap. from the German of Ludwig Fulda. MS. (Fifth Ave. Theatre, Jan. 4, 1897)

NATHAN HALE. 1899. (Hooley's Theatre, Chicago, Jan. 31, 1898; Knickerbocker Theatre, Jan. 2, 1899)

THE MOTH AND THE FLAME. In Moses' *Representative Plays by American Dramatists*, III. (Chestnut St. Theatre, Phila., Feb. 14, 1898; Lyceum Theatre, April 11, 1898)

THE HEAD OF THE FAMILY. With Leo Ditrichstein. Adap. of HASEMANNS TÖCHTER, by Adolph L'Arronge. (Knickerbocker Theatre, Dec. 6, 1898)

THE COWBOY AND THE LADY. c. 1908. (Broad St. Theatre, Phila., March 13, 1899; Duke of York's Theatre, London, June 5, 1899)

BARBARA FRIETCHIE. 1900. (Broad St. Theatre, Phila., Oct. 10, 1899; Criterion Theatre, Oct. 23, 1899)

SAPHO. Dram. of SAPHO, by Alphonse Daudet with scenes from the play by Alphonse Daudet and Adolphe Belot. MS. (Powers Theatre, Chicago, Oct. 31, 1899; Wallack's Theatre, Feb. 16, 1900)

BIBLIOGRAPHY AND PLAY LIST

CAPTAIN JINKS OF THE HORSE MARINES. 1902. (Walnut St. Theatre, Phila., Jan. 7, 1901; Garrick Theatre, Feb. 4, 1901)

THE CLIMBERS. 1906. (Bijou Theatre, Jan. 15, 1901; Comedy Theatre, London, Sept. 5, 1903)

LOVERS' LANE. Boston, 1915. (Manhattan Theatre, Feb. 6, 1901)

THE LAST OF THE DANDIES. (Her Majesty's Theatre, London, Oct. 24, 1901)

THE MARRIAGE GAME. Adap. of LE MARRIAGE D'OLYMPE, by Emile Augier. (Broad St. Theatre, Phila., Sept. 23, 1901)

THE WAY OF THE WORLD. MS. (Hammerstein's Victoria Theatre, Nov. 4, 1901)

THE GIRL AND THE JUDGE. MS. (Lyceum Theatre, Dec. 4, 1901)

THE STUBBORNNESS OF GERALDINE. 1906. (Garrick Theatre, Nov. 3, 1902)

THE GIRL WITH THE GREEN EYES. 1905. (Savoy Theatre, Dec. 25, 1902)

THE BIRD IN THE CAGE. Adap. of DIE HAUBENLERCHE, by Ernst von Wildenbruch. MS. (Bijou Theatre, Jan. 12, 1903)

THE FRISKY MRS. JOHNSON. Adap. of MADAME FLIRT, by Paul Gavault and Georges Beer. (Princess Theatre, Feb. 9, 1903)

HER OWN WAY. 1907. (Star Theatre, Buffalo, Sept. 24, 1903; Garrick Theatre, Sept. 28, 1903; Lyric Theatre, London, April 25, 1905)

MAJOR ANDRÉ. MS. (Savoy Theatre, Nov. 11, 1903)

GLAD OF IT. MS. (Savoy Theatre, Dec. 28, 1903)

THE CORONET OF A DUCHESS. MS. (Garrick Theatre, Sept. 21, 1904)

GRANNY. Adap. of L'AIEULE by Georges Michel. MS. (Lyceum Theatre, Oct. 24, 1904)

COUSIN BILLY. Adap. of LE VOYAGE DE M. PERRICHON, by Eugène Labiche and Edouard Martin. MS. (Criterion Theatre, Jan. 2, 1905)

THE WOMAN IN THE CASE. Boston, 1915. (Herald Square Theatre, Jan. 30, 1905; Garrick Theatre, London, June 2, 1909)

A HISTORY OF THE AMERICAN DRAMA

HER GREAT MATCH. In Quinn's *Representative American Plays*. Editions up to 1930. (Syracuse, Sept. 1, 1905; Criterion Theatre, Sept. 4, 1905)

THE TOAST OF THE TOWN. MS. (Broad St. Theatre, Phila., Oct. 9, 1905; Daly's Theatre, Nov. 27, 1905)

WOLFVILLE. With Willis Steell. Dram. of WOLFVILLE, by A. H. Lewis. MS. (Broad St. Theatre, Phila., Oct. 23, 1905)

THE GIRL WHO HAS EVERYTHING. (Hollis St. Theatre, Boston, March 12, 1906; Liberty Theatre, Dec. 4, 1906)

TODDLES. Adap. of TRIPLEPATTE, by André Godferneaux and Tristan Bernard. MS. (Duke of York's Theatre, London, Sept. 3, 1906; Baltimore, Feb. 24, 1908; Garrick Theatre, March 16, 1908)

THE HOUSE OF MIRTH. Dram. with Edith Wharton of her novel. MS. (Detroit Opera House, Sept. 11, 1906; Savoy Theatre, Oct. 22, 1906)

THE TRUTH. 1907. (Cleveland, Ohio, Oct. 15, 1906; Criterion Theatre, Jan. 7, 1907; Comedy Theatre, London, April 6, 1907; Neues Theater, Berlin, Sept. 24, 1908; Little Theatre, April 14, 1914)

THE STRAIGHT ROAD. MS. (St. Louis, Dec. 23, 1906; Astor Theatre, Jan. 7, 1907)

HER SISTER. With Cosmo Gordon Lennox. MS. (Hudson Theatre, Dec. 24, 1907)

THE HONOR OF THE FAMILY. Adap. of Emile Fabre's dramatization of Balzac's LA RABOUILLEUSE. (Hudson Theatre, Feb. 17, 1908)

GIRLS. Adap. of DIE WELT OHNE MÄNNER, by Alexander Engel and Julius Horst. (Belasco Theatre, Washington, D. C., March 9, 1908; Daly's Theatre, March 23, 1908)

THE BLUE MOUSE. Adap. from the German of Alexander Engel and Julius Horst. (Hyperion Theatre, New Haven, Nov. 25, 1908; Lyric Theatre, Nov. 30, 1908)

A HAPPY MARRIAGE. MS. (Schenectady, Jan. 28, 1909; Garrick Theatre, April 12, 1909)

THE BACHELOR. MS. (Hyperion Theatre, New Haven, March 4, 1909; Maxine Elliott Theatre, March 15, 1909)

THE CITY. Boston, 1915. (Hyperion Theatre, New Haven, Nov. 15, 1909; Lyric Theatre, Dec. 21, 1909)

BIBLIOGRAPHY AND PLAY LIST

Biographical and Critical

Fitch, Clyde, "The Play and the Public." *Smart Set,* XIV (Nov., 1904), 97–100. Rep. in *Plays,* IV, v–xlvii, in revised form.

Bell, Archie, *The Clyde Fitch I Knew.* 1909.

Bernbaum, Martin, "Clyde Fitch, an Appreciation." *Independent,* LXVII (July 15, 1909), 123–131.

Eaton, Walter Prichard, "The Dramatist as Man of Letters. The Case of Clyde Fitch." *Scribner's Magazine,* XLVI (April 1910), 490–497. Rep. in *At the New Theatre and Others,* pp. 258–282.

Lowe, John A., "A Reading List of Clyde Fitch." *Bulletin of Bibliography,* VII (July, 1912), 304.

Moses, Montrose J., and Gerson, Virginia, *Clyde Fitch and His Letters.* Boston, 1924. [The most useful biography]

Phelps, William Lyon, *Essays on Modern Dramatists,* 1921, pp. 142–178.

"The American Stage Loses Clyde Fitch," *Theatre,* X (Oct., 1909), 112.

Steell, Willis, "Clyde Fitch as Collaborator," *Theatre,* X (Dec., 1909), 176–178.

Strang, L. C., *Players and Plays of the Last Quarter Century,* 1902, II, 167–183.

FLAVIN, MARTIN A. ˙

* The Blind Man. 1926. (Garrick Theatre, 1921)

* Casualties. 1926. (Garrick Theatre, 1921)

Children of the Moon. 1924. (Comedy Theatre, Aug. 17, 1923)

* Caleb Stone's Death Watch. 1926. (Carnegie Tech., 1923)

* Brains. In *Brains and Other One-Act Plays,* 1926. (Carnegie Tech., 1924)

Lady of the Rose. 1925. (Forty-ninth St. Theatre, May 19, 1925)

Service for Two. 1927. (Gaiety Theatre, Aug. 30, 1926)

The Criminal Code. 1930. (National Theatre, Oct. 2, 1929)

Broken Dishes. 1930. (Ritz Theatre, Nov. 5, 1929)

CROSSROADS. 1930. (Morosco Theatre, Nov. 11, 1929)
SPINDRIFT. 1930. (Pasadena Community Theatre, 1930)
DANCING DAYS. (Pasadena Community Theatre, 1931)
THE ROAD TO THE CITY. (Detroit Playhouse, 1931)
AMACO. 1933. (Univ. of Minn., 1933)
SUNDAY. (Produced Carmel Community Theatre, 1934)
ACHILLES HAD A HEEL. 1936. (Pasadena Community Theatre,
   April 23, 1935; 44th St. Theatre, Oct. 13, 1935)
TAPESTRY IN GRAY. 1936. (Shubert Theatre, Dec. 28, 1935.)

FORBES, JAMES
THE CHORUS LADY. c. 1920. (Savoy Theatre, Sept. 1, 1906)
THE TRAVELLING SALESMAN. c. 1916. (Washington, March 16,
   1908; Liberty Theatre, Aug. 10, 1908)
THE COMMUTERS. c. 1916. (Criterion Theatre, Aug. 15, 1910)
A RICH MAN'S SON. (Harris Theatre, Nov. 4, 1912)
THE SHOW SHOP. c. 1920. (Hudson Theatre, Dec. 31, 1914)
THE FAMOUS MRS. FAIR. c. 1920. (Academy, Baltimore, Dec.
   15, 1919; Henry Miller Theatre, Dec. 22, 1919)
THE ENDLESS CHAIN. (Cohan Theatre, Sept. 4, 1922)
YOUNG BLOOD. (Ritz Theatre, Nov. 24, 1925)
PRECIOUS. (Royale Theatre, Jan. 14, 1929)

FORD, HARRIET
A GENTLEMAN OF FRANCE. (Grand Opera House, Chicago, Nov.
   5, 1901)
A LITTLE BROTHER TO THE RICH. With J. M. Patterson, q.v.
THE ARGYLE CASE. With Harvey O'Higgins. c. 1927. (At-
   lantic City, N. J., Oct. 17, 1912)
POLYGAMY. With Harvey O'Higgins. MS. (Columbia Thea-
   tre, Washington, D. C., Nov. 1, 1914; Playhouse, Dec. 1,
   1914)
MR. LAZARUS. With Harvey O'Higgins, q.v.
IN THE NEXT ROOM. With Eleanor Robson, q.v.

FRANKEN, ROSE
ANOTHER LANGUAGE. 1932. (Booth Theatre, April 25, 1932)
MR. DOOLEY, JR. With Jane Lewin. 1932.

FYLES, FRANKLIN
THE GIRL I LEFT BEHIND ME. With David Belasco, q.v.
THE GOVERNOR OF KENTUCKY. (Fifth Ave. Theatre, Jan. 21,
   1896)

BIBLIOGRAPHY AND PLAY LIST

A WARD OF FRANCE. With E. W. Presbrey. (Wallack's Theatre, Dec. 13, 1897)

KIT CARSON. (American Theatre, May 27, 1901)

GALE, ZONA

MISS LULU BETT. Dram. of novel of same name. 1921. (Belmont Theatre, Dec. 27, 1920)

MR. PITT. Dram. of novel, BIRTH. 1925. (Thirty-ninth St. Theatre, Jan. 22, 1924)

GRANDMA. 1932.

PAPA LA FLEUR. 1933. Dram. of novel by author.

FAINT PERFUME. 1933. Dram. of novel by author.

GATES, ELEANOR

THE POOR LITTLE RICH GIRL. 1916. (Walnut St. Theatre, Phila., Jan. 7, 1913; Hudson Theatre, July 23, 1913)

WE ARE SEVEN. 1915. (Walnut St. Theatre, Phila., Dec. 8, 1913; Maxine Elliott Theatre, Dec. 24, 1913)

GEDDES, VIRGIL

THE FROG. Paris, 1926. (Boston Stage Society, Jan., 1927)

THE EARTH BETWEEN. 1930. (Provincetown Theatre, March 5, 1929)

BEHIND THE NIGHT. In *The Earth Between,* 1930.

NATIVE GROUND. 1932. (Experimental Theatre, Boston, April 1929)

THE PLOUGHSHARE'S GLEAM. In *Native Ground, A Cycle of Plays,* 1932.

AS THE CROW FLIES. In *Native Ground.*

POCAHONTAS AND THE ELDERS. Chapel Hill, 1933. (Chapel Hill, N. C., 1933)

FOUR COMEDIES FROM THE LIFE OF GEORGE EMERY BLUM. Brookfield, Conn., 1934.

GILLETTE, WILLIAM

THE PROFESSOR. (Madison Square Theatre, June 1, 1881)

ESMERALDA. With Frances Hodgson Burnett. Dram. of story of same name by Mrs. Burnett. 1881. (Madison Square Theatre, Oct. 29, 1881; St. James's Theatre, London, as YOUNG FOLK'S WAYS, Oct. 20, 1883)

THE PRIVATE SECRETARY. Adap. of DER BIBLIOTHEKAR, by G. von Moser. MS. (Comedy Theatre, Sept. 29, 1884, as DIGBY'S SECRETARY)

A HISTORY OF THE AMERICAN DRAMA

HELD BY THE ENEMY. c. 1898. (Criterion Theatre, Brooklyn, Feb. 22, 1886; Madison Square Theatre, Aug. 16, 1886; Princess's Theatre, London, April 2, 1887)

SHE. Dram. of novel by Rider Haggard. (Niblo's Garden, Nov. 29, 1887)

A LEGAL WRECK. Pub. in novel form by author, 1888. (Madison Square Theatre, Aug. 14, 1888)

ROBERT ELSMERE. Dram. of novel by Mrs. Humphry Ward. (Union Square Theatre, April 29, 1889)

ALL THE COMFORTS OF HOME. c. 1897. Adap. of EIN TOLLER EINFALL, by Carl Laufs. (Boston Museum, Boston, March 3, 1890; Proctor's Twenty-third St. Theatre, Sept. 8, 1890; Globe Theatre, London, Jan. 24, 1891)

MR. WILKINSON'S WIDOWS. Adap. of FEU TOUPINEL, by Alexandre Bisson. (Washington, D. C., March 23, 1891; Proctor's Twenty-third St. Theatre, March 30, 1891)

SETTLED OUT OF COURT. Adap. of LA FAMILLE PONT-BIQUET by Alexandre Bisson. (Fifth Ave. Theatre, Aug. 8, 1892)

NINETY DAYS. (Broadway Theatre, Feb. 6, 1893)

TOO MUCH JOHNSON. c. 1912. (Opera House, Holyoke, Mass., Oct. 25, 1894; Standard Theatre, Nov. 26, 1894; Garrick Theatre, London, April 18, 1898)

SECRET SERVICE. c. 1898. Revised form in Quinn's *Representative American Plays*. (Broad St. Theatre, Phila., May 13, 1895; Garrick Theatre, Oct. 5, 1896; Adelphi Theatre, London, May 15, 1897; Renaissance Théâtre, Paris, Oct. 2, 1897)

BECAUSE SHE LOVED HIM SO. Adap. of JALOUSE by Alexandre Bisson and Adolphe Leclerq. MS. (Hyperion Theatre, New Haven, Oct. 28, 1898; Madison Square Theatre, Jan. 16, 1899)

SHERLOCK HOLMES. London, 1922. Rev. 1935. (Star Theatre, Buffalo, Oct. 24, 1899; Garrick Theatre, Nov. 6, 1899; Lyceum Theatre, London, Sept. 2, 1901)

* THE PAINFUL PREDICAMENT OF SHERLOCK HOLMES. (Metropolitan Opera House, March 23, 1905)

CLARICE. MS. (Duke of York's Theatre, London, Sept. 13, 1905; Garrick Theatre, Oct. 16, 1906)

* THE RED OWL. In *One Act Plays for Stage and Study*, 1924. (1907)

BIBLIOGRAPHY AND PLAY LIST

* TICEY; OR, THAT LITTLE AFFAIR OF BOYD'S. (Columbia Theatre, Washington, D. C., June 15, 1908; Liberty Theatre, Dec. 18, 1908)

SAMSON. Adap. of SAMSON, by Henri Bernstein. MS. (Lyceum Theatre, Rochester, Oct. 9, 1908; Criterion Theatre, Oct. 19, 1908)

* THE ROBBER. (Coliseum, London, Aug. 9, 1909)

* AMONG THIEVES. In *One Act Plays for Stage and Study,* Second Series, 1925. (Palace Theatre, London, Sept. 6, 1909)

ELECTRICITY. In *The Drama,* No. 12 (Nov., 1913), 13–123. Repub. c. 1914. (Park Theatre, Boston, Sept. 26, 1910; Lyceum Theatre, Oct. 31, 1910)

THE DREAM MAKER. Dram. of short story by H. E. Merton. (Empire Theatre, Nov. 21, 1921)

WINNIE AND THE WOLVES. Dram. of short stories by Bertram Akey. (Lyric Theatre, Phila., May 21, 1923)

Biographical and Critical

"Mr. William Gillette Surveys the Field." *Harper's Weekly,* Supplement, Feb. 2, 1889.

Gillette, William, "On the Illusion of the First Time in Acting," *Publications of the Dramatic Museum of Columbia University,* Ser. 2, Vol. I, 1915.

Burton, Richard, "William Gillette." *The Drama,* No. 12 (Nov., 1913), 5–11.

Clapp, J. B., and Edgett, E. F., *Plays of the Present.* 1902.

Hapgood, Norman, *The Stage in America,* 1901, pp. 61–79.

S[cott] C[lement], *The Theatre* (London), XVIII (April 2, 1887), 281–283.

GLASPELL, SUSAN

* SUPPRESSED DESIRES. With George Cram Cook. In *Plays,* Boston, 1920. (Wharf Theatre, Provincetown, Summer, 1915)

* TRIFLES. In *Plays,* Boston, 1920. Dram. of her story, "A Jury of Her Peers." (Wharf Theatre, Provincetown, Summer, 1916)

* THE PEOPLE. In *Plays,* Boston, 1920. (Playwrights' Theatre, 1917)

* CLOSE THE BOOK. In *Plays,* Boston, 1920. (Playwrights' Theatre, 1917)

* THE OUTSIDE. In *Plays,* Boston, 1920. (Playwrights' Theatre, 1917–18)

* WOMAN'S HONOR. In *Plays,* Boston, 1920. (Playwrights' Theatre, 1918)

* TICKLESS TIME. With George Cram Cook. In *Plays,* Boston, 1920. (Playwrights' Theatre, 1918)

BERNICE. In *Plays,* Boston, 1920. (Playwrights' Theatre, March 21, 1919)

THE INHERITORS. Boston, 1921. (Playwrights' Theatre, March 21, 1921)

THE VERGE. Boston, 1922. (Playwrights' Theatre, Nov. 14, 1921)

ALISON'S HOUSE. 1930. (Civic Repertory Theatre, Dec. 1, 1930)

THE COMIC ARTIST. With Norman Matson. (Country Playhouse, Westport, Conn., July 13, 1931; Morosco Theatre, April 19, 1933)

Biographical

Glaspell, Susan. *The Road to the Temple, the Life of George Cram Cook.* 1927.

GOODMAN, ARTHUR

IF BOOTH HAD MISSED. 1932. (Maxine Elliott's Theatre, Feb. 4, 1932)

GOODRICH, ARTHUR

YES OR NO. (Murat Theatre, Indianapolis, Oct. 11, 1917; Forty-eighth St. Theatre, Dec. 21, 1917)

SO THIS IS LONDON! c. 1926. (Hudson Theatre, Aug. 30, 1922)

CAPONSACCHI. With Rose A. Palmer. Dram. of THE RING AND THE BOOK, by Robert Browning. 1927. (Murat Theatre, Indianapolis, April 3, 1923; Hampden's Theatre, Oct. 26, 1926)

RICHELIEU. 1930. Adap. of RICHELIEU by Bulwer Lytton. (Hampden's Theatre, Dec. 26, 1929)

BIBLIOGRAPHY AND PLAY LIST

THE PLUTOCRAT. Based on novel by Booth Tarkington. (Vanderbilt Theatre, Feb. 20, 1930)

THE PERFECT MARRIAGE. (Bijou Theatre, Nov. 16, 1932)

MR. GRANT. c. 1934.

GREEN, PAUL

IN AUNT MAHALY'S CABIN. 1925.

THE LORD'S WILL AND OTHER CAROLINA PLAYS. 1925. (By The Carolina Playmakers)

LONESOME ROAD. 1926. Six plays.

IN ABRAHAM'S BOSOM. 1927. (Provincetown Theatre, Dec. 30, 1926)

THE FIELD GOD. 1927. (Werba's Theatre, Brooklyn, April 11, 1927; Greenwich Village Theatre, April 21, 1927)

IN THE VALLEY AND OTHER CAROLINA PLAYS. 1928.

TREAD THE GREEN GRASS. 1931. In *The House of Connelly and Other Plays.*

THE HOUSE OF CONNELLY. 1931. (Martin Beck Theatre, Sept. 28, 1931)

POTTER'S FIELD. 1931. In *The House of Connelly and Other Plays.* (Plymouth Theatre, Boston, April 16, 1934)

ROLL SWEET CHARIOT. 1935. (Cort Theatre, Oct. 2, 1934) (Revision of POTTER'S FIELD)

SHROUD MY BODY DOWN. Iowa City, 1935. (Chapel Hill, N. C., Dec. 7, 1934)

THE ENCHANTED MAZE. (Chapel Hill, N. C., Dec. 6, 1935)

* HYMN TO THE RISING SUN. 1936. (Civic Repertory Theatre, Jan. 12, 1936)

* UNTO SUCH GLORY. (Civic Repertory Theatre, Jan. 12, 1936)

Biographical and Critical

Clark, Barrett H., *Paul Green.* 1928.

GRIBBLE, HARRY WAGSTAFF

MARCH HARES. Cincinnatti, 1923. (Bijou Theatre, August 11, 1921)

MISTER ROMEO. With Wallace A. Manheimer. (Wallack's Theatre, Sept. 5, 1927)

REVOLT. (Vanderbilt Theatre, Oct. 31, 1928)

THE ROYAL VIRGIN. (Booth Theatre, March 17, 1930)

A HISTORY OF THE AMERICAN DRAMA

OLD MAN MURPHY. With Patrick Kearny. (Hudson Theatre, Sept. 14, 1931)

TRICK FOR TRICK. With Vivian Crosby and Shirley Warde. (Sam H. Harris Theatre, Feb. 18, 1932)

THE PERFUMED LADY. (Ambassador Theatre, March 12, 1934)

HAGAN, JAMES

GUNS. (Wallack's Theatre, Aug. 6, 1928)

ONE SUNDAY AFTERNOON. 1933. (Little Theatre, Feb. 15, 1933)

MIDWEST. (Shubert Theatre, Boston, Dec. 31, 1935; Booth Theatre, 1936)

HAMILTON, CLAYTON

THE BIG IDEA. With A. E. Thomas, q.v.

THE BETTER UNDERSTANDING. With A. E. Thomas, q.v.

THIRTY DAYS. With A. E. Thomas, q.v.

FRIEND INDEED. With B. Voight. c. 1926. (Central Park Theatre, April 26, 1926)

HARRIGAN, EDWARD

The autograph MSS. are in possession of the heirs of Edward Harrigan. In addition to plays given, record has been found of seventy-one titles of one-act variety sketches, 1870–79.

* THE PORTER'S TROUBLES. 1875. (Theatre Comique, April 12, 1875)

THE BLUE AND THE GRAY. 1875. (Theatre Comique, Aug. 7, 1876)

DARBY AND LANTY. See DOYLE BROTHERS. (Theatre Comique, Aug. 21, 1876)

* THE EDITOR'S TROUBLES. 1875. (Theatre Comique, Sept. 4, 1876)

IASCAIRE. Auto. MS. (Theatre Comique, Nov. 20, 1876)

OLD LAVENDER. Auto. MS. (Theatre Comique, Sept. 3, 1877)

THE LORGAIRE. Auto. MS. (Theatre Comique, Feb. 18, 1878; in revised form, Dec. 10, 1888)

THE DOYLE BROTHERS. Auto. MS. (Arch St. Theatre, Phila., June 12, 1876; Theatre Comique, Aug. 19, 1878)

THE MULLIGAN GUARD PICNIC. Auto. MS. (Theatre Comique, Sept. 23, 1878; in revised form, Aug. 9, 1880)

THE MULLIGAN GUARD BALL. Auto. MS. (Theatre Comique, Jan. 13, 1879)

356

BIBLIOGRAPHY AND PLAY LIST

THE MULLIGAN GUARD CHOWDER. Auto. MS. (Theatre Comique, Aug. 11, 1879)

THE MULLIGAN GUARDS' CHRISTMAS. Auto. MS. (Theatre Comique, Nov. 17, 1879)

THE MULLIGAN GUARD SURPRISE. Auto. MS. (Theatre Comique, Feb. 16, 1880)

THE MULLIGAN SURPRISE PARTY. Auto. MS. Variant of above.

THE MULLIGAN GUARD NOMINEE. Auto. MS. (Theatre Comique, Nov. 22, 1880)

THE MULLIGANS' SILVER WEDDING. Auto. MS. (Theatre Comique, Feb. 21, 1881)

THE MAJOR. Auto. MS. (New Theatre Comique, Aug. 29, 1881)

SQUATTER SOVEREIGNTY. Auto. MS. (New Theatre Comique, Jan. 9, 1882)

MORDECAI LYONS. (New Theatre Comique, Oct. 26, 1882)

MCSORLEY'S INFLATION. Auto. MS. (New Theatre Comique, Nov. 27, 1882)

THE MUDDY DAY. Auto. MS. (New Theatre Comique, April 2, 1883)

CORDELIA'S ASPIRATIONS. Auto. MS. (partially). (New Theatre Comique, Nov. 5, 1883)

DAN'S TRIBULATIONS. Auto. MS. (New Theatre Comique, April 7, 1884)

INVESTIGATION. MS. (New Theatre Comique, Sept. 1, 1884)

MCALLISTER'S LEGACY. (New Park Theatre, Jan. 5, 1885)

ARE YOU INSURED? MS. (Fourteenth St. Theatre, May 11, 1885)

THE GRIP. Auto. MS. (Harrigan's Park Theatre, Nov. 30, 1885)

THE LEATHER PATCH. MS. (Harrigan's Park Theatre, Feb. 15, 1886)

THE O'REAGANS. Auto. MS. (Harrigan's Park Theatre, Oct. 11, 1886)

MCNOONEY'S VISIT. Auto. MS. (Harrigan's Park Theatre, Jan. 31, 1887; later as 4–11–44, March 21, 1889)

PETE. Auto. MS. (Harrigan's Park Theatre, Nov. 22, 1887)

WADDY GOOGAN. MS. (Harrigan's Park Theatre, Sept. 3, 1888)

A HISTORY OF THE AMERICAN DRAMA

REILLY AND THE FOUR HUNDRED. Auto. MS. (Harrigan's Theatre, Dec. 29, 1890)

THE LAST OF THE HOGANS. MS. (Harrigan's Theatre, Dec. 21, 1891)

THE WOOLEN STOCKING. Auto. MS. (Harrigan's Theatre, Oct. 9, 1893)

NOTORIETY. Auto. MS. (Harrigan's Theatre, Dec. 10, 1894)

MARTY MALONE. Auto. MS. (Bijou Theatre, Aug. 13, 1896)

SARGENT HICKEY. Auto. MS. Variety sketch, revision of LAST OF THE HOGANS. (Proctor's Theatre, 23rd St., Sept. 20, 1897)

UNDER COVER. Auto. MS. (Murray Hill Theatre, Sept. 14, 1903)

THE SIMPLE LIFE. Variety Sketch. (Yorkville Theatre, Jan. 16, 1905)

IN THE NORTH WOODS. MS. [Not produced]

Biographical and Critical

"Mr. Edward Harrigan Speaks." *Harper's Weekly,* Supplement, Feb. 2, 1889.

Harrigan, Edward, *The Mulligans.* [A novel] 1901.

M[ontgomery], G. E., "Edward Harrigan." *The Theatre,* I (1886), 397–398.

Quinn, A. H., "The Perennial Humor of the American Stage." *Yale Review,* XVI (April, 1927), 553–566.

HARTE, BRET

TWO MEN FROM SANDY BAR. Boston, 1876. (Union Square Theatre, Aug. 28, 1876)

AH SIN. With Mark Twain. MS. (National Theatre, Washington, D. C., May 7, 1877; Daly's Fifth Ave. Theatre, July 31, 1877)

SUE. With T. Edgar Pemberton. London, 1902. (Hoyt's Theatre, Sept. 15, 1896; Garrick Theatre, London, June 10, 1898)

Biographical and Critical

The Letters of Bret Harte. Assembled and edited by Geoffrey Bret Harte. Boston, 1926.

Merwin, Henry C., *The Life of Bret Harte.* Boston, 1911.

BIBLIOGRAPHY AND PLAY LIST

Pemberton, T. Edgar, *The Life of Bret Harte.* London, 1903. See pp. 257–295, "In and About Stageland."

Stewart, George H. Jr., *Bret Harte, Argonaut and Exile.* 1931.

HAZELTON, GEORGE COCHRANE, JR.

Mistress Nell. Phila., 1900. (Denver, June, 1900; Bijou Theatre, Oct. 9, 1900)

Captain Molly. (Manhattan Theatre, Sept. 8, 1902)

The Yellow Jacket. With J. H. Benrimo. Indianapolis, c. 1913. (Fulton Theatre, Nov. 4, 1912)

HELLMAN, LILLIAN

The Children's Hour. 1934. (Maxine Elliott Theatre, Nov. 20, 1934)

HERNE, JAMES A.

Shore Acres and Other Plays. Revised by Mrs. James A. Herne. Biographical note by Julie A. Herne. 1928. Shore Acres, Sag Harbor, Hearts of Oak. (MS. are in possession of Mrs. James A. Herne.)

Charles O'Malley. Dram. of Lever's novel. (Maguire's New Theatre, San Francisco, Nov. 11, 1874)

Oliver Twist. Dram. of Dickens' novel. (Maguire's New Theatre, San Francisco, Nov. 26, 1874)

Within an Inch of His Life. With David Belasco. Dram. of story by Gaboriau. A.L.P. (Grand Opera House, San Francisco, Feb. 17, 1879)

Marriage by Moonlight. Later called Hap-hazard. With David Belasco. Acts I, III, IV, V. MS. (Baldwin Theatre, San Francisco, June 30, 1879)

Hearts of Oak. With David Belasco. 1928. (First as Chums, Baldwin Theatre, San Francisco, Sept. 9, 1879; as Hearts of Oak, Hamlin's Theatre, Chicago, Nov. 17, 1879; New Fifth Ave. Theatre, March 29, 1880)

The Minute Men of 1774–75. A.L.P. (Chestnut St. Theatre. Phila., April 6, 1886)

Drifting Apart. A.L.P. under title of Mary, the Fishermen's Child. (People's Theatre, May 7, 1888)

Margaret Fleming. In Quinn's *Representative American Plays.* 1930 ed. (Lynn Theatre, Lynn, Mass., July 4, 1890; Chickering Hall, Boston, May 4, 1891; Palmer's Theatre, Dec. 9, 1891)

A HISTORY OF THE AMERICAN DRAMA

My Colleen. (People's Theatre, May 9, 1892)

Shore Acres. 1928. (First as Shore Acres Subdivision, Mc-Vicker's Theatre, Chicago, May 17–30, 1892; as Uncle Nat, May 30–June 11, 1892; as Shore Acres, Boston Museum, Feb. 20, 1893; Fifth Ave. Theatre, Oct. 30, 1893)

The Reverend Griffith Davenport. A.L.P. (Lafayette Square Theatre, Washington, D. C., Jan. 16, 1899; Herald Square Theatre, Jan. 31, 1899)

Sag Harbor. 1928. (Park Theatre, Boston, Oct. 24, 1899; Republic Theatre, Sept. 27, 1900)

Biographical and Critical

Herne, James A., "Old Stock Days in the Theatre." *Arena,* VI (Sept., 1892), 401–416.

Herne, James A., "Art for Truth's Sake in the Drama." *Arena,* XVII (Feb., 1897), 361–370.

Corbin, John, "Drama." *Harper's Weekly,* XLIII, (Feb. 11 and March 4, 1899), 139, 213. [Griffith Davenport]

Flower, B. O., "Mask or Mirror." *Arena,* VIII (Aug., 1893), 304–313.

Garland, Hamlin, "Mr. and Mrs. Herne." *Arena,* IV (Oct., 1891), 543–560.

Garland, Hamlin, "On the Road with James A. Herne." *Century Magazine,* N. S. LXXXVIII (Aug., 1914), 574–581.

"An Appreciation: James A. Herne, Actor, Dramatist and Man." Articles by Hamlin Garland, J. J. Enneking and B. O. Flower. *Arena,* XXVI (Sept., 1901), 282–291.

Hapgood, Norman. *The Stage in America,* pp. 61–69.

Howells, W. D., Editor's Study, *Harper's Magazine,* LXXXIII (Aug. 1891), 478–479 [Margaret Fleming].

Tiempo, Marco, "James A. Herne in Griffith Davenport." *Arena,* XXII (Sept., 1899), 375–382.

HEYWARD, DOROTHY

Nancy Ann. 1927. (49th St. Theatre, March 31, 1924)

Little Girl Blue. 1931.

HEYWARD, DU BOSE

Porgy. With Dorothy Heyward. 1927. (Guild Theatre, Oct. 10, 1927)

BIBLIOGRAPHY AND PLAY LIST

BRASS ANKLE. 1931. (Masque Theatre, April 23, 1931)

PORGY AND BESS. With music by George Gershwin. (Alvin Theatre, Oct. 10, 1935)

HOOKER, WILLIAM BRIAN

* THE TWO BURGLARS. 1908.

MONA. 1911. (Metropolitan Opera House, March 14, 1912)

FAIRYLAND. New Haven, 1915.

MORVEN AND THE GRAIL. 1915.

CYRANO DE BERGERAC. Adap. of play by Edmond Rostand. 1924. (National Theatre, Nov. 1, 1923)

THE WHITE BIRD. New Haven, 1924.

WHITE EAGLE. Based on THE SQUAW MAN by Edwin Milton Royle. (Musical) (Casino Theatre, Dec. 26, 1927)

THROUGH THE YEARS. (Manhattan Theatre, Jan. 28, 1932)

RUY BLAS. Adap. of play by Victor Hugo. 1931. (Pittsfield, Mass., Oct., 1933)

HOUSUM, ROBERT

THE GYPSY TRAIL. c. 1920. (Plymouth Theatre, Dec. 4, 1917)

A VERY GOOD YOUNG MAN. With Martin Brown. (Plymouth Theatre, Aug. 19, 1918)

* THE CORSICAN LIEUTENANT. In *One-Act Plays for Stage and Study,* Second Series.

SYLVIA RUNS AWAY. New York, n. d.

HOWARD, BRONSON

FANTINE. (Detroit, 1864)

SARATOGA; OR, PISTOLS FOR SEVEN. c. 1870. (Fifth Ave. Theatre, Dec. 21, 1870; Court Theatre, London, as BRIGHTON, May 25, 1874)

DIAMONDS. (Fifth Ave. Theatre, Sept. 3, 1872)

LILLIAN'S LAST LOVE. See THE BANKER'S DAUGHTER.

MOORCROFT; OR, THE DOUBLE WEDDING. Auto. MS. (Fifth Ave. Theatre, Oct. 17, 1874)

ONLY A TRAMP. MS. dated 1878. See BARON RUDOLPH.

HURRICANES. A.L.P. (Hooley's Theatre, Chicago, May 27, 1878; Criterion Theatre, London, as TRUTH, Feb. 8, 1879)

OLD LOVE LETTERS. Priv. printed, 1897. A.L.P. (Park Theatre, Aug. 31, 1878)

THE BANKER'S DAUGHTER. Priv. printed, 1878. A.L.P. (Union Square Theatre, Nov. 30, 1878; Hooley's Theatre, Chicago,

A HISTORY OF THE AMERICAN DRAMA

as LILLIAN'S LAST LOVE, Sept. 4, 1873; Court Theatre, London, as THE OLD LOVE AND THE NEW, Dec. 15, 1879)

WIVES. Adap. of L'ECOLE DES MARIS and L'ECOLE DES FEMMES, by Molière. MS. (Daly's Theatre, Oct. 18, 1879)

BARON RUDOLPH. A.L.P. (Royal Theatre, Hull, England, Aug. 1, 1881; Grand Opera House, Sept. 12, 1881 [see text])

FUN IN A GREEN ROOM. (Booth's Theatre, April 10, 1882)

YOUNG MRS. WINTHROP. c. 1899. (Madison Square Theatre, Oct. 9, 1882; Marylebone Theatre, London, Sept. 21, 1882 [copyright]; Court Theatre, London, Nov. 6, 1884)

ONE OF OUR GIRLS. Priv. printed, 1897. A.L.P. (Lyceum Theatre, Nov. 10, 1885)

MET BY CHANCE. (Lyceum Theatre, Jan. 11, 1887)

THE HENRIETTA. Priv. printed, 1901. In Halline's *American Plays*. (Union Square Theatre, Sept. 26, 1887; Knickerbocker Theatre, Dec. 22, 1913, as THE NEW HENRIETTA)

KNAVE AND QUEEN. With Sir Charles Young. A.L.P.

SHENANDOAH. Priv. printed, 1897. In Quinn's *Representative American Plays*. (Boston Museum, Nov. 19, 1888; Star Theatre, Sept. 9, 1889)

ARISTOCRACY. Priv. printed, 1898. (Palmer's Theatre, Nov. 14, 1892)

PETER STUYVESANT. With Brander Matthews. MS. (Providence, R. I., Sept. 25, 1899; Wallack's Theatre, Oct. 2, 1899)

KATE. 1906.

Biographical and Critical

"Mr. Bronson Howard Illustrates and Defines." *Harper's Weekly*, Supplement, Feb. 2, 1889.

Howard, Bronson, *The Autobiography of a Play*. Reprinted, with an Introduction by Augustus Thomas, by the Dramatic Museum of Columbia University. 1914.

In Memoriam, Bronson Howard. Addresses Delivered at the Memorial Meeting, Oct. 18, 1908. Privately printed by the American Dramatists' Club. 1910. [The authoritative biographical source. Contains: "An Appreciation," by Brander Matthews, based on his article in the *North American Review;* "A Brief Biography," by H. P. Mawson, "The Auto-

BIBLIOGRAPHY AND PLAY LIST

biography of a Play," by Bronson Howard; a list of Howard's plays, with casts]

Archer, William, *English Dramatists of To-day*. London, 1882.

M[ontgomery], G. E., "Bronson Howard," *The Theatre*, I (Aug. 2, 1886), 469–470.

Clark, Barrett H., *A Study of the Modern Drama*, 1925, pp. 362–368.

Matthews, Brander, "Bronson Howard" in *Gateways to Literature*. 1912.

HOWARD, SIDNEY

SWORDS. c. 1921. (National Theatre, Sept. 1, 1921)

S. S. TENACITY. Adap. from French of Charles Vildrac. In *Mod. Cont. Plays*, 1929. (Belmont Theatre, Jan. 2, 1922)

CASANOVA. 1924. Adap. from Spanish of Lorenzo de Azertis. (Empire Theatre, Sept. 26, 1923)

SANCHO PANZA. Adap. from Hungarian of Melchoir Lengyel. (Hudson Theatre, Nov. 26, 1923)

LEXINGTON. Lexington, 1924.

BEWITCHED. With Edward Sheldon. MS. (Allentown, Pa., Sept. 26, 1924)

THEY KNEW WHAT THEY WANTED. 1925. (Garrick Theatre, Nov. 24, 1924)

MICHEL AUCLAIR. Adap. from MICHEL AUCLAIR, by Charles Vildrac. In Leverton's *Plays for the College Theatre*, 1933. (Provincetown Theatre, March 4, 1925)

LUCKY SAM McCARVER. 1926. (Playhouse, Oct. 21, 1925)

THE LAST NIGHT OF DON JUAN. Adap. from Edmond Rostand. (Greenwich Village Theatre, Nov. 9, 1925)

MORALS. With Charles Recht. Adap. of MORALE, by Ludwig Thoma. (Comedy Theatre, Nov. 30, 1925)

NED McCOBB's DAUGHTER. 1926. (John Golden Theatre, Nov. 22, 1926)

THE SILVER CORD. 1927. (John Golden Theatre, Dec. 20, 1926)

SALVATION. With Charles MacArthur. (Empire Theatre, Jan. 31, 1928)

OLYMPIA. Adap. from OLYMPIA by Molnar. (Empire Theatre, Oct. 16, 1928)

HALF GODS. 1930. (Plymouth Theatre, Dec. 21, 1929)

A HISTORY OF THE AMERICAN DRAMA

MARSEILLES. Adap. from MARIUS by Marcel Pagnol. (Henry Miller Theatre, Nov. 17, 1930) (Originally produced in Philadelphia under title of MARIUS)

THE LATE CHRISTOPHER BEAN. 1933. Founded upon PRENEZ GARDE À LA PEINTURE by Rene Fauchois. (Ford's Opera House, Baltimore, Oct. 24, 1932; Henry Miller's Theatre, Oct. 31, 1932)

ALIEN CORN. 1933. (Belasco Theatre, Feb. 20, 1933)

DODSWORTH. Dram. of novel by Sinclair Lewis. 1934. (Garrick Theatre, Philadelphia, Feb. 5, 1934; Shubert Theatre, Feb. 24, 1934)

YELLOW JACK. In collaboration with Paul de Kruif. 1934. (Martin Beck Theatre, March 6, 1934)

GATHER YE ROSEBUDS. With Robert Littell. (Garrick Theatre, Phila., Nov. 28, 1934)

ODE TO LIBERTY. Adap. from LIBERTÉ PROVISOIRE by Michel Duran. (Little Theatre, Jan. 14, 1935)

PATHS OF GLORY. Dram. of novel by Humphrey Cobb. 1935. (Shubert Theatre, New Haven, Sept. 18, 1935; Plymouth Theatre, Sept. 26, 1935)

HOWELLS, WILLIAM DEAN

SAMSON. Adap. of SANSONE by Ippolito D'Aste. 1889. (Olympic Theatre, St. Louis, Oct. 5, 1874; Palmer's Theatre, Oct. 13, 1889)

* THE PARLOR CAR. Boston, 1876.

OUT OF THE QUESTION. Boston, c. 1877.

A COUNTERFEIT PRESENTMENT. Boston, c. 1877. (Grand Opera House, Cincinnati, O., Oct. 11, 1877)

YORICK'S LOVE. Adap. from UN DRAMA NUEVO, by Tamayo y Baus. MS. (Euclid Ave. Opera House, Chicago, Oct. 25, 1878; Lyceum Theatre, London, April 14, 1884)

* THE SLEEPING CAR. Boston, 1883.

* THE REGISTER. Boston, 1884.

* THE ELEVATOR. Boston, 1885.

A FOREGONE CONCLUSION. Dram. of novel of the same name. (Madison Square Theatre, Nov. 18, 1886)

THE AMERICAN CLAIMANT; OR, MULBERRY SELLERS TEN YEARS LATER. With Mark Twain. (Lyceum Theatre, Sept. 23, 1887)

BIBLIOGRAPHY AND PLAY LIST

* THE GARROTERS. 1886. (Avenue Theatre, London, Nov. 30, 1895, as A DANGEROUS RUFFIAN)

A SEA CHANGE; OR, LOVE'S STOWAWAY. Boston, 1888.

* THE MOUSE TRAP. c. 1889. (Queen's Hall, London, bef. 1904 by Mrs. Kendal)

* FIVE O'CLOCK TEA. c. 1889.

* A LIKELY STORY. c. 1889.

* THE ALBANY DEPOT. 1892.

* A LETTER OF INTRODUCTION. 1892.

* UNEXPECTED GUESTS. c. 1893.

* EVENING DRESS. c. 1893.

* A MASTERPIECE OF DIPLOMACY. *Harper's Magazine,* LXXX-VII (Feb., 1894), 371–385.

* A PREVIOUS ENGAGEMENT. 1897.

* BRIDE ROSES. 1900.

* ROOM FORTY-FIVE. 1900.

* INDIAN GIVER. 1900.

* THE SMOKING CAR. Boston, 1900.

* HER OPINION OF HIS STORY. *Harper's Bazaar,* XLI (May, 1907), 429.

* SAVED: AN EMOTIONAL DRAMA. *Harper's Weekly,* LII (Dec., 1908), 22–24.

* A TRUE HERO: MELODRAMA. *Harper's Magazine,* CXIX (Nov., 1909), 866–875.

THE MOTHER AND THE FATHER. 1909.

* PARTING FRIENDS. 1911.

* THE IMPOSSIBLE: A MYSTERY PLAY. *Harper's Magazine,* CXXII (Dec., 1910), 116–125.

* THE NIGHT BEFORE CHRISTMAS. In *The Daughter of the Storage,* 1916.

* SELF-SACRIFICE: A FARCE TRAGEDY. In *The Daughter of the Storage,* 1916.

Biographical and Critical

Howells, W. D., "The New Taste in Theatricals." *Atlantic Monthly,* XXIII (May, 1869), 635–644.

Howells, W. D., Editor's Study. *Harper's Magazine,* LXXIX (June, 1889), 314–319.

A HISTORY OF THE AMERICAN DRAMA

Howells, W. D., "The Recent Dramatic Season." *North American Review*, CLXXII (March, 1901), 468–480.

Cooke, Delmar Gross, *William Dean Howells: A Critical Study.* c. 1922.

Firkins, Oscar W., *William Dean Howells, A Study.* Cambridge, 1924.

Howells, Mildred. *Life in Letters of William Dean Howells.* 2 Vols. 1928.

HOYT, CHARLES HALE

CEZALIA. MS. (Globe Theatre, Boston, 1882?)

A BUNCH OF KEYS. With Willie Edouin. A.L.P. (Newark, N. J., Dec., 1882; San Francisco Music Hall, New York, March 26, 1883)

A RAG BABY. MS. (Haverley's Theatre, Aug. 16, 1884)

A PARLOR MATCH. MS. (Tony Pastor's Opera House, Sept. 22, 1884)

A TIN SOLDIER. MS. (Arch St. Theatre, Phila., Oct. 5, 1885)

THE MAID AND THE MOONSHINER. With Edward Solomon. (Standard Theatre, Aug. 16, 1886)

A HOLE IN THE GROUND. MS. (Arch St. Theatre, Phila., April 18, 1887; Fourteenth St. Theatre, Sept. 12, 1887)

A BRASS MONKEY. MS. (Bijou Theatre, Oct. 15, 1888)

A MIDNIGHT BELL. A.L.P. (Bijou Theatre, March 5, 1889)

A TEXAS STEER. In Moses' *Representative American Dramas.* (Chestnut St. Theatre, Phila., Sept. 29, 1890; Bijou Theatre, Nov. 10, 1890)

A TRIP TO CHINATOWN. A.L.P. (Harlem Opera House, Dec. 8, 1890; Chestnut St. Theatre, Phila., Jan. 26, 1891)

A TEMPERANCE TOWN. A.L.P. (Chestnut St. Theatre, Phila., March 28, 1892; Hoyt's Madison Square Theatre, Sept. 18, 1893)

A MILK WHITE FLAG. A.L.P. (Wilkes-Barre, Pa., Dec. 23, 1893; Hoyt's Theatre, Oct. 8, 1894)

A RUNAWAY COLT. MS. (American Theatre, Dec. 2, 1895)

A BLACK SHEEP. MS. (Chestnut St. Theatre, Phila., Sept. 17, 1894; Hoyt's Theatre, Jan. 6, 1896)

A CONTENTED WOMAN. MS. (Hoyt's Theatre, Jan. 4, 1897)

A STRANGER IN NEW YORK. MS. (Garrick Theatre, Sept. 13, 1897)

BIBLIOGRAPHY AND PLAY LIST

A DAY AND A NIGHT IN NEW YORK. MS. (Garrick Theatre, Aug. 30, 1898)

A DOG IN THE MANGER. MS.

HUGHES, HATCHER

WAKE UP, JONATHAN! With Elmer L. Rice. 1928. (Henry Miller Theatre, Jan. 17, 1921)

HELL-BENT FER HEAVEN. 1924. (Klaw Theatre, Jan. 4, 1924)

RUINT. 1925. (Provincetown Theatre, April 7, 1925)

IT'S A GRAND LIFE. With Alan Williams. (Cort Theatre, Feb. 10, 1930)

JAMES, HENRY

DAISY MILLER. Dram. of novel by author. Boston, 1883.

THE AMERICAN. Dram. of novel by author. (Southport, England, Jan. 3, 1891)

GUY DOMVILLE. Printed as MS. for Private Circulation Only. London, 1894. (St. James's Theatre, London, Jan. 5, 1895)

THE HIGH BID. First written as MRS. GRACEDEW. (Lyceum Theatre, Edinburgh, March 6, 1908)

Theatricals.

> FIRST SERIES. London, 1894. Contains TENANTS and DIS-ENGAGED. (Hudson Theatre, March 11, 1909)
>
> SECOND SERIES. 1895. Contains THE ALBUM and THE REPROBATE.
>
> THE SALOON. Dram. of OWEN WINGRAVE by James. (Little Theatre, London, Jan. 17, 1911)

THE TRAGIC MUSE. Adap. by Herbert Griffith. London, 1927.

Biographical and Critical

Gosse, Edmund, "Henry James." *Scribners' Magazine,* April, 1920.

Matthews, Brander, "Henry James and the Theater." In *Playwrights on Playmaking,* pp. 187–204.

Robins, Elizabeth. Theatre and Friendship. Some Henry James Letters. 1932.

JOHNSON, HALL

RUN, LITTLE CHILDREN. (Lyric Theatre, March 1, 1933)

JOHNSTON, MARY

THE GODDESS OF REASON. Boston. 1907. (Majestic Theatre,

A HISTORY OF THE AMERICAN DRAMA

Boston, Dec. 21, 1908; Daly's Theatre, Feb. 15, 1909)

KAUFMAN, GEORGE S.

SOME ONE IN THE HOUSE. With Larry Evans and Walter Percival. (Knickerbocker Theatre, Sept. 9, 1918)

DULCY. With Marc Connelly. 1921. (Indianapolis, Feb. 14, 1921; Frazee Theatre, Aug. 13, 1921)

TO THE LADIES. With Marc Connelly. In Quinn's *Contemporary American Plays.* (Lyceum Theatre, Rochester, Feb. 13, 1922; Liberty Theatre, Feb. 20, 1922)

MERTON OF THE MOVIES. With Marc Connelly. Dram. of story by H. L. Wilson. c. 1925. (Brooklyn, Oct. 16, 1922; Cort Theatre, Nov. 13, 1922)

THE DEEP TANGLED WILDWOOD. With Marc Connelly. (Frazee Theatre, Nov. 5, 1923)

BEGGAR ON HORSEBACK. With Marc Connelly. 1925. (Broadhurst Theatre, Feb. 12, 1924)

MINICK. With Edna Ferber. Dram. of novel by Edna Ferber. Garden City, 1924. (Booth Theatre, Sept. 24, 1924)

THE BUTTER AND EGG MAN. 1925. (Longacre Theatre, Sept. 23, 1925)

THE GOOD FELLOW. With Herman J. Mankiewicz. 1931. (Playhouse, Oct. 7, 1926)

THE ROYAL FAMILY. With Edna Ferber. 1928. (Selwyn Theatre, Dec. 28, 1927)

ANIMAL CRACKERS. With Morrie Ryskind. Musical Comedy. (44th St. Theatre, Oct. 23, 1928)

THE CHANNEL ROAD. With Alexander Woollcott. (Plymouth Theatre, Oct. 17, 1929)

JUNE MOON. With Ring Lardner. 1931. (Broadhurst Theatre, Oct. 9, 1929)

STRIKE UP THE BAND. Musical Comedy based on Libretto by Kaufman. (Shubert Theatre, Phila.; Times Square Theatre, Jan. 14, 1930)

THE STILL ALARM. One Act Play. 1930. (Music Box Theatre, in THE LITTLE SHOW)

ONCE IN A LIFETIME. 1930. (Nixon's Apollo Theatre, Atlantic City, May 26, 1930; Music Box Theatre, Sept. 24, 1930)

BIBLIOGRAPHY AND PLAY LIST

OF THEE I SING. With Morrie Ryskind. 1932. (Sam H. Harris Theatre, Dec. 26, 1931)

THE BAND WAGON. With Howard Dietz. Revue with music. (Garrick Theatre, Phila., May 25, 1931; New Amsterdam Theatre, June 3, 1931)

DINNER AT EIGHT. With Edna Ferber. 1932. (Music Box Theatre, Oct. 22, 1932)

LET 'EM EAT CAKE. With Morrie Ryskind. A musical comedy in two acts. Music by George Gershwin. Lyrics by Ira Gershwin. (Imperial Theatre, Oct. 21, 1933)

THE DARK TOWER. With Alexander Woollcott. 1934. (Morosco Theatre, Nov. 25, 1933)

MERRILY WE ROLL ALONG. With Moss Hart. 1934. (Music Box Theatre, Sept. 29, 1934)

FIRST LADY. With Katharine Dayton. 1936. (Garrick Theatre, Phila., Nov. 11, 1935; Music Box Theatre, Nov. 25, 1935)

KEARNEY, PATRICK

A MAN'S MAN. 1925. (Fifty-second St. Theatre, Oct. 13, 1925)

AN AMERICAN TRAGEDY. Dram. of novel by Theodore Dreiser. (Longacre Theatre, Oct. 11, 1926)

ELMER GANTRY. Dram. of novel by Sinclair Lewis. (Playhouse, Aug. 7, 1928)

KELLY, GEORGE EDWARD

The Flattering Word and Other One-Act Plays. Boston, 1925. [In vaudeville]

* FINDERS-KEEPERS. 1923.

THE TORCHBEARERS. 1923. (Savoy Theatre, Asbury Park, N. J., Aug. 14, 1922; Forty-eighth St. Theatre, Aug. 29, 1922)

THE SHOW-OFF. Boston, 1924. (Playhouse, Feb. 4, 1924)

CRAIG'S WIFE. Boston, 1926. (Morosco Theatre, Oct. 12, 1925)

DAISY MAYME. Boston, 1927. (Playhouse, Nov. 24, 1926)

A LA CARTE. Musical Revue Sketch. (Martin Beck Theatre, Aug. 1, 1927)

BEHOLD THE BRIDEGROOM. Boston, 1928. (Cort-Jamaica Theatre, Dec. 26, 1927)

MAGGIE THE MAGNIFICENT. (Cort Theatre, Oct. 21, 1929)

TOP O' THE HILL. (Eltinge Theatre, Nov. 26, 1927)

PHILIP GOES FORTH. 1931. (Biltmore Theatre, Jan. 12, 1931)

A HISTORY OF THE AMERICAN DRAMA

KENNEDY, CHARLES RANN

The Servant in the House. 1908. (Duke of York's Theatre, London, March 19, 1907; Savoy Theatre, March 23, 1908)

The Winterfeast. 1908. (Savoy Theatre, Nov. 30, 1908)

The Flower of the Palace of Han. (Little Theatre, March 19, 1912)

* The Terrible Meek. 1912. (Little Theatre, March 19, 1912)

* The Necessary Evil. 1913. (Fine Arts Theatre, Chicago, May 12, 1913)

The Idol Breaker. 1914.

The Rib of the Man. 1917.

The Army with Banners. 1919. (Théâtre du Vieux Colombier, New York, April 9, 1918)

The Fool from the Hills. 1919.

The Chastening. 1922.

The Admiral. 1923.

The Salutation. 1925.

KENYON, CHARLES

Kindling. 1914. (Los Angeles, Calif., July 31, 1911; Daly's Theatre, Dec. 5, 1911)

Husband and Wife. (Forty-fourth St. Theatre, Sept. 21, 1915)

The Claim. With Frank Doré. (Royal Alexandra Theatre, Toronto, Can., May 28, 1917; Fulton Theatre, Oct. 17, 1917)

KINGSLEY, SIDNEY

Men in White. 1933. (Broadhurst Theatre, Sept. 26, 1933)

Dead End. 1936. (Belasco Theatre, Oct. 28, 1935)

KIRKLAND, JOHN M. (JACK)

Frankie and Johnnie. (Republic Theatre, Sept. 25, 1930)

Tobacco Road. Based on novel by Erskine Caldwell. 1934. (Masque Theatre, Dec. 4, 1933)

KILPATRICK, JUDSON

Allatoona. With J. Owen Moore. New York, n. d. (Eagle Theatre, Oct. 22, 1877, First?)

KLEIN, CHARLES

By Proxy. (Boston Museum, June 27, 1892)

The District Attorney. With Harrison Grey Fiske. (American Theatre, Jan. 21, 1895)

370

BIBLIOGRAPHY AND PLAY LIST

Two LITTLE VAGRANTS. Adap. of LES DEUX GOSSES, by Pierre de Courcelles. (Academy of Music, Nov. 23, 1896)

HEARTSEASE. With J. I. C. Clarke. c. 1916. (Garden Theatre, Jan. 11, 1897)

A ROYAL ROGUE. (Broadway Theatre, Dec. 24, 1900)

THE AUCTIONEER. With Lee Arthur. (Hyperion Theatre, New Haven, Conn., Sept. 9, 1901; Bijou Theatre, Sept. 23, 1901)

THE MUSIC MASTER. 1935. (Atlantic City, N. J., Sept. 12, 1904; Belasco Theatre, Sept. 26, 1904)

THE LION AND THE MOUSE. [1916] (Lyceum Theatre, Nov. 20, 1905)

DAUGHTERS OF MEN. [1917] (Astor Theatre, Nov. 19, 1906)

THE THIRD DEGREE. [1917] (Hudson Theatre, Feb. 1, 1909; as FIND THE WOMAN, Garrick Theatre, London, June 17, 1912)

THE NEXT OF KIN. [1917] (Hudson Theatre, Dec. 27, 1909)

THE GAMBLERS. [1916] (Lyric Theatre, Chicago, Sept. 26, 1910)

MAGGIE PEPPER. [1916] (New Haven Opera House, Jan. 30, 1911; Harris Theatre, Aug. 31, 1911)

POTASH AND PERLMUTTER. Dram. of stories by Montague Glass. (Cohan Theatre, Aug. 16, 1913)

THE MONEY MAKERS. (Booth Theatre, Oct. 5, 1914)

Biographical and Critical

Klein, Charles, "Religion, Philosophy and the Drama." *Arena,* XXXVII (May, 1907), 492–497.

KNOBLOCK, EDWARD

THE CLUB BABY. With Laurence Sterner. (Parkhurst Theatre, London, Oct. 14, 1895)

THE SHULAMITE. With Claude Askew. Dram. of novel of same name. (Savoy Theatre, London, May 12, 1906; Lyric Theatre, Oct. 29, 1906)

THE COTTAGE IN THE AIR. Dram. of THE PRINCESS PRISCILLA'S FORTNIGHT, by author of ELIZABETH AND HER GERMAN GARDEN. (New Theatre, Nov. 11, 1909)

THE FAUN. (Daly's Theatre, Jan. 16, 1911)

A HISTORY OF THE AMERICAN DRAMA

KISMET. 1911. (Garrick Theatre, London, April 19, 1911; Knickerbocker Theatre, Dec. 25, 1911)

MILESTONES. With Arnold Bennett. 1912. (Royalty Theatre, London, March 5, 1912; Liberty Theatre, Sept. 17, 1912)

DISCOVERING AMERICA. (Daly's Theatre, Sept. 7, 1912)

THE HEAD-MASTER. With W. T. Coleby. London, 1913. (Playhouse, London, Jan. 22, 1913)

MY LADY'S DRESS. 1916. (Royalty Theatre, London, April 21, 1914; Playhouse, Oct. 10, 1914)

MARIE ODILE. 1915. (Belasco Theatre, Washington, D. C., Jan. 19, 1915; His Majesty's Theatre, London, June 8, 1915)

* A WAR COMMITTEE. London, 1915. (Haymarket Theatre, London, July 2, 1915)

* THE LITTLE SILVER RING. London, 1915. (Theatrical Garden Party, Regent's Park, London, July 20, 1915)

PAGANINI. c. 1915. (Criterion Theatre, Sept. 11, 1916)

TIGER! TIGER! 1924. (Belasco Theatre, Nov. 12, 1918)

ONE. (Savoy Theatre, Asbury Park, July 5, 1920)

THE LULLABY. 1924. (Knickerbocker Theatre, Sept. 17, 1923)

THE GOOD COMPANIONS. With J. B. Priestly. Adap. from Priestly's novel of same name. (Forty-fourth St. Theatre, Oct. 1, 1931)

EVENSONG. With Beverly Nichols. Adap. from novel by Beverly Nichols. (Selwyn Theatre, Jan. 31, 1933)

IF A BODY. With George Rosener. (Biltmore Theatre, April 30, 1935)

KUMMER, CLARE

GOOD GRACIOUS ANNABELLE. c. 1922. (Republic Theatre, Oct. 31, 1916)

A SUCCESSFUL CALAMITY. c. 1922. (Booth Theatre, Feb. 17, 1917)

THE RESCUING ANGEL. 1923. (Hudson Theatre, Oct. 8, 1917)

BE CALM, CAMILLA. c. 1922. (Booth Theatre, Oct. 31, 1918)

ROLLO'S WILD OAT. c. 1922. (Columbia Theatre, Far Rockaway, N. Y., Jan. 30, 1920; Punch and Judy Theatre, Nov. 23, 1920)

THE MOUNTAIN MAN. (Maxine Elliott Theatre, Dec. 12, 1921)

* THE CHORUS REHEARSAL. 1922. (Punch and Judy Theatre, 1921)

BIBLIOGRAPHY AND PLAY LIST

* CHINESE LOVE. 1922. (Punch and Judy Theatre, 1921)
* BRIDGES. 1922. (Punch and Judy Theatre, 1921)
* THE ROBBERY. (Punch and Judy Theatre, 1921)
POMEROY'S PAST. 1926. (Garrick Theatre, Phila., Sept. 18, 1922; Longacre Theatre, April 19, 1926)
* PAPERS. 1927.
* SO'S YOUR OLD ANTIQUE. 1928.
AMOURETTE. (Henry Miller Theatre, Sept. 27, 1933)
HER MASTER'S VOICE. 1934. (Chestnut St. Opera House, Phila., Oct. 2, 1933; Plymouth Theatre, Oct. 23, 1933)

LACY, ERNEST
* CHATTERTON. In *Plays and Sonnets*. Phila., 1900. (Hollis St. Theatre, Boston, 1893; Broadway Theatre, March 26, 1897)
RINALDO, THE DOCTOR OF FLORENCE. In *Plays and Sonnets*. Phila., 1900. (Castle Square Theatre, Boston, Feb. 25, 1895)
THE RAGGED EARL. With Joseph Humphreys. (Academy of Music, Jan. 16, 1899)
THE BARD OF MARY REDCLIFFE. Phila., 1916.

LAVERY, EMMET
THE FIRST LEGION. 1934. (Forty-sixth St. Theatre, Oct. 1, 1934)
MONSIGNOR'S HOUR. In *Stage Magazine,* XIII (1936), 89–99.

LAWRENCE, REGINALD
MEN MUST FIGHT. With S. K. Lawrence. 1933. (Walnut St. Theatre, Phila., April 6, 1931; Lyceum Theatre, Oct. 14, 1932)
IF THIS BE TREASON. With John Haynes Holmes. 1935. (The Music Box Theatre, Sept. 23, 1935)

LEE, HARRY
THE LITTLE POOR MAN. 1922. (Princess Theatre, Aug. 5, 1925)

LLOYD, DAVID DEMAREST
FOR CONGRESS. (Haverley's Theatre, Jan. 10, 1884)
THE WOMAN HATER. 1908. (Denver, Col., July 31, 1886; Newcastle-on-Tyne, England, Sept. 1, 1887)
THE DOMINIE'S DAUGHTER. (Wallack's Theatre, March, 1887)
THE SENATOR. MS. (Chicago Opera House, Sept. 16, 1889)

A HISTORY OF THE AMERICAN DRAMA

LOGAN, (SYKES) OLIVE

SURF. (Arch St. Theatre, Phila., Nov. 4, 1867; Fifth Ave. Theatre, Jan. 12, 1870)

NEWPORT. MS. (Daly's Theatre, Sept. 18, 1879)

LONG, JOHN LUTHER

MADAME BUTTERFLY. With David Belasco. In Quinn's *Representative American Plays*. (Herald Square Theatre, March 5, 1900)

THE DARLING OF THE GODS. With David Belasco. MS. (New National Theatre, Washington, D. C., Nov. 17, 1902)

ADREA. With David Belasco. MS. (Convention Hall, Washington, D. C., Dec. 26, 1904)

THE DRAGON FLY. With E. C. Carpenter. (Garrick Theatre, Phila., 1905)

DOLCE. (Lyric Theatre, Phila., March 24, 1906; Manhattan Theatre, April 24, 1906)

KASSA. (Liberty Theatre, Jan. 23, 1909)

CROWNS. MS. (Provincetown Theatre, Nov. 6, 1922)

MACKAYE, JAMES STEELE

MONALDI. With Francis Durivage. (St. James Theatre, Jan. 8, 1872)

MARRIAGE. Adap. of JULIE by Octave Feuillet. (St. James Theatre, Feb. 12, 1872)

ARKWRIGHT'S WIFE. With Tom Taylor. (Theatre Royal, Leeds, England, July 7, 1873; Boston Museum, Oct., 1874)

ROSE MICHEL. Adap. from the French of Ernest Blum. A.L.P. 1941. (Union Square Theatre, Nov. 23, 1875)

QUEEN AND WOMAN. With J. V. Pritchard. (Brooklyn Theatre, Brooklyn, Feb. 14, 1876)

TWINS. With A. C. Wheeler. (Wallack's Theatre, April 12, 1876)

WON AT LAST. A.L.P. (Wallack's Theatre, Dec. 10, 1877)

THROUGH THE DARK. (Fifth Ave. Theatre, March 10, 1879)

AN IRON WILL. (Low's Opera House, Providence, R. I., Oct. 27, 1879) Rewritten as HAZEL KIRKE, q.v.

HAZEL KIRKE. Priv. printed, 1880. Revised in Quinn's *Representative American Plays*. (Madison Square Theatre, Feb. 4, 1880)

A FOOL'S ERRAND. Dram. of A FOOL'S ERRAND, by Albion W. Tourgée. (Arch St. Theatre, Phila., Oct. 26, 1881)

374

BIBLIOGRAPHY AND PLAY LIST

DAKOLAR. Adap. of LE MAÎTRE DE FORGES, by Georges Ohnet. (Lyceum Theatre, April 6, 1885)

IN SPITE OF ALL. Adap. of ANDREA, by Victorien Sardou. A.L.P. (Lyceum Theatre, Sept. 15, 1885)

RIENZI. Dram. of RIENZI by Bulwer-Lytton. (Albaugh's Opera House, Washington, D. C., Dec. 13, 1886)

ANARCHY. (Academy of Music, Buffalo, N. Y., May 30, 1887) Revised as PAUL KAUVAR.

THE DRAMA OF CIVILIZATION. Pageant. (Madison Square Garden, Nov. 27, 1887)

PAUL KAUVAR. In Moses' *Representative Plays by American Dramatists,* III. (Standard Theatre, Dec. 24, 1887)

A NOBLE ROGUE. (Chicago Opera House, Chicago, July 3, 1888)

AN ARRANT KNAVE. A.L.P. (Chicago Opera House, Chicago, Sept. 30, 1889)

COLONEL TOM. (Tremont Theatre, Boston, Mass., Jan. 20, 1890)

MONEY MAD. (Standard Theatre, April 7, 1890.) Revision of THROUGH THE DARK and A NOBLE ROGUE.

Biographical and Critical

MacKaye, Percy, "Steele MacKaye, Dynamic Artist of the American Theatre." *The Drama,* No. 4 (Nov., 1911), 138–161, and No. 5 (Feb., 1912), 155–173.

MacKaye, Percy, *Epoch, the Life of Steele MacKaye.* 2 Vols., 1927.

MACKAYE, PERCY [WALLACE]

Poems and Plays. 2 Vols. 1916.

Vol. II contains THE CANTERBURY PILGRIMS; JEANNE D'ARC; SAPPHO AND PHAON; THE SCARECROW; and MATER.

A GARLAND TO SYLVIA. 1910. [Written 1896–99]

KINFOLK OF ROBIN HOOD. A Play for Boys, in Four Acts. Founded upon the old English Ballad, *Adam Bell, Clym o' the Clough and William of Cloudesley.* 1926. (Berkeley Lyceum Theatre, May 19, 1901)

FENRIS THE WOLF. 1905.

A HISTORY OF THE AMERICAN DRAMA

SAINT GAUDENS MASQUE-PROLOGUE. 1909. (Cornish, N. H., June 20, 1905)

JEANNE D'ARC. 1906. (Lyric Theatre, Phila., Oct. 15, 1906; Lyric Theatre, Jan. 28, 1907; Waldorf Theatre, London, April 24, 1907)

SAPPHO AND PHAON. 1907. (Opera House, Providence, R. I., Oct. 14, 1907; Lyric Theatre, Oct. 21, 1907)

MATER. 1908. (Van Ness Theatre, San Francisco, Aug. 3, 1908; Savoy Theatre, Sept. 25, 1908; Playhouse, London, June 4, 1915)

THE CANTERBURY PILGRIMS. 1903. (Park Extension Theatre, Savannah, Ga., April 30, 1909. As the Gloucester Pageant, Gloucester, Mass., Aug. 3, 1909. As an opera, Metropolitan Opera House, March 8, 1917)

ANTI-MATRIMONY. 1910. (Theatre, Ann Arbor, Mich., March 10, 1910; Garrick Theatre, Sept. 22, 1910)

THE SCARECROW. 1908. (Middlesex Theatre, Middletown, Conn., Dec. 30, 1910; Garrick Theatre, Jan. 17, 1911; Theatre Royal, Bristol, Eng., Nov. 30, 1914; Deutsches Theater, Berlin, 1914)

Yankee Fantasies. 1912. Including * CHUCK (Coburn Players, Oxford, Ohio, July 17, 1912); * GETTYSBURG (Bijou Theatre, Boston, Jan. 3, 1912); * THE ANTICK (Bandbox Theatre, Oct. 4, 1915); * THE CAT-BOAT; * SAM AVERAGE (Toy Theatre, Boston, Feb. 26, 1912)

A MASQUE OF LABOR. 1912.

SANCTUARY, A BIRD MASQUE 1914. (Meriden, N. H., Sept. 12, 1913)

TOMORROW. 1912. (Little Theatre, Phila., Oct. 31, 1913)

A THOUSAND YEARS AGO. 1914. (Shubert Theatre, Dec. 1, 1913)

SAINT LOUIS: A CIVIC MASQUE. 1914. (St. Louis, May 28, 1914)

THE IMMIGRANTS. 1915.

THE NEW CITIZENSHIP, A CIVIC RITUAL. 1915. (New York, Feb. 14, 1916)

CALIBAN, A COMMUNITY MASQUE. 1916. (New York, May 25, 1916)

THE EVERGREEN TREE. 1917. (Fargo, N. D., Dec. 15, 1917)

BIBLIOGRAPHY AND PLAY LIST

SINBAD THE SAILOR. 1917.

THE ROLL CALL: A MASQUE OF THE RED CROSS. 1918. (Simultaneously, in different places, Dec. 16, 1918)

THE WILL OF SONG. With Harry Barnhart. 1919. (Orange, N. J., May 2, 1919)

RIP VAN WINKLE. 1919. (Auditorium Theatre, Chicago, Jan. 2, 1920)

WASHINGTON, THE MAN WHO MADE US. 1918. (Belasco Theatre, Washington, D. C., Feb. 23, 1920)

THIS FINE-PRETTY WORLD. 1924. (Neighborhood Playhouse, Dec. 26, 1923)

* NAPOLEON CROSSING THE ROCKIES. In *Kentucky Mountain Fantasies,* 1928. (Carnegie Institute, Pittsburgh, May 21, 1924)

KENTUCKY MOUNTAIN FANTASIES. Three Short Plays for an Appalachian Theatre. 1928. Rev. Ed., 1932.—Includes, NAPOLEON CROSSING THE ROCKIES, THE FUNERALIZING OF CRICKNECK, and TIMBER.

WAKEFIELD, A FOLK MASQUE OF AMERICA. Pub. by U. S. Bicentennial Commission. Washington, 1932. (Convention Hall, Washington, D. C., Feb. 21, 1932)

Biographical and Critical

MacKaye, Percy, *A Sketch of His Life, with Bibliography of His Works.* Rep. from the Twenty-fifth Anniversary Report of the Class of 1897, Harvard College. 1922.

MacKaye, Percy, *The Playhouse and the Play.* 1909.

MacKaye, Percy, *The Civic Theatre.* 1912.

MacKaye, Percy, *Community Drama.* Boston, 1917.

MacKaye, Percy, *Epoch, the Life of Steele MacKaye.* 2 Vols. 1927.

PERCY MACKAYE: A SYMPOSIUM ON HIS FIFTIETH BIRTHDAY: 1925. With Foreword by Amy Lowell. Hanover, N. H., 1928.

Dickinson, Thomas H., "The Playwright as Pioneer, Percy MacKaye." *Playwrights of the New American Theater,* pp. 1–55.

Garnier, M., "M. Percy MacKaye." *La Revue du Mois,* April 10, 1909.

Russell, Charles E., *Julia Marlowe, Her Life and Art,* 1927, pp. 416–420 and later.

Doggett, Frank A., *Dipped in Sky.* A study of the Kentucky Mountain Cycle of Percy MacKaye. 1930.

Botkin, B. A., "Folk Speech in the Kentucky Mountain Cycle of Percy MacKaye." Reprint, from *American Speech;* April, 1931. Philadelphia, 1931.

Grover, Edwin Osgood (ed.). *Annals of An Era: Percy MacKaye and The MacKaye Family, 1826–1932.* 1932.

MALTZ, ALBERT

Merry-Go-Round. With George Sklar. (MS. only from French.) (Provincetown Playhouse, April 22, 1932)

Peace on Earth. With George Sklar. 1934. (Civic Repertory Theatre, Nov. 29, 1933)

Black Pit. (Civic Repertory Theatre, March 20, 1935)

* Private Hicks. In *New Theatre Magazine.* 1936. (Civic Repertory Theatre, Jan. 12, 1936)

MANSFIELD, RICHARD

Monsieur. (Madison Square Theatre, July 11, 1887)

Don Juan. 1891. (Garden Theatre, May 18, 1891)

The First Violin. (Meridan Phelps). With J. I. C. Clarke. Dram. of novel by Jessie Fothergill. (Hollis St. Theatre, Boston, April 18, 1898)

Biographical and Critical

Winter, William, *Life and Art of Richard Mansfield.* 2 Vols. 1910.

MATTHEWS, BRANDER

Margery's Lovers. MS. (Royal Court Theatre, London, Feb. 18, 1884; Madison Square Theatre, Jan. 11, 1887)

A Gold Mine. With George H. Jessop. c. 1908. (Cincinnati, 1887; Fifth Ave. Theatre, March 4, 1889)

The Silent System. Boston, 1889.

* This Picture and That. 1894. (Lyceum Theatre, April 15, 1887)

On Probation. With George Jessop. MS. (Decatur, Ill., Sept. 9, 1889; Star Theatre, Nov. 19, 1890)

BIBLIOGRAPHY AND PLAY LIST

* In the Vestibule Limited. c. 1892.
* The Decision of the Court. 1893. (Hermann's Theatre, March 23, 1893)
Peter Stuyvesant. With Bronson Howard, q.v.
Cuttyback's Thunder. Boston, 1902. Adap. of Le Serment d'Horace, by Henri Murger.
* Too Much Smith. Boston, 1902.

Biographical and Critical

Matthews, Brander, *These Many Years: Recollections of a New Yorker.* 1917.
Matthews, Brander, *Comedies for Amateur Acting.* 1880.
For Brander Matthews' Critical Works, see General Bibliography.

MAYER, EDWIN JUSTUS
The Firebrand. 1924. (Morosco Theatre, Oct. 15, 1924)
Children of Darkness. 1929. (Biltmore Theatre, Jan. 7, 1930)

MAYO, FRANK
Pudd'nhead Wilson. Dram. of story by Mark Twain. MS. (Herald Square Theatre, April 15, 1895)

McCABE, JAMES D., Jr.
The Guerillas. Richmond, 1863. (Richmond Varieties, Dec. 22, 1862)

McEVOY, J. P.
The Potters. Chicago, 1924. (Plymouth Theatre, Dec. 25, 1923)
Americana. (Belmont Theatre, July 26, 1926)
God Loves Us. (Maxine Elliott Theatre, Oct. 19, 1926)

McGROARTY, JOHN STEVEN
The Mission Play. (Mission Theatre, San Gabriel, Calif., April 29, 1912)

McGUIRE, WILLIAM ANTHONY
Six Cylinder Love. (Harris Theatre, Aug. 25, 1921)
Twelve Miles Out. (The Playhouse, Nov. 16, 1925)
If I Was Rich. (Eltinge Theatre, Sept. 3, 1926; earlier on road as A Great Little Guy)

A HISTORY OF THE AMERICAN DRAMA

McINTYRE, JOHN T.

STEVE. (Harris Theatre, Sept. 28, 1912)

A YOUNG MAN'S FANCY. (Playhouse, Oct. 15, 1919)

GENIUS AND THE CROWD. With Francis Hill. (Cohan Theatre, Sept. 6, 1920)

McLELLAN, C. M. S.

LEAH KLESCHNA. c. 1920. (Manhattan Theatre, Dec. 12, 1904)

JUDITH ZARAINE. (Astor Theatre, Jan. 16, 1911)

* THE FOUNTAIN. (Princess Theatre, Jan. 31, 1914)

MIDDLETON, GEORGE

* EMBERS [and other one-act plays]. 1911.

* TRADITION [and other one-act plays]. 1913.

* POSSESSION [and other one-act plays]. 1915.

NOWADAYS. 1914.

POLLY WITH A PAST. With Guy Bolton. 1923. (Atlantic City, N. J., June 11, 1917; Belasco Theatre, Sept. 6, 1917)

THE CAVE GIRL. With Guy Bolton. 1925. (Atlantic City, N. J., April 7, 1919)

ADAM AND EVA. With Guy Bolton. 1923. (Longacre Theatre, Sept. 13, 1919)

THE OTHER ROSE. Adap. from French of Edouard Bourdet. (Morosco Theatre, Dec. 20, 1923)

THE ROAD TOGETHER. 1916. (Frazee Theatre, Jan. 17, 1924)

* MASKS [and other one-act plays]. 1920.

BLOOD MONEY. From story by H. H. Van Loon. 1927. (Hudson Theatre, Aug. 22, 1927)

THE BIG POND. With A. E. Thomas. 1930. (Bijou Theatre, Aug. 22, 1928)

HISS! BOOM!! BLAH!!! 1933.

MILLAY, EDNA ST. VINCENT

* THE PRINCESS MARRIES THE PAGE. 1932. (Provincetown Theatre, 1918)

* ARIA DA CAPO. 1921. (Provincetown Theatre, Dec. 1919)

THE LAMP AND THE BELL. 1921.

LAUNZI. Adap. of LAUNZI by Ferenc Molnar. (Plymouth Theatre, Oct. 10, 1923)

THE KING'S HENCHMAN. 1927. Opera, with music by Deems Taylor. (Metropolitan Opera House, Feb. 17, 1927)

BIBLIOGRAPHY AND PLAY LIST

MILLER, JOAQUIN

THE DANITES IN THE SIERRAS. San Francisco, 1882. (Broadway Theatre, Aug. 22, 1877)

FORTY-NINE. San Francisco, 1882. (Haverley's Theatre, Oct. 1, 1881)

AN OREGON IDYLL. In *Poems,* Vol. VI, San Francisco, 1910.

TALLY HO! In *Poems,* Vol. VI, San Francisco, 1910.

MITCHELL, LANGDON ELWYN

SYLVIAN. In *Sylvian and Other Poems.* 1885.

BECKY SHARP. Dram. Thackeray's VANITY FAIR. A.L.P. 1941. (Fifth Ave. Theatre, Sept. 12, 1899)

THE ADVENTURES OF FRANÇOIS. Dram. novel by S. Weir Mitchell. (Park Theatre, Phila., Oct. 20, 1900)

THE KREUTZER SONATA. Adap. from Yiddish of Jacob Gordin. (Lyric Theatre, Sept. 10, 1906)

THE NEW YORK IDEA. Boston, 1908. (Lyric Theatre, Nov. 19, 1906; Kammerspiel Theater, Berlin, Oct. 7, 1916)

THE NEW MARRIAGE. MS. (Empire Theatre, Syracuse, Oct. 19, 1911)

MAJOR PENDENNIS. Dram. Thackeray's novel. (Atlantic City, N. J., Oct. 11, 1916; Criterion Theatre, Oct. 26, 1916)

Biographical and Critical

Archer, William, Criticism of THE NEW YORK IDEA. *London Tribune,* May 27, 1907.

Winter, William, *The Wallet of Time.* 1913. II, 273–286. [Becky Sharp]

MOELLER, PHILIP

HELENA'S HUSBAND. 1915. (Bandbox Theatre, Oct. 4, 1915)

* TWO BLIND BEGGARS AND ONE LESS BLIND. 1918. (Bandbox Theatre, 1915)

MADAME SAND. 1920. (Academy of Music, Baltimore, Oct. 29, 1917; Criterion Theatre, Nov. 19, 1917)

Five Somewhat Historical Plays. 1918. Contains: HELENA'S HUSBAND; THE LITTLE SUPPER; SISTERS OF SUSANNAH; THE ROADHOUSE IN ARDEN; POKEY; OR, THE BEAUTIFUL LEGEND OF THE AMOROUS INDIAN.

A HISTORY OF THE AMERICAN DRAMA

Molière. 1919. (Ford's Theatre, Baltimore, Feb. 24, 1919; Liberty Theatre, March 17, 1919)

Sophie. 1919. (Greenwich Village Theatre, March 2, 1919)

Caprice. Adaptation from play by Sil-Vara. (Guild Theatre, Dec. 31, 1928)

Love Is Not So Simple. Adap. of play by Ladislas Fodor. (Chestnut St. Opera House, Phila., Nov., 1935)

MOODY, WILLIAM VAUGHN

Collected Edition: *Poems and Plays.* 2 Vols. Boston, 1912. Intro. by John M. Manly.

Vol. I: The Fire Bringer; The Masque of Judgment; The Death of Eve.

Vol. II: The Great Divide; The Faith Healer.

The Masque of Judgment. Boston, 1900.

The Fire Bringer. Boston, 1904.

The Great Divide. 1909. (Garrick Theatre, Chicago, April 12, 1906, as A Sabine Woman; Princess Theatre, Oct. 3, 1906; Adelphi Theatre, London, Sept. 15, 1909)

The Faith Healer. Boston, 1909; 1910 (revised). (Century Theatre, St. Louis, March 15, 1909; Savoy Theatre, Jan. 19, 1910)

The Death of Eve. In *Poems and Plays,* Vol. I.

Biographical and Critical

Barr, Nash O., "The Lyrist and Lyric Dramatist." *The Drama,* No. 2. (May, 1911), 177–206.

Caffin, C. H., "The Playwright." *The Drama,* No. 2 (May, 1911), 206–211.

Henry, David D., *William Vaughn Moody: A Study.* Boston, 1934.

Lovett, Robert M., Int. to *Selected Poems of William Vaughn Moody.* Boston, 1931.

MacKaye, Percy, ed., *Letters to Harriet.* Boston, 1935.

Mason, Daniel Gregory, *Some Letters of William Vaughn Moody.* Boston, 1913.

Sinclair, May, "Three American Poets of To-Day." *Atlantic Monthly,* XCVIII (1906), 326–335.

382

BIBLIOGRAPHY AND PLAY LIST

Wolf, Rennold, in *N. Y. Telegraph,* Jan. 20, 1910. [Faith Healer]

MURDOCH, FRANK HITCHCOCK

LIGHT HOUSE CLIFFS. MS. (California, 1870)?

DAVY CROCKETT. A.L.P. (Rochester, N. Y., Sept. 23, 1872; Wood's Museum, June 2, 1873)

BOHEMIA; OR, THE LOTTERY OF ART. (Arch St. Theatre, Phila., Oct. 28, 1872)

ONLY A JEW. (Globe Theatre, Boston, Feb. 24, 1873)

NICHOLS, ANNE

THE GILDED CAGE. (Morosco Theatre, Los Angeles, Calif., Dec. 12, 1920)

JUST MARRIED. With Adelaide Mathews. (Comedy Theatre, April 26, 1921)

ABIE'S IRISH ROSE. (Morosco Theatre, Los Angeles, Calif., March 5, 1922; Fulton Theatre, May 23, 1922; London, April 11, 1927)

Biographical and Critical

Nichols, Anne, "The Story of Abie's Irish Rose." *Theatre,* XL, (July, 1924), 19, 54.

NICHOLSON, KENYON

LOVE IS LIKE THAT. With Behrman, Samuel Nathaniel, q.v.

SALLY AND COMPANY. 1925.

THE BARKER. 1927. (Biltmore Theatre, Jan. 18, 1927)

HERE'S TO YOUR HEALTH. 1927.

EVA THE FIFTH. With John Golden. 1928. (Little Theatre, Aug. 28, 1928)

BEFORE YOU'RE 25. (Maxine Elliott Theatre, Apr. 16, 1929)

TORCH SONG. 1930. (Plymouth Theatre, Aug. 27, 1930)

SAILOR BEWARE. With Charles Robinson. 1933. (Lyceum Theatre, Sept. 28, 1933)

ODETS, CLIFFORD

AWAKE AND SING. 1935. (Belasco Theatre, Feb. 19, 1935)

WAITING FOR LEFTY and UNTIL THE DAY I DIE. In volume with AWAKE AND SING. 1935. (Longacre Theatre, March 26, 1935)

PARADISE LOST. 1936. (Longacre Theatre, Dec. 9, 1935)

A HISTORY OF THE AMERICAN DRAMA

O'HIGGINS, HARVEY

THE ARGYLE CASE. With Harriet Ford, q.v.

POLYGAMY. With Harriet Ford, q.v.

MR. LAZARUS. With Harriet Ford. c. 1926. (Shubert Theatre, Sept. 5, 1916)

O'NEILL, EUGENE GLADSTONE

The Complete Works of Eugene O'Neill. 2 Vols. 1924.

Vol. I: ANNA CHRISTIE, BEYOND THE HORIZON, THE FIRST MAN, DIFF'RENT, GOLD, THE MOON OF THE CARIBBEES, BOUND EAST FOR CARDIFF, THE LONG VOYAGE HOME, IN THE ZONE, and ILE.

Vol. II: THE EMPEROR JONES, THE HAIRY APE, ALL GOD'S CHILLUN GOT WINGS, DESIRE UNDER THE ELMS, WELDED, THE STRAW, THE ROPE, THE DREAMY KID, WHERE THE CROSS IS MADE, and BEFORE BREAKFAST.

The Plays of Eugene O'Neill. Wilderness Edition. 12 Vols. 1934.

* BOUND EAST FOR CARDIFF. In Provincetown Plays, First Series, 1916. (Wharf Theatre, Provincetown, Mass., Summer, 1916; also London, Liverpool, etc.)

* THIRST. Boston, 1914. (Wharf Theatre, Provincetown, Mass., Summer, 1916)

* THE WEB. In Thirst and Other Plays. Boston, 1914.

* WARNINGS. In Thirst and Other Plays. Boston, 1914.

* RECKLESSNESS. In Thirst and Other Plays. Boston, 1914.

* BEFORE BREAKFAST. In Provincetown Plays, Third Series, 1916. (Playwrights' Theatre, Dec. 1, 1916)

* FOG. In Thirst and Other Plays. Boston, 1914. (Playwrights' Theatre, Jan., 1917)

* THE SNIPER. MS. (Playwrights' Theatre, Feb. 16, 1917)

* IN THE ZONE. In The Moon of the Caribbees and Six Other Plays of the Sea. 1919. (Comedy Theatre, Oct. 31, 1917; Everyman Theatre, London, June 15, 1921; also Prague, 1924–25)

* THE LONG VOYAGE HOME. In The Smart Set, LIII (Oct., 1917), 83–94. (Playwrights' Theatre, Nov. 2, 1917; also London, Liverpool)

* ILE. In The Smart Set, LV (May, 1918), 89–100. (Play-

wrights' Theatre, Nov. 30, 1917; also Everyman Theatre, London, April 17, 1922; Rome, etc.)

* THE ROPE. In *The Moon of the Caribbees and Six Other Plays of the Sea.* 1919. (Playwrights' Theatre, April 26, 1918)

* WHERE THE CROSS IS MADE. In *The Moon of the Caribbees and Six Other Plays of the Sea.* 1919. (Playwrights' Theatre, Nov. 22, 1918)

* THE MOON OF THE CARIBBEES. In *The Smart Set,* LV (Aug., 1918), 73–86. Rep. in *The Moon of the Caribbees and Six Other Plays of the Sea.* 1919. (Playwrights' Theatre, Dec. 20, 1918; Volksbühne, Berlin, 1924; also Kiel, Hamburg)

* THE DREAMY KID. In *Theatre Arts Magazine,* IV (Jan., 1920), 41–56. (Playwrights' Theatre, Oct. 31, 1919)

BEYOND THE HORIZON. 1920. (Morosco Theatre, Feb. 2, 1920; Repertory Theatre, London, 1926; also Tokio, Japan)

CHRIS CHRISTOPHERSON. (Atlantic City, N. J., March 8, 1920)

* EXORCISM. (Playwrights' Theatre, March 26, 1920)

THE EMPEROR JONES. *Theatre Arts Magazine,* V (Jan., 1921), 29–59. Rep. in *The Emperor Jones, Diff'rent, The Straw.* 1921. (Playwrights' Theatre, Nov. 1, 1920; also London; Odéon, Paris, Oct. 30, 1923; Berlin, 1924; Prague, 1924–25; Tokio; Italy; Dublin, Jan. 1927)

DIFF'RENT. In *The Emperor Jones, Diff'rent, The Straw.* 1921. (Playwrights' Theatre, Dec. 27, 1920; Everyman Theatre, London, Oct. 4, 1921; also Dublin; Rotterdam)

GOLD. 1920. (Frazee Theatre, June 1, 1921)

ANNA CHRISTIE. In *The Hairy Ape, Anna Christie, The First Man,* 1922. (Vanderbilt Theatre, Nov. 2, 1921; Strand Theatre, London, April 10, 1923; Deutsches Theater, Berlin, Oct. 10, 1923; Sweden, Norway, Denmark, 1923; Barcelona, Vienna, Moscow, 1924; also a tour in Italy; coast cities in Orient)

THE STRAW. In *Emperor Jones, Diff'rent, The Straw.* 1921. (Greenwich Village Theatre, Nov. 10, 1921)

THE FIRST MAN. In *The Hairy Ape, Anna Christie, The First Man.* 1922. (Neighborhood Playhouse, March 4, 1922)

THE HAIRY APE. In *The Hairy Ape, Anna Christie, The First Man.* 1922. (Playwrights' Theatre, March 9, 1922;

Freie Bühne, Berlin, Nov. 1, 1924; Kamerny Theatre, Moscow, 1924; Prague; Melbourne; Italy; London)

WELDED. In *Complete Works,* Vol. II. 1924. (Thirty-ninth St. Theatre, March 17, 1924)

THE ANCIENT MARINER. Dram. of poem by Coleridge. (Provincetown Playhouse, April 6, 1924)

ALL GOD'S CHILLUN GOT WINGS. In *American Mercury,* I (Feb., 1924), 129–148. (Provincetown Playhouse, May 15, 1924)

DESIRE UNDER THE ELMS. In *Complete Works.* Vol. II. 1924. (Greenwich Village Theatre, Nov. 11, 1924; Stavovske Theatre, Prague, Oct. 4, 1925; Berlin)

THE FOUNTAIN. In *The Great God Brown, The Fountain,* etc., 1926. (Greenwich Village Theatre, Dec. 10, 1925)

THE GREAT GOD BROWN. In *The Great God Brown, The Fountain,* etc., 1926. (Greenwich Village Theatre, Jan. 23, 1926)

MARCO MILLIONS. 1927. (Guild Theatre, Jan. 9, 1928)

LAZARUS LAUGHED. 1927. (Community Playhouse, Pasadena, California, April 9, 1928)

STRANGE INTERLUDE. 1928. (John Golden Theatre, Jan. 30, 1928)

DYNAMO. 1929. (Martin Beck, Feb. 11, 1929)

MOURNING BECOMES ELECTRA. 1931. (Guild Theatre, Oct. 26, 1931)

AH WILDERNESS! 1933. (Guild Theatre, Oct. 2, 1933)

DAYS WITHOUT END. 1933. (Henry Miller Theatre, Jan. 8, 1934)

Biographical and Critical

O'Neill, Eugene, "Strindberg and Our Theatre." *Program of the Provincetown Theatre,* No. 1, 1923–24.

O'Neill, Eugene, "Memoranda on Masks." *American Spectator,* Nov., 1932.

O'Neill, Eugene, "Second Thoughts." *American Spectator,* Dec., 1932.

Anonymous, "O'Neill's Plays Abroad." *Program of the Greenwich Village Theatre,* Season 1924–26.

Bone, David W., "The Sea Across the Footlights." *New York Times Book Review,* Jan. 15, 1922.

BIBLIOGRAPHY AND PLAY LIST

Brie, Friedrich, "Eugene O'Neill als Nachfolger der Griechen (Mourning Becomes Electra)." *Germanisch-Romanischen Monatsschrift*, XXI, 46–49. (Jan.–Feb., 1933)

Clark, Barrett H., *Eugene O'Neill*. 1926. Revised 1933. [Indispensable. Bibliography and Lists of Plays to 1933]

Clark, Barrett H., and Sanborn, Ralph, *A Bibliography of the Works of Eugene O'Neill*. 1931.

Clark, Barrett H., "Aeschylus and O'Neill." *English Journal*, XXI (Nov., 1932), 699–710.

Eaton, Walter Prichard, "Eugene O'Neill as a Dramatist." *Theatre Arts Magazine*, IV (Oct., 1920), 286–289.

Hamilton, Clayton, *Conversations on Contemporary Drama*. 1924, pp. 198–218.

Hayes, J. J., "An Irish Emperor Jones." *New York Times*, Feb. 12, 1927.

Quinn, A. H., "Eugene O'Neill, Poet and Mystic," *Scribner's Magazine*, LXXX (Oct., 1926), 368–372.

Sayler, Oliver M., *Our American Theatre*, 1923, pp. 27–43.

Skinner, Richard D., *Eugene O'Neill: A Poet's Quest*. 1935.

Woollcott, Alexander, *Shouts and Murmurs*, 1922, pp. 144–170.

O'NEIL, GEORGE

AMERICAN DREAM. 1933. (Guild Theatre, Feb. 20, 1933)

MOTHER LODE. With Dan Totheroh; q.v.

PARKER, LOTTIE BLAIR

WAY DOWN EAST. Priv. printed, 1899. (Manhattan Theatre, Jan. 19, 1898)

PATTERSON, J. MEDILL

THE FOURTH ESTATE. MS. (Wallack's Theatre, Oct. 8, 1909)

A LITTLE BROTHER TO THE RICH. With Harriet Ford. Dram. of novel by Patterson. (Wallack's Theatre, Dec. 27, 1909)

REBELLION. MS. (Maxine Elliott Theatre, Oct. 3, 1911)

PEABODY, JOSEPHINE PRESTON (Mrs. Lionel Marks)

FORTUNE AND MEN'S EYES. Boston, 1900.

MARLOWE. Boston, 1901. (Radcliffe College, 1905)

THE WINGS. In *Harper's Magazine*, CX (May, 1905), 947–956. Rep. c. 1917. (Toy Theatre, Boston, Jan. 15, 1912)

THE PIPER. Boston, 1910. (Stratford Memorial Theatre, England, July 26, 1910; New Theatre, Jan. 30, 1911)

THE WOLF OF GUBBIO. Boston, 1913.

A HISTORY OF THE AMERICAN DRAMA

The Chameleon. c. 1917.
The Portrait of Mrs. W—. Boston, 1922.

Biographical and Critical

Baker, Christina Hopkinson. Ed., *Diary and Letters of Josephine Preston Peabody.* Boston, 1925.

POLLOCK, CHANNING

The Fool. 1923. (Times Square Theatre, Oct. 23, 1922)

The Enemy. 1925. (Shubert Theatre, New Haven, Conn., June 1, 1925)

Mr. Moneypenny. 1928. (Garrick Theatre, Phila., Sept. 24, 1928)

The House Beautiful. 1931. (Apollo Theatre, March 12, 1931)

Stranglehold. 1934. (Detroit Civic Theatre, Feb. 1, 1932)

RAPHAELSON, SAMSON

The Jazz Singer. 1925. (Century Theatre, April 18, 1927)

Young Love. 1928. (Masque Theatre, Oct. 30, 1928)

The Wooden Slipper. 1934. (Ritz Theatre, Jan. 3, 1934)

Accent on Youth. 1935. (Plymouth Theatre, Dec. 25, 1934)

White Man. 1935. (In Volume with Accent on Youth)

RICE, ELMER E.

On Trial. c. 1919. (Candler Theatre, Aug. 19, 1914)

For the Defence. (Playhouse, Dec. 19, 1919)

Wake up, Jonathan! With Hatcher Hughes, q.v.

The Adding Machine. 1923. (Garrick Theatre, March 19, 1923)

Close Harmony. With Dorothy Parker. 1924 and 1929. (Gaiety Theatre, Dec. 1, 1924)

Cock Robin. With Philip Barry. 1929. (Forty-eighth St. Theatre, Jan. 12, 1928)

The Subway. 1929. (Cherry Lane Theatre, Jan. 25, 1929)

Street Scene. 1929. (Playhouse Theatre, Jan. 10, 1929)

See Naples and Die. 1930. (Vanderbilt Theatre, Sept. 24, 1929)

The Left Bank. 1931. (Little Theatre, Oct. 5, 1931)

Counsellor-at-Law. 1931. (Plymouth Theatre, Nov. 6, 1931)

BIBLIOGRAPHY AND PLAY LIST

THE HOUSE IN BLIND ALLEY. 1932.

BLACK SHEEP. 1938. (Morosco Theatre, Oct. 13, 1932)

WE THE PEOPLE. 1933. (Empire Theatre, Jan. 21, 1933)

JUDGMENT DAY. 1934. (Belasco Theatre, Sept. 12, 1934)

BETWEEN TWO WORLDS. In *Two Plays,* 1935. (Belasco Theatre, Oct. 25, 1934)

NOT FOR CHILDREN. In *Two Plays.* 1935. (London Stage Society, at Fortune Theatre, Nov. 25, 1935; Pasadena Playhouse, Feb. 25, 1936)

RICHMAN, ARTHUR

NOT SO LONG AGO. c. 1924. (Globe Theatre, Atlantic City, N. J., Feb. 29, 1920; Booth Theatre, May 4, 1920)

AMBUSH. 1922. (Garrick Theatre, Oct. 10, 1921)

A SERPENT'S TOOTH. (Asbury Park, N. J., July 31, 1922)

THE AWFUL TRUTH. c. 1930. (Henry Miller's Theatre, Sept. 18, 1922)

A PROUD WOMAN. (Maxine Elliott's Theatre, Nov. 14, 1926)

HEAVY TRAFFIC. (Henry Miller's Theatre, Sept. 5, 1928)

RIGGS, LYNN

BIG LAKE. 1927. (American Laboratory Theatre, April 8, 1927)

RANCOR. (Hedgerow Theatre, Rose Valley, Pa., 1927)

THE DOMINO PARLOR. (Tryout in Newark, N. J., Spring of 1928)

KNIVES FROM SYRIA. 1928.

A LANTERN TO SEE BY. 1928. In *Two Oklahoma Plays.*

SUMP'N LIKE WINGS. 1928. In *Two Oklahoma Plays.*

ROADSIDE. 1930. (Longacre Theatre, Sept. 26, 1930)

THE CHEROKEE NIGHT. 1936. In Vol. with Russet Mantle. (Hedgerow Theatre, Pa., 1930)

GREEN GROW THE LILACS. 1931. (Garrick Theatre, Phila., Dec. 29, 1930; Guild Theatre, Jan. 26, 1931)

RUSSET MANTLE. 1936. (Masque Theatre, Jan. 16, 1936)

RILEY, LAWRENCE

PERSONAL APPEARANCE. 1935. (Henry Miller Theatre, Oct. 17, 1934)

ROBINSON, EDWIN ARLINGTON

VAN ZORN. 1914. (Brooklyn Y.M.C.A., Feb. 26, 1917)

THE PORCUPINE. 1915.

ROBSON, ELEANOR

IN THE NEXT ROOM. With Harriet Ford. Dram. of story by
B. E. Stevenson. c. 1925. (Vanderbilt Theatre, Nov. 27,
1923)

ROYLE, EDWIN MILTON

FRIENDS. MS. (Standard Theatre, May 9, 1892)

CAPTAIN IMPUDENCE. (American Theatre, Jan. 4, 1897; first
produced as MEXICO, Euclid Ave. Opera House, Cleveland,
Ohio, Aug. 26, 1895)

1 + 1 = 3; OR, THE SINS OF THE FATHERS. (Garrick Theatre,
March 1, 1897)

MY WIFE'S HUSBANDS. (Madison Square Theatre, Aug. 24,
1903)

THE SQUAW MAN. MS. (Star Theatre, Buffalo, April 24, 1905;
Wallack's Theatre, Oct. 23, 1905; Lyric Theatre, London,
Jan. 11, 1908 as THE WHITE MAN)

MARRYING MARY. Musical version of MY WIFE'S HUSBANDS.
(Daly's Theatre, Sept. 3, 1906)

CLEO. (Park Theatre, Boston, April 22, 1907)

THE STRUGGLE EVERLASTING. MS. (Opera House, Providence,
R. I., Sept. 23, 1907; Hackett Theatre, Sept. 26, 1907)

THE UNWRITTEN LAW. MS. (Fulton Theatre, Feb. 7, 1913)

AFTERMATH. (Atlantic City, N. J., March 22, 1920)

LAUNCELOT AND ELAINE. MS. (Greenwich Village Theatre,
Sept. 14, 1921)

THE CONQUEROR. (Union Square Theatre, June 18, 1923)

HER WAY OUT. (Gaiety Theatre, June 23, 1924)

SABINE, LILLIAN

THE RISE OF SILAS LAPHAM. Dram. of novel by W. D. Howells.
(Garrick Theatre, Nov. 25, 1919)

SHELDON, EDWARD

SALVATION NELL. MS. (Opera House, Providence, R. I., Nov.
12, 1908; Hackett Theatre, Nov. 17, 1908)

THE NIGGER. 1910. (New Theatre, Dec. 4, 1909)

THE BOSS. In Quinn's *Representative American Plays*. (Garrick Theatre, Detroit, Mich., Jan. 9, 1911; Astor Theatre,
Jan. 30, 1911)

PRINCESS ZIM-ZIM. MS. (Harmanus Bleecker Hall, Albany,
Dec. 4, 1911)

BIBLIOGRAPHY AND PLAY LIST

EGYPT. Priv. printed, 1912. (The Playhouse, Hudson, N. Y., Sept. 18, 1912)

THE HIGH ROAD. Priv. printed, 1912. (His Majesty's Theatre, Montreal, Oct. 14, 1912; Hudson Theatre, Nov. 19, 1912)

ROMANCE. 1914. (Harmanus Bleecker Hall, Albany, Feb. 6, 1913; Maxine Elliott Theatre, Feb. 10, 1913; Devonshire Park Theatre, Eastbourne, Sept. 30, 1915)

THE SONG OF SONGS. Priv. printed, 1914. Dram. of Hermann Sudermann's DAS HOHE LIED. (Atlantic City, N. J., Oct. 29, 1914; Eltinge Theatre, Dec. 22, 1914)

THE GARDEN OF PARADISE. 1915. (Park Theatre, Nov. 28, 1914)

ALICE IN WONDERLAND. MS., dated 1916.

THE LONELY HEART. MS. (Baltimore, Oct. 24, 1921)

BEWITCHED. With Sidney Howard. MS. (Allentown, Pa., Sept. 26, 1924)

LULU BELLE. With Charles MacArthur. (Broad St. Theatre, Phila., Jan. 26, 1926)

MY PRINCESS. Operetta based on play by Sheldon and Dorothy Donnelly, adapted by D. Donnelly. (Shubert Theatre, Oct. 6, 1927)

JENNY. With Margaret Ayer Barnes. (Booth Theatre, Oct. 8, 1929)

DISHONORED LADY. With Margaret Ayer Barnes. (Empire Theatre, Feb. 4, 1930)

SHERWOOD, ROBERT

THE ROAD TO ROME. 1927. (Playhouse Theatre, Jan. 31, 1927)

THE LOVE NEST. Based on story by Ring Lardner. (Comedy Theatre, Dec. 22, 1927)

THE QUEEN'S HUSBAND. 1928. (Playhouse Theatre, Jan. 25, 1928)

WATERLOO BRIDGE. 1930. (Fulton Theatre, Jan. 6, 1930)

THIS IS NEW YORK. 1931. (Providence Opera House, R. I., Nov. 17, 1930; Plymouth Theatre, Nov. 28, 1930)

REUNION IN VIENNA. 1932. (Martin Beck Theatre, Nov. 16, 1931)

THE PETRIFIED FOREST. 1935. (Broadhurst Theatre, Jan. 7, 1935)

A HISTORY OF THE AMERICAN DRAMA

SKLAR, GEORGE

MERRY-GO-ROUND. With Albert Maltz, q.v.

PEACE ON EARTH. With Albert Maltz, q.v.

STEVEDORE. With Paul Peters. 1934. (Civic Repertory Theatre, Apr. 18, 1934)

PARADE. With Paul Peters, and others. (Guild Theatre, May 20, 1935)

SMITH, WINCHELL

BREWSTER'S MILLIONS. With Byron Ongley. Dram. of novel by George Barr McCutcheon. c. 1925. (New Amsterdam Theatre, Dec. 31, 1906)

THE FORTUNE HUNTER. c. 1909. (Gaiety Theatre, Sept. 4, 1909)

THE ONLY SON. MS. (Gaiety Theatre, Oct. 16, 1911)

THE BOOMERANG. With Victor Mapes. c. 1915. (Playhouse, Wilmington, Del., April 5, 1915; Belasco Theatre, Aug. 10, 1915)

TURN TO THE RIGHT. With John E. Hazzard. c. 1916. (Gaiety Theatre, Aug. 18, 1916)

LIGHTNIN'. With Frank Bacon. c. 1918. (Gaiety Theatre, Aug. 26, 1918)

THANK YOU. With Tom Cushing. c. 1922. (Longacre Theatre, Oct. 3, 1921)

STALLINGS, LAURENCE

WHAT PRICE GLORY. With Maxwell Anderson, q.v.

FIRST FLIGHT. With Maxwell Anderson, q.v.

THE BUCCANEER. With Maxwell Anderson, q.v.

DEEP RIVER. (Shubert Theatre, Phila., Sept. 21, 1926)

RAINBOW. (Gallo Theatre, Nov. 21, 1928)

STEELE, WILBUR DANIEL

POST ROAD. With Norma Mitchell. 1933. (Masque Theatre, Dec. 4, 1934)

STEVENSON, CHRISTINE WETHERILL

THE PILGRIMAGE PLAY. (Pilgrimage Theatre, Hollywood, Calif., June 28, 1920)   .

STODDARD, LORIMER

NAPOLEON BONAPARTE. MS. (Herald Square Theatre, Oct. 27, 1894)

IN THE PALACE OF THE KING. With F. Marion Crawford, q.v.

BIBLIOGRAPHY AND PLAY LIST

STRONG, AUSTIN

BUNNY. (Hudson Theatre, Jan. 4, 1916)

THREE WISE FOOLS. Ottawa, 1919. (Criterion Theatre, Oct. 31, 1918)

SEVENTH HEAVEN. c. 1922. (Booth Theatre, Oct. 30, 1922, as HEAVEN; Garrick Theatre, Detroit, Mich., June 7, 1920)

The Drums of Oude—And Other One Act Plays. 1926.

A PLAY WITHOUT A NAME. (Booth Theatre, Nov. 26, 1928)

SULLIVAN, THOMAS RUSSELL

DR. JEKYLL AND MR. HYDE. Dram. of novel by R. L. Stevenson. (Boston Museum, May 9, 1887)

NERO. (Garden Theatre, Sept. 21, 1891)

TARKINGTON, NEWTON BOOTH

MONSIEUR BEAUCAIRE. With E. G. Sutherland. Dram. of MONSIEUR BEAUCAIRE, by Tarkington. In Pence's *Dramas by Present-Day Writers.* c. 1927. (Garrick Theatre, Phila., Oct. 7, 1901; Herald Square Theatre, Dec. 2, 1901)

THE MAN FROM HOME. With Harry Leon Wilson. 1908. (Studebaker Theatre, Chicago, Sept. 29, 1907; Astor Theatre, Aug. 17, 1908)

YOUR HUMBLE SERVANT. With Harry Leon Wilson. (Lyceum Theatre, Rochester, N. Y., Oct. 8, 1909; Garrick Theatre, Jan. 3, 1910)

CAMEO KIRBY. (Hackett Theatre, Dec. 20, 1909)

GETTING A POLISH. With H. L. Wilson. (Wallack's Theatre, Nov. 7, 1910)

* BEAUTY AND THE JACOBIN. 1912. (Comedy Theatre, Nov. 29, 1912)

THE OHIO LADY. Priv. printed, 1916. (Hartman Theatre, Columbus, O., Jan. 24, 1916) Rev. as THE COUNTRY COUSIN.

MR. ANTONIO. (Star Theatre, Buffalo, Sept. 11, 1916; Lyceum Theatre, Sept. 18, 1916)

THE COUNTRY COUSIN. With Julian Street. c. 1921. (Broad St. Theatre, Phila., April 23, 1917) See THE OHIO LADY.

THE GIBSON UPRIGHT. With H. L. Wilson. Garden City. 1919.

CLARENCE. c. 1921. (Apollo Theatre, Atlantic City, N. J., July 7, 1919; Hudson Theatre, Sept. 20, 1919)

UP FROM NOWHERE. With H. L. Wilson. (Comedy Theatre, Sept. 8, 1919)

A HISTORY OF THE AMERICAN DRAMA

Poldekin. (New Haven, Feb. 23, 1920; Park Theatre, Sept. 9, 1920)

The Wren. c. 1922. (Gaiety Theatre, Oct. 10, 1921)

The Intimate Strangers. c. 1921. (Henry Miller Theatre, Nov. 7, 1921)

Rose Briar. (Empire Theatre, Dec. 25, 1922)

Tweedles. With H. L. Wilson. 1924. (Frazee Theatre, Aug. 13, 1923)

Magnolia. (Liberty Theatre, Aug. 27, 1923)

Bimbo the Pirate. 1926.

How's Your Health. With H. L. Wilson. 1930. (Vanderbilt Theatre, Nov. 26, 1929)

Colonel Satan. MS. (Fulton Theatre, Jan. 10, 1931)

Biographical and Critical

Currie, Barton. *Booth Tarkington, A Bibliography.* 1932.

Dickinson, Asa Don, *Booth Tarkington, A Sketch.* Garden City, 1926.

Winter, William, *Life and Art of Richard Mansfield,* II, 149–154. [Beaucaire]

THOMAS, ALBERT ELLSWORTH

Her Husband's Wife. 1914. (Broad St. Theatre, Phila., Feb. 14, 1910; Garrick Theatre, April 9, 1910; New Theatre, London, Sept. 5, 1916)

Thirty Days. With Clayton Hamilton. 1923. (Cort Theatre, Chicago, March 9, 1910)

What the Doctor Ordered. (Astor Theatre, Sept. 20, 1911)

Little Boy Blue. Adap. of Lord Piccolo by Rudolph Schanzer and Carl Lindau. (Fulton Opera House, Lancaster, Pa., Nov. 9, 1911)

The Rainbow. c. 1919. (Liberty Theatre, March 11, 1912)

The Big Idea. With Clayton Hamilton. c. 1917. (Globe Theatre, Nov. 16, 1914; first, as Wanted $22,000, Apollo Theatre, Atlantic City, N. J., June 22, 1914)

Come Out of the Kitchen. Dram. of novel by Alice Duer Miller. c. 1921. (Columbia Theatre, San Francisco, Aug. 14, 1916; Cohan Theatre, Oct. 23, 1916)

The Better Understanding. With Clayton Hamilton. Boston, 1924. (Columbia Theatre, San Francisco, May, 1917)

THE MATINEE HERO. (Vanderbilt Theatre, Oct. 7, 1918)

JUST SUPPOSE. c. 1923. (Academy, Baltimore, Md., May 17, 1920; Henry Miller Theatre, Nov. 1, 1920)

THE CHAMPION. With Thomas Louden. c. 1922. (Longacre Theatre, Jan. 3, 1921)

ONLY THIRTY-EIGHT. Dram. of short story by W. P. Eaton. c. 1922. (Cort Theatre, Sept. 13, 1921)

THE FRENCH DOLL. Adap. from French of Armont and Gerbiddon. (Lyceum Theatre, Feb. 20, 1922)

THE JOLLY ROGER. (National Theatre, Aug. 30, 1923)

SPINDRIFT. Adap. of LE DEMI-MONDE, by Alexander Dumas, fils. (Park Theatre, Boston, March 9, 1925)

LOST. With G. A. Chamberlain, from novel by him. (Mansfield Theatre, March 28, 1927)

THE BIG POND. With George Middleton. 1930. (Bijou Theaatre, Aug. 22, 1928)

VERMONT. (Erlanger's Theatre, Jan. 7, 1929)

HER FRIEND THE KING. With Harrison Rhodes. 1930. (Longacre Theatre, Oct. 7, 1929)

NO MORE LADIES. 1933. (Chestnut St. Opera House., Phila., Dec. 23, 1923; Booth Theatre, Jan. 23, 1934)

THOMAS, AUGUSTUS

ALONE. (Marion Place Dramatic Club, Moberly, Mo., 1875)

THE BIG RISE. (Pickwick Theatre, St. Louis, 1882)

* EDITHA'S BURGLAR. Dram. of story by Frances Hodgson Burnett. MS. (McCullough Dramatic Club, St. Louis, 1883; Lyceum Theatre, Sept. 19, 1887)

* A NEW YEAR'S CALL. (Pope's Theatre, St. Louis, 1883)

* A MAN OF THE WORLD. MS. (Pope's Theatre, St. Louis, 1883; Madison Square Theatre, Oct. 30, 1889)

* A LEAF FROM THE WOODS. (Pope's Theatre, St. Louis, 1883)

* A STUDIO PICTURE. (Pope's Theatre, St. Louis, 1883)

COMBUSTION. With Edgar Smith. (Opera House, Mexico, Mo., 1884)

THE BURGLAR. (Park Theatre, Boston, June 17, 1889; Madison Square Theatre, July 1, 1889)

* A WOMAN OF THE WORLD. (Star Theatre, Aug. 4, 1890)

RECKLESS TEMPLE. (Standard Theatre, Oct. 27, 1890)

* Afterthoughts. (Madison Square Theatre, Nov. 24, 1890)

Alabama. 1898. (Madison Square Theatre, April 1, 1891; Garrick Theatre, London, Sept. 2, 1895)

A Night's Frolic. From the German. (Union Square Theatre, June 10, 1891)

For Money. With Clay M. Greene. (Cleveland, O., Dec., 1891; Star Theatre, Jan. 12, 1892)

Colonel Carter of Cartersville. Dram. of novelette by F. Hopkinson Smith. (Palmer's Theatre, March 22, 1892)

* The Holly Tree Inn. (Union Square Theatre, April 11, 1892)

Surrender. MS. (Columbia Theatre, Boston, Nov. 21, 1892)

* A Proper Impropriety. (Union Square Theatre, 1893?)

In Mizzoura. c. 1916. (Hooley's Theatre, Chicago, Aug. 7, 1893; Fifth Ave. Theatre, Sept. 4, 1893)

New Blood. (McVicker's Theatre, Chicago, July 26, 1894; Palmer's [Broadway] Theatre, Sept. 19, 1894)

* The Music Box. (Lambs Club, 1894)

* The Man Upstairs. Washington, D. C., 1918. Rep. in *One Act Plays for Stage and Study,* 1924. (Hoyt's Theatre, April 9, 1895)

The Capitol. MS. (Standard Theatre, Sept. 9, 1895)

Chimmie Fadden. Dram. of story by E. W. Townsend. (Garden Theatre, Jan. 13, 1896)

The Jucklins. Dram. of story by Opie Read. (Broad St. Theatre, Phila., Dec. 13, 1897)

The Hoosier Doctor. MS. (New National Theatre, Washington, D. C., April 22, 1897; Fourteenth St. Theatre, April 18, 1898)

* That Overcoat. (Hoyt's Theatre, Jan. 7, 1898)

Don't Tell Her Husband. (Columbia Theatre, San Francisco, 1898)

The Meddler. (Wallack's Theatre, Sept. 1, 1898.) Earlier as Don't Tell Her Husband.

Colonel George of Mount Vernon. 1913. (Castle Square Theatre, Boston, Dec. 12, 1898)

The Bonnie Briar Bush. MS. Revision of James MacArthur's dram. of novel by Ian Maclaren. (1901)

Arizona. 1899. (Hamlin's Grand Opera House, Chicago, June

BIBLIOGRAPHY AND PLAY LIST

12, 1899; Herald Square, Sept. 10, 1900; Adelphi Theatre, London, Feb. 3, 1902)

OLIVER GOLDSMITH. c. 1916. (Empire Theatre, Albany, Nov. 30, 1899; Fifth Ave. Theatre, March 19, 1900)

ON THE QUIET. MS. (Madison Square Theatre, Feb. 11, 1901; Comedy Theatre, London, Sept. 27, 1905)

CHAMPAGNE CHARLEY. (Aug., 1901)

COLORADO. MS. (Wallack's Theatre, Nov. 18, 1901)

SOLDIERS OF FORTUNE. Adap. of play by R. H. Davis, based on novel. (Hyperion Theatre, New Haven, Conn., Feb. 17, 1902; Savoy Theatre, March 17, 1902)

THE EARL OF PAWTUCKET. c. 1917. (Madison Square Theatre, Feb. 5, 1903; Playhouse, London, June 25, 1907)

THE OTHER GIRL. c. 1917. (Criterion Theatre, Dec. 29, 1903)

MRS. LEFFINGWELL'S BOOTS. c. 1916. (Savoy Theatre, Jan. 11, 1905)

THE EDUCATION OF MR. PIPP. Dram. of pictures by C. D. Gibson. MS. (Liberty Theatre, Feb. 20, 1905)

DELANCEY. (Empire Theatre, Sept. 4, 1905)

THE EMBASSY BALL. (Hyperion Theatre, New Haven, Conn., Oct. 16, 1905; Daly's Theatre, March 5, 1906)

THE RANGER. (Wallack's Theatre, Sept. 2, 1907)

THE MEMBER FROM OZARK. (Opera House, Detroit, 1907)

THE WITCHING HOUR. c. 1916. (Providence, R. I., Nov. 16, 1907; Hackett Theatre, Nov. 18, 1907)

THE MATINEE IDOL. Adap. of Bernard's HIS LAST LEGS, as a musical comedy. (Daly's Theatre, April 28, 1909)

THE HARVEST MOON. c. 1922. (Garrick Theatre, Oct. 18, 1909)

AS A MAN THINKS. 1911. (Hyperion Theatre, New Haven, Conn., March 4, 1911; Thirty-ninth St. Theatre, March 13, 1911)

THE MODEL. (Illinois Theatre, Chicago, April 8, 1912, as WHEN IT COMES HOME; Harris Theatre, Aug. 31, 1912)

MERE MAN. MS. (Harris Theatre, Nov. 25, 1912)

AT BAY. With George Scarborough. (Thirty-ninth St. Theatre, Oct. 7, 1913)

INDIAN SUMMER. MS. (Buffalo, Sept. 29, 1913; Criterion Theatre, Oct. 27, 1913)

THREE OF HEARTS. (Thirty-ninth St. Theatre, 1913)

THE BATTLE CRY. Dram. of novel by Charles Neville Buck. (Lyric Theatre, Oct. 31, 1914)

THE NIGHTINGALE. (1914)

RIO GRANDE. (Lyric Theatre, Allentown, Pa., Feb. 26, 1916; Empire Theatre, April 4, 1916)

THE COPPERHEAD. In Cohen's *Longer Plays by Modern Authors.* Rep. with Int. by Thomas. c. 1922. (Parson's Theatre, Hartford, Conn., Jan. 22, 1918; Shubert Theatre, Feb. 18, 1918)

THE CRICKET OF PALMY DAYS. 1929. (Playhouse, Oct. 27, 1919)

SPEAK OF THE DEVIL. (As THE BLUE DEVIL, Academy of Music, Baltimore, Md., May 10, 1920; Broad St. Theatre, Phila., May 17, 1920)

* THE TENT OF POMPEY. (1920)

NEMESIS. (Garrick Theatre, Phila., March 21, 1921; Hudson Theatre, April 4, 1921)

STILL WATERS. 1926. (Belasco Theatre, Washington, D. C., Sept. 7, 1925)

Biographical and Critical

Thomas, Augustus, Introduction to *The Autobiography of a Play,* by Bronson Howard, q.v.

Thomas's Introductions, prefaced to the acting editions of his plays, published by Samuel French, contain valuable chapters in dramatic technique.

Thomas, Augustus, *The Print of My Remembrance.* 1922. [Authoritative autobiography]

Winter, William, *The Wallet of Time,* II, 529–557. [Important]

Howells, W. D., *North American Review,* CXXII (March, 1901), 474. [Arizona]

Scott, Clement, *Free Lance* (London), Feb. 15, 1902. [Arizona]

THOMPSON, DENMAN

JOSHUA WHITCOMB. (As variety sketch, Harry Martin's Varieties, Pittsburgh, Feb., 1875; as full-length play, with George W. Ryer, National Theatre, April 3, 1876)

THE OLD HOMESTEAD. With George W. Ryer. (Boston Museum, April 5, 1886; Fourteenth St. Theatre, Jan. 10, 1887)

BIBLIOGRAPHY AND PLAY LIST

THE TWO SISTERS. With George W. Ryer. (Boston Theatre, Sept. 3, 1887)

THE SUNSHINE OF PARADISE ALLEY. With George W. Ryer. (Fourteenth St. Theatre, May 11, 1896)

OUR NEW MINISTER. With George W. Ryer. c. 1900. (1893?)

TOTHEROH, DAN

WILD BIRDS. 1925. (Cherry Lane Playhouse, April 9, 1925)

THE BREAKING OF THE CALM. 1928.

DISTANT DRUMS. 1932. (Belasco Theatre, Jan. 18, 1932)

MOOR BORN. 1934. (Playhouse, April 3, 1934)

MOTHER LODE. With George O'Neil. (Cort Theatre, Dec. 22, 1934)

SEARCHING FOR THE SUN. (Fifty-eighth St. Theatre, Feb. 19, 1936)

TRIPLET, JAMES [REYNOLDS, W. H.]

A SUPPER IN DIXIE. 1865. (McVicker's Theatre, Chicago, 1865?)

TROMBLY, ALBERT EDMUND

MASQUE OF AMERICAN DRAMA. Philadelphia, 1917. (University of Pennsylvania, May, 1917)

TULLY, RICHARD WALTON

THE ROSE OF THE RANCHO. With David Belasco, q.v.

THE BIRD OF PARADISE. MS. (Daly's Theatre, Jan. 8, 1912)

OMAR THE TENTMAKER. MS. (Lyric Theatre, Jan. 13, 1914)

THE FLAME. MS. (Lyric Theatre, Sept. 4, 1916)

TWAIN, MARK

THE GILDED AGE. With G. S. Densmore. (California Theatre, San Francisco, April 23, 1874; Park Theatre, Sept. 16, 1874)

AH SIN. With Bret Harte, q.v.

THE AMERICAN CLAIMANT; OR, MULBERRY SELLERS TEN YEARS LATER. With W. D. Howells. (Lyceum Theatre, Sept. 23, 1887)

Biographical and Critical

Howells, W. D., For criticism of Colonel Sellers see "Drama," *Atlantic Monthly,* XXXV (June, 1875), 749–751.

Matthews, Brander, "Mark Twain and the Theatre." In *Playwrights on Playmaking.* 1923.

Paine, Albert Bigelow, *Mark Twain, a Biography.* 3 Vols., 1912. [Authoritative biography]

VARESI, GILDA

ENTER MADAME. With Dolly Byrne. 1921. (Garrick Theatre, Aug. 16, 1920)

VEILLER, BAYARD

WITHIN THE LAW. c. 1917. (Princess Theatre, Chicago, April 6, 1912; Eltinge Theatre, Sept. 11, 1912)

THE TRIAL OF MARY DUGAN. 1928. (National Theatre, Sept. 19, 1927)

DAMN YOUR HONOR. With Becky Gardiner. (Cosmopolitan Theatre, Dec. 30, 1929)

THAT'S THE WOMAN. (Fulton Theatre, Sept. 3, 1930)

VOLLMER, LULA

SUN-UP. 1925. (Provincetown Theatre, May 24, 1923; Vaudeville Theatre, London, May 4, 1925)

THE SHAME WOMAN. (Greenwich Village Theatre, Oct. 16, 1923)

THE DUNCE BOY. (Daly's Theatre, April 3, 1925)

TRIGGER. (Little Theatre, Dec. 6, 1927)

TROYKA. Adap. from the Hungarian of Imre Fazekas. (Hudson Theatre, April 1, 1930)

SENTINELS. (The Honor and the Glory) MS. (Biltmore Theatre, Dec. 25, 1931)

MOONSHINE AND HONEYSUCKLE. 1934.

WALLACK, LESTER

THE ROMANCE OF A POOR YOUNG MAN. Adap. of LE ROMAN D'UN JEUNE HOMME PAUVRE, by Octave Feuillet. (Wallack's Lyceum, Jan. 24, 1860)

CENTRAL PARK; OR, THE HOUSE WITH TWO DOORS. (Wallack's Lyceum, Feb. 14, 1861)

ROSEDALE; OR, THE RIFLE BALL. Priv. printed, 1890. (Wallack's Theatre, Sept. 30, 1863)

WALTER, EUGENE

SERJEANT JAMES. (Boston Theatre, Aug. 30, 1902). Rev. as BOOTS AND SADDLES.

THE UNDERTOW. (Harlem Opera House, April 22, 1907)

PAID IN FULL. (Montreal, first; Astor Theatre, Feb. 25, 1908)

THE WOLF. (Bijou Theatre, April 18, 1908)

THE EASIEST WAY. Priv. printed, 1908. (Parson's Theatre,

BIBLIOGRAPHY AND PLAY LIST

Hartford, Conn., Dec. 31, 1908; Stuyvesant Theatre, Jan. 19, 1909)

JUST A WIFE. (Colonial Theatre, Cleveland, O., Jan. 17, 1910; Belasco Theatre, Jan. 31, 1910)

BOOTS AND SADDLES. (Albany, Oct. 17, 1910)

THE TRAIL OF THE LONESOME PINE. Dram. of novel by John Fox, Jr. (New Amsterdam Theatre, Jan. 29, 1912)

FINE FEATHERS. MS. (Cort Theatre, Chicago, Aug. 12, 1912; Astor Theatre, Jan. 7, 1913)

JUST A WOMAN. (Forty-eighth St. Theatre, Jan. 17, 1916)

THE LITTLE SHEPHERD OF KINGDOM COME. Dram. of novel by John Fox, Jr. (Belasco Theatre, Washington, D. C., April 3, 1916)

THE KNIFE. (Bijou Theatre, April 12, 1917)

THE ASSASSIN. (New Haven, Conn., May 31, 1917)

NANCY LEE. With H. C. Wilson. (Hudson Theatre, April 9, 1918)

THE CHALLENGE. (Selwyn Theatre, Aug. 5, 1919)

THE MAN'S NAME. With Marjorie Chase. (Republic Theatre, Nov. 15, 1921)

JEALOUSY. 1925. (Maxine Elliott Theatre, Oct. 22, 1928)

Biographical and Critical

Walter, Eugene, *How to Write a Play.* 1925.

WATKINS, MAURINE

CHICAGO. 1927. (Music Box Theatre, Dec. 30, 1926)

REVELRY. Based on novel by Samuel Hopkins Adams. (Masque Theatre, Sept. 12, 1927)

WEXLEY, JOHN

THE LAST MILE. 1929. (Sam H. Harris Theatre, Feb. 13, 1930)

STEEL. MS. by French. (Times Square Theatre, Nov. 17, 1931)

THEY SHALL NOT DIE. 1934. (Royale Theatre, Feb. 21, 1934)

* RUNNING DOGS. (Civic Repertory Theatre, Feb., 1936)

WILLIAMS, JESSE LYNCH

THE STOLEN STORY. Dram. of story by author. Rewritten as novel, THE DAY DREAMER, 1906. (Providence, R. I., April 30, 1906; Garden Theatre, Oct. 2, 1906)

WHY MARRY? Published as AND SO THEY WERE MARRIED.

401

A HISTORY OF THE AMERICAN DRAMA

1914. Revised as acting version of WHY MARRY? in Quinn's
Contemporary American Plays. (Columbus, O., Nov. 1,
1917; Astor Theatre, Dec. 25, 1917)

WHY NOT? Adap. of novelette by author, REMATING TIME.
Boston, 1924. (Forty-eighth St. Theatre, Dec. 25, 1922)

LOVELY LADY. (Belmont Theatre, Oct. 14, 1925)

WOOLF, BENJAMIN E.

OFF TO THE WAR. Boston, 1861. (Boston, 1861)

A NATION'S DESTINY; OR, A GLASS OF WATER. Adap. of Scribe.
(Chestnut St. Theatre, Dec. 18, 1865)

CAUGHT AT LAST. (Chestnut St. Theatre, Phila., Jan. 1, 1866)

AFTER MANY DAYS. (Chestnut St. Theatre, April 29, 1867)

DOWN AT CAPE MAY. (Chestnut St. Theatre, Phila., Nov. 18,
1867)

THE MIGHTY DOLLAR. 1943. (Park Theatre, Sept. 6, 1875)

CLAIRE; OR, MATES AND CHECKMATES. Adap. of LE MAÎTRE DE
FORGES, by Georges Ohnet. (Boston Museum, April 14,
1884)

YOUNG, WILLIAM

PENDRAGON. MS. (Chicago, Dec. 5, 1881; Haverley's Fifth
Ave. Theatre, Feb. 13, 1882)

THE HOUSE OF MAUPRAT. With J. G. Wilson. (1882)

THE RAJAH. 1882. (Madison Square Theatre, June 5, 1883)

JOAN OF ARC. Adap. from JEANNE D'ARC. (Fifth Ave. Theatre,
Dec. 8, 1890)

GANELON. (Broadway Theatre, Jan. 5, 1891)

IF I WERE YOU. (Hermann's Theatre, Dec. 19, 1892)

YOUNG AMERICA. (Columbia Theatre, Boston, Aug. 25, 1894;
Murray Hill Theatre, May, 1897)

BEN HUR. Dram. of novel by Lew Wallace. Priv. printed, 1899.
(Broadway Theatre, Nov. 29, 1899)

THE SPRIGHTLY ROMANCE OF MARSAC. Dram. of novel by M. E.
Seawell. (Republic Theatre, Dec. 3, 1900)

A JAPANESE NIGHTINGALE. Dram. of novel by Onoto Wotanna.
(Daly's Theatre, Nov. 23, 1903)

A HISTORY OF THE AMERICAN DRAMA

Note to Reprinting of Revised Edition

AMERICA'S LOST PLAYS [1]

The following volumes contain plays of the period covered by this history. In the Play List, this series is indicated by "A.L.P."

Volume IV: Miscellaneous

(Edited by the late Isaac Goldberg, completed by Hubert Heffner) *Across the Continent,* by J. J. McCloskey; *Rosedale,* by Lester Wallack; *Davy Crockett,* by Frank Murdoch; *Sam'l of Posen,* by G. H. Jessop; *Our Boarding House,* by Leonard Grover.

Volume VII: James A. Herne

(Edited by Arthur Hobson Quinn)

Drifting Apart; The Minute Men; Within an Inch of His Life; Griffith Davenport (fragment).

Volume VIII: Recent Melodramas

(Edited by Garrett H. Leverton)

A Royal Slave, by Clarence Bennett; *The Great Diamond Robbery,* by Edward W. Alfriend and A. C. Wheeler; *From Rags to Riches,* by Charles A. Taylor; *No Mother to Guide Her,* by Lillian Mortimer; *Billy the Kid,* by Walter Woods.

Volume IX: Charles Hoyt

(Edited by Douglas L. Hunt)

A Bunch of Keys; A Midnight Bell; A Milk White Flag; A Trip to Chinatown; A Temperance Town.

---

[1] *Favorite American Plays of the 19th Century,* edited by Barrett H. Clark (1943), contains nine plays reprinted from the series, and also *The Mighty Dollar,* by B. E. Woolf.

BIBLIOGRAPHY AND PLAY LIST

VOLUME X: BRONSON HOWARD

(Edited by Allan G. Halline)

Knave and Queen (Ivers Dean); Old Love Letters; Hurricanes; Baron Rudolph; The Banker's Daughter; One of Our Girls.

VOLUME XI: STEELE MACKAYE

(Edited by Percy MacKaye)

Rose Michel; Won at Last; In Spite of All; An Arrant Knave.

VOLUME XVI: HISTORICAL AND ROMANTIC PLAYS

(Edited by J. B. Russak)

Monte Cristo (as played by James O'Neill); *Hippolytus,* by Julia Ward Howe; *Mistress Nell,* by George Hazleton; *Becky Sharp,* by Langdon Mitchell; *The Warrens of Virginia,* by William C. deMille.

VOLUME XVII: HENRY C. DEMILLE (IN COLLABORATION WITH DAVID BELASCO AND CHARLES BARNARD)

(Edited by Robert Hamilton Ball)

The Main Line; The Wife; Lord Chumley; The Charity Ball; Men and Women.

VOLUME XVIII: DAVID BELASCO

(Edited by Glenn Hughes and George Savage)

La Belle Russe; The Stranglers of Paris; The Heart of Maryland; The Girl I Left Behind Me; Naughty Anthony.

VOLUME XIX: BARTLEY CAMPBELL

(Edited by Napier Wilt)

The White Slave; My Partner; The Galley Slave; Peril; Fairfax; The Virginian.

VOLUME XX: AUGUSTIN DALY

(Edited by Catherine Sturtevant)

Man and Wife; Divorce; The Big Bonanza; Pique; Needles and Pins.

INDEX

A

Abbey Theatre, II, 260.
Abbott, George. *See* List of Plays.
Abie's Irish Rose, II, 120–122; 383.
About, Edmond, I, 24.
Accent on Youth, II, 388.
Achilles Had a Heel, II, 350.
Adam and Eva, II, 380.
Adam and Eve in the Garden of Eden, II, 321.
Adams, Maude, I, 133; 173; 203; 272; 281–282. II, 4.
Adding Machine, The, II, 110; 388.
Ade, George, II, 4; 113–115. *See also* List of Plays.
Admiral, The, II, 370.
Adrea, I, 183–188. II, 4; 321; 324; 374.
Adventures of François, The, II, 63; 381.
Aeschylus, II, 255; 257.
After Business Hours, I, 32. II, 338.
After Many Days, II, 402.
Aftermath, II, 390.
After the Wedding; or, A Grain of Sand, II, 339.
Afterthoughts, I, 243. II, 396.
Ah Sin, I, 110; 121. II, 358; 399.
Ah, Wilderness!, II, 258–259; 260; 386.
L'Aieule, I, 283.
Akins, Zoë, II, 80; 135; 141–144; 161; 261; 286. *See also* List of Plays.
Alabama, I, 243–245; 262. II, 396.
A la Carte, II, 369.
Aladdin and the Wonderful Lamp, II, 321.
Albany Depot, The, I, 77. II, 365.
Albery, James, I, 49.
Album, The, II, 367.
Aldrich, Louis, I, 122.
Aldrich, Thomas Bailey, I, 66; 141; 205–207. II, 81. *See also* List of Plays.
Alias Jimmy Valentine, II, 319.
Alice in Wonderland, II, 391.
Alien Corn, II, 272; 364.
Alison's House, II, 261; 354.
Alixe, I, 24. II, 335.
Allatoona, I, 216–217. II, 370.

Allen, Viola, I, 58; 209; 215; 271. II, 167.
All God's Chillun Got Wings, II, 162; 188; 206; 386.
All the Comforts of Home, I, 221. II, 352.
Alone, I, 240. II, 395.
Amaco, II, 264; 298; 350.
Ambition, II, 329.
Ambush, II, 216–217; 389.
American, The, (by Daly), I, 22. II, 336.
American, The, (by James), II, 367.
Americana, II, 379.
American Born (by Belasco), I, 167. II, 323.
American Born (by George M. Cohan), II, 116; 118; 331.
American Citizen, An, II, 50.
American Claimant, The; or, Mulberry Sellers Ten Years Later, I, 115. II, 364; 399.
American drama, condition of, after the Civil War, I, 3ff., at the beginning of the Twentieth Century, II, 2–6, during the second decade, 158–164; conferences on, 164; effect of Great War on, 207; perennial vitality of, 301.
American Dramatists and Composers, Society of, I, 64.
American Dramatists Club, I, 64.
American Dream, II, 387.
American Duchess, An, I, 272. II, 346.
American Girl, An, II, 343.
American Idea, The, II, 331.
American Lord, An, II, 326.
Americans Abroad, I, 38. II, 345.
Americans in Paris, I, 39.
American Tragedy, An, II, 369.
Ames, Winthrop, II, 24–25.
Amherst College, I, 265. II, 213.
Among Thieves, I, 234. II, 353.
Amourette, II, 373.
Anarchy, II, 375.
Ancient Mariner, The, II, 185; 386.
Andersen, Hans, II, 94; 95.
Anderson, Maxwell, II, 233–236; 266–271; his use of the supernatural,

INDEX

INDEX

407

INDEX

Broadhurst, George, II, 4; 102–104.
See also List of Plays.
Broadway, II, 90; 111–112; 230; 316; 344.
Broadway Jones, II, 116; 331.
Broadway Theatre, Closing of, I, 4.
Broken Dishes, II, 264; 349.
Broker of Bogota, The, I, 1; 4.
Bronze Statue, The, II, 321.
Brown, Alice, II, 24. *See also* List of Plays.
Browne, Porter E., II, 111. *See also* List of Plays.
Browning, Robert, II, 151.
Brutus, I, 1; 4.
Buccaneer, The, II, 235; 318; 392.
Buchanan, Thompson, II, 75–76. *See also* List of Plays.
Buck, Pearl, II, 252.
Bull Run; or, The Sacking of Fairfax Courthouse, I, 5.
Bulls and Bears, I, 119. II, 328.
Bulwer Lytton, Edward, I, 37.
Bunch of Keys, A, II, 366.
Bundle of Lies, A, II, 339.
Bunny, II, 393.
Buntling Ball, The, II, 345.
Burgess, Neil, I, 162. *See also* List of Plays.
Burglar, The, I, 242; 243. II, 395.
Burnett, Frances Hodgson, I, 208–209; 214–215; 241. II, 240. *See also* List of Plays.
Butcher's Revenge, The; or, The Seven Buckets of Blood, II, 321.
Butter and Egg Man, The, II, 223; 368.
Butterflies, The, I, 203. II, 329.
By Proxy, II, 370.
Byrne, Dolly, II, 157.

C

Caldwell, Erskine, II, 288.
Caleb Stone's Death Watch, II, 349.
Calhoun, A. R., I, 7.
Caliban, A Community Masque, II, 38–40; 48; 376.
California, drama in, I, 7; 164–167. II, 46–47.
California, University of, II, 129; 228; 237.
Campbell, Bartley, I, 118–124; birth and training, 118; directs plays in Chicago, 118–119; career in California of, 119; attends rehearsals of *My Partner* in Berlin, 122; insanity and death of, 124; 165. *See also* List of Plays.

Cameo Kirby, II, 127; 393.
Camilla's Husband, I, 131.
Canterbury Pilgrims, The, II, 5; 28–29, 38; 376.
Capitol, The, I, 104; 262. II, 396.
Caponsacchi, II, 151–152; 354.
Caprice, II, 382.
Captain Courtesy, II, 329.
Captain Impudence, II, 390.
Captain Jinks of the Horse Marines, I, 277. II, 345; 347.
Captain Lettarblair, II, 50.
Captain Molly, II, 359.
Capture of Fort Donelson, The, I, 5.
Carb, David, II, 140.
Carleton, Henry Guy, I, 203. *See also* List of Plays.
Carnegie Institute of Technology, II, 164.
Carolina Playmakers, II, 241; 287.
Carpenter, Edward Childs, II, 152–154. *See also* List of Plays.
Carré, A., I, 272.
Carry On, II, 341.
Carter, Mrs. Leslie, I, 174; 176; 188–189.
Casanova, II, 363.
Case of Becky, The, I, 196.
Casualties, II, 349.
Caught Wet, II, 334.
Cave Girl, The, II, 380.
Cayvan, Georgia, I, 169; 172n.
Cazauran, A. R., I, 48–49.
Central Park; or, The House With Two Doors, I, 38. II, 400.
Cezalia, II, 366.
Challenge, The, II, 153; 330; 401.
Chameleon, The, II, 23; 388.
Champagne Charley, II, 397.
Champion, The, II, 395.
Chanfrau, F. S., I, 105.
Changelings, The, II, 79–80; 344.
Channel Road, The, II, 368.
Charity Ball, The, I, 171–172. II, 323; 343.
Charles Lamb, II, 327.
Charles O'Malley, I, 130. II, 359.
Charles II, I, 1.
Chastening, The, II, 370.
Chatterton, I, 208; 211. II, 373.
Chekhov, Anton, I, 150.
Cherokee Night, The, II, 389.
Cherry Pickers, The, II, 319.
Chicago, II, 111–112; 401.
Children of Darkness, II, 379.
Children of Earth, II, 21; 327.
Children of the Moon, II, 156; 349.
Children's Hour, The, II, 300–301; 359.

INDEX

INDEX

Crosman, Henrietta, I, 190. II, 35; 156.

Cross Roads, II, 264; 350.

Crothers, Rachel, II, 4; 5; 50–61; birth and training, 50–51; her protests against the standards of the world, 52–53; her recognition of woman's responsibility, 54–56; president Stage Women's War Relief, 56; her picture of social life since the Great War, 57–59; her satire on the cult of self-expression, 59–60; her talent, 60–61; her later social comedies, 250–251. *See also* List of Plays.

Crowns, I, 188–189. II, 374.

Cub, The, II, 327.

Cunningham, Leon, II, 237.

Cupid at Vassar, II, 340.

Curse of Cain, The, II, 323.

Curtis, G. W., I, 10.

Cuttyback's Thunder, II, 378.

Cyrano de Bergerac, II, 148; 361.

D

Daddy's Gone A-Hunting, II, 142; 317.

Daisy Mayme, II, 227; 369.

Daisy Miller, II, 367.

Dakolar, II, 375.

Daly, Augustin, I, 1–38; birth, 7; comparison with Dunlap, 7; as dramatic critic, 9; classification of plays of, 13; forms association of managers, 16; opens Daly's Fifth Ave. Theatre, 16; opens New Fifth Ave. Theatre, 16; opens Daly's Theatre, 17; adaptations from French of, 20–26; theory of acting of, 23; adaptations from the German of, 26–32; adaptations from the Spanish of, 32–33; takes his company to London, 34; to Germany, 34; to Paris, 34; first performance of a Shakespearean comedy by an American company in Europe, 34; takes *The Taming of the Shrew* to Paris, 34; produces *As You Like It* in London, 35; nature of his adaptations of Shakespeare, 35; third visit to Paris of, 35; builds theatre in London, 35; adapts Tennyson's *The Foresters,* 35; his adaptation of *Twelfth Night,* 35, of *Much Ado About Nothing,* 35, of *The Merchant of Venice,* 35, of *The Tempest,* 35; last years and death, 36; his achievement, 36; inspiration to later playwrights, 37; 39; 40; 41; 71; 108; 109; 110; 119; 125. II, 1; 74; 108. *See also* List of Plays.

Daly, J. F., I, 7; 25; 30.

Damn Your Honor, II, 400.

Dancing Days, II, 350.

Dangerous Ruffian, A, I, 67.

Danites in the Sierras, The, I, 79; 116–117; 166. II, 381.

Dan's Tribulations, I, 91; 92. II, 357.

Darby and Lanty, I, 85. II, 356.

Dark City, The, I, 13; 17; 18. II, 337.

Dark Tower, The, II, 285; 369.

Darling of the Gods, The, I, 180–183. II, 321; 324; 374.

d'Aste, Ippolito, I, 68.

Daudet, Alphonse, I, 274.

Daughters of Men, II, 5; 104; 371.

Dauvray, Helen, I, 54; 55.

Davenport, E. L., I, 118.

Davenport, Fanny, I, 17; 24; 26.

David Harum, II, 4.

Davis, Donald, II, 252.

Davis, Owen, II, 217–220; 252. *See also* List of Plays.

Davis, R. H., I, 104; 253. *See also* List of Plays.

Davy Crockett, I, 105–108. II, 383.

Dawn of a To-Morrow, The, II, 327.

Day and a Night in New York, A, II, 367.

Days Without End, II, 259–260; 386.

Dayton, Katharine, II, 286.

Dazey, C. T., II, 101–102.

Dead End, II, 299; 370.

Dear Old Darling, II, 252; 332.

Death of Eve, The, II, 10–11; 382.

Deborah, I, 9.

Decision of the Court, The, I, 65. II, 378.

Déclassée, II, 142; 317.

de Courcy, Charles, I, 25.

Deep Purple, The, II, 319.

Deep River, II, 235; 392.

Deep Tangled Wildwood, The, II, 222; 332; 368.

de Koven, Reginald, II, 29; 43; 48.

de Kruif, Paul, II, 274.

De Lancey, II, 4; 397.

Delmonico's; or, Larks up the Hudson, I, 21; 25. II, 335.

De Mille, Cecil, I, 194.

De Mille, Henry C., I, 169–174. *See also* List of Plays.

De Mille, William C., I, 198. *See also* List of Plays.

Denise, I, 23. II, 338.

410

INDEX

411

INDEX

INDEX

413

INDEX

Gillette, William, I, 3; 7; 57; 212–238; his idea of the relation between words and action, 212–213; birth and training, 213; first success as actor, 213; first play, 213; collaboration with Mrs. Burnett, 214; writes the first successful drama of the Civil War, 216; plays "Beene" in *Held by the Enemy*, 218; writes novel based on *A Legal Wreck*, 220; his adaptations from French and German, 221–222; acts in *Too Much Johnson*, 222; in *Secret Service*, 223; in *Sherlock Holmes*, 228; in *Clarice*, 229; his one-act plays, 234; classification of his plays, 235; his dramatizations of fiction, 235; later adaptations of French and German plays, 235–236; plays of, in which he acted, 236; relation of the actor to the playwright, 236–238; his achievement, 237–238; 241; 290. II, 1; 4; 298. *See also* List of Plays.

Gillmore, Margalo, II, 174.

Girl and the Judge, The, I, 277. II, 347.

Girl I Left Behind Me, The, I, 174–176. II, 323; 350.

Girl of the Golden West, The, I, 191–192. II, 321; 324.

Girl Who Has Everything, The, II, 348.

Girl with the Green Eyes, The, I, 279–280. II, 345; 347.

Girls, I, 290. II, 348.

Glad of It, I, 281. II, 347.

Gladiator, The, I, 1; 4. II, 48.

Glance at New York, A, I, 4; 11; 84; 127.

Glaspell, Susan, II, 160; 209–212; 261. *See also* List of Plays.

Glaucus, I, 200.

Goddess of Reason, The, II, 137; 367.

Godferneaux, André, I, 290.

Godfrey, Thomas, II, 48.

God Loves Us, II, 379.

Gods of the Lightning, II, 266; 271; 318.

Going Some, II, 319.

Gold, II, 171; 175; 385.

Gold Mine, A, I, 64. II, 378.

Golden Widow, The, II, 339.

Goldfische, I, 29; 30.

Good Companions, The, II, 372.

Good Earth, The, II, 252; 341.

Good Fellow, The, II, 224; 368.

Good Gracious Annabelle, II, 77; 372.

Goodman, Arthur. *See* List of Plays.

Goodrich, Arthur, II, 151. *See also* List of Plays.

Goodwin, N. C., I, 64; 103; 203; 273. II, 69.

Goose Hangs High, The, II, 237; 320.

Gordon, Ruth, II, 252.

Gossip, II, 346.

Gottschalk, Ferdinand, I, 272; 276.

Governor of Kentucky, The, II, 350.

Governor's Lady, The, I, 196. II, 325.

Governor's Son, The, II, 116; 330.

Gozzi, Carlo, II, 32.

Gran Uale, I, 119. II, 328.

Grand Army Man, A, I, 194. II, 324.

Grandma, II, 351.

Grandmama, II, 339.

Granny, I, 282; 283. II, 347.

Grant's Campaign, I, 7.

Great Divide, The, I, 108. II, 4; 11–13; 51; 195; 382.

Great God Brown, The, II, 190–194; 200; 201; 203; 206; 260; 386.

Greatness, II, 143; 317.

Great Unknown, The, I, 30. II, 339.

Great War, effect on drama of, II, 207.

Greek influence on American drama, II, 189; 251; 252.

Greeks Had a Word for It, II, 317.

Greeley, Horace, I, 117.

Green, Elizabeth Lay, II, 242.

Green, Erma, II, 243.

Green Eyed Monster, The, II, 340.

Green Grow the Lilacs, II, 290; 389.

Green Pastures, The, II, 282–284; 332.

Green, Paul, II, 162; 242–245; his early work for the Carolina Playmakers, 242–243; his studies of the negro, 244–245; his portrayal of social conditions in the South, 286–287; 290. *See also* List of Plays.

Greene, Clay, I, 113; 150.

Griffith Davenport. See *The Reverend Griffith Davenport*.

Griffith Gaunt; or, Jealousy, I, 10. II, 334.

Grip, The, II, 357.

Group Theatre, The, II, 300.

Groves, C., I, 167.

Guerillas, The, I, 6. II, 379.

Guns, II, 356.

Guy Domville, II, 367.

Gypsy, II, 266–267; 318.

Gypsy Trail, The, II, 154; 361.

H

Hackett, J. H., I, 4.

Hackett, James K., I, 210. II, 4.

414

INDEX

Half Gods, II, 271; 363.
Hagan, James, II, 300. *See also* List
of Plays.
Haggard, Rider, I, 220.
Hairy Ape, The, II, 162; 183–184; 200;
201; 202; 204; 206; 385.
Halbe Dichter, I, 31.
Halévy, Ludovic, I, 23.
Hale, Louise Closser, II, 59.
Hamilton, Clayton, II, 74–75. *See
also* List of Plays.
Hamlet, II, 271.
Hampden, Walter, II, 148; 151; 152.
Handkerchief, The, II, 344.
Hanging of Nathan Hale, The, II, 321.
Happy Marriage, A, I, 290. II, 348.
Harding, Ann, II, 216.
Hare, John, I, 215.
Haroun al Raschid, I, 27.
Harrigan, Edward, I, 66; 82–96; birth
and ancestry, 82; training in Cali-
fornia of, 82; appearance with Hart
in New York of, 82; becomes man-
ager of Theatre Comique, 83; of
New Theatre Comique, 83; leases
Park Theatre, 83; separates from
Hart, 83; builds Harrigan's The-
atre, 83; last appearance and death
of, 83; development of his plays
from vaudeville sketches, 83–85; his
Irish characters, 86–96; contrast
with Boucicault, 86; comparison
with Hoyt, 103; 279. II, 1; 113;
136. *See also* List of Plays.
Harris, Joel Chandler, II, 288.
Harrison, Richard, II, 282.
Hart, Moss, II, 284; 285.
Hart, Tony, I, 82–83; 84.
Harte, Bret, I, 14; 20; 38; 66; 108–
114; collaboration with Mark
Twain, 110–111; with T. E. Pember-
ton, 112; 120; 253; 274. II, 106;
108. *See also* List of Plays.
Harvard College, I, 213. II, 25–26;
33; 34; 87; 101; 133; 217; 228.
Harvest, The, I, 270; 272. II, 345.
Harvest Moon, The, I, 255–256. II,
5; 397.
*Hatteras Inlet; or, Our Naval Vic-
tories,* I, 5.
Haunted, The. See *Mourning Be-
comes Electra.*
Haunted House, The, II, 322; 341.
Hauptmann, G., II, 34.
Hawthorne, Nathaniel, II, 33; 201;
203; 204; 205; 260.
Hawthornes, The. See *Shore Acres.*
Hayes, Helen, II, 128; 154; 221; 270.

Hay, John, I, 42; 43; 72.
Hazardous Ground, I, 21. II, 335.
Hazel Kirke, I, 126; 127; 128. II, 374.
Hazelton, George C., II, 131–132.
See also List of Plays.
Head-Master, The, II, 372.
Head of the Family, The, II, 346.
He and She, II, 54–55; 60; 333.
He Knew He Was Right, I, 15–16.
Heart of Maryland, The, I, 176–177.
II, 323.
Heart of Paddy Whack, The, II, 56;
333.
Hearts, II, 328.
Heartsease, II, 371.
Hearts of Oak, I, 129; 133–136; 168.
II, 322; 359.
Heat Lightning, II, 316.
Heavy Traffic, II, 389.
Heir to the Hoorah, The, II, 319.
Held by the Enemy, I, 7; 57; 216–220.
II, 352.
Helena's Husband, II, 137; 381.
Hell-Bent Fer Heaven, II, 248; 367.
Hellman, Lillian, II, 300–301. *See
also* List of Plays.
Henrietta, The, I, 55–57; revival of,
57. II, 362.
Henry Esmond, I, 57.
Herfords, The, II, 54.
Her Friend the King, II, 395.
Her Great Match, I, 283; 285. II, 4;
347.
Her Husband's Wife, I, 25. II, 74;
394.
Her Lord and Master, I, 17.
Her Master's Voice, II, 262; 373.
Here's to Your Health, II, 383.
Herne, Chrystal, I, 157; 258. II, 59;
227.
Herne, James A., I, 66; 125–162; birth,
129; early stage career of, 129–
130; in California, 130ff.; influence
of Dickens on, 130; of Boucicault
on, 130; association with Belasco
130–136; sources of his early plays,
130–133; comes east with *Hearts of
Oak,* 133–134; his theories about
realism, 138–140; writes *Margaret
Fleming* to prove them, 140; quotations from *Margaret Fleming,* 143,
145, 146; employs the "quiet ending" in *Shore Acres,* 149–150; produces *Griffith Davenport* and fails,
150–156; quotations from *Griffith
Davenport,* 153–155; success with
Sag Harbor, 157; death, 157; classification of plays of, 157–158; hu-

415

INDEX

manitarian interests of, 159; significance of *Margaret Fleming* and *Griffith Davenport*, 159–160; character drawing of, 160–161; 197; 198; 212. II, 1. *See* List of Plays.
Herne, Julie, I, 156; 157.
Herne, Mrs. James A., I, 131; 133; 136; 137; 141; 146; 161.
Heroine in Rags, A, I, 119. II, 328.
Her Opinion of His Story, II, 365.
Hero, The, II, 212–214; 344.
Her Own Way, I, 280. II, 4; 345; 347.
Her Sister, I, 289–290. II, 348.
Her Way Out, II, 390.
Heyward, Dorothy, II, 288. *See also* List of Plays.
Heyward, Dubose, II, 288–289; 290; 301. *See also* List of Plays.
Heywood, Thomas, as a character, I, 70.
Hickerson, Harold, II, 266.
High Bid, The, II, 367.
Highest Bidder, The, II, 323.
High Road, The, II, 391.
Higley, Philo, II, 300.
His Grace de Grammont, I, 270. II, 346.
His Majesty, Bunker Bean, II, 79; 343.
Hiss! Boom! Blah! II, 380.
Hitchcock (Murdoch), Frank, I, 105–108.
Hitchcock, Harry, I, 106.
Hit the Trail Holliday, II, 117; 331.
Hohe Lied, Das, II, 94.
Hole in the Ground, A, II, 366.
Holiday, II, 276–277; 320.
Holly Tree Inn, The, II, 396.
Holmes, John Haynes, II, 298.
Holy Terror, A, II, 315.
Homecoming. See *Mourning Becomes Electra.*
Home Fires, II, 341.
Home-Towners, The, II, 331.
Honor, II, 340.
Honor of the Family, The, I, 290. II, 348.
Hooker, Brian, II, 145–148. *See also* List of Plays.
Hoosier Doctor, The, II, 396.
Horizon, I, 13; 14; 16; 18; 38; 108; 109; 125. II, 335.
Horse Shoe Robinson, I, 4.
Horst, Julius, I, 290.
Hospitality, II, 237; 334.
Hotel Universe, II, 277–279; 320.
House Beautiful, The, II, 388.
House in Blind Alley, The, II, 389.
House of Connelly, The, II, 286–287; 355.

House of Mauprat, The, II, 402.
House of Mirth, The, I, 286. II, 348.
House That Jack Built, The, II, 326.
Housewarming, II, 344.
House We Live In, The, II, 319.
Housum, Robert, II, 154. *See also* List of Plays.
Howard, Bronson, I, 1; 3; 36; 38; 39–64; birth, 39; ancestry, 40; his first play, 40; production of *Saratoga* by, 40; sees *Saratoga* in Germany, 41; his literary honesty, 42; his explanation of the laws of dramatic construction, 44–49; writes a new form of social comedy, 52–53; his achievement, 62–63; founds American Dramatists Club, 63; death, 64; 167; 169. II, 1; 62; 74; 100. *See also* List of Plays.
Howard, Leslie, II, 281; 295; 296.
Howard, Sidney, II, 96; 227–233; 271–275; 299. *See also* List of Plays.
Howells, William Dean, I, 66–81; inspires other playwrights, 66; London performances of his plays, 67; professional productions of, 68–74; his achievement, 79–81; collaborates with Mark Twain, I, 115; 125; 138; 140; 148; 158. *See also* List of Plays.
How's Your Health, II, 394.
How to Avoid Drafting, I, 6.
How Women Love; or, The Heart of the Sierras, I, 119. II, 328.
Hoyt, Charles H., I, 96–103; birth and training, 96–97; analysis of his plays, 97ff.; death, 102; his achievement, 102–103. II, 1; 113; 119. *See also* List of Plays.
Hughes, Hatcher, II, 248–249. *See also* List of Plays.
Hull, Henry, II, 288.
Hungary, American drama in, I, 289.
Hunted, The. See *Mourning Becomes Electra.*
Hunter, Glenn, II, 128; 222.
Hurlbert, W. H., I, 39.
Hurricanes, I, 50; 53. II, 361.
Husband and Wife, II, 370.
Huston, Walter, II, 209; 273.
Hutton, Lawrence, I, 14.
Hymn to the Rising Sun, II, 355.

I

Iascaire, I, 85. II, 356.
Ibsen, H., I, 158. II, 34; 35; 217.
Icebound, II, 218–219; 341.

416

INDEX

417

INDEX

INDEX

419

INDEX

an inspirational force, 43–44; 48; 160; 249; 251. *See also* List of Plays.
Madama Butterfly, i, 179.
Madame Butterfly, i, 177–179. ii, 123; 130; 321; 324; 374.
Madame Sand, ii, 137–139; 381.
Madeleine and the Movies, ii, 117; 331.
Madeleine Morel, i, 10. ii, 108; 336.
Maggie Pepper, ii, 105; 371.
Maggie the Magnificent, ii, 265; 369.
Magical City, The, ii, 141–142; 317.
Magnolia, ii, 394.
Maid and the Moonshiner, The, ii, 366.
Main Line, The; or, Rawson's Y, i, 169. ii, 343.
Maison Neuve, La, i, 21; 272.
Major André, i, 280–281. ii, 347.
Major Pendennis, ii, 68; 381.
Major, The, i, 93.
Maltz, Albert. *See* List of Plays.
Man and Wife, i, 19–20. ii, 335.
Man from Home, The, ii, 5; 80; 126–127; 393.
Mannering, Mary, ii, 4.
Man of the Hour, The, ii, 4; 102–103; 326.
Man of the World, A, i, 242. ii, 395.
Mansfield, Richard, i, 200; 203; 204; 205; 266. ii, 4; 18; 126. *See also* List of Plays.
Man's Man, A, ii, 238, 369.
Man's Name, The, ii, 401.
Man's World, A, ii, 5; 52–54; 60; 250; 333.
Man Upstairs, The, ii, 396.
March Hares, ii, 355.
Marco Millions, ii, 194–196; 203; 386.
Margaret Fleming, analysis of and quotations from, i, 140–146; 158. ii, 359.
Margery's Lovers, ii, 378.
Marie Odile, ii, 135; 372.
Mariner's Compass, The, i, 133, 134–136.
Marlowe, ii, 387.
Marlowe, Julia, i, 203; 206; 207; 242; 274. ii, 17–18; 30; 31; 137.
Marquise, La, i, 21.
Marriage, ii, 374.
Marriage, 1892, i, 270.
Marriage by Moonlight, i, 131–133. ii, 322; 359.
Marriage Game, The, ii, 347.
Marryatt, Florence, i, 17.
Marrying Mary, ii, 390.
Mars, Antony, i, 25.
Marse Covington, ii, 115; 316.

Marseilles, ii, 364.
Marshall, Frank, i, 41.
Marty Malone, ii, 358.
Mary of Scotland, ii, 268–270; 318.
Mary, the Fishermen's Child, i, 137–138.
Mary the Third, ii, 58; 334.
Masked Ball, The, i, 272. ii, 345.
Masks, ii, 380.
Mason, John, i, 258. ii, 64.
Massey, Raymond, ii, 252.
Masque of American Drama, ii, 48–49; 399.
Masque of Judgment, The, ii, 7–10; 382.
Masque of Labor, A, ii, 376.
Masterpiece of Diplomacy, A, i, 78. ii, 365.
Mater, ii, 5; 28; 34; 44; 376.
Matinee Hero, The, ii, 395.
Matinee Idol, The, ii, 397.
Matrimony, ii, 328.
Matthews, Brander, i, 14; 43; 57; 61; 64–65. *See also* List of Plays.
Matthison, Edith Wynne, ii, 11; 23; 79.
May Blossom, i, 156; 168. ii, 323.
Mayer, Edwin J. *See* List of Plays.
Mayfair, ii, 345.
Mayo, Frank, i, 106; 108; 115.
Mayor and the Manicure, The, ii, 115; 317.
McAllister's Legacy, ii, 357.
McCabe, J. D., Jr., i, 6.
McEvoy, J. P., ii, 120.
McGroarty, J. S., ii, 45–46.
McGuire, William Anthony, ii, 111; 120. *See also* List of Plays.
McIntyre, John T., ii, 145. *See also* List of Plays.
McLellan, C. M. S., ii, 4; 110–111. *See also* List of Plays.
McNooney's Visit, ii, 357.
McSorley's Inflation, ii, 357.
Meddler, The, ii, 396.
Meilhac, Henri, i, 23.
Mélodrame, ii, 111.
Member from Ozark, The, ii, 397.
Memnon, i, 203. ii, 329.
Men and Women, i, 172–173. ii, 323; 343.
Men in White, ii, 299; 370.
Men Must Fight, ii, 298; 373.
Mercedes, i, 205–206; 211. ii, 317.
Mere Man, ii, 397.
Merington, Marguerite, ii, 50.
Merivale, H. C., i, 167.
Merivale, Philip, ii, 270; 296.

INDEX

Muddy Day, The, I, 93–94. II, 357.
Mulligan Guard, The, I, 87; 88; 96.
Mulligan Guard Ball, The, I, 83; 88–89. II, 356.
Mulligan Guard Chowder, The, I, 89. II, 357.
Mulligan Guard Nominee, The, I, 90. II, 357.
Mulligan Guard Picnic, The, I, 88. II, 356.
Mulligan Guard Surprise, The, I, 89; 91. II, 357.
Mulligan Guards and the Skidmores, The, I, 88.
Mulligan Guards' Christmas, The, I, 89; 91. II, 357.
Mulligans' Silver Wedding, The, I, 90. II, 357.
Mulligan Surprise Party, The, II, 357.
Murdoch, Frank Hitchcock, I, 105–108. *See also* List of Plays.
Murdoch, James E., I, 105; 240.
Murger, Henri, I, 272.
Music Box, The, II, 396.
Music Master, The, II, 104; 371.
My Colleen, I, 150. II, 360.
My Foolish Wife, I, 119. II, 328.
My Geraldine, II, 328.
My Lady's Dress, II, 134; 372.
My Maryland, I, 274.
My Partner, I, 119–122. II, 328.
My Princess, II, 391.
Myself Bettina, II, 52; 333.
Mysterious Inn, The, II, 322.
My Wife's Husbands, II, 390.

N

Nancy and Company, I, 31; 34. II, 338.
Nancy Ann, II, 288; 360.
Nancy Lee, II, 401.
Napoleon Bonaparte, I, 204. II, 392.
Napoleon Crossing the Rockies, II, 29; 377.
Nathan Hale, I, 273. II, 345; 346.
National Guard, The, I, 5.
Nation's Destiny, A; or, A Glass of Water, II, 402.
Native Ground, II, 351.
Naughty Anthony, I, 177. II, 324.
Nazimova, Alla, II, 252; 257.
Necessary Evil, The, II, 370.
Ned McCobb's Daughter, II, 230–232; 363.
Needles and Pins, I, 31. II, 337.
Neighborhood Playhouse, The, II, 39; 160.

Neighbor Jackwood, I, 127.
Nemesis, I, 261. II, 398.
Nero, II, 393.
Nervous Wreck, The, II, 220; 341.
Nettie, II, 115; 316.
New Blood, I, 246. II, 5; 396.
New Brooms, II, 120; 332.
New Citizenship, A Civic Ritual, The, II, 376.
New King Arthur, The, II, 345.
New Magdalen, The, I, 167.
New Marriage, The, II, 67; 381.
Newport, I, 38. II, 374.
New South, The, I, 150.
New Theatre, The (Chicago), II, 3.
New Theatre, The (New York), II, 3; 23; 24; 25; 87; 133.
New Theatre Comique, The, I, 83.
New Year's Call, A, II, 395.
New York and Brooklyn; or, The Poor Sewing Girl, I, 37.
New York Burglars; or, Wedded by Moonlight, I, 37.
New York Fireman, The, I, 4.
New York Idea, The, II, 4; 63–67; 381.
New York in 1860; or, a Hit at the Times, I, 37.
Next of Kin, The, II, 105; 371.
Nice People, II, 57–58; 60; 333.
Nichols, Anne, II, 121–122. *See also* List of Plays.
Nicholson, Kenyon. *See* List of Plays.
Nick of the Woods, I, 4; 105.
Nigger, The, II, 3; 5; 87–88; 390.
Night Before Christmas, The, II, 365.
Nightingale, The, II, 398.
Night Off, A; or, A Page from Balzac, I, 29; 34. II, 338.
Night over Taos, II, 268; 318.
Night's Frolic, A, II, 396.
19th Hole, The, II, 332.
Ninety Days, II, 352.
Ninth Guest, The, II, 341.
Noah, M. M., I, 4.
Noble Rogue, A, II, 375.
No 'Count Boy, The, II, 243.
No More Ladies, II, 395.
No Name, I, 20. II, 335.
North Carolina, University of, II, 241; 243.
North Dakota, University of, II, 233; 240.
Norwood, I, 7.
Nos Bons Villageois, I, 21; 122.
Not for Children, II, 263–264; 389.
Not Guilty, II, 322.
Notoriety, II, 358.

422

INDEX

INDEX

424

INDEX

INDEX

426

INDEX

427

INDEX

INDEX

Tempers and Tempests; or, Extremes Touch, II, 340.
Tempest, Marie, I, 289.
Tempest, The, II, 39.
Tenants, II, 367.
Tent of Pompey, The, II, 398.
Terrible Meek, The, II, 155; 370.
Test Arrow, The, II, 340.
Test Case, A, I, 32. II, 339.
Texas Nightingale, A, II, 143.
Texas Steer, A, II, 366.
Thackeray, William, II, 63; 68.
Thankful Blossom, I, 112.
Thank You, II, 119; 392.
Thank You Doctor, II, 344.
That Imprudent Young Couple, II, 329.
That Overcoat, II, 396.
That's Gratitude, II, 332.
That's the Woman, II, 400.
Theatre, the closing of, during the Civil War, I, 3–4; call for an independent, 141; condition of, in 1900, II, 2–3; civic, 43; community, 45–49; decline in traveling company, 158; commercial spirit in, 159; rivalry of motion picture to, 158, 159; excessive competition in, 159; rise of independent, 160–163; conferences on the American, 164.
Théâtre des Mathurins, II, 272.
Theatre Guild, The, II, 137; 161; 260; 289.
Theatrical Syndicate, The, I, 189.
They Knew What They Wanted, II, 228–229; 363.
They Shall Not Die, II, 297; 401.
Things That Count, The, II, 136; 344.
Third Degree, The, II, 104; 371.
Thirst, II, 162; 168; 384.
Thirty Days, II, 356; 394.
39 East, II, 57; 333.
This Fine-Pretty World, II, 29; 37–38; 249; 377.
This Is New York, II, 391.
This Picture and That, I, 65. II, 378.
This Way Out, II, 332.
Thomas, Albert E., II, 25; 74–75. *See also* List of Plays.
Thomas Augustus, I, 3; 60; 66; 239–264; birth and parentage, 239–240; training, 240–241; his advice to playwrights, 242; newspaper experience of, 242; acts as manager for Julia Marlowe, 242; joins staff of Madison Square Theatre, 243; establishes his reputation with *Alabama,* 243; its social and political

effect, 244–245; treats of the trusts and of politics, 246–248; plays of the West, 248–251; his period of light comedy, 251–252; plays of mental influence, 253–256; treats double standard of morality, 256–258; Civil War plays of, 245, 258–261; personal liberty in plays of, 261–263; his achievement, 262–264. II, 1; 4; 5; 24; 54; 250. *See also* List of Plays.
Thomas, Frankie, II, 300.
Thompson, Denman, I, 128–129. *See also* List of Plays.
Those We Love, II, 316.
Thou Desperate Pilot, II, 317.
Thousand Years Ago, A, II, 28; 32; 376.
Three Bears, II, 330.
Three of Hearts, I, 258. II, 398.
Three of Us, The, II, 51; 333.
Three Men on a Horse, II, 316.
Three Wise Fools, II, 393.
Through Fire, I, 118. II, 328.
Through the Breakers, II, 340.
Through the Dark, II, 374.
Through the Years, II, 361.
Ticey; or, That Little Affair of Boyd's, II, 353.
Tickless Time, II, 354.
Tiger! Tiger!, II, 135; 372.
Timber, II, 377.
Tin Soldier, A, II, 366.
Tiote, II, 337.
Title Mart, The, II, 330.
Toast of the Town, The, I, 271. II, 348.
Tobacco Road, II, 287; 370.
To-day, II, 326.
Toddles, I, 290. II, 348.
Toller Einfall, Ein, I, 221.
Tomorrow, II, 28; 35–36; 376.
Tomorrow and Tomorrow, II, 280; 320.
Tongues of Men, The, II, 153; 330.
To-Night at Twelve, II, 341.
Too Many Boats, II, 341.
Too Many Cooks, II, 119; 332.
Too Much Johnson, II, 352.
Too Much Smith, II, 378.
Top O' the Hill, II, 369.
Torchbearers, The, II, 225; 369.
Torch Song, II, 383.
Torrance, Ridgeley, II, 25.
To the Ladies, II, 220–222; 224; 332; 368.
Totheroh, Dan, II, 237–238; 290–291. *See also* List of Plays.
Tourgee, A., I, 127.

INDEX

INDEX

Wallack, Lester, I, 3; 16; 37; 38; 57. *See also* List of Plays.
Walsh, Blanche, I, 284.
Walter, Eugene, I, 10. II, 5; 105–109. *See also* List of Plays.
War Committee, A, II, 372.
Ward of France, A, II, 351.
Warfield, David, I, 189; 197.
War in Peace, II, 340.
Warnings, II, 168; 384.
Warrens of Virginia, The, II, 343.
Washington, George, plays dealing with, I, 248. II, 41–42; 251; 270.
Washington Square Players, The, II, 39; 137; 141; 161; 236.
Washington, the Man Who Made Us, II, 41–42; 377.
Waterloo Bridge, II, 296; 391.
Watkins, Maurine. *See* List of Plays.
Wave of Life, A, I, 270.
Way Down East, I, 162. II, 387.
Way of the World, The, I, 277. II, 347.
Way We Live, The, II, 337.
We Are Seven, II, 145; 351.
Web, The, II, 168; 384.
Wednesday's Child, II, 301; 319.
Welded, II, 184–185; 386.
Well Known Woman, A, II, 331.
Welt ohne Männer, Die, I, 290.
Wet Blanket, A, II, 338.
We, the People, II, 263; 389.
Wexley, John, II, 296–297. *See also* List of Plays.
Wharton, Edith, I, 286. II, 252; 261.
What Happened to Jones, II, 102; 326.
What Price Glory, II, 234–235; 275; 318; 392.
What Should She Do? or, Jealousy, I, 24. II, 336.
What the Doctor Ordered, II, 394.
What They Think, II, 334.
When Ladies Meet, II, 251; 334.
When Witches Ride, II, 242.
When Your Ship Comes In, II, 330.
Where the Cross is Made, II, 171; 175; 385.
Whiffen, Mrs. Thomas, I, 168; 172.
Whiffen, Thomas, I, 168.
Whispering Friends, II, 331.
Whistling in the Dark, II, 330.
White Bird, The, II, 148; 361.
White Desert, II, 233–234; 318.
White Dresses, II, 244.
White Eagle, II, 361.
White Man, II, 388.
White Sister. The, II, 333.

White Slave, The, I, 123. II, 328.
White Wings, II, 83–84; 320.
Who's Who, II, 342.
Why Marry? II, 69–72; 73; 401.
Why Not? II, 72–74; 75; 402.
Why Smith Left Home, II, 102; 326.
Widow's Son, The, I, 259.
Wife, The, I, 169–171. II, 75; 323; 343.
Wild Birds, II, 237–238; 399.
Wilde, Oscar, I, 54.
Wildfire, II, 326.
Wild Harps Playing, The, II, 320.
Wild Man of Borneo, II, 332.
Williams, Hope, II, 276.
Williams, Jesse Lynch, II, 68–74; 250. *See also* List of Plays.
Willing Performer, The, II, 317.
Will of Song, The, II, 377.
Willow Tree, The, II, 132–133; 326.
Wilson, Francis, I, 283.
Wilson, H. L., II, 222.
Wine, Women and Cards, II, 332.
Wings, The, II, 18; 387.
Winnie and the Wolves, I, 235. II, 353.
Winterfeast, The, II, 155; 370.
Winterset, II, 270–271; 318.
Winter, William, I, 266.
Wisdom Tooth, The, II, 224; 332.
Witching Hour, The, I, 243; 253–255; 263. II, 5; 397.
Within an Inch of His life, II, 322; 359.
Within the Law, II, 111; 400.
Wives, I, 51–52. II, 362.
Wolf, The, II, 106; 400.
Wolf of Gubbio, The, II, 22–23; 387.
Wolf, Pierre, I, 194.
Wolfville, I, 286. II, 348.
Woollcott, Alexander, II, 285.
Woman, The, II, 343.
Woman Hater, The, II, 373.
Woman in the Case, The, I, 283–285. II, 4; 345; 347.
Woman in White, The, I, 20.
Woman of the World, A, II, 395.
Woman's Honor, II, 354.
Woman's Way, A, II, 75–76; 327.
Woman's Won't, A, II, 338.
Won at Last, II, 374.
Wooden Slipper, The, II, 388.
Wooden Spoon, A; or, Perdita's Penates, II, 338.
Woodworth, Samuel, I, 127.
Woolen Stocking, The, II, 358.
Woolf, B. E., I, 6. *See also* List of Plays.
Wren, The, II, 394.
Wrong Mr. Wright, The, II, 326.

INDEX

Wyndham, Sir Charles, I, 41.

Y

Yale University, I, 40. II, 81; 164.
Yankee Fantasies, II, 29; 36; 376.
Yankee in England, A, I, 4.
Yankee Prince, The, II, 331.
Yankee Tourist, The, II, 342.
Ye Earlie Trouble, II, 329.
Yellow Jack, II, 274; 364.
Yellow Jacket, The, II, 132; 326; 359.
Yes or No, II, 354.
Yorick, II, 336.
Yorick's Love, I, 70–72; quotation from, 71–72. II, 364.
You and I, II, 81–82; 320.
Young America, I, 203. II, 402.
Young Blood, II, 350.
Younger Son, The, I, 176. II, 323.

Youngest, The, II, 82; 320.
Young Folks' Ways, I, 215.
Young Love, II, 388.
Young Man's Fancy, A, II, 145; 380.
Young Mrs. Winthrop, I, 52–53; 57. II, 74; 167; 362.
Young, Sir Charles, I, 57.
Young, William, I, 200–203. *See also* List of Plays.
Young Wisdom, II, 56; 333.
Your Fiery Furnace, II, 244.
Your Humble Servant, II, 127; 393.

Z

Zanina; or, The Rover of Cambaye, II, 337.
Zaza, I, 177. II, 324.
Zone Police, The, II, 342.